Contemporary Business

Contemporary Business

Louis E. Boone
The University of Tulsa

David L. Kurtz
Eastern Michigan University

The Dryden Press *Hinsdale, Illinois*

To Jere L. Calmes and Paula Solinger
  who shared our dreams of this book and possessed the insight, patience, and perseverance to turn these dreams into reality

Editorial-Production services by Cobb/Dunlop,
  Publisher Services, Inc.
Photo research by Marcia Kelly
Cover and text design by Caliber
Typesetting by Applied Typographic Systems

Grateful acknowledgment is made to the following publishers, photographers, and agencies for permission to reproduce their photographs in the color photo essay following the Contents.
Page 1: (trees and sun) Dan Morrill/VJK; (buildings and fountain) 1st National Bank of Chicago.   **Page 2:** (butterfly) Dan Morrill/VJK; (airplane) Dan Morrill/VJK; (bird and sun) William Eastman III/Tom Stack & Associates.   **Page 3:** (windmill) Dan Morrill/VJK; (computer) Dan Morrill/VJK; (industrial wheels) W. R. Grace; (tractor wheel) Robert Keeling/VJK; (waterwheel) Vermont Development Dept.   **Page 4:** (tree farming) Dan Morrill/VJK; (wood grain) Dan Morrill/VJK; (log pile) Dan Morrill/VJK; (crate and barrel) Robert Keeling/VJK; (saw mill) Vermont Development Dept.   **Page 5:** (textile pattern) Marimekko textile made in Finland, photograph courtesy of Design Research, Inc., Cambridge; (orange grove) Dan Morrill/VJK; (contour plowing) Grant Heilman; (pine trees) Dan Morrill/VJK; (farm squares) Pfizer, Inc.; (highway stripes) Exxon.   **Page 6:** (chickens) Pfizer, Inc.; (red VW's) Volkswagon of America; (lipsticks) Robert Keeling/VJK; (tulips) Dan Morrill/VJK.   **Page 7** (bees) courtesy Jere Calmes; (crowd) Bob Davis/Tom Stack & Associates; (penguins) Reprinted from the book *Emperor Penguin* by Jean-Claude Deguine. Published in the United Kingdom by Angus & Robertson Ltd. Reprinted by permission from *The Living Wilderness*, spring 1975. Copyright 1975 by The Wilderness Society; (crowd on beach) Dan Morrill/VJK.   **Page 8:** (farmer and bags) Pfizer, Inc.; (grain in hand) Pfizer, Inc.

Preface

Contemporary Business is a student's textbook. It is designed to enlighten, and enchant, the reader as he or she is introduced to the fascinating world of business. The book is both comprehensive and contemporary; it focuses on introducing the student to the many exciting aspects of modern business. Its reading level matches that of the student. Often students complain that most business textbooks are too long, boring, vague, and unrelated to contemporary events. *Contemporary Business* corrects these deficiencies.

Contemporary Business is probably the most ambitious project ever attempted by a publisher of business textbooks. The objective of both the authors and the publisher has been to develop the most comprehensive teaching/learning package ever assembled for a business course. While the textbook is undoubtedly the most critical ingredient in the package, it is only one part. It is supplemented by a thorough *Student Involvement Guide* prepared by Professors Steven L. Shapiro of Queensborough Community College, Roderick D. Powers of Iowa State University, and Joseph T. Straub of Valencia Community College. Additional viewpoints on the business scene are offered in *Readings in Contemporary Business* edited by Professors David E. Grainger of Oakland Community College, Marie R. Hodge of Bowling Green State University, and Raymond Tewell of American River College. The instructor may also choose a film from our film catalogue, use the cassette tapes that are available, or introduce specific business and economic issues in the student's area of the country through the special demographic materials.

Over one hundred people were involved in some way in the development of the *Contemporary Business* package. All are skilled teachers and acknowledged professionals in some aspect of business administration. The authors will be forever indebted to the persons listed on the following pages. We would specifically like to thank Albert Belskus of Eastern Michigan University, Clifford Butt of Suffolk County Community College, Mel Choate of North Seattle Community College, W. R. Christensen of Community College of Denver, Craig Christopherson of Richland College, Frederick L. Davis of Long Beach City College, Lawrence J. Gitman of the University of Tulsa, Bill C. Gunter of E. F. Hutton, Robert W. Hall of Indiana University/Purdue University at Indianapolis, R. Barry Hoover of Brevard Community College, Hans V. Johnson of the University of Texas at San Antonio, Ray L. Jones of East Carolina University, Jagdish R. Kapoor of College of DuPage, George Katz of San Antonio College, Paul N. Keaton of the University of Tennessee at Chattanooga, Lawrence A. Klatt of Florida Atlantic University, Lawrence W. Konopka of Van Winkle & Van Winkle, Xymena Kulsrud and Anne Morrow of the University of Tulsa, R. S. Raymond of Ohio University, Robert Ristau of Eastern Michigan University, Barry Shane of Oregon State University, Daniel J. Sullivan of College of San Mateo, James P. Vomhof of Johnson County Community College, and Gene C. Wunder of Northeast Missouri State University, who prepared some of the original material used in *Contemporary Business*.

Enjoy your first business course. We think it will be one of the most valuable classes you will ever take. Our mission will have been fulfilled if *Contemporary Business* opens some avenues of understanding in our dynamic business environment.

Tulsa, Oklahoma   *Louis E. Boone*
Ypsilanti, Michigan   *David L. Kurtz*
January 1976

Acknowledgments

The authors gratefully acknowledge the contributions of the following people to *Contemporary Business:*

James Agresta
Prince George's Community College

Albert Belskus
Eastern Michigan University

Lester R. Bittel
Madison College

Vencil J. Bixler
Southwest Missouri State
University

Walter A. Bogumil, Jr.
Florida Technological University

Charles E. Boyle
Ferris State College

Eugene F. Brigham
University of Florida

Michael Broida
Miami University

Alena Bullock
Brookdale Community College

Clifford Butt
Suffolk County Community
College

Mel Choate
North Seattle Community College

W. R. Christensen
Community College of Denver

C. W. Christopherson
Richland College

Ronald Copeland
University of South Carolina

James W. Cox
Lane Community College

Robert M. Crowe
Memphis State University

Frederick L. Davis
Long Beach City College

Donald R. Domm
Kent State University

Max E. Douglas
Indiana State University

W. Jack Duncan
University of Alabama in
Birmingham

William D. Evans
Wright State University

Lawrence J. Gitman
University of Tulsa

William F. Glueck
University of Missouri, Columbia

Donald S. Gordon
Illinois Central College

Douglas C. Gordon
Arapahoe Community College

David E. Grainger
Oakland Community College

Rust F. Gray, Jr.
Wright State University

Bill C. Gunter
E. F. Hutton

Thomas G. Gutteridge
State University of New York
at Buffalo

Bill Haggard
Mesa Community College

Robert W. Hall
Indiana University-Purdue
University

Carl E. High
New York City Community College

Darrell D. Hilliker
Suffolk County Community College

Marie R. Hodge
Bowling Green State University

William Holley
Auburn University

Michael M. Homer
Utah Technical College
at Salt Lake

R. Barry Hoover
Brevard Community College

Rate A. Howell
The Ohio State University

J. G. Hunt
Southern Illinois University at
Carbondale

Hans V. Johnson
University of Texas
at San Antonio

Ray L. Jones
East Carolina University

Jagdish R. Kapoor
College of DuPage

George Katz
San Antonio College

Paul N. Keaton
University of Tennessee at
Chattanooga

Lawrence A. Klatt
Florida Atlantic University

Lawrence W. Konopka
Van Winkle & Van Winkle

Xymena Kulsrud
University of Tulsa

Murray P. Leavitt
De Anza College

Jack Mendleson
Arizona State University

Robert Monroe
University of Missouri,
Columbia

Anne Morrow
University of Tulsa

John L. Myers
University of Southern
Colorado

Dale E. Nelson
California State University,
Long Beach

Donald Nelson
College of DuPage

Vincent Orza
South Oklahoma City Junior
College

Jack W. Partlow
Seminole Community College

Michael F. Pauritsch
Moraine Valley Community
College

William G. Perry
Oregon State University

Norman H. Petty
Central Piedmont College

Barbara A. Pletcher
California State University,
Sacramento

Roderick D. Powers
Iowa State University

R, S. Raymond
Ohio University

Robert Ristau
Eastern Michigan University

David C. Roberts
San Joaquin Delta College

Joseph T. Rogers
Peirce Junior College

Art Rose
College of DuPage

Kenneth Schock
West Valley Joint Community
College District

Frank K. Schuhmann
Idaho State University

Daniel Segebarth
Triton College

Barry Shane
Oregon State University

Steven L. Shapiro
Queensborough Community
College

Joseph T. Straub
Valencia Community College

Daniel J. Sullivan
College of San Mateo

Raymond Tewell
American River College

James P. Vomhof
Johnson County Community
College

Bert Weesner
Lansing Community College

Roman L. Weil
Georgia Institute of Technology

Timothy W. Wright
Lakeland Community College

Gene C. Wunder
Northeast Missouri State University

Contents

PART II Organization and Management of the Enterprise 72

PART IV Marketing Management 218

PART VI Quantitative Tools of Management 422

PART VII Additional Dimensions 496

HARMONY OR CONFLICT?

In recent years there has been much discussion concerning American Business and the American ecology. Can business and ecological interests co-exist without being detrimental to each other? We feel each can interact and gain. The following color essay illustrates this thought.

Contemporary Business

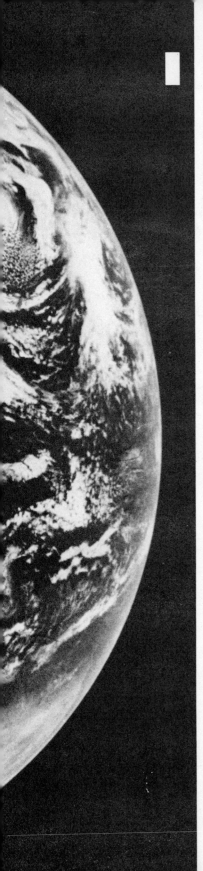

I | Business and Its Environment

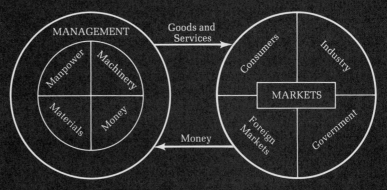

1 The Foundations of Business
2 Social Responsibility and Business
3 Forms of Business Ownership

SOURCE: NASA.

1

The Foundations of Business

"The business of America is business."

—Calvin Coolidge

". . . today's large corporation is responsive to broad social goals because it is managed for the long-run."

—Randell Meyer, President
Exxon Company, U.S.A.

What Chapter 1 Is All About

1. In this chapter you will learn what a business is and how it operates within the free enterprise system.
2. You will learn about the role of the entrepreneur and competition in a free enterprise system.
3. You will understand how the historical development of the American economy influences contemporary business.
4. The different types of alternative economic systems will also be explained in this chapter.
5. You will understand the role of big business in modern society.
6. The study of business will be explained to you in this chapter.
7. A simple diagram will help explain the operation of contemporary business.
8. After reading this chapter, you will understand these terms:

business	production era
profit	marketing concept
free enterprise system	communism
competition	socialism
entrepreneur	mixed economies
"Invisible Hand"	countervailing powers
antitrust laws	5 Ms
private property	perfect competition
factors of production	monopolistic competition
land	oligopoly
labor	monopoly
capital	law of supply and demand
Industrial Revolution	

Alvah C. Roebuck

SOURCE: Sears, Roebuck and Co.

If ever there was an ups and downs businessman, that man was Alvah C. Roebuck, one-half of what was to be the well-known mail-order firm of Sears, Roebuck and Company. In 1887 Richard W. Sears was in business in Chicago, selling watches when he discovered he needed a watch repairman—one with his own tools. Sears put an ad in the newspaper, and that was how Sears and Roebuck met. Sears hired Roebuck, who had travelled from Hammond, Indiana, to answer the ad. The two men began working together, and by 1893 Sears and Roebuck were incorporated, while both men were still in their twenties.

But things did not move along very well. Sears had resigned from the company only to re-enter the partnership a short time later. Then Roebuck sold his part of the business to Sears for $25,000. The decision was made because the company was in debt, but it was a bad time to sell out. Chicago was rapidly growing into the transportation center of the United States, and Sears, Roebuck was expanding its mail-order inventory. Now profits began to boom. Sears offered to give Roebuck his partnership back again. Instead, Roebuck became a salaried employee of the company. He was in and out of the company until he started making motion picture projectors on his own. After he sold the motion picture company he became a Florida real estate agent. That enterprise went "bust" in 1929.

Roebuck returned to Sears, Roebuck as a clerk. Sears was dead, and the company was now under new management. When Roebuck died, in 1948 in his eighties, he had only the stock from the firm's profit-sharing plan to mark his financial affiliation to Sears, Roebuck and Company.

Mention the word "business" to someone and you will get varied respones. Some people think of their jobs; others recall the firms they deal with as consumers. And rightly so! Business is a broad, inclusive term that can be applied to many kinds of enterprises.

What Is Business?

Business can be defined as all profit-directed economic and commercial activities that provide goods and services necessary to a nation's standard of living. Business is the economic pulse of the nation as it strives to increase society's standard of living. Profits are the normal mechanism for motivating these activities. Accountants and business people define **profit** as the difference between revenues (the firm's receipts) and expenses (the company's expenditures).

All businesses must serve their customers in some way if they are to survive in the long run. Some businesses produce tangible products—like Zenith televisions, General Electric light bulbs, and Boeing aircraft. Others provide services—like those offered by Prudential Insurance, Avis car rentals, Columbia Broadcasting System, and Ramada Inns.

The J.M. Smucker Company believes that it best serves society (and its own interests) by manufacturing top-quality jams and preserves.

"With a Name Like Smucker's, It Has To Be Good"

"Orrville just sounds like a small town where they actually make good preserves," according to Paul Smucker. Orrville, Ohio, a small community south of Cleveland, is the headquarters of J.M. Smucker Company, manufacturers of jams, jellies, and preserves. Paul Smucker is the current head of the Smucker organization.

Four generations of Smuckers have built the firm's nationwide reputation for quality. With annual sales exceeding $100 million, the J.M. Smucker Company still follows a rigid adherence to producing only the finest quality products. Paul Smucker says:

I just can't imagine a nicer business to be in. To me, it all starts with what you put in the jar. If it's honest and of good quality—and if you deal that way with your people—then all the rest will come.

While some manufacturers compensate for rising production costs by using lower quality ingredients, Mr. Smucker insists that products bearing his family name maintain their high marks for quality. The company's advertising slogan—"With a name like Smucker's, it has to be good"—reflects its management philosophy. When traveling, Paul Smucker makes it a point to check Smucker displays in supermarkets. If he finds crooked labels or a dirty jar, he always buys it off the shelf, then contacts the manager of the plant that produced the item.

Smucker's is also known for its even handed treatment of employees. Paul Smucker puts it this way: "We're not always out to get maximum earnings for our stockholders, not if that means hurting people in the process."

Source: Everrett Groseclose. "Paul H. Smucker Takes Great Pains to Preserve His Products' Quality," *The Wall Street Journal* (February 3, 1975), pp. 1, 16. Reprinted with permission of *The Wall Street Journal,* © Dow Jones & Company, Inc. 1975. All rights reserved.

If a business (such as a student union) fails to satisfy the needs of its customers, they will turn elsewhere. Then, the business faces the task of changing its operation if it is to survive. Consider one of the latest trends on college campuses.

Big Mac and His Cousins Enroll in College . . .

The University of Cincinnati lost $50,000 on its student union food sales in 1971-1972. So, in 1972-1973, the University brought in LaRosa's Pizzeria and Mr. Jim's Steak House. Food sales shot up 22%. McDonald's arrived the next year, and sales rose another 48%.

Over at Ohio State, the story is similar. The 1974–1975 academic year saw OSU lease student union space to McDonald's, Shakey's Pizza, Findley Sweet Shack, and Fruit Drinks, Inc. Food sales tripled over the previous year.

The Ohio schools are not alone. Western Illinois University doubled its union food sales when it added a Hardee's. The University of Central Arkansas lost money in its union operation until a Minute Man of America franchise arrived.

The colleges adopted a basic concept of business. *Customers (students) must be satisfied, if the organization is to survive and prosper.* Apparently, these student unions could not beat the fast food franchises located off campus, so they joined them!

Source: Jack Magarrell. "Big Mac on Campus," *The Chronicle of Higher Education* (December 2, 1974), p. 6.

The Free Enterprise System

All American businesses—large or small—belong to what is called the free enterprise system. The **free enterprise system** *simply means businesses operate in a dynamic environment where success or failure is determined by how well they match and counter the offerings of competitors.* **Competition** *refers to the battle between businesses for consumer acceptance.* Sales and profits are the yardsticks by which consumer acceptance is measured.

Henry Ford held a considerable lead over his competitors in the automobile industry, but he failed to observe that the need for cheap transportation had been met, and that consumer needs were gradually changing. Ford's competition captured the consumer acceptance that he had gained then lost.

Henry Ford's dream was to produce a car that everyone could afford. He decided to make just one model in order to cut production costs, and thus lower the vehicle's selling price. Ford announced that buyers could get any color they wanted *as long as it is black.* The mass assembly line was introduced in 1913, and further reduced production costs, despite the fact that Ford began paying his employees $5 for an eight-hour shift—an unheard of wage!

Millions of Model T's were produced by the mid-1920's, but Henry Ford was beginning to lose his grasp on the automobile market. Competitors offered color choices, different models, and options that were unavailable from Ford. Marketing had joined production as a key to success in the motor industry, a fact Ford finally realized in 1927. So he closed his plants and began to retool to produce the "Model A." But Ford was never able to regain his once overwhelming lead in the U.S. car market.

Ford Motor Company remained production-oriented during the administrations of Henry Ford and his son, Edsel. In 1945 a youthful grandson, Henry Ford II, began to move the firm into its present position as an innovative, consumer-oriented corporation. Henry

Ford II still leads the company as it faces the problems and challenges of the 1970's.

Competition is a vital mechanism for assuring that the free enterprise system continues to provide Americans with the goods and services that make up the high standard of living in the United States. Even a government-owned business like the U.S. Postal Service must yield to the pressures of competition. Industry's demand for increased efficiency and lower cost bulk mail led to the development of private postal systems.

The Entrepreneur's Role in the Free Enterprise System

An **entrepreneur** *is the risk-taker in the free enterprise system.* This is the person who sees a profitable opportunity and then organizes and operates a business designed to achieve this objective. Profits are the rewards for a successful entrepreneur, but they do not come easily. Herbert H. Dow was involved in several business ventures and met with only modest success until the Dow Chemical Company was founded. Dow's earlier experiences probably created his lifelong habit of using those resources that were immediately available.

Dow Chemical—Yesterday and Today

After eight years involvement with small chemical enterprises, Herbert H. Dow organized the Dow Chemical Company on May 18, 1897. It eventually absorbed other Dow business ventures. . . .

The young company began operation with $200,000 invested by 57 original stockholders (or owners). Forty percent of this money was used to build a plant in Midland, Michigan. Economizing became an obsession with Dow. He and a small crew of employees built the plant, largely from local materials.

Dow adopted two policies that became his legacy to the infant firm. One was his insistance on using readily available materials wherever possible. Local timber built the first plant, and local scrap wood burned in its boilers. Brines from the Midland area were the firm's basic raw material. Dow also believed in hiring and training previously unskilled local labor rather than importing skilled labor from distant places.

Today, Herbert Dow's fledgling enterprise has become a giant, multinational corporation. It is still headquartered in Midland, Michigan. But it now has 50,000 people on the payroll, and its sales exceed $3 billion.

Source: Murray Campbell and Harrison Hatton. *Herbert H. Dow: Pioneer in Creative Chemistry* (Englewood Cliffs, New Jersey, Prentice-Hall, Inc., 1951), pp. 38–46.

Someone must take an economic risk if a business is to meet public needs. But in a few cases the costs and risks are so great that it is impossible for private individuals to perform the task. The space exploration program is an example. The potential payoff is slight when compared to the risks, so the government (through its National

Aeronautics and Space Administration) became the entrepreneur in this venture.

The Operation of the Free Enterprise System

The free enterprise system, or capitalism, is founded on the principle that competition between business firms will best serve the needs of society. Adam Smith, who is often called the *Father of Capitalism*, first described this process in his book *Wealth of Nations*, published in 1776. Smith said that an economy is best regulated by the **Invisible Hand** of competition. By this, Smith meant that *competition among firms would assure that consumers received the best possible products and prices since the less efficient producers would gradually be eliminated from the marketplace.*

The Invisible Hand concept is the basic premise of the free enterprise system. Competition is the primary regulator of our economic life. However, in some cases the public (through its elected representatives) has passed laws designed to strengthen the role of competition. These laws, called **antitrust laws,** *prohibit attempts to monopolize, or dominate, a particular market.* Two antitrust laws, the Sherman Act (1890) and the Clayton Act (1914), are described later in this text. Antitrust legislation outlaws efforts to monopolize markets and preserves the advantages of competition for society.

BASIC RIGHTS OF THE FREE ENTERPRISE SYSTEM
Certain rights are available to citizens living in a free enterprise economy. These rights are crucial to the operation of capitalism.

Private property

The free enterprise system guarantees that people have the right to own, accumulate, buy, sell, and will property. This right includes most forms of property—land, buildings, machinery, and equipment. The right to **private property** is the most fundamental of all rights under the free enterprise system. *Most Americans firmly believe that people should have the right to any property that they work to acquire, and to all profits resulting from such property.*

Profits

The free enterprise system also guarantees that the risk-taker has the rights to all profits (after taxes) that might be earned by the business. The free enterprise system does not guarantee that the business will earn a profit; but if it does, the entrepreneur has a legal and ethical right to it.

Freedom of choice

Under free enterprise everyone has maximum freedom of choice in employment, purchasing decisions, and investments. This right means that a person can go in (or out of) business with a minimum of governmental interference. Anyone can change jobs, negotiate the compensation level, join a labor union, and quit if one so desires. Consumers are offered several choices of bread, furniture, television programs, and magazines.

The freedom of choice is so habitual to us that we sometimes forget its importance. A free enterprise economy tries to maximize human welfare and happiness by providing alternatives. Other systems sometimes limit freedom of choice to accomplish government goals, such as production increases.

Competitive ground rules

The free enterprise system also guarantees that the public retains the right to set ground rules for competitive activity. The government, speaking for the public, passed laws to prohibit "cutthroat" competition, or excessively competitive practices designed to eventually eliminate competition. Other ground rules have been established to prohibit price discrimination; fraudulent dealings in financial markets; and deceptive practices in advertising, packaging, and personal selling.

"You know the lifestyle so many of us dream about — living in a cabin in the woods, doing some pottery, perhaps weaving a wallhanging, and selling it for just enough to buy a week's food, informal meals cooked in a fireplace, no pressure — well, I had enough of that and decided to drop out and become a business executive."

Americans Have Freedom of Choice in Their Career Decisions
SOURCE: Reproduced by permission of Sidney Harris.

The free enterprise system requires certain inputs if it is to operate effectively. Economists call these inputs the factors of production. Not all enterprises require exactly the same combination of these elements. Each business has its own peculiar mix of the four **factors of production:** *land, labor, capital, and entrepreneurship.*

Land *refers to all types of real property,* such as a 10-acre plot of land, a factory on Commerce Street, or a store in a nearby shopping mall. It is a basic resource that is required in any economic system.

Labor is a critical input to the free enterprise system. The term **labor** *refers to everyone who works for a business.* This includes the company president, the production manager, a sales representative, and an assembly line worker.

Capital *is defined as the funds necessary to finance the operation of a business.* Capital can be provided in the form of investments, profits, or loans. This money is then used to build factories, buy raw materials, hire workers, and so forth.

Entrepreneurship

An entrepreneur is the risk-taker in the free enterprise system. In some situations the entrepreneur actively manages the business; in other cases this duty is handed over to a salaried manager.

All four factors of production must receive a financial return if they are to be used in the free enterprise system. These corresponding factor payments are rent, wages, interest, and profit. (*See* Table 1-1).

The specific factor payment that is received varies among industries, but all factors of production are required in some degree for all businesses.

Four basic types of industries exist in a free enterprise system: perfect (or pure) competition, monopolistic competition, oligopoly, and monopoly. Firms fall into one of these four categories depending on the relative competitiveness of a particular industry.

Perfect competition *is a situation where all of the firms in an industry are so small that none of them can individually influence the price charged in the marketplace.* Price is set by total market demand and total market supply. This is the Law of Supply and

Table 1-1
The Factors of
Production and Their
Factor Payments

Factors of Production	Corresponding Factor Payment
Land	Rent
Labor	Wages
Capital	Interest
Entrepreneurship	Profit

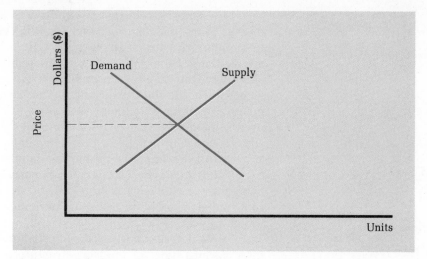

Figure 1-1
Supply and Demand
Determine Price

Demand. **Supply** *is a schedule of what producers will offer in the market at various price levels.* **Demand** *is a schedule showing what consumers will buy at various price levels.* The intersection of the supply and demand curves is the price level that will prevail. (See Figure 1-1.)

Perfect competition also means there is a **similar product,** *one that cannot be differentiated from that of a competitor.* Agriculture is probably the closest example of perfect competition (even though government price-support programs make it somewhat less competitive); and wheat would be a similar product. Finally, the small size of the firms involved in a perfectly competitive market make it relatively easy to enter or leave that market.

Monopolistic competition *is an industry where a few less firms* (than would exist in perfect competition) *produce and sell products that are different from those of their competitors.* Monopolistic competition also gives the firm some power over the price it will charge. A good example is retailing, where the price can vary for different brands of aspirin, toothpaste, or gasoline. The relatively small size of these firms also makes it easy to enter the industry.

Oligopoly *is a market where there are few sellers.* Automobiles and steel are good examples. In some oligopolies the product is similar (steel); in others it is different (automobiles). The entry of new competitors is restricted by the huge investments that are required for market entry. But the primary difference between oligopoly and the markets mentioned previously is that the limited number of sellers gives the oligopolistic firm substantial control over the product's price. In an oligopoly the prices of competitive products are quite similar because substantial price competition would lessen every firm's profit. When Chrysler introduced its price rebate program in 1975, all other U.S. competitors followed suit in order to retain their customers.

Monopoly *is a market situation where there is only one competitor.* Since the Sherman and Clayton Acts prohibited attempts to monopolize markets, nearly all of the monopolies that do exist are regulated monopolies, such as the public utilities. Firms selling electricity, natural gas, or telephone service are usually regulated by an agency of the state government. These agencies have power over many aspects of regulated monopolies, including pricing and the profits that are made. In a pure monopoly the firm would have substantial control over price; but in regulated monopolies pricing is subject to rules imposed by the regulatory body.

There are no directly competitive products in a monopoly, and entry into the industry is restricted by the government. In fact, in some states a public utility must periodically seek voter approval to continue its service.

Table 1-2 summarizes the most important characteristics of these various types of industry structures.

Development of the American Economy

The United States has a fascinating business history. Business has significantly influenced events in other areas such as customs, politics, and even family living. The historical development of the American economy continues to affect the way business operates today.

COLONIAL AMERICA — Colonial America's agricultural society was built on the products of its farms and plantations. The nation's prosperity depended on the success of its latest crop, and most people lived in rural areas. America's cities—quite small in comparison to those of Europe at

Table 1-2 Major Characteristics of Perfect Competition, Monopolistic Competition, Oligopoly, and Monopoly

Type of Industry	Number of Firms	Characteristics Product	Control over Pricing	Ease of Entry
Perfect Competition	Many	Similar	None	Easy
Monopolistic Competition	Many	Different	Some	Relatively Easy
Oligopoly	Few	Similar or Different	Substantial	Difficult
Monopoly	One	No Readily Available Substitute	Usually Regulated by Government	Virtually Impossible

the time—were the marketplaces and residences of craft workers, traders, bankers, and government officials.

But the real economic and political power of the nation was centered in rural America. The population was tied socially, as well as economically, to the land. The American colonies looked to England for manufactured products and capital with which to finance infant industries.

Even after the Revolutionary War (1776–1783), America maintained close economic relations with England. British investors provided much of the money needed to finance the developing business system. This financial influence remained well into the nineteenth century.

THE INDUSTRIAL REVOLUTION

The Industrial Revolution began in England around 1750–1775. The traditional manufacturing system of independent skilled workers each pursuing their specialities was replaced by a *factory system* that mass produced items by bringing large numbers of semiskilled workers together.

The factory system profited from savings that were created by large-scale production (for example, raw materials could often be purchased cheaper in large lots), and the fact that it allowed *specialization of labor* (each worker concentrated on one specific task or job). Production efficiency was improved substantially, and the factory system revolutionized business.

America was soon influenced by these events occurring in England, and the United States began its march toward becoming an industrialized nation. Agriculture became mechanized, and factories sprang up throughout the nation. But most business historians agree that real progress did not occur until railroads provided a fast, economical method of transporting the goods produced by businesses.

The rapid construction of our railroad systems during the 1840's and 1850's was really America's "Industrial Revolution." Not only did the railroads provide the necessary transportation system; they also created the need for expanded quantities of lumber, steel, and real estate.

THE AGE OF THE ENTREPRENEUR

The nineteenth century saw business make sizeable advances in the United States. Eli Whitney introduced the concept of interchangeable parts for firearms. Whitney believed that all parts to his product should be built to the same specifications, which would facilitate mass production. Pack peddlers, the sales personnel of the day, were operating in the Mississippi Valley by about 1800. Financiers became less dependent upon England, and the banking system became better established after some early problems. Inventors seemed to be creating an endless array of commercially feasible products.

People were encouraged to take risks and become entrepreneurs. Vanderbilt, Rockefeller, Morgan, and Carnegie—all became wealthy because of their willingness to take business risks during this period of time. Admittedly, some people were hurt by the speculation that characterized industry during the 1800's; but, on balance, the entrepreneurial spirit of the age did much to advance our business system and raise the American standard of living.

PRODUCTION ERA

The early part of the twentieth century was a period when business managers concentrated almost solely on the firm's production tasks. Industry was under considerable pressure to produce more and more to satisfy growing consumer demand and to correct product shortages.

Work assignments became increasingly specialized. Assembly lines, such as the one introduced by Henry Ford, became common. Owners turned over management responsibilities to a new class of managers, who specialized in operating established businesses rather than in starting new ones.

Marketing tended to be viewed as strictly selling. Fields like consumer research were still not accepted by business. In other words, marketers were those individuals responsible for distribution after the production function had been performed. Business was internally oriented rather than consumer oriented.

THE MARKETING CONCEPT

The post-World War II era has been influenced by an important new concept in management. **The marketing concept** became the prevalent business philosophy. The marketing concept *advocates that all activities and functions of the organization ought to be directed toward the identification and satisfaction of consumer wants.* Thus, a company-wide consumer orientation became the principal goal of the company.

New jobs sprang up throughout the organization. Marketing research departments began to analyze what the consumer would buy before the company produced the item. This concept was in marked contrast to the earlier philosophy of producing a product, then trying to sell it to the consumer. Advertising reached ever larger numbers of consumers and increased the efficiency of the firm's promotional efforts. Today firms must have a strong consumer orientation if they are to remain competitive in the marketplace.

THE 1970's

Challenge after challenge has confronted business throughout the 1970's. Consumer critics have noted several failures in the economic system. Concern over large numbers of industrial accidents resulted in passage of federal legislation concerning occupational safety and health. Financial scandals touched off public demand for greater government regulation in this area of business. Millions of people were shocked by the ecological reports of environmentalists.

The Arab oil embargo made resource conservation and energy-saving programs priority items at management meetings.

These challenges have produced several noticeable trends in the business world. Businesses have become more socially responsible; the impact on society of a business decision is now weighed in most management thinking. Business has also become more conscious of its operating costs. More minorities and women have business careers than formerly. Management continues to struggle with the problem of predicting and then reacting to new government regulations and requirements. Business has also found new markets abroad (such as in Communist nations), but is finding increased competition from foreign producers at home. Later writers may well describe the 1970's as a *Decade of Challenges* for the American business system.

Alternative Economic Systems

Many Americans fail to realize that a large part of the world lives under an economic system other than capitalism. The number of countries with Communist and Socialist systems makes it important to learn the primary features of these alternative economies. We will be concerned with the economic aspects of socialism and communism; political questions are beyond the scope of this book.

COMMUNISM **Communist theory** was the product of Karl Marx, a nineteenth-century economist. Marx believed that the *laboring classes were being exploited by Capitalists (entrepreneurs and managers)*. He said that eventually there would be a class struggle and a new form of society would emerge. Marx labeled his new order *communism*. He believed that the people should own all of a nation's productive capacity, but conceded that the government would have to operate businesses until a classless society could evolve. Communists also adhere to the principle that people should receive according to their needs and give according to their abilities.

A perfect Communist state does not exist, since even the Soviet Union and the People's Republic of China have managerial and professional classes in their societies. These countries are an example of how communism has evolved over the years. Managers and workers now receive incentives for exceeding production quotas. The government has shifted substantial resources into providing more consumer goods. Moscow's GUM department store, for instance, is as modern as any store found in the west.

Communists believe that centralized management of all productive activity results in less waste than the competition of free enterprise. They admit that a consumer's freedom of choice has to be sacrificed in the interests of production efficiency. Capitalists counter with the argument that government-operated industries soon become inefficient bureaucracies because of a lack of employee incentive. Capitalists believe that competition promotes efficiency by providing incentive to achieve and by eliminating inefficient producers.

SOCIALISM **Socialist** economies exist in countries *where the government owns and operates all of the basic industries* such as natural resources, banking, transportation, and large-scale manufacturing. Private ownership still exists in smaller businesses, like shops and restaurants. Socialists believe that major industries are too important to be left in private hands. They argue that government industries are more efficient and serve the public better. Again, the Capitalist counterargument is that state-run industries become massive bureaucracies that are insensitive to consumer needs.

Socialist economies usually follow some master plan for the use of a nation's resources. Workers are free to choose their employment, but the state often encourages people to go into areas where they are needed. Thus, most citizens work for some government enterprise.

MIXED ECONOMIES The term **mixed economy** has become popular in recent years. It is used to describe *economies where there is a mix of socialism and free enterprise.* Sweden and the United Kingdom are often given as examples of nations that still adhere to the basic philosophy of free enterprise but also have a high degree of government ownership. The United Kingdom's coal, steel, and communications industries are governmental enterprises.

Free enterprise proponents often classify these mixed economies as "Socialist" because of the high degree of public ownership. But these countries also have a far larger degree of private ownership than is found in a Socialist nation. In fact, the United States could be considered a mixed economy in that some public utilities are owned by governmental units.

Big Business! Big Labor! Big Government!

The United States is the world's leading industrial power primarily because it has a highly developed system of "big business." Our leading firms are among the world's leading firms. Fourteen of the world's twenty largest companies are U.S. firms.[1]

American industry is extremely diversified. Thousands of business enterprises exist in nearly every conceivable commercial activity. Table 1-3 shows the number of firms in each of our major industries.

Big business has given Americans the highest standard of living ever known in the world. But the size of our business system

Table 1-3
The Number of Firms
in Major American
Industries

Industry	Number of Firms (in thousands)
Agriculture, forestry, and fisheries	3,287
Mining	85
Construction	932
Manufacturing	414
Transportation, communications, electricity, gas	386
Wholesale trade	515
Retail trade	2,298
Finance, insurance, and real estate	1,359
Services	3,053

SOURCE: Adapted from *Statistical Abstract of the U.S.*, 1974.

has also affected other areas of society. Big business created the need for *Big Labor* and *Big Government*. Today, economists and politicians refer to big business, big labor, and big government as the three **countervailing powers** in our nation. *This means that the size and strength of each allows it to balance the economy so that no one sector will ever totally dominate our society.* This unique situation is the leading characteristic of today's American economy.

A later chapter will describe the tremendous growth of the U.S. labor movement. Government has also become big; in fact, many people believe it has become too big. Arch Booth, past president of the Chamber of Commerce of the United States, points out that:

. . . government took 10 percent of the national income in 1929. Today, it takes 40 percent. And if present trends continue, it will take more than half by the late 1980's."[2]

Bigness also raises many complex social and ethical questions. While Americans generally are proud of the high standard of living produced by industry, many raise questions like "How big is too big?", "Should General Motors be split into several corporations?", and "Does Exxon's size allow it to be too profitable?". According to one estimate, there will be only about 300 large firms left in world business by 1988.[3]

The Study of Business: Why? And How?

Many people are actively involved in studying the U.S. business system. Senior business executives are constantly learning how to become more effective managers. Many consumers are examining how business decisions affect their daily lives. Many students are

How Big Is Too Big?

American business may be approaching its own "Age of the Dinosaur." Corporations have been expanding in size and profit-taking, and are now merging or buying into smaller established firms in related industries. This diversification and growth has created a group of big businesses that some critics see as slow moving and unwieldy. Will they become so huge that, in fact, like the dinosaur, corporations will one day become extinct?

In the early 1970's there were about 250 companies in the United States that earned over $1 billion. Many of these same companies have expanded overseas to become multinationals. Companies of this size are able to combine many of the regular costs that are a part of doing business. Shipping of products is just one example. A shipment costs the same whether the delivery truck is half empty or is full. If a number of different products are distributed from and to a central point, filling the truck, shipping costs on each item are lowered. Since urban areas in the United States are growing, distribution of products can be centralized and greater consumer demands for products in such areas can be met more easily and cheaply. The same economies of size can be achieved for such business expenditures as research, advertising, production facilities, and financial management. Big companies can pay for product and market research that smaller companies cannot afford.

But are such companies growing too big to manage? Critics who feel there may not be enough good executives to keep these companies functioning efficiently are answered by those who say that one large company draws on fewer executives than ten independent, small companies. Those in favor of large corporate size say such firms utilize human resources in the best possible way. They can afford to employ good management talent and absorb only that portion of managers needed to run a company well.

Critics of big companies see them as stagnant and inflexible. Because of their large size, big business managers tend to resist change and downgrade creativity, these critics say. Often the demand for a product has already been satisfied, but managers in a large firm do not respond quickly enough to react to changes that will give the company a realistic return on investment.

Critics also see big business as harmful to free enterprise, selling competitive products at lowered prices, putting smaller firms out of business, and then lowering the quality of the product in order to maintain the reduced price. Such critics as Ralph Nader think the consumer pays the penalty for a smaller number of manufacturers for a product.

enrolled in a business administration course.

With this much activity, it is fitting that attention be given to why people study business and how they study it.

WHY STUDY BUSINESS? People study business for a number of reasons. Some plan to enter a business career. Others want to learn how the business system affects them in their roles as wage-earners or consumers. Still others are just curious about what business actually means. Certainly, business affects all of us in some manner, and the more we know about the subject the better we will be able to cope with some of our most common everyday problems. Some specific reasons for studying business are given below.

Career selection

Most students do not spend adequate time in selecting their careers. Many students drift from one curriculum to another and then repeat this pattern when they enter the job market. The study of business allows a student to consider various occupational possibilities. The bulk of these jobs are in private industry, but many similar careers are available in government agencies and in other forms of public employment.

The study of business allows the student to consider various jobs, the work required, available rewards, necessary training, and the relative advantages and disadvantages of each. *Contemporary Business* includes sections describing jobs that can be found in each functional area of business. A separate appendix on career selection appears at the end of the text. This appendix discusses employment trends, sources of jobs, how to find a job, and preparing a resumé.

Self-employment

Some students will decide to work for themselves and establish their own businesses. But business concepts and principles are the same regardless of the size of the firm. Studying business can be an invaluable first step in setting up one's own business.

A self-employed person is someone actively and personally involved in business. A knowledge of successful business practices becomes even more crucial when one is risking one's own funds. The solution—study business!

Tackling the problems of society

Business puts you on the firing line for most of today's pressing societal problems. Resource conservation, pollution, minority hiring and affirmative action programs, consumerism, and industrial safety are problems encountered on a daily basis by the business person.

A business career is likely to put you in a position of responsibility earlier than most other occupations. Many experts believe that business careers are an excellent choice for activists who want to improve the society in which we live.

Better consumer decisions

Business decisions create the consumer decisions we all face. A certain stereo comes with three options for accessory equipment. An executive decides to pass on a recent union wage increase to the consumer by raising a product's price. These are typical business decisions that call for related decision making by consumers.

The study of business provides an appreciation of the background for many consumer decisions. Consumer advocates often point out that an informed consumer is a better consumer.

Business is relevant

Students often argue that some fields of study simply are not relevant to life in the late 1970's. Perhaps this is so! But few students believe that business is not relevant. Regardless of opinions about business, executive behavior, and the free enterprise system, *the study of business is the study of what is happening today!* Business is probably one of the most relevant and fascinating subjects the student will ever study.

HOW TO STUDY BUSINESS

Business can be studied through formal programs of instruction such as those offered at colleges or universities. These programs teach the basic concepts, methods, principles, and practices used in modern business. Formal study of business provides the framework for later experiences which together will build toward a well-rounded management education.

The study of business, or "business administration" as it is often called, has grown more formalized and systematic over the years. In the past, many managers achieved their positions on the basis of practical experience in a given area, rather than on formal study. But times have changed, and formal education in business has become a recognized early step in a business career.

Business leaders from earlier decades would be amazed to see the modern classrooms and instructional methods used by business students in the late 1970's. The study of business has become one of the most popular programs at most colleges and universities. Enrollments in business administration courses have continued to rise despite substantial declines in other educational programs. Projections show that more and more students want to enter this challenging career field.

Don't we have anyone *who took business administration?"*
The Study of Business Allows You To Become a More Effective
Manager

SOURCE: Reproduced by permission of Sidney Harris and *Management Review.*

Business programs are usually organized around various functional areas. Typically, courses are offered in such subjects as accounting, finance, management, personnel, marketing, sales, and data processing. Most business programs require students to take at least one course in each major area of study.

This book, and such courses, will give the student a broad overview of the field of business. The information acquired here will allow for a better selection of business courses in the future.

While students can learn the basics of business in a classroom setting, it is impossible to learn all that an executive needs to know in this manner. Observation, experience, and continued reading and study are necessary to develop a comprehensive business education. This is the informal part of the study of business.

Much can be learned by observing how a retail store is arranged, pausing to watch the cargo-loading operation at a nearby airport or dock, and by touring the assembly line of a local manufacturer. Parttime jobs and summer employment can show the practical side of concepts and principles learned in a classroom. Finally, a well-informed student of the U.S. business system is always seeking up-to-date information. The business world is constantly evolving with major changes occuring every hour. Regular reading of such publications as *The Wall Street Journal, Business Week,* and *Fortune* can be a valuable ingredient in a total business education.

A Diagram of Contemporary Business

It is helpful to visualize contemporary business as a system designed to satisfy the needs of society. Business continues to function only if it achieves consumer acceptance for its products. Firms that fail in this objective will soon disappear from the marketplace.

Figure 1-2 is a simplified diagram of contemporary business. This model shows that a business's objective is to make a profit by serving the needs of its markets. The manager has several variables to control in operating the firm. These variables, the **5 Ms,** are *manpower, materials, money, machinery, and management.*[4] The manager combines these elements into a proper mix to produce goods and services that satisfy markets.

There are four major markets for the products of industry. These are consumers, industry, government, and foreign markets. Some businesses serve all four market segments. Others serve only one or a few of these markets. In any case, the provision of satisfactory goods and services to the markets means that the firm will receive funds necessary to operate the business, pay its taxes, and, perhaps, earn a profit.

The diagram will be used throughout the text. As each part of the business organization is studied, it is useful to relate it to the model shown in Figure 1-2. This will clarify the complex but exciting world of business.

Figure 1-2
A Diagram of
Contemporary Business

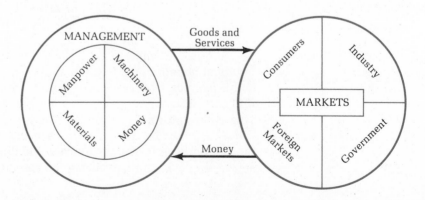

Summary

Business can be defined as all profit-directed economic and commercial activities that provide goods and services necessary to maintain a nation's standard of living. American businesses are part of a free enterprise system where success is determined by competition among firms. An entrepreneur is the risk-taker in this type of economic system. Profits are the rewards for a successful entrepreneur.

Certain basic rights are available to citizens living in a free enterprise economy:

Right to private property.

Legal and ethical right to any profits that might result from an enterprise.

Freedom of choice in purchases, employment, and investments.

The public retains the right to set ground rules for competitive activity.

Four factors of production provide the necessary inputs for the operation of free enterprise. These are land, labor, capital, and entrepreneurship. Each factor receives a payment such as rent, wages, interest, and profits.

Chapter 1 examined the four basic types of industries: perfect competition, monopolistic competition, oligopoly, and monopoly. The chapter also traces the development of the American economy from the Colonial period up to the 1970's.

Many Americans fail to realize that a large part of the world lives under an economic system other than capitalism. The economic features of socialism, communism, and mixed economies were described in this chapter.

Big business dominates many aspects of American industry. Our leading firms are among the world's leading firms. But big business has also led to the development of big labor and big government. As a result, economic size has become a crucial public issue.

Below are several reasons why the study of business is important:

1. It assists in career selection.
2. It gives opportunities for self-employment.
3. It tackles the problems of society.
4. It leads to better consumer decisions.
5. It is one of the most relevant studies in contemporary society.

The actual study of business often begins in a classroom and continues in a less formal manner as the person enters the world of business.

Chapter 1 concludes by presenting a simple diagram that shows how the "5 Ms" of business can be used to reach the four major markets: consumers, industry, government, and foreign markets.

Review questions

1. Identify the following terms:
   a. business
   b. profit
   c. free enterprise system
   d. competition
   e. entrepreneur
   f. "Invisible Hand"
   g. antitrust laws
   h. private property
   i. factors of production
   j. land
   k. labor
   l. capital
   m. perfect competition
   n. monopolistic competition
   o. oligopoly
   p. monopoly
   q. law of supply and demand
   r. Industrial Revolution
   s. production era
   t. marketing concept
   u. communism
   v. socialism
   w. mixed economies
   x. countervailing powers
   y. 5 Ms

2. Comment on the sentence: "All businesses must serve their customers in some way if they are to survive."

3. Explain the entrepreneur's role in the free enterprise system.

4. Outline the basic rights that exist in a free enterprise system.

5. What are the four factors of production?

6. The four basic types of industries are perfect competition, monopolistic competition, oligopoly, and monopoly. Match these types with the businesses listed below:
   a. New York's electrical utility company, Consolidated Edison
   b. J.C. Penney
   c. American Motors
   d. Harold Clawson's 260-acre farm in southern Iowa

7. Trace the historical development of the American economy.

8. Describe the three alternative economic systems discussed in this chapter.

9. List some specific reasons for studying business.

10. Explain the diagram of contemporary business that appears in this chapter.

Discussion questions and exercises

1. Evaluate the pro and con arguments for the controversial issue that appears in this chapter.

2. Make a list of all the "businesses" that serve students on your campus. Then prepare a brief evaluation of how effectively these businesses serve their customers.

3. Prepare a short report on a person who has influenced the development of the American business system.

4. Discuss the following question: "How can government help improve the free enterprise system?"
5. Set up a panel discussion of instructors and advanced students to explain the business curriculum at your school.

Case 1-1
The Growth of Black-owned Business Enterprises

A U.S. Census Bureau Survey reported a 19 percent increase in black-owned businesses in a recent three-year period. Significant gains were recorded in the fields of manufacturing and transportation, areas where there were relatively few black-owned enterprises. An example of one of these new black manufacturers is Archie Williams of Boston, who operates Freedom Electronics Engineering, Inc., and Freedom Die Casting, Inc. Williams' companies sell to customers like I.B.M., Honeywell, NASA, Ford, and General Motors. Combined revenues exceed $1 million annually. Nationally, however, blacks still own less than 2.5 percent of American business. Yet, the U.S. population is 11 percent black.

Questions

1. Why are blacks underrepresented in the ownership structure of American business?
2. What can be done to increase black-owned business enterprises?
3. What role can the study of business play in achieving our national goal of equal opportunity for all citizens?

Source: "Black-owned Business Enterprises Increase," *Tulsa World* (December 12, 1974); "A Model of Black Success in Business," *Business Week* (April 13, 1974), p. 100.

Case 1-2
Business Failures

The Business Failure Record, published by Dun & Bradstreet, surveyed the collapse of 9,345 American businesses in 1973. The leading causes of these business failures were:

incompetence	41 percent
lack of balance in the management team (not well rounded in production, selling, finance, and purchasing)	21.6 percent
lack of experience in a particular field	16.4 percent
general lack of managerial experience	14.1 percent

California led the nation in business failures with 81 bankruptcies per 10,000 firms. It was followed by Oregon, New York, Michigan, the District of Columbia, and New Jersey.

Questions

1. Can most bankruptcies be prevented? If so, by whom?
2. What is Dun & Bradstreet?
3. In your opinion, what are the implications of the Dun & Bradstreet study?
4. Can cases of business failure be useful in the study of business? If so, how?

Source: "Businesses Fail Due to Incompetence, Study Shows," *Advertising Age* (December 2, 1974), p. 73.

2

Social Responsibility and Business

"Mere money making has never been my goal."
—John D. Rockefeller

"When I first heard the slogan, I was just mortified. It's degrading to us."

—Claudia Lampe, stewardess
representative of the Air Line
Pilots Association, upon hearing
Continental Airlines' advertising
slogan, "We really move our tails for
you."

What Chapter 2 Is All About

1. This chapter points out that contemporary business faces a dynamic societal environment that is often difficult to predict.
2. You will learn that the concept of social responsibility has become accepted business policy, but that actual use has lagged in some areas. As a result, there is a real need to develop an effective and efficient method of evaluating a firm's social performance.
3. You will acquire a grasp of the major social issues confronting business: (a) people-oriented management, (b) ecology and environmental protection, (c) consumerism, and (d) the energy crisis and national resource utilization.
4. Chapter 2 will also familiarize you with the ethical questions facing management in its relations with consumers, with other personnel in the company, business associates, and investors and the financial community.
5. After reading this chapter, you should understand these items:

social responsibility   pollution
social issues   consumerism
ethical issues   energy crisis
ecology   cooling-off laws
planned obsolescence

Henry John Heinz

At eight years of age Henry John Heinz was peddling the produce raised in his family's garden in Pittsburgh. Then, as a young man, he established a small food products packing business in Sharpsburg, Pennsylvania. He had already graduated from a business college and was following a traditional business career. In 1872 he moved back to Pittsburgh and did business as Heinz, Noble & Company. Four years later Heinz, his brother, and his cousin organized F. & J. Heinz, which was expanded twelve years later to become H.J. Heinz Company. After the turn of the century the Heinz business was reorganized as a corporation.

What made Heinz an outstanding and unique kind of businessman?

To understand Heinz' contribution it is necessary to look at conditions in the second half of the nineteenth century. By the beginning of the 1870's railroad empires were booming in a post-Civil War era of prosperity. When the expansion ended and the banks failed, railroaders were struck by labor. It was in the summer of 1877, when Heinz was thirty-two years old, that forty people were killed in the Pittsburgh railroad riots and federal troops were called in to keep order.

Heinz was deeply impressed, enough so that he wanted to—and did-establish a community of workers who could feel rewarded and happy in their jobs. At a time when sweatshops, child labor, and industrial accidents were commonplace, Heinz workers had free medical care, a library, classes in cooking and sewing, private lockers in which to keep their belongings, the use of a gym, and free entertainment. Heinz pioneered in creating decent working conditions for his staff. And to the benefit of all people, he was in the forefront of the pure food movement in the United States.

Social responsibility is an important part of modern business. The concept of **social responsibility** *means that management considers social effects, as well as economic effects, in its decisions.* This belief affects all businesses regardless of size, location, or industry. For the NIK-O-LOK Company of Indianapolis, it was business as usual until CEPTIA arrived on the scene. Now NIK-O-LOK is in a lengthy battle with CEPTIA over what the role of social responsibility should be in the pay toilet business.

CEPTIA Challenges the Pay Toilet Industry

The Committee to End Pay Toilets in America (CEPTIA) has a problem. The mere mention of its name makes people snicker. But the committee is actually a serious public action group according to Michael Gessel of Philadelphia, its President. While their purpose may be sincere, the group uses humor to its best advantage. Its official publication, for instance, is entitled "Free Toilet Paper" and features the committee's symbol—a clenched fist rising out of a toilet bowl. CEPTIA, with lifetime dues of a quarter, reports membership of over 1,200 people located in 40 states. The committee regards pay toilets as both inhumane and discriminatory—particularly toward women.

The committee's campaign to convince the public that pay toilets are a socially irresponsible enterprise has achieved several successes. Chicago passed an ordinance banning them in public places such as hotels, restaurants, and stores. The pay locks have also been banned on the Pennsylvania Turnpike, and bills to prohibit them have been introduced in the Massachusetts and Florida legislatures. And California Assembly-woman March Fong smashed a commode on the steps of the state capital to call attention to the issue.

CEPTIA's efforts point out that public action campaigns often encounter well-entrenched profitable business practices. One large firm reports a $50 per month gross from each lock. This can amount to over $30 million annually for the estimated 50,000 restroom stalls in the country. Some "good" locations average $200 per month.

All this is bad news to the people who make and operate pay locks. Indianapolis-based NIK-O-LOK Company, a leading maker of pay toilets, has gone to court in Chicago to challenge the constitutionality of the ordinance there. "Anytime anybody tries to put you out of business, you're worried," says a NIK-O-LOK spokesman.

The future of the pay toilet issue is uncertain. But, in the meantime CEPTIA will probably continue to put forth its message in a manner similar to a recent feature in their official publication. "The Toilet Zone"—a take off on television's "Twilight Zone"—was based on Albert Cury, a mythical pay lock manufacturer whose "creations were the terror of restrooms all across the nation." When Mr. Cury dies, he is condemned to rush panic-stricken through the after-life, lacking the dime that would open one of his own locks. "Until the end of time," the story ends, "Albert Cury could not get in."

Source: Adapted from Bryon C. Calme. "Brother, Can You Spare a Dime? Group Assails Pay Toilets," *The Wall Street Journal* (April 23, 1973), pp. 1, 16. Reprinted with permission of *The Wall Street Journal*, © Dow Jones & Company, Inc. 1973. All rights reserved.

Social Responsibility Questions Facing Business

Contemporary business faces an environment that is often difficult to predict. Consider the now landmark case of Reserve Mining Company.[1] The Silver Bay, Minnesota, plant was opened in 1955 to provide its owners, ARMCO Steel Corporation and Republic Steel Corporation, with a supply of iron ore pellets for their blast furnaces. Before the original operating license was granted to Reserve in 1947 several environmental hearings were held. Both state and federal authorities approved of Reserve's plan to dispose of waste rock in Lake Superior. When the plant opened, several of Reserve's competitors sent their managers through Silver Bay to view its modern dust controls. Reserve Mining also built Silver Bay as a model community. It had a 1974 population of 3,200 (80 percent of whom were dependent upon Reserve for their livelihood).

Silver Bay's tranquility was suddenly disrupted twenty-seven years later when, in April 1974, U.S. District Judge Miles Lord ordered the plant closed as a health hazard. Minnesota and federal authorities had charged that Reserve was polluting Lake Superior with its waste rock and the air from dust emissions. There were fears that the waste rock and dust contained asbestoslike particles that might cause cancer. This had to be balanced against the possible loss of 3,000 jobs and a $350 million capital investment. The 8th U.S. Circuit Court of Appeals reviewed the case. It ruled that Reserve be given "reasonable time" to set up a land disposal for the waste rock, but the air pollution had to end immediately. The U.S. Supreme Court also refused to close Reserve.

The Reserve Mining Company case has now become a classic example of how societal influences can affect business behavior. *The Wall Street Journal* summarized the case this way:

By any yardstick, it is a milestone in the changing environment in which U.S. industry operates these days—a classic illustration of how shifting public opinion, changing laws and new scientific discoveries can make a plant that is perfectly acceptable today an outlawed despoiler of the environment and a threat to public health only a few years down the road.[2]

Social responsibility has become a popular word in today's business vocabulary. Society is calling on private enterprise to be more socially conscious and adopt a higher level of management ethics. Production managers are asked to make assembly-line jobs more meaningful. Personnel officers have been called upon to provide employees with access to personnel files. Retail executives are questioned about their store policies in ghetto areas. And the credit department has to answer charges concerning the invasion of personal privacy.

All organizational levels must deal with these kinds of vital questions. Middle management, production managers, district sales managers, and staff personnel must all be involved in a total company-wide effort to raise the firm's level of business ethics and corporate responsibility.

Most companies have adopted social responsibility as the proper business philosophy. It has become standard corporate policy. But its acceptance at this level does not mean that it has always been put into practice. The divergence between policy and actual practice is a common one in modern business. It can best be overcome by assuring that every policy adopted also contains a set of procedures for putting it into practice.

It is essential for the business person to realize that public outcry for increased social responsibility will not disappear. When industry fails to respond to the challenge posed by society, the public will is typically enforced through other means, namely, the government. Some children's toys have been banned because of their dangerous features. And government now regulates the type of information that may be requested in job applications.

Intelligent managers realize the need for self-regulation by industry. It has become a prerequisite to corporate survival!

How Can We Evaluate Social Performance?

While critics demand higher levels of social responsibility for business, management is faced with the dual problems of *implementation* and *evaluation*. The implementation of socially oriented objectives requires a careful analysis to determine whether the benefits deriving from the action exceed the cost of taking the action. This type of study should be done from the viewpoints of both society and the firm.

Business also faces the question of how to evaluate a firm's social performance. Critics readily point out that the free enterprise system is oriented toward meeting the *quantities* of life, not the quality of life. In other words, modern society tends to confuse new houses, automobiles, dishwashers, color television, and the like with the true "quality of life."

The public even finds it difficult to assess correctly some qualities of life. Corporate profitability is an example. An Opinion Research Corporation survey found that the average person believed that after-tax corporate profits were near 28 percent of sales, while in reality profits were about 4 percent for the 1,000 largest American industrial firms.[3]

Traditional methods of evaluating social performance were usually based on the firm's contribution to national output and the provision of employment opportunities. Items such as weekly wage

SOURCE: "Doonesbury." Copyright, 1975, G. B. Trudeau/distributed by Universal Press Syndicate.

payments were often used as crude measures of social performance. However, this ignores the other areas of business responsibility—industrial safety, assembly-line drudgery, product safety, minority and female hiring, and pollution. Industry is currently unable to answer its critics because it lacks adequate measures of social performance.

Some companies are now developing means of assessing their own performances. No generally accepted format has emerged, but the work is encouraging. Environmental groups, churches, and public interest groups have also attempted to create measures of corporate performance. A *Happiness Index* was developed by a Japanese bank. It included thirty-three factors—such as income, crime, paved roads, parks, and suicide rates. Americans will be happy to know that the Index reported the United States to be 2.53 times happier than Japan.[4]

Early attempts at measuring social responsibility are bound to be subject to many problems and failures. But it is important that this development continue and accelerate in the future. Meaningful social goals are retarded by the lack of an adequate evaluation system for corporate social performance.

A Classification of Social Issues

Both societal and ethical issues are closely related and similar in meaning and impact. Generally, however, social issues are somewhat *broader* in that they are usually directed to all areas of business enterprise. By contrast, it is possible to isolate *specific* ethical issues for various segments of a company. Social issues will be considered here, while business ethics will be dealt with in the section that follows.

There are four major groups of social issues that confront business near the end of the 1970's:

1. people-oriented management
2. ecology and environmental protection
3. consumerism
4. the energy crisis and natural resource utilization.

Nearly all specific societal questions can be put under one of these general topics. Some issues are interrelated. The energy crisis led to concern over the use of petroleum resources, but it also raised important consumerism and ecological issues.

PEOPLE-ORIENTED MANAGEMENT There is a growing concern that business should adopt a more people-oriented concept of management. Many observers fear that management has neglected people in several ways. Women and members of minority groups have been systematically excluded from many positions at both the employee and managerial levels.

The special needs of some consumers have been neglected for too long. The physically handicapped find that they must overcome managerial barriers in order to achieve occupational dignity. Prisoners on parole who have "paid their debt to society" need jobs that will keep them from returning to criminal activity. "Thirty and out" became the battle cry of UAW workers as they sought to limit their number of working years. Coal miners have called for programs to combat "black lung," an occupational disease of their industry.

All of these situations reflect dissatisfaction on the part of people involved in or affected by business organizations. Business, it is argued, has too long been concerned with short-run profitability, machinery, evaluation, and control of corporate personnel, instead of the people involved. Many aspects of concern for social responsibility are aimed at achieving a new concept of management.

People are more productive when they have a sense of participation in the decisions affecting them. Human resource development has become a major organizational objective for many businesses. West German firms have labor representation on management boards. Swedish automobile manufacturers have pioneered the concept of job enrichment for assembly-line workers. American companies have substantially upgraded their equal employment and affirmative action hiring programs.

People-oriented management requires a careful balance between productivity and profitability objectives on the one hand and employee desires on the other. Is the four-day week (four work days of ten hours each) as productive as the traditional five-day, forty-hour week? This is the type of question that must be answered by management. Several human relations questions will be discussed in detail later in this book.

ECOLOGY AND ENVIRONMENTAL PROTECTION

Reserve Mining's story shows what a vital issue ecology and environmental protection can be in modern business. **Ecology,** *the relationship between people and their environment,* is an important managerial consideration from the legal viewpoint as well as from the viewpoint of social responsibility.

Management's original ecology question was **planned obsolescence,** *where products are made less long-lasting than they might otherwise be.* In the automobile industry annual model changes make the previous model obsolete—at least from a styling viewpoint. Product obsolescence does not have an easy solution. One must balance the cost of producing goods that will soon be obsolete with the need to maintain employment. Durability is also a function of production costs, and for many goods it is possible to reach a point where increased durability has priced the product beyond the means of the average buyer.

"You mean that's the _only_ way we can meet the Federal Exhaust Emission Standards?"

SOURCE: *The Wall Street Journal*, January 23, 1974. Reprinted with permission of *The Wall Street Journal*.

Pollution has become the major ecology question of the 1970's. It refers to the *tainting or destroying of a natural environment.* We are constantly being reminded of the dangers of water and air pollution. Automobiles now have elaborate emission-control devices. Smoke-belching factories have been fined and even closed by environmental protection authorities. Municipal water and sewer treatment systems have been upgraded.

Some pollution control programs have been extremely successful. British authorities have reported that fish have even returned to the once polluted Thames River, and an occasional environmental engineer has suggested there might be some hope for the Great Lakes.

Society faces two major questions about pollution. One is whether the benefits of cleaning up a form of pollution are worth the cost involved. A second question is whether consumers are willing to pay now for a future ecological benefit. The public recognizes most pollution problems, but their willingness to pay for corrections is sometimes doubtful. Gulf Oil had to withdraw unleaded gasoline when it first appeared because of low sales.

The advent of disposable packaging has created mountains of plastic containers, throwaway bottles, tin cans, and the like. One study found that 43 percent of roadside litter was a form of disposable packaging.[5] This situation has led to bans on nonreturnable bottles and other regulations on disposable packaging. These are stopgap measures until business (or government) can develop an effective system for recycling used materials. In most cases business possesses the technological know-how required, but lacks an ade-

Air Pollution and the Cost of Doing Business

Just how much will industry and individuals be willing to pay to prevent air pollution? There have been hidden costs as a result of polluted air since the rise of manufacturing in the Industrial Revolution, and these have increased as manufacturing grew in scope and sophistication. Such costs include crop loss and the health of the American people. Perhaps now values are changing, and individuals will be more willing to pay the increased price that prevention of air pollution will require. And that cost will be huge, beginning with the manufacturing of pollution control devices and including manufacturing techniques, maintenance of machinery to safeguard against pollution, and the interest paid on developing new technologies.

High prices, unemployment, and consideration for future generations are just some of the subjects that enter into any discussion of pollution of the environment. How much pollution is to be prevented and how prevention is going to be paid for are central questions.

Part of the problem is the lack of solid research and the confusion over what degree of pollution is really unacceptable. If there is to be no air pollution at all, the costs will be very different than if, for example, 5 percent of air pollution is considered to be acceptable.

Air pollution affects the quality of life and living. Crops and other vegetation can be killed by polluted air; stone buildings can be eroded; and people seem to be more susceptible to lung cancer, emphysema, and heart disease in a polluted environment.

Air pollution is mainly a problem of such industries as automobile manufacturers; electric utilities using high-sulphur content coal; and oil refineries. The problem is complicated by the fact that cleaning up the air over one city or town offers no real solution to the problem. The air over the entire United States, even of the world, must be cleaned up in order to prevent air pollution in any area.

The Clean Air Act of 1970 provides for governmental regulation of such industries as paper and steel mills, the automobile industry, and electrical utilities. But this is not a simple answer. If low-sulphur coal is to be used in a power plant, for example, it must be transported from an area like the Northwest, where the coal is stripmined. Strip mining is itself considered to be a wasteful process, which complicates the fuel supply system when pollution is an important concern. The costs involved in shipping low-sulphur coal causes a rise in the cost of electricity, which the consumer eventually pays. Similarly, pollution control devices and more expensive industrial processes lead to higher manufacturing costs and higher prices for the consumer.

quate method of getting the used items from the consumer back to the manufacturer. Some have proposed that a tax be imposed on all sales to pay for recycling. Others think business should absorb the cost of recycling.

CONSUMERISM   Consumerism is another pressing issue facing business. Business-persons often see the consumer as unpredictable, emotional, and sometimes irrational. Some consumer demands are unusual and unexpected. For example, the Royal National Institute for the Blind recently reported a demand by blind British men for "girlie" magazines printed in Braille.[6] But most of the time consumer demands are not so unusual. *Consumers are becoming more activist and willing to take action against what they see as abuses in the business system.* This trend is known as the **consumerism** movement.

Ralph Nader probably did most to attract public attention to consumer complaints. Nader's book, *Unsafe at Any Speed,* was one of many consumer criticisms leveled against American industry. Some were justified; others were not.

Since the emergence of consumerism in the 1960's various consumer groups have sprung up throughout the country. Some have concentrated on an isolated problem, such as excessive prices by a local service industry, while others are more broadly based. The net effect has been the passage of consumer protection laws covering everything from unethical sales practices to the licensing of repairpeople in some states. There is little doubt that there will be further consumer protection laws passed in the years ahead.

Business would be well advised to heed the warnings of the consumerism movement. Many companies have taken steps to assure that consumer complaints are given a full hearing. The following list of affirmative steps has been suggested:[7]

1. Provide for a high-level, action-oriented contact point within the organization to which consumers can address their grievances.
2. Create advertising strategies that are in line with the consumer's reality.
3. Hold executive-consumer panel discussions on a periodic basis.
4. Reduce after-sale consumer frustration in product servicing.
5. Establish a separate corporate department for consumer issues.

An excellent description of consumer rights was put forth by President John F. Kennedy in 1962 when he stated:

1. The consumer has the right to safety.
2. The consumer has the right to be informed.
3. The consumer has the right to choose.
4. The consumer has the right to be heard.[8]

Much of the post-1962 consumer legislation has been based

on these rights. They are an excellent set of guidelines for business to use in assessing various consumer demands.

THE ENERGY
CRISIS AND
NATIONAL
RESOURCE
UTILIZATION

The energy crisis is also a pressing societal issue. Everyone has had to deal with the inconveniences and annoyances of declining supplies of energy. The government set up a fuel oil allocation plan that forced homeowners to dial thermostats down to 68° from the customary 74°. Office buildings have conserved energy by turning off heat on weekends and reducing lighting. States were forced to reduce their maximum highway speeds to 55 m.p.h. Many firms and public buildings have removed every other light bulb in fixtures in an effort to conserve electricity (and other energy forms required to run electric generators). Oregon led the way in adopting a statewide gasoline rationing plan, while contingency plans for a nationwide, World War II style of gasoline rationing was developed at the federal level.

The energy crisis is a worldwide problem. Holland banned Sunday driving. Great Britain adopted a three-day work week for a while. New Zealand instituted a 50 m.p.h. auto speed limit. Airline schedules were reduced in most parts of the world, including the United States. Energy and natural resource conservation became a major national goal. A Canadian division of Nashua Corporation tried to head off an appeal to Canadian nationalism by labeling its promotional material:

"Printed in U.S.A. to conserve Canadian raw material and energy"[9]

Considerable public debate was devoted to establishing suitable energy policies for future decades. Many of these debates are still unresolved, In some cases, national energy needs clashed with ecological and environmental objectives. One such situation was the Alaskan oil pipeline question, where the nation's gasoline needs had to be balanced against the preservation of the natural environment of our fiftieth state. Figure 2-1 shows the Trans-Alaska Pipeline. Another debate concerned the role that government should play in developing natural resource policies. Congressional legislation was introduced setting up a government corporation to develop petroleum resources on public lands and water. But contrary viewpoints were also offered. Randall Meyer, President of Exxon Company, U.S.A., speaking at Onondago Community College in Syracuse, New York, said:

Perhaps the best way I can illustrate the potential difference between an oil company as seen by private enterprise and as seen by government is to take a look at the government's record in business. Twenty years ago, a penny would move a gallon of oil from Texas to New York by tanker, and a penny would move a postcard from Texas to New York via the U.S.

Figure 2-1 The Trans-Alaska Pipeline

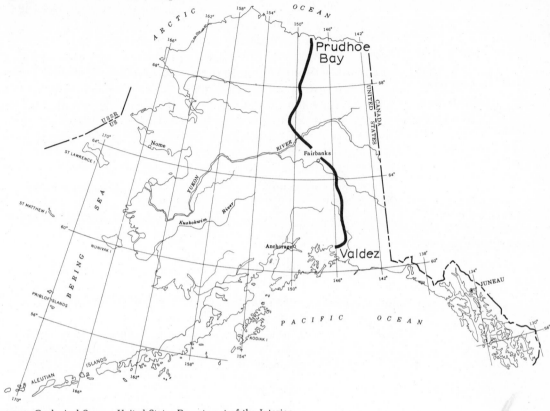

SOURCE: Geological Survey, United States Department of the Interior.
Reproduced with permission.

mails. Today, private enterprise is still moving a gallon of oil from Texas to New York for about a penny a gallon; but the government's postcard will cost you eight cents. I don't think we have any reason to believe the government could run the oil business any better that it ran the old U.S. Post Office.

Shortages have begun to develop in other crucial areas. A paper shortage prompted a "toilet paper scare." Much to the disappointment of thousands of college students a "textbook shortage" never materialized. But some supermarkets gave up double-bagging. The Grand Union supermarket chain offered five trading stamps (or 1¢) for each bag returned or reused.[10]

Hundreds of other products—industrial and consumer—were and still are in short supply. This has required management at all levels to develop effective responses to such problems. Executives, for example, have been forced to set up allocation programs for some products in short supply. This has sometimes meant giving the customer only part of what he or she ordered.

While resource conservation may just now be becoming a part of contemporary life, it is significant to observe that *energy crises* have existed before. Shortages of human and animal muscle power in fourth-century Rome led to the extensive development of water power. Later, in the seventeenth century, firewood shortages brought about the development of coal mining.[11] People have always adapted to depleted energy sources by harnessing new forms of energy. The current crisis has brought a wave of short-term policies and practices to meet the reduced availability of existing energy sources. Over the long run, alternative sources of energy must be discovered (or rediscovered) and developed.

Business Ethics

Management is also required to deal with specific ethical questions that arise in any work environment. There is sometimes a conflict between an ideal decision and one that is practical under given conditions. But it is important that the company engage in some sort of an evaluation of the ethical responsibilities of a decision. Business ethics is becoming increasingly important as society's view of ethical behavior continues to evolve in a post-Watergate era.

The Village Voice Forces Its Readers to Make Moral Decisions

The *Village Voice* puts readers "in the position of making a moral as well as a value judgment" in choosing between reduced or regular rates for subscription renewals. The weekly New York newspaper says it needs the money from regular rates, but concedes there's a case for paying less: "You're only taking advantage of somebody who's asking to be taken advantage of." Results so far: About 80% of renewers opt for reduced rates.

Source: *The Wall Street Journal* (May 2, 1974), p. 1. Reprinted with permission of *The Wall Street Journal*, © Dow Jones & Company, 1974. All rights reserved.

An ethical conflict occurred when a *Harvard Business Review* study put businesspersons in a set of hypothetical situations where some actions would normally be right, others wrong. Half of the sample were asked: "What would you do?"; while the others were asked: "What would the average businessperson do?" The answers to the second question indicated more immoral behavior than responses to the first question. Business people apparently think their peer groups are less moral than they are themselves.[12]

Ethical Questions Facing Business

There are numerous ethical questions that face the modern executive every day. Some of the more frequently encountered ones are discussed in the sections that follow.

RELATIONS WITH CUSTOMERS The possibility of ethical abuses are quite evident in relations with customers. A multitude of package sizes makes price comparison difficult for the consumer. High pressure sales tactics have led to **cooling off laws,** *where a consumer can cancel a sales contract within a certain period of time.* What degree of advertising to children should be acceptable?

Promotional strategy is the basis of most ethical questions involved in relations with consumers. The personal sales process has always been subject to some form of ethical criticism. But in recent years advertising has been subjected to close attention because of its vast reach.

Pricing is an area that has an immediate, direct effect on the consumer. It is also the most regulated aspect of the firm's relations with consumers. Chapter 23 describes many of the laws affecting pricing strategy.

RELATIONS WITH OTHER PERSONNEL IN THE COMPANY These may be some of the most difficult ethical questions to resolve since the eventual decision will affect the person's work environment for years to come. Managers are required to make hiring, promotion, transfer, compensation, and dismissal decisions. Consider the ethical dilemma of a manager forced to make a promotion decision between a rising young executive with potential for further development and a long-service employee nearing retirement who has performed faithfully, if not sensationally, over the years. Promotion of the older person may cause the younger executive to jump to a competitor. Selection of the younger person may be regarded as breaking faith with senior people in the organization. There are complex and vital ethical questions involved in such decisions.

Ethical questions also arise in a manager's relationship with other personnel in the organization. A marketing research director knows that the sales manager needs a certain item of competitive information immediately, but considers the possibility of waiting to present it directly to the marketing vice-president who is returning from overseas next week. The research director reasons that the week's delay will keep the sales manager from claiming credit for the information and possibly misinterpreting its meaning. While most ethical evaluations would disagree with the marketing research director, it is important to point out that this type of personal conflict arises every day in business.

RELATIONS WITH BUSINESS ASSOCIATES

One's relations with business associates is another area of possible ethical conflict. Which conversations violate reasonable business ethics? Or, an executive may ask: "Am I Harold's friend because I like him as a person or because he is sometimes a good source of competitive information?" Many interpersonal relationships in business include important ethical considerations.

Another important question is: "When does a gift and/or business entertainment become a bribe?" Most firms have clear policies prohibiting the outright payment of bribes to purchasing directors, government officials, or a competitor's employees. On some occasions these restrictions have not been effective in stopping ethical abuses, but most of the time they work. However, there is often a very fine line between business gifts and a bribe. Some organizations have prohibited their employees from either giving or receiving any business gift; others have set specified limits on the value of the gifts given to their employees. One guide is the Internal Revenue Service regulation which sets a twenty-five dollar annual limit per recipient. Gifts exceeding twenty-five dollars are not tax deductible.

RELATIONS WITH INVESTORS AND THE FINANCIAL COMMUNITY

Throughout history there have been financial scandals in nearly every era. The financial health of firms has been misrepresented; there have been numerous land swindles; savers have lost millions of dollars due to embezzlement; and nonexistent assets have been reported to the financial community.

Each of these financial abuses has typically been dealt with by government, so that we now have a comprehensive, well-developed set of laws regulating financial affairs. These legal requirements are outlined later in this text. But business management has also moved to a higher level of ethical behavior. Few firms would now permit financial misconduct by their personnel. Professional organizations and societies, such as the Certified Public Accountants, have also worked to improve financial ethics.

Does Student Cheating Lead to Business Cheating?

Many college students suspect that some of their fellow students have cheated on examinations, quizzes, or assignments. There are various degrees and types of cheating, but most of us will agree that all cheating is unethical.

QUESTIONS

1. Suppose a person has cheated in some classwork at your college. Would you hire that person if you were an employer?
2. Does student cheating lead to continued cheating when one enters the business world?

Levels of Social Involvement by Business

The level of social involvement varies from firm to firm. Some firms have just recognized their social responsibilities; others have reached significantly higher levels of social involvement. Five concrete levels of social involvement can be identified:[13]

1. *Recognition that the situation exists.* Some executives do not even recognize that they have certain social responsibilities.
2. *Willingness to assign a social responsibility to an organizational unit.* For example, the Public Affairs Department might be told to check that the firm is meeting specified social responsibilities.
3. *Willingness to act if no corporate resources are involved.* Many managers praise societal objectives until it comes down to a cash outlay; then they view these goals less favorably.
4. *Willingness to make direct corporate commitments.* A higher level of social involvement because it requires financial outlay.
5. *Willingness to restructure corporate decisions, policies, and actions.* The highest stage of development, since it means that the firm is committed to socially responsible decisions.

Future business development may very well depend upon how fast industry moves to higher levels of social involvement. This area should receive managerial priority in the decade ahead.

Summary

Contemporary business faces a dynamic societal environment that is often difficult to predict. Social responsibility has become accepted business policy, but its actual implementation has often lagged. As a result, there is a real need to develop an effective method of evaluating a firm's social performance.

Societal and ethical issues are closely related and similar in meaning and impact. Generally, however, social issues are somewhat broader in that they are usually directed to all areas of business enterprises. By contrast, it is possible to isolate specific ethical issues for various segments of a company.

There are four major groups of social issues confronting business today:

1. people-oriented management
2. ecology and environmental protection
3. consumerism
4. the energy crisis and natural resource utilization.

Ethical questions face management in its relations with consumers, other personnel in the company, business associates, and investors and the financial community.

These are five definite levels of social involvement:

1. recognition that the situation exists
2. willingness to assign social responsibility to an organizational unit
3. willingness to act if no corporate resources are involved
4. willingness to make direct corporate commitments
5. willingness to restructure corporate decisions, policies, and actions.

Review questions

1. Identify the following terms:
   a. social responsibility
   b. social issues
   c. ethical issues
   d. ecology
   e. planned obsolescence
   f. pollution
   g. consumerism
   h. energy crisis
   i. cooling off laws
2. Relate the goals of CEPTIA to the points raised in Chapter 2.
3. Outline what you see as the moral of the Reserve Mining Company story.
4. Discuss the need for social performance measures in business.
5. Outline the four major groups of social issues facing business.
6. What were the basic consumer rights suggested by President Kennedy in 1962?
7. Identify the various ethical questions facing business.
8. How would you answer the questions in the chapter about student cheating?
9. Describe the various levels of social involvement by business.
10. List some reasons why you think social responsibility has become so important in business today.

Discussion questions and exercises

1. Evaluate the pro and con arguments to the controversial issue that appears in this chapter.
2. Describe the major social and ethical issues facing:
   a. automobile manufacturers
   b. real estate developers
   c. detergent manufacturers
   d. drug firms selling birth control products
   e. corporate attorneys.
3. Would H.J. Heinz be considered a socially responsible executive in modern business?
4. Identify two or three social issues facing business in your local area. How have local firms responded to these issues? How have local government agencies and officials responded to these matters?

5. Prepare a two-page paper on what you think is the most important social issue confronting business today.

Case 2-1
"Grass," Profits, and Social Responsibility

A special news flash . . . The President has just signed a bill legalizing the possession and use of marijuana. The bill—known as the Federal Marijuana Control Act—sets up a national board to oversee the sale of pot through licensed dealers. The new board will set strict price controls and ban the sales of marijuana by anyone other than licensed dealers. The manufacture and distribution of pot is expected to be handled by the nation's large tobacco firms.

This news flash has never been broadcast, and many doubt that any action of this nature will ever take place. But it is interesting to consider pot in a business context. The Justice Department estimates that marijuana and hashish sales amount to $1.4 billion annually. A presidential commission reported that one out of every six Americans has tried "grass." At current prices, the retailer's (street dealer's) profit margin is about 85–120 percent.[*]

Many groups have pushed for the decriminalization of marijuana whereby private use would be permitted, but growth, distribution, and sales would continue to be illegal. Decriminalization of pot was recommended by the National Commission on Marijuana and Drug Abuse. A Washington-based lobby, the National Organization for the Reform of Marijuana Law (NORML), is now trying to get the Commission's report implemented. A California group, the California Marijuana Initiative, got the decriminalization issue on the November 1972 state ballot. The initiative failed by a 2-1 margin.[†]

Questions
1. Describe the social issues raised in the case.
2. Should business attempt to influence legislation concerning marijuana?
3. Should cigarette manufacturers and other firms develop business plans in case marijuana is legalized in the future?
4. Who should determine whether a product is socially desirable?

[*]Dan Lewandowski. "A Secret Keynote Address," *M.B.A.* (January 1974), pp. 57–58, 60.
[†]Patrick Anderson. "The Pot Lobby," *The New York Times Magazine* (January 21, 1973), pp. 8–9, 65, 70, 72, 86.

Case 2-2

Business and the Arts

The Business Committee for the Arts reported that in 1973 industry gave $144 million to the arts up from $110 million given in 1970, the last time such a study was completed. Museums and symphony orchestras received the largest share, while film-makers and individual artists received the least. Only 3 percent of the 1,000 firms surveyed were large corporations, yet this group gave 42 percent of the total business support for the arts.

Questions

1. Does business have a responsibility to support the arts?
2. Who should provide the financial support needed by the arts?
3. Why do you think large corporations provided such a high share of the total business contribution to the arts?

Source: "The Arts Got $144 Million from U.S. Business in '73," *The Wall Street Journal* (September 24, 1974), p. 8.

3

Forms of Business Ownership

"Starting this business has been my dream. If I got discouraged easily, I'd never have come this far."

—Harry Marcowitz, President
of American Hydraulic
Paper Cutter, Inc.

What Chapter 3 Is All About

1. This chapter will explain the three basic forms of business ownership and the advantages and disadvantages of each.
2. You will understand how a corporation is organized and operated.
3. You will learn the difference between private ownership, public ownership, and cooperatives.
4. After reading this chapter, you will understand these terms:

sole proprietorship	open corporation
partnership	closed corporation
general partnership	preferred stock
limited partnership	common stock
joint venture	proxy
corporation	cumulative voting
dividend	board of directors
Subchapter S corporation	outside director
domestic corporation	subsidiary
foreign corporation	merger
alien corporation	public ownership
stockholders	cooperative

William Procter

James Gamble

Early in the 1800's debt, civil unrest, and depression forced a host of European immigrants to see the United States as "the land of opportunity." For some, the promise never paid off; for others—like the Procters and the Gemmels—the gamble paid off handsomely.

William Procter's family had come from Herefordshire, England, where his father was a farmer. Young William was apprenticed to a general storekeeper in his home county, and it was there he learned to make candles. Later he moved to Wolverhampton and worked in a dry goods store, before opening his own woolen shop in London. Fire and theft left him in debt and despair; and the United States beckoned. After six weeks on the ocean and six more weeks on a stagecoach and a river boat, the Procters landed and settled in Cincinnati.

James Gamble's family had been named Gemmel until, as fugitives from religious persecution in Scotland, they had fled to Ireland and changed their name. The Gambles also sailed from Europe, traveled by wagon and flatboat and, after almost twelve weeks, landed in Cincinnati. Two years later, in 1821, James Gamble was learning how to make soap. When he met William Procter (whose second wife was Mrs. Gamble's sister), James Gamble was in business for himself.

William Procter had been making, selling, and delivering candles—previously imported to Cincinnati all the way from Philadelphia. In 1837 the father-in-law of both Mr. Procter and Mr. Gamble suggested they form a candle and soap manufacturing partnership. Today the company is known throughout the world as Procter & Gamble. They still make soap, but their product line has been expanded many times over.

Harry Marcowitz satisfied his lifetime dream by founding the firm, American Hydraulic Paper Cutter, Inc., of Elk Grove, Illinois, in April 1974. Marcowitz does not fit the traditional stereotype of a corporation president, as he physically assembles a 6,000-pound industrial paper cutter. Marcowitz and his machinist, Sigmund "Ziggy" Janiszewski, are American Hydraulic Paper Cutter's entire work force. The firm is typical of thousands of American businesses started every year. Marcowitz has worked in a variety of jobs from baby photographer to life insurance salesman. But let's examine how he became president of American Hydraulic Paper Cutter, Inc.

Marcowitz once sold and serviced paper cutters for a now defunct German company. He patterned the machine he constructs after those produced by the German firm. David Kayner, the attorney who handled the legal aspects of setting up American Hydraulic Paper Cutter, donated his services and invested $1,000 in the new enterprise. Other investors include a relative, Ziggy Janiszewski, and Marcowitz's accountant. President Marcowitz has also continued to service the German machines on a parttime basis, and has put nearly all of his earnings back into his infant company.[1]

The situation just outlined is common in the American business system. New companies must decide the form of business ownership which best meets their needs. There are three basic forms of private ownership: *sole proprietorship, partnership,* and *corporation.* Harry Marcowitz chose the corporate form. No one can claim definitely that deciding on one form of ownership is correct or a mistake. Others in the same position, or with slightly different circumstances, may choose another form of business ownership. Selection of a legal form of business organization is a complex and extremely critical decision for any new enterprise.

Forms of Private Ownership

Each of the three forms of private ownership—sole proprietorship, partnership, and corporation—has its own unique advantages and disadvantages. A summary of these features appears in Table 3-2.

Sole Proprietorship

Sole proprietorship was the original form of business ownership. It is also the simplest, since there is no legal distinction between the sole proprietor as an individual and as a business owner. A **sole proprietorship** *is an organization owned, and usually operated, by a single individual.* The assets, earnings, and debts of the sole proprietorship are also the assets, earnings, and debts of the owner.

Today, sole proprietorships are still the most common form of private business ownership in the United States. While they are used in a variety of American industries, sole proprietorships are primarily concentrated in small-scale retailing and service establishments. Barber shops, repair shops—all are likely to be sole proprietorships.

ADVANTAGES OF A SOLE PROPRIETORSHIP

Sole proprietorships offer some unique advantages not found in other forms of business ownership. These include: *retention of all profits, ease of formation and dissolution,* and *ownership flexibility.* All profits (as well as losses) of a sole proprietorship belong to the owner. If the firm is a very profitable one this can be an important advantage. Retention of all profits (and losses) provides sole proprietors with a maximum incentive to operate the business as effectively as possible.

A minimum of legal requirements makes it easy to go into (and out of) business relatively simply. Usually the only legal requirements for starting a sole proprietorship are to register the business's name at the county courthouse (this guarantees that two firms do do not use the same business name), and to take out the necessary licenses. Restaurants, coffee shops, motels, barber shops, retailers, and many repair shops require certain kinds of licenses.

The fact that it is easy to discontinue a business set up as a sole proprietorship is also an attractive feature for some types of enterprises. This is particularly true for businesses that are set up for a limited period of time, and are involved in a minimum of transactions. An example would be someone who imports a shipment of antiques or jewelry from abroad, and then resells the items to local department stores.

Ownership flexibility is another advantage of sole proprietorships. The owner has no one to consult about management decisions. A sole proprietor has complete managerial flexibility. The owner can take prompt action when needed, and preserve complete secrecy where required. Ownership flexibility may also contribute to the proprietor's personal satisfaction as exemplified by the common saying: "I like being my own boss."

DISADVANTAGES OF A SOLE PROPRIETORSHIP

Disadvantages associated with a sole proprietorship include *unlimited financial liability, limits to financing, management deficiencies,* and *lack of continuity.* Since there is no legal distinction between the business and its owner as an individual, the sole proprietor is financially liable for all debts of the business. If the assets of the firm cannot cover its debts, the sole proprietor is required to cover the debts with personal funds. This ownership feature can mean that a sole proprietor is required to sell personal property—such as a home, furniture, and an automobile—to pay off business losses. The unlimited liability of a sole proprietorship can mean financial ruin to an owner if the business fails.

The financial resources of a sole proprietorship are limited to the owner's personal funds and money that can be borrowed. Sole proprietors usually do not have easy access to large amounts of capital because they are typically small businesspeople with limited personal wealth. Banks and other financial institutions are sometimes reluctant to risk loans to organizations of this small size. Financing limits can retard the expansion of some sole proprietorships.

The manager of the sole proprietorship is usually the firm's owner. This person has to be able to handle a wide range of managerial and often operative activities. As the firm grows, its managerial resource is stretched thin, since the sole proprietor cannot usually handle all duties with equal effectiveness. This type of business often has difficulty in attracting employees, particularly managerial personnel. Sole proprietorships offer little hope of promotion (except for the owner's offspring); fewer fringe benefits than can be found in other organizations; and minimal employment security, since the firm can be closed easily if the owner's interest changes. But sole proprietorships do offer employees who want to own their own businesses a chance to learn about a particular type of enterprise.

Sole proprietorships also lack long-term continuity. Deaths, bankruptcy, insanity, imprisonment, retirement, or change in personal interest can terminate a business organized as a sole proprietorship.

Partnership

Partnerships are another form of private business ownership. **Partnerships,** as defined by the Uniform Partnership Act, *are associations of two or more persons who operate a business as co-owners by voluntary legal agreement.* This has been a traditional form of ownership for professional service organizations—such as doctors, lawyers, and dentists.

General partnerships *are established when all partners carry on the business as co-owners.* All partners are liable for the debts of a general partnership. Some states also permit **limited partnerships** *composed of one or more general partners and one or more limited partners.* A **limited partner** *is one whose liability is limited to the amount contributed to the capital of the partnership.*

Joint ventures are another type of partnership. *When two or more people form a temporary business for a specific undertaking, it is called a joint venture.* An example would be a group of investors who import a shipment of high-quality wine from France and then resell it to wine dealers in the United States. Joint ventures have also been used with real estate investments. Joint ventures are distinguished from other partnerships by their lack of continuity.

ADVANTAGES OF PARTNERSHIPS

Partnerships offer these advantages: *ease of formation, complementary management skills,* and *expanded financial capability.* As with sole proprietorships, it is relatively easy to establish a partnership. The legal requirements are minimal and are usually limited to registration of business names and licensing requirements. Limited partners must also comply with state legislation based on the Uniform Limited Partnership Act.

It is usually wise to establish written Articles of Partnership specifying the details of the partners' agreement. This helps to clarify the relationships within the firm, and protects the original agreements upon which the partnership is based.

Complementary managerial skills is a common reason for setting up a partnership. If the people involved were to operate as sole proprietors each would lack some managerial skills, but by combining into a partnership each can offer the firm his or her unique managerial ability. An example would be the general partnership formed by an engineer, accountant, and marketer to produce and sell a particular product or service. William Procter and James Gamble offered their partnership complementary managerial skills. If additional managerial talent is needed in the business, it may be easier to attract such persons as partners rather than simply as employees.

Partnerships also offer expanded financial capability. Additional equity capital is usually available since more than one individual is involved. Partnerships usually have greater access to borrowed funds than do sole proprietorships. Since partners are subject to unlimited financial liability, financial institutions may be more willing to advance loans to partnerships. Involvement of additional owners may also mean that additional sources of loans become available.

DISADVANTAGES OF PARTNERSHIPS

Like other forms of business ownerships, partnerships have some related disadvantages, which include *unlimited financial liability, interpersonal disagreements, lack of continuity,* and *complexity of dissolution.* Partnerships have unlimited financial liability, for each partner is responsible for the debts of the firm. All partners are legally liable for the actions of other partners. This provision involves not only incurring debts in the name of the partnership but also lawsuits resulting from a partner's malpractice. Partners are also required to pay the total debts of a partnership from private sources if necessary. In other words, if the debts of a partnership exceed its assets, then creditors will turn to the personal wealth of the partners. Limited partners only lose the amount of capital they invested in the firm. If only one general partner has any personal wealth, then she or he is subject to paying *all* of the debts of the partnership.

Interpersonal disagreements may also plague partnerships. All partnerships, from barber shops to rock groups, face the problem of both personal and business disagreements among the participants. If these interpersonal disagreements cannot be resolved, the partnership is sometimes best dissolved, since continuation would adversely affect the business.

Continuity of a partnership is disrupted when a partner is no longer able (or willing) to continue in the business association. The partnership agreement is terminated, and a final settlement is then made.

It is not as easy to dissolve a partnership as it is to dissolve a sole proprietorship. A partner cannot simply withdraw his or her investment in the business. The person must find someone (perhaps an existing partner) to buy that interest in the firm and who is acceptable to the remaining partners. So it is sometimes very difficult to transfer an investment in a partnership to another party.

Corporation

In 1819 Chief Justice of the United States Supreme Court John Marshall set forth a classical definition of a corporation. Marshall said a **corporation** *was an artificial being, invisible, intangible, and existing only in contemplation of law.* Corporations are separate legal entities apart from their owners. Since they are legally separate bodies, corporations limit the liability of their owners to the amount that each has invested. Corporate charters are granted through state legislation.

Corporate ownership is represented by shares of stock in the firm. Types of stock and their issuance are discussed later in this chapter. Anyone who holds one or more shares of a corporation's stock is a part owner of the business. These shares can usually be bought and sold readily on the open market.

ADVANTAGES OF CORPORATIONS

Corporate ownership offers considerable advantages, including *limited financial liability, specialized management skills, expanded financial capability,* and *economics of larger scale operation.* Since corporations are considered to be separate legal entities, the stockholders (owners) have limited financial liability. If the firm fails, the stockholders can lose only the amount of their investments. Personal funds of owners are not touched by corporate failures. The limited liability of corporations is clearly designated in the names used by firms throughout the world. American corporations use the designation "Incorporated" or "Inc." Corporate enterprises in Canada and the United Kingdom use "Limited" or "Ltd." In Australia, limited liability is shown by "Proprietary Limited" or "Pty. Ltd." The limited liability of corporations is their most significant advantage over other forms of ownership.

The managerial ability of sole proprietorships and partnerships is usually limited to that provided by the owners. Corporations can more easily obtain specialized managerial skills because they offer longer-term career opportunities for qualified personnel. Employees can concentrate their efforts in some specialized activity, or functional area, because of the corporation's large size.

Expanded financial capability is another advantage of corporate ownership. This factor in turn may allow the corporation to grow and become more efficient than it would if the business were set up as a sole proprietorship or partnership. Since corporate ownership is divided into many small units (shares), it is usually easier to attract capital. People with both large and relatively limited resources can invest their savings in corporations by buying shares of stock. Corporate size and stability also make it easier for corporations to borrow additional funds. Large, financially strong corpora-

Table 3-1 America's Largest Industrial Corporations

Rank	Company	Sales ($000)	Assets ($000)	Rank	Employees Number	Rank
1	Exxon (New York)	42,061,336*	31,332,440	1	133,000†	13
2	General Motors (Detroit)	31,549,546	20,468,100	2	734,000†	1
3	Ford Motor (Dearborn, Mich.)	23,620,600	14,173,600	4	464,731†	2
4	Texaco (New York)	23,255,497	17,176,121	3	76,420	33
5	Mobil Oil (New York)	18,929,033*	14,074,290	5	73,100	37
6	Standard Oil of California (San Francisco)	17,191,186	11,639,996	8	39,540	96
7	Gulf Oil (Pittsburgh)	16,458,000*	12,503,000	7	52,700	59
8	General Electric (Fairfield, Conn.)	13,413,100	9,369,100	10	404,000†	4
9	International Business Machines (Armonk, N.Y.)	12,675,292	14,027,108	6	292,350	5
10	International Tel. & Tel. (New York)	11,154,401	10,696,544	9	409,000	3
11	Chrysler (Highland Park, Mich.)	10,971,416	6,732,756	13	255,929†	6
12	U.S. Steel (New York)	9,186,403	7,717,493	12	187,503†	9
13	Standard Oil (Ind.) (Chicago)	9,085,415*	8,915,190	11	47,217	77
14	Shell Oil (Houston)	7,633,455*	6,128,884	16	32,287	125
15	Western Electric (New York)	7,381,728	5,239,551	18	189,972	8
16	Continental Oil (Stamford, Conn.)	7,041,423	4,673,434	22	41,174	93
17	E.I. du Pont de Nemours (Wilmington, Del.)	6,910,100	5,980,300	17	136,866	12
18	Atlantic Richfield (Los Angeles)	6,739,682*	6,151,608	15	28,771	145
19	Westinghouse Electric (Pittsburgh)	6,466,112	4,301,804	24	199,248†	7
20	Occidental Petroleum (Los Angeles)	5,719,369	3,325,471	32	34,400	112
21	Bethlehem Steel (Bethlehem, Pa.)	5,380,963	4,512,617	23	121,623†	15
22	Union Carbide (New York)	5,320,123	4,882,800	20	109,566	20
23	Goodyear Tire & Rubber (Akron, Ohio)	5,256,247	4,241,626	25	154,166†	10
24	Tenneco (Houston)	5,001,474	6,401,557	14	81,016	29
25	Phillips Petroleum (Bartlesville, Okla.)	4,980,704	4,028,112	28	30,802	132

*Does not include excise taxes.
†Average for the year.

SOURCE: Reprinted by permission from the 1975 Fortune Directory. © Time, Inc.

tions can usually borrow money at rates lower than those smaller businesses must pay.

The larger scale operation permitted by corporate ownership has several advantages associated with it. Employees can specialize in the work activities they perform best. Many projects can be internally financed by transferring money from one part of the corporation to another. Longer manufacturing runs usually mean more efficient production and lower prices, thus attracting more customers. America's leading industrial corporations are listed in Table 3-1.

While corporate size may be an advantage from a business viewpoint, some economists, attorneys, political figures, and business executives have begun to question whether there are limits to which corporate size is an advantage to society. Case 3-1 deals with this important social issue. It is also important to emphasize that corporations are not automatically large-scale businesses, since many very small firms have incorporated.

DISADVANTAGES OF CORPORATIONS

Some disadvantages are also inherent in corporate ownership. Corporations are *the most difficult and costly ownership form to establish;* corporations are usually at a *tax disadvantage;* corporate ownership often faces a multitude of *legal restrictions; the impersonality of corporate management can alienate some employees.* Each state has different incorporation laws, some of which are quite technical and complex. Delaware has traditionally attracted many corporations because it has relatively easy requirements and lower incorporation costs. Establishing a corporation usually requires the services of an attorney, which means that some legal fees must be paid. States also charge incorporation fees that add to the cost of setting up this type of business.

Corporations are subject to federal and state income taxes as separate legal entities. Corporate earnings are taxed; and any **dividends** (*payments from earnings*) to the stockholders are subject to taxation on an individual basis. This effectively amounts to double taxation of corporate earnings from the viewpoint of the stockholders who receive dividends. By contrast, the earnings of sole proprietorships and partnerships are taxed only once, since they are treated as personal income.

SOURCE: Drawing by Donald Reilly; © 1973 The New Yorker Magazine, Inc.

Many states provide tax relief to corporations meeting certain size and stock ownership requirements by recognizing what is known as **Subchapter S Corporations.** A Subchapter S Corporation *can elect to be taxed as a proprietorship and still maintain the advantages of incorporation.*

Corporate ownership also faces a multitude of legal problems not encountered by sole proprietorships and partnerships. Corporate charters restrict the type of business activity in which the corporation can engage. Corporations must also file various reports about their operations. The number of laws and regulations affecting corporations has increased dramatically in recent years.

Big corporations—like other large organizations in government, the military, and religion—sometimes suffer from the impersonality of management. Employees become alienated because they do not feel any close ties with the corporation or its management. Many specialized jobs within a corporation lack a sense of identity with the firm. Some managers lack the initiative and sense of self-achievement found in sole proprietorships and partnerships. Employee morale, productivity, volume, and profitability can all be affected if steps are not taken to reduce this problem.

Current Ownership Structure of American Business

Figure 3-1 shows the actual ownership structure of American business. There are nearly ten million sole proprietorships, by far the most widely used form of business ownership. Corporations rank second, with about 14 percent of businesses using this form of or-

Table 3-2 The Advantages and Disadvantages of Each Form of Private Ownership

Form of Ownership	Sole Proprietorship	Partnership	Corporation
Advantages	1. retention of all profits 2. ease of formation and dissolution 3. ownership flexibility	1. ease of formation 2. complementary management skills 3. expanded financial capability	1. limited financial liability 2. specialized management skills 3. expanded financial capability 4. economics of larger scale operation
Disadvantages	1. unlimited financial liability 2. limits to financing 3. management deficiences 4. lack of continuity	1. unlimited financial liability 2. interpersonal disagreements 3. lack of continuity 4. compex dissolution	1. difficult and costly ownership form to establish 2. tax disadvantage 3. legal restrictions 4. alienation of some employees

Figure 3-1
The Ownership
Structure of American
Business

SOURCE: *Statistical Abstract of the United States,* 1974, p. 476.

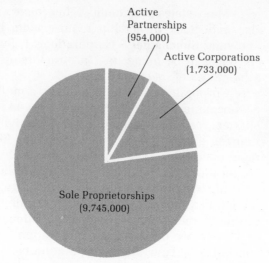

Active Partnerships (954,000)

Active Corporations (1,733,000)

Sole Proprietorships (9,745,000)

ganization. Partnerships are the smallest segment. Furthermore, states have liberalized the requirement that professional service groups must be partnerships, so it seems likely that this form of ownership may decline as more and more professional workers incorporate.

Organizing and Operating a Corporation

Suppose you decided to start a business and believed that a corporation would be the best form of business ownership for your enterprise. How would you go about setting up a corporation?

The first step should be to consult an attorney about your proposed incorporation. While it may be possible to incorporate the business by yourself, most people hire a lawyer so that they can be assured that all necessary requirements are met.

SELECT A STATE Selection of a state in which to incorporate is an extremely important decision, since regulations and incorporation costs vary widely. If you intend to operate primarily within the Commonwealth of Massachusetts, you should probably incorporate in that state. But if your principal business will be in Harris County, Texas, you should probably be a Texas corporation. Aside from the convenience of incorporating in one's home state, if the business involves state contracts many state governments specify that local firms be given preference in state purchases.

Fees, taxes, stock transfer fees, and ownership rights vary widely among the fifty states. Historically, the states of Delaware and New Jersey have offered incorporation advantages to businesses that expect to operate nationwide. But the selection of a state in which to incorporate should be decided only after careful research.

A firm is considered a **domestic corporation** *in the state where it is incorporated. If the firm expects to do business in states other than the state of incorporation, it must register as a* **foreign corporation** *in those states. A corporation organized in another nation is known as an* **alien corporation** *if it operates in the United States.*

INCORPORATING
THE BUSINESS

Figure 3-2 shows the Articles of Incorporation for the State of Illinois. This form must be completed, as per its instructions, and filed with the Secretary of State for Illinois. Most states designate a certain official or state agency to administer incorporations. Usually the Secretary of State is the designated party. Blank articles of incorporation, corporation charters, or incorporation certificates—depending on the terminology used in a particular state—can be obtained from this official or agency.

Figure 3-2
Articles of Incorporation
(Corporation Charter)
for the State of Illinois

FORM B C A-47

BEFORE ATTEMPTING TO EXECUTE THESE BLANKS BE SURE TO READ CAREFULLY
THE INSTRUCTIONS ON THE BACK THEREOF.

(THESE ARTICLES MUST BE FILED IN DUPLICATE)

STATE OF ILLINOIS,

_____COUNTY_____ } ss.

TO MICHAEL J. HOWLETT, Secretary of State

The undersigned,

(Do note write in this space)
Date Paid
Initial License Fee $
Franchise Tax $
Filing Fee $

Clerk $

Name	Number	Street	Address City	State

being one or more natural persons of the age of twenty-one years or more or a corporation, and having subscribed to shares of the corporation to be organized pursuant hereto, for the purpose of forming a corporation under "The Business Corporation Act" of the State of Illinois, do hereby adopt the following Articles of Incorporation:

ARTICLE ONE

The name of the corporation hereby incorporated is:_____

_____

ARTICLE TWO

The *address* of its initial registered office in the State of Illinois is:_____

Street, in the_____of_____(_____) County of_____and
(Zip Code)

the *name* of its initial Registered Agent at *said address* is:_____

ARTICLE THREE

The duration of the corporation is:_____

Corporation charters usually include similar information. California asks for the name of the corporation; the specific business in which the corporation will engage; purposes of the corporation; California county in which the principal office will be located; the number, names, and addresses of the board of directors; the number of shares issued; and names of incorporators. Additional information is required if more than one class of shares is to be issued.

THE
STOCKHOLDERS

Stockholders *are those people who acquire the shares of the corporation.* They are the owners of the corporation. *Some corporations are owned by relatively few stockholders, such as family businesses that have been incorporated.* The few stockholders also control and manage the corporation's activities. These firms are known as **closed corporations.** *But in larger corporations, the ownership is widely diversified.* The term **open corporation** is sometimes used to describe this situation. American Telephone and Telegraph Corporation (AT&T) has 2,934,000 stockholders. These people obviously have little individual control of this giant corporation. But there is a ready market for their shares if they decide to sell. Adequate markets are available for the stock of large corporations, so the individual stockholder can sell the stock more easily than if the shares held were in a small firm with no public market for its stock.

Corporations usually hold an annual stockholders' meeting. The firm's management presents reports on the activities of the firm, and any decisions requiring stockholders' approval are put to a vote. The election of some directors (discussed in the next section), and the choice of an independent public accountant are two matters that must be voted upon at nearly all stockholders' meetings.

Stock is usually classified as common or preferred. **Preferred stock** *has the first claim to the corporation's assets after all debts have been satisfied.* But such shareholders usually do not have voting rights at the stockholder's meetings. **Common stock** *has only a residual claim (after everyone else has been paid) to the firm's assets,* but common stockholders have voting rights in the corporate system. When a vote is taken, each share of common stock is worth one vote. A person with 150 shares has 150 votes. If people cannot attend the stockholders' meetings, they can give their **proxy** to someone else who will be in attendance. A proxy means that *someone else is authorized to vote these shares as the owner has instructed them.* Figure 3-3 shows a proxy statement that was used at a recent stockholders' meeting for the Columbia Broadcasting System.

Small stockholders may have little influence on corporate management. A larger stockholder with 200,000 shares has 200,000 votes for each director's position, while a holder of 50 shares has only 50 votes for each director. As a result, the issue of **cumulative voting** has come before many stockholders' meetings. Cumulative voting *may allow smaller stockholders to have a greater influence*

CBS COMMON STOCK

PROXY FOR ANNUAL MEETING SOLICITED ON BEHALF OF MANAGEMENT

The undersigned hereby appoints WILLIAM S. PALEY, ARTHUR R. TAYLOR and J. A. W. IGLEHART, or any of them, each with power of substitution, attorneys and proxies to vote all shares of common stock which the undersigned is entitled to vote, with all powers which the undersigned would possess if personally present, at the Annual Meeting (including all adjournments thereof) of Shareholders of Columbia Broadcasting System, Inc., to be held Wednesday, April 17, 1974 at 10 AM, in Studio A, WAGA-TV, 1551 Briarcliff Road, N.E., Atlanta, Georgia, as follows:

1. FOR the election of 16 directors. (Any shareholder wishing to do so may withhold authority to vote for directors by drawing a line through the preceding sentence.)

2. FOR ☐ **AGAINST** ☐ the election of Coopers & Lybrand to serve as auditors for CBS. The directors recommend a vote for this proposal.

3. FOR ☐ **AGAINST** ☐ a proposal to change the Corporation's name to CBS INC. The directors recommend a vote for this proposal.

4. FOR ☐ **AGAINST** ☐ a proposal to adopt a Performance Incentive Plan. The directors recommend a vote for this proposal.

5. FOR ☐ **AGAINST** ☐ a shareholder proposal to amend the By-Laws with respect to shareholder proposals omitted from the proxy materials. The directors recommend a vote against this proposal.

6. FOR ☐ **AGAINST** ☐ a shareholder proposal to amend the By-Laws to require notification of the availability of documents relating to program standards and practices. The directors recommend a vote against this proposal.

7. Upon such other business as may properly come before this meeting.

PLEASE NOTE. CHECK HERE ☐ IF YOU PLAN TO ATTEND THE ANNUAL MEETING. AN ADMITTANCE CARD WILL BE SENT TO YOU.

continued, and to be signed, on the other side

THIS PROXY SHALL BE VOTED AS DIRECTED, AND IF NO DIRECTION TO THE CONTRARY IS INDICATED, IT SHALL BE VOTED FOR THE ELECTION OF 16 DIRECTORS, FOR PROPOSALS 2, 3 AND 4, AND AGAINST PROPOSALS 5 AND 6.

PLEASE SIGN HERE exactly as name appears below, indicating, where proper, official position or representative capacity. For joint accounts, each joint owner should sign.

Date:

SHAREHOLDERS ARE REQUESTED TO DATE AND SIGN THIS PROXY AND TO RETURN IT PROMPTLY IN THE ENCLOSED ENVELOPE. NO POSTAGE IS REQUIRED.

Figure 3-3
A CBS Proxy Form
SOURCE: Courtesy of CBS, Inc.

on the selection of directors. If three director positions are to be filled, cumulative voting allows the small stockholder to cast 150 (50 × 3) votes for one person, rather than apportioning the 150 votes among the three positions.

Issues of corporate social responsibility have also come before recent stockholders' meetings. Many churches, labor unions, and college and university trust funds hold common stock investments. The trustees of these organizations have sometimes used their voting power to raise questions about a corporation's social performance.

BOARD OF DIRECTORS The stockholders elect a board of directors who become the governing authority for the corporation. The board elects its own officers, usually a chairman, a vice-chairman, and a secretary. Most states require a minimum of three directors and at least one annual meeting of the board. Most corporations, other than small or closely held ones, have large boards of directors that meet at least quarterly.

A board of directors must authorize major transactions involving the corporation and set overall corporate policy. A board might be concerned with changes in the firm's stock, financing arrangements, dividends, or a major change in corporate holdings. But the most important decision made by a board of directors is the hiring of the corporation's top management. The company's president is an employee of the board of directors. While the board may exert considerable influence on the employment of top executive officers, it usually leaves the selection of other managers to the firm's top executives.

In some corporations the board of directors plays an active role in the management of the organization; this is particularly so in smaller companies. But in most corporations the board acts more as a review panel of management decisions. Most boards are composed of some of the corporation's executives and some **outside directors,** *who are people not employed by the organization.* Sometimes the corporation's president is also the chairman of the board of directors.

TOP MANAGEMENT

Top management, including the president and most vice-presidents, is hired by the board of directors. These executives are then responsible for the actual operation of the corporation, subject to board approval. They make most of the major corporate decisions and delegate other tasks to subordinate managers in the organization. Top management is responsible to the board of directors although they often sit on these boards themselves. State legislation usually defines the duties of some corporate officers such as president, secretary, and treasurer. Still other executive posts are created by the board.

SUBSIDIARY ORGANIZATIONS

Many corporations own other organizations called subsidiaries. Allstate Insurance Company is a subsidiary of Sears, Roebuck and Company. Dryden Press, the publisher of this book, is a division of Holt, Rinehart, and Winston, which is a subsidiary of CBS, Inc.

When a corporation's stock is either wholly or majority owned by another corporation it is a **subsidiary.** *The owner is usually called* **the parent company.** Typically, the management of the subsidiary is appointed by the top executive of the parent company, subject to the approval of the parent's board. Many widely known corporations are actually subsidiaries of still other corporations.

CORPORATE GROWTH

Corporate growth has become a major economic, political, and social issue in recent years. Successful corporations have traditionally been able to expand through effective business-management practices. In some cases, corporations have grown by acquiring other firms. *When one firm buys the assets and liabilities of another company, it is known as a* **merger.**

Americans historically have seen corporate growth as desirable, provided it did not restrain competition. But today some people are questioning the desirability of additional growth. Typically, these critics argue that further enlargement will not significantly improve the firm's productivity, and it may reduce competition in the marketplace. Corporate executives usually reply that significant economies are still available if the firm expands. No general concensus has emerged on this issue, and it is likely that this will remain a critical public issue in the decade ahead.

Alternatives to Private Ownership

While most business organizations are owned privately by individuals or groups of individuals, some are owned by either municipal, state, or federal governments. Parking structures and water systems are often owned by local governments. The Pennsylvania Turnpike Authority operates a vital highway link across that state. The United States government established the Tennessee Valley Authority to provide electricity in that region. The Federal Deposit Insurance Corporation insures bank savings deposits.

The alternative to private ownership is some form of **public ownership.** Public ownership means that *some governmental unit or its agency owns and operates a particular organization on behalf of the population served by that unit.* While public ownership is more common abroad, it has been used in several places and times in the United States.

WHEN PUBLIC OWNERSHIP IS USED
When is public ownership used? Sometimes public ownership comes about when private investors are unwilling to make investments where they believe the possibility of failure is too high. An example of this situation was the rural electrification program in the 1930's which significantly expanded utility lines in less populated areas. In other cases public ownership replaces privately owned organizations that fail. After the Penn Central Railroad financial collapse, there were several proposals to set up a National Passenger Train Corporation. Still other businesses require too large an outlay for any one company—the National Aeronautics and Space Administration (NASA) is an illustration. Some governments have also reasoned that certain activities are too important to public welfare to be entrusted to private ownership. Turnpikes and municipal water systems are examples. Finally, some nations have used public ownership to foster competition. Public companies are put into direct competition with private firms. Both are operated as competitive business enterprises. Canadian National Railroad (publicly

The Issue of Public Power

Imagine the telephone company in a totally competitive situation. Because you like the rates, you lease or buy your telephone from Company A. Your office phone is leased from Company B, because Company B has more outlets in the area where your firm does most of its business. Your friend's phone is from Company C. You would have to install phones from Companies B and C if you wanted to talk to your office or your friend. To prevent a situation like this, public utilities are monopolies, and their monopolistic position is why they are heavily regulated by government.

Recently, utilities have been getting into financial trouble. Their costs have skyrocketed and their earnings have decreased, because overhead costs (labor and energy) have risen. But in order to pass such costs on to the consumer, public utilities must have the permission of local and state governments. At the same time, the quality of service of many utilities appears to be decreasing. With all these problems, why not turn the ownership of utilities over to the government?

Utilities provide such services as water, gas, telephones, and electricity. Consumers want better service at more reasonable rates and resources to be used more efficiently. The supporters of private ownership of utilities say that it would result in a more efficient operation and use of personnel. They believe that public own-

ership of utilities would only lead to public support of such companies through taxation, and, furthermore, that in many instances public utilities would not be paying taxes on their earnings, depriving the government of one source of revenue.

Those who see public ownership of utilities as harmful say that since many decisions made are political rather than economic, the costs of operation would not be a primary concern of a public company. Privately owned utilities, however, would be geared to competition, so research and development (investigating more efficient technologies) would be important to them. Consumers also have greater influence on private companies, because they can show dissatisfaction by buying less or none of the service.

Those in favor of public ownership of utilities believe that such companies generally provide services at lower rates than privately owned companies. Public companies, for instance, tend to have lower executive salaries, lower financing costs (that is, lower interest rates because of public or tax-backed loans), fewer advertising and public relations expenditures, and lower taxation. Supporters of public ownership of utilities also believe that labor-management relations are better than in privately owned companies and that interruption of services due to strikes is minimized.

owned) competes with Canadian Pacific Railroad (privately owned) in a wide range of travel activities. Trans-Australia Airlines (publicly owned) competes against Ansett Airlines of Australia (privately owned). The operation of publicly owned organizations also varies. Some strive to be "profitable" for their governmental units; others are viewed entirely as public services that operate at—sometimes—considerable loss. Canadian National Railroad and Trans-Australia Airlines are economically viable organizations, while Japan's well-publicized train system requires a substantial government subsidy to its own revenues. Subsidies are also common in many publicly owned bus systems in the United States.

COOPERATIVES— A SECOND ALTERNATIVE TO PRIVATE OWNERSHIP

Another alternative to private ownership is collective ownership of a production, storage, transportation, or marketing activity. **Cooperatives** *are organizations where private ownership is maintained, but all of the owners band together to collectively own and operate all or part of their industries.* Cooperatives are often used where there are a large number of small producers so that a collective organization will make them more competitive in the marketplace. The well-known "Sunkist" brand is used to identify the products of the California Fruit Grower's Exchange, a cooperative. Some cooperatives have become large economic units that exert considerable power. The Mesta was a Spanish sheep-owners' cooperative formed in the 1200's. By the sixteenth century it was the biggest economic organization in Spain, and herded 3 million sheep. Its size allowed it to exert considerable influence on government policy.[2] By contrast,

"We're a nonprofit organization—we don't intend to be, but we are!"

Some Privately Owned Businesses Are Also Nonprofit Organizations
SOURCE: "*Grin and Bear It*" by Lichty and Wagner, courtesy of Field Newspaper Syndicate.

cooperatives have never reached significant proportions in the United States. American businesses have traditionally operated as independent economic entities.

Summary

Selection of a legal form of business organization is a complex and extremely critical decision for any enterprise. There are three forms of private business ownership: sole proprietorship, partnership, and corporation.

The advantages of a sole proprietorship are retention of all profits, ease of formation and dissolution, and ownership flexibility. Its disadvantages are unlimited financial liability, limits to financing, management deficiences, and lack of continuity.

Partnerships offer these advantages: ease of formation, complementary management skills, and expanded financial capability. The disadvantages are unlimited financial liability, interpersonal disagreements, lack of continuity, and complex dissolution.

Advantages of corporations include limited financial liability, specialized management skills, expanded financial capability, economies of larger scale operation. The disadvantages are the difficulty and cost of establishing this form of ownership, the tax disadvantage, legal restriction, alienation of some employees.

This chapter also examined current ownership structure and how to organize and operate a corporation. Consideration was given to the selection of a state in which to incorporate; the actual incorporation process; the role of stockholders, boards of directors, top management, and subsidiary organizations; and corporate growth.

An alternative to such forms of business organization is public ownership, where a government unit or its agency owns and operates a particular organization on behalf of the population served by that unit. Another alternative to private ownership is a cooperative, where there is collective ownership of a production, storage, transportation, or marketing activity.

Review questions

1. Identify the following terms:
   - a. sole proprietorship
   - b. partnership
   - c. general partnership
   - d. limited partnership
   - e. joint venture
   - f. corporation
   - g. dividend
   - h. Subchapter S corporation
   - i. domestic corporation
   - j. foreign corporation
   - k. alien corporation
   - l. stockholders
   - m. open corporation
   - n. closed corporation
   - o. preferred stock
   - p. common stock
   - q. proxy
   - r. board of directors

s. outside director   v. merger
t. subsidiary   w. public ownership
u. cumulative voting   x. cooperative.

2. After reading this chapter, why do you believe Harry Marcowitz incorporated his paper cutter business rather than setting it up as a sole proprietorship or partnership?
3. Identify the advantages and disadvantages of the three forms of business ownership.
4. Carefully read the story of how Procter & Gamble was formed. In your opinion, why did these two men work together so well?
5. Distinguish between a general partner and a limited partner.
6. What is the most commonly used form of business ownership? Why?
7. List the steps in the incorporation process.
8. What is a subsidiary? List all of the subsidiary companies that operate in your area. Where are their parent companies located?
9. What is the status of cooperatives in the United States?
10. Assume that you are involved in establishing the following businesses. What form of business ownership would you employ?
    a. roadside fruit stand (assume you own an orchard)
    b. barber shop
    c. management consulting firm
    d. small foundry.

Discussion questions and exercises

1. Evaluate pro and con arguments of the controversial issue that appears in this chapter.
2. In November, 1974, the Justice Department began a legal battle against the American Telephone and Telegraph Corporation. It accused AT & T of monopolizing the telecommunications industry. The Justice Department specifically asked that Western Electric, AT & T's manufacturing subsidiary, be split into competing companies. The suit also asked that the regional telephone system be split from the firm's long-distance business. The Justice Department estimated that with appeals the case could go on for ten years before a settlement was reached.*

    What is the status of this suit? What is your opinion of the case? Outline a brief case for both the Justice Department and the corporation's defense attorneys.
3. Ask a local attorney to speak to your class about how one goes about setting up a corporation in your state.

---

*"U.S. Govt. Sues Giant Company," *The Age* (November 22, 1974), p. 115; "Monopoly Move Hits ATT Shares," *The Age* (November 23, 1974), p. 27.

4. Secure announcements of future stockholder meetings of corporations located in your area. Analyze the types of issues which are scheduled to be debated at these meetings. Can you make any generalizations about these issues?
5. Invite a director of a firm in your area to speak to the class. Ask this person to describe how the firm's board of directors operates, and to describe his personal philosophy of the role of the board of directors in corporate affairs.

Case 3-1
The Industrial Reorganization Act

In 1974 the United States Senate Anti-Trust and Monopoly Sub-Committee began hearing testimony on the Industrial Reorganization Act introduced by Senator Philip A. Hart of Michigan. This proposed legislation would break up large corporations in **concentrated industries,** *those dominated by relatively few manufacturers.* Hart believes that firms should be considered monopolies and subject to court-ordered reorganization designed to increase competition if: (a.) four or less firms have 50 percent or more of an industry's sales; or (b.) two companies or more have not engaged in substantial price competition during a three-year period.

A staff report prepared for the Senate group argued that the large automobile manufacturers should divest themselves of divisions involved in producing other means of transportation. The study also suggested that the three major automobile producers be split "into a balanced group of competing auto, truck, bus and rail firms" so as to achieve a more effective national transportation system.

Questions

1. What is your opinion of Senator Hart's proposed legislation?
2. Is corporate size related to public welfare? Why? Why not?
3. If you spoke for General Motors, how would you respond to the proposed Industrial Reorganization Act?

Sources: Saul Friedman. "GM's Nazi Ties Cited in Anti-trust Hearing," *Detroit Free Press* (March 3, 1974), p. 16-F; "Jail for More Price Fixers?" *Time* (November 11, 1974), p. 65.

Case 3-2
Vinalhaven Light and Power Company

Vinalhaven Light and Power Company, one of the nation's smallest utility companies, is situated on a picturesque island sixteen miles off the central Maine coast. The company serves 1,500 residents on the island and nearby North Haven Island. Herbert Patterson is the president and majority stockholder of Vinalhaven Power and Light. He is also office manager and diesel mechanic in the firm that employs only ten people. Vinalhaven Power and Light Company was formed in 1914, but failed in 1918. Patterson's father then took over its management and eventually accumulated a 51 percent ownership. Herbert Patterson inherited the firm in 1963.

Vinalhaven was a profitable concern for many years, but its situation worsened because of a variety of factors. There was an increased power demand by the residents of the area, particularly during the summer months when the island's population doubles or triples. The company is so short of funds that it is required to pay cash for fuel. Old generators have failed, causing numerous blackouts, voltage cutbacks, and power surges. On one occasion Patterson tried to restore the island's power by borrowing a generator from the Maine National Guard, but it would not start. The company's dependency on diesel generators requires it to charge about 60 percent more than mainland utilities. The island's situation is complicated by the fact that while a cable to the mainland would allow it to be served by Central Maine Power Company, this would cost an estimated $1 million.

Vinalhaven Power and Light Company lost about $25,000 in 1973. As of 1974 the company was $55,000 in debt. Patterson was turned down for another bank loan. In 1974 he told a *Wall Street Journal* reporter that he would like to sell the firm. "They've only got to knock once," he promised.

Questions

1. Describe the form of business ownership used by Vinalhaven Light and Power Company. Is this similar to that found in other utilities?
2. Should the governor of Maine propose public ownership of this utility?
3. What would you do if you were Patterson?

Source: David Gunpert. "Here is One Utility That Makes Con Ed Look Like a Winner," *The Wall Street Journal* (May 23, 1974), pp. 1, 21. Reprinted with permission of *The Wall Street Journal*, © Dow Jones & Company, 1974. All rights reserved.

II

Organization and Management of the Enterprise

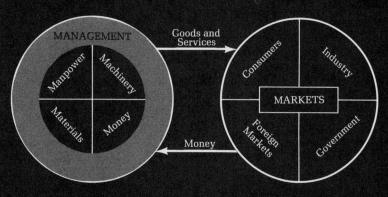

SOURCE: Ellis Herwig/Stock, Boston.

4

Introduction to Management

"All mankind is divided into three classes: those who are immovable; those who are movable; and those who move."

—Benjamin Franklin

"Never tell people how to do things. Tell them what to do and they will surprise you with their ingenuity."

—General George Patton

What Chapter 4 Is All About

1. In this chapter, you will learn that management is important in all types of organizations—both profit-seeking firms and nonprofit organizations.
2. You will understand the basic functions performed by all managers—planning, organizing, directing, and controlling.
3. You will be able to identify the three levels of managers in a firm, and you should be able to state which of the managerial functions are likely to be more important to each management level.
4. You should recognize the importance of objectives in establishing standards by which management performance is measured.
5. You will be able to compare and contrast the three basic leadership styles.
6. After reading this chapter, you should understand these terms:

management	planning
management pyramid	organizing
top management	directing
middle management	controlling
supervisory	autocratic leader
management	democratic leader
objectives	free rein leader

Walter "Smokey" Alston

The quick image of the manager of a Big League baseball team is a fast-talking, gum-chewing, loud-voiced, hard-hitting man who spends as much time screaming at the umpire as he does prepping his players. "Smokey" Alston, sixty-plus-year-old manager of the Los Angeles Dodgers, doesn't fit that image at all. Six feet two inches, freckle-faced, and a chunky 210 pounds, Alston comes closest to the traditional ball-club skipper when seen with his ever present cigarette and chewing gum. But his image is most like that of the traditional businessman.

After Alston earned a bachelor of science degree, he played ball for the East Dixie League at a time when you either played well or left the team. He began managing baseball teams over thirty years ago, and in that time developed a style that is relaxed, patient, and low-keyed. He treats his players like grown men, expecting them to stay in shape because it is good for the game and not because their manager is disciplining them. Although time pressures mean Alston must provide negative criticism of the way players handle themselves in a game, he tries to delay serious disciplining of his team for at least a day. That helps him control his temper and allows the players and the manager to talk about mistakes in privacy.

Always available to his players, cool under pressure, and supportive of the men whose talent he values, Alston is warm and logical, but baseball means a lot to him and he becomes tense and anxious during a game.

Alston's management style—his emphasis on team spirit and his evaluation of players—has resulted in twenty-plus seasons with the Dodgers, longer with one club than anyone except Connie Mack and John McGraw—and that on a year-to-year contract.

W alter Alston, Mick Jagger, and Henry Ford II have at least one thing in common: They are all managers. Alston pilots the Los Angeles Dodgers; Jagger leads the Rolling Stones; and Ford is chief executive officer at Ford Motor Company. Other managers preside over the local Red Cross office, city governments (many cities are led by a city manager), and colleges or universities.

What Is Management?

Management may be defined as *the achievement of objectives through people and other resources.* The manager's job is to combine human and technical resources in such a way that the objectives of the organization are achieved. Managers do not produce a finished product; they are not directly involved in production. Instead, they direct the efforts of others toward company goals by combining

"I FIRED THEM ALL. 2,437 OF THEM. I'LL GO IT ALONE."

The Manager Achieves Objectives *through People and Other Resources*

SOURCE: Reproduced by permission of the artist, Sidney Harris and *Saturday Review*.

available resources—employees, raw materials, financial resources, factories, and equipment. Management is the critical ingredient in the **Five Ms,** the basic resources of any firm (see Figure 4-1): *management, manpower, materials, money, and machinery.* The task of management is to efficiently combine the other four resources to achieve organizational objectives.

MANAGEMENT PRINCIPLES ARE UNIVERSAL

The management principles and concepts discussed in this section are universally applicable. They are fundamental not only to profit-seeking firms, such as Schwinn and Kentucky Fried Chicken, but also to nonprofit organizations. The local hospital administrator, the head of the United Fund, and the PTA president all perform managerial functions.

Figure 4-1
The Five Ms—Basic
Resources of the
Organization

Business is only one form of enterprise. It is distinguished from the March of Dimes organization only in terms of objectives. Businesses are *profit-oriented,* while such nonprofit organizations as hospitals, city government, and charitable agencies are *service-oriented.* But both benefit from effective management.

THE MANAGEMENT PYRAMID

The local McDonald's franchise has a very simple organization: a manager and an assistant manager or two. In contrast, Columbia Record Company has a president, several vice-presidents, department heads, plant managers, supervisors, and foremen. Are all of these people managers?

The answer is yes. Since all of them are engaged in combining human and other resources to achieve company objectives, they are all managers.

There are various levels of managers, who together form a **management pyramid.** This pyramid is *the hierarchy, or levels, of management in an organization.* As Figure 4-2 indicates, management of a firm may be divided into three categories: *top manage-*

Figure 4-2
The Management
Pyramid

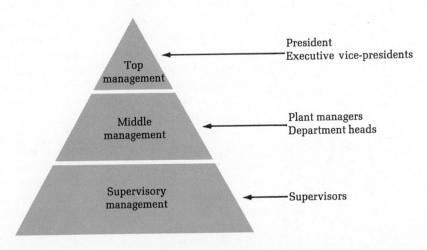

ment, *middle management,* and *supervisory management.* Although all three categories contain managers, each level of the management pyramid stresses different activities.

The highest level of the management pyramid is comprised of the president and other key company executives. This is the **top management** of the company. They devote their time to developing long-range plans for the company. They make such broad decisions as whether to manufacture new products, purchase smaller companies, or begin international operations. A considerable amount of their time is directed to activities *outside* the organization, involving government and community affairs.

Top Management Receives Top Pay

Persons in top management positions are highly paid. The consulting firm McKinsey & Company conducted an executive-compensation survey of companies whose annual sales for the year 1974 exceed 1 billion dollars. The average pay of chief executives—including salary, bonus, and other cash considerations—is listed below:

Industry	Pay	Industry	Pay
Motor vehicles	$440,000	Textiles	$292,000
Pharmaceuticals	435,000	Food products	290,000
Rubber, plastic products	391,000	Household appliances	273,000
Office machines	375,000	Paper, allied products	269,000
Petroleum	360,000	Retail trade	269,000
Soaps, cosmetics	354,000	Steel	269,000
Tobacco	346,000	Railroad transportation	255,000
Alcoholic beverages	342,000	Air transportation	239,000
Electrical products	333,000	Apparel	195,000
Chemicals	328,000	Retail food chains	186,000
Building products	297,000	Utilities	184,000

SOURCE: McKinsey & Company, Inc. Annual Executive Compensation Survey. Reprinted by permission of McKinsey & Company, Inc.

Middle management is *the second level of the management pyramid, and includes such executives as plant managers and department heads.* Middle management is more involved in specific operations within the organization. It is responsible for developing specific plans and procedures to implement the broader plans of top management. Middle management might be involved in such activities as determining the number of salespeople for a particular territory, operating a branch of a department store chain, selecting equipment for a new facility, and developing techniques for evaluating the performances of employees.

Supervisory management is *the third level of the management pyramid, and includes supervisors* who are directly responsible for the details of assigning workers to specific jobs, evaluating daily—and even hourly—performance. They are in direct and continuing contact with production personnel and are responsible for putting into action the plans developed by middle management.

Importance of Objectives

The old axiom—"If you don't know where you are going, *any* road will get you there"—applies to business as well as to individuals. Both businesses and individuals need definite objectives in order to be successful. **Objectives** serve as *guideposts for managers in defining standards of what the organization should accomplish in such areas as profitability, customer service, and social responsibility.* Plans can be developed that are designed to accomplish these objectives. Performance can continually be evaluated in terms of how well the organization is moving in the direction of its objectives.

OBJECTIVES SERVE AS STANDARDS

Objectives become types of standards for the manager. They define excellence in organizational performance. Without objectives to serve as standards, the manager possesses no tools for evaluating performance; no means of deciding whether work is good or bad, satisfactory or disappointing. These objectives provide not only a definite statement of what the organization wants to accomplish but they become a means of evaluating actual performance. Should performance prove unsatisfactory, management may take corrective action to refocus the organization in the direction of its objectives.

EXAMPLES OF OBJECTIVES

The belief that "the purpose of a business is to make a profit" is accepted by most people—both defenders and critics of business. Newspaper accounts of the success of Walt Disney Enterprises or Levi Strauss are typically stated in terms of annual earnings, the most straightforward measure of business performance.

But a statement that profits are the *only* objective of a business is clearly misleading. Profits are obviously necessary for the survival of the firm. Companies must be profitable in order to attract additional capital and to satisfy owners with an adequate return for their invested funds. But other objectives are equally important. Unless the company provides a service to its customers through the production and marketing of needed goods and services, profits will not be made.

The mere existence of a firm results in the achievement of a number of **social objectives.** These may include such areas as *providing job opportunities, paying good wages, making plants and offices good places in which to work, offering job training for the hard-core unemployed, and being a good corporate citizen of the community.* Figure 4-3 describes the objectives of Johnson & Johnson, the maker of Band-Aids, baby oil, and cotton swabs.

Figure 4-3
The Objectives of
Johnson & Johnson

Our Credo

WE BELIEVE THAT OUR FIRST RESPONSIBILITY IS TO THE DOCTORS, NURSES, HOSPITALS,
MOTHERS, AND ALL OTHERS WHO USE OUR PRODUCTS.
OUR PRODUCTS MUST ALWAYS BE OF THE HIGHEST QUALITY.
WE MUST CONSTANTLY STRIVE TO REDUCE THE COST OF THESE PRODUCTS.
OUR ORDERS MUST BE PROMPTLY AND ACCURATELY FILLED.
OUR DEALERS MUST MAKE A FAIR PROFIT.

OUR SECOND RESPONSIBILITY IS TO THOSE WHO WORK WITH US —
THE MEN AND WOMEN IN OUR PLANTS AND OFFICES.
THEY MUST HAVE A SENSE OF SECURITY IN THEIR JOBS.
WAGES MUST BE FAIR AND ADEQUATE,
MANAGEMENT JUST, HOURS REASONABLE, AND WORKING CONDITIONS CLEAN AND ORDERLY.
EMPLOYEES SHOULD HAVE AN ORGANIZED SYSTEM FOR SUGGESTIONS AND COMPLAINTS.
SUPERVISORS AND DEPARTMENT HEADS MUST BE QUALIFIED AND FAIR MINDED.
THERE MUST BE OPPORTUNITY FOR ADVANCEMENT — FOR THOSE QUALIFIED
AND EACH PERSON MUST BE CONSIDERED AN INDIVIDUAL
STANDING ON HIS OWN DIGNITY AND MERIT

OUR THIRD RESPONSIBILITY IS TO OUR MANAGEMENT.
OUR EXECUTIVES MUST BE PERSONS OF TALENT, EDUCATION, EXPERIENCE AND ABILITY.
THEY MUST BE PERSONS OF COMMON SENSE AND FULL UNDERSTANDING.

OUR FOURTH RESPONSIBILITY IS TO THE COMMUNITIES IN WHICH WE LIVE.
WE MUST BE A GOOD CITIZEN — SUPPORT GOOD WORKS AND CHARITY,
AND BEAR OUR FAIR SHARE OF TAXES.
WE MUST MAINTAIN IN GOOD ORDER THE PROPERTY WE ARE PRIVILEGED TO USE.
WE MUST PARTICIPATE IN PROMOTION OF CIVIC IMPROVEMENT,
HEALTH, EDUCATION AND GOOD GOVERNMENT,
AND ACQUAINT THE COMMUNITY WITH OUR ACTIVITIES.

OUR FIFTH AND LAST RESPONSIBILITY IS TO OUR STOCKHOLDERS.
BUSINESS MUST MAKE A SOUND PROFIT.
RESERVES MUST BE CREATED, RESEARCH MUST BE CARRIED ON,
ADVENTUROUS PROGRAMS DEVELOPED, AND MISTAKES PAID FOR.
ADVERSE TIMES MUST BE PROVIDED FOR, ADEQUATE TAXES PAID, NEW MACHINES PURCHASED,
NEW PLANTS BUILT, NEW PRODUCTS LAUNCHED, AND NEW SALES PLANS DEVELOPED.
WE MUST EXPERIMENT WITH NEW IDEAS.
WHEN THESE THINGS HAVE BEEN DONE THE STOCKHOLDER SHOULD RECEIVE A FAIR RETURN.
WE ARE DETERMINED WITH THE HELP OF GOD'S GRACE,
TO FULFILL THESE OBLIGATIONS TO THE BEST OF OUR ABILITY.

Johnson & Johnson

SOURCE: Reproduced by permission of Johnson & Johnson.

How Much Emphasis Should Business Place on Societal Objectives?

Accompanying the growth of corporations in the United States is the growing concern among some individuals and organizations for the quality of life. Consumerism, pollution, and equality for minorities and women are concrete forms of such concern. Should a better society be one of the goals of big business, and, if so, to what degree and for what reasons should social welfare be of interest to an individual company? Should not social priorities be the exclusive concern of government, educators, the church, and individuals?

Some advocates of business involvement in social concerns see this as a kind of debt owed to society by the successful company and business person. Society has enabled such people to be successful, so they should give something back to society. Others see support of societal objectives as good for business. A better society would result in a better economic climate and thus, a better marketplace.

Although most companies offer similar salary ranges and benefits, a company that pays attention to the good of society should have an edge in attracting superior employees. An understanding of societal objectives gives executives and workers a broad viewpoint and knowledge that can be applied to better business practice. If business does not take responsibility for including societal objectives among its priorities, then government may well begin to regulate business in order to force it to do so.

But those who are against including social concerns as a business goal say that such a corporate policy can be threatening to managers. Managers who feel that the best people have been hired to fill jobs in their departments and then realize that all of these employees are white males between the ages of thirty and forty, may feel that their freedom to hire is being taken away, if corporate policy directs them to begin hiring minorities and women. What will the real cost of hiring be if such people are untrained or undertrained and not yet ready to assume management responsibility or to do the job? A directive of this kind seems to take away the managers' traditional freedom to hire and fire. Or, for example, what would be the added costs to a firm if an executive is given six months' leave to teach in a ghetto school?

Managers who do not want to participate in fulfilling social responsibilities are deprived of independence not to do so once social welfare becomes a company objective. Shareholders in a corporation and owners of a business, too, are deprived of a portion of their profits that would be spent on social concerns.

Figure 4-4
The Production Process

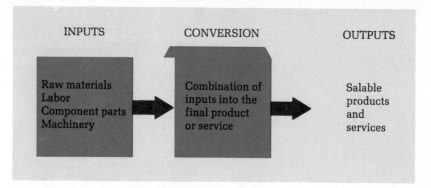

INPUTS   CONVERSION   OUTPUTS

Raw materials   Combination of   Salable
Labor   inputs into the   products
Component parts   final product   and
Machinery   or service   services

Management Functions

Management has already been defined as the achievement of objectives through people and other resources. This definition implies that management is a **process;** that is, *a series of actions that results in a certain end.* Figure 4-4 shows the workings of a manufacturing firm. A series of inputs in the form of raw materials, machinery, workers, and other ingredients are converted into finished products designed to satisfy the firm's customers. Completion of this process allows the firm to achieve its objectives.

Managers perform four basic functions: *planning, organizing, directing,* and *controlling.** These are the activities in which managers must be skilled if they are to accomplish their work.

Although Figure 4-5 shows four separate managerial functions, it is important to note that the functions are not separate and distinct. All four are interdependent, and the manager must coordinate them. As managers develop plans, they will also be involved in organizing to carry out these plans. Methods of controlling the operations will also be considered during the planning process. Coordination of these functions leads to the accomplishment of organizational objectives.

It should be emphasized that all of these functions are performed by *all* levels of the management pyramid. Although top management may devote more time to planning, while supervisory managers spend more time on the directing function, the three levels are involved to some extent with all of the functions of management.

PLANNING   **Planning** *is the management function of anticipating the future and determining the courses of action to achieve company objectives.*

*It should be pointed out that management writers differ on both the number of management functions and the specific lists of functions. Writers who choose to define the specific functions more narrowly include such functions as staffing, communicating, motivating, innovating, coordinating, and evaluating. Each of these functions must be accompanied by managers. The four functions listed here are assumed to encompass these more specific functions.

Figure 4-5
The Functions of
Management

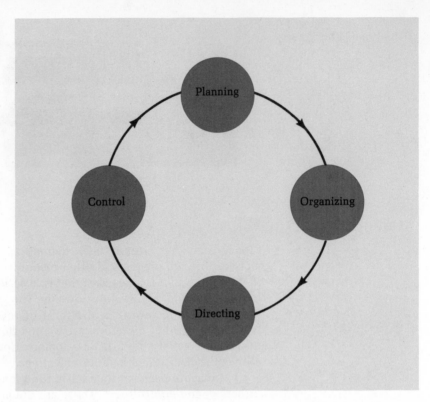

It encompasses decisions about what activities the organization should perform; how big it should be; what production, marketing, and financial strategies it should use in reaching its objectives; and what resources are needed to accomplish its goals. Planning involves the determination of courses of action to answer the questions of what should be done, by whom, where, when, and how. In the same way an architect designs a blueprint, the manager constructs a plan for the organizational activities necessary to reach objectives.

The planning process

The planning process includes several steps. Figure 4-6 shows how planning progresses through each one.

The following business example describes the stages of the planning process.

The Sturdivant Meat-packing Company

The Sturdivant Meat-packing Company is a leading firm in the meat-packing industry, with annual sales in excess of $600 million. Its brand name is well known in canned meat products and in frozen meats. Although the brand is highly regarded by consumers, the management of Sturdivant has recently become increasingly concerned about the growing price dif-

Figure 4-6
Steps in the Planning
Process

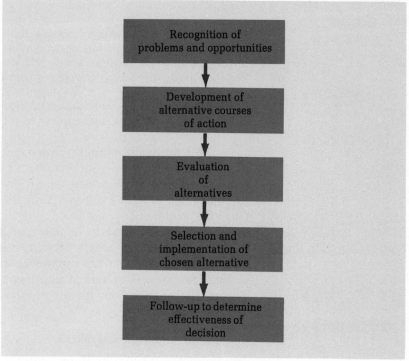

Recognition of
problems and opportunities

Development of
alternative courses
of action

Evaluation
of
alternatives

Selection and
implementation of
chosen alternative

Follow-up to determine
effectiveness of
decision

"Son, the Marshak Co. has taken us over, lock, stock and barrel. And old man Marshak—he's adopted you."

Managers Must Be Prepared To Cope with Change

SOURCE: Reproduced by permission of the artist, Sidney Harris.

85 INTRODUCTION TO MANAGEMENT

ference between domestic and imported meats. Large food chains are increasingly turning to the marketing of meat products under their own brand names, often at prices as much as 10 to 15 percent less than national brands through volume purchases from countries such as Argentina. Imported meat is identical in quality with domestic meats because of U.S. Department of Agriculture grading requirements.

Consumers appear to be gradually turning away from the Sturdivant brand because of the price differential. Sturdivant has been approached by two South American meat suppliers to contract for future beef imports.

The Sturdivant example illustrates some of the steps in the planning process. Sturdivant first learned of the problem (and potential opportunity) by observing the actions of retail chain stores and by comparing company sales with organizational goals for the year. Once the problem is determined, alternative courses of action are listed and then evaluated. In this case such factors as consumer reactions to imported meats, labeling requirements, and dependability of the South American suppliers may be involved. Information on these factors will enable management to assess the merits of the various alternatives. Finally, one of the alternatives will be chosen and put into action.

Planning is a continual process

The statement, "The only thing constant is change," is undeniably true in the business world of the 1970's. Business conditions change; laws change; organizations change. Managers must continually monitor their operations and the business environment, and make any necessary adjustments to their plans. This continual analysis and comparison of actual performance with company objectives allows the manager to make corrections and adjustments to plans before problems become crises. Otherwise, managers may be forced to devote all of their energies to emergency planning and "firefighting" in order to meet short-term emergencies. Successful accomplishment of other managerial functions is unlikely without sound and continuous planning.

ORGANIZING   Once plans have been developed, the next step is typically that of organization. **Organizing** may be defined as *the means by which management blends human and material resources through the design of a formal structure of tasks and authority.* It involves classifying and dividing work into manageable units. Organizing includes these three steps:

1. determining specific work activities necessary to accomplish organizational objectives
2. grouping work activities into a logical pattern or structure
3. assigning the activities to specific positions and people.

Organization in a Commune?

Most people view communes as pastoral settings where people ignore such worldly considerations as money, planning, organizing, and the other trappings of modern society. But communal failures have resulted in a concern for learning from past mistakes. Conferences have been held at which representatives from the nation's two thousand communes have exchanged ideas of effective management, the formation of cooperative buying groups, trade agreements, and communications systems.

The 35-member Twin Oaks commune, located on 123 acres near Louisa, Virginia, is operated as a corporation. Its organizational structure rivals many large companies.

For Twin Oaks members, the commune's businesslike methods begin with a contract executed before joining. Under this agreement members either lend or donate money to Twin Oaks at the time of membership; and after three years members are expected to turn over all their assets as outright donations to the community . . .

Members are paid in "labor credits" for their various chores; the more distasteful the task, the higher its credit rating and the less time needed to earn the weekly quota of 40 credits. (Dish-washing, for example, is thought by most members to be undesirable and rates 1.4 credits an hour; more desirable tasks rate only one credit an hour.) Overseeing the awarding of credits and other administrative tasks are managers—one for every communal sector (including the garden, pets and construction, among others)—who are appointed by a *board of planners* that acts much like a corporate board.

The planners at Twin Oaks consult with the membership as a whole prior to making decisions, but unanimity of opinion isn't required. "Group consensus becomes a silly forum for people fond of their own voices," a spokesman says. "My solution: Let them talk—then have experienced and responsible people make decisions."

Source: "What's This? Distasteful as It Is, Many Communes Turn to Business Techniques," *The Wall Street Journal* (December 12, 1971). Reprinted with permission of *The Wall Street Journal,* © Dow Jones & Company, Inc. 1971. All rights reserved.

Included in the organizing function are the important steps of **staffing** the organization with *competent employees who are capable of performing the necessary activities and the assignment of authority and responsibility to each individual.* The staffing area is the subject of Chapter 7 of this book, while Chapter 5 is devoted to the subject of the organizing function.

DIRECTING Once plans have been formulated and an organization has been created and staffed, the task becomes one of directing people to achieve organization goals. **Directing** may be formally defined as *the accomplishment of organizational objectives by guiding and motivating subordinates.* It includes making work assignments, explaining procedures, issuing orders, and seeing that mistakes are corrected.

The directing function is particularly important at the supervisory management level since the greatest number of employees are concentrated at this level. If the supervisors are to accomplish this task of "getting things done through people," they must be effective leaders.

Directing is also sometimes referred to as *motivating, leading, guiding,* or *human relations.* It is the *people* function of management and is discussed at length in Chapter 6 of this book.

CONTROLLING **Controlling** is *the management function involved in evaluating the organization's performance to determine whether it is accomplishing its objectives.* Controlling is linked closely to planning; in fact, the basic purpose of controlling is the determination of how successful the planning function has been.

The three basic steps in controlling are:

1. setting standards
2. collecting information to discover any deviations from standards
3. taking corrective action to bring any deviations that might occur into line.

A home automatic heating system provides a good illustration of the controlling function, as shown in Figure 4-7. Once the objective of a temperature setting (perhaps 68° Fahrenheit) has been established, information about the actual temperature in the house is collected and compared with the objective, and a decision is made based upon this comparison. If the temperature drops below an

Figure 4-7
A Temperature Control
System

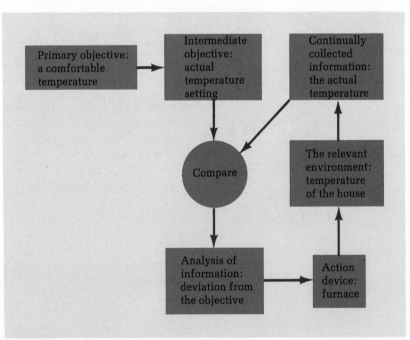

SOURCE: Reprinted by permission of John Wiley & Sons, Inc. from Bertram Schoner and Kenneth P. Uhl, *Marketing Research: Information Systems and Decision Making.* Copyright © 1975 John Wiley & Sons, Inc.

ORGANIZATION AND MANAGEMENT OF THE ENTERPRISE

established figure, the decision is made to activate the furnace until the temperature reaches some established level. On the other hand, a high temperature may result in a decision to turn off the furnace and start the cooling system.

Deviation from the firm's goals of profitability, return on investment, or market share may require changes in price structures, new sources of raw materials, changes in production methods, a new package design, or numerous other alternatives. The firm's control system must provide the necessary information—from sales records, production cost figures, financial data, or marketing research studies —to uncover deviations from organizational goals. This information then becomes the key ingredient for revisions in plans, and the cycle of planning/organizing/directing/controlling continues.

Management Functions and the Management Pyramid

Earlier in the chapter it was pointed out that all four management functions are performed at all levels of management. But as Figure 4-8 indicates, the amount of time devoted to each function varies for each management level. Top management performs more planning than does the supervisory management level. On the other hand, supervisors at the third rung of the management pyramid will devote more of their time to directing and controlling.

Leadership

Managers achieve organizational objectives by being good leaders. Good leadership can motivate individuals and groups to higher levels of achievement. But what is good leadership?

Various attempts have been made to identify the traits of a good leader. Although the various listings differ, three traits are usually present. These traits are *empathy*, *self-awareness*, and *objectivity in dealing with others*. Each is illustrated in Figure 4-9.

DOES AGE MATTER? While most persons associate leadership with experience, history sometimes reflects a different story. Alexander the Great won some of his most important victories at eighteen. At twenty-nine, Senator Charles Percy was president of Bell and Howell. The Maharaj Ji had attracted millions of devoted followers at the age of sixteen. Experience was not a barrier for these persons.

Figure 4-8
Relative Amount of Time Spent on Each Management Function by Different Levels of Management

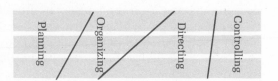

Top management

Middle management

Supervisory management

Figure 4-9
The Traits of a Good
Leader

A good leader should possess:

1. *Empathy.* Placing myself in his or her shoes.
   "How does the worker view this new rule?"
   "Will the worker be able to see its value if I explain it this way?"
   "Whom does the worker trust, and whom does he or she fear?"

2. *Self-awareness.* Knowing oneself:
   "What are my strengths? My weaknesses?"
   "What do my people think of me?"
   "Do they consider me fair and objective?"
   "Am I too gruff in dealing with others?"

3. *Objectivity in interpersonal relations.*
   "Am I objective in dealing with my subordinates or do I react too emotionally?"
   "Do I maintain a detached view in reacting to subordinates' behavior?"
   "Can I be empathetic and objective at the same time?"

LEADERSHIP STYLES

An effective leader recognizes that there are wide variations in leadership styles. Some leaders will emphasize the power of their position to compel the performance of subordinates. Some leaders make decisions on their own, rather than consulting their subordinates. Others allow their subordinates to participate in decision making.

The three basic leadership styles are:

1. autocratic
2. free rein
3. democratic.

Autocratic leaders *make decisions on their own without consulting others.* **Democratic leaders** *involve their subordinates in making decisions.* An autocratic sales manager provides sales personnel with specific sales quotas; a democratic manager allows them to *participate* in setting quotas. **Free rein leaders** *believe in minimal supervision and leave most decisions to be made by their subordinates.* Figure 4-10 illustrates this continuum of leadership styles.

WHICH LEADERSHIP STYLE IS BEST?

The answer to this question is: "It depends!" The best leadership style will vary, depending on three elements: *the leader, the followers,* and *the situation.* Some leaders do not possess the personality necessary to encourage—or even allow—subordinates to participate in decision making. Also, some followers do not have the ability—or desire—to assume the responsibilities involved in decision making. And the particular situation will affect what type of leadership style will be most effective. Problems requiring immediate solutions may have to be handled without consultation of subordinates. With less time pressure, participative decision making may be desirable.

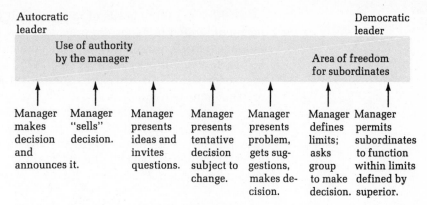

Figure 4-10
Continuum of
Leadership Behavior

Autocratic leader — Democratic leader

Use of authority by the manager — Area of freedom for subordinates

| Manager makes decision and announces it. | Manager "sells" decision. | Manager presents ideas and invites questions. | Manager presents tentative decision subject to change. | Manager presents problem, gets suggestions, makes decision. | Manager defines limits; asks group to make decision. | Manager permits subordinates to function within limits defined by superior. |

SOURCE: Adapted from Robert Tannenbaum and Warren H. Schmidt, "How to Choose a Leadership Pattern," *Harvard Business Review* (May–June 1973), p. 164. Reprinted with permission.

A normally democratic leader may be forced to be autocratic in making a decision concerning a 10 percent reduction in staff personnel. The employees are not likely to be called into conference and consulted on who should go!

In general, managers are increasingly adopting the democratic style of leadership. Workers who are involved in decision making generally feel that they are more involved in the overall organization, and are motivated to contribute more to organizational objectives.

Should the Leadership Style Depend upon the Situation?

After devoting many years of research into the best types of leader, Professor Fred Feidler concluded that *no one best style of leadership exists.* He feels that the most effective leadership style will depend upon the power held by the leader, the difficulty of the tasks involved, and the characteristics of the workers.

Feidler argues that situations that are either extremely easy or extremely difficult are best handled by leaders who emphasize task accomplishment. Situations of moderate difficulty are best handled by leaders who emphasize participation and good working relations with subordinates.

Source: Fred Feidler, *A Theory of Leadership Effectiveness* (New York: McGraw-Hill, Inc., 1967).

Summary

Management is the achievement of objectives through people and other resources. It is the critical ingredient in the Five Ms of an organization: management, manpower, materials, money, and machinery. Management principles are universal; they apply equally to profit and nonprofit organizations.

There are three levels of management in most firms: *top management,* which includes the president and vice-presidents; *middle management,* which includes plant managers and key department heads; and *supervisory management,* which is made up of first-line managers such as supervisors. These three levels constitute the management pyramid.

Definite organizational objectives are needed by managers in performing their functions. These objectives serve as standards, and their pursuit is the basis of all management efforts. Common organizational objectives include profitability, market share, and such societal aims as providing employment and being a good corporate citizen.

Managers perform four basic functions in attempting to achieve company objectives:

1. planning
2. organizing
3. directing
4. controlling.

Plans serve as blueprints for future courses of action. *Organizing* involves grouping work into logical patterns and assigning tasks to specific workers. *Directing* involves matching performance with organizational goals. It is the people function of management. *Controlling* deals with evaluating actual performance to determine whether the organization is accomplishing its objectives. Control involves setting standards, collecting information to discover any deviations from standards, and taking corrective action to bring any deviation into line.

Although all management levels are involved in each of the managerial functions, top management devotes more of its time to the planning and organizing functions, while the lower levels are more involved with directing and controlling.

Effective leaders are likely to possess three traits: empathy (or the ability of the leader to look at the situation from another's point of view), self-awareness, and objectivity. The three basic leadership styles are autocratic, free rein, and democratic. The best leadership style depends on three elements: the leader, the followers, and the situation. The general trend is to more participation of subordinates in decisions that affect them.

Review questions

1. Identify the following terms:
   a. management
   b. management pyramid
   c. top management
   d. middle management
   e. supervisory management
   f. objectives
   g. planning
   h. organizing

i. directing   l. democratic leader
j. controlling   m. free rein leader
k. autocratic leader

2. How do managers achieve objectives through people and other resources?
3. "Management principles are universal." Comment.
4. Outline the organization of the management pyramid.
5. Why are objectives important to managers?
6. Identify and define the four basic functions of management.
7. Describe the steps in the planning process.
8. What are the three basic steps of controlling?
9. What traits are usually associated with effective leadership?
10. Identify and explain the three basic leadership styles.

Discussion questions and exercises

1. Evaluate the pro and con arguments to the controversial issue that appears in this chapter.
2. How much should a corporation president be paid? How should the salary be determined?
3. How would you describe your own leadership style? Has your approach been successful in leadership situations you have faced?
4. Consider a club, sports team, or other group to which you belong. Describe how the basic functions of management have been performed in this group. Has the group's management been effective in accomplishing its objectives? Why, or why not?
5. Develop a written plan for accomplishing some personal objective. (You will want to consider the four basic steps in the planning process.)

Case 4-1
Kockums—An Innovative Swedish Shipbuilder

Kockums, a Swedish builder of supertankers, faced critical personnel problems in 1969. Labor turnover was running at about 50 percent a year, and productivity was down. The firm's management first turned to efficiency experts who pushed for greater worker output, which angered Kockums' production workers.

Finally, in desperation, Nils-Hugo Hallenborg, the firm's chief executive, took a unique action. He turned the problem over to the union and asked union officials to determine the solution. They agreed to tackle the problem and produced a public report that was highly critical of Kockums' management. They also asked for specific changes in working conditions.

Hallenborg again startled observers by implementing the union report. Wages based on the number of units produced were replaced by hourly rates that now average $5.36 per hour. Additional medical staff was hired. Safety standards were upgraded. Saunas were provided. Social workers were made available to deal with a worker's personal problems. Vacation cabins were built in Scandinavia, Western Europe, and Africa.

Kockums has also tried to give production workers more responsibility. Joint management-labor committees now schedule the construction of the six or so supertankers built annually. The firm acknowledged that jobs that are basically "dirty" cannot be changed. But management has worked to improve nearly everything around these jobs.

Kockums' employees have enthusiastically supported these reforms. Worker output is up and turnover is now under 20 percent a year. Kockums' personnel director puts it this way: "People like to work when they know why they are working."

Questions

1. Do you think Kockums' approach would work in a large U.S. manufacturing firm? Why, or why not?
2. In your opinion, why did Hallenborg's strategy prove effective?
3. Relate the situation at Kockums to what you learned in Chapter 4 of this book.

Source: Bowen Northrup. "More Swedish Firms Attempt to 'Enrich' Production-line Jobs," *The Wall Street Journal* (October 25, 1974). Used with permission. Reprinted with permission of *The Wall Street Journal,* © Dow Jones & Company, Inc. 1974. All rights reserved.

Case 4-2
Management—Japanese Style

Japanese firms have made major investments in the United States in recent years. Japanese-managed factories are now found throughout the country.

Some Americans employed by these firms have had a difficult time adjusting to the Japanese style of management. Japanese workers identify more closely with their companies than they do with their communities. Some even wear company jackets to work. Japanese managers take special steps to keep their employees happy, and workers feel that they are lifetime employees of the firm. Firings and layoffs are rare. Japanese managers are accustomed to making decisions through group agreement and find it difficult to say "no" to their subordinates. Problem-solving meetings are frequent and usually last for several hours.

Japanese managers also keep close contact with their employees. Yoshinori Kitano, president of YKK Zipper in Macon, Georgia, works in a company windbreaker similar to that worn by all YKK employees. His desk is jammed into an open area used by many of his subordinates. Kitano spends at least an hour a day working as a machine operator.

Questions

1. How would you describe the Japanese style of management?
2. What is your opinion of this Japanese management style?
3. What type of problems would you expect Japanese managers to encounter in the United States?

Source: Louis Kraar. "The Japanese Are Coming—With Their Own Style of Management," *Fortune* (March 1975), pp. 116ff. Used with permission.

5

The Role of Organization

"An organization chart strangles profits and stifles people."
—Robert Townsend

". . . the easiest course would be for me to blame those to whom I delegated the responsibility . . . In any organization the man at the top must bear the responsibility. That responsibility, therefore, belongs here in this office. I accept it."

—Richard M. Nixon

What Chapter 5 Is All About

1. In this chapter you will learn about the need for a formal organization structure and what is involved in building this structure.
2. You will be able to evaluate the four basic forms of organization: line, functional, line-and-staff, and committee.
3. You will understand the meanings of authority and responsibility.
4. You will know the factors that determine how many workers a supervisor should manage.
5. You will be able to explain Parkinson's Law and how to avoid it.
6. You will be aware of both the strengths and weaknesses of organizational charts.
7. You will recognize the function of informal organizations in a firm.
8. After reading this chapter, you should understand these terms:

organization	Parkinson's Law
departmentalization	line organization
delegation	line-and-staff
responsibility	organization
authority	functional organization
accountability	committee organization
span of control	organization chart
decentralization	informal organization

When young Vito Corleone came to the United States from his home in Sicily, he carried only a small parcel of clothes and his identification tags. Almost half a decade later he controlled a huge empire, commanded an army of men, and had amassed a fortune. There was no room in Don Vito's organization for sharing of power; it was an absolute dictatorship, and he was the dictator. What benefits he gave were given out of his volunteered generosity and his paternalism.

The influence of authority figures was an old story to Vito Corleone. In Sicily he had seen his whole family wiped out by a local chieftain and had barely escaped with his life. In New York he had worked hard, only to see his job handed to a relative of an extortionist who controlled the neighborhood. So Vito made friends and kept his own counsel. But his was not a loyal and blind obedience to those who commanded the mean streets in the Italian ghetto where he lived.

Vito coldly and logically saw crime as the only way he could get what he wanted. But what he stole was to be his; he refused to "share" with the local boss. Vito was without morals, but he acted out of what he saw as necessity, as the men around him acted. His mind was clever and calculating. While building a reputation for helping others weaker than himself (who were no threat to him), for fairness and courage, he left behind him debts to be repaid—at some time in the future. His influence grew as the not-to-be forgotten debts mounted. He knew when to allow his adversaries to back gracefully out of a stalemate, but he always held the winning hand—"an offer no one could refuse." Ruthless, a strategist of great foresight, Vito Corleone survived the bullet wounds inflicted by the "hit men" of a rival Family and died at home.

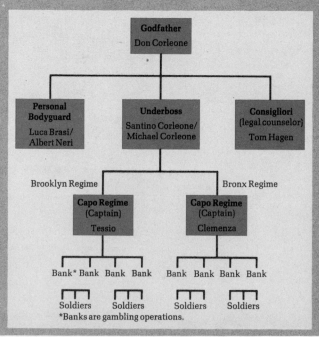

"Our New Accounts Department will be pleased to accept your deposit."

"Since this is the first day of class, let's talk about how the course will be organized . . ."

"The hive contains soldiers, workers, drones, and the queen . . ."

"You will be assigned to Personnel this summer . . ."

W e are constantly confronted with organization in a bewildering variety of activities. Sports teams and social organizations, religious groups and work activities—all include organization. Even groups of animals—such as bees, ants, baboons, and beavers—have organization.

Much of the success of a business depends on organization. Some established structure is required to see that the manager's plans are carried out.

What Are Organizations?

Organization may be defined simply as *a structured process in which people interact to accomplish objectives.* Note that three key elements are present:

1. human interaction
2. goal-directed activity
3. structure.

ORGANIZATIONS ARE AS OLD AS MANKIND

The need for organization to accomplish goals efficiently has long been recognized by humans. In *Exodus* Moses grappled with the problem of how to get things done, and received this advice from his father-in-law:

The thing that thou doest is not good. Thou wilt surely wilt away, both thou and this people with thee; for this thing is too heavy for thee—thou are not able to perform it thyself alone.

Hearken now unto my voice, I will give thee counsel . . . thou shalt provide out of the people able men . . . and place such over them (the people), to be rulers of thousands, rulers of hundreds, rulers of fifties, and rulers of tens. And let them judge the people at all seasons. And it shall be that every great matter they shall bring unto thee, but every small matter they shall judge themselves. So shall it be easier for thyself, and they shall bear the burden with thee.

If thou shalt do this thing, and God command thee so, then thou shall be able to endure, and all this people shall also go to their place in peace.

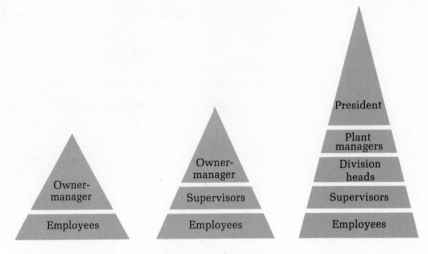

ORGANIZATION PROBLEMS INCREASE AS THE FIRM GROWS

For small businesses, the organizing function is rather simple. The owner-manager of the local dry-cleaning firm employs a few people to sell, to launder and dry-clean clothing, and to make deliveries. The owner usually handles the necessary purchases of detergents, plastic wrappers, and other materials; assigns jobs to employees; and personally directs the operation of the business.

But as a company grows, the need for organization increases as Figure 5-1 illustrates. With increased size comes specialization and a larger number of employees. Rather than a single salesperson, the organization employs a large sales force; rather than one bookkeeper, the firm has a sizeable accounting department. The large number of personnel and accompanying specialization make it impossible for one person to supervise all operations individually. Some formal organization is necessary—as the manager faces the same organizational problems that once confronted Moses.

Organizational Structure

Although the small dry-cleaning firm experiences fewer organizational problems than the larger company, both have established a formal *structure* to insure that people perform tasks designed to accomplish company objectives. Specific duties are assigned to wrappers, cleaners, and other personnel in the dry-cleaning company, for example.

Organizational structure focuses first upon the *activities* necessary to reach goals. Management must analyze the sequence of jobs that are to be performed. Then people with both an interest and the necessary qualifications for performing the jobs are employed. *Coordination* of the activities of each worker is another important responsibility of management, since employees must "pull together" if the firm is to operate smoothly.

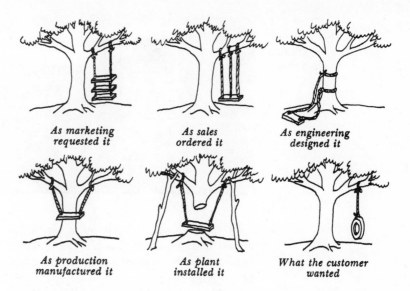

As marketing
requested it

As sales
ordered it

As engineering
designed it

As production
manufactured it

As plant
installed it

What the customer
wanted

Departmental Structure Aids Management in the Coordination of Company Activities

SOURCE: Reproduced by special permission from *Parts Pups*.

Well-defined organizational structure should also contribute to *employee morale*. When the employee knows exactly what is expected on the job, who the supervisor is, and how the work fits into the total organizational structure, the *esprit de corps* of a harmonious, loyal work force is likely to exist.

Building the Organizational Structure

The structure of the formal organization is based on an analysis of the three key elements of any organization: human interaction, work activities, and objectives. Management must coordinate the activities of workers in accomplishing organizational objectives.

But viewing a list of company objectives does not specifically show the mechanic that production machinery should be regularly inspected and any defects repaired. The company objective reads: *to provide our customers with quality products at competitive prices.*

Company objectives are broad in nature and do not reflect specifically on each individual work activity. Consequently, these objectives must be broken down into specific goals for each worker in the organization. Figure 5-2 illustrates this *hierarchy of organizational objectives.*

HIERARCHY OF OBJECTIVES Objectives exist in a hierarchy, extending from the overall objectives of the firm to specific objectives established for each employee. The broader goals of profitability, sales, market share, and service must be broken down into objectives for each division, for

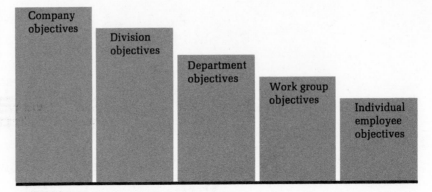

Figure 5-2
The Hierarchy of
Organizational
Objectives

Company objectives

Division objectives

Department objectives

Work group objectives

Individual employee objectives

each factory, each department, each work group, and each individual worker. Once this has been accomplished, each worker can view his or her contribution to accomplishing the total organizational goals.

The number of levels in the hierarchy depends on the size and complexity of the firm. Smaller firms usually have fewer levels of objectives than do larger companies.

DEPARTMENTALI-ZATION

Building an organizational structure begins with an analysis of the major activities of the organization. In most firms these activities would consist of production, marketing, and finance. Each of these activities would be assigned to separate departments in the firm, with both managers and employees.

Departmentalization is *the subdivision of work activities into units within the organization.* A marketing department may be headed by a marketing vice-president, and would include sales, advertising, and market research. The personnel department would include such areas as recruitment, training, employee benefits, and industrial relations.

Five major forms of departmentalization exist. General Motors subdivides its organizational structure on the basis of *products*—the Chevrolet, Pontiac, Oldsmobile, Buick, and Cadillac divisions. The Bell Telephone System is subdivided on a *geographic* basis; so are many railroads, chain stores, and gas and oil distributors. Many sporting-goods stores subdivide on a *customer* basis, with a wholesale operation serving school systems and a retail division to serve retail customers. A fourth form of departmentalization is by *function.* The production department will consist of the areas of manufacturing, purchasing, research and development, quality control, and production engineering. An oil company, such as Mobil or Exxon, may be divided into exploration, production, refining, marketing, and finance departments. The final kind of departmentalization is by *process.* For example, the manufacturing of a product may include cutting the material on a lathe, heat-treating it, cutting it

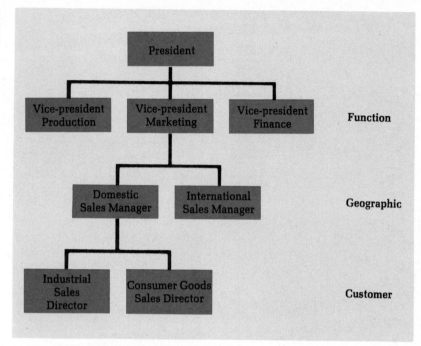

into its final shape, and painting it. These activities would be included in one department.

As Figure 5-3 indicates, a number of different bases for departmentalization may be used within the same company. The
decisions on which bases to use are made by balancing the advantages and disadvantages of each base. The experience and judgment of top management come into play in such decisions.

**AUTHORITY AND
RESPONSIBILITY**

As the organization grows, the manager must assign some actiyities
to subordinates in order to have time to devote to managerial functions. *The act of assigning part of the manager's activities to subordinates is called* **delegation.**

In delegating activities, the manager assigns a **responsibility**
to subordinates to perform the tasks assigned to them. Responsibility
may be defined as *the obligation of a subordinate to perform assigned duties.* Along with responsibility must go **authority,** *the
power to act and make decisions in carrying out assignments.*
Authority and responsibility must be balanced so that subordinates
are capable of carrying out their assigned tasks. Delegation of sufficient authority to fulfill the subordinate's responsibility in turn
makes the subordinate **accountable** to the supervisor for results.
Accountability is *the act of holding a manager liable for carrying
out activities for which he or she has the necessary authority and
responsibility.* This relationship is illustrated in Figure 5-4.

Figure 5-4
The Delegation Process

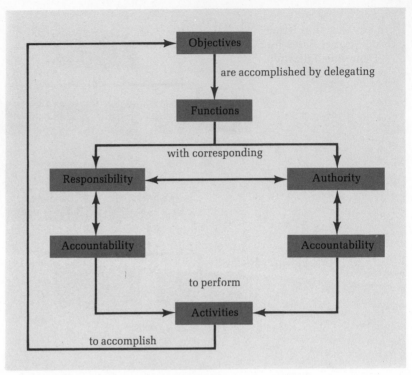

SOURCE: Robert D. Hay, *Introduction to Business* (New York: Holt, Rinehart and Winston, 1968), p. 102. Copyright © 1968 by Holt, Rinehart and Winston, Inc. Reprinted by permission of Holt, Rinehart and Winston, Inc.

Even though the manager delegates authority to his subordinates, the *final responsibility rests with him*. It is therefore incumbent upon the manager to select qualified subordinates who are capable of performing the delegated tasks.

HOW MANY SUBORDINATES CAN A MANAGER SUPERVISE?

One of the reasons for departmentalization is that managers are limited in the number of activities they can perform and the number of subordinates they can effectively supervise. The **span of control** *is the optimum number of subordinates a manager can effectively manage.*

Although the optimum number will vary from one firm to the next, many management writers agree that top management should directly supervise no more than four to eight people. Supervisory managers who direct workers performing relatively routine tasks are capable of effectively managing a much larger number.

The critical factors in determining the optimum span of control are the *type of work, training of workers, ability of the manager,* and the *effectiveness of communications*. An experienced supervisor, who manages trained workers performing routine tasks with clear guidelines as to what is expected of them, can effectively manage a much larger number of subordinates than the Vice-president of Marketing or Production can.

Communications Problems Often Grow as the Size of the Organization Increases

A colonel issued the following order to his executive officer:

Tomorrow evening at approximately 2000 hours Halley's Comet will be visible in this area, an event which occurs only once every 75 years. Have the men fall out in the battalion area in fatigues, and I will explain this rare phenomenon to them. In case of rain, we will not be able to see anything, so assemble the men in the theater and I will show them films of it.

Executive officer to company commander:

By order of the Colonel, tomorrow at 2000 hours, Halley's Comet will appear above the battalion area. If it rains, fall the men out in fatigues, then march to the theater where this rare phenomenon will take place, something which occurs only once every 75 years.

Company commander to lieutenant:

By order of the Colonel be in fatigues at 2000 hours tomorrow evening, the phenomenal Halley's Comet will appear in the theater. In case of rain, in the battalion area, the Colonel will give another order, something which occurs once every 75 years.

Lieutenant to sergeant:

Tomorrow at 2000 hours, the Colonel will appear in the theater with Halley's Comet, something which happens every 75 years if it rains, the Colonel will order the comet into the battalion area.

Sergeant to squad:

When it rains tomorrow at 2000 hours, the phenomenal 75-year-old General Halley, accompanied by the Colonel, will drive his comet through the battalion area theater in fatigues.

Source: *DS Letter,* Vol. 1, No. 3 (1971), from a speech by Dan Bellus. Reprinted by permission of the publisher Didactic Systems, Inc., Box 457, Cranford, New Jersey 07016.

CENTRALIZATION VERSUS DECENTRALIZATION

A fundamental question of delegation is that of **decentralization.** How much authority is the manager willing to disperse throughout the organization? *Managers who disperse only the slightest amount of authority operate on a* **centralized** management philosophy. Proponents of the centralization philosophy feel that they can control and coordinate company activities more effectively by retaining most of the authority.

Some managers emphasize **decentralization.** This means they follow *the practice of dispersing great amounts of authority to subordinates.* This allows middle and supervisory management more leeway in making decisions than they would have under a centralization philosophy. Middle managers in a decentralized operation are more likely to make many financial, production, and personnel decisions themselves, without the necessity of obtaining prior approval from their superiors. As more decisions are made by subordinates, higher-level managers are freed to devote additional time to more important problems.

Too Much Decentralization Can Prove Disastrous

Some companies have carried decentralization too far—with almost fatal results. Unless control procedures have been developed to keep top management informed of major decisions, the practice of giving subordinate managers the power to make key decisions can prove very costly. The greatest loss incurred by a private company in the history of the United States occurred for this reason.

The Convair Division of General Dynamics Corporation acquired so much authority that it was able to lose $480 million on the poorly controlled Convair 880 and 990 jet airplane program. This huge loss almost bankrupted General Dynamics Corporation.*

*The history of the Convair Division is described in a lively manner in Richard Austin Smith. *Corporations in Crisis* (New York: Doubleday Anchor Books, 1966), pp. 67–112.

AVOIDING UNNECESSARY ORGANIZATIONAL GROWTH

As the size and complexity of the organization increases, the tendency to add additional supervisory personnel and specialists also increases. This tendency is natural as decentralization occurs and as managers recognize their limited span of control. The organizational planner must, however, be convinced of the need for additional personnel, or new layers of managers and dozens of technical advisers may be added to the company with very little accompanying increase in production output or efficiency.

The British historian-philosopher C. Northcote Parkinson expressed this tendency in his book **Parkinson's Law:** *"Work expands so as to fill the time available for its completion."*[1]

Parkinson applied this law to organizations by illustrating how the number of employees in a firm increases over a period of time regardless of the amount of work to be done. He pointed out that in 1914 the British navy was the most powerful in the world and contained 4,366 officials. By 1967 the "practically powerless" British navy was managed by more than 33,000 civil servants. As the British Empire shrunk rapidly, in the period from 1935 to 1954, the number of officials in the British Colonial Office grew from 372 to 1,661, an average annual increase of nearly 6 percent.

The British government possesses no monopoly on continued organizational growth. The U.S. Department of Agriculture payroll contains one official for every 24 farmers. And the proportions are even more significant at the Bureau of Indian Affairs. A tongue-in-cheek story tells of the BIA official sobbing uncontrollably in his office at the Washington headquarters. When asked about the nature of his problem he responded, "My Indian died!"

Why does this tendency to add employees at a faster rate than the work to be done occur? According to Parkinson, it can be blamed on:

1. the selfish desire of managers to build empires by adding additional subordinates

2. the paperwork created by the employment of additional workers.

Preventing (or minimizing) the occurrence of Parkinson's Law requires top management to be constantly vigilant and to give an honest appraisal of the need for each proposed new position.

Forms of Organization Structure

Any group possessing common goals is an organization. But business organizations may be classified according to the nature of the authority relationships within their internal structures. Although four forms of organizational structure will be discussed in this text, only two forms are in common use today: **line** and **line-and-staff.** A third form, **functional organization,** is a transition from pure line organizations to the line-and-staff form. The final form is the **committee organization,** which exists in many companies, but only rarely as the sole type; it is instead typically used as a suborganizational form within a line or line-and-staff structure.

LINE ORGANIZATION— EVERY MANAGER AN EXPERT

The line organization is the oldest and simplest form of organizational structure. Caesar's legions used this form; so did the Roman Catholic Church. Figure 5-5 illustrates the line organization.

Line organization is *the organizational structure based on a direct flow of authority from the chief executive to subordinates.* It is illustrated by the familiar story of the general who informs the colonel, who tells the major, who instructs the captain, who orders

Figure 5-5
The Line Form of Organization Used by the Catholic Church

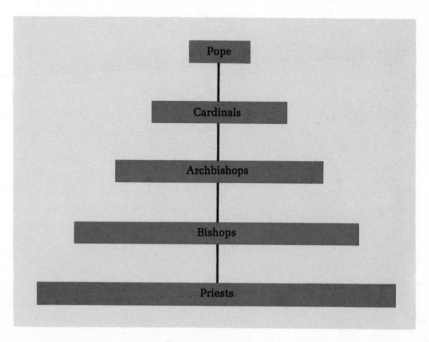

the lieutenant, who yells at the sergeant, who makes an unprintable request of the private, who carries out the order—or else.

The line form is simple; the chain of command is clear; and buck-passing is extremely difficult. Decisions may be made quickly, since the manager can act without consulting anyone other than his or her immediate superior.

But some obvious defects exist with line organization. Each manager has complete responsibility for a number of activities and cannot possibly be an expert in all of them. The supervisor is therefore forced to become a jack-of-all-trades.

The defects become very apparent in medium- and large-sized firms. The pure line form fails to provide specialized skills so vital in modern industry. Executives are overburdened with administrative details and paperwork and have little time to devote to planning.

In evaluating the strengths and weaknesses of the line form, the obvious conclusion is that this structure is ineffective in all but the smallest organizations. Beauty shops, cleaning plants, "Mom and Pop" grocery stores, and local law firms can operate effectively with a simple line structure. CBS, American Motors, and General Electric cannot.

FUNCTIONAL ORGANIZATION— ATTEMPTING TO SOLVE THE LINE ORGANIZATION'S LACK OF SPECIALIZATION

The functional organization form was developed by the *father of scientific management*, Frederick Taylor, who was attempting to overcome the basic weakness of the line organizational form: the concentration of too many duties on a single manager. Taylor divided the work of a supervisor into areas such as the components shown in Figure 5-6. Then he appointed a separate supervisor to be responsible for each activity. This made each worker responsible to a specialist in each activity—repair and maintenance, routing, inspection, training, and time and credit. The functional organization did not increase the number of managers; it simply grouped them differently. Under the line form each supervisor would occasionally be responsible for training. Under the functional form a specialist was placed in charge of all training and was given full authority and responsibility for this activity.

The **functional organization** *is the organizational structure based on a direct flow of authority for each work activity or function.* This form suffers from one critical deficiency: It creates a situation where workers have *more than one boss at the same level.* Even though each boss should possess authority only in the area of specialization, overlapping and conflict are inevitable. And when problems occur, it is extremely difficult to locate the person at fault. With too many masters, production may be slowed, rather than speeded up, and disciplinary problems are difficult to handle. The problems of this form are so great that it no longer exists in most organizations. But the functional organization form did serve a

Figure 5-6
The Functional
Organization of
Frederick Taylor

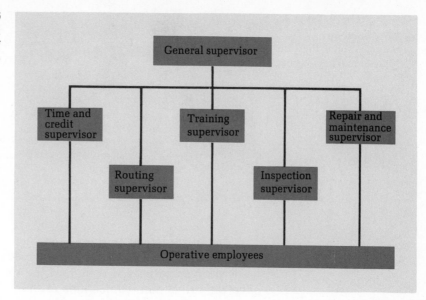

purpose in forcing management to focus on the need for developing an organizational structure that would overcome the shortcomings of the pure line form.

**LINE-AND-STAFF
ORGANIZATION—
COMBINING
THE MERITS OF
THE LINE AND
FUNCTIONAL
ORGANIZATION
FORMS**

The next logical step in organizational structure is to combine the strengths of the two kinds of organization. The **line-and-staff organization** is *the organizational structure which combines the direct flow of authority present in the line organization with staff departments which serve, advise, and support the line departments.* Line departments are involved directly in decisions which affect the operation of the organization. Staff departments lend specialized technical support. As Figure 5-7 shows, workers receive daily supervision from a line manager, while obtaining specialized advice and suggestions from staff personnel.

Figure 5-7
The Line-and-Staff
Organization

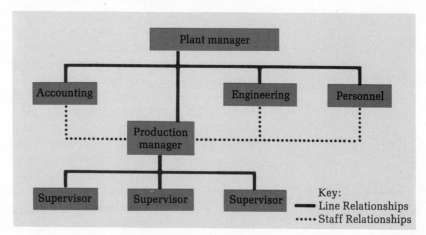

Table 5-1
Five Examples of Staff
Managers and the Line
Managers They Advise

Staff Manager	Line Managers Served
Controller	Performs financial analyses and makes recommendations to the president and other high-level executives.
Advertising Manager	Assists the marketing director in developing the firm's advertising strategy.
Director of Research	Collects information and advises the firm's president, vice-presidents, and general managers.
Legal Counsel	Advises top management of the company.
Director of Engineering	Advises top management on technical and engineering matters.

For all practical purposes the line-and-staff structure is the only organizational form capable of meeting the requirements of modern organizations. It combines the rapid decision making and effective, direct communications of the line organization with the expert knowledge needed to direct diverse and widespread activities of the functional organization.

The major difference between a line manager and a staff manager is in their *authority relationships*. The purpose of the staff is to make recommendations and to advise the line manager. Staff managers do not possess the authority to give orders or to compel the line manager to take action. Although staff managers do have the necessary line authority to supervise their own departments, their basic function is to provide expert advice for the line manager. Table 5-1 illustrates some staff personnel and their activities.

COMMITTEE ORGANIZATION

Committee organization is *the organizational structure where authority and responsibility are jointly held by a group of individuals rather than by a single manager*. It is not proposed as a separate structure for the entire organization but is typically incorporated into the regular line-and-staff structure.

In the area of new-product introductions, the most common organizational arrangement is the new-product committee. This committee is typically composed of representatives of top management in such areas as marketing, finance, manufacturing, engineering, research, and accounting. In major corporations, such as the 3 M Company, the inclusion of representatives from the various areas involved in developing new products should improve planning, since diverse perspectives—production, marketing, finance—are considered. Also, company morale should be strengthened, since all areas participate in decision making.

But committees tend to be slow and generally conservative, and decisions are often made by compromise based on conflicting interests rather than by choosing the best decision. The definition of

"The motion to take immediate and decisive action was tabled until next meeting. . . ."

Committees Are Often Slow in Making Decisions

SOURCE: *The Wall Street Journal*, March 18, 1975. Reprinted with permission from *The Wall Street Journal*.

a camel as a horse designed by a committee may be descriptive of some committee decisions.

COMPARING THE FOUR FORMS OF ORGANIZATION

Although most large companies are organized on a line-and-staff basis, the line organization is usually the best form for many smaller businesses. The committee form is also used to a limited extent in most major corporations, and such departments as legal may be organized on a functional basis. Table 5-2 compares the strengths and weaknesses of the four forms.

Methods of Formalization

Most companies show the *formal outline of the authority and responsibility relationships in an organization* through an **organization chart.** Such charts provide all employees with a visual statement of these relationships.

ORGANIZATION CHARTS

One of the tangible evidences of organizational structure in most companies is the presence of an organizational chart. The chart allows each person in the company to see how the work relates to the overall operation of the company and to see exactly to whom he or she reports. *The chart is the blueprint of the organization, indicating lines of authority within the organization.* Staff relationships as well as line ones are shown, as are all permanent committees.

Since the organization chart specifies each area of responsibility and authority, it can also help in *coordinating activities.* But

Table 5-2 Comparison of Line, Functional, Line-and-Staff, and Committee Organization

	Advantages	Disadvantages
Line Organization	1. Simple and easy for both workers and managers to understand 2. Clear delegation of authority and responsibility for each area 3. Quick decisions 4. Direct communications	1. No specialization 2. Overburdens top executives with administrative details
Functional Organization	1. Allows the benefits of specialization 2. Expert advice is available for each worker 3. Reduces managerial workload	1. Workers may have more than one boss 2. Discipline may break down unless authority is clearly defined 3. Conflict may arise due to overlapping of authority
Line-and-Staff Organization	1. Makes use of specialists who advise line managers 2. Employees report to one superior	1. Unless relationships are clear, conflict may arise between line and staff 2. Staff managers can only make recommendations to line managers
Committee Organization	1. Combined judgment of several executives in diverse areas 2. Improved morale through participation in decision making	1. Committees are often slow in making decisions 2. Decisions may be compromises rather than the best decisions

the chart reflects the organization at one point in time, and it should be revised and updated periodically to reflect changing conditions.

Robert Townsend, former president of Avis and author of the business satire *Up the Organization,* strongly endorses the need for *flexible* organizational charts which reflect a dynamic organization:

. . . draw them in pencil. Never formalize, print, and circulate them . . . A chart demoralizes people. Nobody thinks of himself as below other people . . .

In the best organizations people see themselves working in a circle as if around one table. One of the positions is designated chief executive officer, because somebody has to make all those tactical decisions that enable an organization to keep working . . .[2]

Although most organizational charts are constructed in the shape of a pyramid extending downward from the board of directors or the president, some firms have accepted Townsend's recommendations and construct their organization charts in a circle. Figure 5-8 shows how a circular chart might be constructed.

The Informal Organization

In addition to the formal lines of authority and responsibility shown on the organizational chart, informal channels of communications and contacts also exist. The **informal organization** *is a self-grouping*

Figure 5-8
A Circular Organization
Chart

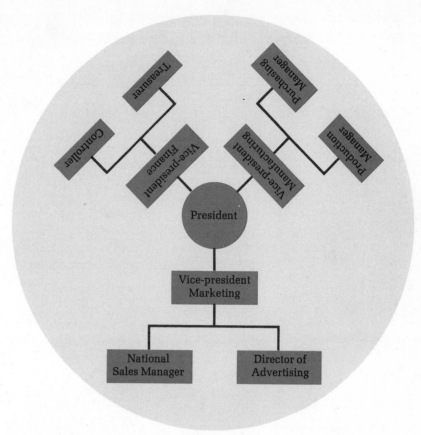

Treasurer

Purchasing Manager

Controller

Vice-president Finance

Vice-president Manufacturing

Production Manager

President

Vice-president Marketing

National Sales Manager

Director of Advertising

of employees in the organization who possess informal channels of communications and contacts. The type of organization is not formally planned; it develops out of the interactions of people.

Formal organization is the creation of management; informal organizations are the result of social and communications relationships. Groups of workers often cut across the formal organizational structure, and informal relations exist at both managerial and employee levels. Supervisors from a number of departments may take coffee breaks together to discuss mutual interests and problems—both company and personal ones. Two machinists, a drill press operator, a receiving clerk, and a supervisor may form the company basketball team. They regularly interact and discuss company operations. The results of their talks are often communicated to other workers in their work areas.

Even though the informal organization is not shown on the organizational chart, managers should be aware of its existence. It may even be possible to make use of the informal organization in accomplishing organizational objectives. One example is the use of the **grapevine**—*the informal communications network found in most organizations.* In his studies of the grapevine Professor Keith

Should Executives Reveal Their Illnesses?

Stress and its handicapping by-products seem to be one of the facts of life among today's business executives. Not too long ago stress seemed to be confined to corporate presidents in the form of ulcers. But the recent recession either has revealed the greater incidence of illness among executives at all levels of business, or has increased the amount and degree of such problems.

Should executives talk about their illnesses, mental or physical? Will companies, industry, and the economy be turned on their ears if executives are frank about their personal health problems?

In the United States it has been assumed that among business executives good health, especially good mental health, is common. To be sick in the all-male executive environment of the past was shameful, because it was equated with weakness. In a country where the rugged frontier has always been a part of the national life, where something fresh has been necessarily something good, being ill and worn out has been something to be concealed.

When illness is not acknowledged or is hidden, it is often left untreated and probably will only grow worse. Most often treatment of either a physical or a mental problem leads to improved health and improved functioning. When a health problem is ignored, it can be channeled into destructive directions for both the individual and the firm: absenteeism, poor productivity, drug use, or bad management.

When illness is hidden, the rumor mill may operate to the confusion and anxiety of employees and executives. Speculation based on rumor can often do more harm than facing up to real health problems and sharing them with bosses and other employees.

Even for those who feel that an executive's privacy is more important than the willingness to share problems with those around him or her on the job, neglect of an illness is no answer. As long as the illness is being treated, the individual's right to keep personal concerns private is a basic one in the United States. The security of employees can be undermined if they find out their boss is ill, and some employees may even leave the company. Although some bosses do understand and sympathize with the executive who has a health problem, others will allow it to influence their decisions concerning the responsibilities, training, and promotion of the executive, even when treatment is being given and the executive's health is improving. This is particularly the case when mental illness is involved. Many bosses do not understand mental illness and tend to see it as incurable or recurring. It is better to keep it hidden, some say, even if functioning is impaired and added stress is suffered through such concealment.

Davis has found it to be 80 to 90 percent accurate in transmitting noncontroversial information. Since this information travels by word of mouth, the grapevine is faster than formal communications.[3] Recognition of its existence and how it works may enable managers to use the grapevine as a supplement to formal communications channels in dispersing information and in minimizing rumors and incorrect information.

Summary

Organizations provide the necessary structure for managers to work toward the accomplishment of company objectives. The need for structure increases as businesses grow in size. As the numbers of subordinates increase, the responsibility of coordinating their activities through a formal structure also increases.

Formal organizational structure is based upon an analysis of the three key elements of an organization: human interaction, work activities, and objectives. Once the activities of the organization have been analyzed, they are grouped into units within the organization. This process of departmentalization may be based on one of five forms: products, geography, customers, functions, or processes.

Developing a formal organizational structure means that the chief executive must delegate the necessary authority and responsibility to accomplish their assignments to subordinates. They in turn are held accountable to their supervisors for the accomplishment of these assigned duties.

The optimum number of subordinates that can be effectively supervised by a manager is known as the span of control, which is determined by such factors as type of work being done, training of subordinates, abilities of the manager, and effectiveness of communications.

Four forms of organization structure have been used: line, functional, line-and-staff, and committee. The line organization is the simplest form, but it suffers from a lack of specialization by management. The functional organization solves the problem of specialization by appointing managers for each specialized activity. This form suffers from the potential problem of multiple bosses for each worker. The most common organization structure is the line-and-staff form, which incorporates the strengths of both line and functional organizational structures by assigning authority to line managers and adding staff specialists to provide information and advice. The committee form of organization is rarely used as the sole organizational structure, but is usually incorporated to some extent within the line-and-staff structure. Group decision making provides varied inputs to the decision-making process, since a committee may be composed of representatives of a number of areas in the organization. It also insures that each of these areas will be represented in the decision-making process. But it is relatively slow in making decisions, which may often simply be compromises between conflicting interests.

The organizational chart is a blueprint of the authority relationships within the organization. It shows functions, formal channels of communication, and line-and-staff relationships. It also indicates the responsibility, authority, and accountability relationships within the firm; but it does not reflect the informal groups or lines of communication that exist.

Review questions

1. Identify the following terms:
   a. organization
   b. departmentalization
   c. delegation
   d. authority
   e. responsibility
   f. accountability
   g. span of control
   h. decentralization
   i. Parkinson's law
   j. line organization
   k. line-and-staff organization
   l. functional organization
   m. committee organization
   n. organization chart
   o. informal organization
2. What are the purposes of a formal organization structure?
3. What is departmentalization? What major forms of departmentalization exist?
4. Why is it important that authority and responsibility be balanced in an organization?
5. Identify the determinants of the optimum span of control.
6. Distinguish between centralization and decentralization. Under what circumstances might each be preferred?
7. List the four types of formal organization.
8. Summarize the major advantages and disadvantages of each type of formal organizational structure.
9. What are the major purposes of an organizational chart?
10. Explain the concept of the informal organization. How does it differ from the formal organization?

Discussion questions and exercises

1. Evaluate the pro and con arguments to the controversial issue that appears in this chapter.
2. Give an example of a firm in your state that should use each of the following forms of departmentalization and explain why each form was chosen:
   a. products
   b. geographic
   c. customer
   d. functional
   e. process

3. Suggest some ways in which Parkinson's Law might be prevented.
4. Draw an organizational chart for your college. Indicate which positions are primarily *line* and which are primarily *staff*.
5. Although the Du Pont organization is a major exception, the committee structure is rarely used as a separate structure for an entire organization. Suggest several specific ways of improving the committee form of organizational structure.

Case 5-1
Mitbestimmung

Mitbestimmung is a German word meaning "have a voice in." It also represents a well-known industrial practice in West Germany and other European countries. *Mitbestimmung* began in the West German coal industry after World War II when workers gained the right to sit on industry supervisory boards. The practice has continued and expanded in recent years. For example, Norwegian workers are now allowed to select up to one-third of a firm's board of directors.

Questions

1. Do you think *Mitbestimmung* would be successful in the United States? Why, or why not?
2. Should this practice be introduced on an experimental basis by American firms? Defend your answer.
3. How would you feel about working in a company where this practice existed? Discuss.

Source: "Workers on the Board," *Time* (May 19, 1975), p. 57.

Case 5-2

The Organization of a Professional Sports Team

Professional sports teams in football, baseball, basketball, tennis, and hockey are business enterprises that use a simplified organizational structure. While not all sports or teams follow exactly the same pattern, most professional teams are owned by wealthy individuals (many of whom are millionaires) who enjoy being involved with a particular sport. The owner(s) usually makes major policy decisions, but a hired general manager handles other managerial duties. The general manager oversees the business side of the operation—such as ticket sales, travel, contracts for facilities, equipment, vendors, and personnel matters. The general manager usually has responsibility for player personnel decisions—as in trades, drafts of new players, and assignment of personnel to minor leagues. The field manager, or head coach, is in charge of the team's actual performance. This person assists the general manager in matters concerning players. In some cases the general manager is also the field manager. Other personnel employed by professional teams include team physicians, assistant coaches, trainers, equipment managers, secretaries, scouts, and ticket sales personnel.

Questions

1. Describe the strengths and weaknesses of the organizational structure of a professional sports team.
2. Draw an organization chart for a professional sports team.
3. Can you think of similar organizational structures in other businesses?

6

Human Relations in Management

"... fairness and decency for American workers means more than simply keeping them alive and safe from injury and disease. It means an effort to make it possible for workers to live not just as robots or machines, but as men and women who are human beings. Additionally, making the assembly line more human and humane is a large and difficult task, but it is at the heart of everything we mean by social justice in America."

—Senator Edward Kennedy

"Let them eat cake!"

—Marie Antoinette

What Chapter 6 Is All About

1. In this chapter you will explore different types of needs, and learn what motivates people.
2. You will be able to describe a Theory X manager and contrast him or her with a Theory Y manager.
3. You will be able to analyze a particular job and point out the factors that could serve as motivators.
4. You will understand the importance of good morale in achieving productivity and the factors involved in producing it.
5. You should be able to outline the steps involved in installing a Management by Objectives program.
6. After reading this chapter, you should understand these terms:

Hawthorne studies
needs
physiological needs
safety needs
social needs
esteem needs
self-actualization needs

Theory X
Theory Y
motivational factors
morale
management by
    objectives
job enrichment

Robert Townsend

SOURCE: Alfred A. Knopf.

Is it possible to have a sense of humor *and* a successful career in business? Robert Townsend, author of *Up the Organization* or "How to stop the corporation from stifling people and strangling profits," has credentials such as senior vice-president, chairman, director, and chief executive officer of a number of large U.S. corporations. These have included Avis Rent-a-Car, American Express, and Dun & Bradstreet.

Wit, a sharp mind, and clearheadedness mark the career and writings of Townsend, a direct descendant of George Washington's Chief of Intelligence. Following his own belief that no one should head a company for more than six years, Townsend left Avis in 1965, when it was sold to ITT, and after he had built the company from a multi-million dollar loser to a multi-million dollar profit maker. While Townsend seems to contradict all or most of the passwords of corporation life, his good common sense and his ability to face reality paid off in both profit and pleasure for himself and for others. He believes in people and in rewarding them for doing a good job. He advises business people to fight nonsense (meaning the waste of time and effort that often exist in business—especially big business), fight for justice, have fun, and thank people for their efforts. For business-women he has a special recommendation: ". . . don't admit you know shorthand or typing (although they're good skills to have). You may end up in a dead end secretarial spot."

Now in nonretirement, Townsend runs the *Congressional Monitor*, a daily newsletter that reports on pending legislation and hearings in the U.S. Congress, does some consulting for businesses and institutions, and makes investments in small businesses, while sitting comfortably at home on Long Island, New York, with his self-made fortune.

In 1927 Elton Mayo and a group of researchers from Harvard University traveled to Chicago to explore the relationship between changes in physical working conditions and employee productivity. They chose the Hawthorne Plant of Western Electric as the subject of their research. The **Hawthorne Studies** were *a series of investigations which revealed that money and job security are not the only source of employee motivation; they led to the development of the human relations approach to motivation.*

Asking such questions as: "What is the effect of different intensities of light on employee output?" "How will varying noise levels change worker productivity?", the researchers sought answers by setting up controlled experiments in the relay assembly section of the plant. A group of six female workers was provided with sufficient lighting; then the amount of light was reduced. Mayo and his colleagues were baffled to discover that reducing the amount of light had almost no effect on productivity—in some cases output actually rose. The light intensity was further reduced to about the intensity of moonlight, and again production increased!

(Mayo and his colleagues) swooned at their desks . . . Because of some mysterious X which had thrust itself into the experiment, this group of six girls was pouring 25 per cent more relays into the chutes . . .

What was this X? The research staff pulled themselves together and began looking for it. They conferred, argued, studied, and presently they found it. It wasn't in the physical production end of the factory at all. It was in the girls themselves. It was an attitude, the way the girls now felt about their work and their group. By segregating them into a little world of their own, by asking their help and cooperation, the investigators had given the young women a new sense of their own value. Their whole attitude changed from that of separate cogs in a machine to that of a congenial team helping the company solve a significant problem.

They had found stability, a place where they belonged, and work whose purpose they could clearly see. And so they worked faster and better than they ever had in their lives. The two functions of a factory had joined into one harmonious whole.[1]

What Motivates Workers?

The Hawthorne studies revolutionized management's approach to direction (or motivation) of employees. Prior to the Hawthorne investigation, most organizations had used *money* as the primary means of motivating workers. Satisfactory wages and job security were assumed to satisfy employees and motivate them to work faster and more efficiently in pursuit of overall organizational objectives. The importance of the Hawthorne findings lies not in denying the importance of money as a motivator but in emphasizing the presence of a number of other sources of employee motivation.

THE WORKER IS
A WANTING
ANIMAL

Each individual is motivated to take action designed to satisfy needs. A **need** is simply *the lack of something useful*. **Motives** are *inner states that direct the individual toward the goal of satisfying a felt need*. The individual is *moved* (the root word for motive) to take action to reduce a state of tension and return to a condition of equilibrium. This motivation process is described in Figure 6-1.

A Ladder of Human Needs

The psychologist Abraham H. Maslow has developed a widely accepted list of human needs. His list is based on two important assumptions:

1. People are wanting animals whose needs depend on what they already possess. A satisfied need is not a motivator; only those needs that have not been satisfied can influence behavior.

Figure 6-1
The Process of
Motivation

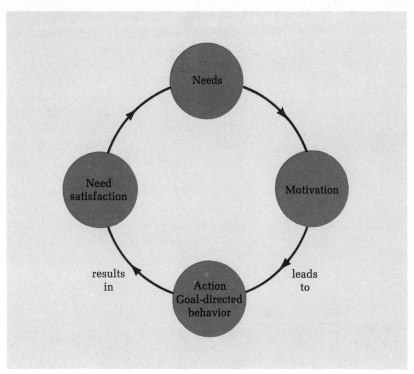

SOURCE: Adapted by permission from James H. Donnelly, Jr., James L. Gibson and John M. Ivancevich, *Fundamentals of Management* (Dallas: Business Publications, Inc., 1975), p. 130.

2. People's needs are arranged in a hierarchy of importance. Once one need has been at least partially satisfied, another emerges and demands satisfaction.[2]

    Figure 6-2 shows the ladder of human needs arranged in order of their importance to the individual. Priority is assigned to the basic physiological needs.

Figure 6-2
The Ladder of
Human Needs

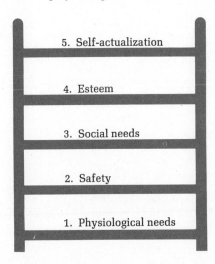

5. Self-actualization

4. Esteem

3. Social needs

2. Safety

1. Physiological needs

PHYSIOLOGICAL NEEDS
: **Physiological needs** are *the primary needs for food, shelter, and clothing that are present in all humans,* and must be satisfied before the individual can consider higher-order needs. A hungry person is possessed by the need to obtain food. Other needs are ignored.

But once the physiological needs are at least partially satisfied, other needs come into the picture. Since minimum wage laws and union wage contracts have forced wage levels upward so that most families can afford to satisfy their basic needs, the higher-order needs are likely to play a greater role in worker motivation today.

SAFETY NEEDS
: The second-level **safety needs** include *protection from physical harm, the need for job security, and avoidance of the unexpected.* Gratification of these needs may take the form of guaranteed annual wages, life insurance, the purchase of radial tires, obeying job safety rules, or membership in the company health club.

SOCIAL NEEDS
: Satisfaction of physiological and safety needs leads to the third rung on the ladder, **social needs:** *the desire to be accepted by members of the family and other individuals and groups.* The individual

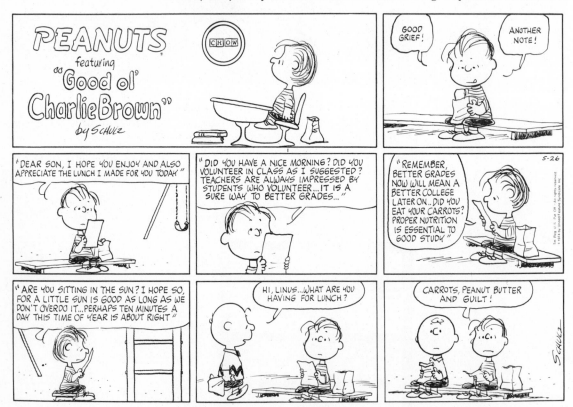

Linus Satisfies Third-order Needs by Obeying the Many Rules Developed by His Mother

ESTEEM NEEDS

The needs near the top of the ladder, **esteem needs,** are more difficult to satisfy. At this level is *the need to feel a sense of accomplishment, achievement, and respect from others.* The competitive need to excel—to better the performance of others—is an almost universal human trait.

The esteem need is closely related to belongingness needs. But at this level the individual desires not just acceptance but also recognition and respect. There is a desire to "stand out" from the crowd in some area.

SELF-ACTUALIZATION NEEDS

The top rung on the ladder of human needs is **self-actualization.** This is *the need for fulfillment, for realizing one's own potential, to use one's talents and capabilities totally.*

Maslow defines self-actualization this way: "The healthy man is primarily motivated by his needs to develop and actualize his fullest potentialities and capacities. What man *can* be, he *must* be."

The famous author Robert Louis Stevenson was describing self-actualization when he wrote ". . . to be what we are, and to become what we are capable of becoming, is the only end of life." For Bob Hope, self-actualization may mean being the best-loved American comedian. The approximately 200 new entries in each revised edition of the *Guinness Book of World Records* represents individuals daring to accomplish what no person has done before.

Jonathan Livingston Seagull, the feathered hero of a best-selling book, expressed the need for self-actualization in this way: "Instead of our drab slogging forth and back to the fishing boats, there's a reason to life! We can lift ourselves out of ignorance. We can be free. We can learn to fly!"[3]

APPLYING THE NEEDS CONCEPT

Maslow points out that a satisfied need is no longer a motivator. Once the physiological needs are satisfied, the individual is concerned with higher-order needs. There will obviously be periods motivated by the need to relieve thirst or hunger, but an individual's interest is most often directed toward the satisfaction of safety, belongingness, and the other needs on the ladder.

American business organizations have been extremely successful in satisfying the lower-order physiological and safety needs. The traditional view of workers as an ingredient in the productive process—a *machine* like the lathes, drill presses, and other equipment—led management to motivate workers with money. The Hawthorne studies showed that people are people, that the employee's social and psychological needs may prove just as effective as motivators as money. Managers had to reconsider their assumptions about employees and how best to motivate them.

Evaluating Theory *X*—Do People Hate Work?

The *traditional managerial assumptions that employees dislike work and must be coerced, controlled, or threatened to motivate them to work* is called **Theory *X*.** These assumptions include:

1. The average human being has an inherent dislike of work and will avoid it if possible.
2. Because of this human characteristic of dislike of work, most people must be coerced, controlled, directed, or threatened with punishment to get them to put forth adequate effort toward the achievement of organizational objectives.
3. The average human being prefers to be directed, wishes to avoid responsibility, has relatively little ambition, and wants security above all.[4]

The traditional view of workers—if true—is a rather depressing indictment of human nature. Managers who accept such a view may choose to direct their subordinates through close and constant observations, continually holding over them the threat of disciplinary action and demanding that they closely follow company policies and procedures.

Replacing Theory *X* with Theory *Y*

Theory X appears to have a critical deficiency. It focuses strictly on physiological and safety needs, while ignoring the higher-order needs. If people behave in the manner described by Theory X, the reason for their behavior may be that the organization only partially satisfies their needs. If the organization can enable individuals to satisfy their social, esteem, and self-actualization needs, new behavior patterns should develop. In addition different assumptions about employees must be made. **Theory *Y*** contains a *new set of managerial assumptions that workers do not dislike work and that, under proper conditions, they will accept and seek out responsibilities in order to fulfill their social, esteem, and self-actualization needs.* These new assumptions include:

Lucy Van Pelt—the Ultimate Theory X Manager

SOURCE: © 1963 United Feature Syndicate, Inc.

1. Workers do not inherently dislike work. The expenditure of physical and mental effort in work is as natural as play or rest.
2. Employees do not want to be rigidly controlled and threatened with punishment.
3. The average worker will, under proper conditions, not only accept but will actually seek responsibility.
4. Employees desire to satisfy social, esteem, and self-actualization needs in addition to security needs.[5]

Unlike the traditional management philosophy which relied on external control and constant supervision, Theory Y emphasizes self-control and direction. Its implementation requires a totally different managerial strategy.

A Theory *Y* Army?

Behold the modern Dutch fighting man. It is a sight that makes many an old professional soldier want to cry.

The hair, long and lank, spills from beneath the helmet. The uniform is rumpled, the demeanor cheerful and offhand. When our hero goes on a field march, he may wear sneakers rather than combat boots; they are more comfortable. Does he salute officers? Hardly ever.

This is how *The Wall Street Journal* described the modern Dutch army. A military union has brought about profound changes in the life of the Dutch soldier. Soldiers in the Netherlands now earn overtime pay when they spend weekends on guard duty or maneuvers in the field. Late-evening personnel checks in the barracks and morning reveille have ended. The recruit gets up when he wants to, so long as he reports for work on time.

Quality of the food in military camps has improved. The requirement for wearing uniforms at meals was dropped. Then the issue of saluting was considered. "A strange way of contact between people," was how one Dutch sergeant described the practice. Now salutes are exchanged only in formal appointments between an officer and an enlisted man or in formal ceremonies.

Source: Adapted from Bowen Northrup. "This Is an Army? Well, It Has Arms, Marches—Sort Of," *The Wall Street Journal* (October 1, 1974), p. 1. Reprinted with permission of *The Wall Street Journal,* © Dow Jones & Company, 1974. All rights reserved.

Two decades ago the psychologist Frederick Herzberg conducted a study of various job factors as sources of satisfaction and dissatisfaction in human motivation. Based on his research, Herzberg reached two conclusions:

1. There are some characteristics of a job, called **maintenance factors,** that are necessary to maintain a desired level of satisfaction. These include *such job-related factors as salary, working conditions, and job security, which must be present in order to avoid worker dissatisfaction, but which are not strong motivators when they are present.* If they are absent or inadequate, they are likely to serve as *dissatisfiers.*

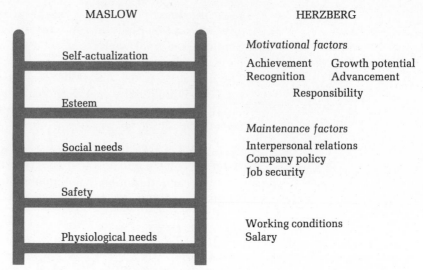

Figure 6-3
Comparing Herzberg
and Maslow

MASLOW

HERZBERG

Self-actualization

Esteem

Social needs

Safety

Physiological needs

Motivational factors

Achievement Growth potential
Recognition Advancement
        Responsibility

Maintenance factors

Interpersonal relations
Company policy
Job security

Working conditions
Salary

SOURCE: Adapted from Keith Davis, *Human Behavior at Work* (New York: McGraw-Hill, 1972), p. 59.

2. There are other job-centered **motivational factors**—*such job-related characteristics as the work itself, recognition, responsibility, advancement, and growth potential which are the key sources of employee motivation.*

Although such maintenance factors as money are extremely important when they are lacking, they are of low motivational value when they are present in adequate amounts.

It is obvious that the key motivational factors are related to *the job itself.* The supervisor does not motivate the worker with an additional coffee break; the supervisor further involves the worker in the job itself.[6]

As Figure 6-3 shows, there is a great deal of similarity between Herzberg's two factors and Maslow's ladder of human needs. Herzberg's message is that the lower-rung needs have already been satisfied for most workers and the manager must focus on primary motivators—the higher-level needs.

WHICH FACTORS INFLUENCE EMPLOYEE MORALE?

Morale is *the mental attitude of employees toward their companies and their jobs.* High morale is a sign of a well-managed organization. The worker's attitude toward the job will obviously affect the kind of job that will be done.

One of the most obvious signs of poor manager-worker relations is poor morale. Poor morale lurks behind absenteeism, employee turnover, slowdowns, and wildcat strikes. It also shows up in lower productivity, employee grievances, and transfers.

But often management's view of what leads to high employee morale is incorrect. One research study compared the ranking of managers and workers on the relative importance of various morale factors. Table 6-1 shows how management ranked these factors.

Table 6-1
Factors Leading to High
Morale According to
Management

Morale Item	Management Ranking
Good wages	1
Job security	2
Promotion and growth with company	3
Good working conditions	4
Interesting work	5
Management loyalty to workers	6
Tactful disciplining	7
Full appreciation for work done	8
Sympathetic understanding of personal problems	9
Feeling "in" on things	10

SOURCE: Reprinted by permission from Paul Hersey and Kenneth H. Blanchard. *Management of Organizational Behavior* (Englewood Cliffs, N.J.: Prentice-Hall, Inc., 1972), p. 39.

Table 6-2
Factors Leading to High
Morale According to
Workers

Morale Item	Employee Ranking
Full appreciation for work done	1
Feeling "in" on things	2
Sympathetic understanding of personal problems	3
Job security	4
Good wages	5
Interesting work	6
Promotion and growth with company	7
Management loyalty to workers	8
Good working conditions	9
Tactful disciplining	10

SOURCE: Reprinted by permission from Paul Hersey and Kenneth H. Blanchard. *Management of Organizational Behavior* (Englewood Cliffs, N.J.: Prentice-Hall, Inc., 1972). p. 39.

According to Table 6-1 managers placed the chief emphasis on the lower-order needs of money and job security. But Table 6-2 reveals a quite different ranking by employees.

Opinions differed significantly on the importance of such items as job security and credit and recognition. Other differences in rankings were present on the importance of fair pay, promotion, and understanding of personal problems.

HAPPINESS DOES NOT ALWAYS EQUAL HIGH MORALE

The maintenance of high morale means more than keeping employees happy. A two-day work week, longer vacations, or almost continuous coffee breaks could easily result in producing happy employees. But morale results from an environment in which workers may obtain satisfaction from their work and are motivated to excel in their assigned duties. The presence of high morale should lead to more productive workers. And management must create a work environment that will result in high employee morale.

Management Techniques Designed to Improve Motivation

Two management techniques are widely used today in an attempt to improve the overall motivation and performance of workers. These techniques are **management by objectives** and **job enrichment.**

MANAGEMENT
BY OBJECTIVES The Management by Objectives (MBO) approach was first proposed in the early 1950's by Peter Drucker, who described it in this way:

> . . . the objectives of the district manager's job should be clearly defined by the contribution he and his district sales force have to make to the sales department, the objectives of the project engineer's job by the contribution he, his engineers and draftsmen make to the engineering department . . . This requires each manager to develop and set the objectives of his unit himself. Higher management must, of course, reserve the power to approve or disapprove his objectives. But their development is part of a manager's responsibility; indeed, it is his first responsibility . . . [7]

Thus, **Management by Objectives** is *a program designed to improve employees' motivation through their participation in setting individual goals and in knowing in advance precisely how they will be evaluated.*

Five steps in an MBO program

Figure 6-4 illustrates the five-step sequence of most MBO programs:

1. The subordinate discusses the description of the job individually with the superior.
2. Short-term performance goals are established.
3. The subordinate meets regularly with the superior to discuss progress toward the goals.
4. Intermediate checkpoints are established to measure progress toward the goals.
5. At the end of a defined period, superior and subordinate together evaluate the results of the subordinate's efforts.

Management by Objectives involves mutual goal-setting by manager and employee. Both superior and subordinate must reach an understanding about the subordinate's major area of responsibility and what constitutes an acceptable level of performance. These understandings form the basis of the subordinate's goals for the next planning period, such as the next six months.

Goals should be in numerical terms whenever possible. Such objectives as "reducing scrap losses by 5 percent" or "increasing sales of mini-calculators by 15 percent" are examples. Once these goals are established and agreed upon, the subordinate has the responsibility of achieving them.

During the interim period the employee may check often with the supervisor. At the end of the period a formal progress review is

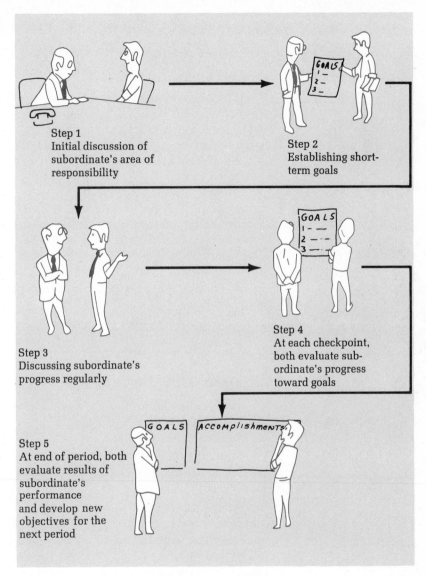

Figure 6-4
The Management by
Objectives Sequence

Step 1
Initial discussion of
subordinate's area of
responsibility

Step 2
Establishing short-
term goals

Step 3
Discussing subordinate's
progress regularly

Step 4
At each checkpoint,
both evaluate sub-
ordinate's progress
toward goals

Step 5
At end of period, both
evaluate results of
subordinate's
performance
and develop new
objectives for the
next period

conducted. Both the employee and the manager will discuss performance and determine whether the goals were achieved. New
goals will then be established for the next period.

Benefits of an MBO program

The chief purpose of Management by Objectives is *to improve
motivation of employees through participation in setting individual
goals.* Workers know both the job to be done and precisely how they
will be evaluated.

An MBO program should improve morale through improved
communications between individual employees and their superiors.

Workers should be able to relate individual performances to overall organizational goals through an MBO program. Finally, MBO can serve as a basis for decisions about salary increases and promotions.

MBO at all levels

MBO is not limited to any one level in the organization. It should probably begin with the president of the company, who should set some personal job objectives in consultation with the board of directors of the company. The process should then proceed throughout the organization and extend to every employee.

MBO for everyone?

Experience with MBO programs indicates that they have merit if used with judgment and a great deal of planning. Since changes may have to be made in such areas as the degree of communication between superiors and subordinates and the number of personal contacts, managers must be conditioned. MBO will succeed only at levels where personnel feel comfortable with it and are willing to participate.

Management must recognize the fact that in many organizations worker goals are constantly changing. In such instances it will be especially difficult to measure results accurately.

JOB ENRICHMENT
An assembly-line job is likely to have these characteristics:

1. a mechanically controlled work pace
2. repetitiveness
3. minimum skill requirements
4. use of predetermined tools and techniques
5. minute subdivision of product and the need for only surface mental attention.[8]

Such a worker—who cannot control his work pace, cannot use judgment, and is not challenged to improve his skills above a minimal level—is likely to be poorly motivated at best and suffer from alienation at worst. These job characteristics often lead to what is popularly called the blue-collar blues.

Job enrichment builds on the ideas of Herzberg by emphasizing the characteristics of the job as the key source of employee motivation. **Job enrichment** may be defined as *giving the workers more authority to plan their work and decide how it is to be accomplished and allowing them to learn new related skills or trade jobs with others.* Job enrichment focuses on motivational factors by designing work that will satisfy individual as well as company needs.

Herzberg explains job enrichment this way:

[job enrichment] seeks to improve both task efficiency and human satisfaction by means of building into people's jobs . . . greater scope for personal achievement and recognition, more challenging and responsible work, and more opportunity for individual advancement and growth. It is concerned only incidentally with matters such as pay and working conditions, organizational structure, communications, and training, important and necessary though these may be in their own right.[9]

How can jobs be enriched?

A number of companies are using job enrichment with excellent results.

Chrysler assembly line workers now get the chance to road test cars to help spot quality defects. In one Detroit assembly plant, Chrysler formed a workers' "damage committee" to check welding operations of car bodies. One worker wrote management after his week of moving around the department: "Since that week, I see metal damage, missing welds, and forming fits I never noticed before. This . . . gives me a whole new outlook on body building . . . a sense of real satisfaction . . . using my eyes and mind instead of just my hands."[10]

Two Swedish automobile manufacturers, Volvo and Saab, began a program of job enrichment in 1971. Rather than stationing each worker on an assembly line to perform one task or a few monotonous operations on each car as it passed by, they decided to have parts brought to the cars and then installed by semiautonomous groups of workers.

When General Foods Corporation built its new plant in Topeka, Kansas, to process and package Gaines dog-food products, they designed the production process with job enrichment in mind. Workers were free to schedule their own hours for starting and stopping work. Production was built around three teams: one to process products, one to package and ship products, and one to handle supporting office services.

The members rotate through the team's various jobs. A man on the packaging and shipping team may operate the forklift truck one day and bag "Gravy Train" the next. Undesirable jobs are rotated; executive parking spaces do not exist. Team members screen job applicants and make employment decisions; they draw up work rules. Quality-control responsibility is shared by the two production teams. No custodians are on the payroll; each person keeps his or her own work area clean. The results: higher product quality; lower operating costs; little absenteeism; and productivity per worker averaging 40 percent higher than similar, conventionally managed plants.[11]

Job enrichment for everyone?

Like MBO programs, attempts at job enrichment have not been completely successful. After introducing job-enrichment programs in nineteen areas at AT&T, management reported that nine were "outstandingly successful," one was a complete flop, and the re-

Is Job Enrichment an Attempt by Management to Exploit Workers by Motivating Them to Work Harder?

Business executives in the United States have only recently identified, or named, another aspect of the management equation. It is the development of human resources, those people who work on assembly lines or in offices to produce a product or service that the company sells.

Large U.S. companies whose management is concerned with the quality of work have begun to see human resources as an important part of the business organization. Company managers have become aware of the importance of motivating employees to do their best on the job, to see their work as worth doing.

Advocates of job enrichment believe that using such management techniques as involving the individual or a team of individuals in decision making, providing the individual or team with a minimum of supervision, or granting at least a degree of independence in getting the job done are answers to stopwatch management mentality. If workers are bored, go unchallenged, and never see what they have achieved, they will be alienated and unmotivated. Alcoholism and absenteeism may result, and productivity will decline. Redefining jobs and providing workers with tasks that are goal-oriented should result in variety and increased interest.

Workers will receive a feeling of fulfillment and satisfaction, along with a paycheck.

But many labor unions see job enrichment simply as a way of keeping unions out of industry. If workers can be satisfied through job enrichment, the union's function of upgrading working conditions becomes unnecessary. Rather than having unions negotiate for better working conditions, management-imposed methods of job enrichment (and the limitations of what management is willing to grant the individual worker) would be established. According to the opponents of job enrichment, if job productivity increases through job enrichment, fewer workers would be needed and the work force would be reduced, which would result in increased unemployment.

For many who believe that the United States is approaching the ultimate in technical know-how and super-mechanization, the answer to improving job conditions lies not in proper management of human resources but in better use of leisure time and improving life in general. Rather than getting more productivity out of fewer workers by redesigning jobs or enlarging responsibilities, many union leaders and others see social benefits and economic rewards as goals for the future.

maining nine were "moderately successful."[12] A series of interviews with asembly-line workers in a television plant revealed that the workers did not view their jobs as either frustrating or dissatisfying.[13] One researcher even discovered that some workers preferred routine jobs because it gave them more time to daydream or talk with their fellow employees without hurting their productivity.[14]

Prospects for more job enrichment are good

Although job-enrichment programs continue to be relatively rare, the accomplishments in a number of industries and companies of varying sizes are indications of the merits of such programs. Even though such programs are not always successful, their numbers will undoubtedly grow during the next decade. More and more managers are recognizing that such programs allow an integration of individual goals with those of the organization.

Summary

The beginnings of the human relations movement and the emphasis on employee motivations can be traced to the Hawthorne studies of the 1920's. These studies revealed that employee attitudes and interpersonal relations were important sources of motivation. Although wages and job security are important requirements for all workers, other human needs are present and require satisfaction as well.

Maslow has proposed a ladder of human needs extending from the basic physiological needs for water, food, and sex to (2) safety, (3) social needs, (4) esteem, and (5) self-actualization. He pointed out that satisfied needs are not motivators. Since union contracts, social security, and other benefits have contributed to the satisfaction of lower-order needs, the focus of most individuals is on satisfaction of the top three rungs on the needs ladder.

The traditional Theory X manager views workers as lazy, disliking work, and requiring close and constant supervision. The new assumptions about workers are termed Theory Y, and assume that employees desire to satisfy social, esteem, and self-actualization needs through work as well as through other activities. Theory Y emphasizes employee self-control and direction.

The keys to good employee morale appear to lie in job-centered motivational factors, such as the work itself, the potential for achievement, recognition, responsibility, advancement, and growth. Two management techniques designed to improve employee motivation were discussed in this chapter: management by objectives and job enrichment.

Management by Objectives focuses on employee participation in establishing individual work goals. Both manager and employee agree upon goals and each participates in evaluating the achievement of predetermined objectives. Employees know where they stand at all times and precisely what is expected of them and on what basis they will be evaluated.

Job enrichment focuses on increasing the motivational factors of jobs. It seeks to eliminate worker alienation by making work more interesting, as well as more efficient, by developing employee skills and by increasing individual worker responsibility in the job.

Review questions

1. Identify the following terms:
   a. Hawthorne studies
   b. needs
   c. motives
   d. physiological needs
   e. safety needs
   f. social needs
   g. esteem needs
   h. self-actualization needs
   i. Theory X
   j. Theory Y
   k. maintenance factors
   l. motivational factors
   m. morale
   n. management by objectives
   o. job enrichment
2. How did the Hawthorne studies revolutionize management's approach to employee motivation?
3. Describe the process of motivation.
4. Outline Abraham Maslow's theory of human needs.
5. What does Frederick Herzberg mean by "dissatisfiers"?
6. List the factors that influence employee morale.
7. Outline the five steps in an MBO program.
8. Can you think of any situations where job enrichment programs would not be effective? List them and explain your reasoning.
9. How would you classify the management of today's Dutch army (as described in this chapter)?
10. Do you think the Dutch army described in this chapter would be effective in an emergency? Why, or why not?

Discussion questions and exercises

1. Evaluate the pro and con arguments to the controversial issue that appears in this chapter.
2. Describe a recent decision you have made. What factors motivated you in making this decision?
3. Consider your most recent (or current) job supervisor. Would you describe this person as a Theory X or a Theory Y manager? Why do you think your superior has adopted this management approach?
4. Design an MBO program for the successful completion of some class you are now taking.
5. Prepare a brief report on job enrichment. Show instances where it has been successful, and cases where it is ineffective.

Case 6-1
The Company That Gives Its Employees the Business

In late 1974 Texasgulf, Inc., a major sulphur and metals supplier, decided to really give its employees the business. Texasgulf distributed 40,000 shares of its stock to the firm's 4,000 employees. Another 50,000 shares were scheduled for distribution to employees over the following five years. Each employee was scheduled to receive from one to fifty shares, depending on his or her years of service.

Charles F. Fogarty, chairman of Texasgulf, said the program was designed "to promote a better understanding of our free enterprise system and of the common interests of employees, shareowners, and governments in the company's continuing growth."

Questions

1. Is this free stock-distribution program designed to appeal to *maintenance* factors or *motivational* factors?
2. How should this program result in improved employee morale?
3. Are there any possible disadvantages to such a program?

Source: "Texasgulf to Distribute Stock to All Employees," *The Wall Street Journal* (October 31, 1974), p. 5. Reprinted with permission of *The Wall Street Journal,* © Dow Jones & Company, Inc., 1974. All rights reserved.

Case 6-2
Intermatic, Inc.

Intermatic, Inc., a timer and heater producer based in Spring Grove, Illinois, has been a leader in some aspects of labor-management relations. The firm's president, Jim Miller, once paid ten employees $50 each as winners of a year-long "I quit smoking" program. Two years later Miller offered to pay three dollars for each pound an employee lost. This program was limited to those workers who were fifteen pounds or more overweight, and 144 of the 500 employees signed up.

Questions

1. Do you think companies should have programs of a social nature such as Intermatic's?
2. What other programs might Miller consider?

Source: "3 Tons of Fat at $3 a Pound," *Detroit News* (March 31, 1975), p. 1.

Careers in Management

Management offers an exciting array of career opportunities for the person who has the leadership qualities and the professional preparation to deal with the complex problems facing a modern executive. A 1973 Gallup Poll showed that the percentage of young people (under thirty years of age) citing "Business Executive" as their preferred occupation had tripled since a similar poll was taken in 1962.* Effective managers have numerous career paths available to them because they can move from one industry or economic sector to another. Most experts believe that managerial ability is transferable from one enterprise to another. Good industrial executives can effectively apply their abilities in service industries, federal agencies, or hospitals, for example.

It must be remembered that most management positions require considerable practical experience. Management is not a beginning job; it is a position that you work toward as you acquire experience.

The Bureau of Labor Statistics has projected annual job openings to 1985. Their forecasts for some selected management jobs appear below:

Job Projections to 1985

Career	Latest Employment (1972 Estimate)	Annual Average of Job Openings to 1985
City managers	2,500	150
Supervisors	1,400,000	58,000
Hospital administrators	17,000	1,600
Hotel managers and assistants	110,000	7,500

SOURCE: *Occupational Manpower and Training Needs* (Washington, D.C.: Bureau of Labor Statistics, 1974).

Here are some of the careers in management that are available to you:

General Management

After obtaining substantial practical experience some people move into general management positions. Titles can range anywhere from President to Vice-president to General Manager. These positions involve the management of activities that cross functional areas. For example, a general manager of an automobile dealership has over-

Detroit Free Press (December 2, 1973), p. 14-F.

	all responsibility for sales (new and used vehicles), leasing and service, finance and personnel.
Department Head	A department head is the manager of an organizational unit. An office manager is a department head. A marketing manager or production manager is also a department head. These positions usually require experience in the areas that are to be managed.
Supervisor	Supervisors are managers of a part of a department. This is the first level of management, and it involves direct supervision of employees. The supervisor in a quality control department is an example of this kind of job.
Public Administrator	A public administrator is a manager of a department, bureau, agency, or other governmental unit. Public administrators also work in hospitals and other nonprofit institutions. Many areas now employ professional public administrators to manage the operations of local government. Federal and state governments also require a large number of public administrators to manage their units and departments.
Administrative Assistant	Administrative assistants are staff personnel who are working directly for general management. They often hold the title "Assistant to _____". Sometimes these positions are used as a training ground for people expected to advance to a general management position in the firm.

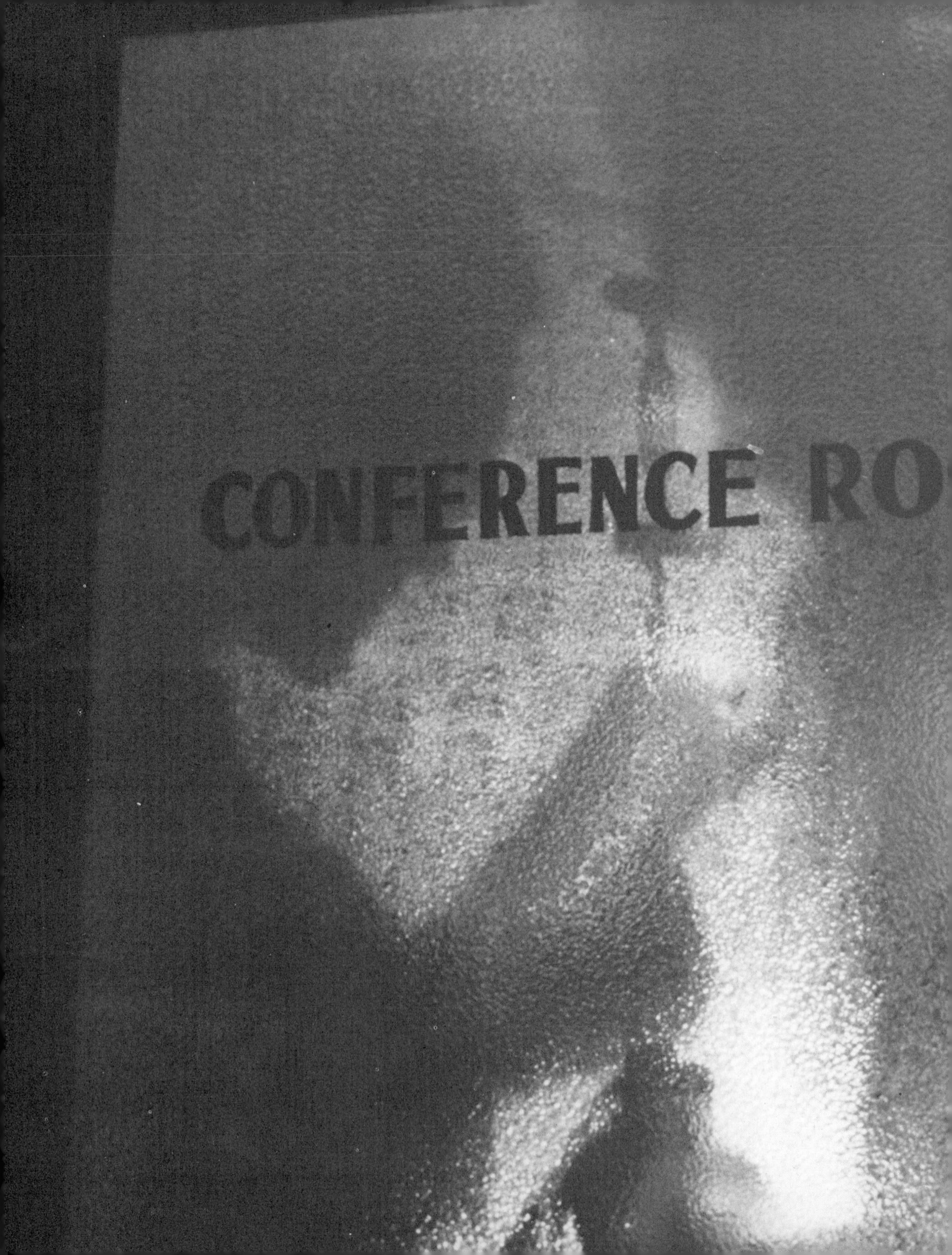
CONFERENCE RO

III
Management of Human Resources and Production

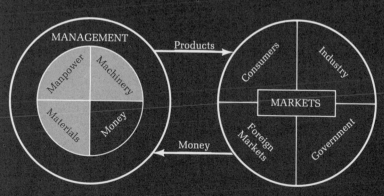

MANAGEMENT

Manpower   Machinery

Materials   Money

Products →

← Money

Consumers   Industry

MARKETS

Foreign Markets   Government

SOURCE: De Palma/Monkmeyer.

7

Human Resources Management

"It is not the scarcity of money, but the scarcity of men and talents, which make a state weak."

—Voltaire

"The trouble with personnel experts is that they use gimmicks borrowed from manufacturing: . . . recruiting, selecting, indoctrinating and training machinery, job rotation, and appraisal programs. And this manufacturing of men is about as effective as Dr. Frankenstein was."

—Robert Townsend

What Chapter 7 Is All About

1. Chapter 7 looks at human resources management at two levels: the functions of a specialized personnel department and the continuing responsibilities of all departments for the effective use of human resources.
2. In this chapter you will study the steps in the selection process and be able to see how each contributes to selecting the right person for the job.
3. You should be able to evaluate the different methods of training employees and present and potential managers.
4. Since different workers are paid wages on different bases, you should be able to identify the different forms of wages and explain when each form should be used.
5. You should be able to discuss the different types of employee benefits and the changes that are likely to occur in future fringe benefit programs.
6. After reading this chapter, you should understand these terms:

personnel management	transfer
job analysis	separation
job description	layoff
job specification	termination
EEOC	wage
on-the-job training	salary
classroom training	job evaluation
apprenticeship	piece wage
training program	time wage
vestibule schools	bonus
job rotation	profit-sharing
coaching	fringe benefits
promotion	OSHA

George S. Patton, Jr.

It would have been no surprise to George Patton that he was the subject of a major Hollywood film, for his life was intense, power-filled, and dramatic. He was commissioned in the Cavalry in 1909 after graduation from West Point, and he never lost the romantic posture associated with the Cavalry: carrying a riding crop and wearing matched ivory-handled revolvers. Even his personal motto—"Grab 'em by the nose and kick 'em in the tail"—comes from this service branch.

Patton's courage, energy, and drive made him a valuable officer. His knowledge of military tactics and campaigns often put him and his men in the first line of battle—where Patton, at least, wanted to be. "Old Blood and Guts," as he was called, was an example for men who took pride in a brave commander, a man's man. Those he bullied went along with him out of fear.

Right from the outset Patton's military career was theatrical. He was General John J. Pershing's aide in the Punitive Expedition into Mexico, in pursuit of the bandit Pancho Villa. Patton followed Pershing to France in World War I, where the young officer commanded a tank brigade. Tanks were than a new weapon. In the Meuse-Argonne sector Patton was wounded and was later awarded the Distinguished Service Cross for "conspicuous courage, coolness, energy, and intelligence in directing the advance of his brigade." During the next twenty years of peace Patton learned, was promoted, and waited. In 1940 he created the toughest division in the Army, the 2nd Armored, which took part in the North African campaign. Patton later commanded the 7th Army during the invasion of Sicily.

Always controversial, Patton was criticized by both his commander, General Dwight D. Eisenhower, and press people for slapping two hospitalized shell-shocked soldiers, whom he suspected of being cowards and faking illness. While he did not die with his boots on, Patton also did not die in bed. A 1945 car accident in Germany ended his life.

The emphasis of this chapter is on people—the human element—in accomplishing the goals of an organization. The acquisition, training, motivation, and retention of qualified personnel is a critical factor in determining the success or failure of a business.

One hundred years ago companies hired workers by posting a notice outside the gate stating that perhaps four workers would be hired the following day. The notice might list skills—a mechanic, a carpenter—or it might simply list the number of workers needed. The next morning people would appear at the front gate—a small number in prosperous times, large crowds in periods of unemployment—and the workers would be chosen. The choices were often arbitrary; the

Figure 7-1
Rules for Clerks
—in 1882

Rules for Clerks

1. This store must be opened at Sunrise. No mistake. Open 6 o'clock A.M. Summer and Winter. Close about 8:30 or 9 P.M. the year round.

2. Store must be swept—dusted—doors and windows opened—lamps filled, trimmed and chimneys cleaned—counters, base shelves and show cases dusted—pens made—a pail of water also the coal must be brought in before breakfast, if there is time to do it and attend to all the customers who call.

3. The store is not to be opened on the Sabbath day unless absolutely necessary and then only for a few minutes.

4. Should the store be opened on Sunday the clerks must go in alone and get tobacco for customers in need.

5. The clerk who is in the habit of smoking Spanish Cigars—being shaved at the barbers—going to dancing parties and other places of amusement and being out late at night—will assuredly give his employer reason to be ever suspicious of his integrity and honesty.

6. Clerks are allowed to smoke in the store provided they do not wait on women with a "stogie" in the mouth.

7. Each clerk must pay not less than $5.00 per year to the Church and must attend Sunday School regularly.

8. Men clerks are given one evening a week off for courting and two if they go to prayer meeting.

9. After the 14 hours in the store the leisure hours should be spent mostly in reading.

SOURCE: Reprinted by permission from Delbert J. Duncan, Charles F. Phillips, and Stanley C. Hollander. *Modern Retailing Management* (Homewood, Ill.: Richard D. Irwin, Inc., 1972), p. 182.

first four in the line might be selected or the four persons who looked the strongest or the healthiest.

Workers operated by a set of specific rules. One amusing list prepared many years ago is shown in Figure 7-1.

What Is Personnel Management?

Personnel management can be viewed in two ways. In the narrowest sense it refers to the functions and operations of a single department in the firm, the personnel department. Most firms with 200 or more employees establish a separate department and assign to it the responsibility and authority for selecting and training personnel. A typical personnel department is illustrated in Figure 7-2.

In a broader sense personnel management involves the entire organization. Even though a special staff department has been established, general management must also be involved in the process of training and developing workers, evaluating their performances, and motivating them to work well. **Personnel management** may be defined as *the recruitment, selection, development, and motivation of human resources.*

Figure 7-2
Organization of a
Typical Personnel
Department

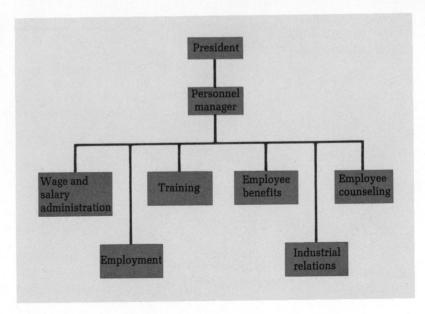

Employee Selection

The personnel manager plays a crucial role in selecting personnel. The guiding philosophy is: "Don't fit a square peg into a round hole!" Adding new employees is a costly process. Recruitment costs are high. Various interviews and tests are often conducted before new workers are chosen. Medical examinations at company expense are commonly required for applications. Training expenses are part of the cost, and an inefficient worker wastes money. The personnel manager must insure that potential employees possess the necessary qualifications for the job.

JOB ANALYSIS, JOB DESCRIPTIONS, AND JOB SPECIFICATIONS

In order to effectively match jobs with qualified people, the personnel manager uses three techniques: job analysis, job description, and job specification.

Job analysis is *a systematic detailed study of jobs, consisting of identifying and examining the elements and characteristics of each job and the requirements of the person assigned to the job.* From job analysis, the personnel department develops the **job description,** *which is a document describing the objectives of a job, the work to be performed, the responsibilities involved, skills needed, the relationship of the job to other jobs, and its working conditions.* Next a **job specification** is prepared. *This is a document describing the special qualifications required of a worker who fills a particular job.* The specification lists requirements for experience, education, special skills, and other expected physical requirements.

The job description and job requirement are typically combined into one document. Figure 7-3 illustrates how the two areas

Figure 7-3
A Combined Job
Description and Job
Specifications for Delta
Air Lines Flight
Attendants

JOB DESCRIPTION FOR FLIGHT ATTENDANT:

Performs or assists in the performance of all cabin service to enroute passengers or grants service to delayed or cancelled passengers in a resourceful and gracious manner, and shall include responsibility to apply these services for the welfare, comfort, enjoyment, and safety of passengers. Airline flight attendants have a public relations as well as a service job. Their responsibility is to care for the passengers on their flight in such a way that passengers will prefer Delta Air Lines over any other mode of transportation.

JOB SPECIFICATIONS:

AGE: 20 years minimum
HEIGHT: 5′ 2″ to 6′ 0″
WEIGHT: In proportion to height
MARITAL STATUS: Single; or widowed; or divorced
EDUCATION: Two years college preferred or business equivalent
VISION: Good vision; contact lenses are permitted if have been worn successfully for six months, and uncorrected vision is at least 20/100 with no astigmatism. (Glasses are not permitted.)

The main qualities Delta interviewers look for in Flight Attendant applicants are a neat, wholesome appearance and the ability to project themselves and their personality.

SOURCE: Reprinted by permission of Delta Air Lines.

specify both the description of the work involved and the necessary requirements for a worker who fills the job. This document combining the job description and job specification is invaluable to the personnel department when seeking qualified applicants for job openings. Although these documents were first used in factory jobs, they are common today in retail stores, offices, banks, and almost any large organization.

AVOID SEXISM IN JOB TITLES Numerous legislative acts in the United States—both federal and state—have been passed to prohibit job specifications which limit employment to males. In the Soviet Union 90 percent of all physicians are women. Women comprise 70 percent of the overhead crane operators in Sweden. Employers are prohibited from excluding females from job considerations unless they can demonstrate that the job requires physical skills not possessed by women.

Table 7-1
Changes in Job Titles:
1956 to 1976

Former Job Title	New Job Title
Fireman	Firefighter
Policeman	Police officer
Mailman	Mail carrier
Salesman	Sales person
Foreman	Supervisor
Bus Boy	Dining room attendant
Housewife	Homemaker
Congressman	Member of Congress/Representative
Cameraman	Camera operator
Stewardess	Flight attendant
Headmaster	Principal
Cleaning lady/maid	Housekeeper
Song and dance man	Song and dance person

One well-known result of these laws is the elimination of sex distinctions in the "Help Wanted" sections of newspapers. A second result is the change in job titles. When the U.S. Department of Labor revised its *Dictionary of Occupational Titles* in 1976 in order to remove sexist job titles, nearly 3,500 of the 35,000 listings had to be changed. Table 7-1 lists some of the revisions.

RECRUITMENT   After the job description and job specification are prepared, the next step in the selection process is the recruitment of qualified employees. Personnel departments use two sources of candidates for a specific job—internal and external.

Most firms have a policy of **hiring from "within"**—*first considering their own employees for new job openings.* Since the personnel department maintains a current file of all employees, these records may be quickly screened to determine whether any employees possess the necessary qualifications for a new opening.

Not only is the use of employees to fill new job vacancies a relatively inexpensive method of recruitment, it also contributes to good employee morale. The railroad industry has long been known for its policy of filling job vacancies from existing workers whenever possible. The statement of a personnel manager for one railroad summarized this policy: "When a president retires or dies, we hire a new office boy."

All firms must utilize external sources to some extent in filling vacancies or in adding new employees to fill newly created jobs. The company may not have qualified employees to fill a certain position, or better qualified people may be available from outside the firm. External sources of job applicants include college recruiting; advertising in newspapers and professional journals; public employment agencies, such as the state employment service; private employment agencies; vocational schools; workers recommended by employees; labor unions; and unsolicited applications. In ob-

"Can't those Equal Opportunity people leave well enough alone??"

SOURCE: Reprinted with permission from *The Wall Street Journal*.

taining candidates for top-management positions the firm may use specialized executive recruiting firms or advertise in *The Wall Street Journal* or the business section of such newspapers as *The New York Times*.

THE SCREENING PROCESS

Once the job applications have been located, the next step involves screening. At this stage the decision is made as to which candidate is best fitted for the job. The first step of the screening process is to have the applicant complete an application form. This formal application is then used to determine whether the applicant meets the general qualifications for the position. The application form will include biographical questions—such as the applicant's name, address, type of work desired, education, experience, and personal references.

The EEOC—Federal Guardian Against Discrimination in Employment

The *Civil Rights Act of 1964* ruled that discriminatory practices were illegal. Title VII of the Act covered discrimination in employment and set up the **Equal Employment Opportunity Commission** (EEOC) to police this part of the Act. The EEOC is a *federal commission created to increase job* *opportunities for women and minorities, and to assist in ending job discrimination based on race, religion, color, sex, or national origin in hiring, promotion, firing, compensation, and other terms and conditions of employment.*

The EEOC has been further strengthened by the passage of the *Equal Pay Act of 1963*, the *Age Discrimination in Employment Act of 1967*, the *Equal Employment Opportunity Act of 1972*, and numerous presidential executive orders. These acts apply to private employers of fifteen or more, private and public educational institutions, state and local governments, and labor unions with fifteen or more members.

The EEOC assists employers in setting up *affirmative action* programs to increase job opportunities for women and minorities. Such programs include analysis of the present work force and setting of specific hiring and promotion goals, with target dates in areas where women and minorities are underutilized.

Penalties for violations can also be imposed. The largest penalty to date has been the consent decree signed by AT&T. Approximately $15 million in back wages were paid to persons who had suffered due to discriminatory practices, and an estimated $50 million in annual payments is being paid by AT&T for promotion and wage adjustments to women and minority groups.

SOURCE: *Affirmative Action and Equal Employment: A Guidebook for Employers* (Washington, D.C.: U.S. Equal Employment Opportunity Commission, 1974).

EMPLOYEE TESTING— MEASURING APTITUDE, ABILITIES, AND PERHAPS PERSONALITY

Employee testing makes the selection process more efficient. Careful studies determine the tests to be used in measuring the aptitude and abilities required for each job. Some companies with testing programs also administer personality tests.

Testing serves two main purposes: It helps to eliminate those applicants who are not suited for a particular job, and it aids in predicting those candidates who are likely to become successful employees.

Do tests discriminate?

Employee testing is a controversial issue in the 1970's since a number of courts have ruled that some intelligence tests are culturally biased and do not predict job success. Since the Civil Rights Act of 1964 prohibits the use of tests which would produce discrimination in hiring workers, considerable effort is being expended in evaluating the objectivity of tests currently being used and in designing bias-free tests.

The Chitlin' Test

Black sociologist Adrian Dove developed the Counterbalance General Intelligence Test (The Chitlin' Test)—"a half-serious idea to show that we're just not talking the same language." Many of the thirty items on the test would make the white, middle-class child feel "culturally deprived."

For example:

1. A "handkerchief head" is:
   - (a) a cool cat
   - (b) a porter
   - (c) an Uncle Tom
   - (d) a hoddi
   - (e) a preacher

2. Which word is most out of place here?
   - (a) splib
   - (b) blood
   - (c) grey
   - (d) spook
   - (e) black

3. A "gas head" is a person who has a:
   - (a) fast-moving car
   - (b) stable of "lace"
   - (c) "Process"
   - (d) habit of stealing cars
   - (e) long jail record for arson

4. Bo Diddley is a:
   - (a) game for children
   - (b) down-home cheap wine
   - (c) down-home singer
   - (d) new dance
   - (e) Moejoe call

5. If a pimp is up tight with a woman who gets state aid, what does he mean when he talks about "Mother's Day"?
   - (a) second Sunday in May
   - (b) third Sunday in June
   - (c) the first of every month
   - (d) none of these
   - (e) first and fifteenth of every month

6. T-Bone Walker got famous for playing:
   - (a) trombone
   - (b) piano
   - (c) T-flute
   - (d) guitar
   - (e) ham-bone

(The correct answers: C for Questions 1–5; D for Question 6.)

SOURCE: Copyright Newsweek, Inc., 1968, reprinted by permission.

INTERVIEWING— FACE-TO-FACE CONTACT WITH THE JOB APPLICANT

The job applicant's first formal contact with a company is usually through an interview. This face-to-face contact between the prospective employee and a company representative is another step in the screening of candidates for the job. Trained interviewers are able to obtain considerable insight into the prospective employee's goals, attitudes toward others and self, and motivations.

The line manager for whom the prospective employee will work may also interview him or her at this stage. Since the line manager will make the ultimate hiring decision (or at least participate jointly in the decision with the personnel department), it is sound practice to involve the manager in the screening process.

If the interviewer or the line manager feels that the applicant is unsuitable, they will say so at this stage. If the applicant appears to be acceptable and has satisfactory references, she or he may be subject to a physical examination prior to employment.

Should Job Quotas for Minorities and Women Exist?

In the early 1970's the U.S. government began to enforce federal goals and timetables for the hiring and promotion of minorities and women. The Equal Employment Opportunity Commission (EEOC) and other government agencies have required companies to commit themselves to affirmative action programs that are designed to overcome past discrimination against minorities and women. Failure to meet the goals has led to million-dollar fines in cases involving such large companies as AT&T and the Bank of America. Minorities and women have also begun to have higher expectations for hiring and promotions.

Along with consideration of the threat of fines, costly legal and research fees and stricter enforcement of EEOC standards are the real-life problems of meeting job quotas for minorities and women.

Finding qualified people is one problem that goes hand in hand with training employees in a short period of time for promotion within a firm. Very often people already employed by a company cannot be promoted because they do not have the background or experience to move into the job. The alternative sometimes is to promote them and let them fail.

Many supervisors are inexperienced in dealing with minority members or women in a particular job, and the process of becoming accustomed to different kinds of people is painful and slow for both sides.

In some cases equipment used on the job must be redesigned before women can use it. This was the case with the safety belts worn by telephone workers when climbing poles. The belts were simply too big for most women, and new equipment had to be ordered and made before women could take these jobs.

Some union leaders see affirmative action programs as striking a blow against basic union doctrines, such as seniority. In their view this in itself is a kind of discrimination against older union members.

Because the pool of trained minorities and women for many kinds of jobs is extremely small (for example, the limited number of black female engineers), there tends to be highly competitive bidding for a few qualified people among many large firms.

Those who believe in job quotas for minorities and women feel that affirmative action must be seen as part of the cost of doing business. If there are not enough qualified people available, then others must be trained to be qualified at company expense, if necessary. When minorities and women are promoted, they should be supported with all the resources of the company, including consciousness raising for executives and peers and developing an awareness of the problems involved. Discrimination is illegal, as well as unjust, and the cost of job bias can be prohibitive.

Figure 7-4
Steps in the Employee
Selection Process

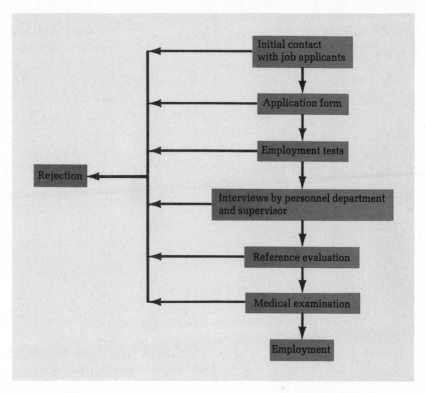

THE PHYSICAL EXAMINATION— INSURING THAT THE APPLICANT IS PHYSICALLY CAPABLE OF PERFORMING THE JOB

Most firms include a medical examination as part of the employee selection process for certain jobs. The examination determines whether the employee meets the physical requirements for the job. It also is designed to protect the company against future claims of disability which were present at the time of employment. In such European countries as France, Belgium, and the Netherlands, pre-employment physical examinations are required by law.

ORIENTATION OF EMPLOYEES

Once the employee is hired, she or he is subject to an orientation period. Orientation is the joint responsibility of the personnel department and the department in which the employee will work. Orientation will likely include a tour of the plant and a meeting with the department head and the new employee's immediate supervisor. The personnel department will provide the new worker with a copy of the employee manual, which explains such company rules as vacation policy, absenteeism, rest periods, lunch breaks, and available employee benefits. The supervisor is responsible for introducing the new employee to fellow workers and explaining the operations of the department in detail and how the job fits into the operations of the department.

A new employee in a large firm must be put at ease by the supervisor and shown that he or she is needed. The negative, lonely feelings that often accompany the first days on a new job may lead to frustration, negative attitudes, and poor job performance. The orientation program is designed to convey this sense of belonging and the feeling of the employee's personal worth to the organization. While the personnel department will provide the new employee with information about company history, its products, and its employee benefits, the responsibility for developing a sense of importance and belonging is primarily the function of the new worker's immediate supervisor and the other employees in the department.

Employee Training

A second major function of the personnel department is the development of a well-trained labor force. Employee training should be viewed as a continuing process which lasts as long as the employee is with the company. Two types of employee training programs are common: *on-the-job training* and some form of *classroom training*.

ON-THE-JOB TRAINING— LEARNING BY DOING

For relatively simple jobs most training is done **on the job.** This kind of *employee training program is based on the new worker actually performing the work involved under the guidance of an experienced employee.* The experienced worker serves as a source of advice and makes suggestions in teaching the new worker efficient methods of performing the job.

A variation of on-the-job training is the use of **apprenticeship training.** Such programs are used in jobs requiring long periods of training and high levels of skill. In these *training programs the new worker serves as an apprentice for a period of two to four years to a trained worker*—a carpenter, welder, electrician, tool and die maker, machinist, or plumber. Employers often use apprenticeship programs in cooperation with trade unions to insure that skill standards are maintained in these trades.

CLASSROOM TRAINING— LEARNING BEFORE DOING

In more difficult jobs, where a high level of skill is involved or where the employee's work must be closely coordinated with the work of others, some form of classroom training is used. In this environment the employee can acquire the necessary skills at his or her own pace without experiencing the pressures of the actual job environment. Also, the possibility of wasted materials and time by the new employee on the job is eliminated through proper training *prior to* assignment in a particular job.

Classroom training *programs use classroom techniques to teach new employees difficult jobs requiring high levels of skill.* Such training may consist of lectures, conferences, use of films and other audiovisual aids, programmed instruction, or special machines. Some companies establish **vestibule schools** *where workers are given instructions on the operation of equipment similar to the equipment used in their jobs.* The vestibule school is a facsimile of the actual work area, with a duplication of the jobs and machinery found in the plant. New employees are trained in the proper methods of performing a particular job and have an opportunity to become accustomed to the work before actually entering the department.

MANAGEMENT DEVELOPMENT PROGRAMS While job training is as old as recorded history, most management development programs have been established within the last twenty-five years. Management development programs are designed to improve the skills of present managers and to broaden their knowledge; they also provide training for employees who appear to have management potential.

Management development programs usually include formal courses of study and often are conducted off the company premises. Such companies as General Motors and Texaco have established formal institutes resembling colleges that offer specific programs for current and potential managers. New managers for McDonalds Corporation are required to complete a three-week intensive program at Hamburger University, McDonalds' training facility in suburban Chicago.

Other forms of management development programs include **job rotation,** *to familarize junior executives with the various operations of the firm and the contributions of each department,* and **coaching** of a junior executive by a member of senior management, *having the junior executive work directly under the senior executive.*

EMPLOYEE COUNSELING Usually the employee will discuss individual problems with an immediate supervisor. But, increasingly, personnel departments are adding trained specialists to assist workers in solving family or financial problems.

Another aspect of employee counseling deals with performance evaluation. While the task of performance evaluation is the chief responsibility of the line supervisor, workers occasionally feel that they have been treated unfairly or that performance standards are too high. One worker reported that performance appraisal in his department appeared to be based on the system shown in Table 7-2.

One of the chief advantages of the *Management by Objectives* program discussed in Chapter 6 is that it provides the employee with specific information on precisely how performance will be evaluated. Since the employee participates in goal-setting, there is no uncertainty about what constitutes satisfactory performance.

Promotion, Transfers, Layoffs, and Separations

Over a period of time many employees will receive promotions, transfers, or will be terminated. While four out of every five of the employees of the U.S. Postal System are still employed in their entry positions, most business organizations experience employee movement over a period of time.

Table 7-2 Guide to Employee Performance Appraisal

	Performance Degrees				
Performance Factors	*Far Exceeds Job Requirements (1)*	*Exceeds Job Requirements (2)*	*Meets Job Requirements (3)*	*Needs Some Improvement (4)*	*Does Not Meet Minimum Requirements (5)*
Quality	Leaps tall buildings with a single bound	Must take running start to leap over tall building	Can only leap over a short or medium building with no spires	Crashes into buildings when attempting to jump over them	Cannot recognize buildings at all, much less jump
Timeliness	Is faster than a speeding bullet	Is as fast as a speeding bullet	Not quite as fast as a speeding bullet	Would you believe a slow bullet?	Wounds self with bullets when attempting to shoot gun
Initiative	Is stronger than a locomotive	Is stronger than a bull elephant	Is stronger than a bull	Shoots the bull	Smells like a bull
Adaptability	Walks on water consistently	Walks on water in emergencies	Washes with water	Drinks water	Passes water in emergencies
Communication	Talks with God	Talks with the Angels	Talks to himself	Argues with himself	Loses those arguments

SOURCE: Reprinted with permission of Macmillan Publishing Co., Inc. from *The New Management* by Robert M. Fulmer. Copyright © 1974 by Robert M. Fulmer.

Promotion refers to *the upward movement in the organization to positions of greater authority and responsibility and higher salaries.* While most promotions are based on employee performance, some companies and many labor unions prefer to base promotion on **seniority,** *the length of time the employee has worked at a particular job or in a particular department.* Most managers agree that seniority should be the basis for promotion only when two candidates for promotion possess equal qualifications.

Transfers refer to *horizontal movements in the organization at about the same wage and the same level in the organization.* Transfers may involve shifting workers into new jobs that appear to be more interesting or the movement of a worker to a new department where skills possessed by the worker are required.

Separations include *resignations, retirements, and layoffs.* Resignations result when employees find better-paying positions or when they move to other cities. Many large firms have compulsory retirement programs, and require employees to retire at age sixty-five. This practice is controversial, however, and has been called discriminatory in several court rulings.

Age Discrimination in Employment Act Protects Older Workers*

In 1967, Congress passed the **Age Discrimination in Employment Act** to prevent discrimination in firing or refusing to hire workers over age 40. One provision of the Act makes it unlawful for an employer "to fail or refuse to hire or to discharge any individual or otherwise discriminate against any individual with respect to his compensation, terms, conditions, or privileges of employment because of such individual's age."

Critics of age discrimination practices have long argued that experience and maturity of older workers and increased loyalty to the firm more than compensates for the higher wages they receive as compared with new workers. They also point out that many of the major contributions of such notables as Galileo, Freud, Edison, Baruch, and Shaw occurred beyond the age of 60.

Approximately 37 million workers, or 40 percent of the total work force, are in the 40 to 65 age category. The law applies to private employers of 25 or more workers.

The largest settlement made in the first seven years of the Act occurred when Standard Oil Company of California agreed to pay 2 million dollars in back pay to 160 former employees, and to rehire 120 of them. More than 200 lawsuits have been filed by the Labor Department charging age discrimination.

*For additional information on how the law affects older workers, see "Fired for Being 'Too Old'? Government is On Your Side," *U.S. News & World Report* (June 3, 1974), pp. 75–76.

Layoffs differ from terminations in that layoffs are considered to be *temporary separations due to business slowdowns*. Most employers lay off workers on a seniority basis, letting the newly hired employees go first. When business conditions improve, these workers are the first to be rehired.

Terminations, or discharges, are *permanent separations resulting from inability to perform the work, repeated violation of work rules, excessive absenteeism, elimination of jobs, or the closing of production facilities*. Well-run personnel departments have specific employee discipline policies which have been explained to all workers. Table 7-3 illustrates some typical penalties. The violation of work rules typically results in an oral reprimand in the case of first offenses. Further violations lead to written reprimands and, ultimately, discharge.

Since the termination of an employee represents the failure of the selection process and substantial costs for the company, most firms conduct investigations of each termination and separation to uncover the cause of failure. These experiences should serve to improve the company selection process in the future.

Table 7-3
Typical Penalties in
Order of Severity

Penalties for Violating Company Work Rules
1. Oral warning
2. Written warning
3. Suspension for a specified length of time
4. Demotion to a less desirable job
5. Termination

How One Company Helped Its Employees Find New Jobs

When Pan American World Airways, Inc., drastically reduced its work force in 1974 in an attempt to cut losses, it accepted the responsibility for assisting these loyal employees find new jobs. One tangible example of Pan Am's attempts to help was this classified advertisement which appeared in a number of newspapers:

Source: Reproduced by permission from Pan American World Airways, Inc.

Employee Compensation

One of the most difficult functions of personnel management is the development and operation of a fair and equitable compensation system. Since labor costs represent a sizeable percentage of total product costs, too-high wages may result in products that are too high-priced to compete in the marketplace. On the other hand, inadequate wages lead to excessive employee turnover, poor morale, and inefficient production. A satisfactory compensation program should attract well-qualified workers, keep them satisfied in their jobs, and inspire them to produce.

The terms *wages* and *salaries* are often used interchangeably, but they do have slightly different meanings. **Wages** are *employee compensation based on the number of hours worked.* **Salaries** are *employee compensation calculated on a weekly, monthly, or annual* *basis. Salaries are generally used to compensate white-collar workers* such as clerks, executives, and professional employees. Wages usually refer to pay for production employees and maintenance personnel.

The company's wage policy is typically based on five factors:

1. wages paid by other companies in the area who compete for the same labor
2. government legislation
3. the cost of living
4. ability of the company to pay
5. productivity of the workers.

JOB EVALUATIONS DETERMINE WAGE LEVELS FOR DIFFERENT JOBS In developing compensation programs the personnel department conducts **job evaluations.** This is *a method of determining wage levels for different jobs by comparing each job on the basis of skill requirements, education, responsibilities, and physical requirements.* A monetary scale is then determined for each job. This process attempts to eliminate wage inequities that may exist among jobs. Although the personnel department does not set the specific wages paid to employees, it does recommend to line officials rates based on its job evaluation and surveys of comparable wages paid by other firms in the area for similar jobs.

ALTERNATIVE WAGE PLANS Wages paid to employees are based on the *amount of output produced by the worker* (**a piece wage**), *the amount of time spent on the job* (**a time wage**), or some **incentive** added to a time wage or piece wage to *reward the employee with extras (such as time off or bonus money) for exceptional performance.*

Time wages are usually paid to secretaries, executives, assembly-line workers, and maintenance personnel. They are easy to compute, quickly understood, and simple to administer. A time wage plan assumes a satisfactory performance level, but there is no incentive for outstanding performance by the employee.

Skilled craftsworkers may be paid on a piece-rate basis for each unit of output produced. The wage might be based on individual output or the production of an entire department. The practice of compensating salespeople with a commission based on sales is an example of the piece-wage form of compensation. The piece-rate payment plan not only includes an incentive for increased output but it also encourages workers to supervise their own activities. This plan operates well in departments where the work is standardized and the output of each employee or each department can be accurately measured.

In order to increase worker productivity, incentive wages are frequently added to a basic time or piece wage. Salespersons are often paid a combination base salary (time wage) and a commission.

Incentive Wages Encourage Superior Performance

SOURCE: "Funky Winkerbean" by Tom Batiuk, courtesy of Field Newspaper Syndicate.

Bonuses *represent an addition to a time or piece wage to provide incentive for employees to increase productivity.* They are occasionally used to reward employees for exceptional performance. Eastman Kodak employees receive annual bonuses equal to the amount of dividends paid to company stockholders. **Profit-sharing** plans are increasingly used to increase the feeling of belongingness for employees. *This is a type of incentive wage program where a percentage of company profits are distributed to employees involved in producing those profits.* When United Airlines reported significantly higher earnings in 1974, $1 million was distributed to the firm's employees as their share in the company's success. The creation of a partnership between employees and the firm increases employee morale and more harmonious working relationships between management and labor.

Employee Benefits

The typical business organization of the 1970's furnishes many benefits to employees and their families in addition to the payment of wages and salaries. These benefits are typically administered by the personnel department. **Fringe benefits** may be defined as *non-monetary employee benefits such as pension plans, health and life insurance, sick-leave pay, credit unions, and health and safety programs.* Many large companies employ a doctor and nurses as part of their staffs to investigate working conditions and treat minor illnesses and any job-related accident. Some companies sponsor recreation programs including golf, baseball, or bowling teams and hobby groups, and maintain separate recreational areas. The latest figures of the U.S. Chamber of Commerce show that wages account for only three-fourths of a worker's earnings; the other fourth is in the form of fringe benefits, which averaged over $3,200 per employee in the United States in 1975.

The Occupational Safety and Health Act of 1970

The Occupational Safety and Health Act went into effect on April 28, 1971. The **Occupational Safety and Health Administration** (OSHA) is *a federal administering body created by the Occupational Safety and Health Act of 1970 to assure safe and healthful working conditions for the American labor force.* All employers are covered by OSHA except governmental bodies and those firms covered by specific employment acts such as the Coal Mine Health and Safety Act.

Special emphasis is placed on improving safety conditions in five industries with injury rates more than double the national average of 15.2 disabling injuries per million employee hours worked. These industries are *longshoring* (69.9 injuries per million employee hours), *meat and meat products* (43.1 injuries), *roofing and sheet metal* (43.0 injuries), *lumber and wood products* (34.1 injuries) and *miscellaneous transportation equipment*—particularly manufacturers of mobile homes, campers, and snowmobiles (33.3 injuries).

The employer is responsible for knowing all mandatory standards under the Act. Employers must develop and put into action a plan including inspection of work facilities, removal of all hazards, promotion of job safety, and provide reports to OSHA. All employees must be informed of their rights and responsibilities under the provisions of OSHA.

The Act is enforced by inspections conducted by trained professionals in the occupational safety and health fields. Such inspections are conducted during normal working hours without prior notice. They include a walk-around inspection of work facilities and an examination of all required OSHA records. This is followed by a departure briefing outlining any violations that might be present and the corrective action recommended.

Four categories of violations may result from the inspection. The *de-minimus* is a minor violation not directly job related. A *non-serious* violation is similar to the *de-minimus* violation but is directly job-related, and can carry a penalty up to $1,000. A *serious* violation is one in which the probability of serious injury or death exists and is subject to penalties in excess of $1,000. An *imminent danger* violation is one in which the virtual certainty of serious injury exists and the penalty is assessed by the Federal Court System.

For any penalty assessed, the employer has appeal rights such as an informal hearing with the district or area OSHA director or, in more serious matters, a formal hearing by the Occupational Safety and Health Review Board. These rights are outlined in the Act itself.

Source: *All about OSHA* (Washington, D.C.: U.S. Department of Labor).

In 1976, most Americans worked a maximum of 175 days out of the 366. By 1986 the 175 work days may be reduced to 125 through shorter work weeks, longer vacations, and additional paid holidays. Other future fringe benefits are likely to include such items as portable retirement programs that can be transferred from one job to the next, the option of early retirement at age fifty-five, guaranteed lifetime employment, educational benefits for both the employee and her or his family, and a guaranteed annual wage.

Summary

Human resources management may be viewed in two ways. One way is to approach the subject through the eyes of the personnel department, which is responsible for handling such matters as developing job descriptions and job specifications, screening job applicants, developing and administering testing programs, interviewing prospective employees, training new employees, and administering employee compensation programs and various employee benefits programs.

A second—and more complete—description of the human resources management function involves a recognition that effective personnel management is the responsibility of every line manager. Although many of the specialized tasks involved in locating, training, and compensating employees are assigned as a staff function to the personnel department, the ultimate responsibility for selection, motivation, and retention of qualified workers remains with the line manager.

The specialists in the personnel department are involved with all aspects of employee selection, training, and development. The selection process includes such steps as locating potential employees, the evaluation of each applicant's completed application form and references, the administering of employment tests, a medical examination, and interviews by personnel employees and by the job applicant's supervisor. Job orientation is typically at least partly the responsibility of the personnel department.

The company will use one of two basic types of training programs: on-the-job and in the classroom. On-the-job training by an experienced worker is typically used with jobs that are relatively simple, while more complex jobs may be taught through a formal classroom training program. Human resources management also involves the development and administering of various types of management development programs for current and potential executives.

Employee compensation is another responsibility of the company. Wages can be based on the amount of output of the worker (piece wages) or the amount of time spent on the job (time wages). In addition, incentive wages, such as bonuses or profit-sharing programs, are often added to a time-piece wage in order to reward superior performance and to boost employee morale by sharing the results of the company's success.

An increasingly important function of human resources management is in the area of employee benefits. Such fringe benefits as pension plans, insurance programs, health and safety programs, credit unions, and sick-leave pay are typically administered by the personnel department.

Review questions

1. Identify the following terms:
   a. personnel management
   b. job analysis
   c. job description
   d. job specification
   e. EEOC
   f. on-the-job training
   g. classroom training
   h. apprenticeship training
   i. wage
   j. salary
   k. job evaluation
   l. piece wage
   m. time wage
   n. bonus
   o. profit-sharing
   p. fringe benefits
   q. OSHA
2. Draw an organization chart for a personnel department.
3. Outline the employee selection process.
4. Why do many firms follow a policy of hiring from within?
5. "Employee training should be viewed as a continuing process." Why?
6. Explain the basic criteria for promotion in most companies.
7. Outline the typical penalties for violating company work rules.
8. List the major factors that influence a company's wage policy.
9. Outline the alternative wage plans discussed in this chapter.
10. Describe the typical fringe benefits enjoyed in industry in the United States.

Discussion questions and exercises

1. Evaluate the pro and con arguments to the controversial issue that appears in this chapter.
2. Prepare a brief report on the use of psychological testing in the employee selection process.
3. What is your opinion of Pan American's decision to help laid-off personnel find new jobs? Does a company have an obligation to undertake this task? Why, or why not?
4. Interview an executive at a local firm and write a brief report, including information on how the firm goes about hiring new employees.
5. Discuss the type of compensation plan you would recommend for:
   a. watch repair personnel
   b. retail sales personnel
   c. assembly-line worker in a refrigerator factory
   d. professional athletes
   Justify your opinions to the class.

Case 7-1
Coronary—The Price of Success?

Many executives around the world have a life style that may lead to a coronary (heart) attack. Emotional stress, heavy lunches, little exercise, and sometimes excessive drinking can lead to health problems for executives. Studies indicate that heart attack deaths in twenty-five to forty-four-year-old American males have risen 14 percent since 1950.

Questions

1. Can coronaries among executives be considered a problem of human resource management? If so, how?
2. Do companies have any responsibility for the health of their executives?
3. What can a company do to reduce the risk of heart attacks among its management?

Source: George Negus. "How to Avoid the 'Ultimate Penalty' for Getting on in Business," *The Australian Financial Review* (August 8, 1974), pp. 2–3.

Case 7-2
Pravda Reports a "Brain Drain"

Pravda, Russia's Communist Party newspaper, has complained recently that Capitalist nations have benefited from a "brain drain" from less-developed countries. *Pravda* reports that 150,000 scientists, doctors, and engineers emigrated to the United States during 1950–1970, saving the United States the $3 to $6 million that would have been required to train these specialists.

Questions

1. Why do you think so many foreign professionals emigrated to the United States?
2. *Pravda* views human resources management in terms of a national and international perspective. Should the U.S. government have such a view? What should the national policies of the United States in the area of human resource management be?
3. How does the reported "brain drain" affect U.S. companies?
4. Does a "brain drain" exist *within* the United States?

Source: Detroit News (March 30, 1975), p. 3-C.

8

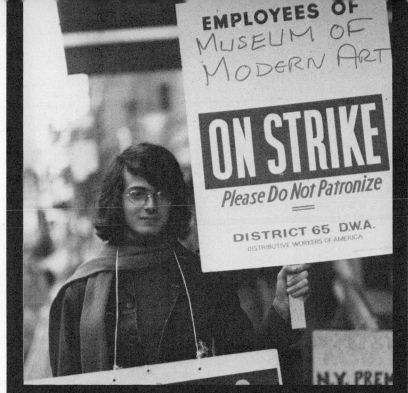

Labor-Management Relations

When Samuel Gompers, the colorful first president of the American Federation of Labor, was asked what the goals of his union were, he responded with one word: "More!"

The following conversation took place between a Ford Motor official and the late United Auto Workers president, Walter Reuther. The Ford official was escorting Reuther through an ultramodern auto plant. He stopped, pointed toward several automatically controlled machines, and turned to the UAW president.

Ford official: "How are you union people going to collect union dues from these guys?"
Walter Reuther: "How are you going to get them to buy Fords?"

What Chapter 8 Is All About

1. Chapter 8 views the worker as a member of an organized group. You should be able to explain why labor unions were first organized and what their chief objectives are: wages, hours, and decent working conditions.
2. You should be able to identify the major federal laws affecting labor unions and the key provisions of each law.
3. Both labor and management have sources of power or "weapons." You will be able to explain these weapons, and show how each might be used.
4. Unions have, until now, attracted members primarily from the ranks of blue-collar workers. Where will the new union members of the 1980's be recruited?
5. After reading this chapter, you should understand these terms:

labor union	right-to-work laws
craft union	Landrum-Griffin Act
industrial union	collective bargaining
American Federation of Labor	mediation
Congress of Industrial	arbitration
Organizations	grievance
Norris-La Guardia Act	strike
Wagner Act	picketing
Fair Labor Standards Act	boycott
Taft-Hartley Act	lockout
closed shop	injunction
union shop	employers' associations
agency shop	

Walter Reuther

SOURCE: United Press International.

Labor unions came into full legitimacy in the United States when the Wagner Act of 1935 made them collective bargaining agents for labor. That was almost thirty years after Walter Reuther, founder of Local 174 of the United Automobile Workers (UAW), was born. Reuther's father was a labor organizer. Reuther himself was fired from his first job as an apprentice tool-and-diemaker in West Virginia while still a teenager. He had been fired for organizing a protest against working holidays and Sundays. Reuther moved to Detroit and worked for General Motors and Ford while completing his high-school education and taking night courses at Wayne State University.

Once again union activity cost Reuther his job, and once again he moved. This time he went to Europe and the Far East, where for three years he toured by bicycle and worked for more than a year in an auto plant in the U.S.S.R. When he returned to the United States, Reuther went back to Detroit to become president of the UAW local he had founded.

Sit-down strikes and violence in the late 1930's eventually led to a recognition of the UAW by GM, Chrysler, and finally, Ford. Though World War II brought a kind of peace to Reuther (he served the U.S. government in maintaining the war effort), world peace renewed his battles for labor. After a UAW strike in 1945 and 1946, wage increases and better working conditions were won. But in 1948 Reuther's right hand was crippled as a result of a gunshot wound, and his brother Victor, also a union member, lost an eye in an attack on Reuther's home.

In the early 1950's Reuther became president of the CIO. Always a man of principle, he saw the value in a merger of the CIO and the AFL and used his influence to push it through—a merger that was split when Reuther pulled out the UAW and joined it with the Teamsters as independent unions. He died in an airplane crash in 1970, just two years later.

Ninety minutes remained before sunrise on the morning of July 6, 1892, when the warning steam whistle sounded in the little town of Homestead, Pennsylvania. Sentries ran through the town shouting, "The Pinkertons are coming!" By the time the two barges loaded with 300 Pinkerton detectives approached the landing, a crowd of 10,000 awaited them.

The Pinkertons had been hired by the manager of the Carnegie Steel Company to break the strike at Andrew Carnegie's Homestead factory. Since the local members of the Amalgamated Association of Iron and Steel Workers controlled much of the town, and some 1,000 pickets patrolled the Works, the Pinkertons decided to use the Monongahela River to surprise the strikers. But as the barges passed Pittsburgh shortly after 3 A.M., a union lookout telegraphed an advance warning.

The Pinkertons were armed with Winchester repeating rifles. The strikers on the landing carried an assortment of weapons, including rifles, shotguns, pistols, and revolvers. Those with no guns were armed with sticks, rocks, and nailed clubs. The battle raged all day until the Pinkertons finally surrendered. Forty strikers had been shot and nine died. Seven Pinkertons had been killed and nearly all of the survivors had been injured, either by gunfire or by the strikers' rocks and clubs.

The strike was finally ended by the appearance of 8,000 National Guardsmen. The 4,000 original strikers were replaced by new employees and only 400 of them were ever rehired.[1]

The battle at Homestead is only one in a long list of bloody confrontations between management and organized labor in the United States. American labor history contains the names of such battles as the Haymarket Riot, the Battle of the Overpass, the Ludlow, Colorado strife, and the bloody 1934 Auto-Lite strike at the Toledo plant. More often the disagreements were resolved in court.

Many famous labor leaders came into prominence during the late 1800's and early 1900's, before labor unions were recognized as legal by the federal government. Samuel Gompers, Joe Hill, Walter Reuther, John L. Lewis, and George Meany are well-known for their roles in the growth of the American labor movement.

What Is a Labor Union?

A **labor union** is *a group of workers who have banded together to achieve common goals involving the key areas of wages, hours, and working conditions.* Two types of labor unions exist in the United States: craft and industrial unions. **Craft unions** are *labor unions consisting of skilled workers in a specific craft or trade.* They exist for such artisans as carpenters, painters, machinists, and printers.

While craft unions focus on a specific trade, **industrial unions** are *labor unions consisting of all of the workers in a given industry, regardless of their occupations or skill levels.* Industrial unions include the United Auto Workers, the United Mine Workers, and the Amalgamated Clothing Workers Union.

Why Are Labor Unions Needed?

The Industrial Revolution brought the advantages of specialization and the division of labor. These factors produced increased efficiency, since each worker could specialize in some aspect of the production process and become proficient at the work. The combination of numerous workers in producing goods resulted in increased output over the previous handicraft methods of production. The factory system converted the jack-of-all-trades into a specialist.

**"For years he had me believing his
union wouldn't let him do housework."**

The Objectives of Labor Unions Include Wages, Hours, and Working
Conditions
SOURCE: *The Wall Street Journal*, March 19, 1975. Reprinted with permission from the *Wall
Street Journal.*

But industrial workers of the nineteenth and the early twentieth centuries discovered that the Industrial Revolution had produced a more sinister impact on their lives. Specialization had
resulted in their dependence on the factory for their livelihood. In
prosperous times they were assured of employment. But when
depressions came, they were out of work. Unemployment insurance
was a subject for dreamers and the poorhouses represented reality
for unemployed workers.

Working conditions were often bad. Work days were long; and
safety standards were nonexistent in many factories.

Working Conditions in the Nineteenth Century

At the beginning of the nineteenth century, the lot of the average working-
man was not an enviable one. Working conditions were unbelievably
wretched in terms of today's standards. Young boys and girls were pressed
into the work force to earn a few pennies to help their families. In Boston
in 1830, two-fifths of the total employed were children. The entire cotton
and woolen industries were based on the exploitation of young female
labor. Hours of work were from daybreak to dark, and wages were low. In
the spinning and weaving mills of New Jersey, children earned an average
of a little more than a dollar a week. Imprisonment for debt was common.

By the end of the century, the work week was typically 60 hours, but
in some industries, such as in steel, it was 72 or even 84 hours—seven 12-
hour days a week. Working conditions were frequently unsafe, and child
labor was common.

Source: James A. Barnes. *Wealth of the American People: A History of Their Economic Life*
(New York: Prentice-Hall, Inc., 1949), pp. 286–290.

Workers gradually learned that through bargaining as a unified group they could obtain improvements in job security and better wages and working conditions. The organized efforts of Philadelphia printers in 1786 resulted in the first minimum wage in America—one dollar a day. One hundred years later New York City streetcar conductors banded together in successful negotiations that reduced their work day from seventeen to twelve hours. In 1973 negotiations by representatives of the American and National League Players Association resulted in a requirement that baseball club owners obtain the approval of veteran players with ten or more years of experience with the same team before they are traded.

A Brief Look at the History of Labor Unions in America

Although the history of trade unionism in the United States can be traced back prior even to the Declaration of Independence, early unions were loose-knit local organizations that served primarily as friendship organizations or benevolent societies to help fellow workers in need. Such unions were typically short-lived. They usually grew during prosperous times and suffered severely when depressions came.

The first truly national union was the *Knights of Labor,* founded in 1869. By 1886 its membership exceeded 700,000 workers, but it was soon split into factions. One group had revolutionary aims: It wanted the government to take over production. A second faction wanted the union to continue to focus on improving the economic well-being of union members, and opposed the Socialist tendencies of some union members. This faction merged with a group of other unaffiliated craft unions in 1886 to form the **American Federation of Labor** (**AFL**), to become *a national union made up of affiliated individual craft unions.*

The AFL's president was a dynamic man named Samuel Gompers, who believed that labor unions should operate within the framework of the economic system and who was totally opposed to socialism. In 1903 he stated:

I want to tell you, Socialists, that I have studied your philosophy; read your works on economics . . . I have heard your orators and watched the work of your movement the world over. I have kept close watch upon your doctrines for thirty years; have been closely associated with many of you, and know how you think and what you propose. I know, too, what you have up your sleeve. And I want to say that I am entirely at variance with your philosophy. I declare it to you, I am not only at variance with your doctrines, but with your philosophy. Economically, you are unsound; socially, you are wrong; industrially, you are an impossibility.[2]

Gomper's bread-and-butter concept of unionism kept the labor movement focused on the critical objectives of wages, hours, and working conditions. The AFL grew rapidly, and by 1920 three out of every four organized workers were AFL members. The anthem of the labor movement was the song, "Solidarity Forever."

Solidarity Forever!

(Sung to the tune of "Battle Hymn of the Republic.")

When the Union's inspiration through the workers' blood shall run,
There can be no power greater anywhere beneath the sun
Yet what force on earth is weaker than the feeble strength of one?
But the Union makes us strong.

Chorus:

Solidarity forever!
Solidarity forever!
Solidarity forever!
For the Union makes us strong.

Is there aught we hold in common with the greedy parasite
Who would lash us into serfdom and would crush us with his might?
Is there anything left for us but to organize and fight?
For the Union makes us strong.

It is we who plowed the prairies; built the cities where they trade;
Dug the mines and built the workshops; endless miles of railroad laid.
Now we stand, outcast and starving, mid the wonders we have made;
But the Union makes us strong.

All the world that's owned by idle drones, is ours and ours alone.
We have laid the wide foundations; built it skyward stone by stone.
It is ours, not to slave in, but to master and to own.
While the Union makes us strong.

They have taken untold millions that they never toiled to earn.
But without our brain and muscle not a single wheel can turn.
We can break their haughty power; gain our freedom when we learn
That the Union makes us strong.

In our hands is placed a power greater than their hoarded gold;
Greater than the might of armies, magnified a thousand-fold.
We can bring to birth the new world from the ashes of the old.
For the Union makes us strong.

Union growth was slow in the period between 1920 and 1935. The philosophy of organizing labor along craft lines that had accounted for the AFL's forty-year growth record led to difficulties, since there were few nonunion skilled craftsmen left to organize.

Several unions in the AFL began to organize workers in mass-production automobile and steel industries. Successes in organizing the communications, mining, newspaper, steel, rubber, and automobile industries resulted in the formation of a new group called the **Congress of Industrial Organization (CIO)**. The CIO is *a national union made up of affiliated individual industrial unions.* This new technique of organizing entire industries, rather than individual crafts, was so successful that the CIO soon rivaled the AFL in size.

In 1955 the two groups were united under the presidency of George Meany. By 1976 more than 200 separate unions existed in the United States, approximately one-half of which were affiliated with the AFL-CIO. Figure 8-1 shows the organization of the AFL-CIO.

Two major national unions that are not affiliated with the AFL-CIO are the 2 million-member International Brotherhood of Teamsters, which was expelled in 1957 for alleged corruption, and the United Auto Workers, which left the Federation in 1968 due to disagreements between Meany and the then-UAW president Walter Reuther.

SUB—The United Auto Workers'
Answer to a Guaranteed Annual Wage

The concept of a guaranteed annual wage has long been a goal of labor unions as a means of providing income stability to industrial workers. In 1955 contract negotiations between the United Auto Workers and the Big Three auto manufacturers (Ford, General Motors, and Chrysler Corporation) resulted in the adoption of a new plan called *Supplementary Unemployment Benefits* (SUB).

Under this plan, the company sets aside an amount ranging from seven to twelve cents per worker hour in the SUB fund. During periods of low production and when the auto plants close each year for new model changeovers, the SUB fund pays the laid-off employees an amount based on their current hourly wages. Each employee must first file for unemployment benefits; then SUB will pay an additional amount which, when added to the unemployment benefits, will total 95 percent of the worker's current take home pay. At the height of the layoffs in 1975, General Motors was paying out $9 million a week from its SUB fund and Ford and Chrysler were each paying out $5 million weekly.

The SUB fund is no remedy for long-term unemployment, however. In early 1975 both the GM and Chrysler SUB funds were depleted. The average laid-off GM worker had been living on $176 a week, including $92 from the SUB fund. Most of them continued to receive an average $84 a week in state unemployment benefits. As workers were recalled, the funds were replenished by company contributions.

Source: Associated Press (May 9, 1975).

By 1976 some 20 million American workers—or 23 percent of the labor force—belonged to a labor union. Unions are particularly strong among blue-collar workers, and in such industries as construction and transportation four out of every five blue-collar workers are union members. The twenty largest unions are listed in Table 8-1.

Labor Legislation[3]

U.S. government attitudes toward unionism have varied considerably during the past century. These shifting attitudes can be seen in the major pieces of legislation enacted during this period.

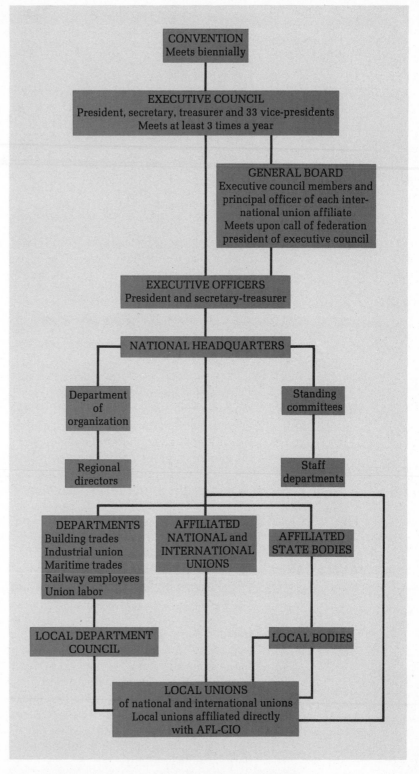

Figure 8-1
Organization of the
AFL-CIO

CONVENTION
Meets biennially

EXECUTIVE COUNCIL
President, secretary, treasurer and 33 vice-presidents
Meets at least 3 times a year

GENERAL BOARD
Executive council members and
principal officer of each international union affiliate
Meets upon call of federation
president of executive council

EXECUTIVE OFFICERS
President and secretary-treasurer

NATIONAL HEADQUARTERS

Department
of
organization

Standing
committees

Regional
directors

Staff
departments

DEPARTMENTS
Building trades
Industrial union
Maritime trades
Railway employees
Union labor

**AFFILIATED
NATIONAL and
INTERNATIONAL
UNIONS**

**AFFILIATED
STATE BODIES**

**LOCAL DEPARTMENT
COUNCIL**

LOCAL BODIES

LOCAL UNIONS
of national and international unions
Local unions affiliated directly
with AFL-CIO

Table 8-1
The Twenty Largest
Unions in the
United States

Union	Number of Members
Teamsters	1.9 million
Automobile Workers	1.4 million
Steelworkers	1.4 million
Electrical Workers (IBEW)	957,000
Carpenters	829,000
Machinists	758,000
Retail Clerks	633,000
Laborers	600,000
State, County, and Municipal	529,000
Meat Cutters	524,000
Service Employees	484,000
Hotel and Restaurant	458,000
Communications Workers	443,000
Ladies' Garment Workers	428,000
Operating Engineers	402,000
Paperworkers	389,000
Clothing Workers	365,000
Musicians	315,000
Government (AFGE)	293,000
Electrical (IUE)	290,000

SOURCE: *Statistical Abstract of the United States* (Washington, D.C.: Government Printing Office, 1974).

THE NORRIS-LA GUARDIA ACT

The **Norris-La Guardia Act** (1932) is *early federal legislation aimed at protecting unions through greatly reducing management's ability to obtain injunctions to halt union activities.* Employers had always found it very easy to obtain court decrees forbidding strikes, peaceful picketing, and even membership drives. Such injunctions, once obtained, automatically made the union a wrongdoer in the eyes of the law if it continued these activities vital to union effectiveness.

THE WAGNER ACT—ORGANIZED LABOR'S MAGNA CARTA

Congress also passed the *National Labor Relations Act,* or **Wagner Act** (1935), which *made collective bargaining legal and required employers to bargain with the elected representatives of their employees.* Prior to this time union activities were often ruled as violations of the Sherman Act, which prohibited "attempts to monopolize."

Not only did the Wagner Act make collective bargaining legal it *ordered* employers to bargain with the agents of their workers if a majority of them elected to be represented by a union. A National Labor Relations Board was set up to supervise union elections and to prohibit unfair labor practices by management. These unfair labor practices included such activities as firing workers for joining a union, refusing to hire workers who were sympathetic to unions, threatening to close the firm if workers joined a union, interfering with or dominating the administration of a union, and refusing to bargain with a union.

FAIR LABOR STANDARDS ACT— ESTABLISHING A MINIMUM WAGE

The **Fair Labor Standards Act** of 1938 continued the wave of pro-union legislation. It *set a federal minimum wage and maximum basic hours for workers employed in industries engaged in interstate commerce. It also outlawed the use of child labor.* The first minimum wage was set at twenty-five cents an hour, with exceptions for farm workers and retail employees. By 1976 the minimum wage had increased to $2.30 an hour. The law allows workers to stay on the job longer than the maximum weekly limit, but only on the basis of overtime pay.

THE TAFT-HARTLEY ACT— THE PENDULUM SWINGS

Government support of organized labor produced a generation of growth for the unions. One by one, the industrial giants—Ford, General Motors, U.S. Steel—were unionized. For the first time in history they recognized a CIO union as their workers' bargaining agent. Union membership jumped from below 3 million in 1933 to almost 15 million by 1945. In that year union members represented 36 percent of all nonagricultural employment. This figure has never been reached since.

The Wagner Act of 1935 focused on unfair labor practices *by employers.* It said nothing about unfair practices *on the part of labor.* These were the subject of the **Taft-Hartley Act** (1947), passed by Congress over the veto of President Harry Truman. This piece of *federal legislation was designed to balance the power of unions and management by prohibiting the closed shop and a number of unfair union practices.* The Act was passed against the background of a postwar wave of strikes, as the now-giant unions for the first time learned to make full use of their strength. Paralyzing strikes in steel, coal, and shipping alarmed the public. So did **jurisdictional** strikes, resulting not from disputes with employers but from *two unions fighting each other for jurisdiction over a group of workers.* Labor, it was argued, had been given an overdose of power. To counter this the new Act outlawed the closed shop (discussed in the next section), but did not outlaw the union shop. A number of other unfair union practices were also prohibited.

THE CLOSED SHOP, THE UNION SHOP, AND THE AGENCY SHOP

The **closed shop** is *an employment agreement whereby management agrees not to hire nonunion workers.* Before workers could be hired, they had to become union members. And they had to continue to be union members as a condition of their employment. The closed shop was considered an essential ingredient of union security. If all workers were union members, the union was assured of recognition by the employer. The union also had unquestionable power to make requests concerning wages and working conditions. And since all employees enjoyed the benefits of union contracts, it was felt that they should all support the union.

Employers argued that a fundamental principle of freedom was violated if people were forced to join an organization as a condition of employment. They also argued that since they could hire only union members, the best, most qualified workers might not be hired. Finally, employers contended that union leaders, with a guaranteed membership, were likely to become irresponsible and deal dishonestly with their members. Apparently, Congress favored these arguments, since the Taft-Hartley Act made the closed shop illegal.

The **union shop** *is an employment agreement whereby any qualified employee may be hired, but they must join the union within a specified time period.*

The **agency shop** *is an employment agreement whereby any qualified employees may be hired, but nonunion workers must pay the union a fee equal to union dues.* Such an arrangement eliminates "free riders," who benefit from union negotiations without supporting the union financially.

The Taft-Hartley Act contained a clause whereby *state laws outlawing the union shop* could be passed. A total of nineteen states, located mainly in the South and the Great Plains, passed these **right-to-work laws.** Figure 8-2 shows the right-to-work states in which compulsory union membership is illegal.

Other unfair union practices outlawed by the Taft-Hartley Act include refusal of the union to bargain with the employer, **feather-bedding** (*a mild form of extortion where workers are paid for work not done*), striking without sixty days' notice, and **secondary boycotts** (*where unions refuse to buy or handle products produced by another union or worker group*).

Figure 8-2
States with Right-to-work Laws (Shaded Areas)

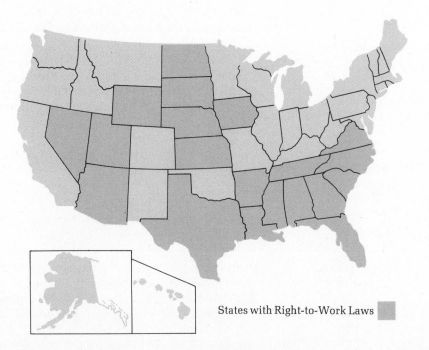

States with Right-to-Work Laws

Has Anyone Seen Napoleon?

Most writers cite the railroad fireman on diesel locomotives as the best current example of featherbedding. But Robert Townsend found an even better example in England:

The British created a civil service job in 1803 calling for a man to stand on the Cliffs of Dover with a spyglass. He was supposed to ring a bell if he saw Napoleon coming. The job was abolished in 1945.

Source: Robert Townsend. *Up the Organization* (New York: Alfred A. Knopf, Inc., 1970), p. 93.

Under the Taft-Hartley Act employers may sue unions for breach of contract and may engage (without coercion) in antiunion activities. Unions must make financial reports to their members and disclose their officers' salaries; they cannot use dues for political contributions nor charge excessive initiation fees. The Act also allowed the President of the United States to ask for court suspension for eighty days of strikes that "imperil the national health and safety." At the end of this cooling-off period, there must be a secret union ballot on the latest company offer.

THE LANDRUM-GRIFFIN ACT—DISCLOSING INFORMATION ABOUT UNION AFFAIRS

The Taft-Hartley Act was amended in 1959 by the **Landrum-Griffin Act.** It is *federal legislation requiring regularly scheduled elections of union officers by secret ballot and increased regulation of the handling of union funds.* The Act was passed against a background of hearings by the McClellan Senate committee investigating labor racketeering. The committee had exposed "gangsterism, bribery, and hoodlumism" in the affairs of some unions. Several union leaders had taken union funds for personal use; had accepted payoffs from employers for union protection; and were even involved in blackmail, arson, and murder. The Act established regulations requiring regularly scheduled elections of union officers and the use of secret ballots. It required that officials handling union funds be bonded, and imposed federal penalties for embezzlement of these funds.

The Collective Bargaining Process

The primary objective of a labor union is the improvement of wages, hours, and working conditions for its members. These goals are achieved primarily through the process of **collective bargaining,** which may be formally defined as *a process of negotiation between management and union representatives for the purpose of arriving at mutually acceptable wages and working conditions for employees.*

Once a union is accepted by a majority of the workers in a firm, it is certified by the National Labor Relations Board and must be recognized by the firm's management as the legal collective-bargaining agent for all employees. The stage is then set for representatives of the union and management to meet formally at the bargaining table to work out a collective bargaining agreement or contract. Union contracts typically cover a two or three-year period. The contract is often the result of days and even weeks of discussions, disagreements, compromises, and eventual agreement. Once agreement has been reached, union members must vote to accept or reject the contract. If the contract is rejected, union representatives may resume the bargaining process with management representatives, or the union members may strike to obtain their demands.

The contract, once ratified by the union membership, becomes the legally binding agreement for all labor-management relations during the period of time specified by the agreement. It typically includes such areas as wages, industrial relations, and methods of settling labor-management disputes. Some contracts are only a few pages in length, while others may run more than two hundred pages. Table 8-2 lists topics typically included in a union contract.

Table 8-2
Topics Usually Included in a Union Contract

Union Contract

I. *Union Activities and Responsibilities*
    A. Dues collection
    B. Union bulletin boards
    C. Union officers
    D. Wildcat strikes and slowdowns

II. *Wages*
    A. Job evaluation
    B. Wage structure
    C. General wage adjustments
    D. Wage incentives
    E. Time studies
    F. Shift differentials and bonuses

III. *Hours of Work*
    A. Regular hours of work
    B. Vacations
    C. Holidays
    D. Overtime rules
    E. Rest periods

IV. *Insurance*
    A. Medical and life insurance
    B. Pensions

V. *Employee Job Rights and Seniority*
    A. Seniority regulations
    B. Transfers
    C. Promotions
    D. Layoffs
    E. Recalls

VI. *Grievance Handling and Arbitration*

Settling Union-Management Disputes—Arbitration and Mediation

Although strikes make newspaper headlines, nineteen out of every twenty union-management negotiations result in a signed agreement without a work stoppage. There are approximately 150,000 union contracts currently in force in the United States. Of these, 147,000 were the result of successful negotiations with no work stoppages taking place.

MEDIATION
When negotiations do break down, disagreements between union and management representatives may be settled by **mediation.** This is *the process of bringing in a third party, called a mediator, to make recommendations for the settlement of labor-management differences.*

The Taft-Hartley Act requires labor and management to notify each other of desired changes in union contracts sixty days before such contracts expire. They must also notify a special agency, the Federal Mediation and Conciliation Service, within thirty days after that, if a new contract has not been accepted. The Service has a staff of several hundred mediators to assist in settling union-management disagreements affecting interstate commerce. In addition, such states as New York, Pennsylvania, and California have their own mediation agencies.

Although the mediator will not serve as a decision maker, union and management representatives can be assisted in reaching an agreement by the mediator's suggestions, advice, and compromise solutions. Since the confidence and trust of both sides must be given the mediator, impartiality is essential. Mediators are often selected from the ranks of community social or political leaders, attorneys, professors, or distinguished national figures.

ARBITRATION
The final step in settling union-management differences is **arbitration.** This is *the process of bringing in a third party, called the arbitrator, who renders a binding decision in a labor-management dispute.* The mediator does not do so. The process of arbitration involves the use of an impartial third party who is acceptable to both sides and whose decision is binding and legally enforceable. In essence, *the arbitrator acts as a judge.* After listening to both sides of the argument, the arbitrator makes a decision. This is called **voluntary arbitration,** *since both union and management representatives made the decision to present their unresolved issues to an impartial third party.* Ninety percent of all union contracts call for the use of arbitration if union and management representatives fail to reach an agreement.

On occasions *a third party, usually the federal government, will require management and labor to submit to* **compulsory ar-**

"Gentlemen, instead of trying to mediate this thing, why don't you just slug it out?"

SOURCE: Reprinted by permission of the publisher from *Management Review*, © 1967 by the American Management Association.

bitration. Although it is rarely used in the United States, there is considerable interest in compulsory arbitration as a means of eliminating prolonged strikes affecting major industries and threatening to disrupt the economy.

Grievance Procedures

The union contract represents an agreement that serves as a guide to relations between the firm's management and its employees. The rights of each party are stated in the agreement. But no contract—no matter how detailed—will completely eliminate the possibility of disagreements.

Differences of opinion may arise on how to interpret a particular clause in the contract. Management may interpret the layoff policy of the contract as based on seniority for each work shift. The union interpretation may be that the layoff policy is based on the seniority of all employees. Such differences may be the beginning of a **grievance.**

A grievance—whether by a single worker or by the entire union—is an *employee or union complaint that management is violating some provision of the union contract.* Since grievance handling is the primary source of contact between union officials and management from the signing of one contract to the next, the way in which grievances are resolved plays a major role in the relationship between the employer and the union.

Figure 8-3
Five Steps in the
Grievance Procedures
(Grievances Not Settled
at One Level Are
Carried to the Next
Level)

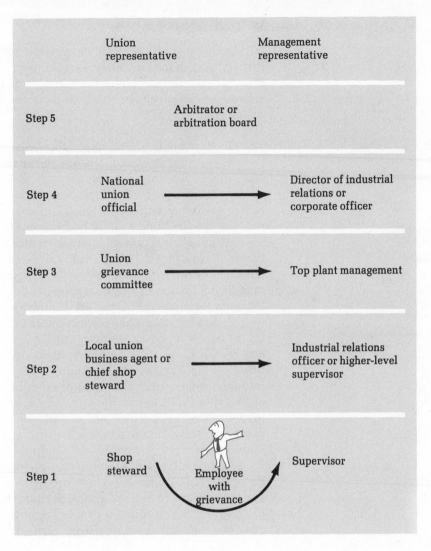

Since grievances are likely to arise over such matters as transfers, work assignments, and seniority, almost all union contracts require that these complaints be submitted to a formal grievance procedure. Figure 8-3 shows the five steps involved in a typical grievance procedure.

As Figure 8-3 indicates, the employee's grievance is first submitted by the union representative (the shop steward) to the immediate supervisor. If the complaint is corrected, it goes no further. But if no satisfactory agreement is reached, a higher union official may take the grievance to a higher manager. Should the highest company officer not settle the grievance, it is then submitted to an outside arbitration panel for a final and binding decision.

Weapons of Unions and Management

Although most differences between labor and management are settled through the collective bargaining process or through a formal grievance procedure, both unions and management will occasionally resort to tools of power to make their demands known (see Table 8-3).

UNION WEAPONS   The chief weapons of unions are the strike, picketing, and boycotts.

The **strike,** or walkout, is one of the most effective tools of the labor union. It involves *the temporary work stoppage by employees until a dispute has been settled or a contract has been signed.* Since striking workers will not be paid, unions establish **strike funds** *to pay the workers and enable them to continue the strike.*

Although the power to strike is the ultimate weapon of the union, it is not used lightly. In many cases the threat of a strike is almost as effective as an actual work stoppage. The actual number of man-days lost due to strikes represents only one-half of 1 percent—less than the amount of time lost from work due to the common cold.

Picketing is another effective form of union pressure. Picketing is *the practice of workers marching at the entrances of the employer's plant as a public protest against some management practice.* As long as the picketing does not involve violence or intimidation, the practice is protected under the constitutional right of free speech. Picketing may take place for a number of reasons. It may accompany a strike or be a protest for alleged unfair labor practices. Since union workers will usually refuse to cross picket lines, the firm may be unable to obtain deliveries or other services.

A **boycott** is *an attempt to stop the purchase of goods or services from a company.* There are two kinds of boycotts: primary and secondary. In the case of a **primary boycott,** *union members are told not to patronize a firm being boycotted.* Some unions will even fine members who buy from such a firm. A **secondary boycott**

Table 8-3
The Weapons of Unions
and Management

Form	How Used
Union Weapons	
Strike	Refusal to work
Picketing	Discourage patrons of the firm
Boycott	Refuse to do business with the firm
Management Weapons	
Lockout	Refuse workers entry to the plant
Injunction	Stop union actions, such as strikes, by obtaining a court order
Employers' association	Cooperative, united effort in dealing with labor unions

is used when *a supplier of the boycotted company is threatened with a strike unless it ceases to do business with the first boycotted firm.*

In the late 1960's César Chavez, head of the United Farm Workers Organizing Committee, became nationally known for his efforts to organize farm laborers. His best-known technique was a call for a nationwide boycott of grapes picked by nonunion workers. Housewives throughout the United States joined in this secondary boycott by purchasing only those grapes in produce boxes marked with an Aztec thunderbird, the Farm Workers union symbol. Although the Taft-Hartley and Landrum-Griffin acts make most secondary boycotts illegal, farm workers are not covered by these acts.

MANAGEMENT WEAPONS Management also has weapons for dealing with organized labor. In the past it used the **lockout** to counter the threats of unions to strike. The lockout is, in effect, *a management strike to bring pressure on union members by closing the firm.* The lockout is rarely used today, unless a strike has been called which has partially shut a plant down.

Injunctions are sometimes obtained by management to prevent picketing or certain unfair union practices. Injunctions are *court orders prohibiting some practice.* Prior to the passage of the Norris-La Guardia Act, injunctions were used frequently to prohibit all types of strikes. Since then, their use has been limited to restrain violence, restrict picketing, and prevent damage to company property.

Some employers make cooperative efforts to present a united front in dealing with labor unions. These **employers' associations** may even act as negotiators for individual employers who want to reach agreements with labor unions. In some industries characterized by many small firms and a single large union, there is an increasing tendency for industry-wide bargaining between the union and a single representative of the industry employers. Although they do not negotiate contracts, the National Association of Manufacturers and the United States Chamber of Commerce are examples of employers' associations. Both of these associations present the views of their members on key issues.

The Future of Organized Labor

The last two decades have witnessed a lack of union growth. From a peak membership of 36 percent of the nonagricultural labor force in the United States in 1945, union members now represent only 23 percent of nonfarm employment. In addition, the prospects for increasing union membership from traditional blue-collar occupations and industries are bleak for two reasons.

First, most blue-collar workers have already been organized. It has been pointed out in this book that almost every employee of the automobile, steel, aerospace, paper, rubber, and brewing industries is a union member. In cities such as Pittsburgh, Seattle, and Detroit, nine out of every ten manufacturing workers are currently members of unions. The days of masses of unorganized blue-collar workers are gone. Union organizers must look to new directions for additional members.

How Unemployment Affected Membership in One Union

The recession that began in 1974 hit the automobile industry particularly hard. By 1975 the unemployment rate in the Detroit area approached 20 percent. Auto plant employment had plunged 30 percent in fifteen months, as new car sales dropped 25 percent below their record 1973 pace. More than 200,000 workers of the Big Three automakers had lost their jobs.

The effects of the recession and resulting unemployment quickly spread to the United Auto Workers. In January of 1974 the UAW membership rolls listed 1.6 million. Twelve months later it had dropped to 1.3 million—a decline of 18 percent. Union income from monthly dues declined by 10 percent over the same time period.

The second problem is that job-growth projections, shown in Figure 8-4, illustrate that blue-collar ranks—the source of union membership strength in the past—will lessen in importance in the future. As factories become more automated, the demand for blue-collar workers decreases.

As a result of the decline in blue-collar jobs, labor unions are refocusing their organizing efforts on public workers and white-collar workers.

Prior to President John F. Kennedy's executive order of 1962, *federal employees* were prohibited from union membership. Since that time more than 50 percent of all federal employees have joined

Figure 8-4
Projected Percentage
Increase in Occupations:
1970–1980

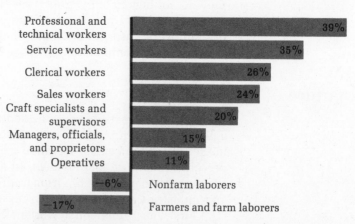

Professional and technical workers	39%
Service workers	35%
Clerical workers	26%
Sales workers	24%
Craft specialists and supervisors	20%
Managers, officials, and proprietors	15%
Operatives	11%
Nonfarm laborers	−6%
Farmers and farm laborers	−17%

SOURCE: U.S. Department of Labor, *Manpower Report of the President* (Washington, D.C.: U.S. Government Printing Office, 1972), p. 259.

Should Public Employees Have the Right to Strike?

In recent years public employees—those professionals and workers who are employed by the city, the state, and the federal government—have used the same tactics in making demands for better working conditions as workers employed by private companies. At one time government employment represented unquestioned security, and there seemed to be no need for the ultimate labor weapon—the strike. Government workers could negotiate salary scales, hours and conditions of employment, benefits, and so on. Recently, however, the situation has changed.

New York City, for example, has been forced to lay off thousands of police, firefighters, and sanitation workers while struggling to keep itself from fiscal ruin. With the threat of bankruptcy clawing at its throat, the city has done what private enterprise would do in similar circumstances—cut its expenditures, which has included trimming the city payroll.

Experts who believe that the functions of public employees (such as teachers, transport and welfare workers, sewage and street maintenance people, and water supply workers, as well as the police, firefighters, and sanitation workers) are too vital to be disrupted, also say that these workers must not be allowed to strike. They believe that the business of government is to render services, not to make a profit. If profit is not the object of such services, then salary raises and costly benefit packages for government workers must be considered in this light. Yet even if the expenses cannot be met by government, the services must not be interrupted by striking public employees, for this would not be in the public interest. Government has few options, beyond raising taxes, for obtaining more money with which to pay service staffs. The government cannot go out of business or move to another locality where labor is cheaper, as a private enterprise can. Therefore, it must make do with relatively little freedom at the bargaining table. Government cannot improve the situation very much, and even the little that can be done must be approved by city, state, or federal legislators who are elected by the public and serve the public interest.

Labor unions, on the other hand, maintain that there is no difference between workers in public and private enterprise. Food deliveries and utilities are as vital to the public as, for example, the police. Yet other industries negotiate settlements and can utilize the paralyzing threat of a strike if and when that becomes necessary. Since government and labor are both members of the public, negotiations for the benefit of labor should be possible. But labor's basic weapon, the strike, must be permissible or public workers have no strength at the bargaining table.

unions. Although they are not allowed to strike, they do have the right to bargain collectively. In some instances, such as the postal workers strike of 1970, government employees have resorted to strikes to reinforce their demands for pay increases. Although a few union leaders were jailed for this illegal strike, the wage demands were met.

State and municipal employees have been other targets for union organizing attempts. Strikes have spread to such occupations as police officers and firefighters, sanitation workers, doctors and hospital employees, zookeepers, and even prison guards, as these workers sought a dramatic means of obtaining higher wages and employee benefits. Mass "sick calls" are often used when strikes are prohibited by law. The "blue flu" was the popular name attached to strikes by police officers in the early 1970's.

Public school teachers have used strikes as a means of exerting pressure on state and local officials to meet their demands. While more than 200,000 teachers have joined the American Federation of Teachers, the most powerful teachers' association is the National Education Association (NEA), with more than 1 million members. The NEA, in essence, functions as a labor union, since it has called for strikes and pickets to enforce teacher demands and has acted as a bargaining agent for public school teachers and some college faculties.

Organizing attempts are also focused on *agricultural workers* and *white-collar employees*. To date less than 50,000 agricultural and fishing workers are union members. White-collar union membership is estimated to be approximately 3.4 million, or one-sixth of all white-collar workers in the United States.

The success of organizing attempts in these areas—public employees, agricultural workers, and white-collar employees—will ultimately determine whether American labor unions will continue to grow or whether they have already reached their membership peak.

Summary

Labor unions have a long and sometimes violent history in the United States. Although they existed even before the Declaration of Independence, they were typically small, weak, and usually short-lived. Serious attempts to form national unions in the late 1800's and the early part of the twentieth century were met with fierce resistance by both management and government. Courts often ruled that organizing attempts constituted "attempts to monopolize" and violated antitrust laws.

The development of the American Federation of Labor under the leadership of Samuel Gompers focused union goals on three "bread-and-butter" issues: improvements in wages, hours, and working conditions. The two decades following the passage of the Wagner Act represented the Golden Era for union growth; in 1945 union members represented 36 percent of all nonagricultural workers in the United States. During this period the Congress of Industrial Organizations experienced considerable success in organizing the automobile, mining, and steel industries. In 1955 the AFL and CIO merged their 18 million members under the presidency of George Meany.

The Wagner Act has been called the *Magna Carta* of the union movement. It required management to bargain collectively with the duly elected representatives of its employees and outlawed a number of unfair management practices. In order to balance the power between labor and management, Congress passed the Taft-Hartley Act in 1947 and the Landrum-Griffin Act in 1959 to outlaw a number of unfair practices on the part of labor unions.

A collective bargaining agreement, or contract, is the basis of relations between management and a union. It specifies agreements concerning such areas as wages, hours of work, employee rights and seniority provisions, and grievance handling. The contract is the result of negotiations between representatives of both management and labor. Occasionally, when negotiations break down, a third party—a mediator or an arbitrator—will join the negotiations to assist in reaching an agreement. The mediator offers advice and makes recommendations; the arbitrator listens to both sides and then makes a decision which becomes binding on both sides.

Future union growth will result primarily from organizing attempts in three areas: public employees, agricultural workers, and white-collar employees. Since most of the union membership comes from the blue-collar ranks, these three relatively unorganized groups of workers represent the greatest source of future union members.

Review questions

1. Identify the following terms:
   a. labor union
   b. craft union
   c. industrial union
   d. American Federation of Labor
   e. Congress of Industrial Organizations
   f. Norris-La Guardia Act
   g. Wagner Act
   h. Taft-Hartley Act
   i. Landrum-Griffin Act
   j. closed shop
   k. union shop
   l. agency shop
   m. right to work laws
   n. collective bargaining
   o. mediation
   p. arbitration
   q. grievance
   r. strike
   s. picketing
   t. boycott
   u. lockout
   v. injunction
   w. employers' associations

2. Trace the development of labor unions in industrialized society.
3. Briefly outline the history of labor unions in the United States.
4. What is the AFL-CIO?
5. What are SUB benefits?
6. Trace the development of labor legislation in the United States.
7. What is meant by these labor-management terms?
   a. featherbedding
   b. secondary boycotts
   c. "cooling off period"
8. Describe the collective bargaining process.
9. Outline the steps in the grievance procedure.
10. What do you think is the future of organized labor in the United States?

Discussion questions and exercises

1. Evaluate the pro and con arguments to the controversial issue that appears in this chapter.
2. Douglas A. Fraser, vice-president of the United Auto Workers, told one student group that: "One of the secrets to successful bargaining is never say 'never.'"* What do you think Fraser meant by this statement?
3. West Germany uses a very humanitarian approach to the unemployed. Jobless workers receive written invitations to mandatory monthly visits to the local labor office. Conferences with employment counselors are held in private offices. Unemployment checks are mailed from a Nuremberg computer center. As a result, there are no long lines at German unemployment offices.† Comment on the West German approach.
4. Invite a local labor leader to speak to your class about how his or her union operates.
5. Secure a collective bargaining agreement from a firm. Then divide the class into a management and a labor bargaining team, and conduct a simulated bargaining session for the next contract. Your instructor will act as moderator and set some ground rules for the bargaining.

*Quoted in Micki Maynard. "UAW VP Fraser Speaks on Bargaining," Eastern Echo (March 10, 1975), p. 1.

†This approach is described in Richard F. Janssen. "In Europe, the Jobless Get Special Treatment to Minimize the Unrest," The Wall Street Journal (May 28, 1975), p. 1.

Case 8-1
Paying Workers to Quit

Volkswagen and Opel, General Motors' German subsidiary, both used a unique method for reducing the size of their work force during a sales downturn. The two firms offered cash bonuses to employees willing to give up their jobs. Volkswagen offered payments ranging from $1,960 to $3,525, while Opel paid $2,145 to $3,900 to quitting workers.

Questions

1. Why would Opel and Volkswagen choose such an unusual method of terminating workers?
2. What benefits in employee morale may result from these actions?
3. What possible future problems might arise from the decision to pay workers to quit their jobs?

Source: "GM Opel Unit, Like VW, Entices Workers to Quit," *The Wall Street Journal* (July 3, 1974).

Case 8-2
Providing an Incentive to Reach Bargaining Agreements

The union contract between a local of the Upholsterers Union and the Dunbar Furniture Corporation of Berne, Indiana, contains an unusual provision: an incentive for both management and labor to reach an agreement.

Once the old contract expires, union members continue to work. Half of their pay and a matching amount from the employer goes into the bank. If a new contract is agreed upon within six weeks after the old contract expires, the money is returned to each party. If no settlement is reached in six weeks the percentage of the money that will be returned to each party is progressively reduced, with the remainder going to local public-service projects.

If no settlement is reached by the twelfth week all of the money in the bank goes to such projects. Only then can a strike take place.

Questions

1. As a union member, would you favor such a provision in your contract? What are the advantages of such a provision? What disadvantages can you see?
2. As a management representative, would you favor such a provision?

9

Production
Management

"Everything is more complicated than it seems."
"Nothing ever gets done as quickly as it should."
"If anything can go wrong, it will."
"If you play with a thing long enough you will break it."
— *Murphy's Laws*

What Chapter 9 Is All About

1. In Chapter 9 you will learn the meaning of *utility* and how production creates utility for the firm's customers.
2. You will be able to consider a plant in your city and analyze the plant location factors that were most important in its location decision.
3. You will be able to discuss the advantages and disadvantages of keeping large amounts of inventory on hand.
4. Assume that you are responsible for production control for a ballpoint pen manufacturer. After reading Chapter 9 you will be able to illustrate the importance of each step in the production control process.
5. After reading this chapter, you should understand these terms:

utility	production planning
form utility	routing
production	scheduling
production management	PERT
industrial park	critical path
reciprocity	dispatching
inventory control	follow up
production control	quality control

Berry Gordy, Jr.

One of the most famous aspects of American culture is its native black American music. First spirituals, then jazz, and now rock and soul have been played and adopted by people all over the world. For a long time, though, none of the blacks involved with this music were making it financially; that is, until Berry Gordy, Jr., ex-boxer and Ford auto worker, founded Hitsville USA. In 1953, when Gordy got out of the army, he opened a record store in his native Detroit. Because he liked jazz, he invested his small capital in records by such performers as Charlie Parker and Stan Kenton. But that was not what his customers wanted. They wanted rhythm and blues, and Gordy did not have the money to stock a whole new line of black music. He went bankrupt.

Gordy wrote some songs while he worked as a plasterer for his father. These were recorded by Gordy himself and a group of musicians in a rented studio. The resulting masters were then sold—when possible—to a record company that would manufacture and distribute them. Then, in 1959, with $700 borrowed from his family, Gordy began to manufacture and sell his own records on the Hitsville USA label. The next year William Robinson, as Smokey Robinson and the Miracles, wrote and recorded "Shop Around," Gordy's first big million-copy hit. A few years after that, one of the Miracles introduced Gordy to eleven-year-old Steveland Morris. The youngster was signed to a contract and began recording for Gordy as Stevie Wonder. Another name change proved equally lucky when Hitsville became Motown (for "motor town," Detroit).

It may be that Gordy's shoestring beginnings have made him cautious. Whatever the reason, for a very long time Motown has kept down its overhead, with headquarters in a group of old houses on Detroit's West Grand Boulevard before moving to Los Angeles. The emphasis is not on trimmings but on talent and hits. Gordy is a fast learner, as the success of Motown and its enterprises has proved.

Henry Ford was obsessed with a burning question: Could the motor car be converted from a plaything of the rich to a replacement for the horse of the common man? In 1893, when Ford built his first horseless carriage, the typical price tag was $9,000. Every piece of the automobile was hand-designed and the emphasis was on high prices for limited production runs.

Ford saw a different strategy. If the horseless carriage could be mass-produced, a firm could earn small profits on each car sold and reduce the price of a car to fit the budget of most American families. Ford found a solution in using vanadium steel for automobile bodies and adding a fast-moving assembly line. Specialists were hired, trained, and assigned specific duties on the line. Worker morale was boosted tremendously through the adoption of an eight-hour day. Ford shocked American industry by paying his employees $5 a day, more than doubling the prevailing wages in similar industries. And his strategy worked. By 1908 his Model T carried a price tag of $850. In 1926 the price had dropped to $284. By that time nearly 15 million Model Ts had been sold.

But Ford was destined to make numerous mistakes in the future. His refusal to add such technological improvements as hydraulic brakes and a six-cylinder engine to the Model T paved the way for General Motors and Chrysler to make major inroads on Ford's share of the automobile market. He ignored important marketing considerations, and his competitors capitalized on these deficiencies. His militant opposition to unionization left scars on Ford union-management relations for years. Yet Henry Ford was a production genius. And he left a mark on American industry that is still visible today.[1]

What Is Production?

Society allows businesses to operate only so long as the businesses make a contribution to its members. By producing and marketing desired goods and services, businesses satisfy this societal commitment. They create what economists call **utility,** which may be defined as *the want-satisfying power of a product or service.* There are four basic kinds of utility—form, time, place, and ownership.

Time, place, and ownership utility are created by marketing. They are created when products are available to the consumer at a convenient location when he wants to buy them and facilities are available where title to the products may be transferred to him at the time of purchase.

Form utility is *the creation of utility through the conversion of raw materials and other inputs into finished products or services.* Glass, steel, fabrics, rubber, and other components are combined to form a new Fiat or Pinto. Plastics and papers are molded to produce a Frisbee. Cotton, thread, and buttons are converted into Arrow shirts. The creation of form utility is the responsibility of the production function of the firm and is the subject of this chapter.

The Products for Sale under the Golden Arches at McDonald's

Two allbeefpattiesspecialsaucelettucecheesepicklesonionsonasesameseedbun. That phrase presented to Americans through a 50-million dollar advertising campaign immediately produces the image of Ronald McDonald and the golden arches of McDonald's. Today McDonald's ranks as the nation's largest dispenser of meals. A company survey revealed that carrot-topped Ronald McDonald could be identified by 96 percent of American schoolchildren, ranking him second only to Santa Claus. The McDonald's sign OVER ** BILLION SOLD increases by another billion every three or four months.

Led by its dynamic 70-plus year-old chairman Ray Kroc, McDonald's has passed the $1 billion mark in sales in its nearly 3,000 outlets—not counting the hundreds of restaurants being opened throughout the rest of the world from Western Europe to Japan and Australia. Kroc built his $500 million fortune by taking a familiar American institution—the greasy-spoon hamburger joint—and transforming it into a computerized, standardized, premeasured, superclean production machine efficient enough to give even the chiefs of General Motors food for thought.

McDonald's creates form, time, place, and ownership utility through a rigidly controlled menu. The original burger-shake-fries choices have been expanded over the years, but only after thorough testing. The double hamburger and double cheesburger were added in 1963, the fish sandwich in 1964, apple pie in 1967, the Big Mac in 1968, and Eggs McMuffin came on the scene in 1972.

Don't expect to buy a pack of cigarettes at McDonald's. As Chairman Kroc points out, "We made sure that no McDonald's became a hangout. We didn't allow cigarette machines, newspaper racks, not even a pay telephone. We still don't. We made the hamburger joint a dignified, clean place with a wholesome atmosphere."

McDonald's remains as one of the few places left where a customer can buy a meal for one dollar or less. The local operator usually expects to simply break even on the sale of a hamburger; his highest profits come from French fries, soft drinks, and the extra nickel a customer pays for a cheeseburger.

Source: "The Burger that Conquered the Country" (September 17, 1973). Reprinted by permission from *Time*, The Weekly Newsmagazine; Copyright Time Inc.

Production may be defined as *the use of people and machinery to convert materials into finished products or services.* This conversion of raw materials into finished products—or combination of such component parts as spark plugs, lights, tires, and metal tubing into a Kawasaki—creates form utility. Figure 9-1 illustrates the

Figure 9-1
The Production Process

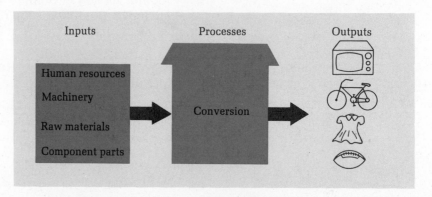

production process whereby manpower and machinery are used to convert raw materials and component parts into finished products.

The conversion process may involve major changes in raw materials or a simple combining of finished parts. Pillsbury's cake mixes are the result of transforming a number of ingredients—wheat into flour; addition of sugar, eggs, nuts, and other inputs. The butcher performs his production function by reducing a side of beef to ground beef, steaks, and chuck roasts. General Motors combines Firestone tires, AC spark plugs, a Delco battery, and 15,000 other components to complete a new Vega. But all of these processes result in the creation of form utility.

PRODUCTION AND POLLUTION

An undesirable output of many production processes is **pollution,** which may take many forms: *air pollution; pollution of lakes, rivers, and the oceans; and noise pollution.* Such activities as strip mining have produced extensive damage in West Virginia, Kentucky, Illinois, and other ore-producing states. Major oil spills in California and along the Gulf Coast have killed thousands of fish and birds and damaged beaches. Discharges from chemical producers have also meant death to fish in a number of state waters. Atmospheric dis-

"It's not my factory that's polluting the lake. . . . It's all those dead fish that're doing it."

SOURCE: *Playboy* Magazine, August 1974, p. 193. Reproduced by special permission of *Playboy* Magazine; copyright © 1974 by Playboy.

charges by lead smelters have endangered the health of nearby residents. These undesirable outputs have resulted in the enactment of numerous state and federal laws designed to protect the environment. Efforts by manufacturers to stop pollution have resulted in the investment of billions of dollars in equipment to halt pollution.

What Is Involved in Production Management?

Obviously the process of converting inputs into finished goods and services must be managed. This, then, is the task of **production management:** *to manage the use of manpower and machinery in converting materials into finished products.*

Inside a Big Mac

top bun

chopped onions

meat patty

pickle slices

secret sauce and shredded lettuce

middle bun

chopped onions

meat patty

cheese

secret sauce and shredded lettuce

bottom bun

Filling an Order at McDonald's

A good place to start describing the production process at McDonald's is with the product itself. The McDonald's burger is a machine-stamped 1.6 ounce patty, .221 inches thick and 3.875 inches wide when raw; next comes .25 ounces of onion, a pickle slice, and splats of ketchup and mustard. The entire ingredients rest on a 4.25-inch bun.

At every McDonald's outlet, winking lights on the grills tell the counterpersons exactly when to flip over the hamburgers. Once done, the burgers can be held under infra-red warming lights for up to ten minutes, no more: After that, any burgers that have not been ordered must be thrown away. Deep fryers continuously adjust to the moisture in every potato stick to make sure that French fries come out with a uniform degree of brownness; specially designed scoops make it almost physically impossible for an employee to stuff more or fewer French fries into a paper bag than headquarters specifies for a single order. The whole process is dedicated to speed—turning out a burger, fries, and a shake in 50 seconds.

Professor Theodore Levitt of the Harvard Business School described McDonald's as "a machine that produces, with the help of totally unskilled machine tenders, a highly polished product. Everything is built integrally into the machine itself, into the technology of the system. The only choice available to the attendant is to operate it exactly as the designers intended."

Source: "The Burger that Conquered the Country" (September 17, 1973). Reprinted by permission from *Time,* The Weekly Newsmagazine; Copyright Time Inc.

Production management is responsible for three major activities. *First, production managers must make plans for production inputs.* This involves determining the necessary inputs required in the firm's operations. It includes such decisions as product planning; plant location; and providing for adequate supplies of raw materials, labor, power, and machinery. These plans must be completed before the conversion process from raw material to finished product can begin.

The second responsibility of production management involves installation of the necessary production inputs. This includes the decisions for the actual design of the plant and the choice of the best types of machines to be used. It also includes arranging the production machinery and deciding upon the most efficient flow of work in the plant.

The third activity of production managers is to coordinate the production process. This concerns the actual production processes in the factory—routing of materials to the right place, developing work schedules, and assigning work to specific employees. The objective is to promote efficiency through coordination of the production processes to insure that they run smoothly.

Production Planning

Two Oklahomans invented the Stairchair—a special wheelchair designed to assist many of the 500,000 Americans currently confined to a wheelchair in solving a major problem: overcoming the barriers of curbs, stairs, and uneven land. The Stairchair is equipped with bulldozer-like treads and has the ability to climb even the steepest stairs.

But before the new wheelchair could be mass-produced and marketed, dozens of activities had to be completed. Three prototypes were assembled in the inventor's machine shop and given to wheelchair users for testing. Marketing research studies were begun to determine the reactions of potential consumers—both individuals and institutions, such as hospitals, nursing homes, and airports—to the new product. Decisions had to be made about the location of the production facility and the capacity required. A number of components were used in the Stairchair and suppliers had to be contacted. Employees had to be hired and trained. The assembly line had to be designed, and material flows within the plant decided upon. All of these plans had to be made prior to beginning full-scale production of the new product.

PRODUCT PLANNING A firm's total planning begins with the choice of products it wants to offer its customers. Plant location, machinery purchases, pricing decisions, and selection of retail outlets are all based on product planning. In a very real sense *the sole economic justification for the firm's existence is the production and marketing of want-satisfying products.*

In most firms product planning is the joint responsibility of both the production and marketing departments. Since the product must be designed in such a manner as to produce consumer satisfaction, marketing research studies are used to obtain consumer reactions to proposed products, to test prototypes of new products, and to estimate the potential sales and profitability of the new product. The production department is primarily concerned with converting the original product concept into the final product, and in designing production facilities to produce this new product as efficiently as possible. The new product must not only be accepted by consumers, it must also be produced economically to assure an acceptable return on company funds invested in the project. Product planning is an important and complex subject, and is discussed in detail in Chapter 10.

Plant Location

On a forty-mile stretch of the Mississippi River between Baton Rouge and New Orleans, some fifty chemical plants have been built. (See Figure 9-2.) Gates Rubber Company discovered that it could distribute its tires to every customer in the United States within three days by using two locations—Denver and Cincinnati.

One of the major production decisions is the choice of plant locations. The decision typically represents a long-term commitment and a substantial investment. A poor location poses severe problems in attempting to compete with better-located competitors. It should not be surprising that such companies as Texaco, McDonald's, and Scottish Inns list location as a primary consideration when building new outlets.

WHAT CONSTITUTES A GOOD PLANT LOCATION?

The choice of a plant location is typically divided into two stages:

1. selection of a community in which the plant will be located
2. choice of a specific site within the community.

The choice of a best location should be made following a consideration of such factors as proximity to raw materials, proximity to markets, availability of labor, transportation, power, local regulations, and community living conditions.

Proximity to raw materials

When raw materials are large and heavy, manufacturing firms often locate their plants near the source of these inputs. Production facilities for sheetrock are usually located in close proximity to where the major ingredient, gypsum, is mined. Mined gypsum must be dehydrated immediately to eliminate the need to transport the water in it. Trees are processed into wood products near forests, thereby eliminating the cost of transporting those parts of the log that become waste materials. Since 50,000 gallons of water are required to produce one ton of paper, the paper mills of International Paper Co., St. Regis, Georgia-Pacific, and Container Corporation of America must be located in areas where large quantities of clean, low-cost water are available.

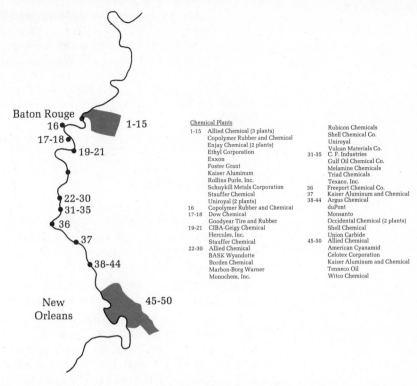

Figure 9-2
The Fifty Chemical Plants Located on the 40-Mile Stretch of the Mississippi River between Baton Rouge and New Orleans

Chemical Plants

1-15	Allied Chemical (3 plants)
	Copolymer Rubber and Chemical
	Enjay Chemical (2 plants)
	Ethyl Corporation
	Exxon
	Foster Grant
	Kaiser Aluminum
	Rollins Purle, Inc.
	Schuykill Metals Corporation
	Stauffer Chemical
	Uniroyal (2 plants)
16	Copolymer Rubber and Chemical
17-18	Dow Chemical
	Goodyear Tire and Rubber
19-21	CIBA-Geigy Chemical
	Hercules, Inc.
	Stauffer Chemical
22-30	Allied Chemical
	BASK Wyandotte
	Borden Chemical
	Marbon-Borg Warner
	Monochem, Inc.

	Rubicon Chemicals
	Shell Chemical Co.
	Uniroyal
	Vulcan Materials Co.
31-35	C. F. Industries
	Gulf Oil Chemical Co.
	Melamine Chemicals
	Triad Chemicals
	Texaco, Inc.
36	Freeport Chemical Co.
37	Kaiser Aluminum and Chemical
38-44	Argus Chemical
	duPont
	Monsanto
	Occidental Chemical (2 plants)
	Shell Chemical
	Union Carbide
45-50	Allied Chemical
	American Cyanamid
	Celotex Corporation
	Kaiser Aluminum and Chemical
	Tenneco Oil
	Witco Chemical

SOURCE: Reprinted from *American Business,* Third Edition, by Ferdinand M. Mauser and David J. Schwartz, © 1966, 1970, 1974, by Harcourt Brace Javanovich, Inc., adapted and reproduced with their permission.

Proximity to markets

If transportation costs for raw materials are not a significant part of total production costs, the plant is likely to be located near markets in which the final products are sold. A nearby location allows the manufacturer to provide fast, convenient service for its customers. Many automobile components manufacturers are located in the metropolitan Detroit area so as to provide quick service for auto-assembly plants.

Where Should the New McDonald's Be Built?

Since the average McDonald's outlet generates annual sales in excess of $500,000 per year and earns its operator around $70,000 before taxes, it should not be surprising that the home office receives thousands of requests for licenses each year. It accepts only about 10 percent of them.

The typical licensee must invest an average of $150,000 and complete courses at Hamburger U. in Oak Brook, Illinois, a suburb of Chicago. In order to earn his "Bachelor of Hamburgerology, with a minor in French fries," the licensee must take courses covering everything from how to scrape a grill to how to keep books.

For his license fee, the licensee gets expertise in store location. Headquarters executives will choose the sites, buy (or sometimes lease) the land, arrange for construction of the store, and rent it with equipment to the licensee for 8.5 percent of gross sales, plus a 3 percent annual franchise fee. The site should have a population of 30,000 to draw customers from. While outlets have traditionally been built in the suburbs, new outlets are being built in downtown locations and even on college campuses.

Source: "The Burger that Conquered the Country" (September 17, 1973). Reprinted by permission from *Time*, The Weekly Newsmagazine; Copyright Time Inc.

Availability of labor

A third consideration in the location of production facilities is the availability of a qualified labor force. One early problem facing Litton Industries' giant Ingalls shipbuilding complex in the little Gulf Coast town of Pascagoula, Mississippi, was the lack of sufficient numbers of skilled workers. Many electronics firms are located in the Boston area with its concentration of skilled technicians. The same is true for Akron (tires), Hartford (insurance), Pittsburgh (steel), and Seattle (aircraft).

When unskilled workers can be used, the manufacturer has a much greater number of alternative locations. Many manufacturing plants employing unskilled labor have located in the South, where wage rates have historically been below those of the North. In the worldwide search for inexpensive labor, a number of manufacturers of electrical equipment have recently begun to manufacture parts in the United States, ship them in unassembled form to the island of Taiwan, have them assembled there by low-cost workers, and then ship them back to the United States for inclusion in a finished product.

Transportation

Most manufacturing plants use transportation facilities to ship raw materials to the plant and to transport finished products to customers. At most locations the producer will have the choice of a number of transportation alternatives, such as trucks, railroads, waterways, and air freight. Availability of numerous alternatives may result in increased competition and lower rates for transportation users.

Power

The aluminum industry began in the Tennessee Valley because the manufacture of aluminum requires great amounts of electric power. Cheap electricity provided by the Tennessee Valley Authority allows aluminum manufacturers to produce their product at a price ranging from three to four cents lower than the cost of an identical plant in Baltimore or Philadelphia, where electrical rates are substantially higher. For such industries as chemicals, aluminum, and fertilizers, availability of inexpensive power supplies are a major consideration in plant location.

Local regulations

Another factor to consider in plant location is local and state taxes. Local and state governments typically impose real estate taxes on factories, equipment, and inventories. Sales taxes and income taxes may also be imposed. Such taxes vary considerably from state to state and city to city, and should be considered in the location decision. Some states and cities attempt to entice manufacturers into their areas by granting low taxes or temporary exemptions from taxation. However, low taxes may also mean inadequate municipal services. Taxes must therefore be considered together with the availability and quality of needed city services.

Until recently, most communities actively competed in attracting industry which would produce new jobs and population growth. In recent years a countertrend has developed, as many communities are rejecting the notion that all growth is beneficial. Most local officials are aware that more jobs also produce more demands on the public school system, more traffic congestion, increased likelihood of industrial pollution, and added pressures on police and fire departments. This awareness has resulted in numerous location constraints for the manufacturer.

Both community and state pressures in Maine and New Hampshire prevented the construction of oil refineries in New England. Construction of a Miami jetport partially located on the edge of the Everglades was blocked by environmentalists. In 1971 Delaware passed the Delaware Coastal Zone Act, preventing heavy manufacturing industry from locating within two miles of the state's 115-mile coastline. The entire state of Oregon has sought to halt the flow of new residents, and legislators have discussed the choice of the mosquito as Oregon's state bird. State and community attitudes will often play a role in a plant location decision.

Community living conditions

A final consideration in factory location would include such factors as the quality of the community, as measured by its school system, colleges, cultural programs, fire and police protection, climate, and community attitudes toward the new factory.

The final decision on plant location should be based upon a careful evaluation of all the factors discussed here. Management must weigh each of these factors in the light of its own individual needs. Table 9-1 summarizes these considerations.

Table 9-1
Factors to Be
Considered in the Plant
Location Decision

Location Factor	Examples of Companies That Are Most Affected
Transportation	
Proximity to markets	Colonial Baking Company (perishable products)
Proximity to raw materials	U.S. Gypsum
Availability of transportation alternatives	Brick manufacturers
Human Factors	
Labor supply	B.F. Goodrich
Local regulations	Hercules (manufacturer of explosives)
Community living conditions	Firms located in such cities as Denver, Princeton, Ann Arbor, Tulsa, and Phoenix
Physical Factors	
Water supply	International Paper Company
Power	Kaiser Aluminum

CHOOSING A SITE

Once a community has been selected, a specific site must be chosen. Before this site can be selected, a number of factors must be considered: zoning regulations; availability of sufficient land; cost of the land; existence of shipping facilities, such as railroad sidings, roads, and dock facilities; and construction costs.

Most cities have developed **industrial parks,** which are *planned site locations that provide necessary zoning, land, shipping facilities, and waste disposal outlets.* Industrial parks are created to entice manufacturers to locate new plants in the area by providing maximum cooperation between the firm and the local governing bodies of the community.

Figure 9-3 shows a proposed industrial park between Houston and Galveston, Texas, and illustrates the strengths of these planned parks. The land is correctly zoned for industrial production and contains a sufficient area for large facilities. Note also the availability of rail, water, and highway transportation.

Putting the Plan into Operation

Once the product decisions have been made, production facilities have been developed, the necessary machinery has been purchased, and the most efficient plant layout has been determined, management must implement the production plan. Raw materials and component parts that will serve as production ingredients must be purchased, inventory levels must be decided upon and controlled, and production schedules must be put into operation. Each of these activities must be performed efficiently if the production plan is to succeed.

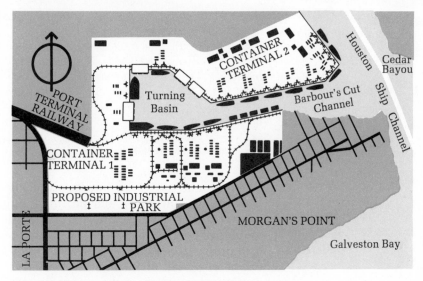

SOURCE: Reproduced through the courtesy of *Port of Houston Magazine*.

PURCHASING DECISIONS

The objectives of purchasing are summarized as *to buy the right materials in the right amounts at the right time for the right price.* To achieve this goal the purchasing department must:

1. precisely determine the correct materials to purchase
2. select the best supplier
3. develop an efficient ordering system.

Too many people define the term *quality* as *high quality*. But quality costs money. And the purchase of higher than necessary quality materials may affect the ability of the company's products to compete on a price basis with competitive products. A minimum quality level is obviously necessary to allow the product to perform its necessary functions. But the precise quality levels necessary on materials to be purchased should be specified in order to assist in the purchasing process.

Purchasing Raw Materials for the Telephone Is a Worldwide Job

Most people think of the telephone as an American institution, but it's a regular United Nations when it comes to the materials it takes to make a phone.

To give you an idea of where the purchasing agent at the phone company has to look for needed materials, let's examine the telephone. The chromium used to make your finger stop on the dial comes from Africa. Nickel used in springs is mined in Canada and Norway. Indonesian or Malayan rubber finds several uses, including the phone's feet.

Of course most of the materials are mined, grown, or made in the United States. Some of these include brass for the bells, carbon for the mouthpiece, plastics that house the insides, and steel that forms a variety of parts.

Some of the materials seem a little unlikely for a telephone. Cotton acts as an accoustical barrier in the handset. Wax fills capacitators and insulators. There's even a trace of gold and silver in the transmitter. And don't forget the paper your number's printed on. Other materials include aluminum, cobalt, copper, lacquer, lead, petroleum, rayon, silicon, tin, and zinc.

Source: Don Davis. "Your Telephone: A Mulligan Stew of Materials," *Telephone Talk* (St. Louis: Southwestern Bell, 1975).

MAJOR PURCHASES TAKE TIME AND INVOLVE MANY DECISION MAKERS

Where major purchases are involved, the period of negotiations between the purchaser and potential suppliers may take several weeks or even months, and the buying decision may rest with a number of persons in the firm. The choice of a supplier for industrial drill presses, for example, may be made jointly by the production, engineering, and maintenance departments, as well as by the purchasing agent. Each of these departments has a different point of view which must be reconciled in making a purchasing decision. The computer purchase decision shown in Figure 9-4 begins with the department head in the calculations section. This group head then informs the factory purchasing agent, who discusses company needs with salespeople representing three suppliers. The salespeople meet with the calculations department head, who makes a tentative decision to purchase from Supplier C. The decision is next considered, in turn, by the associate research director, the research director, the plant engineer, and the controller, as well as the corporate director of purchasing, before the order is placed. In all, the decision takes two years from conception to order placement.

Raw materials and component parts are often purchased for long periods on a contractual basis. A manufacturing operation requires a continual supply of materials, and a one- or two-year contract with a supplier insures a steady supply of raw materials or supplies as they are needed.

SELECTING THE RIGHT SUPPLIER

The choice of a supplier will usually be made by comparing quality, prices, availability, and services offered by competing companies. In many cases quality and price will be virtually identical between suppliers, and the choice of suppliers will be based on such factors as the firm's experience with each, speed of delivery of orders, warranties on purchases, and other services provided by the supplier.

RECIPROCITY— YOU BUY FROM ME AND I'LL BUY FROM YOU

A highly controversial practice in a number of industries is **reciprocity,** *the extension of purchasing preferences to those suppliers who are also customers.* Reciprocal agreements are particularly common in the chemical, steel, rubber, paint, and petroleum industries. Even though the purchasing department might desire the freedom of using

Figure 9-4
The Decision to
Purchase a Computer

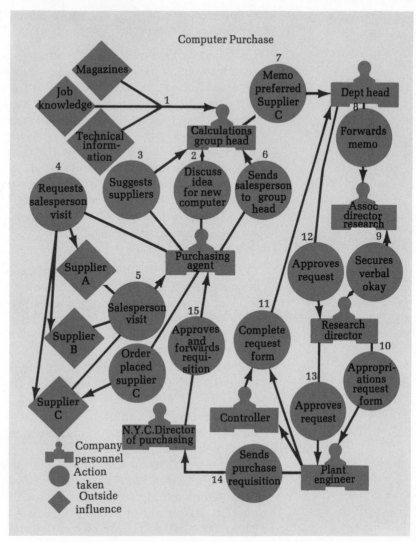

SOURCE: From "Who really makes the purchasing decision," by Murray Harding, *Industrial Marketing,* September, 1966, copyright 1966, by Advertising Publications Inc., Chicago, Illinois.

suppliers of its own choosing, guaranteed sales are strong incentives for reciprocity, particularly in cases where prices and the quality of competing offerings are similar. Both the Federal Trade Commission and the U.S. Department of Justice frown upon reciprocity resulting in the reduction of competition.

INVENTORY CONTROL

Inventory control *balances the need to have available supplies of inventory on hand to meet demand with the costs involved in carrying the inventory.* Development of an efficient ordering system results from a balancing of two needs:

1. the need to maintain sufficient supplies of raw materials and components on hand to meet production needs

2. the need to minimize inventory on hand to reduce the costs of *carrying* inventory.

The financial costs of carrying inventory are the funds tied up in the inventory which cannot be used in other activities of the business. Other expenses are involved in storing inventory—warehousing, taxes, insurance, and maintenance. If the inventory on hand is excessive, these expenditures represent waste.

But a lack of needed raw materials or parts will often mean lost production. And delays in production may mean unhappy customers if these production delays result in late delivery of promised merchandise. Firms lose business when they gain a reputation for an inability to meet promised delivery dates. These two costs should be balanced to produce acceptable inventory levels.

Control of the Production Process

Throughout this chapter production has been viewed as a *process of converting inputs into finished products.* First, plans are made for production inputs—the products to be produced; location of manufacturing plants; sources of raw materials, labor, power, and machinery. Next, the production plans are implemented through the purchase of materials and machinery and the employment of a trained work force to convert the inputs into salable products. The final step in the production process is *control.*

WHAT IS
PRODUCTION
CONTROL?

Production control can be seen as *a well-defined set of procedures for coordinating manpower, materials, and machinery for providing maximum production efficiency.*

Suppose that the Little Rock Timex factory has been assigned the production of 800,000 watches during the month of October. Production control executives then break this down to a daily production assignment of 40,000 for each of the twenty working days. The next steps would involve a determination of the number of workers, raw materials, parts, and machines that would be needed to meet this production schedule.

THE FIVE STEPS
IN PRODUCTION
CONTROL

Production control can be thought of as a five-step sequence. The order in which these five steps usually occur are *planning, routing, scheduling, dispatching,* and *follow up.*

Planning

Planning is that *phase of production control that determines the amount of resources needed to produce a certain amount of products.* This phase would include a determination of the amounts of raw materials and components required. If the needed amounts are not available in inventory, purchase requisitions for these materials would be sent to the purchasing department, in order that they could be on hand when needed. Similar determinations would be made to insure that the necessary machines and workers are available when needed.

The Metric System Is Creeping in on the U.S.

Steadily, without much fanfare, the U.S. is adopting the metric system—the standard of weights and measures used by most of the world. Leading the shift are businesses—especially those competing abroad—educators, and some federal agencies.

Also, a new push is getting under way in Congress to make metrics the official system for the nation within a decade. It's a legislative issue, debated now and again for almost 150 years, that may finally be resolved.

General Motors, the nation's largest manufacturer, is swinging to a policy of designing all new parts in metrics. The giant firm wants to harmonize production for all GM plants around the world. In the U.S., it will affect about 40,000 of GM's suppliers.

Pintos and Mustangs equipped with 2.3-liter engines are being powered by motors designed entirely in metrics. An estimated 30 to 40 percent of Ford's production is in foreign markets where metrics are the standard. A shift in the U.S. will make parts interchangeable.

Big international firms such as Caterpillar Tractor, John Deere, International Harvester and IBM have been using metrics for years in foreign trade. They are now working on plans to use more of the same specifications in the U.S.

Before long, shoppers may be buying clothing and textiles with sizes in centimeters, and meters, rather than in inches and yards. Sears Roebuck, J. C. Penney, and Levi Strauss, among others, are now studying the impact of such changes.

Some canned and packaged foods will soon be carrying metric equivalents to ounces and pounds on their labels. Seven-Up now comes in one-half liter and liter bottles as a substitute for pints and quarts. By 1979, all wine sold in the U.S. will be in metric bottles. . . .

At least 14 States are in the early stages of preparing classwork in metrics. Six have enacted laws calling for the metric system to be taught. In California, all elementary-school texts must include metrics. Maryland has a six-year program of instruction to shift to the new system. . . .

Kilometers, as well as miles, are cropping up on highway signs as several states try out the new system. Some television and radio stations are reporting temperatures in both Fahrenheit and Celsius (or Centigrade) degrees.*

The current American measuring system is a holdover from England—which has already switched to the metric system. The mile, for instance, is one thousand paces stepped off by a Roman soldier. A yard, according to legend, is the distance from King Edgar's nose to the end of his outstretched hand. An acre represents the amount of ground that a yoke of oxen can plow in a day.

The *metric system* is based upon the decimal system of tens and multiples of 10. These multiples include *deca* (10), *hecto* (100), *kilo* (1,000), and *myria* (10,000). Fractions are *deci* (1/10th), *centi* (1/100th), and *milli* (1/1,000th). A centimeter, therefore, is 1/100th of a meter.

Conversion costs will undoubtedly be high. Estimates run as high as $11 billion. But supporters of the switch argue that it will save teacher's time now being used to explain the much more complicated current system and will also eliminate the need to manufacture products in two versions—those for domestic consumption and those using metric measures for international consumers. Such a change should also increase export sales by smaller American firms who cannot afford to produce two sets of products for different markets.

Refusal to convert to the metric system would isolate U.S. manufacturing from the rest of the industrialized nations. The only nations that have not already begun to convert to metrics are Brunei, Burma, Liberia, the Yemen Arab Republic, and the Yemen People's Democratic Republic.

*Source: Reprinted from "The Metric System Is Creeping in on U.S.," U.S. News & World Report (March 3, 1975), p. 54. Copyright 1975 U.S. News & World Report, Inc.

Routing

Routing is that *phase of production control that determines the sequence of work throughout the plant.* It specifies where and by whom in the shop each aspect of production will be performed.

Scheduling

Scheduling is that *phase of production control that is involved in developing timetables that specify how much time each operation in the production process takes.* Efficient scheduling will insure that delivery schedules are met and that productive resources are efficiently used.

Scheduling is extremely important for a manufacturer of complex products with large numbers of parts or production stages. A Timex watch may contain dozens of component parts and each part must be available at the right place, at the right time, and in the right amounts if the production process is to function smoothly.

Production Scheduling Techniques To solve the problems of effective scheduling for complex products a number of methods have been devised. A commonly used *scheduling technique designed for such complex products as ships or new airplane designs* is PERT (**Program Evaluation and Review Technique**). PERT was first developed for military uses in producing guided missiles for the Polaris nuclear submarine, but was quickly modified for use by industry. Figure 9-5 shows a simplified PERT diagram.

PERT *is designed to minimize production delays by coordinating all aspects of the production task.* The heavy line in Figure 9-6 shows the **critical path**—*the sequence of operations in the* PERT *diagram that requires the longest time for completion.* The other operations that can be completed before they are needed by operations on the critical path have some slack time and are therefore not critical. Noncritical operations may be performed early, or they may be delayed until later in the production process. Some workers and machinery may be assigned to critical path tasks early, then

Figure 9-5
Simplified PERT
Diagram for a Nuclear
Submarine

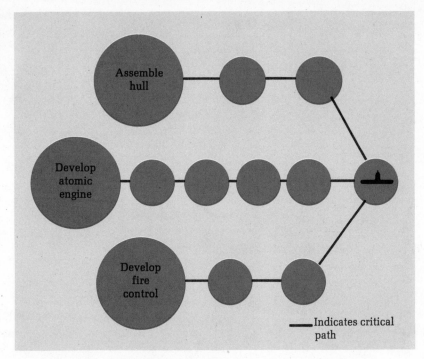

Assemble
hull

Develop
atomic
engine

Develop
fire
control

—— Indicates critical
path

reassigned to noncritical operations as these are needed.

In actual practice a PERT network may consist of thousands of events and cover months of time. Complex computer programs are used in developing the network and in finding the critical path among the maze of events and activities.

Dispatching

Dispatching is *that phase of production control that issues instructions to each department on what work is to be done and the time allowed for its completion.* The dispatcher authorizes the performance of certain jobs, provides instructions for their performance, and lists priorities for each job.

Follow up

Since even the best plans sometimes go awry, some means of **follow up** must be available to keep management aware of problems as they arise. Follow up is *that phase of production control that spots problems in the production process and informs management of needed adjustments.* These problems come in many forms: a machine malfunction, delays in shipment of vital materials, or employee absenteeism may result in production delays. These delays must be reported to production control so that adjustments in production schedules can be made. A delay in the delivery of a particular component may require new assignments by the dispatcher to work areas affected by this delay.

Can Assembly-line Work Really Be Made More Meaningful or Enriching?

When Henry Ford introduced the first assembly line in 1913, it was considered the ultimate in rapid and inexpensive manufacturing techniques. With workers positioned at one station, parts and partially completed products were brought to them to be worked on. Each operation was simplified as much as possible to increase worker efficiency and speed.

Later, the assembly-line technique was improved by mechanical devices added to the human operations. This was called *automation*. By positioning the parts for the human operator or the equipment used and by removing scrap, speed and efficiency were increased even further.

Lately cybernetics has been introduced to the assembly line. This means that computers do some of the controlling and mechanical work formerly done entirely by human hands.

Speed and efficiency have been the aim of those who design assembly-line programs: more product in fewer hours with less expense. But efficiency has broken down, and something has gone wrong. The human beings who work on the assembly line are often bored and alienated. They are subject to alcoholism, drug use, and absenteeism. And, in some cases, assembly-line workers have engaged in active sabotage of the system.

Human resource engineers and psychologists have been investigating the problem, hoping to stem these symptoms by making assembly-line work more meaningful. Some of the tiresome tasks have been taken over by machines. But the machines—their unfailing accuracy, the pace at which they work, and the workers' dependence on them—are part of the problem.

Many managers are also concerned with the psychological support of an individual worker. They want an assembly-line worker to feel that he or she can participate in the design and structure of individual jobs. By helping to make such decisions as the scheduling of product either as an individual or in a team situation, they argue that workers will feel a greater responsibility on the job and be motivated to do well. Getting feedback (comments on the work they are doing or helpful suggestions on how to do the job better or make it easier) is also suggested for promoting positive attitudes on the part of workers. Job rotation, where team members do each other's jobs for part of the time, gives variety to an otherwise repetitive series of tasks.

Some authorities maintain that assembly-line work simply lacks challenge. No matter what is done to change this, the job itself, worked on year after year, is boring. The answer lies in a shorter work day and week, more frequent breaks, longer and more vacations, and larger rewards, such as pay raises, greater benefits, and earlier retirement. For these people, a good life outside the plant is earned by well-paid time on the job.

QUALITY CONTROL   **Quality control** involves the *measuring of products against estab-lished quality standards.* Such checks are necessary to spot defec-tive products that are occasionally produced and to see that they are not shipped to the firm's customers. Measuring devices for monitor-ing quality levels of the firm's output involve visual inspection, electronic sensors, and X-rays. This particular aspect of production control may occasionally result in changing production practices. A high rate of rejected products can lead to required changes in equipment, raw materials used in the products, or additional train-ing for workers who are employed in the production process.

Quality Control at McDonald's

At McDonald's, quality control is summed up in the initials QSC (for Quality, Service, Cleanliness), a set of letters that every McDonald's em-ployee learns quickly.

Cleanliness is required from the licensees. Periodic unannounced inspections are designed to produce spotless outlets. These roving inspec-tors (called *field supervisors*) make sure that the restaurant floor is mopped at proper intervals and the parking lot is tidied up hourly.

Quality control begins with raw material purchases that meet rigid headquarters specifications. The hamburger patty must be "pure" beef—that is, no lungs, hearts, cereal, soybeans, or other filler—with no more than 19 percent fat content. This compares favorably with the more than 30 percent fat in some competing hamburgers. The bun must have a higher-than-normal sugar content for faster browning.

Once the product has been prepared to national specifications, qual-ity is further assured by the discarding of hamburgers that remain unsold after ten minutes. Coffee can be no more than 30 minutes old.

Source: "The Burger that Conquered the Country" (September 17, 1973). Reprinted by permis-sion from *Time*, The Weekly Newsmagazine; Copyright Time Inc.

Summary

Production creates form utility by converting raw materials and component parts into finished products. Production management is responsible for three major activities: *developing plans for pro-duction inputs, installing necessary production inputs and im-plementing production plans,* and *coordinating and controlling the production process.*

Production planning begins with a decision on what products will be produced. This is a major company decision, since the firm fulfills its commitments to society by producing and marketing want-satisfying products. A second major decision involves select-ing a plant location. A number of factors must be considered in selecting the best location, including proximity to raw materials, proximity to markets, availability of labor, transportation, power, local regulations, and community living conditions.

Once product and plant location and layout decisions have been made, management must implement the production plan. This involves purchase of raw materials and components, inventory control, and the implementation of production schedules. Those responsible for purchasing attempt to buy the right materials in the right amounts at the right time for the right price. Once quality levels for materials have been determined, suppliers are contacted and orders are placed. The task of inventory control is to balance two factors: the need to maintain adequate supplies to meet production requirements and the need to minimize funds invested in inventory.

Production control attempts to provide maximum productive efficiency through the coordination of manpower, materials, and machinery. The production control process consists of five steps: planning, routing, scheduling, dispatching, and follow up—including quality control. Coordination of each of these phases should result in improved production efficiency and lower production costs.

Review questions

1. Identify the following terms:
   a. utility
   b. form utility
   c. production
   d. industrial park
   e. reciprocity
   f. inventory control
   g. production control
   h. PERT
   i. critical path
   j. quality control
2. What utility is produced by the production function?
3. Outline the production process.
4. What is involved in production planning?
5. Discuss the factors that influence plant location decisions.
6. Describe the decision-making process involved in purchasing.
7. What costs must be considered in setting up an inventory control system?
8. List the basic steps in production control.
9. How has the metric system influenced production management in the United States?
10. Draw a PERT diagram for the completion of the course for which this book is being used.

Discussion questions and exercises

1. Evaluate the pro and con arguments to the controversial issue that appear.
2. Visit a local factory and observe the production operation in the plant. Then prepare a brief report on what you have learned.
3. Chapter 9 describes the production of a Big Mac, but other fast-food franchises also have effective production methods. Go to another franchise and observe their manufacturing operation.

Then prepare a report on what you have observed. You might consider looking at "nonhamburger" operations like Taco-Bell, Kentucky Fried Chicken, Bonanza, Ponderosa, Shakey's Pizza, Fish and Chips, and the like.

4. Interview an executive at a local plant. Find out why this firm decided to locate in your particular area, and then report your findings to the class.

5. Assume that you were responsible for locating a new McDonald's outlet in your area. Where would you locate the store, and why?

Case 9-1
The Broom Industry

The U.S. broom industry got its start when Benjamin Franklin introduced a plant into the country called broom corn, which is similar in appearance to ordinary corn. The industry flourished in New England and upstate New York in the early 1800's. Later, broom manufacturing shifted westward to near Arcola and Mattoon, Illinois, while the farming and hand harvesting of broom corn spread throughout the nation.

Upon arrival at the plant, broom corn must be sorted according to length and quality. Bundles are then given to "winders," who construct the brooms. A machine holds the broom handle and turns it, while at the same time securing the straw with a length of steel wire. But an employee must guide the wire with a special blade and furnish the wire turns by hand. Broom-making is demanding work; it requires skill, close attention, and is sometimes painful. Broom-makers receive a piece wage, and experts can make from twelve to fifteen dozen high-quality brooms or up to thirty dozen inexpensive brooms, a day. Daily earnings can be as much as $50.

After it is wound, a broom goes to the "stitcher," who machine sews the upper part of the broom to hold the corn fibers rigid. Finally, the broom is trimmed to make the bottom even and ready for use. One source reports that since 1876 the only technological innovation in the industry has been the replacement of foot treadles with electrically powered machines.

Current average annual production is about 2.6 million brooms. But labor and material costs are rising; vacuum cleaners have cut into the market; and broom-corn brooms are facing competition from brooms made of synthetic fibers. High-grade brooms, selling at $3 to $4, face severe competition from inexpensive ones priced at about $1. And as older broom-makers die, and small shops close, some manufacturers believe that the industry is gradually losing its expertise. Attempts at automation, such as a mechanical broom-corn harvester, have failed.

Questions

1. What is your opinion about the broom-corn broom industry's long-term future?
2. Can you identify other industries with problems similar to the broom industry?
3. What suggestions would you offer a broom manufacturer?

Source: Everett Groseclose. "This Handmade Item Costs Just $1 to $4. But Who Needs It?" *The Wall Street Journal* (April 23, 1974), pp. 1, 16. Reprinted with permission of *The Wall Street Journal*, © Dow Jones & Company, Inc. 1974. All rights reserved.

Case 9-2
Vlasic Foods, Inc.

Vlasic Foods, Inc., based in a Detroit suburb, sells $60 million worth of pickles, peppers, relishes, and sauerkrauts each year. The firm began as a pickle distributor to the local Polish community during the 1930's. It expanded into other products when it bought a sauerkraut plant in 1959. Vlasic now has plants in Delaware, New York, Pennsylvania, Mississippi, and Michigan.

Vlasic produces two types of pickles. The first type, the *processed dill,* is really a cucumber cured in barrels of salt and spices. After curing, the dill is then either sweetened or soured on the basis of its use and size. The second variety is a *fresh-packed pickle.* This product is a cucumber that is pickled in its own bottle.

Questions

1. What type of production problems might be encountered at Vlasic Foods?
2. Draw a PERT diagram for a processed dill.

Source: Christopher Willcox. "Top Pickle," *Detroit News* (February 16, 1975), p. G-1.

Careers in Human Resource Management and Production Management

Human resource management involves people management. Admittedly, all managers must deal with people regardless of the functional areas with which they are associated. But executives directly involved in human resource management have primary responsibility for the administration of people-related activities, such as employment, wages and salaries, health and safety, and the like.

The Bureau of Labor Statistics has projected annual job openings to 1985. Their forecasts for some selected jobs in human resource management and production management appear below:

Job Projections to 1985

Career	Latest Employment (1972 Estimate)	Annual Average of Job Openings to 1985
College-placement officers	3,800	200
Employment counselors	8,500	800
Industrial engineers	125,000	7,400
Inspectors	725,000	44,700
Personnel workers	240,000	20,800
Psychologists	57,000	4,300

SOURCE: *Occupational Manpower and Training Needs* (Washington, D.C.: Bureau of Labor Statistics, 1974).

Here are some of the careers in human resource and production management that are available to you:

Personnel Manager

A personnel manager has overall responsibility for the personnel function. This includes recruiting, hiring, training, wage and salary administration, health and safety, and so forth. The personnel manager is usually the chief executive involved in human resource management. Sometimes this person is called "Vice-President of Personnel."

Director of Industrial Relations

This person is usually management's representative in dealings with labor unions. The Director of Industrial Relations is often the spokesperson for management during collective bargaining. In some firms the Director of Industrial Relations also performs the duties described above for the Personnel Manager.

Union Executive

Many labor unions are starting to employ people with a management education as union executives. While most union leaders still come from the rank and file, more professional managers are entering this field. A labor union career provides many interesting challenges in human resource management.

Wage and Salary Administrator

Wage and salary administrators are in charge of the compensation plans used in the organization. They are responsible for setting up compensation plans designed to meet organizational goals. These people then administer the plans and study their effectiveness, so timely revisions can be made when they are required.

Industrial Counselor (or Psychologist)

Many large firms have added counselors to their personnel departments. These people counsel and advise employees and management on work, career, and personal problems. Industrial counselors are also involved in areas such as selection procedures for new employees. Many times such people are qualified industrial psychologists. Others hold degrees in guidance and counseling. To be effective, industrial counselors must have a firm business background so they can appreciate the problems they may encounter.

Production Manager

A production manager is responsible for the actual manufacturing of a product. This job would include engineering, production control, quality control, and other administrative duties. The person is sometimes called the "Plant Manager."

IV Marketing Management

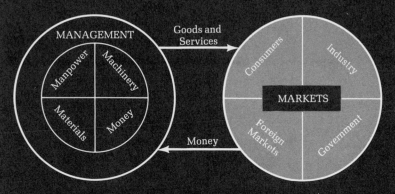

MANAGEMENT — Goods and Services → MARKETS ← Money

Manpower | Machinery
Materials | Money

Consumers | Industry
Foreign Markets | Government

SOURCE: The White Stag Beetleboard.

10

Marketing: Matching Consumer Needs with Product Offerings

"Marketing is the delivery of a standard of living."

—Paul Mazur

What Chapter 10 Is All About

1. In this chapter you will learn the types of utility created by marketing.
2. You will be able to distinguish between consumer and industrial markets, and to identify the major characteristics of these markets.
3. You will understand how market targets are selected through marketing research.
4. You will be able to identify the four strategies that compose the marketing mix.
5. You will learn how products may be classified, and how they fit into the life-cycle concept.
6. The identification of products will also be explained in this chapter.
7. After reading this chapter, you should understand these terms:

marketing	marketing research
time utility	marketing mix
place utility	convenience goods
ownership utility	shopping goods
marketing concept	specialty goods
consumer goods	capital items
industrial goods	expense items
market segmentation	product life cycle
zero population growth	brand names
market target	private brands

Mary Wells Lawrence

SOURCE: Booke & Company, Inc.

As one of the founders and chief executive officers of Wells, Rich, Greene, Inc., a top advertising agency, Mary Wells Lawrence has proven herself to be the star performer that many of her colleagues in retailing and advertising always suspected her to be. A graduate of the Carnegie Institute of Technology, Mary Wells came to New York City to work for Macy's department store in 1950.

After becoming the store's manager of fashion advertising, Wells decided that advertising was what she wanted to do. Before she was thirty years old she had gone to work for the innovative advertising agency, Doyle Dane Bernbach. As Doyle Dane's copy chief and a vice-president, Wells was earning a top salary when she decided she really wanted to be in charge. She switched to Interpublic's branch, Jack Tinker & Partners, in 1964, and created a series of highly successful and attention-getting campaigns. But it was Braniff International that really clicked for Wells. Talking Braniff President Harding L. Lawrence into redesigning the Braniff planes inside and out, Wells developed the slogan "The End of the Plain Plane," painted the great metal monsters in bright colors, and clothed the flight attendants in Pucci uniforms. Braniff shed its old conservative image and gained the attention of the flying public.

Wells took the Braniff account with her when she established her own agency with Richard Rich and Stewart Greene. The agency ranked in the top fifty agencies in the United States within six months of its founding. Wells herself is one of the hundred highest paid people in U.S. industry. She married Lawrence in 1967.

In addition to creativity and drive, Wells credits most of her success to her good track record. The fact that she is a top executive who is also a woman seems incidental to her proven ability.

$\mathbf{M}$arketing and production are the two basic functions of any business firm. All organizations must produce and market a product or service for use by its consumers. **Marketing** can be defined as *"the performance of business activities that direct the flow of goods and services from producer to consumer or user."*[1] Marketing activities are one of the most vital elements of contemporary business.[2]

Creating Utility for the Consumer

A business must create **utility,** the *want-satisfying power of a product or service,* for its consumers. There are four kinds of utility—form, time, place, and ownership.

Form utility, as described in Chapter 9, is *created when the business firm converts raw materials into finished products.* The creation of form utility is the job of the firm's production function. The other three kinds of utility—time, place, and ownership—are created by marketing.

Time utility refers to *having the product available when the consumer wants to buy.* This requires effective marketing research to determine what items the consumer will desire at some future date.

Place utility is created by *having the product available to the consumer at a convenient location when the person wants to buy.*

Marketers also create **ownership utility** by arranging for the *transfer of title from seller to buyer.*

The highly successful introduction of the American Motors Buyer Protection Plan shows how a firm's production and marketing efforts produced utility for AMC buyers.

American Motors Buyer Protection Plan

In early 1971 American Motors Corporation was faced with a declining penetration of the automobile market. The firm's management established a task force to develop a plan for switching General Motors, Ford, and Chrysler buyers to American Motors products. The task force was given only nine months to formulate and launch their competitive strategy.

Marketing research found that consumers held a basic mistrust of U.S. automobile manufacturers. The public wanted a reliable, trouble-free, quality car. And they sought evidence that the car would meet these standards.

The task force decided on an unconditional guarantee backed by better predelivery service, loaner cars to drive when customers had to leave their cars at a dealership overnight, and a direct line to the factory to assist in customer-factory communications. The American Motors Buyer Protection Plan was born.

Consumer research showed that prior to being exposed to the buyer protection concept, only 27 percent of those interviewed indicated they might consider an AMC product. After exposure, the figure was 75 percent. Before exposure to the program, 4 percent said they would definitely consider AMC. After exposure, this figure reached 20 percent.

The planners realized that the Buyer Protection Plan had to be more than a promotional gimmick. AMC's production effort had to be equal to the task. Additional quality controls and tests had to be performed at the factory. Dealers had to be compensated to recheck the automobiles. AMC management also saw that they could improve quality on the assembly line, beyond investing in manufacturing recommended improvements. Factory personnel were persuaded that the Buyer Protection Plan—if it worked—would mean higher sales for American Motors and greater security for them.

The first few months after the introduction of the Buyer Protection Plan were uneventful for AMC. But things were happening. Customers who had a warranty problem came back to the dealership for repairs. They found that the repairs were made quickly, without any hassle, and the dealer did not want to be paid. Even loaner cars were available. AMC dealers reported many startled customers, and word-of-mouth promotion took over.

American Motors' sales figures increased remarkably over the next few years. Most of this sales increase was attributed to the Buyer Protection Plan. Research showed that one out of four persons who visited an AMC dealer did so because of the Buyer Protection Plan. Eighty-two percent of the AMC shoppers knew about the plan before visiting the showroom, and 47 percent said it was important in prompting their visit. Four out of five buyers said the Buyer Protection Plan was an important reason for selecting an AMC product.

Source: Adapted from Cyril Freeman. "Buyer Protection Plan: Biggest Automobile Innovation in Years." *Advertising Age* (July 8, 1974), pp. 39–40.

The Marketing Concept

During the early decades of this century production management dominated corporate thinking. Manufacturers stressed production of quality products and then looked for people to purchase their output. Here is how Robert J. Keith, late board chairman, described The Pillsbury Company of this era:

We are professional flour millers. Blessed with a supply of the finest North American wheat, plenty of water power, and excellent milling machinery, we produce flour of the highest quality. Our basic function is to mill high-quality flour, and of course (and almost incidentally), we must hire salesmen to sell it, just as we hire accountants to keep our books.[3]

Today, the ability to produce a quality product is simply not enough to achieve success. The product must be effectively marketed.

Most modern firms follow what has been called the **marketing concept.** Introduced in Chapter 1, the marketing concept says that *a firm should adopt a company-wide consumer orientation with the goal of achieving long-run profits.* This policy does not mean that marketing personnel will dominate the firm, but it does say that all areas of the business should try to satisfy consumer wants and needs. Most observers believe that the adoption of the marketing concept has resulted in a greater consumer orientation by business in the United States.

What Is a Market?

A market consists of people, whether they are consumers, company purchasing agents, or purchasing specialists for a government—local, state, or federal.

But people alone do not make a market. Many people may desire the new $75,000 colonial house on Valley Drive, but not everyone can afford it. A market requires not only people but also *pur-*

"You the party called about her refrigerator?"

Prompt, Efficient Service Is Part of the Marketing Concept

SOURCE: *The Wall Street Journal*, July 6, 1973. Reprinted with permission from *The Wall Street Journal*.

chasing power and the *authority to buy.* One of the first rules that the successful salesperson learns is to determine what person in the organization has the authority to make a purchase decision. Too many hours have been wasted convincing the director of purchasing about the merits of a firm's products when the ultimate buying decision actually rests with the design engineer.

CONSUMER AND INDUSTRIAL MARKETS OFTEN DIFFER

Products may be classified as consumer or industrial goods. **Consumer goods** are *those products and services purchased by the ultimate consumer for his or her own use.* **Industrial goods** are *purchased to be used, either directly or indirectly, in the production of other goods for resale.* Most of the products you buy—pizza, toothpaste, clothes—are consumer goods. Raw cotton is an industrial good for Burlington Industries; rubber is a raw material for General Tire.

A classification problem seems to exist in certain cases where the same product has different uses. The purchase of a new set of tires by your neighbor clearly is a consumer good; yet when bought by General Motors the tires become part of a new Vega destined for sale and are classified as industrial goods. The key to the proper classification lies in the purchaser and the reasons for buying the good. A typewriter that serves as a Christmas gift for a college student is a consumer good; the same typewriter is an industrial good when used in the order-processing department of RCA.

MARKET SEGMENTATION
The world is too large and filled with too many diverse people for the marketing manager to construct a marketing plan designed to satisfy *all* of them. Even a mass-market product such as toothpaste is aimed at a specific segment of the population. Stripe was developed for children; Crest focuses on tooth decay prevention; and Ultra Brite hints at greater sex appeal.

The travel trailer manufacturer who decides to produce and market one vehicle to satisfy everyone quickly encounters decisions concerning color, styling, and inclusion of various options. In attempting to satisfy everyone, the firm is forced to make compromises and discovers that it does not satisfy *anyone* very well. Other firms which appeal to the economy-oriented consumer or the long-distance traveler or other segments capture this firm's market by satisfying the needs of smaller market targets which have greater similarities among its members. This process of *taking the total market and dividing it into groups with similar characteristics* is called **market segmentation.**

Market Characteristics

Marketers must know about the characteristics of the markets they serve. These include existing population and income patterns, market location factors, and consumption patterns.

POPULATION AND INCOME
Even though the United States has attained the highest standard of living in the history of the world, its population is small compared with the rest of the world. Of the world's four billion residents, less than 6 percent live in the United States. But the United States possesses 38 percent of the world's income. India has more than double the U.S. population, but its inhabitants must live on a per person income of less than $100 a year.

The U.S. population has experienced substantial growth since the 1600's; the current population stands at over 210 million people. However, proponents of **zero population growth** (*that point where live births equal the current death rate*) were pleased to discover that the birth rate had fallen to its lowest point in the twentieth century in the year 1971. The trend toward smaller families has forced marketers to change some of their strategies. Some baby powder advertisements, for example, now stress the product's use by adults.

MARKET LOCATION
The population of the United States, like that of the rest of the world, is not distributed evenly but is concentrated in large metropolitan states such as New York, Pennsylvania, California, Ohio,

Michigan, and Illinois. The population is continuously shifting. Some states grow, while others lose population.

A migration from the farm to the city has been in progress since 1800. The ten largest metropolitan areas (New York is the largest of these) represent about one-fourth of the total population of the United States. Each of these metropolitan areas contains more residents than the combined populations of Alaska, Wyoming, Idaho, and Montana.

GROWTH OF THE YOUTH AND SENIOR CITIZEN MARKET SEGMENTS

The population of the United States is expected to grow by 13 percent during the 1970's, but this growth will be concentrated in two age groups—young adults between the ages of twenty and thirty-four and persons aged sixty-five and older. Both of these markets are important in contemporary business.

The young adult segment includes young marrieds with demands for housing; products like automobiles, washing machines, and televisions; recreation; as well as baby clothes, food, and associated purchases. This group will account for nearly half of the growth in the population to 1981.

Not so many years ago the senior citizen market was of little importance, since few people reached retirement age. At the present time, however, some 10 percent of the total population is sixty-five or older in the United States. It is not only comforting for this year's male retiree to learn that at age sixty-five his life expectancy is another fourteen years but it also represents a profitable market for American business.

CONSUMPTION PATTERNS VARY BY AGE GROUPS

Figure 10-1 shows 1981 population projections by age groups. Each age group has different consumption patterns, and marketers must design their strategies accordingly.

Levi Strauss has been extremely successful in aiming at the young adult market; toy manufacturers appeal primarily to youngsters (an attempt is made to reach them via commercials on Saturday morning television cartoon shows). Table 10-1 shows some of the types of merchandise most often purchased by or for various age groups.

INCOME AND EXPENDITURE PATTERNS

Earlier in this book, purchasing power was shown to be a key part of a market. A very common method of segmenting consumer markets is on the basis of income. Some large retailers offer their shoppers three qualities of merchandise—good, better, and best—at three different prices.

Income distribution in most countries is shaped like a pyramid, with a small percentage of households having high incomes and the majority of families earning a very small income. In 1935, 78 percent of all families in the United States had incomes of less than $2,000, and more than nine out of every ten families earned less than $3,000.

MARKETING: MATCHING CONSUMER NEEDS WITH PRODUCT OFFERINGS

Figure 10-1
The Age Mix
of Americans
Is Changing

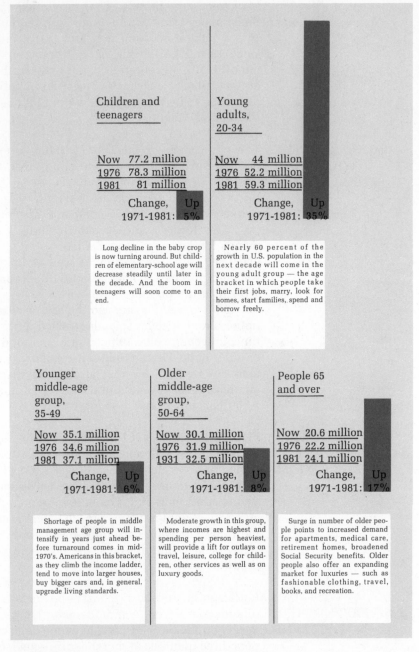

Children and
teenagers

Now   77.2 million
1976 78.3 million
1981   81 million
Change,   Up
1971-1981: 5%

Long decline in the baby crop is now turning around. But children of elementary-school age will decrease steadily until later in the decade. And the boom in teenagers will soon come to an end.

Young
adults,
20-34

Now   44 million
1976 52.2 million
1981 59.3 million
Change,   Up
1971-1981: 35%

Nearly 60 percent of the growth in U.S. population in the next decade will come in the young adult group — the age bracket in which people take their first jobs, marry, look for homes, start families, spend and borrow freely.

Younger
middle-age
group,
35-49

Now 35.1 million
1976 34.6 million
1981 37.1 million
Change,   Up
1971-1981: 6%

Shortage of people in middle management age group will intensify in years just ahead before turnaround comes in mid-1970's. Americans in this bracket, as they climb the income ladder, tend to move into larger houses, buy bigger cars and, in general, upgrade living standards.

Older
middle-age
group,
50-64

Now 30.1 million
1976 31.9 million
1931 32.5 million
Change,   Up
1971-1981: 8%

Moderate growth in this group, where incomes are highest and spending per person heaviest, will provide a lift for outlays on travel, leisure, college for children, other services as well as on luxury goods.

People 65
and over

Now 20.6 million
1976 22.2 million
1981 24.1 million
Change,   Up
1971-1981: 17%

Surge in number of older people points to increased demand for apartments, medical care, retirement homes, broadened Social Security benefits. Older people also offer an expanding market for luxuries — such as fashionable clothing, travel, books, and recreation.

SOURCE: Reprinted from *U.S. News & World Report* (January 17, 1972), pp. 16 & 17. Copyright 1972 U.S. News & World Report, Inc.

But in recent years the income pyramid has overturned! By 1970 nearly 50 percent of the households in the United States earned $10,000 or more. The number of families in the $10,000 to $15,000

Table 10-1
Merchandise Purchased
by Consumer
Age Groups

Years of Age	Name of Age Group	Merchandise Purchased
0–5	Young children	Baby food, toys, nursery furniture, children's wear.
6–19	School children (including teenagers)	Clothing, sports equipment, phonograph records, school supplies, food, cosmetics, used cars.
20–34	Young adults	Automobiles, furniture, houses, clothing, recreational equipment. Purchasers for younger age segments.
35–50	Younger middle age	Larger homes, bigger autos, second cars, new furniture, recreational equipment.
50–64	Empty nest (no children at home)	Recreational items, purchases for young marrieds and infants.
65 and over	Retired	Medical services, travel, drugs, purchases for younger age groups.

income range nearly tripled—to 28.5 percent in the ten years between 1960 and 1970—and the lower-income segments shrunk rapidly. Higher incomes for the typical household mean more spending power.[4] Marketers must keep track of income and expenditure patterns if they are to achieve their objectives.

Selecting Market Targets through Marketing Research

The key to effective marketing lies in locating unsatisfied customers. These customers may not be purchasing goods because they are not currently available; or they may be buying products that give them only limited satisfaction. In this case they are likely to switch quickly to new products with more complete satisfactions. These unsatisfied segments should be the targets for consumer-oriented companies. Rosoff's Restaurant in New York City, for example, provides braille menus for blind patrons.[5]

A **market target** is *the group of consumers toward which the firm decides to direct its marketing effort.* Sometimes a firm has several market targets for a given product.

The selection of market targets requires considerable research in order to identify those groups that are most likely to buy an item. **Marketing research** can be defined as *"the systematic gathering, recording, and analyzing of data about problems relating to the marketing of goods and services."*[6] Marketing researchers use a variety of approaches to identify market targets. These approaches include the analysis of published data, surveys, consumer panels, direct observation of buying behavior, personal interviews, and the like. These approaches will be discussed further in Chapter 20.

Marketers need to know about consumer motivation before making business plans. Let's look at what happened in a situation where Ford didn't have a "better idea."

The Edsel

In 1954 Ford Motor Company matched General Motors in market share of the low-priced auto segment. The Ford car had about 25 percent of the market, Chevrolet had another 25 percent, the Buick-Oldsmobile-Pontiac (or "B-O-P") cars a third 25 percent share, and the remaining 25 percent was divided among all other car makes. It appeared certain that any substantial Ford gains would have to come from the B-O-Ps.

Ford, headed by Lewis Crusoe, put together the following marketing plan:

1. The 1957 and 1958 Ford cars (longer, wider, and more highly styled than any car ever introduced in the low-price field, and with two separate body shells) were to attack the Chevrolet at the low end of the GM line.
2. The Mark II Continental (priced at $10,000) and the 1958 Lincoln (a huge, dramatically styled automobile) were to take on the Cadillac at the high end of the GM line.
3. Three entries were planned against the B-O-P cars. First, a four-passenger version of the highly successful Thunderbird would be introduced in 1958. Second, the Mercury line would be completely restyled with a special model called the Turnpike Cruiser. Third was the Edsel.

The results are known to almost everyone. The Edsel, the Mark II Continental, the 1958 Lincoln, the 1958 Mercury, and the 1958 Ford were all product failures. Only the 1958 four-passenger Thunderbird was a marketing success.

What went wrong? Different authorities offer different reasons. Some feel the Edsel was poorly named (but others list Buick as perhaps the ugliest word in the language and Oldsmobile as a silly name). Others point to the "bugs" in the first Edsels and the subsequent image deterioration. Most seem to agree that the problems lie in the changes in the automobile market. The American love affair with the automobile was undergoing its first rumblings of disenchantment in the late 1950's. The recession of 1958 reduced auto sales substantially and tail fins, chrome, and other trappings of the 1957–1959 cars were increasingly rejected by purchasers who, in 1959, purchased enough American Motors Ramblers to rank that car Number 3 behind Ford and Chevrolet in the United States.

Source: Adapted from William H. Reynolds. "The Edsel Ten Years Later," *Business Horizons* (Fall 1967), pp. 39–46.

The failure of Edsel did not result from an inadequate market. It did not fail because of a lack of consumer income, education, or any of the other variables often used in segmenting markets. It failed because of a misunderstanding of the motivations of consumers. Unfortunately, knowing consumer motivations is perhaps the most difficult task in marketing. Marketing research studies can provide data used in analyzing the buying habits of consumers:

1. *Who* buys?
2. *When* does one buy?
3. *Where* does one buy?
4. *What* does one buy?
5. *How* does one buy?

But answers to the question: "*Why* does one buy (or not buy)?" are much more difficult to uncover.

The Marketing Mix

Once marketing research has identified the firm's market targets a suitable plan has to be made to reach these selected market segments. Marketing decision making can be classified into four strategies:

1. Product strategy
2. Distribution strategy
3. Promotional strategy
4. Pricing strategy

The combination of these four strategy elements forms the **marketing mix,** *the blending of product, channels, promotion, and price to satisfy chosen consumer segments.* It is the total package (or mix) that determines the degree of marketing success. (See Figure 10-2.)

Product planning includes *decisions about package design, branding, trademarks, warranties, guarantees, product life cycles, and new product development.* **Distribution channels** are *the paths a good or service follows from producer to consumer.* **Marketing channels** include such middlemen as *wholesalers and retailers.*

Promotional strategy involves *personal selling, advertising, and sales promotion tools.* These elements must be skillfully blended to produce effective communication between the firm and the marketplace.

Pricing strategy, one of the most difficult parts of marketing decision making, deals with *the methods of setting profitable and justified prices.* Governmental regulations and public opinion must also be considered in pricing decisions.

The marketing mix is the mechanism that allows business to match consumer needs with product offerings. This chapter has already examined how consumer needs are identified, and it will conclude by looking at product strategy. The other three elements of the marketing mix—distribution strategy, promotional strategy, and pricing strategy—will be discussed in Chapters 11 to 13.

Do Large Firms Have the Power to Sell Inferior Products through Superior Marketing Efforts

Large firms that manufacture and distribute a line of products in the United States and abroad have become increasingly marketing oriented. Along with emphasis on the design and control of the cost of a product, such firms have hired researchers to deal with the specific segments of a market and to analyze the competition for the firm's product. Marketing attempts to identify consumer needs and wants and to match product offerings to satisfy these needs.

Some social critics feel that consumers can be manipulated into buying what they do not need, and that a demand for a product can be artificially created. By appealing to individual anxieties (for example, the desire to belong to a particular group or to be sexually attractive), a well-designed marketing program that reaches a majority of the people for whom it was designed can sell a product regardless of its quality. If marketing can convince the customer that a product satisfies certain needs, for instance, to make a person look younger, then it will be bought even though the results are not what was claimed.

By using market research to pick out the desires of a given portion of consumers and then creating a demand for the product, superior marketing techniques can produce a wasteful and witless purchasing pattern, critics claim. By differentiating a product through marketing alone, even though the actual difference is nonexistent, high-powered marketing can cause the consumer to pay attention to the item and buy it.

Others maintain that, although a customer may purchase an inferior product once, due to curiosity or perceived need, experience of the product will determine whether it will ever be bought again. In some cases excessive marketing has caused consumers simply to be irritated through overexposure. They may avoid the product that they felt had to be overpriced because of its expensive marketing and advertising campaign. Often the public's attention is not engaged, and marketing efforts are simply put out of the consumer's mind. Or the climate changes, and needs change along with it. This has been the case with large cars, which were sold as providing higher status to the owner. In a time of gas shortages small cars with more mileage to the gallon outsell large cars.

The federal government has also played a part in protecting the unwary consumer by legislating for truth in advertising. Consumer advocates, such as Ralph Nader and Consumer Reports, not only warn against poor product quality but publish investigative reports that tell consumers what to expect from a product.

Figure 10-2
The Elements of
the Marketing Mix
Focus on the Consumer

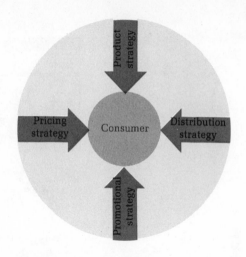

Classifying Products

Marketers have found it useful to classify products, since each requires a different competitive strategy. Products may be classified as either consumer goods or industrial goods, depending on the purchaser of the particular item. Each of these categories can then be subdivided.

CLASSIFYING CONSUMER GOODS

Although a number of classifications have been suggested for consumer goods, the system most often used contains three subcategories: convenience goods, shopping goods, and specialty goods. This system is based on consumer buying habits, and has been used for over fifty years.

Convenience goods are *those products the consumer seeks to purchase frequently, immediately, and with a minimum of effort.* Items stocked in twenty-four-hour convenience stores, vending machines, and the local newsstand are usually convenience goods. Newspapers, chewing gum, magazines, milk, beer, bread, and cigarettes are all convenience goods.

Shopping goods are *purchased only after the consumer has made comparisons of competing goods on such bases as price, quality, style, and color in competing stores.* The young couple intent on buying a new color television may visit many stores, examine perhaps dozens of television sets, and may spend days in making the final decision. They follow a regular routine from store to store in surveying competing offerings, and ultimately select the set that most appeals to them.

The **specialty goods** purchaser is well aware of what he or she wants and is willing to make a special effort to obtain it. A specialty good has *no reasonable substitute in the mind of the buyer.* The nearest Leica camera dealer may be twenty miles away, but the camera enthusiast will go to that store to obtain what he or she may consider to be the best in cameras.

"Say, that is a tricky thing to put together. Why don't we let the *buyer* assemble it?"

Some Products Come Ready to Assemble

SOURCE: *The Wall Street Journal*, July 22, 1974. Reprinted with permission from *The Wall Street Journal*.

This classification of consumer goods may differ according to the buyer. A shopping good for one person may be a convenience good for another.

CLASSIFYING INDUSTRIAL PRODUCTS   The industrial market is comprised of manufacturers, utilities, government agencies, contractors, mining firms, wholesalers, retailers, insurance and real estate firms, and institutions such as schools or hospitals that buy goods and services for use in producing other products for resale. In total the industrial market accounts for the purchase of some 50 percent of all manufactured goods in the United States. The industrial market is concentrated geographically with a limited number of buyers.

Industrial goods can be classified as capital items and expense items. **Capital items** are *those industrial products that are relatively long-lived and usually involve large sums of money.* Examples would include factories, machinery, a new DC-10 for United Airlines, and diesel locomotives for AMTRAK. **Expense items** are usually *less costly industrial products than capital items, and are consumed within a year of their purchase.* Light bulbs, pencils, and lubricating oil would be examples.

The Product Life Cycle

Products, like people, pass through *a series of stages from their initial appearance to death.* This is the **product life cycle.** Humans progress from infancy to childhood to adult status to retirement age to death. The typical path of products from their introduction to eventual deletion is depicted in Figure 10-3.

Figure 10-3
Stages in the
Product Life Cycle

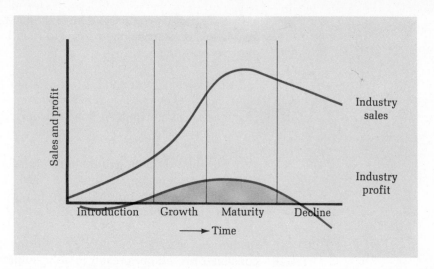

THE
INTRODUCTORY
STAGE

In the early stages of the product life cycle the firm attempts to secure demand for its new market entry. Since the product is not known to the consumer, promotional campaigns highlight its features. Promotion may also be directed toward distributors in the channel to persuade them to carry the product.

As Figure 10-3 indicates, losses are common during the introductory stage of the product life cycle due to heavy promotion expenses and extensive research and development expenses. But the groundwork is being laid for future profits.

The Sniff Test

Commercial introduction of new products is usually preceded by careful testing to be sure that the item meets the needs of the marketplace. Procter & Gamble is an example of a firm that goes through elaborate measures to ensure product acceptability. In the company's Hair Care Evaluation Center, women have half their hair washed with a new shampoo and half with their regular brand. To analyze detergent performance, technicians in a P & G Laboratory wash the laundry of five hundred employees every week. But, some tests become a little bizarre. Employees sampling a new toothpaste or mouthwash enter a laboratory where they breathe through a hole in the wall. A researcher on the other side sniffs their breaths to judge the product's effectiveness. A new deodorant is tested similarly by a professional armpit-sniffer.

Source: Peter Vanderwicken. "P & G's Secret Ingredient," *Fortune* (July 1974), p. 77.

THE GROWTH
STAGE

Sales volume rises rapidly during the growth stage of the product life cycle, as new customers make initial purchases and repurchases are made by the early buyers of the product. Word-of-mouth and mass advertising persuade hesitant buyers to make trial purchases.

The firm begins to realize profits from its investment. Procter & Gamble, for instance, expects to recover development and marketing costs of a product and have it become profitable within three years. Success causes other firms to rush into the market with competitive products.

THE MATURITY STAGE Industry sales continue to grow during the early part of the maturity stage, but they eventually reach a plateau as the backlog of potential customers is exhausted. At this point a large number of competitors have entered the market, and profits decline as competition intensifies.

For the first time available products exceed industry demand. Companies attempting to increase sales and market share must do so at the expense of competitors. As competition grows, competitors tend to cut prices in an attempt to attract new buyers.

THE DECLINE STAGE In the final stage of the product's life new innovations or shifting consumer preferences result in an absolute decline in total industry sales. Safety razors and electric shavers replace the straight razor; Frisbees replace Superballs as the latest fad; and black-and-white televisions are exchanged for color sets. As Figure 10-4 indicates, the decline stage of the old product is also the growth stage for a new product.

Industry profits decline, and in some cases actually become negative as sales fall and firms cut prices in a bid for the dwindling market. Manufacturers gradually begin to leave the industry in search of more profitable products.

An A.C. Nielsen Company study concluded that 85 percent of all new brands can expect that their market share will decline rapidly within a three-year period. As a result manufacturers often

Figure 10-4
Overlap of Life
Cycles for Products
A and B

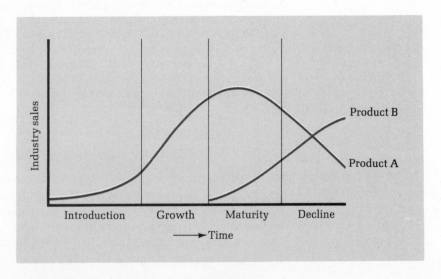

try to delay the eventual product withdrawal by new product or package designs or a fresh promotional campaign. But the Nielsen study reports that brand revivals only succeed for fifteen months on the average.[8]

LIFE CYCLE STAGES OF VARIOUS PRODUCTS

Well-known consumer products can be observed in various stages of the product life cycles. Examples can be seen in Figure 10-5.

Businesspersons should consider the life-cycle stages in the development of marketing plans for products. Effective marketers know that different competitive strategies are required for products which are at different life-cycle stages.

Identifying Products

Brand names have been *used to identify products.* Almost every product contains a means of identification for the buyer. Every five-year-old can spot McDonald's Golden Arches among other fast-food franchises. The California Fruit Growers Exchange brands their oranges with the name Sunkist. The purchasing agent for a construction firm can examine a piece of sheet steel and find the name and symbol for Bethlehem Steel. Brand identification of the firm's products is often a major decision area for the marketing manager.

Brands and Brand Names

Brands are important in developing a product's image. Once consumers are aware of a particular brand, its appearance becomes advertising for the firm. The RCA symbol is instant advertising to shoppers who spot it in a store. Successful branding is also a means of escaping some price competition. Although any chemist will confirm that all aspirin contains the same amount of the chemical *acetylsalicylic acid,* Bayer aspirin has developed so strong a reputation that it can market its aspirin at a higher price than competitive products.

Good brand names are easy to pronounce, recognize, and remember. Short names like Gulf, Crest, Bic, and Kodak meet these requirements. Multinational marketing firms face a real problem in selecting brand names in that an excellent brand name in one country may prove disastrous in another. Every language has "o" and "k" sounds, and "okay" has become an international word. Every language also has a short "a," so that Coca-Cola and Texaco are pronounceable in any tongue. But an advertising campaign for E-Z washing machines failed in the United Kingdom because the British pronounce z as "zed."

Brand names should give the right image to the buyer. The Craftsman name used on Sears' line of quality tools produces the

Figure 10-5
Life-Cycle Stages
of Various Products

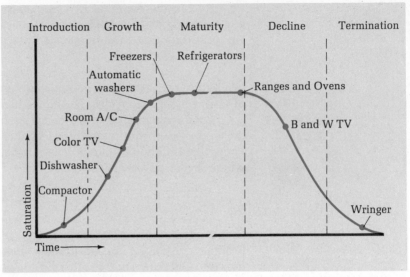

Introduction   Growth   Maturity   Decline   Termination

Freezers | Refrigerators |

Automatic washers — Ranges and Ovens

Room A/C —

Color TV —

Dishwasher —   B and W TV

Compactor

Wringer

Saturation

Time →

SOURCE: John E. Smallwood. "The Product Life Cycle: A Key to Strategic Marketing Planning," *MSU Business Topics* (Winter 1973), p. 30. Reprinted by permission of the publisher, Division of Research, Graduate School of Business Administration, Michigan State University.

correct image. Accutron suggests the quality of the high-priced and accurate timepiece by Bulova. Gorham Company, a highly regarded maker of sterling tableware, used its reputation and high consumer awareness of the Gorham name to introduce china and crystal lines in 1970 and a giftware line in 1972.[9]

Brands must not contain words in general use—such as television, automobile, or suntan lotion. These are *generic* words which describe a type of product and may not be used exclusively by any company.

If a type of product becomes generally known by a certain brand name, it can cause the company that successfully developed it the loss of the name. When this occurs, the brand name may be ruled to be generic, and the original owner loses an exclusive claim to it. Generic names like aspirin, cola, nylon, kerosene, linoleum, and shredded wheat were once brand names.

There is a difference in brand names that are legally judged to be generic and those that are generic in the eyes of many consumers. Jello-O is a brand name owned exclusively by General Foods. But to most grocery purchasers the name Jello-O is the descriptive generic name for gelatin desserts. Legal brand names such as Formica, Xerox, Frigidaire, Kodak, Styrofoam, Kleenex, Scotch tape, Fiberglas, Band-Aid, and Jeep are often used by consumers as descriptive names.

To prevent their brand names from being ruled as descriptive and available for general use, most brand owners take deliberate steps to inform the public of the exclusive ownership of the name.

The Coca-Cola Company uses ®, the symbol for registration, immediately after the name Coca-Cola and Coke. It also sends letters to newspapers, novelists, and nonfiction writers who use the name Coke with a lower-case first letter informing them that the name is owned by Coca-Cola. These companies face the pleasant task of attempting to retain exclusive rights to brand names that are known throughout the world.

Not all brand names belong to manufacturers. Some are the property of retailers or distributors. **Private brands** (often known as house, distributor, or retailer labels) are *products that are not identified as to manufacturer but carry the retailer's label.* Private brands have been around since 1859 when the Great Atlantic & Pacific Tea Company began making its own baking powder. Today, A & P supermarkets carry over 1,300 private-label products.[10] Sears' house brand now accounts for over 90 percent of this large retailer's annual volume.[11]

Branding and brand names are the primary ways that businesses can identify their products in the marketplace. Marketers must spend considerable time and effort in selecting brand names that will enhance the image of their product offerings to consumers.

Summary

Marketing and production are the two basic functions of any business firm. Production creates form utility; while marketing provides time, place, and ownership utilities. Marketing gets the product to the right place at the right time, and then arranges the transfer of ownership from seller to buyer.

Most modern firms have adopted the marketing concept. This management philosophy says that there should be a company-wide consumer orientation with the goal of achieving long-run profits.

Products may be classified as consumer goods or industrial goods. Consumer goods are those products and services purchased by the ultimate consumer for his or her own use. Industrial goods are purchased to be used, either directly or indirectly, in the production of other goods for resale. Both consumer and industrial goods may also be subclassified. Marketers sometimes divide their markets into segments on the basis of market characteristics. The process of designing separate marketing plans for different market segments is known as market segmentation.

A market target is the group of consumers toward which the firm decides to direct its marketing effort. Marketing research is used to identify those market targets that are most likely to buy an item. Once the market targets have been identified, the businessperson must design a marketing mix composed of four kinds of plans: product strategy, distribution strategy, promotional strategy, and pricing strategy.

All products pass through four stages in their life cycles. The stages—introduction, growth, maturity, and decline—are described in this chapter. A discussion of brands and brand names, and how these are used to identify products, concludes the chapter.

Review questions

1. Identify the following terms:

   a. marketing
   b. time utility
   c. place utility
   d. ownership utility
   e. marketing concept
   f. consumer goods
   g. industrial goods
   h. market segmentation
   i. zero population growth
   j. market target
   k. marketing research
   l. marketing mix
   m. convenience goods
   n. shopping goods
   o. specialty goods
   p. capital items
   q. expense items
   r. product life cycle
   s. brand names
   t. private brands

2. Describe how marketing creates utility for the consumer.
3. Distinguish between consumer and industrial markets.
4. Outline how the concept of market segmentation might be used in the marketing of:

   a. beer
   b. a headache remedy
   c. pocket calculators.

5. How has the population shift from rural to urban-suburban areas affected marketing decision making?
6. Assume you are a Japanese executive for a firm that is considering marketing a line of canned fish products in the United States. What type of market information would you want to have about the U.S. market? Discuss.
7. Comment on the use of marketing research to select market targets.
8. List the last five items that you have purchased. Then classify them as convenience, shopping, or specialty goods. Explain why you classified these products as you did.
9. Consider the products shown in Figure 10-5. Explain how the marketing strategies vary for products at different stages of the product life cycle.
10. Suggest a brand name for the following new products:

    a. a development of exclusive homesites
    b. a brand of low-lead gasoline
    c. an extra durable, single-edged razor blade
    d. a portable drill that is considerably faster than its competition.

    Defend your suggestions.

Discussion questions and exercises

1. Evaluate the pro and con arguments to the controversial issue that appears in this chapter.
2. Figure 10-5 shows ranges and ovens to be at the end of the maturity stage of the product life cycle, but several innovations have been developed in this area. How would you describe Amana's "Radar Range" and Corning's "Smooth Top Range" in relation to the product life cycle?
3. Prepare a report evaluating the warranty offers of all automobile manufacturers that have a dealership in your area. Note the difference between the programs, as well as the benefits and disadvantages of each plan. What would you conclude from this study?
4. Many beer drinkers believe they can distinguish between different brands. Yet, some research studies have shown that people are unable to identify brands on the basis of taste. Discuss what this situation implies for brewery executives.
5. Prepare a case history of a firm which you feel successfully matched consumer needs with a new product offering. Also prepare a case of where a firm failed in this objective.

Case 10-1
Catfish: Marketing a Dixie Delicacy

Prior to 1960 catfish farming was practically nonexistent in the United States. By 1963, however, the numbers of acres devoted to raising catfish (*ictalurus punctatus*) had reached 2,400. Most of this new aquabusiness was centered in the Mississippi Delta, where many farms contained the compact clay soil which makes ideal fish ponds. By 1966 total acreage was 15,000, and by 1973 over 60,000 acres of water on 2,400 farms were being used to raise channel catfish. Mississippi and Arkansas accounted for about 75 percent of this total. The remainder was divided among Louisiana, Alabama, Georgia, Tennessee, Kentucky, Indiana, Illinois, Missouri, California, Texas, and Kansas. Because catfish prefer water no cooler than 60 degrees Fahrenheit, with an optimum temperature of 80 degrees, they grow more slowly north of the Mason-Dixon Line.

Catfish have an excellent "food conversion ratio," which is an important element in farming. Only 1.85 pounds of high protein food pellets are required to produce a pound of catfish. By contrast, a pound of chicken requires 2.25 pounds of feed; and a pound of beef requires 8 pounds of feed. Fish farming fits into the annual cycle of other crops and yields a return on investment equal to rice, soybeans, or cotton. Fingerlings [the name for young catfish] grow to market size in a year. The ponds are stocked in March or April with fish about six inches long weighing about four ounces. They are fed daily until Thanksgiving with pellets made of fishmeal, soybean meal, and alfalfa.[1]

In 1973 the Catfish Farmers of America, a trade association with 600 members, headquartered in Little Rock, Arkansas, outlined for its members some of the problems which must be solved before the industry could reach its full potential:

1. The image of catfish as a food delicacy needed to be improved. Many people outside of the South, particularly in the Northeast, believed catfish to be dirty, unhealthful scavengers. Dr. R.A. Collins, Professor of Biology at the University of Central Arkansas, Conway, Arkansas, said: "Farm-raised catfish, which are virtually the only kind sold today, are fed a prepared diet that is high in protein and which produces excellent, nutritious catfish meat. What's more, farm-raised catfish are free of the pollution often found in natural streams."

2. Catfish were not widely displayed in supermarkets nor featured in grocery and restaurant advertisements. Catfish were not marketed throughout the year by producers, as shown by the following table:

Approximate Volume of Catfish Marketed During a Year

January	13%	July	4%
February	20%	August	4%
March	9%	September	7%
April	4%	October	12%
May	1%	November	13%
June	2%	December	11%

"Catfish Processing: A Rising Southern Industry," Agricultural Economic Report No. 224, Economic Research Service (Washington, D.C.: U.S. Department of Agriculture, April 1972).

After the fish had grown to market size—1 to 1 1/2 pounds—they did not need to be sold immediately. Their food supply could be decreased while they were in holding ponds. As cold weather approached, the fish stopped growing and consumed little food during the winter. Thus a farmer could market his fish at any time between October and March, whenever the price was right. Prices to producers were lowest in November and December and highest in July and August. There were not enough farmers in each region to ensure a uniform supply and dependable delivery throughout the year. Also the farmers wanted to sell all or a large part of their crops at one time. Thus a farmer might have 50,000 pounds of catfish to sell once a year. Under these conditions supermarkets and restaurants were reluctant to feature catfish in their advertising.

3. Another problem was the establishment of a federal grade standard for catfish. There were no criteria for determining whether a product qualified for the Department of Agriculture Grade A label.

4. The division of governmental authority over the industry was another problem. The Catfish Farmers of America had asked Congress to place such authority solely with the Department of Agriculture, instead of spreading it between the Departments of Commerce and the Interior.

Prior to 1974 the Catfish Farmers of America had concentrated on solving production problems by promoting research and development of the technical aspects of the industry and they had been successful in this. In 1970 about 6,000,000 pounds of catfish—live weight—were sold to processing firms. This increased to 12,000,000 pounds in 1971, to 17,000,000 pounds in 1972, and to over 24,000,000 in 1973. About half of this was sold frozen and half as fresh. The processors contracted with farmers for their output, helped the farmers harvest their fish by sending their tank trucks to transport them alive, processed[2] them and delivered the fresh and frozen fish of various sizes and in different types of packages to stores and restaurants typically within a fifty-mile radius of the plant. They sold to other stores and restaurants through brokers and distributors. About 2 percent of their output was sold at the plant at the retail price to local customers for their personal use.

As catfish farming increased, recreational (pay-to-fish) and local food markets were saturated so that increased market shares went to consumers who ate in restaurants and bought the fish in supermarkets. Six of the sixteen processing plants were located in Arkansas, Louisiana, and Mississippi and processed 51 percent of the total. The other ten plants—located in Georgia, North and South Carolina, Alabama, Florida, and Tennessee—processed the other 49 percent.

In 1973 and 1974 the trade association had furnished the fish for the catfish dinner given annually by the Louisiana delegation of the U.S. House of Representatives in Washington, D.C., for all other members. This was an effort to create a newsworthy event to promote this Dixie delicacy by getting publicity in national and local media.

The trade association believed that catfish farming had a great potential in the United States and wanted to develop it. Saltwater fishing along U.S. coasts has declined drastically in the early 1970's because of the modern, highly mechanized foreign fishing fleets that operated freely only twelve miles from U.S. shores.[3] Ocean fish had become higher priced as a result of this scarcity. Farm-raised catfish might be a significant source of fishery products for U.S. consumers. It had a long shelf life—up to one year when frozen—and consumers liked it not only for its sweet meat but also because it was high in protein and low in cholesterol.

Questions

1. Outline the marketing problems faced by the catfish-farming industry.
2. As a marketing consultant, what would you recommend as a marketing program to the trade association?

This case was prepared by Professor Robert S. Raymond of Ohio University. Used with permission.

Footnotes

1 "Farmers Try Crops of Catfish," *Columbus Dispatch* (Columbus, Ohio, November 12, 1972), p. 20.
2 This was less than half of the total produced in the United States. The fish were skinned by hand, then beheaded with a bandsaw, and finally gutted and cleaned by hand. The offal products amounted to 40–45 percent of the live weight of the fish. There was no economic use for it.
3 Robert H. Boyle. "At the Rate We're Going, Goodby Fish," *Sports Illustrated* (September 24, 1973), p. 36.

Case 10-2
Adolph Coors Company

There are few products that dominate their markets as does Coors Banquet Beer, which has had a compounded volume growth rate of 12 percent annually. Many famous people including important political figures have gone to great trouble to ensure that their refrigerators were stocked with Coors Beer.

Coors Banquet Beer is the only brand produced by the Adolph Coors Company of Golden, Colorado. The product is marketed only in eleven southwestern states, but is one of the nation's four best-selling beers. It has 41 percent of the California market, compared with only 18 percent for Anheuser-Busch. Coors has achieved an amazing 68 percent of the Oklahoma market.

Company sources attribute Coors' success to product quality, boasting that it "is the most expensively brewed beer in the world." Many beer experts regard Coors as the best American beer. The firm is constantly attempting to develop improved strains of barley for malting. Most hops used at Coors are imported from Germany. Coors is not pasteurized and contains no preservatives or chemical additives to hasten aging. The Coors brewing process takes considerably longer than that of most other major brewers. But the firm's distribution system is so efficient that a bottle of Coors Banquet Beer is shipped cold to prevent deterioration over an average of 900 miles.

Questions

1. How would you classify Coors Banquet Beer? Why?
2. Should Coors expand its market beyond its eleven-state service area?
3. In addition to product quality, what other factors are evident in Coors' success?

Source: The Coors story is discussed in William Bulkeley, "Colorado's Coors Family Has Built an Empire on One Brand of Beer," *The Wall Street Journal* (October 26, 1973), pp. 1, 10.

Marketing Channels and Physical Distribution

"Any article that does not fit well, is not the proper color or quality, does not please the folks at home, or for any reason is not perfectly satisfactory, should be brought back at once, and if returned as purchased within 10 days, we will refund the money. It is our intention always to give value for value in every sale we make, and those who are not pleased with what they buy do us a positive favor to return the goods and get their money back."

—John Wanamaker (circa 1865)

What Chapter 11 Is All About

1. In this chapter you will learn of the value created by the distribution function through primary marketing channels.
2. You will be able to identify, and then understand, the functions of the channel middlemen.
3. You will understand the different degrees of market coverage.
4. You will become aware of the role of the physical distribution system.
5. After reading this chapter you will understand these terms:

marketing channels	sales branches
middlemen	sales offices
wholesalers	wheel of retailing
retailers	scrambled merchandising
industrial distributors	physical distribution
merchant wholesalers	materials handling
agent wholesalers	

Harold Stanley Marcus

It could be said of Stanley Marcus, former chairman of Neiman-Marcus, that he had it made. As the bosses' son, Marcus had a lot going for him when he started working at the famous Dallas specialty store in 1926. There were other fringe benefits for Marcus as well. His father, aunt, and uncle-in-law had had the foresight to establish their store in Texas in a growth area that was to boom when oil was discovered in east Texas in the early 1930's. The single store has multiplied to seven, mostly in Texas, but with branches in Atlanta, St. Louis, and Bal Harbour. Two more out-of-state branches are now being built—in Northbrook, Illinois, and Chevy Chase, Maryland. Others have been announced for California and Illinois. Neiman-Marcus itself was purchased by Carter-Hawley-Hale when it was operating at about $63 million. It has been a good investment for Carter-Hawley-Hale; its most recent profit figure was announced at $125 million.

But Stanley Marcus has paid his dues. He worked summers in Neiman-Marcus between academic years at Amherst, Harvard, and the Harvard Business School. He has bought product for almost every department in the store, from underwear to fur coats. He succeeded his father, Herbert, as president of the store in 1950, and became chairman in 1973. Interested in art, music, books, and good food and wines, Marcus takes Neiman-Marcus very seriously. Applying his own taste, he sees the store as carrying items of elegance—whatever the price. And sometimes the price is astronomical. Famous for special merchandise featured in its Christmas catalogue, which Marcus helped to create, Neiman-Marcus has sold His and Her airplanes and a Noah's ark for the pessimist to match oak seedlings for the optimist. For Marcus, the store is more than a retail specialty shop. It is an institution. Neiman-Marcus' customers tend to agree.

Marketing channels and physical distribution are constantly changing. New channels and marketing institutions replace older methods of distribution which fade into oblivion. Some of these new market entries use established facilities in bringing about change. Early discounters started in abandoned movie theaters and vacant textile mills in New England.

A recent example of shifting distribution patterns in the United States is that of gasoline retailing. Thousands of service stations which have been operating with only a tiny profit have been closed as a result of gasoline shortages and distribution shifts by major oil companies. These valuable locations now offer considerable marketing opportunities to other forms of retailing. "Mr. Donut" opened fifty new outlets in 1973; fifteen of them were abandoned gasoline stations. In 1974 another fifty converted service stations became part of the doughnut chain. "Mr. Donut" reports that it costs $80,000–$90,000 to convert a former service station into an outlet, compared to $115,000–$135,000 for a new one.[1]

This chapter will examine existing channels and distribution patterns, as well as the changing aspects of this vital component of marketing management. A thorough understanding of distribution trends is necessary in modern business.

Importance of Distribution

All organizations perform a distribution function. General Motors uses Chevrolet, Buick, Oldsmobile, Pontiac, Cadillac, and GMC dealers. Del Monte products are distributed in supermarkets and convenience stores across the United States. The government of India has been distributing birth control information in an attempt to better the nation's economic status. Business and public organizations alike must distribute the product or service they are producing and marketing.

The *distribution function* is vital to the economic well-being of society because it provides the products and services desired by the consumer **at the right time and in the right place!** Economists often use the terms time, place, and ownership utilities to describe the value contributed by distribution. In other words, the marketer contributes to a product's value by getting the item to the right place when the consumer wants to buy it, and then provides the mechanism for transferring the ownership. Firms who fail to perform the distribution function effectively usually become business failures.

Distribution also provides considerable employment opportunities. Sales personnel at a J.C. Penney store, check-out clerks at the Grand Union supermarket, Coca-Cola route drivers, stevedores, salespersons, teamsters, and forklift operators are all involved in distribution. Still others are involved in servicing the products provided through a distribution network. Most people involved in distribution are classified as **service personnel,** meaning that their *role is to provide a service to some other section of the economy.* Over 50 percent of the labor force is now involved in service-related occupations. Many of these jobs are highly paid and *approach professional status.*

Channels of Distribution

Marketing channels are *the paths goods—and the title to these goods—follow from producer to consumer.*[2] Hundreds of different channels are used to distribute the output of U.S. manufacturing and

"You may as well go home and get some rest. If there's any change—we'll call you."

Service Personnel Play a Vital Role in Our Business Systems

SOURCE: *The Wall Street Journal*, February 26, 1974. Reprinted with permission from *The Wall Street Journal*.

service industries. Canned food products usually go through wholesalers and retailers to reach the consumer. Some vacuum cleaners and encyclopedias are sold direct to the consumer. No single channel is always correct; channel selection depends upon the circumstances of the market and consumer needs. The best channel for reaching the consumer may vary over time. The channel for distributing beer has changed from taverns to supermarkets. Channels shift, and effective marketers must be aware of consumer needs so that their distribution methods may be kept up-to-date.

Middlemen *are the organizations that operate within a channel of distribution.* These firms perform some type of distribution function and assist the operation of the channel. The two prime categories of middlemen are wholesalers and retailers. **Wholesalers** *are firms that sell to retailers and other wholesalers, or to industrial users, but only occasionally and in small amounts to ultimate users.* **Retailers** *are those firms that sell to persons for their own use, rather than for resale.*

PRIMARY DISTRIBUTION CHANNELS

The primary channels of distribution are shown in Figure 11-1. The channels numbered 1-4 are typical in the distribution of consumer goods; while channels 5-6 are common for industrial goods.

Figure 11-1
The Primary Channels
of Distribution

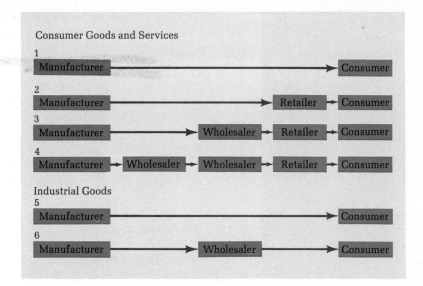

Consumer Goods and Services

1 Manufacturer → Consumer

2 Manufacturer → Retailer → Consumer

3 Manufacturer → Wholesaler → Retailer → Consumer

4 Manufacturer → Wholesaler → Wholesaler → Retailer → Consumer

Industrial Goods

5 Manufacturer → Consumer

6 Manufacturer → Wholesaler → Consumer

Channel No. 1   A direct channel from producer to consumer is used for all services, but only about 5 percent of products. Users include Avon Products, Fuller Brush, Electrolux, Kirby, and many encyclopedia publishers.

Channel No. 2   Some manufacturers distribute their products directly to retailers. The clothing industry has many producers who sell directly to retailers through their own sales forces. Some manufacturers set up their own retail outlets in order to maintain better control over their channels.

Channel No. 3   The traditional channel for consumer goods. It is used by the thousands of small manufacturers who cannot afford to maintain an extensive field sales force to reach the retailing sector, so these companies rely on wholesalers for this function. In some cases these manufacturers maintain technical advisers to assist retailers and to secure marketing information. But they are not directly involved in the selling effort.   .

Channel No. 4   Multiple wholesalers are common in the distribution of agricultural and petroleum products. An extra wholesaling level is required to divide, sort, and distribute bulky items.

Channel No. 5   Direct channels are the most commonly used approach to distributing industrial goods. This channel is used for nearly all industrial products except accessory equipment and operating supplies.

Channel No. 6 *Wholesalers of industrial goods* are often called **industrial distributors.** This indirect channel is used for small accessory equipment and operating supplies that are produced in relatively large lots but are sold in small quantities.

MULTIPLE CHANNELS

The selection of a particular channel of distribution depends on the market segment the manufacturer is attempting to reach. If the product can be marketed in more than one consumer segment, then multiple distribution channels may be required. In fact, multiple marketing channels have become increasingly popular in recent years. Tire manufacturers attempt to reach one part of the replacement tire market by using wholesalers to distribute their products to service stations and independent garages. At the same time the tire manufacturer may operate its own chain of retail outlets to reach the rest of the replacement market. The Original Equipment Market (O.E.M.) is the automobile manufacturer. This is typically reached through the tire manufacturer's own specialized sales force. Still another direct channel would be to the institutional market, such as government motor pools, the Defense Department, taxi companies, and motor vehicle fleet managers.

Channels should be chosen on the basis of the markets they serve. Great care should be taken in the crucial marketing decision. Multiple distribution channels are likely to become even more widespread as marketers try to obtain a competitive advantage in selected consumer segments.

Channel Members

Channel middlemen perform various marketing activities. They store, transport, and distribute products. They are often involved in the grading and classification of bulk products. Middlemen perform both a sales and a buying function. By buying a manufacturer's output, they provide the necessary cash flow for the producer to pay workers and buy new equipment. By selling, they provide consumers or other middlemen with want-satisfying products.

Middlemen are able to enter a channel of distribution because they can perform some activities more efficiently than the manufacturer or other channel members. The relative efficiency of middlemen changes over time, and some have to be replaced. But it is important to observe that someone must perform these vital marketing functions. Marketers considering a channel change should study the functions currently performed in the channel, and then assess how these activities will be handled in a revised distribution channel.

The two major categories of channel middlemen are wholesalers and retailers. Each of these broad classifications have numerous subgroups.

Wholesaling

Channel members who sell to retailers, other channel members, or industrial users, but only occasionally and in small amounts to ultimate users, are called wholesalers. They are important members of many marketing channels, particularly those for consumer goods. Wholesalers provide a variety of services, depending upon the needs of a particular channel. These services include:

1. maintaining a sales force
2. storage
3. delivery
4. credit to the buyer
5. financial assistance to the manufacturer
6. product servicing
7. sales promotional work
8. market information.[3]

Some channel member has to provide these services, and in some channels they are best performed by wholesalers.

The major types of wholesaling are shown in Figure 11-2. Some wholesaling operations are owned by manufacturers; others are independent businesses.

INDEPENDENT
WHOLESALERS
Independent wholesalers can be subclassified as either merchant wholesalers or agent middlemen. **Merchant wholesalers** *take legal title to the goods; while* **agent wholesalers** *may take possession of the goods, but not legal title.* Agent wholesalers usually perform fewer services than merchant wholesalers, and typically act as some type of sales agent.

Figure 11-2
Major Types
of Wholesalers

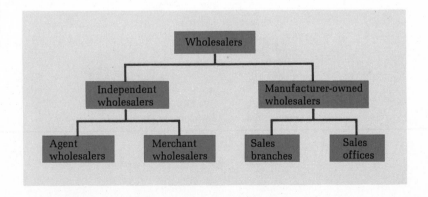

MANUFACTURER-OWNED WHOLESALERS

Manufacturers' sales branches and offices produce 33 percent of the total wholesale volume, yet number only 9 percent of all wholesaling establishments.[4] Manufacturer-owned wholesalers tend to be large-volume middlemen specializing in complex, perishable, or intensely competitive products requiring considerable promotional efforts. They are a growing segment of wholesaling.

Sales branches *stock the items they distribute and process orders from that inventory.* Sales branches are common in the chemical, petroleum products, motor vehicle, and machinery and equipment industries. A **sales office** is exactly what the term says—*an office for sales persons.* Sales offices do not maintain inventories, but do provide close local contacts for potential purchasers.

Retailing

L.L. Bean, Inc., of Freeport, Maine, is a unique, highly successful retailer founded in 1913 when Leon Leonard Bean used a $400 loan to begin selling a hunting shoe that he had designed. Today, L.L. Bean, Inc., employs about four hundred people and has sales of approximately $20 million annually. The firm sells outdoor equipment and clothing to a million customers each year, 80 percent through its mail-order catalogue. L.L. Bean products and its reputation are so highly respected that thousands of people make the trek to Freeport. Bean's famous money-back guarantee has even been extended to include a $1.75 shirt produced thirty-two years ago, but never worn. L.L. Bean, Inc., operates a retail salesroom on the third floor of an old wooden building. The salesroom, staffed by retired game wardens (who tell great hunting and fishing stories), operates twenty-four hours a day, 365 days a year.[5]

Retailers are the final link in the distribution chain. Since they are normally the only channel members with direct customer contact it is exceedingly important that retailers maintain a close

Table 11-1
Ten Largest General
Merchandise Retailers
in the United States,
1973

Rank	Company	Sales ($000)
1	Sears, Roebuck and Company	$12,306,229
2	J.C. Penney	6,243,577
3	S.S. Kresge	4,633,223
4	Montgomery Ward	4,077,415
5	F.W. Woolworth	3,722,107
6	Federated Department Stores	2,962,057
7	W.T. Grant	1,849,802
8	Allied Stores	1,598,301
9	May Department Stores	1,554,641
10	McGrory Corporation	1,424,018

SOURCE: *Advertising Age* (September 30, 1974).

identity with their customers. L.L. Bean, Inc., has done this extremely well over many years. But often other retailers fail because they lack genuine consumer orientation. Nearly all of us have remarked: "They always seem as if they are doing you a favor to sell you something" about some store in our area. Retailers must be genuinely concerned about their customers if they are to prosper in the long run.

SIZE OF THE
RETAILING SECTOR

A recent survey reported that there were 1,657,600 stores in the United States, or one for every 125 residents.[6] The top ten general merchandise retailers in 1973 are shown in Table 11-1.

Employment of Women and Minority Groups in Retailing—A Mixed Record

A 1974 study of major retail chains by the Council on Economic Priorities concluded "The major problem facing women (in retailing) is that they continue to be slotted in sales work, where they hold 80% of the jobs. Only 36% of officials and managers—including supervisors—are women, though this is up slightly from 35% in 1971." The report also concluded that minorities continue to be "underrepresented in all categories except the most menial sales, clerical, blue-collar and service categories."

Sears, Roebuck, J.C. Penney, Montgomery Ward, S.S. Kresge, and W.T. Grant were included in the survey. The retail chains said they were making considerable effort to hire more women and minorities, and would continue their efforts in the future.

Source: Based on "Study Hits Retailer on the Roles Given Women, Minorities," *The Wall Street Journal* (October 29, 1974), p. 16. Used by permission of *The Wall Street Journal* and the Council on Economic Priorities.

RETAILING
CONCEPTS

Retail institutions are subject to constant change as new stores appear to replace older establishments. This change process, called the **wheel of retailing**,[7] suggests that the retail structure is continually evolving as new retailers enter the market by offering lower prices through a reduction in services. These new entries gradually add services as they grow; and they then become the targets for a new competitive assault. Supermarkets and discount houses gained their initial market footholds because of low price, limited-service appeals.[8]

The wheel of retailing sometimes makes it difficult to adequately describe some retailers. Today's attractive K-Mart stores with good lighting, wide aisles, adequate paved parking, and services (such as BankAmericard purchases) are totally different from those early discounters that often operated in quonset huts set on unpaved lots in declining factory districts.

Another factor that makes it difficult to classify retailers is the trend toward **scrambled merchandising.** Many retailers have sought to preserve or increase their sales volumes by *diversifying the prod-*

DO YOUR HAIR, MA'AM?

The Scrambled Merchandising Concept Also Applies to Service Stations

SOURCE: Lubliner/Saltz, New York. Reprinted with permission from *Advertising Age*, April 21, 1975.

ucts they offer for sale. Drug stores added soda fountains, then such items as magazines and newspapers. Now drug stores have become major retailers of cameras, greeting cards, liquor, tobacco products, cosmetics, and toys. Service stations offer a bewildering array of products—party ice, soft drinks, and sometimes toys. Some discount stores have added pharmaceutical departments. The trend toward scrambled merchandising continues in all types of retailing.

TYPES OF RETAILERS

While it is becoming more difficult to classify stores, the following general categories are usually acknowledged:

General Stores — The earliest type of retailers; they can still be found in some localities offering a wide variety of general merchandise.

Department Stores — A.T. Stewart, built in 1863, was the first department store in the United States. Department stores now account for over 10 percent of all American retail sales. The primary strength of department stores has always been the variety of products that they offer. Macy's in New York City provides about 400,000 items in its 168 selling departments.

Specialty Store — Some retailers follow a marketing strategy of offering a complete selection in a narrow range of merchandise. By specializing their product offerings, these stores can concentrate on specific consumer segments, and provide specialized technical knowledge and/or servicing. Camera and jewelry stores are examples.

Chain Stores

About a third of all retail sales are generated by chain stores, which can be defined as two or more centrally owned and managed stores that offer the same product lines. Chain organization is common among shoe stores, department stores, and variety stores (such as the traditional "5 and 10 cent" stores). Many major chain store organizations operate on an international basis.

Discount House

Most retail discounters have emerged since World War II. The traditional market entry was through lower prices allowed by fewer customer services. But, following the wheel of retailing pattern, some of today's discount houses are beginning to resemble general merchandise retailers. Despite definitional problems, statistics indicate that discount houses are a growing segment of retailing.

Vending Machines

Vending machines are an excellent method of retailing various types of consumer goods. Candy, cigarettes, soft drinks, ice, fruit, ice cream, chewing gum, sandwiches, coffee, milk, and hot chocolate are all available through vending machines. Even entertainment has been packaged for vending operations beginning with "juke boxes" and "pinball machines." A modern version is the Video Game, such as "Pong." Approximately 50,000 coin-operated video games were sold in 1973. Consumers pump $250 million annually into slots to play these games.[9]

Hypermarché

There are more than 1,000 hypermarchés in Europe; and they are now appearing in North America. These are giant food and general merchandise discount stores. With prices 10–15 percent below normal retail levels, the typical hypermarché does $35 million in sales annually. Some European hypermarchés have sold $70 million worth of goods in a single year.[10]

Market Coverage

There is usually only one Chevrolet dealer in your immediate area, but there may be several retail outlets that sell General Electric products. Coca-Cola can be found everywhere—supermarkets, neighborhood convenience stores, service stations, vending machines, restaurants, and coffee shops. Various types of products require different kinds of coverage. Three categories of market coverage exist: intensive distribution, selective distribution, and exclusive distribution.

INTENSIVE DISTRIBUTION

An **intensive distribution** strategy is where *the marketer tries to place a product in nearly every available outlet.* Tobacco products, chewing gum, newspapers, soft drinks, *TV Guide,* and many other low-priced convenience products are available in numerous locations convenient to the purchaser. Saturation market coverage usually requires that wholesalers be used to achieve a maximum distribution effort.

EXCLUSIVE DISTRIBUTION

Exclusive distribution is the exact opposite of intensive distribution. Here the *manufacturer gives a retailer or wholesaler the exclusive rights to sell its products in a specific geographical area.* Manufacturers sometimes set up very effective distribution systems in foreign markets by granting resident firms an exclusive license to import (or manufacture) their products. Automobile companies are probably the best examples of exclusive distribution in domestic markets. An exclusive distribution contract allows the retailer to carry an adequate inventory and provide good service facilities that might not be possible if competitive dealers existed in the area. Since the dealer is assured of a guaranteed sales area, he or she is often more likely to make expensive investments in the business. In return, the manufacturer wants the dealer to develop a quality image and effectively promote its products.

SELECTIVE DISTRIBUTION

Selective distribution is a degree of market coverage somewhere between intensive distribution and exclusive distribution. *A limited number of retailers are selected to distribute the firm's product lines.* Television and electrical appliances are often handled in this manner. The manufacturer hopes to develop a close working relationship with a limited number of dealers. Manufacturers often split advertising expenses with their dealers. Extensive servicing and training facilities are also usually maintained to help the retailer do a better job of distributing the manufacturer's product.

Physical Distribution

The distribution system in the United States also includes the function of **physical distribution,** *the actual movement of goods from the producer to the user.* For many years this was a neglected aspect of business management. But since the late 1950's physical distribution has become extremely important in business. Several noticeable trends have occurred. The costs of transportation and maintaining inventory have increased substantially, and are now about 20 percent of the nation's total output. Product lines have been broadened to offer wider consumer choices. This has put a strain on some distribution networks. Management has sought more efficient inventory practices so as to avoid out-of-stock problems and reduce the financing costs associated with maintaining large inventories. Many experts believe that it may no longer be possible to gain significant cost savings in production. In short, production systems may be near to maximum efficiency given the present technology. This makes physical distribution a prime candidate for further efficiency improvements.

All of these trends are responsible for making physical distribution a more critical aspect of modern business. Major gains in efficiency are possible for firms that carefully study their own (and alternative) physical distribution systems.

The Russian Wheat Deal—A Physical Distribution Disaster

Many top government officials and economists thought a deal to sell 19 million tons of grain to the Soviet Union would help the American economy. But the deal did not turn out too well for the U.S. government.

The U.S. agreed to hold to the $1.63 price existing at the time of the sale. However, by the time the wheat actually cleared our distribution system the price was $4.00 a bushel, and the government had to make up the difference to U.S. wheat suppliers.

How did our distribution system let us down? First a dispute over which country's ships would carry the grain caused a delay of several months. A second factor was that half of the 30,000 railway cars used to haul the grain were open-topped. The grain became rain-soaked porridge and could not be loaded onto the ships except by hand. These distribution problems ended up delaying spring fertilizer shipments, worsened an East Coast lumber shortage, and hampered spring grain harvest hauls.

Source: Edward O. Gaylord and Daniel Chapman. "The Many Faces of Product Distribution," *Marketing Times* (May/June 1974), p. 6. Used by permission.

TOTAL COST APPROACH

The study of physical distribution should include all factors involved in moving goods, rather than concentrate on individual aspects of the overall process. The objective of the physical distribution effort is to maximize the level of customer service, so *total costs* should be considered.

Physical distribution costs are often interrelated in that a change in one element may affect other parts of the physical distribution mix. Lower inventory levels might reduce warehousing costs, but result in increases in transportation and order-processing costs. The total cost approach emphasizes that the interrelationship of these costs should be considered in any physical distribution strategy.

TRANSPORTATION COMPANIES

Transportation companies can be classified into three basic types:

1. common carriers
2. contract carriers
3. private carriers.

A **common carrier** *offers to perform services for the general public within a particular line of business.* Examples would be a truck line operating in an area where general merchandise is handled. The line would be expected to serve all the people in that area who offer them general merchandise to haul. However, they would not be required to handle such things as liquid petroleum gas or aviation gasoline. If the common carrier did handle liquid petroleum gas or aviation gasoline it would not be required to handle all the liquid petroleum gas or aviation gas offered to it.

Common carriers usually have certain monopoly or semi-monopoly rights to serve an area. In exchange for these rights they have a responsibility to furnish regular service. Some examples of common carriers are United Airlines, Penn-Central Railroad, and Consolidated Freightways.

Contract carriers *transport goods for hire by individual contract or agreement.* Contract carriers do not offer to perform services for the general public, but usually offer services that meet the special needs of customers. By law, they may be limited to the number of customers they service. Contract carriers are most frequently engaged in business as owner/operator motor carriers. Usually they solicit large shipments from one shipper to one recipient.

Private carriers *carry their own property in their own vehicles.* Examples of private carriers would be Safeway Stores, U.S. Steel, and some mines which operate their own railroads.

TRANSPORTATION MODES

The cost of using a transportation mode is usually related to the speed at which the mode operates. Fast transportation modes typically cost more than slower methods.

Senator Proxmire Doesn't Like Hitchhiking Study

Wisconsin's Senator Proxmire has criticized a year-long, $15,870 study conducted with federal funds. The study, funded by the National Science Foundation, was entitled "Hitchhiking—A Viable Alternative to a Multimodal Transportation System."

Source: The Wall Street Journal (March 7, 1975), p. 1.

Air transportation

Ten percent of all intercity passenger service is handled by the airlines. Seventy-five percent of long-distance passenger transportation, as well as a large part of relatively short-range intercity traffic, has been taken over by the air carriers. Airlines are second only to the passenger automobile in the number of passengers carried. Speed is the principal factor in these growth statistics. However, the near abandonment by the railroads of their passenger service has been another important factor. The airlines depend on their passenger services for the greater part of their revenue—well in excess of 90 percent of their total revenue.

The certificated airlines of the United States are all common carriers. Some of them, and a group of carriers known as supplemental carriers, engage in charter work, which is a form of contract carriage. Many business organizations own or lease aircraft which are operated to transport their personnel or, in some instances, their freight. This is defined as private carriage.

While still dwarfed by other transportation modes, domestic air freight has become increasingly important in recent years. Air freight is usually limited to valuable and/or perishable products because of the mode's relatively high cost. Live lobsters are flown from the seashore to inland cities. Detroit automobile manufacturers ship critical parts to assembly plants by air. In some cases air freight costs are offset by lower inventory costs and more efficient manufacturing operations.

Rail transportation

About 40 percent of all domestic intercity freight is carried by the railroads. Most railroads are common carriers. None are contract carriers. A very few—owned and operated by mining companies, lumbering operations, and very large industries like steel mills—are private carriers.

Carload freight is the kind of freight that railroads prefer to handle. This is freight that is offered to them in shipper-loaded cars to be delivered to someone who will unload the cars. It requires little paperwork and no handling of the freight on the part of the railroad. Freight handling is the most costly part of any carrier's service, both from the standpoint of personnel needed as well as the possibilities of loss and damage.

Companion services to carload freight are the containerization and trailer-on-flatcar (piggyback) services. In each of these cases the physical handling and loading of the freight in the containers and trailers is done by the shipper and the recipient. Carload shipping usually costs less than one-half as much as less-than-carload freight.

Railroads also offer trainload services to shippers of bulk commodities, such as coal and iron ore. Some trains of this type never stop, using continuous loading and unloading equipment.

Highway carriers

Highway carriers are divided into common carriers, contract carriers, and private carriers. The principal advantage the highway carrier has over the other modes of transportation is *flexibility*. Wherever there is a road, a highway carrier can operate, as contrasted to the railroad's dependence on rails and the air carrier's dependence on an airport large enough to accommodate large aircraft.

Highway carriers are most efficient when they move freight for distances of up to 350 miles, even though there are a number of transcontinental highway carriers moving freight coast to coast. For distances over 350 miles, the highway carrier tends to lose its advantage to the railroads.

The typical highway common carrier has pickup and delivery equipment which picks up at the store door of the shipper, then delivers the freight to a freight terminal, where it is loaded into larger trucks to be taken to a freight terminal in another city. There it is unloaded and delivered by smaller delivery vehicles.

Highway common carriers may have monopoly rights or semi-monopoly rights to operate in certain areas and carry certain types of merchandise. However, for these rights they have the responsibility of maintaining regularly scheduled services.

Contract highway carriers can frequently offer lower rates than common carriers because they are serving a limited number of customers, and because they are dealing in volume-type of shipments and are not required by law to offer regularly scheduled services. Contract carriers work when a load is ready, but do not have to operate when they do not have a profitable load.

There are many private highway carrier operations. Wholesale grocery companies, supermarket chains, department stores, manufacturing establishments, mining companies—all may engage in private carrier operations when they transport their goods.

Water transportation

Water transportation is one of the least costly of all modes of transportation. Water transportation can be classified as:

1. international or offshore
2. intercoastal
3. coastal
4. inland waterway.

International transportation, that between the United States and foreign countries, carries the bulk of the exports and imports of the United States. It is carried in both United States flagships and foreign flagships. The U.S. government has subsidized both shipbuilding and the U.S. offshore shipping industry in the interests of national defense.

Intercoastal shipping is offered by steamship companies operating between the Atlantic and Pacific coasts, and Gulf of Mexico ports and the Pacific Coast. Intercoastal service is limited to U.S. flagships. These companies operate as common carriers, serving the general public and maintaining regular schedules. They frequently have limited monopoly rights to perform these services. They are subject to government regulation. U.S. law forbids foreign carriers from transporting passengers or freight between ports in the United States.

At one time coastal steamship service was a very important part of the total transportation system of the United States. However, with the advent of improved rail and highway services, both passenger and freight, there is little coastal steamship service still in existence. Probably most of the service remaining is involved with private transportation. One example is the oil company tankers that carry their company's products from one coastal terminal to another.

About 16 percent of the volume of domestic intercity freight is handled through the inland waterways of the United States. This system of waterways includes the Mississippi, Ohio, Tennessee, and other rivers; inland canals; and the Great Lakes. Much of this traffic, especially on the rivers and canals, is handled in barges pushed by mammoth tugs. Great Lakes traffic is handled by specially built steamers. This low-cost type of transportation lends itself mainly to the hauling of bulky, low-value commodities.

Pipelines

More than 22 percent of intercity freight is handled by pipelines. These convey primarily petroleum products ranging from crude oil to highly refined products and natural gas. Some successful experiments have been made in handling other bulk commodities, such as coal. This is accomplished by grinding the commodities into small pieces and mixing in water to form what is called *slurry*, which can be pumped through the pipelines. Pipelines can transport many liquids and gases much cheaper and faster than other modes of transportation.

Should Government Subsidies Be Used to Solve the Railroad Problem?

From the 1850's to beyond the turn of the century railroads were at the heart of U.S. commerce. Long-distance freight haulage was almost always done by rail, although a few river transports were in operation. The network of highways that now covers the United States had not yet been built, and truck freight shipments were made for short distances only.

Then, through taxation, interstate highways were constructed by the government, which subsidized the trucking industry. Because of these roads, trucks could get to many areas where no railroad lines existed, and today truck revenues exceed those of railroads by about five to one. Cargo airplanes were also put into service for fast shipment of perishable and valuable goods. At the same time, many railroads ignored what was happening and neither updated their technology nor made the necessary cutbacks to match their operating losses. By putting new equipment into service and cutting back on branch lines that were seldom used and duplicated lines between cities, the railroads might have been able to regain a profitable position, at least concerning long-distance and large tonnage freight.

Some feel that government regulations relating to railroad service and discriminating taxation of railroad properties have crippled the industry in the United States. These critics say that it is now the railroads' turn to be supported by government, and that legislation should be passed to eliminate underutilized and duplicated lines. Along with government agencies that are subsidizing the restructuring of railroad systems (such as the Northeast's Conrail, which has merged the Penn Central and six other railroads), proposals have been made for overseeing the amount of traffic on light-density lines. If these lines are not to be abandoned, then some form of subsidy may have to be offered by government.

Many of those who see the railroads as floundering beyond help because of poor service, union restrictions, and outmoded technology offer nationalization of railroads as a solution. If this takes place, railroads will be supported by tax dollars, one more item to be added to the national budget.

For those who want to see the continuance of privately owned railroads, grants are the answer to the system's indebtedness. Such government grants could be used to modernize railroad equipment and be repaid over the long run by a small surcharge collected from shippers. If cost and convenience were allowed to regulate shipping, then freight for short hauls and frequent deliveries could be handled by truckers, whereas long, heavy hauls could be handled by the more efficient rail system.

Freight forwarders

Freight forwarders are different from the carriers considered earlier in this chapter. They do not own any of the equipment used in intercity carriage of freight. They are common carriers who purchase bulk space from carriers, such as the airlines and railroads, by lease or contract and resell this space to small-volume shippers. The freight forwarder picks up the merchandise at the establishment of the shipper, takes care of the billing, and loads the merchandise into the equipment of the carrier which is being used. The freight forwarder also delivers the merchandise at its destination.

The shipper has the advantage of a better, less expensive service, and the carriers do not have to handle all the small shipments or the billing. A further advantage of freight forwarding is the ability of the freight forwarder to know at all times just where each piece of freight is when it is in transit. No other mode of transportation can do this with respect to small shipments. This is an instance where the *addition* of a middleman saves money for everyone and makes for improved service.

MATERIALS HANDLING

Once a product has been transported from its place of manufacture to the consumer, the physical distribution task becomes one of moving the item within the customer's warehouse, terminal, factory, or store. These activities are referred to as **materials handling**.

Two recent innovations have improved materials handling in many firms. Unitizing refers to combining as many packages as possible into one load that is usually handled by a forklift truck. Unitizing is sometimes done by steel bands or shrink packing, where the packages are covered with a plastic sheet and then heated. When the plastic cools, it shrinks and binds the packages together.

Containerization puts packages into a form that is relatively easy to transfer. Some containers are designed to be carried via rail, truck, or ship. These containers might be taken to a rail terminal on a flatbed truck, then placed on a flatbed railway car to be hauled to a seaport where they can be loaded on an overseas freighter. Containerization has significantly reduced materials handling costs for many products.

Summary

All organizations perform a distribution function. A product or service's value is enhanced by having it available at the right time and in the right place. Distribution also provides considerable employment opportunities.

Marketing channels are the paths that goods and services follow to the final user. Some channels involve middlemen, such as wholesalers and retailers; others are direct from manufacturers to the consumers. Multiple channels are sometimes used to reach different market segments.

Various channel middlemen are described in this chapter. Channel members who sell to retailers and other channel members or industrial users, but only occasionally and in small amounts to ultimate users, are called wholesalers. Retailers, by contrast, are channel middlemen who sell direct to consumers.

Three categories of market coverage exist: intensive distribution, selective distribution, and exclusive distribution. These market coverages are described in the chapter.

Physical distribution, the actual physical movement of goods from producer to user, is also an important part of the marketing channel. The objective of the physical distribution effort is to maximize the level of customer service, therefore total costs must be considered.

The chapter concludes with a discussion of transportation companies, transportation modes, and materials handling.

Review questions

1. Identify the following terms:
   - a. marketing channels
   - b. middlemen
   - c. industrial distributors
   - d. wholesalers
   - e. merchant wholesalers
   - f. agent wholesalers
   - g. sales branches
   - h. sales offices
   - i. wheel of retailing
   - j. scrambled merchandising
   - k. physical distribution
   - l. materials handling
2. Outline the primary channels of distribution.
3. Why would a firm ever use multiple channels of distribution?
4. Manufacturer-owned wholesalers tend to be large-volume middlemen. Why?
5. What is the primary difference between merchant wholesalers and agent wholesalers?
6. Outline the various types of retail establishments. Which ones appear to be declining? Growing?
7. What types of market coverage would be best for:
   - a. electronic calculators
   - b. bubble gum
   - c. men's cologne
   - d. bulldozers and other earth-moving equipment
8. What is meant by the *total cost approach* to physical distribution?
9. Differentiate between common, contract, and private carriers.
10. What transportation mode would you suggest for:
    - a. sheet steel
    - b. natural gas
    - c. premium electronic components
    - d. Kellogg's cereal

Discussion questions and exercises

1. Evaluate the pro and con arguments to the controversial issue that appears in this chapter.
2. "The functions performed by channel middlemen cannot be eliminated." Comment.
3. Assume that you were the chief executive officer of a large retail chain. How would you improve the status of female and minority employees? Discuss.
4. The New Zealand government introduced a bill that grades used cars, and requires dealers to provide full warranty coverage within certain mileage and age limits. Warranties for cars less than five years old and with less than 100,000 kilometers (62,500 miles) of use were set at "5,000 kilometers (3,125 miles) or three months." Warranties for older vehicles were for shorter periods of use. Used-car dealers could avoid giving these warranties only by listing all the defects of a car at the time of the sale.* How do you think this legislation would affect retail automobile dealers? Would a similar law be appropriate in the United States?
5. Prepare a report on the physical distribution system used by a company in your area. Can you suggest any way(s) to improve the firm's physical distribution efficiency?

*Source: "Used Cars in NZ Must Be Guaranteed," The Age (November 1, 1974), p. 7.

Case 11-1

Montgomery Ward and Company

Montgomery Ward and Company started as a Chicago mail-order business in 1872. The firm offered lower prices than other Chicago merchants and provided a money-back guarantee. Ward's acquired a favorable reputation in those days and became one of the leading retailers in the United States.

But in the 1970's Wards is trying to deal with the "Monkey Ward" label hung on it by other retailers years ago. While Sears and Penney's expanded after World War II, Ward's management hoarded its cash and waited for another depression when, it was reasoned, construction costs would drop. As Table 11-1 indicates, Ward's is now the fourth largest general merchandiser, but only a third the size of Sears. While Ward's remains a very profitable company with a good growth record, some of the firm's officials openly worry about its public image.

Questions

1. What is your personal image of Montgomery Ward? On what do you base your opinion?
2. What would you do to improve Ward's image?

Source: Ellen Hume. "'Monkey' Ward Trying to Shake Its Stodgy Nuts-and-bolts Image," *Detroit Free Press* (May 5, 1974), pp. 11D, 14D.

Case 11-2

GiftAmerica

GiftAmerica, a Western Union subsidiary, was called "the most successful innovation in retail merchandising since the introduction of the supermarket 40 years ago" when it was introduced in 1973. The company sold a seventeen-item line of gifts (with an average retail price of $25) via 4,500 retailers spread throughout the United States. Western Union's start-up costs for the new operation were estimated to be $28.5 million.

The subsidiary was intended to tap the annual $3 billion market in gifts of $12 or more shipped intercity by persons with household incomes exceeding $10,000. Management believed some $5,000,000 to $10,000,000 of these sales were "last minute" purchases requiring immediate delivery. Consumers were told they could select gifts illustrated in ads, telephone a central toll-free number, and have the gift wrapped and delivered virtually overnight. Use of the Western Union system provided efficient distribution, and heavy advertising expenditures built strong brand recognitions for the firm.

Yet, in the first twelve months of operations, GiftAmerica achieved only about 9 percent of its unit forecast. Action had to be taken. So on September 1, 1974, Western Union management approved plans to restructure GiftAmerica's marketing concept. The revised strategy was to leave the retailing to others, broaden the product line, and allow the otherwise profitable company to retreat into its own area of competence. GiftAmerica executives hoped to sign two or three major retail chains, several promotion-minded national advertisers, plus a couple of catalogue mail-order firms as participants in the subsidiary. Retailers in the system were to offer a wider selection than the original seventeen items from their regular retail lines to customers as part of GiftAmerica's "National Gift Service." Meanwhile, national advertisers were to promote selected items as GiftAmerica selections, which, upon customer order, could be sent immediately anywhere in the nation.

Questions

1. Is GiftAmerica a viable retailing opportunity for Western Union?
2. What marketing problem do you see in the GiftAmerica operation? Discuss.
3. Do you think management's revised retailing plan is adequate? Why or why not?
4. What would you have done if you were the chief executive at the firm?

Source: Based on Bob Donath. "GiftAmerica's Woes Laid to Lack of Marketing Know-how." *Advertising Age* (September 2, 1974), pp. 3, 43.

12

Promotional Strategy

"*If I were starting life all over again, I would go into the advertising business; it has risen with evergrowing rapidity to the dignity of an art.*"

—*Franklin D. Roosevelt*

What Chapter 12 Is All About

1. In this chapter you will learn that most organizations use some type of promotional strategy in order to reach their goals.
2. You will understand the objectives of promotion.
3. You will learn about the basic elements of promotional strategy.
4. You will be able to identify alternative promotional strategies.
5. After reading this chapter you will understand these terms:

promotional strategy	canned sales presentation
positioning	prospect
advertising	qualifying
product advertising	closing
institutional advertising	key accounts
comparative advertising	P.O.P.
personal selling	specialty advertising

Benjamin Feldman

Benjamin Feldman is the exact opposite of Willie Loman, exhausted and wearied company representative in *Death of a Salesman*. Feldman has sold more than $460 million of life insurance in his thirty-three-year history with the New York Life Insurance Company.

Born in New York City in 1912, Feldman grew up in Salineville, Ohio. He left high school when he was sixteen years old in order to work in his father's produce business. Over a decade later he went to work as a debit insurance agent before joining New York Life.

In 1948 Feldman received his Chartered Life Underwriter certificate, two years after reaching his first million-dollar sales year. Since that time Feldman has been a member of the Million Dollar Round Table, an international organization of the most successful sales people in the insurance business.

Feldman lives in Ohio and works out of the Youngstown General Office. There are 8,500 agents working for New York Life, and Feldman has been first in sales volume since 1955. In two of those years, 1970 and 1973, he racked up $50 million in sales, and in 1971 he beat his own record with a monumental sales figure of over $65 million.

He has been featured as a supersalesman in such books as *The Incomparable Salesmen* and *The Feldman Method*.

Most organizations use some type of promotional strategy to reach their goals. **Promotional strategy** is *the function of informing, persuading, and influencing a consumer decision.* Benson and Hedges's creative advertising campaign showing their 100-millimeter cigarette getting bent up when car windows and elevator doors close allowed it to achieve the leading share of this particular cigarette market.[1] By contrast, the State of Oregon has used an "unselling Oregon" promotional strategy in order to reduce the number of new residents coming into the state and to preserve its resources and environmental programs. It included such novel ideas as promoting the mosquito as the state bird, and boasting of Oregon's one-day summer. But some critics have suspected that the strategy was actually intended to attract new industry and residents rather than discourage them.[2*]

Faced with a declining share of the soft drink market, The Seven-Up Company launched a major promotional campaign a few years ago. Their promotional effort was aimed at the twelve to twenty-four age group, the heaviest consumers of soft drinks. Research showed 7UP was weak with this age group, but strong with

*Reprinted with permission from Oregon Ungreeting Card Co., Eugene, Oregon 97402.

older people who used the product primarily as a cocktail mixer. The now familiar "The Uncola" trademark, heavily advertised, created a new image for 7UP, and convinced people it was on UN-traditional soft drink. They were able to reverse its sales decline through an innovative promotional strategy.[3]*

Objectives of Promotional Strategy

Promotional strategy objectives vary among organizations. Some use promotion to expand their markets, others to hold their current positions. Still other firms use promotion to present a corporate viewpoint on a public issue. An organization can have multiple promotional objectives.

Promotion Can Be Used to Present a Corporate Viewpoint

Mobil Oil Corporation used a newspaper advertisement to tell the public how it contributed $100,000 to public television's "Sesame Street." Mobil also warned that tight financial conditions might cause the extinction of "Big Bird," which prompted some California school children to send Mobil a donation of 1,334 pennies.

Source: Michael Corner. "Mobil's Advocacy Ads Lead a Growing Trend, Draw Praise, Customers," *The Wall Street Journal* (May 14, 1975).

Most sources identify these specific promotional objectives or goals:

1. provide information
2. increase sales
3. position the product
4. stabilize sales.

PROVIDE INFORMATION Most advertisements in the early days of promotional campaigns were designed to inform the public of a product's availability in an era characterized by short supply of many items. Criers made public announcements of the cargo carried by vessels newly arrived in Colonial American ports. General stores on the frontier of a nation advancing westward inserted advertisements in weekly newspapers. These advertisements essentially listed the contents of the latest shipment from the East.

Today, a major portion of advertising in the United States is still informational in nature. A large section of Wednesday's or Thursday's newspaper consists of advertising telling consumers what products are being featured by stores (and at what prices) for weekend shopping. Health insurance advertisements in supplements to Sunday newspapers emphasize information about rising hospital

*Reprinted with permission from The Seven-Up Company, St. Louis, Missouri.

costs. Industrial salespersons keep buyers aware of the latest technological advancement in a particular field.

Providing information about product availability, prices, or related data has always been of primary importance to marketing and promotional strategy. Marketers realize that nearly all promotional messages must carry some informational content in what may be referred to as promotion's educational role.

Advertising, personal selling, and other facets of promotional strategy are responsible for moving products from the manufacturer to the consumer in our economy. An effective promotional strategy is required if a firm hopes to increase its sales.

The Seven-Up Company's trademark "The Uncola" and the advertising campaign connected with it, described earlier, is an example of a promotional strategy that achieved the objective of increasing sales. ACE, the unique salesman described in Case 12-2, also increased sales for his employer.

POSITION THE PRODUCT   Promotional strategy has been used to "position" a product in certain markets. **Positioning** is *the strategy of concentrating on specific market segments rather than on trying to achieve a broader appeal.* This requires the marketer to identify the market segments that would be likely users of the product. Promotional strategy is then brought into play to differentiate the item, so that it appeals to these market segments.

Positioning is also often used for products that are not leaders in their particular fields. Faced with a Listerine widely accepted for control of bad breath but characterized by medicinal flavor and odor, Scope offered itself as providing "minty fresh breath" instead of "medicine breath."

INCREASE SALES   The ultimate promotional goal for most firms is increased sales.

But there are other bases for positioning a product. In a classic promotional campaign Avis positioned itself against Hertz with the theme: "Avis is only number two in rent-a-cars, so why go with us? We try harder."*

How Would You Do It?

Consider this possibility for positioning a new razor blade. A survey of thirty college campuses found that razor blade usage is now higher among females than males (85 percent versus 77 percent).*

Since most razor blade promotions have a decided masculine appeal, it would seem that a new blade might be positioned in the female segment. But, how would one go about doing this? First, female-oriented promotion

*Avis Rent a Car System Inc.

would have to be developed. Then the marketer would need to seek out a medium for getting these messages to college-aged women.

For example, a study by Opinion Research Corporation found that the leading publications read by young women between the ages of twelve and twenty-four were *TV Guide* (10.8 million) and *Reader's Digest* (5.8 million). Other publications with readership of over 4 million were *Good Housekeeping*, *McCall's*, *Seventeen*, and *Better Homes and Gardens*.[†]

*"Personal Care Items Popular with Collegians, Survey Finds," *Advertising Age* (October 21, 1974), p. 66.
[†]*Advertising Age* (August 26, 1974), p. 206.

STABILIZE SALES   Sales stabilization is another promotional strategy goal. Sales contests offering prizes (such as vacation trips, color televisions, and scholarships) to sales personnel who meet certain goals are usually held during slack sales periods of the year. Sales promotion materials—such as calendars, pens, and the like—are often distributed to stimulate sales during off-peak periods. Despite shortages of antifreeze in 1974, Union Carbide still advertised its Prestone brand heavily. Robert Cassidy, Union Carbide's marketing director, has pointed out that a company should advertise when times are difficult: "We have a valuable consumer franchise and we don't intend to give it up as long as we can supply the product."[4]

A stable sales pattern allows the firm to do better financial, purchasing, and market planning; even out the production cycle; and reduce some management and production costs. The correct use of promotional strategy can be a valuable tool in accomplishing these objectives.

The Three Elements of a Promotional Strategy

Promotional strategy consists of three distinct elements:

1. advertising
2. personal selling
3. sales promotion.

Each of these elements is important in developing a promotional strategy.

Advertising

Advertising can be defined as a *nonpersonal sales presentation usually directed to a large number of potential customers*. It uses various media—newspapers, magazines, television, radio, direct mail, and outdoor advertising—to relay promotional messages to today's widespread markets. Newspapers receive the largest single share of total advertising revenues.

The leading national advertisers in the United States include

Table 12-1 Twenty Leading National Advertisers

Company	$ Media total	Magazines	Newspaper supplements	Network television	Spot television	Network radio	Outdoor
1. Procter & Gamble Co.	$245,186.1	$9,939.6	$762.8	$145,743.3	$88,740.4	$ —	$ —
2. General Foods Corp.	140,929.7	12,352.6	3,012.9	76,519.6	48,954.5	—	90.1
3. Bristol-Myers Co.	121,618.0	20,707.7	818.2	77,005.7	21,835.9	1,250.5	—
4. American Home Products Corp.	118,228.1	4,997.4	167.8	79,323.0	32,381.7	1,240.4	117.8
5. General Motors Corp.	115,265.2	32,889.1	494.4	57,463.4	20,744.4	1,785.1	1,888.8
6. Colgate-Palmolive Co.	88,272.9	8,535.8	815.6	43,547.5	32,920.3	2,418.7	34.0
7. Lever Brothers Co.	86,550.1	5,120.8	330.2	44,973.3	36,083.4	—	42.4
8. Sterling Drug Inc.	79,756.9	7,139.4	366.8	60,787.5	7,622.2	3,841.0	—
9. Sears, Roebuck & Co.	79,744.9	12,652.3	244.3	42,052.6	24,332.9	360.2	102.6
10. Ford Motor Co.	75,467.2	11,365.4	188.9	40,000.5	20,315.6	2,197.0	1,399.8
11. R. J. Reynolds Industries	69,397.5	29,141.6	17,924.7	5,430.3	1,362.6	—	15,538.3
12. Warner-Lambert Co.	63,290.9	580.3	292.1	48,760.2	12,562.0	1,096.3	—
13. Philip Morris Inc.	63,010.3	27,518.5	8,659.5	7,090.5	6,936.9	—	12,804.9
14. General Mills Inc.	60,953.5	7,978.3	519.9	30,286.4	22,106.7	60.4	1.8
15. Gillette Co.	60,733.9	5,063.8	104.8	45,389.1	9,970.4	205.8	—
16. Ralston Purina Co.	60,109.8	5,800.5	1,496.2	37,624.3	14,782.2	—	406.6
17. Heublein Inc.	55,575.8	9,107.5	155.0	17,874.5	23,869.4	—	4,569.4
18. British-American Tobacco Co. Ltd.	55,378.4	30,380.0	7,260.9	2,486.5	4,008.4	—	11,242.6
19. American Telephone & Telegraph Co.	49,964.8	14,688.9	6.0	18,628.2	15,766.2	352.8	522.7
20. Kraftco Corp.	49,782.8	11,810.8	570.3	23,251.5	13,184.4	696.1	269.7

SOURCE: *Advertising Age* (May 12, 1975), p. 76. Used with permission.

familiar names such as Polaroid, Revlon, Procter & Gamble, and General Mills. But the hundred leading national advertisers also includes the United States government. Foreign-controlled firms— Nissan Motor Company Ltd. (makers of Datsun) and Toyota Motor Company Ltd.—also qualify as leading advertisers in the United States. A listing of twenty leading national advertisers appears in Table 12-1.

Total U.S. advertising expenditures are approaching $30 billion annually, with an average yearly growth rate of more than 6 percent in recent years. This means that nearly $150 is spent in advertising each year for every person in the United States. A recent study based on Internal Revenue sources showed that advertising expenditures averaged 1.08 percent of sales for 217 product or service classifications. The range was from iron-ore mining with zero reported advertising expenditure to soaps, cleaners, and toilet goods which spent 8.95 percent of sales revenue on advertising.[5] The advertising expenditures for major industry groupings are shown in Table 12-2.

TYPES OF ADVERTISING There are two basic types of advertising: product and institutional. **Product advertising** involves *the nonpersonal selling of a good or service.*

Industry	Percent
Total active corporation returns	1.08
Agriculture, forestry and fisheries	0.31
Mining	0.17
Contract construction	0.20
Manufacturing	1.36
Transportation, communication, electric, gas, and sanitary services	0.48
Wholesale and retail trade	1.01
Finance, insurance, and real estate	0.29
Services	1.43

SOURCE: *Advertising Age* (September 30, 1974), p., 76.

The "Goodrich, Not Goodyear" Campaign

Patrick C. Ross, the chief executive at B.F. Goodrich, believes that advertising policy is a top management responsibility that cannot be delegated. He became personally involved in the development of Goodrich's successful "Goodrich, Not Goodyear" advertising campaigns.

Goodrich's market research showed two important facts:

1. Consumers are reluctant to buy tires, and regard the purchase process as a nuisance. Consumers know very little about tires or their value.

"Get in there and show them why they pay you five grand just to shave on TV."

Advertising Can Be Very Expensive

SOURCE: *The Wall Street Journal*, August 2, 1973. Reprinted with permission from *The Wall Street Journal*.

2. Consumers could not differentiate between Goodyear and Goodrich; and since Goodyear spent more on advertising, they usually got credit for innovations.

Separate research by Grey Advertising, Goodrich's ad agency, confirmed the name confusion problem. Grey recommended that Goodrich either change its name or confront the name confusion problem in its advertising program.

Ross opted for the "Goodrich, Not Goodyear" advertising campaign that put him before television cameras attempting to clear up the name confusion, increase Goodrich's radial brand awareness, and position his company as the leader in radials (they were the first to introduce the U.S. radial). Ross was quick to point out:

. . . I did not approve the campaign because of the talent that was selected. As a matter of fact one of our competitors said it was a shame we couldn't afford professional talent.

The results of the "Goodrich, Not Goodyear" campaign were astounding. Average recall of the commercials shot up to 50 percent, compared with Goodrich's normal 10 percent. Even though Goodyear continued to spend more on its advertising program, Goodrich's proven recall outscored theirs on nearly a five to one basis. Other audience statistics show that consumers now recognize B.F. Goodrich as the leading innovator in the industry. Consumer brand preference for Goodrich also improved remarkably.

Source: Adapted from Patrick C. Ross. "Goodrich, Not Goodyear Works at Telling It Straight," *Advertising Age* (October 7, 1974), pp. 63–69.

Institutional advertising concerns *the promotion of a concept, idea, philosophy, or good will of an industry, company, organization, or governmental entity.* "Guns Don't Kill People, People Kill People" is a theme utilized as part of the Firearms Safety Education program of the National Rifle Association of America.*

The California Prune Advisory Board took an innovative approach to institutional advertising.

The California Prune Advisory Board

California growers, who supply most of the nation's prune needs, realized they were on the wrong track when per capita consumption declined to one pound a year in 1969 from 2.1 pounds in 1945. The problems were many, concedes Harold Brogger, California Prune Advisory Board marketing director. Among them were the fact that prunes "were sold mainly as a laxative" and that "they were a wrinkled fruit, associated with old age."

So the Prune Board launched a "funny fruit" campaign in late 1971 with radio ads punctuated with laughter whenever prunes are mentioned. Result: Prune sales rose 10 percent in fiscal 1972 only to drop in 1973 when bad weather and other factors left growers with less than half their usual 160,000-ton crop. But prune people count on a return to fiscal 1972 gains . . .

*Reprinted with permission from the National Rifle Association of America.

Figure 12-1
Relationship between
Advertising and the
Product Life Cycle

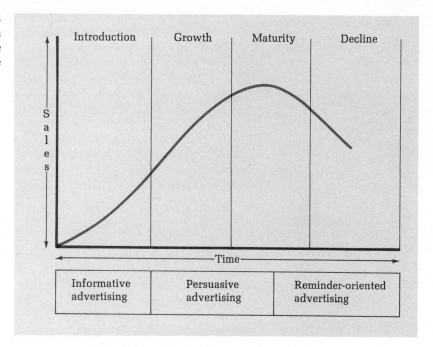

What's more, they claim consumer awareness of prunes has increased 20 percent because of the ad campaign. What about prunes' poor image? Says Mr. Brogger, "there's too much history to expect it to be obliterated in three years, but people's attitudes toward prunes have probably improved."

Source: *The Wall Street Journal* (February 21, 1974), p. 1. Reprinted with permission of *The Wall Street Journal,* © Dow Jones & Company, Inc. 1974. All rights reserved.

RELATIONSHIP BETWEEN ADVERTISING AND THE PRODUCT LIFE CYCLE

Advertising strategy for a product varies according to its stage in the product life cycle (*see* Figure 12-1). **Informative advertising** is intended *to build initial demand for a product;* and is used in the introductory phase of the product life cycle. New toothpaste and shampoos are introduced to consumers through advertising.

The Australian Tourist Commission designed an informative promotional campaign to get young Australians to explore their country. The campaign was based on a free, youth-oriented booklet, *Australia—A Land of Things to Do,* that listed hostels, watering holes (of the alcoholic variety), places to crash, surfing beaches, and the like.

Persuasive advertising attempts *to improve the competitive status of a product, institution, or concept.* It is used in the growth and maturity stages of the product life cycle. "Virginia is for Lovers"* is a persuasive institutional advertising theme.

*Reprinted with permission from the Virginia State Travel Service (6 North Sixth Street, Richmond, Virginia 23219).

Should Television Advertising Directed at Children Be Banned?

Children across the country spend long periods of time in front of television sets; some spend as much as six hours a day. Before children are old enough to go to school, they are watching during the day. For them the television set takes the place of a parent or caretaker. When they are older, children often watch "the tube" instead of doing homework or reading. In this respect they are not very different from adults.

Although many critics are primarily concerned with the violence on television that children see and imitate, such organizations as Action for Children's Television (ACT) are also concerned with the quality of advertising on television, especially since children are young enough not to be able to distinguish between the "fiction" part of the program and the ads.

Critics see advertising directed at children as setting up a pattern of wants that may continue into adult life. The fact that these often are not real *needs* is part of the problem. If children demand that their families buy a particular cereal because they see and hear it advertised on a favorite program, family disorganization can result. Children who demand to know why the cereal is not eaten at home probably are not old enough to understand that their parents object to the cereal because it is too

sugary and does not provide good nutrition. Children from low-income families who see expensive toys on television, particulary around holiday times, may recognize that the family cannot afford such items, but that will not make them feel any better.

Television advertising can also reinforce aggressive and competitive tendencies in children who want to be first with an item. Critics declare such advertising is unethical and distasteful. Federal agencies have taken the position that television advertising directed at children should be self-regulated by the broadcasting industry in its own interest.

Others believe that parents and caretakers should assume responsibility for their children's television viewing, since they control their children. Without advertising, which sponsors children's programs of high quality, many good programs with educational and socially desirable content would not be aired.

Furthermore, these supporters believe that certain kinds of ads teach good habits—how to brush your teeth properly, for instance. And other advertisements allow children to enjoy the fantasies that the ads project. The critics, however, add that children are more sophisticated than adults realize and that they can discriminate between ads and content.

One of the latest trends in persuasive product advertising is to *make direct comparisons with competitive products.* The use of **comparative advertising** has been encouraged by the Federal Trade Commission, the regulatory agency involved in such matters. Carte Blanche, the credit card firm, now advertises that "as good as American Express is, it isn't enough"; then goes on to cite the advantages of its card. It is uncertain at this point what the long-run status of comparative advertising will be in the United States and abroad. But its use has certainly changed forever the veiled comparisons that used to be made with "Product X."[6]

Reminder-oriented advertising is used in the late maturity and decline stages of the product life cycle. Reminder-oriented advertising attempts *to keep a product's name in front of the consumer, or to remind people of a concept's or institution's importance in our society.* Soft drinks, beer, toothpaste, and cigarettes are examples of products that use reminder-oriented advertising. FMC Corporation of Chicago has created an advertisement that says: "Suddenly the World Sees a Future for Coal."* Even police cars in some areas of the United States carry reminder-oriented themes, such as: "To Protect and to Serve."

Personal Selling

Personal selling is defined as *a promotional presentation made on a person-to-person basis with a potential buyer.* Selling was the original method of promotion, and it now employs about 10 percent of the U.S. labor force. The cost of selling averages about 12.5 cents of every sales dollar.[7]

The sales function of most companies is changing rapidly. In some cases the change has only been cosmetic, such as when the title "salesperson" is changed to "sales representative," but the job function remains the same. Yet many companies are making significant changes in their sales forces. Sales duties have been expanded, and in some cases the function itself has actually changed. For instance, the energy crisis and shortages of some raw materials have involved sales personnel in the problems of allocating insufficient supplies. Salespersons should be advisors to their customers, helping them to utilize the items they buy more efficiently. For example, Energy Consulting Services is the new name for Consumers Power Company's (Jackson, Michigan) marketing department.[8]

SALES TASKS   A salesperson's work can vary significantly from one company or situation to another. Three basic sales tasks can be identified:

*Reprinted with permission from FMC Corporation, Chicago.

1. order-receiving
2. creative selling
3. missionary sales.

Most sales personnel perform all three tasks to some degree. A salesperson of a highly technical product may be doing 55 percent in missionary sales, 40 percent in creative selling, and 5 percent in order-receiving. By contrast, some retail salespeople may be doing 70 percent in order-receiving, 15 percent in creative selling, and 15 percent in missionary selling. Marketers often use these three sales tasks as a method of classifying a particular sales job. The designation is based on the *primary* task that is performed by the salesperson.

Order-receiving

Order-receiving involves *the simple processing of an order.* Customer needs are identified, then pointed out to the consumer, and the order is processed. Route sales personnel for such consumer products as bread, milk, and soft drinks are examples. Sales personnel check a store's stock level, report the inventory level to the store manager, and complete the purchase.

Most sales jobs have at least a minor order-receiving function. It becomes the primary duty in cases where needs are readily identified and acknowledged by the customer. Consider Danny McNaughton's sales position in Belfast, Ireland. He works for the Chicago-based Combined Insurance Company of America. During the peak of the Belfast riots McNaughton sold 208 new personal accident

"Our ad said no salesman would call — I am a Consumer Advisory Consultant!"

The Sales Job Has Changed Considerably in Recent Years

SOURCE: *The Wall Street Journal,* June 5, 1974. Reprinted with permission from *The Wall Street Journal.*

income protection policies in a week, averaging one sale every twelve minutes of his working day.[9] Belfast residents readily acknowledged the need for McNaughton's product!

Creative selling

Sales representatives for most industrial goods and some consumer goods are involved in **creative selling.** This is *a persuasive type of promotional presentation.* Creative selling is used when the benefits of using a product are not readily apparent, and/or the purchase is based on a careful analysis of alternatives. New product selling is a situation where the salesperson must be very creative if initial orders are to be secured.

Missionary sales

The **missionary sales** task is *an indirect form of selling where the representative markets the good will of a company and/or provides technical or operational assistance to the customer.* For example, many technically-based organizations, such as I.B.M. and Xerox, provide systems specialists who consult with their customers. These people are problem-solvers and sometimes work on situations not directly involving their employer's products.

THE SALES PROCESS Years ago sales personnel memorized a sales talk provided by their employers. These **canned sales presentations,** as they are called, were intended *to provide all the information that the customer needed to make a purchase decision.* The entire sales process was viewed as a situation where the prospective customer was passive and ready to buy if the correct sales formula could be found and presented by the representative.

Contemporary selling recognizes that the interaction between buyers and sellers rules out canned presentations in all but the simplest of sales situations. Modern sales personnel usually follow a sequential pattern, but the actual presentation will vary according to the circumstances. Seven steps can be identified in the sales process:

1. prospecting and qualifying
2. approach
3. presentation
4. demonstration
5. handling objections
6. closing
7. follow-up.

Prospecting and Qualifying Prospecting is the task of identifying potential customers. These may come from many sources: previous customers, friends, business associates, neighbors, other sales personnel, nonsales employees in the firm, and the like. **Prospects,** as *potential customers* are called, must then be qualified with respect to their financial ability and their authority to buy.

Approach   Salespersons should carefully prepare their approaches to potential customers. All available information about the prospect should be collected and analyzed. Sales representatives should always remember that the initial impression given to prospects often indicates their future attitudes.

Presentation   The presentation stage is when the salesperson transmits a promotional message. The usual method is to describe the product's major features, highlight its advantages, and to conclude by citing examples of consumer satisfaction.

Demonstration   Demonstrations allow the prospect to become involved in the presentation. They supplement, support, and reinforce the message that the sales representative has been communicating to the prospective buyer.

Handling Objections   Many salespeople fear objections from the prospect because they view them as a rebuke to their sales presentations. Actually, salespersons should welcome objections because they allow them to present additional sales points and to answer any questions that the consumer has about the product.

Closing   Closing is the critical point in selling. This is when the seller actually asks the prospect for an order. Several effective closing techniques have been identified. Sometimes the salesperson simply asks the prospect directly. At other times alternative purchases are proposed. And in some cases the salesperson does something that implies the sale has already been completed, such as walking toward a cash register. This forces the prospect to say "no," if he or she does not want to complete the sale.

Follow-up   Post-sales activities are very important in determining whether a new customer will become a repeat customer. After the prospect has agreed to buy, the salesperson should complete the order-processing quickly and efficiently, and assure the customer about the purchase decision. Later, the representative should check with the customer to see that the product is performing satisfactorily.

SALES MANAGEMENT   Consider a management problem faced by Procter & Gamble. They have a field sales force numbering several thousand representatives. The sheer size of the Procter & Gamble sales force would trigger numerous organizational, personnel selection, training, motivation, supervision, and evaluation questions. But all sales forces—regardless of size—face similar circumstances. Such problems must be

Figure 12-2
Typical Sales
Management
Organization for
a Large Company

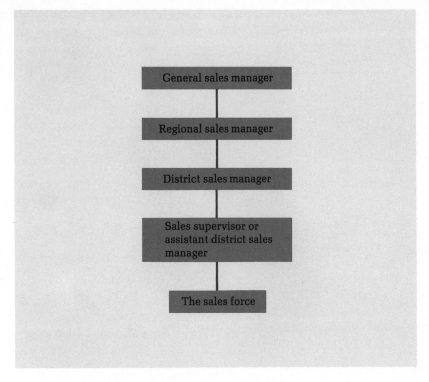

solved if the sales force is to be truly effective and achieve the firm's promotional strategy objectives.

A company's sales function is supervised by multiple layers of sales managers. Advancement to such positions are usually from the field sales force. The sales management organizational structure follows a format somewhat along the lines shown in Figure 12-2.

The general sales manager usually has national, and sometimes international, responsibilities. The market is then broken down into one or more levels, such as regions and districts. The exact terminology varies from company to company. Alternative organizational structures sometimes break the total market down into product or customer classifications. Figure 12-2 uses the title sales supervisor (or assistant district sales manager) to indicate the final level of management responsibility. Positions of this nature are often held by senior sales personnel who are responsible for **key accounts** (*major customers*), and who assume managerial duties such as sales training.

Sales managers are required to perform various managerial tasks. These are shown in Figure 12-3. They must analyze the organization's sales personnel needs and then recruit the appropriate number of candidates, who are then screened for eventual selection. Sales managers are closely involved in the training and development of sales personnel and the organizational structure that is employed.

Figure 12-3
The Sales
Management Tasks

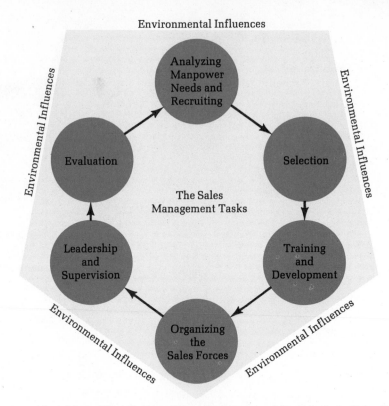

SOURCE: Adapted from Albert H. Dunn, Eugene M. Johnson, and David L. Kurtz, *Sales Management: Concepts, Practices, and Cases* (Morristown, N.J.: General Learning Press, 1974), p. 45.

Leadership and supervision are a natural part of the sales management role. Finally, sales managers must be involved in the evaluation of their sales forces and in making recommendations on salary adjustments, promotions, and dismissals. All sales management tasks are performed subject to the environmental influences that exist in competitive business surroundings.

Sales Promotion

Sales promotion can be defined as *those forms of promotion other than advertising and personal selling that increase sales through nonrecurrent selling efforts.* Sales-promotion techniques are used to enhance and supplement the firm's sales or advertising efforts. They are supporting, one-time aspects of a firm's promotional strategy.

POINT-OF-
PURCHASE
ADVERTISING

Point-of-purchase advertising, or P.O.P. as it is called, includes *displays and demonstrations promoting an item at a time and place near the place of the actual purchase decision,* such as in a retail store. P.O.P. can be very effective in continuing a theme developed in some other aspect of the firm's promotional strategy.[10] For example, the L'eggs displays in supermarkets revolutionized the pantyhose industry.

SPECIALTY ADVERTISING **Specialty advertising** includes such items as pens, calendars, and ash trays that are *valued at less than $4 and are imprinted with the donor's company*.[11] Actually, specialty advertising has been around for years. Artisans in the Middle Ages gave knights wooden pegs (bearing the artisan's name) to use in hanging up their armor.[12]

TRADE SHOWS **Trade shows** are often used to promote products to various resellers in the distribution channel. Retailers and wholesalers attend various trade conventions and shows *where manufacturers exhibit their different lines*. Trade shows are very important in the toy, furniture, and fashion industries. They have also been used to promote the products of one nation to buyers in another country. Eastern European countries have done this very effectively in recent years.

SAMPLES, COUPONS, PREMIUMS, AND TRADING STAMPS **Samples** are *free gifts of products used in an attempt to get public acceptance of the products that will result in future sales*. Samples are particularly useful in the promotion of new products. **Coupons** are *advertising inserts or package inclusions that are redeemable for price discounts with retailers*. They offer a small price discount, and can be helpful in getting a consumer to try a new or different product. **Premiums** are *small gifts that are provided when a consumer buys a product*. They can also be helpful in introducing a new product, or getting consumers to try a different brand. **Trading stamps** are similar to premiums in that they are *redeemable for additional merchandise*. Historically, trading stamps have been used to build loyalty to a certain retailer or supplier.

PROMOTIONAL CONTESTS **Promotional contests** offering *cash or merchandise as prizes* are also considered sales promotion techniques. Promotional contests are useful in getting consumers to consider new products. They are usually designed by specialists in this field.

Selecting a Promotional Strategy

The selection of a promotional strategy is dependent upon a number of variables. The basic decision is whether an organization is going to emphasize advertising or personal selling in the strategy. Sales promotion techniques are nearly always used in a supporting role to either personal selling or advertising.

ALTERNATIVE PROMOTIONAL ACTIVITIES Marketers can use either a pushing or a pulling promotional strategy to achieve their goals. A **pushing strategy** is a *sales-oriented approach*. The product or product line is promoted to the middlemen (wholesalers and retailers) in the marketing channels. Sales personnel explain to the middlemen why it would be desirable to carry this particular item in their inventories. The middlemen are usually offered special discounts, promotional materials, and **cooperative advertising allowances** (*where the manufacturer shares the cost of local advertising of the product or line*). All of these are designed to motivate the middlemen to push the product to his or her customers.

A **pulling strategy** attempts to *stimulate final user demand for the product or product line.* This is done primarily through advertising and sales promotion appeals. Most advertising is aimed at the ultimate consumer. When the consumer asks the retailer for the product, the retailer will in turn request the item from a supplier. This results in pulling the product through the marketing channel. The marketer hopes that strong consumer demand will literally *pull* the product through the channel by forcing middlemen to carry the item.

Most marketing situations require the use of both strategies, although the relative mix can vary. Many consumer products are heavily dependent upon a pulling strategy; while most industrial products emphasize a pushing strategy.

Summary

Most organizations use some type of promotional strategy to reach their goals. Promotional strategy has four specific objectives or goals:

1. provide information
2. increase sales
3. position the product
4. stabilize sales.

There are three distinct elements of promotional strategy:

1. advertising
2. personal selling
3. sales promotion.

Advertising can be defined as a nonpersonal sales presentation usually directed to a large number of potential customers. Personal selling is a promotional presentation made on a person-to-person basis with a potential buyer. Sales promotion includes the supporting, nonrecurrent aspects of a firm's promotional strategy such as specialty advertising, point-of-purchase advertising, and promotional contests.

This chapter has examined the role of advertising, types of advertising, sales tasks, the selling process, sales management, and various sales promotion techniques. It concluded with a discussion concerning the selection of alternative promotional strategies.

Review questions

1. Identify the following terms:
   a. promotional strategy
   b. positioning
   c. advertising
   d. product advertising
   e. institutional advertising
   f. comparative advertising
   g. personal selling
   h. canned sales presentation
   i. prospect
   j. qualifying
   k. closing
   l. key accounts
   m. P.O.P.

2. Outline the objectives of promotional strategy.

3. As a class project try to find examples of advertisements used by each of the leading national advertisers listed in Table 12-1.

4. Relate the various types of advertising that are used in modern business to the product life cycle.

5. What is the primary sales task involved in the following occupations:
   a. selling typewriters to local business firms
   b. counter personnel at Burger Chef
   c. representative for an outdoor advertising firm
   d. industrial salesperson representing Dow Chemical.

6. Describe the steps in the selling process.

7. Outline the six tasks of sales management.

8. What type of sales promotion technique would you use (if any) in these businesses:
   a. independent insurance agent
   b. Chevrolet dealer
   c. cocktail lounge
   d. grocery wholesaler.

9. Differentiate between a pushing and a pulling promotional strategy.

10. Would you emphasize personal selling or advertising to promote these products:
    a. drill press
    b. imported transistor radios
    c. specialty steel products sold to manufacturers
    d. funeral services.

Discussion questions and exercises

1. Evaluate the pro and con arguments to the controversial issue that appears in this chapter.

2. The Federal Trade Commission proposed a ban on television advertisements that featured premiums in such products as cereal. The FTC argued that these items have wide appeal to children, and detract from the real merits of the product. What is your

opinion of this argument? (One way to discuss this question is to set up a class debate between the alternative viewpoints.)

3. How would you go about positioning a razor blade for college-aged women?

4. Divide the class into three groups identified as A, B, and C. Then set up a role-playing exercise in which each student in Group A sells a product to someone in Group B. Group C is responsible for providing a critique of each of the sales interviews. Then rotate the roles among the three groups. For instance, B becomes the sellers, C the prospects, and A provides the critique. Continue this process for three rounds so everyone will have had a chance to play each role.

5. *Advertising Age* (September 16, 1974, p. 92) reported a survey indicating that men are the primary decision makers in 65 percent of all automobile purchases. How would this fact affect the prospecting and qualifying efforts of a retail salesperson? Discuss.

Case 12-1

Four-Walling *American Wilderness*

American Wilderness was one of the lowest-cost movies ever produced in the United States. The movie consisted of nature footage shot by Arthur Dubs on his hunting trips. It cost Dubs' firm, Pacific International Enterprises of Wedford, Oregon, about $50,000 to shoot and splice the film with its narrative. *American Wilderness* grossed over $10.5 million for Pacific International which Dubs claims is the all-time record for returns over costs on a movie.

Based on the success of *American Wilderness,* Pacific International bought additional nature footage for $168,000, and issued this as *Vanishing Wilderness.* This film grossed nearly $13 million.

Dubs' strategy is based on what has come to be called "four-walling." This approach is a complete reversal of the traditional system of promoting movies. The standard way is to introduce an expensively-produced movie in one or two theaters in various cities around the country. The distributor counts on good critical reviews of the picture, so that it can be shown in several theaters in each city—so-called "red carpet exhibition." Later, if the movie proves successful, it is featured in neighborhood theaters in what is called "showcase exhibition."

Advertising costs in this strategy are shared between the distributor and the theater owner. The distributor gets a minimum of 30–35 percent of the gross receipts, and up to 70 percent if the picture is very successful.

The term "four-walling" is based on the fact that movie promoters go to one city at a time and rent every theater available at a flat rate. Then every available dollar goes into an advertising blitz designed to pull in as many people as possible in a one- to two-week period, before the promoters depart for another town. Four-wall movie distributors usually follow these guidelines:

1. Do not spend over $300,000 in making the movie.
2. Stick to G-rated or GP material to keep full access to all advertising media and all theaters.
3. Make the television commercials first, then build the rest of the picture around them. The commercials are what count.
4. Distribute the movie in one television market at a time, to save expenditure for prints and personnel.
5. Move from the smallest television market on your itinerary to the biggest, so you are test-marketing your advertising techniques at the lowest cost.
6. Rent only low-cost theaters. Usually, a $3,000 per week rental should be tops.
7. Rent the maximum possible number of theaters in the area that meet budget requirements.
8. The best four-wall months are November, January, and February when television ratings are highest and movie audiences lowest. That way the commercials are most effective and the theater rentals cheapest.

Pacific International is not the only firm following a four-wall strategy. Others include American National Enterprises and Sun International Enterprises; recently major movie studios have adopted four-walling techniques, particularly on second releases of a film. *Billy Jack, Poseidon Adventure,* and *The Exorcist* were promoted in this manner.

Questions

1. Have you seen any of these "four-walled" movies?

American Wilderness	*Brother of the Wind*
Vanishing Wilderness	*Cougar Country*
Alaska Safari	*North Country*
Chariot of the Gods	*Cry of the Wild*
Toklat	*The Great American Cowboy*

   What was your impression of the film?
2. What is your opinion of the advertising blitz used in a "four-walling" strategy? Discuss.
3. Can you identify any other possible application of a "four-wall" promotional strategy?

Source: Based on Jonathan Kwitny. "In Four-walling, the Way You Sell the Movie is More Important than the Way You Make It," *The Wall Street Journal* (September 3, 1974), p. 26. Reprinted with permission of *The Wall Street Journal,* © Dow Jones & Company, Inc. 1974. All rights reserved.

Case 12-2

"My Name is ACE and I Represent the All Steel Pipe and Tube Company of St. Louis"

Improved sales productivity has always been an objective of sales managers. It is a particularly important goal during times of rising sales costs.

One of the best ways to improve sales force productivity is to direct calls to people who have a high likelihood of buying. This strategy requires that much of the original prospecting effort be done by others. As a result, some firms have set up special prospecting forces of parttime employees like housewives and students. These people give an initial, standardized sales presentation and try to assess prospect interest. If the interviewee appears to be interested, a follow-up call is made by one of the company's sales representatives.

Ennis Business Forms has adopted an interesting modification of this prospecting strategy. Ennis uses a miniature robot to spot prospects. These robots are twelve inches high and are mailed to sales leads in attaché cases. They are equipped with a recorded message, a brochure, printing samples, and request cards to be sent back to Ennis. Real "live" sales representatives follow up with interested prospects.

But Ennis is not the only firm employing a robot sales force. The All Steel Pipe and Tube Company of St. Louis uses a force of eighteen-inch robots named "ACE" to present a seven-minute recorded sales message. "ACE" has proven so successful that the robots are currently closing about 25 percent of "calls to key customers."

Questions

1. Assume you are the purchasing director for a company that might use the products of either Ennis Business Forms or The All Steel Pipe and Tool Company. How would you react to receiving a robot in the mail?
2. Will ACE ever completely replace "flesh and blood" salespeople in your opinion? Discuss.
3. Comment on the advantages and disadvantages of using a special prospecting force rather than regular salespeople.

Source: The use of these robots is described in "The Battle to Boost Sales Productivity," *Business Week* (February 12, 1972), pp. 68–69; "Now: The Ersatz Salesman," *SME Forum* (September 1973), pp. 3–4; and *The Wall Street Journal* (March 22, 1973), p. 1.

13

Prices and Pricing Strategy

"We budget quarterly and plug virtually every pricing factor into the computer."

—Donald W. Fuller,
President of Microdata Corporation

"[Today] a man making $20,000 a year can barely afford to buy a $40,000 house."

—Atlanta Builder Lewis Canker,
Former President of the National Association of Home Builders

What Chapter 13 Is All About

1. This chapter demonstrates the societal and business importance of pricing.
2. You will be able to identify the pricing objectives of different types of businesses.
3. You will understand why inflation is the most critical topic in pricing today, and how consumers and businesses are attempting to combat it.
4. You will learn how prices are actually determined by marketers.
5. New product pricing, price lining, price-quality relationships, and psychological pricing will become familiar to you.
6. After reading this chapter, you should understand these terms:

price	supply curve
inflation	mark-up
demand-pull inflation	stock turnover
cost-push inflation	fixed costs
stagflation	variable costs
demand curve	odd pricing

Jim Augustus
("Catfish") Hunter

A country boy from Perquimans County, North Carolina, Jim ("Catfish") Hunter likes to hunt, fish, and play baseball. Since 1975 Catfish Hunter also has been the highest paid player in baseball history.

Major league baseball scouts had known about Hunter since 1965, when he was pitching for Perquimans High School. At that time a hunting accident caused Hunter to lose the little toe of his right foot. During the baseball season that followed, Hunter seemed to have lost some of his star quality. He pitched well, but not startlingly so. Clyde Kluttz, scouting for the Kansas City A's, persuaded owner Charles O. Finley to sign Hunter for about $50,000. At the Mayo Clinic, where Kluttz took the young player, shotgun pellets previously left in the foot by the doctor who first attended him were removed. Now he was really ready to pitch.

With a record of World Series and All-Star games made while he was with the A's both in Kansas City and in Oakland, California, Hunter decided he wanted security for his family after he was too old to play baseball. At twenty-eight he left the A's when an impartial arbitrator declared him to be a free agent, despite the legal battle put up by A's owner Charley Finley. Hunter became one of the rare major league baseball players who was able to transform the theory of supply and demand into reality, as one club representative after another traveled to North Carolina during the winter of 1974–1975 with contract offers. Hunter accepted the offer of a five-year contract from the New York Yankees estimated to be worth $3.75 million, with an annual salary of about $200,000 and a bonus of $1 million. The Yankees had outbid the other teams interested in acquiring a pitcher of Hunter's star quality. Hunter's earnings with the A's in 1974 had amounted to $100,000 and he had won twenty-five games.

Hunter took with him his talent as a pitcher and his nickname, given to him by Finley when he heard that young Jimmy would not eat any fish but catfish. The pitcher left behind him a very angry former owner and the number 27. For the Yankees Hunter plays as Number 29.

Prices are a standard topic of conversation around the world. This is particularly true during times when prices seem to change almost daily. Families complain about rising meat, sugar, and vegetable prices. Farmers argue that livestock and wheat prices are too low to support their families. Businesspersons are busy improving production efficiency in order to hold down costs and their retail prices.

Recently inflation has boosted food prices to unparalleled highs. The U.S. Department of Agriculture estimates that a "liberal cost" diet for a twenty to thirty-four-year-old male is about $2.64 per day. The U.S. Department of Defense spends $2.28 per day on food for each soldier. This is in remarkable contrast to the Continental

Army of 1776 that allowed 11¢ per day for enlisted personnel and 33¢ for officers. George Washington was allowed the enormous sum of $5.28 daily. The American Medical Association reports that the 1776 ration included more meat than our modern diets do:

1 pound of fresh beef
or salt fish

3/4 of a pound of pork
or 20 ounces of salt beef

1 pound of bread
1 pint of milk

Experts say that the 1776 enlisted man's ration would now cost about $3.00 per day, and was deficient in Vitamins A and C.[1]

It seems likely that Colonial housewives, soldiers, farmers, businessmen, and consumers also complained about "high prices." The whole concept of prices and pricing has always been a much discussed, but little understood, topic. This chapter seeks to explain prices and to show the role of pricing in the modern business system.

The Meaning and Importance of Prices

The value of any item—consumer product, industrial product, or service—is its exchange value in the marketplace. An item is worth only what someone else is willing to pay for it. In a primitive society the exchange value may be determined by trading a good for some other commodity. A horse might be worth two coins; twelve apples might be worth two loaves of bread. More advanced societies use money as the medium of exchange. But in either case, a product's **price** *is its exchange value.*

All goods offer some utility, or want-satisfying, power. Individual preferences determine how much utility a consumer will associate with a particular good or service. Leisure-time pursuits might be valued highly by one person, while the next-door neighbor assigns a higher priority to acquiring real assets—such as property, automobiles, and household furnishings.

Consumers face an allocation problem. They have a limited amount of money and a variety of possible uses for it. The price system helps us make these allocation decisions. A person might

"There's a gentleman from the medical association to see you, Doctor."

Would a Lower Price Persuade Someone to Give Up a New Set of Golf Clubs for an Appendectomy?

SOURCE: Reprinted with permission from the May 20, 1974 issue of *Advertising Age*. Copyright 1974 by Crain Communications Inc.

prefer a new color television to a vacation; but if the price of the television set were to rise, the consumer might reconsider and allocate his limited funds to the vacation trip.

Prices help to direct the overall economic system. A firm uses various factors of production (such as land, labor, and capital) based on the relative prices received by such factors. High wage rates may cause a firm to install new labor-saving machinery. Similarly, high interest rates may lead management to decide against a new capital expenditure. Prices and the volume sold also determine the revenue received by the firm, and influence its profits.

Everyone recognizes the importance that prices play in our daily lives. But no one has ever determined what is the *correct* price for any situation. Early philosophers struggled with the issue as they tried to define a just price. Today consumers may want lower retail prices, yet some also complain of the lack of retail service. All services—such as gift wrapping, delivery, and credit—have some amount of costs associated with them, and these costs must be covered by higher prices. The unanswered question is how do we balance these prices and costs?

Pricing Objectives

Management attempts to accomplish certain objectives through its pricing decisions. Research has shown that multiple pricing objectives are common among many firms.[2] Some companies try to maximize their profits by pricing a new technological innovation very high. Others may use low prices to attract new business. A Miami funeral home now offers a cash-and-carry cremation service. The firm collects the deceased, arranges the cremation, and returns the ashes to the relatives in a cardboard box—all for less than $150![3]

There are three basic categories of pricing objectives. These are:

1. profitability objectives
2. volume objectives
3. social and ethical considerations, status quo objectives, and image goals.

Profitability objectives include profit maximization and target return goals. Volume objectives are stated in terms of either sales maximization or market share goals.

PROFITABILITY OBJECTIVES

Most firms have some type of profitability objective for their pricing strategy. Management knows that:

$$\text{Profit} = \text{revenue} - \text{expenses},$$

and that revenue is a result of the selling prices and the quantity sold:

$$\text{Total revenue} = \text{price} \times \text{quantity sold.}$$

Some firms may try to maximize profits by increasing their prices to the point where a disproportionate decrease appears in the number of units sold. A 10 percent price hike that results in only 8 percent volume decline increases profitability. But a 5 percent price rise that reduces the number of units sold by 6 percent is unprofitable.

Profit maximization is the basis of much of economic theory. However, it is often difficult to apply in practice, and many firms have turned to a simpler profitability objective—*target return* goals. U.S. Steel seeks an 8 percent return on investment (after taxes). General Electric tries to obtain a 7 percent profit (after taxes) on each sales dollar.[4] Most target return pricing goals state the desired profitability in terms of a return on either sales or investment.

VOLUME OBJECTIVES

Another description of pricing behavior is the *sales maximization concept.*[5] This says that management sets a minimum level of profitability that is acceptable and then tries to maximize sales as long as the profitability level is met. Sales expansion is viewed as being more important to the firm's long-term competitive position than are short-run profits.

A second volume objective is *market share,* or the percentage of a market controlled by a certain company or product. U.S. Steel has a target market share of 30 percent.[6] Still other companies seek to maintain or expand their market shares for particular products or product lines. Several brewers have added seven-ounce bottles in an attempt to reach the female market. Anheuser-Busch, Schmidt's, and Miller Brewing have joined the Latrobe Brewing Company of Pennsylvania which has marketed seven-ounce bottles of Rolling Rock beer since 1939. Anheuser-Busch even advertised its Michelob version, Mich VII, in *Women's Day* magazine.[7]

The Great Maine-New Hampshire Liquor Price War

Both New Hampshire and Maine operate state-owned liquor stores. Traditionally, the New Hampshire stores have maintained low liquor prices, while Maine's have been among the highest in the U.S. Many Maine residents regularly buy in New Hampshire. In fact, New Hampshire sells about $100,000,000 in its 58 stores annually, while Maine, with a larger population, only manages $40,000,000 per year in its 88 stores.

In May 1971, the Maine legislature retaliated by deciding to build a discount liquor store at Kittery only four miles from New Hampshire's Portsmouth store (the largest in the state). Maine legislators reasoned that the strategic location at Kittery and competitive prices would stop the out-migration of Maine liquor buyers. But, the lawmakers were in for a surprise!

The Kittery store opened in July 1973, and did over $2,000,000 in sales in the first four months. Still, Maine officials are far from happy. The fact that Kittery prices are significantly cheaper than the state's other 87 stores brought on numerous charges of price discrimination by citizens in other parts of the state. Editorial writers throughout Maine assailed the state's dual pricing policy.

During the same period, the Portsmouth, New Hampshire, store reported a 5 percent increase in volume. Maine residents continued to buy their spirits in New Hampshire. An Augusta woman told a reporter "If I'm going to have to drive 109 miles, I might as well go four more." Consumer resentments to Maine's pricing policy remains widespread in the state.

THE OBVIOUS QUESTION   Who is buying all of the liquor at Maine's Kittery Store?

THE ANSWER   Maine restaurant and cocktail lounge operators who are required to sell only Maine-bought liquor. Where they used to buy at stores near their establishments, they now travel to Kittery to take advantage of Maine's dual price system.

Source: David Gumpert. "Wherein the State of Maine Gets Lessons in Pricing Strategy," *The Wall Street Journal* (November 16, 1973), p. 1. Reprinted with permission of *The Wall Street Journal* © Dow Jones & Company, Inc. 1973. All rights reserved.

Market share objectives have become popular for several reasons:

1. They are easily measured, and can be used by management in evaluating company performance.
2. Managers believe that higher sales leads to higher profits because of *economies of scale* (on a per unit basis, it is cheaper to produce 1,000 ballpoint pens than it is to produce a dozen).
3. Many managers possess a psychological drive to grow. Organizational growth is seen as personal growth by some people.

OTHER OBJECTIVES

Other objectives—not related to profitability or sales volume—are important in the pricing decisions of some firms. These include:

1. social and ethical considerations
2. status quo objectives
3. image goals.

Social and ethical considerations play an important role in some pricing situations. For example, the prices of some products and services are based on the person's ability to pay a certain price. Medical insurance premiums, union dues, and retirement fund contributions are often related to the income of the payers. It seems reasonable to believe that social and ethical considerations will be even more important in future pricing strategies.

Firms may possess *status quo* pricing objectives. They are inclined to follow the leader. When one firm sets a price, everyone in the vicinity goes along. These companies seek stable prices that will allow them to put their competitive efforts into other areas, such as product design or promotion.

Neiman-Marcus, Tiffany, and Chanel No. 5—all illustrate the use of *image goals* in pricing strategy. Their price structures are set to reflect the quality of the merchandise. By contrast, a discount house seeks to achieve a consumer image of "good value at low prices." In many cases a firm's pricing may be an integral part of the overall image the company wishes to put forth.

Prices and Inflation

Inflation (which can be *defined either in terms of rising prices or the decreased purchasing power of a nation's currency*) characterizes today's prices. Inflation has often been a critical economic problem. Consider the situation in post-World War I Europe. Both victors and losers suffered the agony of unprecedented inflation. In Austria and Hungary the currency fell to 1/15,000th of its former worth. Poland's ratio was 1/2,000,000th; while Russia's money dropped to 1/50,000th million of its prewar value. But the greatest inflation was reserved for Germany's postwar government, where the currency circulation reached hundreds of millions of marks. Consider these German prices:

$$1 \text{ egg} = 80,000 \text{ million marks}$$
$$1 \text{ match} = 900 \text{ million marks}$$
$$1 \text{ newspaper} = 2,000 \text{ million marks}$$

When the German mark reached the unbelievable ratio of 1/1,000,-000,000,000th of its prewar value, the government was finally able to stabilize its worth by mortgaging all agricultural land and industrial and business firms.

In only one other time in history did inflation reach worse proportions than the Germany of the 1920's. The aftermath of World War II left Hungary's 1931 gold-based money equal to 130 billion new paper units.[8]

Compared to these examples of inflation, the price rises of the 1970's seem miniscule. Nevertheless, inflation has become a serious economic problem throughout the modern world. Everywhere people discuss prices—at supermarkets, commuter trains and buses, hairdressers, bowling alleys, and eating places.

The two traditional reasons for inflation are the demand-pull and cost-push explanations. **Demand-pull inflation** occurs when *there is too much money relative to the products available.* Once maximum production is reached, increased consumer demand simply bids the prices higher. **Cost-push inflation** results from *rising costs* (labor, raw materials, interest rates, and the like) *that are passed on to the consumer.*

Unfortunately, few people can actually agree on the causes of inflation. A 1974 Gallup poll reported that 45 percent of U.S. citizens saw government as the primary cause of inflation; while 25 percent blamed labor; and 10 percent cited business.[9]

Unemployment has approached 9 percent of the U.S. labor force at the same time that rapid inflation is eating away the purchasing power of earnings. Cost pressures have forced prices up, even though demand was down. This has caused significant problems for the business community, as well as for consumers. Economists now use the term **stagflation** to describe the *dual economic problems of high unemployment and a rapidly rising price level.*

CONSUMER
RESPONSES
TO INFLATION

Rising consumer prices have forced people to make a number of changes in their daily lives. Meat extenders—like soy beans—were used when meat prices went to record levels. Combination soy bean-hamburger products have become common at the supermarket's meat counter. High housing costs have forced many people to seek alternatives to single-unit houses. Housing experts now believe that single-family units will make up only one-third of all housing starts by 1990.[10] Other Americans have turned to consumer credit as a means of countering inflation. The argument that "we had better buy it now, because it will be 10–20 percent higher next year" makes sense to a lot of people. The increased use of credit has created other economic problems. More than 160,000 U.S. families now go bankrupt every year.[11]

Inflation calls for adjustments on the part of the consumer. But for the most part, Americans have reacted sensibly to blunt the effects of inflation. They have cut expenses where possible and delayed purchases. Consumers have also become more activist, and have begun to take direct action where they see a pricing abuse. When sugar prices tripled in 1974, a Michigan housewife suggested a nationwide sugar boycott on a Detroit radio station. Minutes later the station was swamped with telephone calls supporting such a move.[12] Similar actions will no doubt result from continued inflation.

MANAGEMENT RESPONSES TO INFLATION

Businesspersons must also deal with the rising price spiral. Higher costs must be absorbed or passed on to the consumer in the form of higher prices. Management has had to adopt more innovative responses to the problem of inflation. Some companies now charge for what was once provided free. A San Antonio beauty shop asks patrons to either return or pay for pins left in their hair. Some service stations are charging for road maps. Cleveland's Silver Garter Saloon has discontinued free pizza on Friday nights.[13] Other companies have reduced production and operating costs, and offered a smaller range of product options. Huffman Manufacturing Company, the bicycle maker, now allows retailers only thirty days to pay for the bicycles they order.[14] Rising postage rates have forced publications like *Esquire, Ladies' Home Journal, Fortune,* and *The Wall Street Journal* to trim their sizes and/or use lighter-weight paper.[15]

Firms have also switched to substitute components and suppliers to counteract inflation. Huffman switched to domestic suppliers when foreign prices of bicycle parts began to rise rapidly. The firm's annual report is being printed on cheaper paper. Coca-Cola now uses corn syrup as a replacement for 25 percent of the sugar in its noncola drinks.[16]

As costs continue to go up, it is obvious that management will have to find other ways to keep prices competitive in the marketplace. Consumers appreciate and patronize firms that help them offset the effects of inflation. In some cases they actually expand markets. Southwest Airlines introduced a $13 fare between Dallas and San Antonio—half the previous rate. When Braniff Airways followed Southwest's lead, air traffic between the two cities doubled.[17]

Who Should Bear the Cost of Inflation?

When there is a shortage of goods relative to the supply of money and credit (purchasing power), inflation results. Inflation tends to discourage saving and to wipe out what savings do exist. The dollar becomes devalued, and the cost of living goes up. The amount of inflation is measured by the Consumer Price Index of the Bureau of Labor Statistics on the basis of "changes in prices of goods and services by urban wage earners and clerical workers, including families and single persons." Prices are measured in comparison with the years 1957–1959.

With the prices of food, rent, clothes, cars, public transportation, and medical care all rising, it would seem that the general public, and particularly the poor and those persons on fixed incomes (such as retired people and the elderly), are paying the cost of inflation. Because they are not able to buy certain kinds of medical care, for example, they must go without any. Yet Medicare and Medicaid, health clinics, and welfare agencies often supply the care that the individual cannot purchase, perhaps even if costs were to go down. The diet of poor families and others changes in an inflationary period, as does the kind of housing, clothing, and transportation they buy. Some goods (convenience foods, for instance) go unbought in any volume; others (like flour for homemade bread and cake) are sold more readily. Demand alters consumer patterns.

During an inflationary period labor makes demands for wage hikes to cover the cost of living increases. If such pay raises are granted by management, very often fewer people will be employed to do the same work, which adds to rising unemployment. The business that cannot fire any of its staff and is forced into providing higher salaries has no choice but to raise prices for its goods or services. This in turn makes the product more expensive to the consumer, who may be one of the workers being given a raise by the company.

Suppliers of raw materials also experience many of the problems that other firms endure. As their costs rise, they will charge the manufacturers who use their materials a higher price, which inflates the price of the end product. Rather than making an exhorbitant profit, the manufacturer is simply supplying a demand at a market price.

Some economists believe that the law of supply and demand will effectively remedy an inflationary situation. Others believe that more government control of the money supply and bank credit is needed.

Organization of the Pricing Activity

While pricing is usually regarded as a function of marketing, it is also an activity that requires considerable inputs from other areas in the company. Accounting and financial managers have always played a major role in the pricing task by providing the sales and cost data necessary for good pricing decisions. Production and industrial engineering personnel play similarly important roles. The data processing department is usually in charge of the firm's computer-based marketing information system which provides up-to-date information needed in pricing. For instance, Zale Corporation, the Dallas-based jewelry chain, uses a daily computer printout showing cost and other data on all its inventory items.[18]

It is important for managers—at all levels—to realize the total importance of pricing and the contribution that can be made to correct pricing by various areas in the organization.

Inflation has caused modifications in the pricing organization of many companies. Some firms have moved the pricing responsibility higher in the organization. Ducommon, Inc., a Los Angeles metal and electronics distributor, has created a pricing "czar" who monitors all price changes. But the primary change has been that marketing executives now treat pricing as a *continual* responsibility rather than a one-time decision for the period under consideration. In this sense inflation has probably improved the efficiency of the overall marketing effort.

Price Determination

Economic theory, assuming a profit maximization objective, says that market price will be set where the amount of a product desired at a given price is equal to the amount that suppliers will provide at that price. Thus, the amount demanded and the amount supplied are in balance, or equilibrium. In other words, there is a *schedule of amounts that will be demanded at different price levels*—the **demand curve.** Five thousand pounds of an industrial chemical might be sold at $3 per pound; a price increase to $4 per pound might reduce sales to 3,200 pounds; and a $5 per pound price might result in sales of only 2,000 pounds as some would-be customers decide to accept less expensive substitutes or to wait for prices to be reduced.

Correspondingly, there is a schedule that shows *the amounts that will be offered in the market at certain prices.* This is called the **supply curve.** The intersection of these two curves is the equilibrium price that will exist in the marketplace for a particular good or service.

Figure 13-1
Demand and
Supply Curves

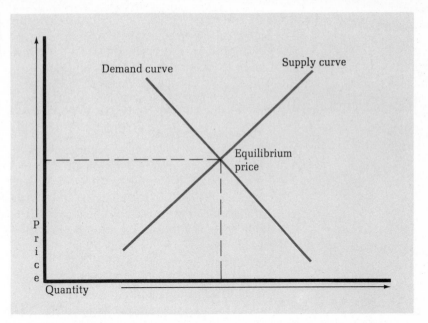

**PRACTICAL
PRICE SETTING**

The economic analysis just discussed is correct in regards to the overall market for a product. But managers face the problem of setting the price of their individual brands based on limited information. Anticipating the amounts of a product that will be bought at a certain price is very difficult. So business has tended to adopt cost-based pricing formulas. While these are simpler and easier to use, executives have to be flexible in applying them to any one situation. Cost-based pricing starts by totaling all the costs associated with offering an item in the market. These include production, transportation, distribution, and marketing expenses. Then *the marketer adds a factor for profit and other expenses not previously considered.* This is known as the **mark-up.**

Mark-up *is the amount that is added to cost to determine the market price:*

$$\text{Mark-up percentage} = \frac{\text{Amount added to cost}}{\text{Price}}$$

If a game in a toy store were priced at $3.00 with an invoice cost of $2.00 (the amount the store pays for the game), then the mark-up percentage would be 33 1/3 percent (1.00 ÷ 3.00).

The firm's mark-up should be related to its **stock turnover,** or *the number of times the average inventory is sold annually.* Mark-ups should be lower for products with stock turnover figures above the industry average, and higher for items with low turnover figures:

$$\text{Stock turnover} = \frac{\text{Sales (or cost of goods sold)*}}{\text{Average inventory}}$$

*Note: Sales is used if the inventory is recorded at retail value; the cost of goods sold is used if inventories are recorded at cost.

305 PRICES AND PRICING STRATEGY

Marketers must be flexible and willing to adjust their mark-ups (and prices) in accordance with the demand for their products. Both costs and market demand must be considered in arriving at the price to be charged to the customer.

Breakeven Analysis—An Aid to Better Pricing Decisions

Marketers often use breakeven analysis as a method of determining the minimum sales volume that is necessary at a certain price level. This involves a consideration of various costs and total revenue. Total cost (TC) is composed of total variable cost (TVC) and total fixed costs (TFC). **Fixed costs** are *those that remain stable regardless of the sales level achieved* (such as the firm's insurance costs). **Variable costs** are *those that change with the level of production* (such as labor and raw material costs). Total revenue is determined by price and the volume sold.

Figure 13-2 shows the calculation of the **breakeven point,** *the level of sales that will cover all of the company's costs* (both fixed and variable). Anything beyond the breakeven point would be profit.

Breakeven points can also be found by using a simple formula:

$$\text{Breakeven point (in units)} = \frac{\text{Total fixed cost}}{\text{Per unit contribution to fixed cost}}.$$

A product selling for $20 with a variable cost of $14 per item, produces a $6 per unit contribution to fixed costs. If total fixed costs are $42,000, then the firm must sell 7,000 units to break even:

$$\text{Breakeven (in units)} = \frac{\$42,000}{\$6} = 7{,}000 \text{ units.}$$

Marketers can compare the breakeven consequences of various prices in this manner. Different prices produce different breakeven points, which can then be compared with what the firm's marketing research shows is the most likely sales volume. This comparison will give an indication of a realistic market price.

New Product Pricing

Pampers, the paper baby diaper, failed in its original market test because of pricing. Later, it became Procter & Gamble's second best-selling brand (the detergent Tide is first). When it was first introduced, Pampers sold for about ten cents each. This was more than the per use cost of buying a cloth diaper and washing it. When Pampers bombed in the marketplace, Procter & Gamble reduced production costs to the point where Pampers could be priced at six cents each, and the product became a household word in families with infants.[19]

Figure 13-2
Breakeven Analysis

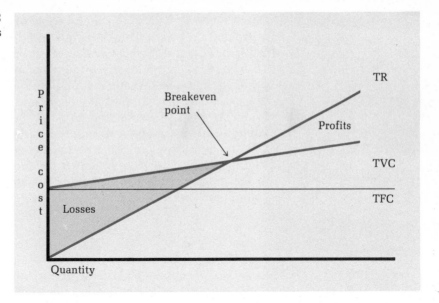

Procter & Gamble's experience with Pampers shows how difficult it is to select a price for a new product line. All such pricing decisions are risky; it is usually best to field test possible alternative prices with a sample group of consumers. Once the product is actually launched, it is difficult to modify its price during the introductory period.

New product pricing can take one of two alternative strategies. One is to *price the new product relatively high compared to substitute goods, and then gradually lower it.* Du Pont, which offers many specialty items, has traditionally followed such a pattern.[20] Du Pont's polyester fiber, Dacron, was sold at $2.25 a pound in 1953. It now goes for about 40¢. Similarly, the price of Quiana, a synthetic silklike fiber, has fallen 35 percent in five years. This alternative is known as a **skimming price policy,** and is used where the market is segmented on a price basis. In other words, some may buy an item at $10; another, larger group will buy if it is priced at $7.50; and a still larger group will buy if the item sells for $6.00. Color television and electronic calculators are examples of where this policy has been used effectively. Today's best-selling ballpoint pen sells for 25¢, but when this product was first introduced after World War II it sold for about $20. A skimming price policy allows the firm to recover its costs rapidly by maximizing the revenue it receives. But the policy has a disadvantage in that early profits tend to attract competition, and this puts eventual pressure on prices.

Soaps and toothpastes are often introduced using a **penetration price policy.** This means *the new product is priced low relative to substitute items in order to secure wide market acceptance.* Later it is hoped that brand acceptance will allow the firm to raise prices.

Dow Chemical, which sells many commodity products, tends to be a penetration pricer. Dow attempts to build its market share with lower prices, and then stay in a certain market for a long time.

Penetration pricing discourages competition because of its low profits. It can also provide competitive opportunities against users of a skimming price policy. Wella-Balsam hair conditioner was introduced at $1.98 (compared to $1.19 for regular cream rinses). Alberto-Culver Company countered with Alberto-Balsam at $1.49 and an advertising budget ten times the size of the one supporting Wella-Balsam. The Alberto-Culver product overtook Wella-Balsam in ten months, and now accounts for about 55–60 percent of hair conditioner sales.

Price Lining

Price lining occurs when *a seller decides to offer merchandise at a limited number of prices, rather than pricing each item individually.* For instance, a boutique might offer lines of women's sportswear priced at $60, $90, and $110. Price lining is a common marketing practice among retailers. The original five-and-ten-cent stores were an example of its early use.

As a pricing strategy the concept of price lining prevents the confusion common to situations where all items are priced individually. The pricing function is more easily managed. But marketers must clearly identify the market segments to which they are appealing. Three "high price" lines might not be appropriate to a store located in an area of young married couples.

A disadvantage of price lining is that it is sometimes difficult to alter the price ranges once they are set. This may be a crucial factor during a period of inflation when the firm must either raise the price of the line or reduce its quality. Consumers may resist either of these decisions. Price lining can be useful, but its implementation must be considered carefully.

Price-Quality Relationships

Numerous research studies have shown that the consumers' perception of product quality is related closely to the item's price. The higher the price of the product, the better the consumer perceives its quality. One study asked four hundred respondents what terms they associated with the word *expensive*. Two-thirds of the replies referred to high quality—such as *best* or *superior*.[21]

Most marketers believe that the price-quality relationship exists over a relatively wide range of prices. It also appears that there are extreme prices that can be viewed as either *too expensive* or *too cheap*. Marketing managers need to study and experiment with prices for their own particular products. The price-quality relationship can be of key importance to a firm's pricing strategy.

"Take three dollars worth every four hours."

Does a Price-Quality Relationship Exist in Pharmaceutical Pricing?

SOURCE: *The Wall Street Journal*, June 28, 1974. Reprinted with permission from *The Wall Street Journal*.

Psychological Pricing

Many marketers feel that certain prices are more appealing to buyers than others. Psychological pricing is widely used by industry throughout the world. The image pricing goals mentioned earlier are an example of psychological pricing.

Have you ever wondered why retailers use prices like $39.95, $18.98, or $9.99? Why don't the stores use $40, $19, or $10 instead? Years ago **odd pricing** (as *this practice is called*) was employed to force clerks to make change. This was before the age of cash registers, so odd pricing served as a cash control technique for retailers. It is now a common technique in retail pricing. Many retailers believe that odd prices are more attractive to consumers than even ones. In fact, some stores have now begun to use prices ending in 2, 3, 4, or 7 to avoid the look of ordinary prices like $5.95, $10.98, and $19.99. The "new" prices are more likely to be $2.22, $6.53, or $10.94.

Summary

Prices can be defined as the exchange value of a good or service in an economy. Prices are an important factor in a society because they help determine society's allocation of economic resources.

Pricing goals include profit objectives (profit maximization and target return objectives); volume objectives (sales maximization and market share objectives); and a third group of objectives that includes social and ethical considerations, status quo objectives, and image goals.

Chapter 13 identifies inflation as the most critical topic in pricing today. Its causes and effects are examined along with the ways consumers and businesses have tried to deal with it.

The economic theory of pricing is considered as background for a discussion on how prices are actually set in business. The demand and supply curves, which intersect at the equilibrium price in the marketplace for a given good or service, are described. Mark-ups, stock turnover, and breakeven analysis are also explained in Chapter 13. Other pricing topics discussed here include new product pricing, price lining, price-quality relationships, and psychological pricing.

Review questions

1. Identify the following terms:

   a. price
   b. inflation
   c. demand-pull inflation
   d. cost-push inflation
   e. stagflation
   f. demand curve

   g. supply curve
   h. mark-up
   i. stock turnover
   j. fixed costs
   k. variable costs
   l. odd pricing

2. Why is pricing so important in contemporary society? Discuss this question from both business and societal viewpoints.

3. Outline the major pricing objectives sought by industry.

4. "The firm's mark-up should be related to its sales turnover." Comment.

5. If a new automobile were "Sticker Priced" at $5,600, and was priced to the dealer at $4,200, what would the dealer's mark-up be?

6. Assume that a local music shop carried a record inventory of $15,000 and had annual sales of $120,000. What would its stock turnover be?

7. Assume that a product sells for $10 with a variable cost of $6 per unit. If total fixed costs were $38,000 for this product, then how many units would the firm have to sell to break even?

8. Contrast the skimming and penetration viewpoints toward new product pricing. Can you make any generalization about the types of products or market situations that would be most suitable to each strategy?

9. "The consumer's perception of quality is closely related to the item's price." Comment.

10. What is meant by price lining?

Discussion questions and exercises

1. Evaluate the pro and con arguments to the controversial issue that appears in this chapter.
2. As a class project interview five or six consumers in your area. Ask these people:
   a. Has inflation affected your lifestyle?
   b. If so, how has it affected you?
   c. How have you attempted to cope with rising prices?
3. Interview executives at several local firms (preferably firms that operate in different industries). Ask them how prices are determined in their particular companies. Then prepare a class report on what you have learned.
4. Spend some time looking at prices used by businesses in your area. Conduct a class discussion about the use of psychological pricing.
5. Assume that you have just been appointed marketing manager for a new World Hockey League franchise. Your team will be using an arena with 3,000 first-class seats; 5,000 regular seats; and 2,000 seats behind the nets. How would you go about setting the seat prices?

Case 13-1

METRO, Seattle's Transit Service

The pricing of public services has always been a very complex question, since profitability is sometimes a secondary goal. Consider the case of METRO, Seattle's transit service. Thanks to a $64,000 appropriation from the City Council, all bus rides in a 105-block area of downtown Seattle were free for a trial period from September 1973 to August 1974.

"Magic Carpet Service," as the free transportation was called, doubled the number of bus riders to about 11,000 daily. This pricing experiment, the first of its kind, was designed to persuade people not to drive in the downtown Seattle area. Multiple objectives were involved:

1. to ease downtown traffic conditions
2. to reduce air pollution
3. to encourage consumers to shop downtown.

And although it was not an original objective of the plan, "Magic Carpet Service" also helped reduce gasoline consumption during the energy crunch.

Seattle's mayor believes free transit could cut downtown auto traffic by 20 percent. John Gilmore of the Downtown Seattle Development Association reports that restaurants and retailers have experienced significant increases in patronage. In fact, Gilmore's Association decided to help promote "Magic Carpet Service" with radio and newspaper advertising.

Questions

1. Prepare a report on what has happened to METRO since August 1974.
2. Do you think Seattle's City Council and METRO were justified in making public transit a free service in downtown Seattle? Why, or why not?
3. What public policy issues are raised by METRO's pricing strategy?
4. Are you aware of similar pricing policies being used for other public services? Comment.

Seattle's free buses are discussed in William Ecenbarger. "Seattle's No-fare Buses Catch-On," *Detroit Free Press* (June 9, 1974), p. 13-A; and William Wong. "Seattle's Free Buses Revitalize Downtown Area: They Save Gas, Cut Traffic and Spread Goodwill," *The Wall Street Journal* (February 12, 1974), p. 28.

Case 13-2

Pricing in a Chinese Restaurant

Chinese restaurants, traditionally inexpensive dining spots, have been affected by inflation the same as most other businesses. Customers now pay twenty-five cents or more for the bowl of rice that was once provided free. Menu prices for most items have also gone up.

Alphonse Chan, president of the San Francisco Chinatown Chinese Restaurant Association, says his own Nam Yuen Restaurant is paying $38.50 for a 100-pound sack of rice, up from $12.50 a year ago. Monosodium glutamate, a basic flavoring ingredient, has jumped 150% in price in six months while cooking oils have tripled, he says. Imported ingredients such as bamboo shoots and water chestnuts have gone up about a third in the past several months.

Chinese restaurant managers confront some critical questions of pricing strategy. Should they:

1. Raise all menu prices?
2. Raise *selected* menu prices?
3. Charge for rice that was once provided free?
4. Absorb the increased costs?

Questions

1. Which pricing decision would you elect to follow? Why?
2. What other pricing alternatives exist?
3. Survey restaurants in your area. Do they face the same type of pricing problems? If so, how have they handled the problem?

The Wall Street Journal (April 25, 1974), p. 1.

Careers in Marketing

Marketing includes many exciting, dynamic fields—such as advertising, marketing research, personal selling, and physical distribution management. These are all growing employment areas. Many beginning marketers start as sales personnel, then move into other positions as they gain experience.

MARKETERS ARE THE COMPANY TO MOST PEOPLE Your impression of an airline is usually based on its reservations personnel, ticket agents, and flight attendants. You do not directly observe the work of mechanics, pilots, and operations personnel. The people you see, and on whom your impression is based, are all part of the airline's marketing function.

The Bureau of Labor Statistics has projected annual job openings to 1985. Their forecasts for some selected marketing jobs appear below.

Job Projections to 1985

Career	Latest Employment (1972 Estimate)	Annual Average of Job Openings to 1985
Airline flight attendants	39,000	8,000
Automobile salesworkers	131,000	4,600
Manufacturers' salesworkers	423,000	20,000
Public relations workers	87,000	5,000
Real estate salesworkers and brokers	349,000	25,000
Retail trade salesworkers	2,778,000	190,000
Traffic agents and clerks (civil aviation)	59,000	7,000
Wholesale trade salesworkers	668,000	31,000

SOURCE: *Occupational Manpower and Training Needs* (Washington, D.C.: Bureau of Labor Statistics, 1974).

Here are some of the careers in marketing that are available to you:

Marketing Manager

A marketing manager, or marketing director, has overall responsibility for all phases of the marketing function. A marketing manager is the highest position within the marketing function. Sometimes this person is called "Vice-president of Marketing."

Advertising Director

An advertising director is the person responsible for all aspects of the firm's advertising program. When part of the program is handled by outside agencies, the firm's advertising director is responsible for the contractual relationship with the agency.

Advertising Account Executive

An account executive works for an advertising agency. This person is assigned to handle one or more of the agency's accounts. An account executive is in charge of all advertising plans submitted to the clients.

Market Researcher

Market researchers analyze information and data on consumers and on buying behavior. These people identify facts and trends that might be relevant in developing an improved competitive strategy for the firm.

Sales Manager

Sales managers are the persons in charge of a group of sales representatives or the entire sales force. In some cases they are also involved in selling to big accounts. But a sales manager's primary job is seeing that the firm's sales personnel perform effectively.

Sales Representative

Sales representatives are the people who handle the personal selling aspects of the firm's marketing program. They call on prospective buyers, explain the firm's products, and solicit orders. They are also responsible for seeing that customers are satisfied with their purchases and become repeat buyers.

Physical Distribution Manager

Also called a "Traffic Manager," the physical distribution manager is responsible for seeing that the firm's physical distribution function is performed effectively. Duties include transportation, shipping, warehousing, and the like.

Buyer

Buyers procure merchandise for retail stores. They usually specialize by products or departments. In other words, there is a furniture buyer, a sportswear buyer, and so forth.

Operations Manager

An operations manager is the person responsible for the nonmerchandise-related activities of retailing. Duties might include supervision of receiving, shipping, delivery, service, security, and inventory control departments.

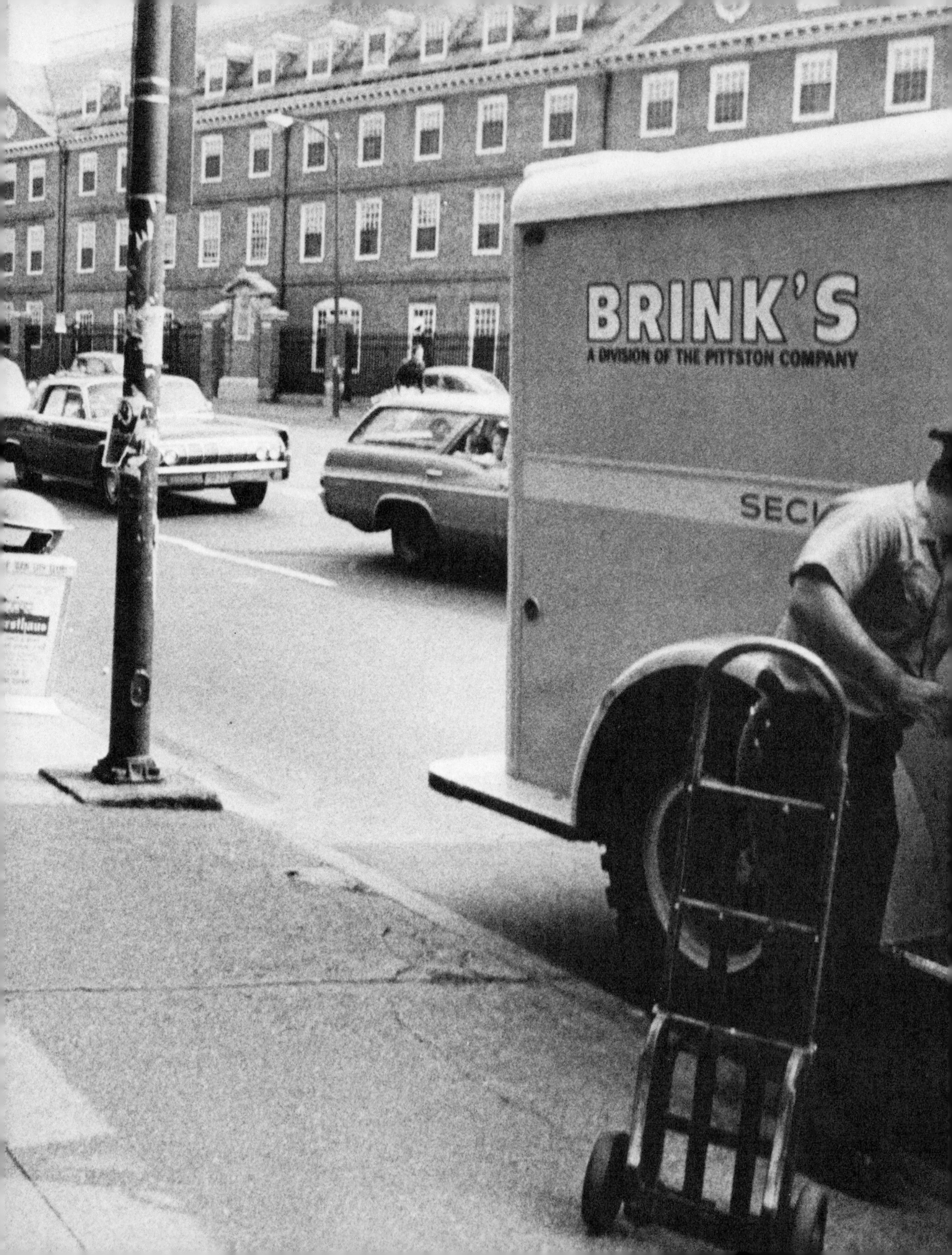
BRINK'S
A DIVISION OF THE PITTSTON COMPANY

V Financing the Enterprise

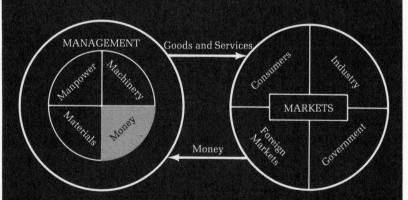

14

Money and the American Banking System

"The lack of money is the root of all evil."

—George Bernard Shaw

SOURCE: Michael Blate.

What Chapter 14 Is All About

1. An alternative to the money system is a system of barter. After reading this chapter you should be able to explain the advantages of money over a barter system.
2. Think about the characteristics that a good money form should possess, and evaluate the use of gold coins as money.
3. Consider each of the functions of money. Why are *all three* functions necessary?
4. You should be able to explain the operations of the Federal Reserve System and how it can increase or reduce the money supply.
5. The Federal Deposit Insurance Corporation is another important component of our banking system. You will be able to explain its purpose and chief functions.
6. After reading this chapter, you should understand these terms:

money
medium of exchange
unit of account
store of value
liquidity
currency
demand deposits
near-money
time deposits
state bank

national bank
Federal Reserve System
reserve requirement
open market operations
discount rate
check
Federal Deposit Insurance
  Corporation
electronic banking
savings and loan association

Alexander Hamilton

As an American statesman, Alexander Hamilton was largely responsible for establishing the credit of the fledgling United States of America and giving its system financial stability. Hamilton was born early in 1755 on the British island of Nevis in the Caribbean, the illegitimate son of a French Huguenot mother and a Scottish father. With little education (he began working as a clerk for a trading firm on St. Croix when he was eleven years old) he went to the colonies for some formal schooling. He spent several years at King's College (now known as Columbia University) without getting a degree and then joined the Revolutionary forces in 1776. Hamilton served as Washington's right-hand man for five years as a military strategist, army reformer, and economist, and drafted some of George Washington's most important letters to Congress and the states.

In 1782 Hamilton set up a law practice. During that same year, he participated in the Continental Congress and was instrumental in calling for the Constitutional Convention. His articles in *The Federalist* and many of his speeches helped to secure the adoption of the Constitution by the states.

In 1789 Hamilton was appointed first Secretary of the Treasury serving under President George Washington. He provided financial guidance during his six years in office, which carried the new nation through a very critical period. The government assumed state debts, as well as providing additional funds through newly established import duties, taxes on liquor and other domestic products. His efforts resulted in the formation of the first national bank and the founding of the first mint in the United States.

During John Adams' presidency, Hamilton was appointed inspector general and second in command of the U.S. Army. When he turned on Adams during the presidential campaign of 1800, Hamilton not only lost his military posts but unexpectedly helped elect Jefferson to the presidency. His political rivalry with Aaron Burr led to his being challenged to a duel by Burr in 1804. Hamilton died from Burr's bullet the day after the duel was fought.

Ask anyone to define money and the person will probably respond: "It's the coins in my pocket and the folding kind I wish I had in my wallet and whatever is currently in my checking account." And a banker would agree: All of those are money.

Money is also one of the most fascinating subjects for both the individual and businessperson. Everyone seems to need money.

Money bewitches people. They fret for it, and they sweat for it. They devise most ingenious ways to get it, and most ingenious ways to get rid of it. Money is the only commodity that is good for nothing but to be gotten rid of. It will not feed you, clothe you, shelter you, or amuse you unless you spend it or invest it. It imparts value only in parting. People will do almost anything for money, and money will do almost anything for people. Money is a captivating, circulating, masquerading puzzle.[1]

Money Comes in Different Shapes and Sizes

Money has not always been the same to all people. Historically, objects of value were used as money. These goods might be referred to as *full-bodied money* since they had usefulness quite separate from their use as money. Cattle have often been used this way. A cow was valuable since it could produce milk, butter, cheese, or could be converted eventually into meat and hide. But its owner could also trade the cow for a wagon. The list of products that have served as money is long, and includes such diverse items as wool, pepper, tea, fishhooks, tobacco, shells, feathers, salt (from which came "salary" and "being worth one's salt"), boats, sharks' teeth, cocoa beans, wampum beads, woodpecker scalps, and precious metals. For a number of reasons precious metals gained wide acceptance as money. As early as 2000 B.C., gold and silver were being used as money. Gold coins were used in the United States as money until 1933.

WHAT CHARACTERISTICS SHOULD MONEY POSSESS? Most of the early forms of money possessed a number of serious disadvantages. Cattle are poor forms of money for the owner who wants a loaf of bread and a pound of cheese. To perform its necessary functions, money should be *divisible, portable, durable, have a stable value, and be difficult to counterfeit.*

Divisibility

The owner of the cow who learns that the loaf of bread on his shopping list is priced at one-fiftieth cow is faced with a major divisibility dilemma. So also were the owners of the other items used as money. But gold and silver coins could be minted in different sizes with differing values in order to facilitate the exchange process.

Spanish gold doubloons were *literally* divided into pieces of eight. The dollar can be converted into pennies, nickels, dimes, and quarters. The pound sterling of the United Kingdom is worth one hundred pence. A French franc is valued at one hundred centimes. The German deutsche mark can be traded for one hundred pfennigs. And these forms of money can easily be exchanged for goods ranging from Wrigley's chewing gum to a Porsche 914.

Portable

The inhabitants of the little island community of Yap chose a unique form of money: huge round stones weighing several hundred pounds. Since the stone money was often placed at the door of its owner,

Figure 14-1
Examples of
Paper Money
From the Past

EXAMPLES OF PAPER MONEY FROM THE PAST

One of the largest denomination notes ever issued. This Hungarian inflation currency, the 10 quintillion pengo note, was issued in 1946. Ten quintillion is written 10,000,000,000,000,-000,000.

The oldest known paper currency. It was issued in China during the Ming Dynasty between 1368 and 1399.

Confederate money. This $20 note was issued in Richmond on February 17, 1864.

U.S. silver certificate of 1886. Note that it is backed by a deposit of five silver dollars payable to the bearer on demand.

Front and back of a three-pence note issued by the Colonial government. One of the printers was a soon-to-be statesman named B. Franklin.

SOURCE: The Chase Manhattan Bank Numismatic Collection. Reproduced with permission.

the wealth of the inhabitant was known to every passerby. But Yap stone money lacked an important characteristic: *portability*. The process of trading the stones for needed goods and services was difficult at best.

Today's modern paper currency is light in weight and facilitates the exchange process. United States paper money comes in denominations ranging from $1 to $10,000.

Durable

Durability is a third important characteristic of money. A monetary system using butter or cheese faces the durability problem in a matter of weeks. Although coins and paper currency will wear out over time, they are simply replaced with crisp new dollars and shiny new coins by the U.S. Treasury. One dollar bills have an average life of eighteen months.

Stable in value

A good money system should have a stable value. If the value of money fluctuates, people become unwilling to trade goods and services for it. Inflation is, therefore, a serious concern for governments. When people fear that their money will lose much of its value in the future, they begin to abandon it and look for safer means of storing their wealth. Where once they accepted dollars or francs, they may now demand gold coins or store their wealth in the form of land, jewelry, or other physical goods. In the case of *runaway inflation*, where the value of money may decrease 20 percent or more in a single year, people increasingly return to a barter system, exchanging their output for the output of others.

Difficult to counterfeit

If you hold a dollar bill to the light you will notice small red and blue silk threads imbedded in the paper. Their purpose is to make

"I don't think they'll reduce the counterfeiting charge just because you used recycled paper."

SOURCE: *The Wall Street Journal*, March 8, 1974. Reprinted with permission from *The Wall Street Journal*.

counterfeiting difficult. Theft of currency plates from government mints is a frequent plot for espionage and mystery novels and movies, since such crimes could result in undermining a nation's monetary system. The production and distribution of counterfeit money could ruin the value of legitimate money. For this reason all governments make counterfeiting a serious crime and take elaborate steps to prevent its occurrence.

WHAT ARE THE FUNCTIONS OF MONEY?

Money can be defined as *anything which is generally accepted as a means of paying for goods and services.* It serves as a **medium of exchange,** which is *the function performed by money in eliminating the need for a barter system.* Rather than the complicated process of trading wheat directly for gasoline or clothing, the farmer sells the wheat, then uses the money from this sale in making purchases.

Secondly, money functions as a **unit of account.** This is *the function performed when money serves as a common denominator for measuring the value of all products and services.* A new car is worth $5,500, a certain cut of beef has a value of $2 a pound, and a 40-yard-line ticket to the Miami Dolphins' game costs $8. Using money as a common denominator aids in comparing widely different products and services.

The third function of money is to act as a temporary **store of value.** This is when *money is used to store accumulated wealth until it is needed to make new purchases.* Wealth can also be held as stocks and bonds, real estate, antiques, works of art, houses, precious gems, or any other kind of valuable goods. The advantage of storing value in goods other than money is that they may produce additional income in the form of dividends, interest payments, rent, or through increases in their value. Paintings by Renoir, Monet, and van Gogh, and the Western art of Russell and Remington have greatly increased in value over the past twenty years.

But money offers one substantial advantage as a store of value: It is highly liquid. **Liquidity** is *the speed at which items may be exchanged for money.* An asset is said to be liquid if it can be obtained and disposed of quickly and easily.[2]

The van Gogh painting may increase in value, but its owner can obtain money for it only after a purchaser is found. In order to exchange bonds for money, the owner must contact a broker and pay a commission. And the possibility always exists that the value of the bond may be less than when it was first purchased. The owner's choice may be to:

1. hold the bond until maturity, at which time the corporation or government agency which issued the bond will pay the total amount of the bond and interest, or
2. sell the bond at a loss in order to obtain more liquid dollars.

Table 14-1
Money in Circulation

Money	Billions of Dollars	Percent of Total
Coins	$ 8	3
Paper Money	69	24
Demand Deposits	210	73
Total	$287	100

SOURCE: *Treasury Bulletin* (April 1975), p. 20.

In addition to the liquidity problem, many nonmoney stores of value involve storage and insurance costs.

There are disadvantages in holding money, particularly in inflationary times. If prices double, all of those dollar bills under the mattress will buy only half the clothes and movie tickets when they're pulled out to be spent. Also, money earns no interest for its owner. Its chief advantage is that it is immediately available for use in purchasing products or in paying debts.

COMPOSITION OF THE MONEY SUPPLY

The U.S. money supply is divided into three categories: *coins, paper money,* and *demand deposits* (or checking accounts). Table 14-1 shows the amount of each category currently in circulation.

Coins

Metal coins ranging from copper pennies to (partially) silver dollars are used for numerous small purchases and are the life blood of both vending machines and parking meters. Unless the value of the metal in the coins is less than the face value of the coins, they will often be melted down for sale as bullion. Such practices are illegal, but they do occur in such cases as pre-1965 dimes, quarters, and half-dollars. The rising prices of silver and copper resulted in the introduction of "sandwich" dimes, quarters, and half-dollars made of nickel and copper, and a reduction in the percentage of the copper content of post-1974 pennies.

Paper money

Paper money in the form of $1 bills, $5 bills (even a few $2 bills), and so on make up approximately one-fourth of the U.S. money supply. If you examine a dollar bill you will note the term *Federal Reserve Note* across the top, indicating that it was issued by the Federal Reserve Banks with the authorization of Congress. Practically all of the paper money in circulation is in the form of Federal Reserve Notes. Slightly less than 1 percent of U.S. paper money is in other forms (such as Silver Certificates and United States Notes), and virtually all of these are held by collectors. These *two components of the money supply—coins and paper money—are usually called* **currency.**

The Faces on American Currency

Every trivia expert can recall that the portraits of Washington, Lincoln, and Hamilton appear on $1, $5, and $10 bills, respectively. But whose faces adorn the other denominations? Each of the approximately 70 million $2 bills in circulation bear the likeness of Thomas Jefferson. Andrew Jackson appears on each $20; Ulysses S. Grant is on the $50; and the portrait of Benjamin Franklin adorns the $100.

Larger-size denominations are seldom seen—except in commercial bank currency exhibits. Although this large-denomination currency is used primarily in transactions between the Treasury Department and the Federal Reserve System, each bears a portrait of an American president or statesman. President William McKinley appears on the $500; President Cleveland is on the $1,000; and the $5,000 bears the likeness of President James Madison. The portrait of Salmon P. Chase appears on the $10,000, and Woodrow Wilson is on the rarely seen $100,000 bill.

The portraits of these noted Americans appear on the faces of U.S. currency. The backs are typically reserved for famous buildings. The embellishments on the backs of currency, in numerical order, are the *Great Seal of the United States* ($1), *Monticello* ($2), the *Lincoln Memorial* ($5), the *U.S. Treasury* ($10), the *White House* ($20), the *Capitol* ($50), and *Independence Hall* ($100). The backs of larger-sized bills are adorned with ornate denominational markings.

Demand deposits

Approximately three-fourths of the money supply in the United States is in the form of **demand deposits,** *the technical term for checking accounts.* Demand deposits are considered as part of the money supply since they are in fact *promises* by banks to immediately pay to the depositor any amount of money requested—so long as this does not exceed the amount in the person's checking account.

Nearly 95 percent of the financial transactions in the United States are conducted with checks rather than currency. There are several explanations for the frequent use of checks. A check is a more *convenient* form of payment for large or odd-numbered purchases. Payment by check for a $90 sports coat ($93.60 assuming a 4 percent sales tax) is more convenient than paying the clerk four twenties, a ten, three ones, two quarters, and a dime. Also, the use of a checkbook *reduces the possibility of theft or loss of currency.* Payment by mail is also easier when checks, rather than currency, are used. Even though an estimated 40 percent of the American people still deal almost exclusively in cash, the use of checkbook money offers the advantages of convenience and safety.[3]

Should the Dollar Be Backed by Gold?

After World War I the price of a loaf of bread in Germany was 1 billion marks. Those Germans who had invested in gold bullion not only held a safe hedge against this kind of runaway inflation but also preserved their capital. Middle Eastern nations and India are known to be buying gold. At the same time, the production of gold in South Africa and elsewhere is going down.

In 1934 the official price of gold in the United States rose from just over $20 an ounce to $35 an ounce. In 1971 the price rose another $3 an ounce. Since then, the price of gold has gone up sharply; public and private debt in the United States has risen; and savings in the form of bonds, insurance, and annuities have declined in value. In March of 1973 gold backing of the dollar was cut. In today's economy the government holds only about 3 percent of gold to back the dollar.

With gold prices floating freely, in an upward spiraling direction, the United States finds itself caught between inflation and recession. When the dollar dropped in value in the international money market, the prices of U.S. goods and services went up—both at home and abroad.

A dollar not backed by gold gives the government a legal right to issue as many dollars as the Federal Reserve System feels are needed. With an increase in the money supply, more buying can be expected. As a consequence, prices rise and inflation occurs and grows worse as more paper money is printed. Even while this happens, however, demand for products and services goes down because of these rising prices, making the necessities of life more expensive along with all other goods.

If the dollar must legally be backed by gold at some specified price, then the government is limited in issuing paper money. When the money supply stops, recession takes over, because without purchasing power the economy slows down. Some economists believe that in this situation the dollar would reach its real value and gain realistic purchasing power for consumers.

Without any gold backing, the dollar would depreciate in relation to gold-backed European currencies, such as the Swiss franc and the German mark. Fixed-dollar amounts, such as those held in savings accounts, bonds, and insurance policies, would be without real value if inflation continues and the dollar drops in value.

In either case—whether the dollar is backed by gold and the money supply is limited, or whether inflation brings money not backed by gold into a more realistic price structure for goods and services—the United States is caught in a dilemma. Recovery from inflation that is worldwide is a complicated matter. Some predict worsening inflation, depression, and even civil disorder. Others look to sophisticated monetary policies as a way out of the problem.

"Do you mean to tell me you don't carry any cash at all – even for emergencies like this?"

SOURCE: *The Wall Street Journal*, February 28, 1974. Reprinted with permission from *The Wall Street Journal*.

The "Inconvenience" of Checking Accounts

Many students will argue that a checking account is a most *inconvenient* form of money. Almost everyone has discovered himself or herself in need of funds in a strange town or in an unfamiliar store, and learned with dismay that the store would not cash a check. This is a common problem for students who are often residing temporarily in new cities with neither a local permanent address nor a local employer. Many colleges have established check-cashing services to assist students in converting demand deposits into currency.

While such instances do represent inconveniences, they are actually no worse a problem than trying to cash a $100 bill at a convenience food store or gas station after 10 P.M. or on Sunday.

NEAR-MONIES In addition to the money supply there are a number of assets that are almost, but not quite, money. These include such assets as **time deposits** (*the technical name for savings accounts*) at banks or savings and loan associations and United States government bonds. These assets are called **near-monies** because they are *assets, such as savings accounts, that are almost as liquid as checking accounts, but that cannot be used directly as mediums of exchange.**

*Some types of savings accounts permit the bank to require one or two months' notice prior to withdrawal. In practice, however, these time deposits are available immediately for conversion into currency or a checking account. Early withdrawal on savings accounts other than passbook accounts subjects the owner to a penalty in the form of loss of some of the interest already accrued.

Near-monies, unlike currency and demand deposits, earn interest for their owners. Savings accounts pay interest rates ranging from 5 to approximately 8 percent; while government bonds pay interest of 5 to 10 percent, depending on the value of the bond and its date of maturity.

A basic reason for not including near-monies in the money supply is that *they cannot be used directly as a medium of exchange.* One cannot ordinarily write a check on a savings account, although a few innovative banks are experimenting with this idea.

Plastic Money as a Substitute for Cash

The era of *plastic money* has arrived. With growing frequency, Americans are using credit cards as substitutes for cash.

At least half of all American families holds one or more credit cards. More than 17 million families use three or more cards and about 6 million families use nine or more. American consumers owe $50 billion on open-end accounts of all types, or roughly $400 per family.

A major reason for the tremendous increase in credit-card business is the amazing growth in the use of bank cards—particularly those issued by Master Charge and BankAmericard which together claim more than 50 million cardholders. About 10,000 banks in the U.S. offer credit-card services.

While credit cards have traditionally been used for such travel-related purchases as airline tickets, gasoline purchases, auto rentals, and motel charges, retail-store charge cards continue to be the most widely used type of credit cards in the United States.

But new areas of credit card use are rapidly developing. In California, a holder of a credit card can pay property taxes, state income taxes, motor-vehicle license fees—even car and home insurance—by simply making a phone call.

Doctors and dentists, hospitals, colleges and universities, utilities, and even mortuaries are accepting credit cards for payment in many parts of the country. Some churches and political parties hand out "pledge" cards with spaces for credit-card numbers.

Even though department store charge cards and bank credit cards are usually provided at no charge to consumers (unlike American Express, Diners Club, and Carte Blanche which charge a $20 annual membership fee), they generally do lead to higher retail prices. Goods and services at many stores that honor the cards are priced higher to cover the service cost charged by the credit-card companies. These fees range from 2 to 9 percent.*

*For more details on the growth of credit card usage in America, see "It's Getting Hard to Live Without a Credit Card," *U.S. News & World* Report (October 8, 1974), pp. 57–60; "Using Credit Cards to Buy the Groceries," *Business Week* (November 9, 1974), p. 50; and "Recession Catches Up with Credit Cards," *Business Week* (February 17, 1975), p. 47.

Our Banking System

The heart of the American banking system are the approximately 14,000 *commercial banks.* Most are **state banks,** *commercial banks that were chartered by individual states.* Approximately one-third

Table 14-2
The Fifteen Largest
Banks in the
United States

Bank Name and Location	Deposits in Billions
Bank of America (San Francisco)	$51.2
First National City Bank (New York)	45.0
Chase Manhattan (New York)	34.5
Manufacturers Hanover (New York)	21.2
Morgan Guaranty (New York)	19.8
Chemical Bank (New York)	17.6
Bankers Trust (New York)	16.2
First National (Chicago)	15.3
Continental Illinois (Chicago)	15.1
Security Pacific National (Los Angeles)	13.0
Wells Fargo (San Francisco)	9.8
Crocker National (San Francisco)	8.6
Irving Trust (New York)	8.5
United California (Los Angeles)	7.8
Mellon Bank (Pittsburgh)	7.4

SOURCE: Reprinted by permission from *The American Banker* (February 27, 1975).

of American banks are *commercial banks chartered by the federal government.* These are called **national banks.** These tend to be larger in size, and they hold approximately 60 percent of the total deposits in commercial banks. While the regulations affecting state and national banks vary slightly, there is, in practice, little difference between the two types from the viewpoint of the individual depositor or borrower.

Table 14-2 lists the fifteen largest banks in the United States. The Bank of America in California is the nation's largest bank with deposits of more than $51 billion. Almost one hundred banks in the United States each have total deposits of more than $1 billion.

How Much Is One Billion Dollars?

Students of business and economics become so accustomed to seeing terms like billions of dollars that they often have no conception of just how much money they are discussing. But suppose that you were given the task of spending $1 billion. At the rate of $100 thousand per day, *you would be spending money for more than twenty-six years!*

THE FUNCTIONS
OF COMMERCIAL
BANKS

Commercial banks perform two basic functions:

1. They hold the deposits of individuals and business firms in the form of checking or savings accounts.
2. They use these funds to make loans to both individuals and businesses. Commercial banks are profit-making business enterprises.

Like frisbee manufacturers, bankers buy inputs, massage them a bit, burn a little incense, say the magic words, and out pops some output from the oven. If their luck holds, they can sell the finished product for more than it cost to buy the raw materials and process them through the assembly line.

For a banker, the raw material is money. He buys it at a long counter he sets up in the store, then rushes around to the back, polishing it on his sleeve as he goes, sits down behind a huge desk (a little out of breath), and sells it as soon as he can to someone else . . .

About the only way you can tell whether a banker is buying money or selling it is to observe him in his native habitat and see whether he's standing up or sitting down. For some unknown reason, probably an inherited trait, bankers always stand up when they buy money (take your deposit), but invariably sit down when they sell it (make loans or buy securities).[4]

Figure 14-2 shows how commercial banks perform these two basic functions.

The Coming of the Federal Reserve System

Banks use deposits as the basis of loans which they make to individual and business borrowers. Since their income is derived from loans, banks will lend most of the currency obtained from their checking and savings account depositors to borrowers at interest rates higher than the rates paid to their savings account depositors. Approximately 15 percent of the total deposits will be kept on hand at the bank or at the nearest Federal Reserve district bank to cover withdrawals; the remainder is used for loans to others.

Figure 14-2
The Operations of
Commercial Banks

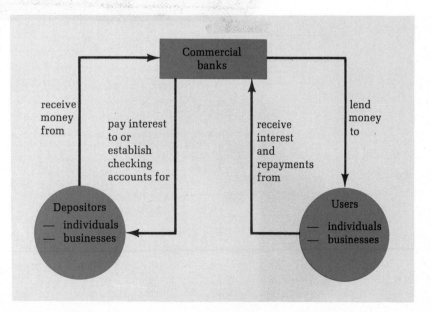

What would happen if all of the bank's depositors decided to withdraw their funds at once? The bank would be unable to return the depositors' money—unless they could borrow the needed funds from another bank. But if the demand for currency instead of checking and savings accounts spread to other banks, the result would be a *bank panic*. Banks would have to close their doors (this was sometimes called a *bank holiday*) until they could obtain loan payments from their borrowers. Such panics in the past often resulted in the failure of numerous commercial banks and plunged the economy into a major depression.

Economic depressions occurred four times in the United States between the end of the Civil War and 1907, and most of them began with bank panics. The severe depression of 1907 prompted Congress to appoint a commission to study the American banking system and to make recommendations for changes. The commission's recommendations became the basis of the *Federal Reserve Act*, which in 1913 established the *Federal Reserve System*.

The Federal Reserve System

Two days before Christmas, 1913, President Woodrow Wilson signed the Federal Reserve Act which created the **Federal Reserve System.** This is a *system of controlling banking in the United States through twelve regional banks controlled by the Board of Governors.* As Figure 14-3 indicates, ten of the twelve regions are further divided into several districts.

In practice, the Federal Reserve System (or the "Fed") is a *banker's bank* holding the deposits of member banks, acting as a clearing house for checks, and regulating the commercial banking system.

Figure 14-3
Map of the
Federal Reserve System

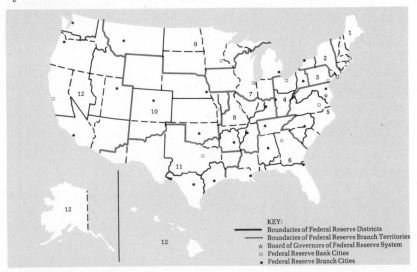

KEY:
——— Boundaries of Federal Reserve Districts
——— Boundaries of Federal Reserve Branch Territories
☆ Board of Governors of Federal Reserve System
□ Federal Reserve Bank Cities
● Federal Reserve Branch Cities

The System is controlled by the Board of Governors in Washington, D.C. The Board consists of seven members appointed by the President and confirmed by the Senate. Political pressures are reduced by a fourteen-year term of office for each member, with one term expiring every two years.

All national banks are required to be members of the Federal Reserve System; membership is optional for state-chartered banks. In all, there are approximately 6,000 member banks.

Control of the Money Supply: Basic Function of the Federal Reserve System

The essential function of the Federal Reserve System is *to control the supply of credit and money in order to promote economic growth and a stable dollar, both at home and in international markets.*[5] It performs this function through the use of three important tools: *reserve requirements, open market operations,* and the *discount rate.*

RESERVE REQUIREMENTS

The strongest weapon in the Federal Reserve System's arsenal of tools in controlling the money supply is the **reserve requirement.** This is the *percentage of a bank's checking and savings accounts that must be kept in the bank or as deposits at the local Federal Reserve District Bank.* By changing the percentage of required reserves, the Federal Reserve System can directly affect the amount of money available for use in making loans. Should the Board of Governors of the Federal Reserve System choose to stimulate the economy by increasing the amount of funds available for borrowing, they can lower the reserve requirement.

Changing the reserve requirement is such a powerful means of changing the money supply that it is not used frequently. Even a 1 percent variation in the reserve requirements means a fluctuation of billions of dollars in the money supply. Because of this the Board of Governors rely more often on the other two weapons at their disposal—open market operations and changes in the discount rate.

OPEN MARKET OPERATIONS

A far more common method of control of the money supply by the Federal Reserve System is through its **open market operations,** *the technique of controlling the money supply by the purchase and sale of government bonds.* When the Board of Governors decides to increase the money supply, they buy government bonds on the open market. The exchange of money for bonds places more money in the economy and makes it available to member banks. A decision to sell bonds would serve to reduce the overall money supply.

Control of the money supply through open market operations is often exercised by the Board when small adjustments are desired.

In addition, these operations do not produce the psychological effect that often results from an announcement of a change in reserve requirements. Such announcements make newspaper headlines and would be widely interpreted by commercial banks, businesspeople, and the stock market as a signal by the Federal Reserve System of "tight" or "easier" money.

THE DISCOUNT RATE Earlier in this text the Federal Reserve Banks were referred to as "bankers' banks." One of the functions they perform is making loans to member banks. When banks need extra money to lend they turn to the Federal Reserve Bank and present either IOUs drawn against themselves or promissory notes from their borrowers. *The interest rate charged by the Federal Reserve System on loans to member banks* is called the **discount rate.**

Commercial banks will choose to borrow from the Federal Reserve System when the discount rate is low, as compared with other sources of funds. A high discount rate may motivate bankers to reduce the number of new loans to individuals and businesses due to the higher costs of obtaining loanable funds.

The Federal Reserve Banks may choose to stimulate the economy by reducing the discount rate. Since the rate will be viewed as a *cost* by commercial banks, a rate reduction encourages commercial banks to increase the number of loans to individual and business loans.

Use of the discount rate as a method for controlling the money supply has declined steadily over the past fifty years. The discount rate, like the reserve requirement, is a blunt instrument with a considerable impact on commercial banking. Over the years open market operations have been increasingly used as a more flexible means of expanding and contracting the money supply. The main use of the discount rate in recent years has been to *communicate* to banks and to the general public the attitude of the Board of Governers concerning the money supply. An announcement of a reduction in the discount rate would be interpreted by commercial banks and the general public as an indication by the Federal Reserve Board of Governors that the money supply should be increased and credit should be expanded.

Table 14-3 shows how each of the tools of the Federal Reserve System can be used to stimulate or "cool off" the economy.

Table 14-3
The Tools of the Federal System and How They Affect the Economy

Federal Reserve System Tools	Stimulate Economy	Slow the Economy
Reserve requirement	Lower	Raise
Open market operations	Buy	Sell
Discount rate	Lower	Raise

Figure 14-4
A Sample Check

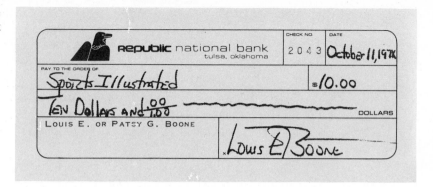

Check Processing: Role of the Federal Reserve System

Figure 14-4 is a **check.** A check may be defined as *a piece of paper addressed to one's bank on which is written a legal authorization to withdraw a specified amount of money from one's account, and to pay that amount to someone else.*

In this case Louis E. Boone has authorized the Republic National Bank of Tulsa, Oklahoma, to reduce his checking account by $10 by paying this amount to *Sports Illustrated* magazine for renewing his subscription. If both parties have checking accounts in the same bank, check processing becomes a simple matter of increasing the checking account of *Sports Illustrated* by $10 and reducing Boone's account by that amount.

But suppose *Sports Illustrated's* publisher, Time, Inc., has a checking account in Chicago. Now the Federal Reserve System enters the picture to act as collector for intercity transactions. The Federal Reserve handles millions of checks every day. Figure 14-5 shows the journey of the check through the System. Whenever you write a check, you can trace the route through the Federal Reserve System it has taken by examining the endorsement stamps on the back of the check.

The FDIC—Providing Insurance for Depositors

Prior to 1934 bank failures were both common and catastrophic for depositors. In the depression year of 1933 alone, nearly 4,000 banks collapsed.[6] Both individuals and businesses feared the loss of their deposits and looked for means of protecting them.

The **Federal Deposit Insurance Corporation** (FDIC) began operating on January 1, 1934. It insures depositors' accounts up to a maximum of $40,000 and sets requirements for sound banking practices. All commercial banks who are members of the Federal Reserve System must subscribe to the FDIC. Most nonmember banks are also covered. In fact, only about 300 commercial banks in the entire United States are not covered.

Figure 14-5
Journey of a
Check through the
Federal Reserve System

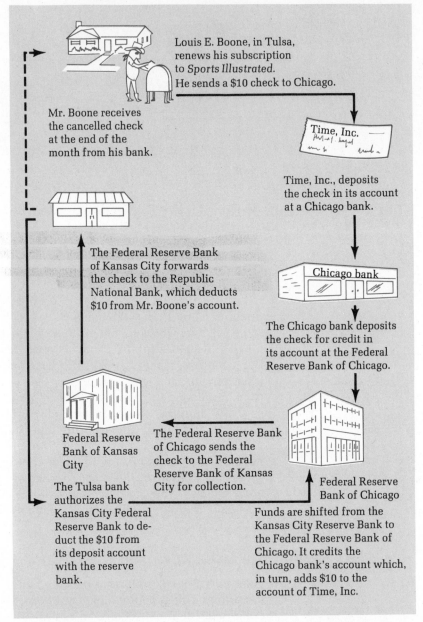

Louis E. Boone, in Tulsa, renews his subscription to *Sports Illustrated*. He sends a $10 check to Chicago.

Mr. Boone receives the cancelled check at the end of the month from his bank.

Time, Inc.

Time, Inc., deposits the check in its account at a Chicago bank.

The Federal Reserve Bank of Kansas City forwards the check to the Republic National Bank, which deducts $10 from Mr. Boone's account.

Chicago bank

The Chicago bank deposits the check for credit in its account at the Federal Reserve Bank of Chicago.

Federal Reserve Bank of Kansas City

The Federal Reserve Bank of Chicago sends the check to the Federal Reserve Bank of Kansas City for collection.

The Tulsa bank authorizes the Kansas City Federal Reserve Bank to deduct the $10 from its deposit account with the reserve bank.

Federal Reserve Bank of Chicago

Funds are shifted from the Kansas City Reserve Bank to the Federal Reserve Bank of Chicago. It credits the Chicago bank's account which, in turn, adds $10 to the account of Time, Inc.

Insurance coverage cannot be increased by holding accounts in a different name or by opening accounts in other branches of the same bank. Deposits in different banks are separately insured, however, so there is no limit to the number of $40,000 deposits that would be fully protected in different banks in the same town or scattered throughout the country.

The FDIC has made major contributions to improving the stability of the American commercial banking system. Since it began operations only about 650 banks have failed. The number of bank failures had dropped to six a year in 1973, and to three in 1974.

When the Franklin National Bank of New York, the twentieth largest bank in the United States, failed in 1974, the FDIC quickly stepped in and arranged for the European-American Bank & Trust Company to take over their banking operations. Depositors lost no money, and consumer installment loans were continued by European-American. As far as the general public was concerned, only the name of the bank had changed.[7] Such actions by the FDIC and the Federal Reserve System contribute to the general public's confidence in the banking system by guaranteeing the savings of depositors.

Electronic Banking

In a single year Americans will write more than 25 billion checks. The huge costs associated with processing these checks have led banks to explore a number of methods of reducing the number of checks being written.

Many banks now provide **electronic banking,** *a computerized system of reducing check-writing through electronic depositing and withdrawal of funds.* This includes automatic twenty-four-hour banking stations where holders of specially coded bank cards can make deposits, cash withdrawals, or payments of utility bills. Automatic cash dispensers are being installed in shopping centers, major department stores, and even in supermarkets—the place where consumers write the greatest number of checks. The cash dispenser is connected to the bank's computer, which checks the validity of the card, reduces the cardholder's checking account by the amount of the cash requested, and provides the requested cash withdrawal and a printed receipt—all within one minute.

For a number of years banks have provided preauthorized payments whereby the consumer could automatically pay utility bills, home mortgage payments, and even insurance payments by allowing creditors to bill the bank. The consumer's checking account was automatically reduced by the amount of the payments, and a receipt showing the exact amount of each bill paid was then mailed to the consumer at the end of the month. Some employers automatically deposit employee pay checks in the banks of their choice. Such services provide maximum consumer convenience and also improve the efficiency of banking operations.[8]

Other Financial Institutions

A number of financial institutions, other than commercial banks, exist as both sources and uses of funds. **Savings and loan associations** and **mutual banks** *accept time deposits from investors and pay* interest at rates that are slightly higher than those paid by commercial banks. These deposits are then used to purchase corporate bonds, home mortgages, and government securities. Nearly half of all new homes are financed by funds from savings and loan associations.

Approximately 30 percent of the nation's 5,500 savings and loan associations are incorporated under federal regulations and must use the term *federal* in their names. The remaining 70 percent are state-chartered. Deposits are insured by the Federal Savings and Loan Corporation (FSLIC).

The deposits of most mutual banks are insured by the Federal Deposit Insurance Corporation (FDIC). Mutual banks are similar to savings and loan associations and are located primarily in the northeastern section of the United States.

The nation's 22,000 **credit unions** serve as *sources for short-term consumer loans at competitive rates for their members.* Credit unions are typically sponsored by a company, union, professional, or religious group and pay interest to their member depositors. Credit unions today have outstanding loans of almost $20 billion.

Other sources of funds include insurance companies and pension funds. **Insurance companies** are *major sources of long-term loans for corporate borrowings, commercial real estate mortgages on major commercial buildings and shopping centers, and government bonds.* These funds are generated through premiums paid by policy-holders. **Pension funds** are established to *guarantee members a regular monthly income upon retirement or on reaching a certain age.* Total assets of all private, state, and local government pension plans are approximately $300 billion. Most pension funds invest surplus cash in corporate securities.

Summary

Money serves as the lubricant for modern industrial society. In order to perform its necessary functions, money should possess the following characteristics: divisibility, portability, durability, a stable value, and difficulty of counterfeiting. These characteristics allow money to perform its functions of acting as a medium of exchange, a unit of account (or common denominator of measuring value of different products), and a temporary store of value.

The money supply is composed of three ingredients: coins, paper money, and demand deposits (or checking accounts). Demand deposits make up the great majority of the American money supply. In addition, such items as savings accounts and United States government bonds are called near-monies. Since they cannot be used directly as a medium of exchange, they are not money. But they are highly liquid and can easily be converted to money.

The heart of the American banking system are the 14,000 commercial banks, which serve two important functions: They hold the deposits of individuals and business firms, and they use these funds to make loans to others.

The regulation of the commercial banking system is the responsibility of the Federal Reserve System, which has three major weapons that can be used to control the money supply: the reserve requirement, open market operations, and the discount rate. Increases in the reserve requirement or the discount rate have the effect of reducing the money supply. Reduction of these rates will have the opposite effect. Open market operations—the purchase and sale of government bonds—is the most commonly used tool. Purchases of government bonds by the Federal Reserve System has the effect of placing more money into circulation in the economy. Sales of bonds act to reduce the money supply. Another function of the Federal Reserve System is to assist in processing checks written on different commercial banks throughout the United States.

The Federal Deposit Insurance Corporation (FDIC) is another agency which regulates the banking system. The FDIC establishes rules for sound banking practices and also insures deposits up to a maximum of $40,000. The FDIC has substantially reduced the number of bank failures and, through insuring deposits, has strengthened the general public's confidence in the American banking system.

Other financial institutions include savings and loan associations and mutual banks. These institutions serve as both sources and uses of funds by paying interest to depositers and making loans for residential and commercial buildings, and purchasing corporate bonds and government securities. Credit unions, insurance companies, and pension funds are other important sources of funds.

Review questions

1. Identify the following terms:
   a. money
   b. medium of exchange
   c. unit of account
   d. store of value
   e. liquidity
   f. currency
   g. demand deposits
   h. near-money
   i. time deposits
   j. state bank
   k. national bank
   l. Federal Reserve System
   m. reserve requirement
   n. open market operations
   o. discount rate
   p. check
   q. Federal Deposit Insurance Corporation
   r. electronic banking
   s. savings and loan association
2. What characteristics should money possess?
3. What are the functions of money?
4. Describe the composition of the money supply in the United States.
5. Why are 95 percent of the financial transactions in the United States conducted with checks rather than currency?

6. Why are near-monies not included in the money supply?
7. Outline the organization of the U.S. banking system.
8. Describe the operation of a commercial bank.
9. Discuss the development and functions of the Federal Reserve System.
10. Outline how checks are processed by the banking system in the United States.

Discussion questions and exercises

1. Evaluate the pro and con arguments to the controversial issue that appears in this chapter.
2. Invite a local banking executive to speak to your class. Ask the executive to explain the role that his or her bank plays in the local community.
3. Prepare a brief report on the different types of money that have been used throughout history.
4. Prepare a brief report on the most recent economic policy actions of the Federal Reserve System. This will require you to do careful research in recent newspaper and magazine accounts of Federal Reserve decisions.
5. Ask a local bank for permission to watch its operation for a few hours. Then report to the class on what you have observed.

Case 14-1
The Treasurer of the United States

Look at the bottom left-hand corner of a dollar bill and you will probably see one of these signatures:

□ Francine I. Neff
□ Acosta Romana Banuelos
□ Dorothy Andrews Kobis.

All of these women have served recently as Treasurer of the United States, a $36,000-a-year post.

By tradition (not law) the Treasurer's signature appears on U.S. currency along with that of the Secretary of the Treasury. Since 1949 the Treasurer's post has been filled by a woman active in the political party of the President of the United States. Aside from a signature for U.S. currency, the Treasurer's only other duties are to promote the purchase of U.S. Savings Bonds and to act as a spokesperson for administrative policy.

Questions

1. Do you think we should have a Treasurer of the United States? Why, or why not?
2. What other functions could be assigned to the Treasurer?
3. Do you approve of the way in which the position has traditionally been filled?

Source: Timothy D. Schellhardt. "U.S. Treasurer Has BIG Job—So Says the U.S. Treasurer," *The Wall Street Journal* (March 18, 1975), pp. 1, 30.

Case 14-2
"Will that Be BankAmericard or Cashcard?"

Many observers have pointed out the the United States has become a credit-card economy. The widespread use of credit cards is an important feature of modern retailing.

Credit-card companies charge retailers from 2 to 9 percent for handling their charge sales. This cost is then passed on to consumers in the form of higher prices. Both cash and credit-card customers pay the higher prices. Many people consider this practice to be discriminatory to cash purchasers. The result has been the formation of such cash-discount organizations as United International Club in Los Angeles and Equity Club International of Jenkintown, Pennsylvania. These plans provide 3 to 10 percent discounts at participating retailers when the cardholder pays by check or in cash.

Questions

1. Do you think charge cards result in discriminatory pricing?
2. Would you be interested in obtaining a cash card? Why, or why not?

Source: "Any Hope for the Cash Customer?" *U.S. News & World Report* (October 8, 1973), p. 60.

15

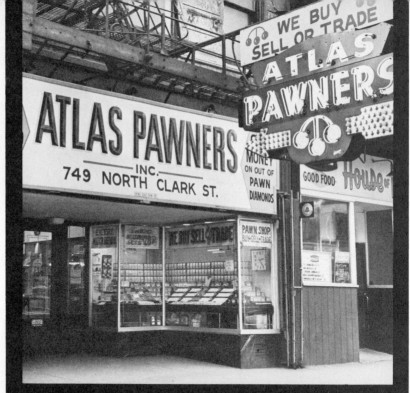

Financial Management: Obtaining and Using Money

"If you owe $50, you're a delinquent account.
If you owe $50,000, you're a small businessman.
If you owe $50 million, you're a corporation.
If you owe $50 billion, you're the government."

—L.T. White

SOURCE: United Press International.

What Chapter 15 Is All About

1. In this chapter, you will meet the financial manager and learn about the important functions the financial executive performs in the operation of the firm.
2. Money is the life blood of any business firm. You should be able to explain how money is used by the firm, both for short-term and long-term purposes.
3. The three basic sources of funds for the business should also be familiar to you.
4. You should be able to identify likely sources of short-term funds for the firm.
5. Occasionally, funds are needed for long-term investments. Where are the most likely sources of funds for these cash needs?
6. After reading this chapter, you should understand these terms:

financial manager	trade credit
finance	cash discount
short term	promissory note
long term	prime interest rate
current assets	line of credit
fixed assets	revolving credit
treasury bill	agreement
commercial paper	factor
certificate of deposit	floor-planning
inventory turnover	bond
debt capital	leverage
equity capital	stock

Stanley Goldblum

SOURCE: Los Angeles
Times Photo.

Within a twenty-five year period Stanley Goldblum managed to become many things—war surplus dealer, mutual-funds insurance clerk, millionaire, and convicted felon.

Equity Funding was incorporated in Delaware in 1960 to sell a package of life insurance policies and mutual fund shares. Customers' monthly payments went into the mutual fund, and the company loaned up to 45 percent of the fund's value as payment on the life insurance premiums.

By selling life insurance policies and mutual funds, Equity Funding reached a total income of over $150 million by 1972; and forecasts showed increasing sales and profits. By that time the corporation also owned savings and loan associations, brokerages, and was involved in real estate, oil and gas, and cattle deals.

When acquisition talks with First Executive Corporation, an insurance company, were broken off in the spring of 1972, Equity Funding's stock declined sharply, and the Securities and Exchange Commission suspended trading on its stock. Then it was discovered that the company had been defrauded of about $2 billion in phony insurance policies that had been resold over the past ten years. A grand jury indictment of some of its officers was handed down late in 1973.

Equity Funding's history had not been peaceful. In 1964 one of its partners sued for damages, and lost. In 1967 one of its subsidiary officers pleaded guilty to bribing a state insurance department representative. In 1973 the company went bankrupt.

Just before the Equity Funding scandal broke, President Goldblum offered 50,000 of his own shares to the market, a sale which was not completed. In 1975 Goldblum pleaded guilty to charges of conspiracy and mail fraud and was sentenced to eight years in prison and a fine of $20,000.

Every weekday morning an employee of the First National Bank in St. Louis boards the early flight to Chicago with a suitcase containing about $15 million in checks.[1] Sound suspicious? Actually the employee is practicing sound financial management. The checks have been written to large corporate depositors of the St. Louis bank and were drawn on major banks in Chicago. Instead of clearing the checks through the Federal Reserve System, as described in Chapter 16, the bank employee delivers the checks directly to the Chicago banks, speeding the check-processing period by one day.

Why go through all this bother just to speed up the system by one day? Although depositors immediately add to their checkbooks any amounts deposited in their banks, the bank doesn't do this. Instead, it waits two or three days until the check clears. This can prove embarrassing to the individual who discovers that a checking account is overdrawn even though a paycheck was deposited earlier that same day. For the large corporation receiving checks totaling hundreds of thousands of dollars on a regular basis, a faster check-processing system means money. At current interest rates saving one day in processing $1 million in deposits *is worth $350!* So, by flying $15 million in checks directly to Chicago for clearing, the St. Louis bank is saving more than $5,000 per day for its depositors.

The Financial Manager—Guardian of the Firm's Purse Strings

On numerous occasions this text has stressed the two primary functions which must be performed by a business in satisfying its customers: production and marketing of want-satisfying products and services. But a third—and equally critical—function is performed. Unless adequate funds are available for the purchase of raw materials, machinery, and production and marketing personnel, management may find itself in bankruptcy proceedings.

The two chief functions of the financial manager are deciding upon sources and uses of funds. Simply stated, **financial managers** *are responsible for both raising and spending money.* They must have funds available to make purchases and pay bills as they come due. They must evaluate alternative sources of funds in deciding upon the least expensive sources. Their responsibilities also extend to continually monitoring the level of the firm's cash, inventories, and unpaid bills in order to insure that excessive funds are not tied up in these items. Although many of these areas are not under the direct control of financial managers, they must act as "watchdogs" in order to be sure that cash is being used efficiently.

WHAT IS FINANCE?　　**Finance** may be defined as *the business function of effectively obtaining and using funds.* Deciding upon the best source of funds and how they should be used are the key ingredients of the company's financial plan. Figure 15-1 illustrates these two ingredients.

LOANS UNLIMITED

"You're putting me on."

SOURCE: *The Wall Street Journal*, July 28, 1975. Reprinted with permission from *The Wall Street Journal*.

Figure 15-1
The Financial Manager
and the Two Key
Ingredients of the
Financial Plan

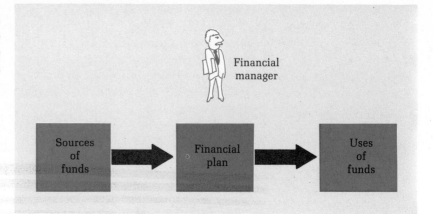

Financial
manager

| Sources of funds | → | Financial plan | → | Uses of funds |

Uses of Funds

A useful method of classifying cash expenditures is in terms of *short-term and long-term* uses. Short-term uses are often referred to as **current assets.** Assets means *items of value* and short term indicates that the assets *are expected to be converted into cash within a period of one year.*

Short-term funds are critical in the day-to-day operations of the business firm, since they provide the firm with the ability to pay bills, extend credit, and promptly deliver merchandise to its customers. The largest dollar investment of many firms takes the form of *long-term* or **fixed assets.** The key long-term uses of funds are for *items of value which are not expected to be converted into cash within a one-year time period.* Such items would include purchases of land, plant, and equipment. Figure 15-2 focuses on the part of the financial plan devoted to uses of funds.

SHORT-TERM USES OF FUNDS

Cash—the ultimate in liquidity

Some of the firm's funds will be held in the form of cash. The majority of this cash is held as a deposit in the firm's checking account for use in paying bills and meeting payrolls. But since the firm cannot receive any interest from cash and checking accounts, the financial manager will try to avoid carrying large balances in the checking account.

The general principle that underlies the financial manager's cash management duty is to minimize the amount of cash required for business operations. Since the firm earns no return on idle money, minimizing the amount of these funds will allow other funds to be used in other interest-producing investments. In order to minimize the firm's cash needs the financial manager should *pay bills as late as possible and collect money as quickly as possible.* As long as these actions can be made without damaging the firm's credit standing, they lead to efficient cash management.

Figure 15-2
Uses of Funds

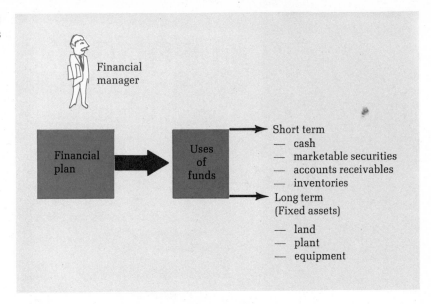

Corporate Savings Accounts Are Severely Restricted at Commercial Banks

A suggestion often made concerning the issue of balancing liquidity and earning a return on funds is that the corporation should deposit its cash in savings accounts—rather than checking accounts. On the surface this compromise appears to allow quick access to funds (liquidity) and also earn some returns on deposited funds. However, this alternative is available only with some major restrictions.

Corporations can draw interest on deposits in commercial banks only if they agree to leave the funds on deposit for ninety-day periods. Withdrawals can only be made within ten days of each calendar quarter. These restrictions exist in order to protect the bank from the possibility of a large depositor (the corporation) withdrawing large amounts of funds at one time. Such a withdrawal might exhaust the amount of funds on hand at the bank, and jeopardize its legal reserve position.

The advertisement of the First National Bank in St. Louis shown in Figure 15-3 emphasizes the efficient management of cash.

Marketable securities as substitutes for cash

Since the financial manager is performing a balancing act between liquidity and profitability, an alternative to holding excessive amounts of cash is to invest cash in the purchase of *marketable securities*. These are often considered "near-money" since they are, by definition, marketable and can be easily converted into cash. The financial manager has a number of different types of marketable securities available for purchase. Three of the most common types are treasury bills, commercial paper, and certificates of deposit.

Figure 15-3
Efficient Cash
Management

THE FIRST NATIONAL BANK CASH MANAGEMENT SYSTEM.

IN

OUT

THE COLLECTOR.

In a cash management system, a few hours' difference could actually mean a difference of two days or more.

At First National Bank in St. Louis, with our First Union Group affiliations, we can put those few hours on your side.

For one thing, mail flows faster in St. Louis than it does almost anywhere else in the country. So money generally reaches a First National lock box sooner.

For another, Missouri is the only state which has two Federal Reserve District Headquarters: at St. Louis and Kansas City. Through our First Union Group of banks, we're on the spot in both places.

So we can offer you a new concept in lock box banking.

Two cities work for you to reduce mail and clearing float in Mid-America. Your funds

THE DISBURSER.

can thus be collected and concentrated into one account swiftly. Automatically.

And when it comes to disbursing your money, you can take advantage of our beneficial disbursement points throughout Missouri.

At First National Bank in St. Louis, that's how we put time on your side.

Our collection system can beat a clearing deadline by an hour. And give you additional money for an extra day.

Our disbursal system, including zero balance accounts, can allow you a day longer to work with your money.

Fast coming in. Slow going out.

In effective cash management, isn't that what it's all about?

Talk it over with us soon. Just call Bob Schmidt, Cash Management Division, at (314) 342-6611.

First National Bank in St.Louis FDIC
We put time on your side.

SOURCE: Courtesy of First National Bank in St. Louis.

United States Treasury Bills **Treasury bills** are issued each week on a competitive bid basis to the highest bidder. Most of them are short-term U.S. Treasury borrowings, usually for 91 or 182 days—although one-year bills are occasionally sold. In most instances the smallest denomination of treasury bills is $10,000. Recently, treasury bills have been sold in denominations as small as $1,000 to allow individual investors to purchase them. Since treasury bills are issues of the U.S. government they are considered virtually riskless. Due to their riskless nature and the ease of resale, treasury bills are probably the most popular marketable security.

Commercial Paper   **Commercial paper** consists of *short-term promissory notes issued by major corporations with very high credit standings.* Commercial paper may have maturities of anywhere from 3 to 270 days. Since commercial paper is riskier than treasury bills, it pays the purchaser a higher rate of interest. The smallest denomination is normally $25,000.

Certificates of Deposit   **Certificates of Deposit** (CD) are *short-term notes issued by commercial banks.* The size of the note and the maturity date are often tailored to the needs of the investor. Minimum maturities of thirty days are quite common, and CDs are easily resold. Normally, the smallest denomination is $100,000. The CD interest rate is typically higher than treasury bills, but below that of commercial paper.

Accounts receivable—credit sales to the firm's customers

In order to retain their present customers and attract new ones, most companies find it necessary to allow at least some credit purchases. For many firms accounts receivable may make up from 15 to 20 percent of all assets. Accounts receivable involve investment by the firm, and a great deal of attention is normally devoted to the efficient management of credit sales. The decision of whether to sell on credit to a firm will usually be based on past dealings with the company and on financial information provided by such credit-rating agencies as Dun & Bradstreet and Retail Credit Company. Figure 15-4 shows a sample Dun & Bradstreet report.

The firm's objective in this area is to collect accounts promptly while still allowing credit terms that will attract the desired level of sales. Since accounts receivable represent sales for which payment has yet to be received, it represents a use of funds. The company has its money invested in products which it no longer owns.

Typical Collection Procedures for a Firm

Step 1. *Letters to overdue customers.* After an account receivable becomes overdue for a certain length of time the firm normally sends a polite letter reminding the customer of the obligation. If the account is not paid within a certain period of time after sending the letter, a second—more demanding—letter is sent. This letter may be followed by a third letter, if necessary.

Step 2. *Telephone calls.* If the use of letters is unsuccessful, the firm's credit manager may call the customer and personally request immediate payment. If the customer has a reasonable explanation, arrangements may be made to extend the payment period.

Step 3. *Personal visits.* This technique is much more common at the consumer credit level, but it may be used by industrial suppliers. Sending a collector, who can confront the customer face to face, may be a very effective collection procedure.

Figure 15-4
Sample of a Typical
Dun & Bradstreet
Report

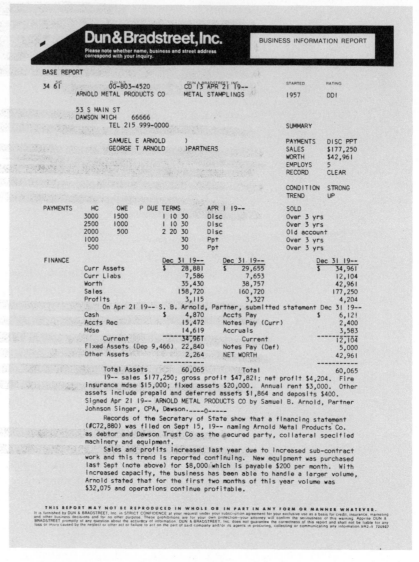

SOURCE: Reproduced by permission of Dun & Bradstreet, Inc.

Alternative Step 3. *Collection agency.* Some firms turn uncollectible accounts over to a collection agency. The fees for this collection method are typically high. Often the firm may receive only fifty cents for each dollar collected.

Step 4. *Legal action.* This represents the most stringent step in the collection process. It is an alternative to the use of a collection agency. In addition to being expensive, direct legal action may result in forcing the debtor firm into bankruptcy, eliminating the possibility of future business with the customer while still not necessarily guaranteeing the receipt of all the delinquent funds.

Inventory—a major use of cash

The subject of inventory management was first discussed in Chapter 9. Since most firms hold inventory in order to satisfy customer demands quickly, inventory represents a major dollar investment. Cash is continuously invested in raw materials, work-in-process (goods in various stages of production), and in finished goods inventory.

The amount of money invested in inventory may vary during the year. The local Sears store will increase its inventories considerably just before the Christmas selling period and reduce its inventories beginning on December 26th. When the next selling season approaches, inventories will again increase.

Inventory as an Investment

Inventory is obviously an investment in the sense that it requires the firm to tie up its money. A useful technique for illustrating the investment nature of inventory is **inventory turnover.** Inventory turnover represents *the number of times the average amount of a firm's inventory is used (or sold) each year.* A high rate of inventory turnover means that the firm can reduce the amount of investment for inventory. Let's see how this works.

The Dryden Press is currently evaluating its textbook inventory in order to determine how much money it will save by increasing inventory turnover from four to six times a year. The increase in turnover is possible through the use of a new, fully automated method of filling book orders within twenty-four hours after they are received.

Dryden expects to continue to move $1.2 million in books through the inventories next year. The average amount of inventory carried under the current and new plans can be calculated by dividing the annual sales by the turnover rate:

$$\text{New plan} \qquad \frac{\$1.2 \text{ million}}{6} = \$200,000$$

$$\text{Old plan} \qquad \frac{\$1.2 \text{ million}}{4} = \$300,000$$

Use of the new plan means that Dryden will tie up only $200,000 in inventory instead of the current average investment of $300,000. Since the extra $100,000 is free from inventory, it can be used elsewhere. If Dryden can earn 7 percent on the $100,000, the reduction in average inventory investment will produce $7,000 (7 percent times $100,000) in new profits. Dryden's management now fully understands that inventory is a major investment.

LONG-TERM USES OF FUNDS For many companies, particularly manufacturing firms, the largest dollar investments take the form of long-term or fixed assets. Fixed assets are required by the manufacturer to be used in producing saleable products. Fixed assets include *land, plant,* and *equipment.*

Size of Purchase	Decision-Making Authority
More than $200,000	Board of directors or specified top management committee
$90,000 to $199,000	President and/or chairman of the board of directors
$30,000 to $89,000	Vice-president in charge of a division
$5,000 to $29,000	Plant manager
Less than $5,000	Persons specified by plant manager

Land owned by the firm is considered to be a fixed asset with an unlimited life. As a result, the firm receives no tax benefits for income tax purposes. *Plant* refers to buildings owned by the firm. Since buildings are likely to deteriorate over time, their owners are allowed to deduct a certain percentage of the purchase price from income each year. These deductions are commonly called depreciation and they result in lowering the firm's tax payments. *Equipment* refers to all items used in production—from drill presses to forklift trucks. Since equipment is also expected to depreciate with use, business firms are permitted to deduct depreciation on their tax forms, thereby reducing the amount of taxes they pay.

Since each of the fixed assets is likely to represent major purchases, the financial manager usually plays a major role in the decision process associated with these purchases.

Who has the authority to purchase fixed assets?

Companies typically delegate fixed-asset purchasing authority on the basis of certain dollar limits. These arrangements usually make major purchases the responsibility of the board of directors, while lesser purchases are delegated to lower levels in the organization. Table 15-1 illustrates how fixed-asset purchasing authority might be delegated in a typical company.

Table 15-1 indicates that as the dollar value of the purchase decreases, the decision-making authority moves to lower levels in the organization. The actual breakdown of this decision-making authority will differ for each company.

Sources of Funds

So far we have focused on the second half of our definition of finance: *effective uses of funds*. But every bit as vital to the firm's financial plan is the choice of the best *sources of needed funds*. As Figure 15-5 shows, the financial manager has three basic sources: borrowing (or debt capital), stock issues (or equity capital), or plowing back earnings to finance future growth.

Figure 15-5
Sources of Funds

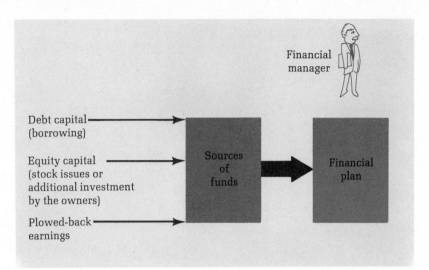

DEBT VERSUS EQUITY

Unless the financial manager is able to generate adequate funds through plowing-back earnings, the manager will be forced to choose between *funds provided by borrowing* (**debt capital**) or obtaining them through *funds provided by the firm's owners through purchases of stock* (**equity capital**). Debt and equity may be compared on the basis of four factors:

1. maturity
2. claim on assets
3. claim on income
4. right to a voice in the management of the firm.

Table 15-2 uses these factors to compare debt and equity.

SHORT-TERM SOURCES OF FUNDS

Just as *uses* of funds were divided into short and long term, it is also convenient to distinguish between short- and long-term *sources* of funds. Short-term sources are those that must be repaid within a one-year period. The phrase *long term* indicates a period of time greater than one year. The four major sources of short-term loans for business firms are:

1. trade credit
2. unsecured bank loans
3. commercial paper
4. secured short-term loans.

Trade credit

One of the short-term uses of funds mentioned earlier in the chapter was for financing of credit sales. Most firms not only sell on credit they also make *sales or purchases on credit*, or *open account*. These

Table 15-2   Comparison of Debt and Equity Financing

Factor	Debt	Equity
Maturity	Has a specific date when it must be repaid.	Has no maturity date.
Claim on assets	Company lenders have prior claims on assets.	Stockholders have claims only after claims to lenders have been paid.
Claim on income	Lenders have prior claim on a fixed amount of interest, which must be paid before dividends can be paid to stockholders. Interest payments are a contractual obligation of the borrowing firm.	Stockholders have a residual claim after all creditors have been paid. While common stockholders may receive large dividends when the company prospers, dividends are paid only when the board of directors of the firm chooses. Dividends are *not* a contractual obligation of the firm.
Right to a voice in management	Lenders are creditors—not owners. They have no voice in company affairs unless interest payments are not received.	Stockholders are the owners of the company and most are given a voice in the operation of the firm. Common stockholders normally have voting rights, while preferred stockholders generally are not given this privilege.

open account purchases, called **trade credit,** represent the major source of short-term financing by most business firms.

Trade credit typically does not involve a formal contract. When the purchaser accepts shipped merchandise, the purchaser in effect agrees to pay the supplier for the goods. The credit terms are stated on the supplier's *invoice* (or bill) which accompanies the shipment.

Why Purchasers Should Always Take Advantage of Cash Discounts

The supplier's invoice will include credit terms. These terms list the period of time credit is extended; the size of the discount offered if the purchaser, will pay cash; and the date the credit period begins. The **cash discount** is the reduction of the purchase price of products, provided the purchaser pays for the goods within a specific time period.

A typical supplier's credit terms may be stated as: 2/10 net 30. The purchaser would read these terms as "A 2 percent discount will be allowed if I pay the invoice within ten days. Otherwise the bill is due in thirty days."

But why should the firm always pay quickly in order to take advantage of the 2 percent discount? Assume the local Pizza Hut was extended credit terms of 2/10 net 30 on a $1,000 paper supplies purchase made March 16th. If the Pizza Hut manager decides to take the discount he will pay $980 ($1,000 less 2 percent) on March 25th. If he decides to ignore the discount offer he will pay $1,000 on April 15th.

The manager's decision not to take the discount means that he is paying $20 to keep his money for an extra twenty days (March 26th to April 15th). Since there are slightly more than 18 twenty-day periods in a year, the interest cost—on an annual basis—amounts to *more than 36 percent!* If the Pizza Hut manager (or any other financial manager) is wise, he will even borrow money from his bank, if necessary, to take advantage of cash discounts.

Unsecured bank loans

A second major source of short-term loans are unsecured loans from commercial banks. The loans are called *unsecured* since the firm does not pledge any of its assets, such as accounts receivable or inventory, as collateral for the loan. The commercial bank makes its short-term loans based upon previous experience in dealing with the firm and the firm's credit reputation. Banks lend unsecured short-term funds in three basic forms:

1. promissory notes
2. lines of credit
3. revolving credit agreements.

Promissory Notes   A **promissory note** is a *traditional bank loan whereby the borrower signs a note stating the terms of the loan, including its length and the interest rate charged.* Such a loan is

"Your signature is all that's required. Cross my heart and hope to die isn't necessary."

Commercial Banks Are Common Sources of Short-term Loans

SOURCE: *The Wall Street Journal,* March 19, 1974. Adapted and reprinted with permission from *The Wall Street Journal.*

Figure 15-6
A Promissory Note

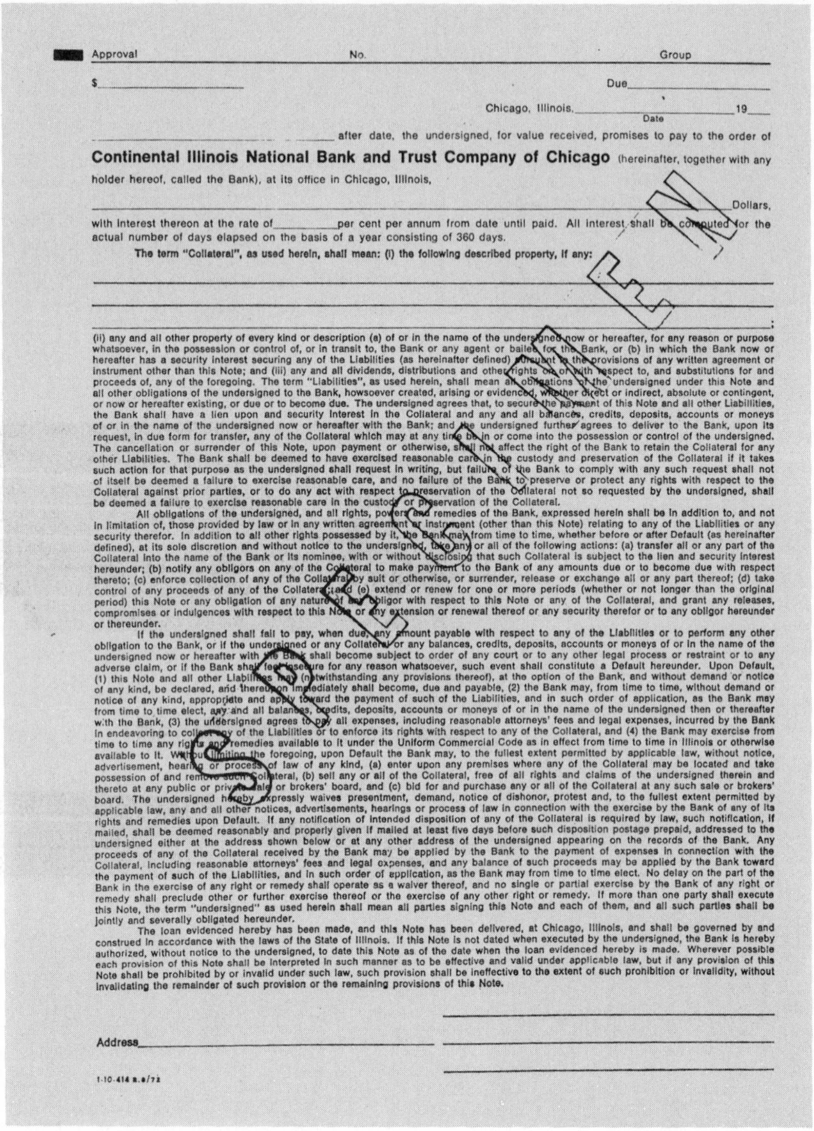

SOURCE: Courtesy of CBS, Inc.

for a specific purpose, such as a temporary increase in inventories for the "Back to School" sales season. Figure 15-6 shows a typical promissory note. The note states the terms of the loan, including the length of time for which the loan is made, and the interest rate charged. Most promissory notes have maturities of from thirty to ninety days.

For major business firms, with high credit standings, the interest rate will be at or near the prime rate. The **prime interest rate** is the *lowest rate of interest charged by commercial banks for* short-term loans to major corporations with extremely high credit standings. The prime rate will shift based upon availability of funds and demand for short-term funds. Changes in the Federal Reserve discount rate usually produce similar changes in the prime rate. Each fluctuation of the prime rate usually makes news headlines, since it indicates the relative availability of funds.

Line of Credit A **line of credit** is an agreement between a commercial bank and a business firm that states the amount of unsecured short-term credit the bank will make available to the borrower—provided the bank has enough funds available for lending. A line of credit agreement is not a guaranteed loan. It typically represents a one-year agreement indicating that if the bank has enough available funds it will allow the firm to borrow the maximum amount of money stated in the agreement. The presence of a line of credit speeds the borrowing process for both the bank and the borrowing firm, since the bank does not have to examine the credit-worthiness of the firm each time it borrows money. Instead, the customer's credit is evaluated and approved in advance.

Bank Credit Cards—Lines of Credit for Individuals

The Bank of America and its affiliated commercial banks who issue Bank-Americards provide a service similar to a line of credit for individual cardholders. Each cardholder is allowed to make credit purchases of up to the authorized amount. Similar services are provided to Master Charge cardholders.

The services even extend to the purchase of money from the local bank servicing the bank card. Cardholders may automatically withdraw $50 to $100 with no credit checks.

Revolving Credit Agreement A **revolving credit agreement** is simply a guaranteed line of credit. The commercial bank guarantees the borrower that the amount of the credit agreement will be available to the borrower. Since availability of funds is guaranteed, a commitment fee is usually charged. The fee applies to the unused balance of the revolving credit agreement.

Commercial paper

Commercial paper, discussed earlier in this chapter, may be both a use of cash for firms with excess funds and a source of funds for major corporations attempting to raise money.

Commercial paper is a short-term promissory note issued by major firms with high credit standings. Since commercial paper is unsecured and is backed only by the reputation of the issuing firm, only very large firms with unquestioned financial stability are able to issue it. Even with large companies risk is present. Holders of Penn Central commercial paper found these unsecured loans were worth very little when the ailing railroad giant defaulted on several million dollars' worth of commercial paper in the early 1970's. Commercial paper is typically sold in denominations of $25,000 with a nine-month maturity or less. The use of commercial paper to raise funds directly from large lenders is usually 1 or 2 percent cheaper than the use of short-term bank loans.

Secured short-term loans

As the firm continues to borrow money it will soon reach a limit beyond which no additional unsecured loans will be made. Many companies—especially smaller firms—are unable to obtain any short-term unsecured money. For them, secured loans are their only sources of short-term borrowed funds.

Secured loans require the borrower to pledge such collateral as accounts receivable or inventory. An agreement is made between lender and borrower which lists the amount of the loan, the interest rate and due date, and the collateral pledged by the borrower. A copy of this agreement is filed in a public office in the state, usually a state or county office. By filing the agreement future lenders are provided with information as to what assets of the borrower are free to be used as collateral.

Commercial banks and such commercial finance companies as CIT Financial Corporation and Commercial Credit Corporation will usually extend loans backed by pledges of accounts receivables or inventory. Both of these assets are usually highly liquid and, therefore, are an attractive form of short-term loan collateral.

Factoring—outright sale of accounts receivables

Instead of using accounts receivables as collateral for loans, some firms sell them to a **factor.** This *financial institution will purchase—at a discount—the accounts receivables of such retailers as furniture and appliance dealers*, where credit sales are common. By selling the accounts receivable to a factor, such as the Walter Heller Company, every sale becomes a "cash" sale and the retailer is freed from the necessity of collecting payments from customers.

In many instances the sales finance company performs the role of a factor. Some commercial banks will also act as factors. When accounts receivables are factored, they are sold at a discount. The factor typically assumes all credit risks. Once the factor has purchased the accounts, customers are notified to make future payments directly to the factor. Although factoring is an expensive method of raising short-term funds, it is often used in retailing because it reduces the need for continuing recordkeeping and for maintaining a collection department.

Floor-planning—the automobile dealer's friend

The automobile industry uses a special type of financing called **floor-planning.** This is *the practice of retailers handling expensive* *items—such as automobiles, furniture, and appliances—by obtaining funds through the assignment of title to their inventories to financing agencies in return for short-term loans.*

When an auto dealer receives a shipment of new cars, an agreement is signed with a local commercial bank or other financing agency for the amount of the shipment. Title to the cars passes to the lender. The inventory, which consists of relatively expensive automobiles, remains in the hands of the borrowing dealer. The lender will periodically check the dealer's inventory in order to make sure that all of the required collateral is still in the hands of the borrower. As cars are sold, a portion of the sales price plus interest is paid to the lender. Some automobile manufacturers allow their financing subsidiaries to make floor-plan loans. The local Chevrolet dealer may have the alternative of floor-planning through a local commercial bank or through General Motors Acceptance Corporation (GMAC), the financial subsidiary of General Motors. Floor-planning is also practiced by many furniture and appliance retailers, since they must make large investments in inventories consisting of identifiable items that are relatively expensive.

LONG-TERM SOURCES OF FUNDS

While short-term sources of cash prove satisfactory in financing current needs for cash or inventory, major purchases of land, plant, and equipment require funds for a much longer period of time. The business firm has several possible long-term financing sources available. The major alternatives are:

1. long-term loans
2. bonds
3. equity financing.

Long-term loans

Long-term loans are made by various financial institutions to business firms. These loans are most often made to purchase machinery and equipment. They generally have maturities of five to twelve years; shorter maturities are available, but minimum five-year maturities are most common. Long-term loans may be made by such financial institutions as commercial banks, insurance companies, and pension funds. Some long-term loans are made by the U.S. Small Business Administration. In some cases, equipment manufacturers allow their customers to make credit purchases over a period of several years.

The cost of long-term financing is generally higher than short-term loans, due to greater uncertainty about the future. Long-term financing agreements will include the length of time for the loan, the interest rate, timing of the payments, and the dollar amount of the required payments. Quarterly interest payments are normally required.

Figure 15-7 A Corporate Bond Issued by CBS

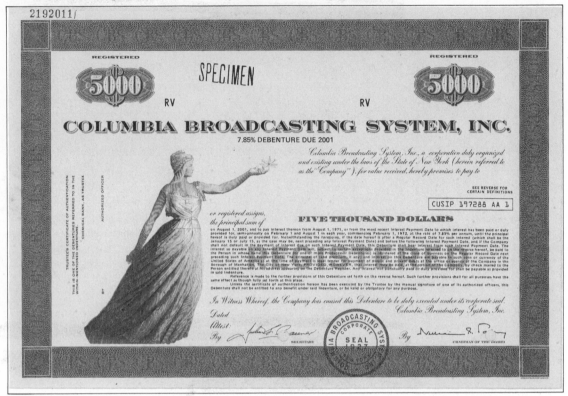

SOURCE: Courtesy of CBS, Inc.

Sales of bonds

The **bond** represents a method of *long-term borrowing by corporations or government agencies.* The corporate bond is issued according to the terms of a legal contract called the *bond indenture,* which contains the provisions of the loan: its amount, interest rate, and maturity date for the bond. Figure 15-7 shows a bond issued by CBS, Inc.

Bonds are typically sold in denominations of $1,000. They are purchased by commercial banks, insurance companies, pension funds, and even individuals. Bonds, like stocks, are actively traded, and may be bought and sold through any stock-brokerage house. Their current market prices are quoted daily in the financial sections of newspapers.

Corporate bonds have essential characteristics as long-term loans. Issuing bonds to raise money is generally reserved only for those larger companies with a regional or national reputation.

How borrowed funds produce leverage

Raising needed cash by borrowing allows the firm to benefit from the principle of **leverage,** *a technique of increasing the rate of return on*

Table 15-3 Simplified Income Statements for the Leverage Corporation and the Equity Corporation

The Leverage Corporation		The Equity Corporation	
Common stock	$ 10,000	Common stock	$100,000
Bonds (at 10% interest)	90,000	Bonds	-0-
	$100,000		$100,000
Earnings	$ 30,000	Earnings	$ 30,000
Less bond interest	9,000	Less bond interest	-0-
	$ 21,000		$ 30,000
Return to stockholders:	$\frac{\$ 21,000}{\$ 10,000} = 210\%$	Return to stockholders:	$\frac{\$ 30,000}{\$100,000} = 30\%$

investment through the use of borrowed funds. Leverage works this way: Table 15-3 shows two identical firms who chose to raise money in different ways. The Leverage Corporation obtained 90 percent of its funds through issuing bonds. The Equity Corporation raised all of its needed funds through the sale of shares of stock in the firm. Although each company earned the same profits, stockholders of The Leverage Corporation earned a 210 percent return on their $10,000 investment—even after paying $9,000 in interest to bondholders. The $30,000 earned by The Equity Corporation represents only a 30 percent return on its stockholders' investment of $100,000.

As long as earnings exceed interest payments on borrowed funds, the application of leverage allows the firm to increase the rate of return on stockholders' investments. *But leverage also works in reverse.* If company earnings drop to $5,000 in the example, The Equity Corporation will earn a 5 percent return on its stockholders' investment. But since bondholders must be paid $9,000 in interest at The Leverage Corporation, what appeared to be a $5,000 gain is actually a $4,000 loss for its stockholders.

Equity funds

Equity funds are *obtained from the sale of stock in the company or by reinvesting company earnings.* Both of these funds differ from debt since there is no maturity date.

Sale of ownership shares is an important company decision and is the subject of Chapter 16. Sales of stock provide cash inflows for the firm—and a share in ownership by stock purchasers. Since these shares are usually traded on organized security exchanges, stockholders may easily transfer their stock through sales on these exchanges.

The sources of equity funds for the company include *sales of stock* and *retained earnings.* Not all firms use each of these sources. Stock sales are possible only for corporations. Each must be evalu-

Should State and Municipal Bonds Be Exempt from Income Taxes?

The state and city taxes you pay (sales, real estate, and, in some cases, income tax, for example) are used to run the state and municipal governments where you live. If you have never thought about who pays the bill for the governor's or the mayor's salary and other governmental expenses, the answer is you do—at least in part. But collecting taxes takes a long time, and in the relatively short term, states and cities may issue bonds to tide them over a period when taxes are still uncollected. These bonds allow the government to borrow money from bond buyers for immediate financing needs. Such bonds may have one maturity date, at which time the face value of the bond must be repaid; or they may have serial dates, whereby a certain portion of the bond has to be repaid each year until the total face value is reached.

Interest on state and municipal bonds is tax exempt. Owners of these bonds pay no income taxes on interest received. The tax exemption aspect of state and municipal bonds is what makes them attractive to buyers who can afford the investment. But the drawing power of such bonds also supports the independence of local government and encourages initiative. Without bond sales, taxes would have to be raised or alternative means of financing of local governments would have to be found.

If the tax exemption of these bonds were to be halted, the interest rate would have to increase in order to attract buyers. Some observers argue that this would eliminate the "inherent discrimination" of such types of bonds. Otherwise, some corporate borrowers argue that interest on all bonds—both government and corporate—should be tax exempt.

Persons opposed to changing the tax exempt status of these bonds argue that if local bonds were less frequently purchased because of reduced profitability, the federal government would probably have to come to the assistance of at least some states and cities. This would mean more federal control and less local control.

Local resources would also have to be allocated on the basis of federal grants, which would take away still more initiative from local government. The classic balance of local and state versus the federal legislative process would be undermined, leaving the federal sector holding the purse strings and most of the power.

The example of a fiscally crippled New York City opens the question of federal willingness to aid local communities and adds another dimension to the puzzle of local financing. Taxation and belt-tightening fiscal policies seem to indicate the direction in which local governments will have to move, if and when bond issues go without buyers.

ated by the financial manager of a business as a possible source of long-term financing.

Sales of Stock The sale of **stock**—*both preferred and common*—represents the true source of equity funds to the business firm. Stocks may be defined as *shares of ownership in the corporation*. The stockholders are considered the real owners of the firm, since they are not guaranteed any dividend payment. The stockholder can receive dividends only after payment to the bondholders of the company. Even then, any dividend payment must be decided on by the board of directors of the firm. Subject to certain legal requirements, firms may sell stock to raise new funds.

Retained Earnings Another source of funds results from reinvesting earnings in the firm. A company may have funds available after paying all claims, including taxes. One choice is to distribute the earnings to stockholders in the form of cash dividends. But generally, not all earnings are paid out as dividends. At least a portion of company earnings are kept to finance future growth. Rapidly growing firms retain most of their earnings. A company such as Walt Disney Enterprises typically distributes less than 10 percent of its annual earnings in the form of dividends. On the other hand, such mature public utilities as AT & T pay out as much as 80 percent of their profits in the form of dividends.

Summary

This chapter has focused on the role of the financial manager in the operation of the firm. Finance is defined as the business function of effectively obtaining and using funds. The firm's financial plan must include a systematic approach to the acquisition of funds and the best uses of these funds.

Uses of funds may be distinguished by time. Short term uses are purchases of assets which will be converted into cash within a one-year period. Long term uses are for purchasing assets which will be used for more than one year. Short term uses of funds include cash, marketable securities, accounts receivables, and inventory. Long-term funds are used to purchase such fixed assets as land, plant, and equipment.

Sources of funds include borrowing (debt capital), sale of stock in the firm (equity capital), and reinvesting company earnings. Short-term sources available to the financial manager include use of trade credit provided by suppliers, unsecured banks loans, commercial paper, and secured short-term loans. Secured loans are those which are backed by pledges of such company assets as accounts receivables or inventory. Some firms sell their accounts receivables directly to financial institutions called factors. These factors purchase the accounts at a discount from such retailers as furniture stores and appliance dealers.

Long-term sources of funds include long-term loans, bonds, and equity financing. Both long-term loans and the sale of bonds represent debt (or borrowed) capital. Equity financing—whether acquired from the sale of stock or the plowing back of company earnings—represents ownership capital.

Review questions

1. Identify the following terms:

a. finance	k. cash discount
b. current assets	l. promissory note
c. fixed assets	m. prime interest rate
d. treasury bill	n. line of credit
e. commercial paper	o. revolving credit agreement
f. certificate of deposit	p. factor
g. inventory turnover	q. floor-planning
h. equity capital	r. bond
i. debt capital	s. leverage
j. trade credit	t. stock

2. What does a financial manager do?
3. What are the two key ingredients of the financial plan?
4. Outline the uses of funds.
5. What role do firms like Dun & Bradstreet and Retail Credit Company play in financial management?
6. Outline the usual collection procedures employed by a firm.
7. Outline the sources of funds.
8. Compare debt and equity financing.
9. How do borrowed funds produce leverage?
10. What is meant by the term "retained earnings"?

Discussion questions and exercises

1. Evaluate the pro and con arguments to the controversial issue that appears in this chapter.
2. A survey by the Financial Institutions Bureau of the Michigan Department of Commerce found that the majority of the state's banks, savings and loan associations, and credit unions considered married men to be the lowest risk group when it came to repaying loans. Next came married women, single men, single women, divorced men, and divorced women in that order.* Conduct a class discussion on the implications of this survey.
3. Ask a local banker to explain his or her bank's procedures in evaluating a loan application from a small businessperson.
4. Ask a local securities broker to talk to your class about the use of corporate bonds by firms.

*Norman Howard. "Women Called More Risky than Men for Credit," *Detroit News* (May 30, 1975), p. 6-E.

5. Do research and then prepare a brief report on the various certificate of deposit plans available from local banks.

Case 15-1
The Great American Debt

Debts in the United States total about $2.7 trillion, or $12,700 for each American. Our per capita debt is more than double our per capita income. Business debt is 55 percent of the total. Federal, state, and local government debt accounts for 23 percent, and the remaining 22 percent of indebtedness is individual debt.

Questions

1. Should the immense debt described above be considered a threat to the economic security of the United States?
2. Identify the types of debt incurred by business, government, and individuals. Should any of these debts be avoided?
3. Is debt a positive or negative feature of our economy? Explain your answer.

Source: Detroit News (March 9, 1975), p. E-1.

Case 15-2
GM Borrows $600 Million

General Motors Corporation's decision to spend an estimated $2 billion to develop a new small car product line shocked financial analysts in 1975. GM's last major borrowing had occurred in 1953.

GM decided to borrow $600 million, while at the same time reducing its dividend. At the time of GM's decision Arvid F. Jouppi, an industry analyst, estimated the firm's debt-to-equity ratio to be 5 percent.

Questions

1. Do you agree with GM's method of raising the $2 billion needed to bring out the new line of small cars?
2. How would you advise GM to obtain the $600 million loan it requires? Give the reasons for your answer.

Source: Christopher Willcox. "Auto Analyst 'Jolted' by GM Financing," Detroit News (March 9, 1975), p. 1-G.

16

The Securities Markets

"A bull can make money in Wall Street; a bear can make money in Wall Street; but a hog never can."

—Anonymous

SOURCE: New York Stock Exchange

What Chapter 16 Is All About

1. In this chapter you will learn about securities. You should be able to distinguish between common stock, preferred stock, and bonds, and be able to identify reasons why an investor might prefer each type of security.
2. Investors seek one or more of three basic objectives. You will consider each objective and then learn to recommend the types of securities that should be purchased by a person seeking a specific objective.
3. You should be able to explain the steps involved in purchasing a security listed on the New York Stock Exchange.
4. When you look at the financial pages of your newspaper you should be able to explain the meaning of the information included in a stock quotation.
5. Investors are protected by several state and federal laws. You should be aware of the major features of each of the laws.
6. After reading this chapter, you should be familiar with these terms:

par value	callable bond
book value	yield
market value	stock exchange
pre-emptive right	over-the-counter market
preferred stock	market order
convertible preferred	limit order
stock	round lot
maturity date	odd lot
secured bond	bull
debenture	bear
convertible bond	price-earnings ratio
bond indenture	mutual funds
serial bond	blue-sky laws
sinking-fund bond	Securities Act of 1933
bond trustee	Securities Exchange Act of 1934

Joseph P. Kennedy

SOURCE: Wide World Photos.

Although many people think of Joseph P. Kennedy as Ambassador to the Court of St. James or as the father of President John F. Kennedy or Robert F. Kennedy, few realize that he retired from banking and the stock exchange in 1929 at the age of forty. Thereafter he devoted himself to his family and to public service. In 1934 he became the first chairman of the Securities and Exchange Commission under President Franklin D. Roosevelt.

A Harvard graduate, Kennedy borrowed money from his father to invest in and become president of a bank at the age of twenty-five. He married Rose Fitzgerald, daughter of a Boston mayor, the following year and established the dynasty that was to include a president, three senators and an attorney general. In Hollywood in the 1920's, Kennedy parlayed a chain of nickelodeons (theaters where movies were shown for five cents) into a clear $5 million profit. He speculated on Wall Street but pulled out just before the crash and never went back into the market.

Turning to politics and the nation's capital, Kennedy contributed heavily to Franklin D. Roosevelt's 1932 presidential campaign. As the SEC chairman, he was instrumental in outlawing many of the practices that he had used to acquire his own wealth. His reforms were necessary, but he did not endear himself to the financial community he had left.

By 1938 Kennedy was named ambassador to England. His conviction that Hitler could be appeased and that World War II could be prevented was turned upside down when Hitler invaded Poland.

Supporting his son Jack's presidential campaign in 1960, Kennedy was nevertheless kept in the background by political advisors who felt that the crusty old Irishman was too controversial a figure. When he died late in 1969, at the age of eighty-one, he had already outlived three of his sons.

The telephone call from his stockbroker came at 9:45 on the morning of April 16, 1968. Seibert Gold was very pleased with the news of the new stock. He had enjoyed a profitable two years buying **new issues** (*stock issued for the first time by corporations seeking to raise equity funds*). In fact, he had just mailed a sizeable check to the Internal Revenue Service district office the day before to pay the federal government's share of profits he had made on his last year's stock market activities.

During the past three years purchasers of new issues were almost guaranteed profits when they sold their stock. Almost every new stock immediately rose above the issuing price. And this new stock sounded particularly intriguing. It's name was Minnie Pearl's Chicken Systems. "Seib, Minnie Pearl's is bound to be another

Kentucky Fried Chicken," said broker Jeffrey Sharp. "The issue price is $20, and I can get you a hundred shares. But you'd better grab it. You know I would never steer a fraternity brother wrong."

"Jeff, you've got a deal! I'll see about mortgaging the Beetle and have the two grand to you in four days."

Seib was so excited he immediately mailed in a subscription to *The Wall Street Journal* and read it religiously each day. Minnie Pearl's stock was issued in May 1968 and the price rose to $30, to $35, and on to $40 per share. Seib's original $2,000 investment had already doubled, and still the stock continued to climb in price. Within a year it had shot up to a peak price of $68 a share, but Seib, who now considered himself a genius of Wall Street, continued to read his *Wall Street Journal* and wait.

By the end of 1968 the founders of Minnie Pearl's Chicken Systems had sold over 1,200 franchises. A year later the number of franchises had grown to 1,600. But the founders were apparently more skilled at selling franchises than fried chicken. Even though the franchises numbered 1,600, only 263 stores had opened. In 1969 even the name of the firm changed. Minnie Pearl's became Performance Systems, Inc.

Investors began to recognize that the new chicken franchise was not exactly a carbon copy of Colonel Sanders' operation. Losses continued and the stock price nosedived.

Seib was torn with indecision. He feared selling at the lower price, since each day he expected the stock price to rise. After all, at its peak his stock had been worth $6,800! Not knowing what to do, he did nothing. Today, Seib still holds his 100 shares. The current price is 12 1/2¢ per share. Seib's $2,000 investment is now worth $12.50.

Securities: Stocks and Bonds

In Chapter 15 two sources of funding were mentioned for long-term capital: equity capital and debt capital. Equity capital takes the form of *stocks—shares of ownership in the corporation.* Long-term debt capital exists in the form of corporate *bonds.*

COMMON STOCK

Holders of common stock are the true owners of a corporation. They vote on major company decisions—such as purchases of other companies or the election of members of the company board of directors. They benefit from company success, and they risk the loss of all of their investment if the company fails.

Common stock is sold on either a par or no-par value basis. The *value printed on the stock certificates of some companies is* called its **par value.** In some states a par value is used as the basis for paying state incorporation taxes. Since the par value is highly arbitrary, most corporations now issue **no-par value** stock. In either

Figure 16-1 A Stock Certificate

SOURCE: Courtesy CBS, Inc. Reproduced with permission.

case, the total number of shares outstanding represents the total ownership of the firm, and the value of an individual stockholder's investment is based upon the number of shares owned rather than on an arbitrary par value.

Sometimes confusion results over two other types of value: *book value* and *market value*. **Market value** is easily determined by referring to the financial page of the daily newspaper. It is simply *the price at which a stock is currently selling*. This will usually vary from day to day, depending upon company earnings and investor expectations concerning future prospects for the firm. **Book value** can be determined by *subtracting what the company owes (its liabilities) from its assets minus the value of any preferred stock.* When this net figure is divided by the number of shares of common stock, the book value of each share is known.

PRE-EMPTIVE RIGHTS— PROTECTION AGAINST DILUTION OF OWNERSHIP

What happens when the corporation decides to raise additional long-term funds through the sale of additional stock? In most cases *current stockholders are given the opportunity to purchase a proportionate share of new stock issues.* This is called the **pre-emptive right** of stockholders. Unless this right exists, a stockholder with 6 percent of the stock in a company would find his share of the comp-

FINANCING THE ENTERPRISE

pany diluted to 3 percent, should the corporation decide to double the amount of stock.

PREFERRED STOCK

In addition to common stock, many corporations—such as Du Pont, General Mills, the Union Pacific Railroad, and RCA—issue **preferred stock,** *whose owners receive preference in being paid dividends, but who do not normally have voting rights.* Preferred stockholders often also have a claim on the assets of the corporation prior to any claim by common stockholders, should the company be dissolved.

In return for these rights preferred stockholders usually do not have voting rights. Even when voting rights exist for preferred stockholders, these rights are typically limited to such important proposals as mergers, sale of company property, or dissolving the company.

Although preferred stockholders are granted certain privileges over common stockholders, they are still considered owners of the firm and dividends are not guaranteed. Preferred stock may be cumulative or noncumulative. In the case of cumulative preferred stock, preferred stockholders must be paid a dividend for each year before dividends may be paid to common stockholders. Should the board of directors of RCA decide to omit the $3.50 dividend to their preferred shareholders in one year due to adverse earnings, they cannot pay dividends to their common stockholders the following year until they pay out dividends of $7 to each preferred stockholder. Any omitted dividend automatically accumulates and must be paid *before* common stockholders can receive dividends.

Preferred stock is often issued with a conversion privilege. Occidental Petroleum Company has an issue of $3.60 preferred stock. Holders of the stock receive $3.60 in dividends annually (assuming they are paid). Their **convertible preferred stock** also gives them *the option of having the preferred stock converted into common stock at a stated price.*

Preferred stock is usually issued to attract more conservative investors who are likely to purchase the stock due to the preferences over common stock. Although preferred stock represents equity capital, many investors consider it as a compromise between the purchase of bonds and common stock.

BONDS

Bondholders are creditors—not owners—of the corporation. Bonds were first introduced in Chapter 15 as a means of obtaining long-term debt capital for the corporation. They are also sources of funds for governmental units—at the municipal, state, and federal levels. Bonds are issued in denominations of $1,000, $5,000, or even $50,000, and indicate a definite rate of interest to be paid to the bondholder and *the date at which a loan must be repaid* (the **maturity date).** Since bondholders are creditors of the corporation, they have a prior claim on the firm's assets to any claims of preferred and common stockholders in the event of dissolution of the firm.

Types of bonds

The potential bondholder has a variety of types of bonds from which to select. Some bonds are **secured** in the sense that they are *backed by specific pledges of company assets*—either real property or such personal property as furniture, machinery, or even stocks and bonds of other companies owned by the borrowing firm. Railroads, which often raise 40 to 45 percent of their long-term funds through issuing bonds, often use rolling stock (locomotives and rail cars) as collateral.

Other companies issue **debentures,** *bonds backed by the reputation of the issuing corporation rather than by specific pledges of assets.* Only major corporations with extremely sound financial reputations can find buyers for debentures. AT & T, the parent company of the Bell Telephone system, has successfully raised billions of dollars from debentures in the past thirty years. Bond purchasers have been willing to buy AT & T unsecured bonds because of their faith in the ability of the issuing company.

In order to entice more speculative purchasers, **convertible bonds** are sometimes issued. These are *bonds with the option of being converted into a specific number of shares of common stock.* The number of shares of stock exchanged for each bond is included in the **bond indenture** (*the legal contract containing all provisions of the bond*). A $1,000 bond might be convertible into 50 shares of

"*What's a debenture?*"

common stock. If the common stock is selling at $18 when the bonds are issued, the conversion privilege has no value. But should the stock rise in price to $30, the value of the bond has increased to $1,500.

How bonds are retired

Since bonds have a maturity date the issuing corporation must have the necessary funds available to repay the principal when bonds mature. The two most common methods of repayment are:

1. serial bonds
2. sinking-fund bonds.

In the case of **serial bonds** the corporations simply *issue a large number of bonds which mature at different dates.* If the Greyhound Corporation decides to issue $4.5 million in serial bonds for a thirty-year period, the maturity dates may be established in such a manner that no bonds mature for the first fifteen years. Beginning with the sixteenth year, $300,000 in bonds would mature each year until all of the bonds are repaid at the end of the thirty-year period. Serial bonds are often issued by city governments as sources of funds.

A variation of the concept of serial bonds is the use of **sinking-fund bonds.** Under this plan, the *issuing corporation makes annual deposits of funds for use in redeeming the bonds when they mature.* These deposits are made with the **bond trustee** (usually a *major bank with the responsibility of representing bondholders*). The deposit must be large enough so that the deposits plus accrued interest will be sufficient to redeem the bonds when they mature.

Many bonds have **callable** provisions. Such *provisions allow the issuing corporation to redeem bonds prior to their maturity dates if a premium is paid.* For instance, a twenty-year bond may not be callable for the first ten years. Between eleven and fifteen years it could be called at a premium of perhaps $50, and between sixteen and twenty years it can be called at its face value.

Table 16-1 summarizes the characteristics of some of the most important types of bonds.

Why Do People Invest?

Chapter 15 focused on the reasons why businesses issue securities. These two sources, equity capital and debt capital, provide the necessary funds to allow business growth. But why do people purchase stocks and bonds?

SPECULATION— LARGE GAINS IN A SHORT TIME

For some people the motivation for purchasing stocks is **speculation.** *They hope to make a large profit on their stocks within a short time period.* This speculation may take the form of high-risk stocks. They

Table 16-1
Types and
Characteristics
of Bonds

Types of Bonds	Characteristics
Secured bonds	Bonds which are backed by specific pledges of company assets—real or personal property
Unsecured bonds (debentures)	Bonds which are not backed with specific pledges of assets but by the financial reputation of the issuing corporation
Convertible bonds	Bonds which can be converted into common stock at the option of the bondholder
Serial bonds	A large issue of bonds, parts of which mature at different dates
Sinking-fund bonds	Deposits of sufficient funds by the corporation with the bond trustee each year to redeem the bonds when they mature
Callable (or redeemable) bonds	The option given to the issuing corporation to redeem the bonds (usually at a premium) prior to their maturity date

may buy low-priced *penny stocks* (so-called because *they sell for less than a dollar per share*) and pray that their 50¢ stock will soar to $5, giving them ten times the amount of their purchase price in return. Such penny stocks include inactive uranium mining companies, Canadian exploration companies, and numerous small oil drilling firms. Most of them show no profits and have little prospect of future profits.

THREE GOALS FOR INVESTORS
In contrast to the speculator, the investor purchases stocks and bonds that assure some safety for the investment and will provide satisfactory dividends and interest as payment for the risk taken. They may also be interested in *growth—increases in the value of stock due to successes of the company.* The objective of the investor will be one or more of these three goals:

1. safety of the investment
2. income
3. growth in the value of the investment.

How $300 Turned into $3 Million

Most investors dream of an investment such as Dave Thurmond's great grandfather made more than 60 years ago. Mr. Thurmond decided to invest $300 dollars (at $1 per share) in a little sandpaper manufacturer called the Minnesota Mining and Manufacturing Company. By the time Dave Thurmond inherited the stock, its original value had increased from $300 to nearly $3 million! In addition, Dave Thurmond received approximately $100,000 a year in dividends. As someone once remarked: "Thrift is an important virtue; especially in an ancestor."

**"For short-term gains, I recommend
Blueboy in the fifth   at Hialeah ! "**

Quick Profits Are the Speculator's Dream

SOURCE: *The Wall Street Journal*, September 16, 1974. Reprinted with permission from *The Wall Street Journal*.

Finding growth industries and growth companies

The investor who chooses *growth* as a primary goal will select companies whose earnings have increased and are expected to continue to grow at a rate faster than that of other companies. The purchaser of growth stocks is likely to own shares of companies in such industries as electronics, drugs, and energy. These companies will typically pay out only small amounts in the form of dividends. Most of their earnings are reinvested in the company to finance further growth. The investor should benefit from this growth through increases in the value of the shares owned in such companies.

Income as a goal—which companies pay dividiends consistently?

Other investors use stocks and bonds as a means of supplementing their incomes. When *income* is the major goal the investor concentrates on the *dividends* of prospective companies. Since dividends are paid from company earnings the investor will consider the company's past record for paying dividends, its current profitability, and its prospects for future earnings. The purchaser of income stocks is likely to own shares of companies in such industries as banking, insurance, and public utilities. Table 16-2 lists twelve examples of companies that have paid dividends consistently for more than one hundred years.

Yield—the investor's return from securities

The *income received from securities* is called the investor's return or **yield**. Yield is expressed as a percent. Assume that a potential

Company	Year Dividend Payments Began
Bank of New York Co., Inc.	1784
First National Boston Corporation	1784
First National City Corporation	1813
J.P. Morgan & Co., Inc.	1840
Chase Manhattan Corporation	1848
Washington Gas Light Co.	1852
Cincinnati Gas & Electric Co.	1853
Scovill Manufacturing Co.	1856
Singer Company	1863
Travelers Corporation	1866
Pullman Incorporated	1867
CNA Financial Corporation	1873

SOURCE: 1974 (or 1975) *Fact Book*, p. 27. Reprinted by permission of the New York Stock Exchange.

investor plans to purchase $1,500 in stocks. He is interested in four companies: B.F. Goodrich, Walt Disney Productions, McDonalds, and MidSouth Utilities. Their recent market prices and dividend rates are:

Company	Recent Market Price	Recent Annual Dividend
B.F. Goodrich	$18	$1.12
Walt Disney Productions	$50	.12
McDonalds	$55	none
MidSouth Utilities	$13	1.26

The yield (*annual dividend divided by the current market price*) for B.F. Goodrich is 6.2 percent, for Disney is less than one-half of 1 percent, and for MidSouth Utilities is almost 10 percent. McDonalds' stock has no yield, since the company does not pay dividends. For the investor seeking immediate income from securities, a utilities stock such as MidSouth may be appropriate.

It should be noted that the yield from a particular security will vary. If the market price changes, so will the yield. When dividend payments are increased or decreased, the yield changes. Should the market price of MidSouth Utilities rise to $18, the yield for a prospective investor would be 7, rather than 9.7, percent. Even though the $1.26 dividend return remains the same, the yield changes.

Safety of principal as an investment goal

In many cases investors are unwilling to risk the potential reverses of common stock. Neither their blood pressures nor their bank accounts are willing to endure such fluctuations as those that occur-

Table 16-3
Comparison of
Securities with
Investment Objectives

	Investment Objectives		
Security	*Safety*	*Income*	*Growth*
Bonds	Best	Very steady	Usually none
Preferred stocks	Good	Steady	Variable
Common stocks	Least	Variable	Best

SOURCE: *How To Invest*. Reprinted by permission from Merrill Lynch, Pierce, Fenner & Smith, Inc. (New York: Merrill Lynch, Pierce, Fenner & Smith, Inc., 1971), p. 21.

red between early 1973 and late 1974. In that twenty-four-month period such glamour stocks as Xerox sank from 170 to 55; IBM from 340 to 172; Eastman Kodak from 152 to 62; McDonalds from 76 to 33; and Polaroid saw its market value *drop 82 percent* as the price fell from 90 to 16! Investors whose primary investment objective is safety for their original investments are likely to purchase high quality bonds and preferred stocks. These securities offer the greatest protection for the investor, and are most likely to continue to pay a good return on the investment.

Most investors are likely to have more than one of these investment goals. Investors who emphasize safety of principal may buy preferred stocks, which may grow in market value. An investor who buys growth stocks may choose stocks paying at least a 3 percent yield in order to receive some short-term return on the investment. Table 16-3 is a useful guide for evaluating stocks and bonds in terms of the three investment objectives.

A Profile of the American Investor

A study by the New York Stock Exchange reveals that an average of one in every four adult Americans now owns shares of common stock. This compares with one in sixteen in 1952. The majority of stockholders have annual incomes of less than $15,000 per year.

For thirteen years, between 1956 and 1969, women stockholders had outnumbered men. But in 1970 the percentage of male stockholders had climbed to 50.1 percent of the nearly 31 million individual stockholders in the United States. The 45-to-54 group is the largest group of individual investors, accounting for one-fourth of the total.

The individual investor is most likely to own one or more of the popular stocks listed in Table 16-4. These ten companies have the largest numbers of stockholders in the United States.

The Securities Exchanges

Securities exchanges are the market places for stocks and bonds. The **stock exchanges** are *the locations at which stocks and bonds are bought and sold*. Although the securities of corporations are

Company	Number of Stockholders
American Telephone & Telegraph	2,934,000
General Motors	1,283,000
Exxon Corporation	725,000
International Business Machines	557,000
General Electric	537,000
General Telephone and Electronics	430,000
Ford Motor Company	341,000
Gulf Oil	333,000
Texaco Inc.	310,000
Consolidated Edison	308,000

Source: The New York Stock Exchange. *1974 Fact Book,* pp. 35, 50.

traded, the corporations themselves are not directly involved, and they receive no proceeds from the sales. The securities traded at organized exchanges have already been issued by corporations. The sales are between individual and corporate investors.

THE NEW YORK STOCK EXCHANGE (NYSE)

When investors talk about the stock market they are usually referring to the New York Stock Exchange. "The Big Board," as it is sometimes called, is the largest and best known of all stock exchanges. In order to transact business on the NYSE a brokerage firm must be a member. There are 1,366 "seats," and potential members must purchase seats from current members and be approved by the thirty-three-member governing board of NYSE. Memberships have varied considerably in price, ranging from a high of $615,000 in 1929 to a low of $17,000 in 1942.

Approximately 2,000 stocks and 1,200 bonds are **listed** (*traded*) on the NYSE. These securities represent 90 percent of the market value of all outstanding stocks in the United States. In addition to the ten companies listed in Table 16-4, the NYSE-listed stocks include such major corporations as Sears, RCA, Mobil Oil, DuPont, Xerox, Eastman Kodak, and TWA. Such foreign stocks as the Canadian Pacific (Canada), KLM Royal Dutch Airlines (Netherlands), Sony (Japan), ASA Limited (South Africa), and British Petroleum (United Kingdom) are also listed.

Requirements for Listing on the New York Stock Exchange

To qualify for listing on the NYSE a company must meet the following minimum standards:

1. annual earnings must be at least $2.5 million before taxes
2. at least 1 million shares must be publicly held

3. at least 2,000 investors must hold 100 shares or more
4. the outstanding common stock must have a market value of at least $16 million
5. the company must have net tangible assets of at least $16 million.

Once these requirements are met, the governing board determines whether the securities of a particular corporation will be listed on a case-by-case basis.

Source: The New York Stock Exchange. *1974 Fact Book*, p. 30.

THE AMERICAN STOCK EXCHANGE (AMEX)

Second in size and importance to the New York Stock Exchange is the American Stock Exchange. The AMEX, as it is called, is also located in New York and has approximately five hundred full members and four hundred associate members. Approximately 1,000 stocks are traded on the AMEX. These include such well-known companies as Tiffany's, STP Corporation, the New York Times, Hormel Meat Packing, and Bic Pen.

REGIONAL AND LOCAL EXCHANGES

In addition to the two major exchanges, a number of regional and local exchanges operate throughout the United States. The largest of the regional exchanges is the Midwest Exchange in Chicago. Others include the Philadelphia-Baltimore-Washington Stock Exchange, the Cincinnati Stock Exchange, and the Pacific Coast Stock Exchange, which has operations in both San Francisco and Los Angeles. Local exchanges operate in Boston, Pittsburgh, Detroit, Salt Lake City, Richmond, Spokane, Honolulu, Colorado Springs, and Wheeling.

Approximately five hundred companies are listed on each of the regional exchanges; each of the local exchanges usually list slightly more than one hundred firms. These exchanges were originally established to trade the shares of smaller firms operating within a limited geographic area. While many of the listed companies continue to be smaller corporations, the regional exchanges now list many of the major corporations. As the volume of trading on the regional exchanges increased, larger firms decided to list their shares there. Today about half of all of the companies listed on the New York Stock Exchange are also listed on one or more regional exchanges.

FOREIGN STOCK EXCHANGES

Stock exchanges are not an American creation. The world's oldest exchange is the Amsterdam Stock Exchange, which began operations in 1611. The London Stock Exchange, which lists more than 10,000 stocks, traces its beginnings to prior to the American Revolutionary War. Other important foreign exchanges are located in Paris, Tokyo, Zurich, Frankfort, Johannesburg, Melbourne, Copenhagen, Montreal, and Toronto. Major American corporations are frequently listed and traded on foreign exchanges.

THE OVER-THE-COUNTER MARKET (OTC)

The investor who decides that the "Uncola" campaign means unquestioned growth for the Seven-Up Bottling Company will not find the stock listed on the New York Exchange. It is not on the American Stock Exchange or on any of the other regional exchanges. Seven-Up is one of the nearly 60,000 securities traded on the **over-the-counter (OTC) market.**

Actually, the OTC market is not a real place at all. It is simply a method of *trading unlisted securities outside the organized securities exchanges.* It is a network of approximately 5,000 brokers scattered throughout the United States who buy and sell unlisted stocks and bonds over the telephone. These brokers are in regular contact with one another, and the prices of the securities they trade are established by supply and demand.

In 1975, most OTC transactions were also quoted on *ticker tapes*—the electronic screens in the offices of stock brokerage firms that had previously shown only trades of listed securities. At the suggestion of the Securities and Exchange Commission, the Consolidated Tape network carried quotations for the approximately 2,000 issues on the NYSE and other markets. OTC trades are indicated by the letter T following the price of the transaction. The letter M is used to indicate the Midwest Stock Exchange, X for the Philadelphia-Baltimore-Washington Exchange, C for the Cincinnati Stock Exchange, and P for the Pacific Coast Exchange. Both OTC dealers and investors can now determine instantly the current prices of issues.[1]

Security dealers in the OTC market will often purchase shares in their own names. When a prospective buyer appears, the shares are then sold at a profit. If the broker has none of the wanted shares in inventory, the broker will call other brokers to make purchases at the lowest possible price for resale.

The OTC market includes trading in the shares of most insurance companies, banks, municipal bonds issued by cities and states, many government bonds, and a number of stocks of industrial firms. These include such companies as Anheuser Busch, Sea World, Mary Kay Cosmetics, American Express, Pizza Inn, Snap on Tools, Taco Bell, Fotomat, and Pabst Brewing Company.

How Securities Are Bought and Sold

Should you decide to invest the $1,000 your grandmother presented to you as a birthday present, you would first contact a **stockbroker.** A stockbroker, or account executive, is *a middleman who buys and sells securities for clients.* If you do not already have a stockbroker, you would probably contact one of the stock brokerage firms listed in the "Yellow Pages" of your local telephone directory. Most cities have offices of such major brokerage firms as Merrill Lynch, E.F. Hutton, and Bache & Company, as well as smaller firms.

Once you have contacted a broker, your next step would be to

Figure 16-2
How a Ticker
Tape Is Read

EK	MCD	XRX	GM	T	XON
93 1/2	5s44 1/8	71 3/4	42 1/8	10s49 3/4	2s73 5/8

How many stocks can you identify? Some of the abbreviations are easily recognizable and others offer no clue as to their identity. Under each abbreviation is shown the current sales price for the stock and the number of shares involved in each transaction. Shares are traded in lots of 100; if more than 100 shares are involved, the ticket tape will indicate the size of the transaction. The 5s shown under the symbol MCD indicates that 500 shares were traded. Here is how the tape is read:

100 shares of Eastman Kodak at $93.50
500 shares of McDonalds at $44.125
100 shares of Xerox at $71.75
100 shares of General Motors at $42.125
1,000 shares of American Telephone & Telegraph at $49.75
200 shares of Exxon at $73.625

meet with him (only about 1 percent of the nation's stockbrokers are women) to discuss your investment objectives. Then you and your broker would discuss a number of stocks and bonds that appear to meet your investment goals.

If Exxon common stock appears to meet your joint goals of income and growth, the broker would determine the current market price of the stock by typing the Exxon symbol (XON) on an electronic device at his desk. These devices—called Telequote, Ultronic Stockmaster, or Quotron—are linked to the national stock exchanges in New York and can provide immediate information on current stock prices, dividends paid, and the high and low prices for the year. Many brokerage firms also have **ticker tapes,** *large screens that electronically display actual securities transactions on the New York and American Stock Exchanges within seconds after they take place.* In many cities with cable television service, one of the channels shows the ticker tape—providing maximum convenience and immediate information for the investor-viewer. Figure 16-2 shows a segment of a ticker tape.

PLACING AN
ORDER

If the investor decides to purchase Exxon common stock, he or she instructs the broker, who then teletypes the order to the firm's member on the floor of the New York Stock Exchange. The New York representative goes directly to the location on the floor of the Exchange where Exxon is traded and attempts to make the purchase.

Market orders and limit orders

An investor request that a stock purchase be made at the current market price is a **market order.** The NYSE floor member will quickly make the purchase on a "best price" basis, and the investor will be notified of the purchase price within a matter of minutes.

On the other hand, an *investor request that a stock purchase*

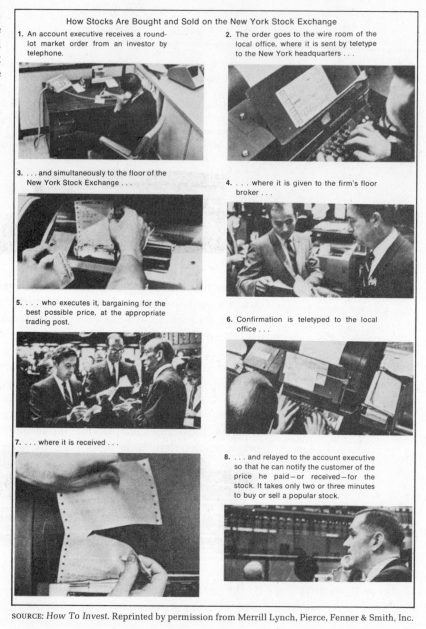

How Stocks Are Bought and Sold on the New York Stock Exchange

1. An account executive receives a round-lot market order from an investor by telephone.

2. The order goes to the wire room of the local office, where it is sent by teletype to the New York headquarters . . .

3. . . . and simultaneously to the floor of the New York Stock Exchange . . .

4. . . . where it is given to the firm's floor broker . . .

5. . . . who executes it, bargaining for the best possible price, at the appropriate trading post.

6. Confirmation is teletyped to the local office . . .

7. . . . where it is received . . .

8. . . . and relayed to the account executive so that he can notify the customer of the price he paid—or received—for the stock. It takes only two or three minutes to buy or sell a popular stock.

SOURCE: *How To Invest.* Reprinted by permission from Merrill Lynch, Pierce, Fenner & Smith, Inc.

or sale be made at a specified price is a **limit order.** In this case a notation of the limit order is made at the post which handles the stock transactions, and should the price drop to the specified price, the purchase will be made.

Round lots and odd lots

As Figure 16-2 indicates, stock trading is conducted in *quantities of* one hundred shares. These are called **round lots.** But one hundred shares of Exxon will cost more than $7,000. How can you invest your $1,000 in Exxon stock?

The answer is through **odd-lot purchases.** *Purchase or sales of less than one hundred shares of stock* are grouped together to make up one or more round lots. The stocks are then distributed to the various odd-lot purchasers when the transaction is completed.

Bulls and Bears

These two frequently mentioned stock market terms refer to investor attitudes. **Bulls** are *investors who expect stock prices to rise.* They buy securities in anticipation of the increased market prices. When stock market prices continue to rise, market observers call it a bull market.

Bears are *investors who expect stock prices to decline.* They are likely to sell their securities, since they expect market prices to fall. When market prices steadily decline, the market is labeled a bear market.

THE COST OF TRADING Buyers and sellers of securities pay commissions to the brokerage firm in payment for their services. Prior to April 1, 1974, the New York Stock Exchange used this minimum commission rate schedule for round lot transactions:

Money Involved	Percent of Money Involved	Plus Stated Amount
Under $100	As mutually agreed	—
$100 but under $800	2.0%	$ 6.40
$800 but under $2,500	1.3%	$12.00
$2,500 and above	0.9%	$22.00

An order to purchase one hundred shares of General Motors at 32 would be calculated as:

Cost of stock: $3,200 (100 shares at $32 each)

Commission: $40.80 (.9% of $3,200 = $28.80; $28.80 plus $22 = $40.80).

The NYSE also established a maximum commission of $65 on any order of one hundred shares. Commissions on transactions are now established on the basis of negotiation between the client and the brokerage firm, but the rate schedule shown is similar to current commissions. Commissions on large trades have declined considerably, however, due to increased price competition. Commissions on transactions by large business investors such as insurance companies, mutual funds, and pension funds have dropped as much as 50 percent due to the increased competition among brokerage firms for this business.

Prior to October 20, 1975, odd-lot purchasers were required to pay an additional 12-1/2¢ commission on each share purchased. This additional fee was charged as payment for the additional costs involved in handling odd-lot transactions.

Reading the Financial News

At least two or three pages of most major daily newspapers are devoted to reporting current financial news. This news typically focuses on the previous day's securities transactions. Stocks and bonds traded on the NYSE and AMEX are listed alphabetically in the newspaper. Information is provided on the volume of sales and the price of each security.

STOCK QUOTATIONS

Figure 16-4 is reproduced from *The Wall Street Journal,* a newspaper published each weekday which contains detailed information on financial and business news.

To see how to read these stock quotations, let's focus on the first stock: Abbott Laboratories. The highest price for Abbott in 1975 has been $78.00 per share; the low was $46.50. Abbott pays

Figure 16-4
Stock and Bond Quotations from *The Wall Street Journal*

Stocks

–1975– High	Low	Stocks	Div.	P-E Ratio	Sales 100s	High	Low	Close	Net Chg.
		– A–A–A –							
78	46½	AbbLab	1.44	17	142	78	76½	78	+ 1
45¾	33¼	ACF In	2.60	9	37	45¼	44⅝	45⅛	+ ¼
10⅜	7	AcmeClv	.50	5	26	9½	9¼	9¼	– ¼
4⅛	1¾	AdmDg	.04e	9	53	3¾	3⅝	3¾	.....
10½	7¾	AdmEx	.77e	...	11	10⅜	10¼	10⅜	+ ⅛
4	2⅛	Adms Millis		...	17	4¼	3⅞	4¼	+ ¼
9⅜	3¼	Addressog		86	77	8⅝	8⅜	8⅝	+ ⅛
10	7¼	AdvInv	.28e	...	13	9	8⅞	8⅞	– ⅛
29⅜	20	AetnaLf	1.08	12	424	27¾	27¼	27½	.....
7	4¾	Aguirre Co		7	5	5⅞	5¾	5¾	– ¼
12	6⅞	Ahmans	.20	7	61	10½	10¼	10⅜	+ ⅛
4⅝	1⅝	Aileen Inc		10	18	4¼	4⅛	4⅛	– ⅛
79⅜	44¾	AirPrd	.20b	19	103	78	75¼	75¼	– 3
13⅜	4⅞	AirbnFrt	.50	10	48	11¾	11¼	11⅝	+ ⅛
23⅜	10½	AircoInc	.90	7	193	23	22	23	+ ¼
2¾	1	AJ Industris		6	103	2¾	2⅝	2¾	+ ⅛
17¼	10½	Akzona	1.20	40	308	16⅜	15⅞	15⅞	– ¼
13⅜	7⅞	Ala Gas	1.18	7	12	12¾	12½	12½	– ⅛
17⅝	9	Alaska Intrs		11	36	16¾	16¼	16¼	– ½
19⅝	13⅞	AlbanyIn	.60	7	10	18	17⅝	18	+ ⅜
8¼	4⅝	AlbertoC	.36	21	48	8	7¾	7¾	– ¼
19⅜	12¼	Albertsn	.60	10	82	19⅞	19½	19⅞	+ ½
26	18⅞	AlcanAlu	.80	7	404	25⅞	25⅜	25½	– ¼
12⅝	7½	AlcoStd	.48	4	57	12¼	11⅞	11⅞	+ ⅛
29	15¼	AlconLb	.24	26	40	26½	26	26⅛	+ ⅝
6½	2½	Alexdrs	.16e	12	183	6⅜	6⅛	6¼	– ⅛
6⅜	3	Alison Mtg		22	121	5¼	4⅛	5	+ ⅞
11⅜	6⅞	AllegCp	.45e	10	27	10⅛	9⅞	9⅞	– ¼
26⅞	20⅜	AllgLud	1.80	3	41	25⅛	24⅞	25⅛	– ⅛
36⅞	31⅝	AllgLud	pf 3	...	3	35⅛	35⅛	35⅛	+ ⅛
18¾	12⅞	AllgPw	1.52	9	73	17½	16¾	17⅛	+ ¼
9⅝	4⅛	AllenGrp	.40	12	83	10½	9¼	10½	+ 1
42	27	AlldCh	1.80	8	224	37⅝	36⅜	37⅛	+ ⅛
15⅜	8⅝	AlldMnt	.54	9	29	14⅞	14¾	14⅞	+ ⅛
15⅜	12½	AlldProd	1	5	25	14⅜	13⅞	14¼	+ ⅜
40¾	15⅞	AlldStr	1.50	9	215	40	39⅝	39¾	.....
4	2⅛	Alld Supmkt		...	25	2¾	2⅝	2⅝	– ⅛
11¾	6⅝	AllisChal	.26	6	276	11¾	11⅛	11⅝	+ ⅜
8	5⅛	AllrtAut	.56	7	2	7½	7½	7½	+ ⅛
12½	7⅜	Alpha Pl	.72	5	1	11⅞	11⅞	11⅞	.....
50¼	27⅛	Alcoa	1.34	10	133	46½	45½	46¼	+ ¼
46⅞	26¾	AmalgSug	3	3	65	38¾	37⅛	38¾	+ 1¾
56¼	28¾	Amax	1.75	9	139	53⅛	52¼	53	+ ½
135½	77	Amax	pf5.25	...	1	129¼	129¼	129¼	– ¾
15	6	AMBAC	.60	7	91	14⅜	14	14⅜	+ ¼
5⅛	3	Amcord	.26	7	18	4¾	4⅝	4¾	.....
18¾	13¼	Amerce	1.20	5	5	17½	17⅛	17½	+ ⅛
22⅜	15⅛	A Hess	.30b	4	288	21¼	20⅝	21⅛	+ ⅜
55½	42	A Hes	pf3.50	...	39	53⅞	52	53⅛	+ ⅝
21¾	7⅜	AAirFilt	.44	13	118	21½	20½	20¾	– ¼
10⅛	5⅛	Am Airlin		29	679	9¼	9	9⅛	.....
14¾	3¾	A Baker	.40	...	13	14⅜	14⅛	14⅜	+ ¼
42⅜	30½	A Brnds	2.68	8	100	42⅛	41½	41¾	.....
27⅜	13⅛	AmBdcst	.80	8	837	23¾	22¼	22⅝	– 1¼
11⅜	5	AmBldM	.36	8	1	10⅞	10⅞	10⅞	.....
34½	28	A Can	2.20a	6	107	30⅞	30⅜	30½	– ½
[illegible]	1½	AmCen Mtg		...	4	2¼	2¼	2¼	.....
[illegible]	[illegible]	A Chain	1.20	6	3	17⅞	17⅞	17⅞	+ ⅛
[illegible]	[illegible]	A Cyan	1.50	8	543	27½	27⅛	27¼	– ⅛
[illegible]	[illegible]	[illegible]mDist	.12p	69	4	8¼	8¼	8¼	– ¼
[illegible]	[illegible]	[illegible]sTel	.52	13	42	28⅛	27½	27¾	.....
[illegible]	[illegible]	[illegible]alVt		...	2	4½	4½	4½	– ⅛
[illegible]	[illegible]	[illegible]f.84a		...	2	12½	12½	12½	+ ⅛
[illegible]	[illegible]	[illegible]		[illegible]	[illegible]	20¼	20	20⅛	+ ⅛

Bonds

CORPORATION BONDS
Volume, $21,950,000

Bonds	Cur Yld	Vol	High	Low	Close	Net Chg
AddM 9⅜95	12.	2	74	74	74	.....
AirRe 3⅞87	cv	20	83⅞	83¾	83⅞	+ ⅛
AlaB 10½99	10.	25	102⅛	102⅛	102⅛	+ ⅛
AlaP 9¾s04	10.	15	97⅜	97	97	– ⅜
AlaP 9s2000	9.6	8	93	93	93	.....
AlaP 8⅞s03	9.9	29	88¾	88	88¾	+ ¼
AlaP 7¾s02	10.	10	75⅛	75⅛	75⅛	+ 1⅛
Alaska 6s96	cv	6	80½	80¼	80½	+ ½
Alison 8¾79	14.	10	59	57⅞	59	+ 1½
AlldC 9s2000	9.0	5	99⅞	99⅞	99⅞	.....
AlldCh 8⅜83	8.3	5	100¼	100¼	100¼	+ ¼
AldCh 6.6s93	7.9	20	82¾	82¾	82¾	.....
AlldCh 3½78	3.8	2	91⅞	91⅞	91⅞	.....
AlldPd 7s84	9.3	1	75	75	75	– 1
AlldSt 4½92	cv	15	91	90½	90½	– ½
AldSu 5¾87	cv	5	43⅝	43	43⅝	.....
Al[illegible] 9.45s2000	9.2	8	102¼	102¼	102¼	– ¼
Alcoa 9s95	9.0	3	99	99	99	– ½
AMAX 9⅜	9.3	10	100	100	100	– 1
AMAX 8½84	8.4	40	100¼	100¼	100¼	– ¼
AMAX 8s86	8.8	17	91¼	90¾	90¾	– 1¼
Amerce 5s92	cv	10	64½	64½	64½	+ ½
AAirln 11s88	11.	26	100	99	99	+ ⅝
AAirl 4¼s92	cv	27	48	47½	48	.....
ABrnd 9⅝79	9.1	40	105¼	104⅝	104⅝	– ⅜
ABrnd 8⅛85	8.2	5	98½	98½	98½	.....
ACan 4¾s90	6.8	5	69¼	69¼	69¼	+ ⅛
AForP 5s30	10.	5	47	46	46	– 1½
AFoP 4.8s87	7.9	5	60½	60½	60½	+ 1
AHoist 5½93	cv	20	79⅝	79	79	– ½
AInvt 9½s76	9.6	5	98⅞	98⅞	98⅞	– ⅛
AMF 4¼s81	cv	16	78	78	78	.....
AMed 9½98	13.	5	69¾	69¾	69¾	.....
AMedcp 5s97	cv	33	49½	49½	49½	+ ½
AmMot 6s88	cv	322	70	69	69¼	+ ¼
ASug 5.3s93	7.7	2	68¾	68¾	68¾	.....
ATT 8.80s05	8.7	290	101	100¼	100⅝	+ ⅛
ATT 8¾2000	8.6	352	101⅝	101⅜	101⅜	+ ⅛
ATT 8.7s02	8.7	88	100½	99¾	99¾	– ¼
ATT 8⅝s07	8.7	148	98⅞	98⅝	98¾	+ ⅜
ATT 7¾s82	7.8	102	98⅜	98⅛	98⅜	+ ¼
ATT 7.75s77	7.6	73	101⅝	101⅛	101½	+ ⅛
ATT 7⅛s03	8.3	25	86	85½	85½	.....
ATT 7s01	8.2	25	85	84½	85	+ ¾
ATT 6½s79	6.8	34	95½	94¾	94¾	– ¾
ATT 4⅜s85	5.7	16	76	75⅛	76	+ ½
ATT 3⅞s90	6.1	16	63¾	63	63	– ½
ATT 3¼s84	4.7	15	69	69	69	– ½
ATT 2⅞s87	4.7	10	60½	60	60	– ½
ATT 2¾s75	2.7	5	98⅞	98⅞	98⅞	.....
[illegible]	[illegible]	[illegible]	[illegible]	[illegible]	81½	+ 1¼

SOURCE: Reprinted with permission of *The Wall Street Journal,* © Dow Jones & Company, 1975.

annual dividends of $1.44. The **price-earnings ratio** (*current market price divided by the annual earnings per share*) is 17. A total of 1,700 shares changed owners in the day's trading. The highest price paid for the stock was $78, while the lowest price was $76.50. When the trading stopped for the day Abbott was being traded for $78, which amounted to $1 more than the closing price on the previous day.

A careful inspection of the sample quotations reveals some additional information. The symbol *pf* following the Allegheny Ludlum listing indicates *preferred stock*. Lower-case letters following the dividend listings on some stocks refer the reader to special information at the bottom of the page. For example, the symbol *e* following the Adams Drug dividend listing of 4¢ means that this is the dividend payment for the previous twelve months.

BOND QUOTATIONS

The right half of Figure 16-4 shows a number of bond quotations. To see how bond quotations are read, let's focus on the Alcoa bond. Since most bonds are issued in denominations of $1,000, bond prices must be read differently from stock prices. Although the closing price for Alcoa reads 99, this does not mean $99. Since the bond prices are quoted as a percentage of the $1,000 price, 99 means $990.

The symbols to the right of the Alcoa name indicate that the bonds pay an annual interest rate of 9 percent, and the maturity date for the bond issue is 1995. Since the bond is currently selling at a discount below its original $1,000 face value, the *yield* is 9.1 percent—slightly greater than the 9.0 percent stated interest rate. The Air Research bond shows the symbol *c.v.* instead of a yield, indicating that it is a convertible bond.

A total of $3,000 worth of the Alcoa bond was traded during the day with no variation in the $990 price. The closing bond price was $5 less than the previous day's closing price.

Stock Averages

A usual feature of most daily newscasts is a report of current stock averages. The two most familiar stock averages are the *Dow-Jones Averages* and the *Standard & Poor's Index*. Both types are indices that have been developed to reflect the general activity of the stock market.

The Dow-Jones Averages are actually three different indices. They are based upon the market prices of 30 industrial, 20 transportation, and 15 utility stocks. The Standard & Poor's Index is developed from the market performance of 425 industrial, 25 rail, and 50 utility stocks.

The Dow-Jones Industrials include a cross-section of major corporations such as AT & T, DuPont, Procter & Gamble, General

Electric, Eastman Kodak, and Sears. While individual stocks may rise when the Dow-Jones Index falls, the Index does provide a general measure of market activity for a given time period.

Mutual Funds—An Alternative Approach to Investing

Many investors who recognize that they have neither the time nor the knowledge to continually analyze stock market developments decide to concentrate their investments in **mutual funds.** These are *companies that sell shares of stock in their own companies in order to raise money to invest in the securities of other firms.* In so doing, they obtain *diversification* in their portfolio of stocks and the *professional management* of the mutual fund. The investor who buys shares of stock in a mutual fund becomes part owner of a large number of companies. Instead of owning one or two different stocks, the investor spreads the risk over dozens of different securities.

The second advantage of mutual funds is that they are managed by trained, experienced professionals. Their careers are based upon success in analyzing the securities markets and specific industries and companies. *Mutual funds attempt to accomplish for the individual investor what he or she might do with enough time, inclination, background, experience, and enough money to spread the investment among many businesses.*[2]

Nearly 9 million Americans currently own shares in one or more of the 600 mutual funds. By 1974 mutual funds assets had grown to more than $46 billion.[3]

Just as individual investor goals differ, so do the objectives of different mutual funds. Some are **growth funds**, which *emphasize the purchase of growth companies.* **Income funds** *emphasize high dividends.* Other *funds diversify their holdings* by purchasing all types of securities—common and preferred stocks, as well as bonds. These are called **balanced funds. Specialty funds** *concentrate on particular industries*, such as gold, real estate, or banking.

Regulating Securities Transactions

Both states and the federal government have passed legislation regulating the sale of securities. Early laws were passed at the state level, beginning with Kansas in 1911. When the proposed law was under consideration, one state legislator remarked that some unscrupulous securities promotors would even sell stock in the "blue sky." And the name **blue-sky law** was quickly applied to these *early state laws regulating securities transactions.* Eventually, every state except Nevada passed laws designed to protect stock purchasers.

Should New Laws Be Passed to Give Small Investors Access to "Inside Information"?

For those individuals and institutions that "play" the stock market, earning money by profiting in the market is a very serious game. It helps to have statistical data and reliable information so that a buy or sell decision is based on something more than vague feelings or an astrologer's predictions.

Information such as stock market listings, annual company reports, *The Wall Street Journal*, and many financially oriented magazines and newspaper columns is needed by the investor who seeks to make some money in the stock market. To those who "want to make a killing," information—preferably inside information—is vital.

As in many other kinds of businesses the market lives on gossip. Tips are its life blood. But whether or not any of these rumors circulating among brokers and investors is true is the basic question.

The Securities and Exchange Commission (SEC) has declared that research is the foundation of the securities business. Financial analysts are constantly obtaining raw data published by the companies listed on the stock exchanges. Yet the SEC also bans the circulation of materials to certain clients if the general investing public does not have access to these same materials. This distinction between disclosed and undisclosed information is at the heart of the argument about inside trading of stocks and bonds.

Those in favor of allowing inside information to be circulated point out that stock analysts routinely give their clients private information that the general public does not have. Keeping their clients well informed is part of their job; it is why they are hired by investors in the first place. It is unrealistic to try to prevent such information from influencing trading on the stock exchange. In fact, analysts who use only published information when advising their clients are not doing their job or performing a real service.

In a case in which a well-informed broker interprets easily available information for clients in light of the strategy of a corporation he or she has been following for several years, the broker might be said to have special information not available to the public, yet this is a matter of the broker's own expertise.

Critics of inside trading see it as elitist. If special information is leaked to certain brokers, for instance, it can result in a run to buy or sell the stock of a specific company. In such a case insiders save a great deal of money by selling before a panic occurs or they make money by buying low before a stock rises in price. If a selling panic occurs, insiders might even dump enough of a company's stock in a short period of time to force it to go under when orderly selling might have kept it afloat.

These laws typically require that most securities sold in the state be registered with an appropriate state official—usually the secretary of state. Annual licenses are usually required for securities dealers and salespeople. But additional protection was needed for interstate sale of securities.

SECURITIES ACT OF 1933

The **Securities Act of 1933** has been called the *Truth in Securities Act. This federal law is designed to protect investors through requiring full disclosure of relevant financial information by companies desiring to sell new stock or bond issues to the general public.* This information takes two forms: a registration statement, containing detailed company information which is filed with the Securities and Exchange Commission, and a *condensed version of the registration statement* in a booklet called a **prospectus,** which must be furnished to each purchaser.

THE SECURITIES EXCHANGE ACT OF 1934

One year after the passage of the Securities Act of 1933, Congress enacted the **Securities Exchange Act of 1934.** This *federal law created the Securities and Exchange Commission (SEC) to regulate the national stock exchanges.* All companies with securities listed on the NYSE or the AMEX are required to file registration statements with the SEC, and to update them annually. Brokerage firms and individual brokers are regulated by the SEC, and brokers selling listed securities are required to pass an examination.

OTHER FEDERAL LEGISLATION

The **Maloney Act of 1938** served as an amendment to the Securities Exchange Act of 1934 and authorized *self-regulation of over-the-counter securities operations.* This led to the creation of the **National Association of Securities Dealers** (NASD), which is *responsible for regulating OTC businesses.* Written examinations are now required of all new brokers and dealers selling OTC securities.

The **Investment Company Act of 1940** brought the *mutual fund industry under the jurisdiction of the SEC.* Mutual funds are now required to register with the SEC.

These state and federal laws have resulted in increased protection for America's 30 million individual investors from the securities trading abuses and stock manipulations which occurred prior to the 1930's.

Summary

Chapter 15 focused on the need to obtain funds and use them wisely in the operation of the firm. In this chapter long-term sources of funds are discussed from the point of view of the individual or corporate investor who purchases corporate securities.

Speculators make securities purchases in the hope of large profits within a very short time period. The investor purchases stocks and bonds to achieve one or more of the following objectives:

1. safety of the original investment
2. income
3. growth in the value of the original investment.

Bonds provide maximum safety; common stocks carry the most risk. Although bonds usually provide no growth, they do give a steady income. Common stocks are likely to be purchased by investors seeking growth. Preferred stocks, although representing ownership in the firm, are considered by many investors as a compromise investment between common stocks and bond purchases.

Common and preferred stocks and the bonds of most major corporations are traded through organized securities exchanges. Unlisted stocks of smaller industrial companies, banks, insurance firms, and government bonds are traded on the over-the-counter market through a network of 5,000 securities dealers and brokers located in cities throughout the United States.

Securities purchases and sales are handled by a trained specialist called a stockbroker or account executive. The stockbroker receives a commission for the services given in handling these transactions. Current prices of securities, sales volume, and information on dividends are reported in the financial sections of most daily newspapers and in such financial newspapers as *The Wall Street Journal*.

Investors who are unwilling or unable to spend the necessary time to analyze individual companies, and who want to spread their investment risks by owning a number of different companies, may choose to purchase shares of mutual funds. These are professionally managed investment companies that own shares in a large number of different companies. The investor who purchases shares in a mutual fund has partial ownership of these many companies.

The Securities Act of 1933 and the Securities Exchange Act of 1934 provide the mechanism for regulating organized securities exchanges and for protecting investors by requiring disclosure of relevant financial information from companies that issue stocks and bonds. The Securities and Exchange Commission (SEC), created by the Securities Exchange Act of 1934, enforces these Acts and also regulates brokerage firms and individual brokers. Other legislative acts have extended the SEC's powers to include the regulation of mutual funds.

Review questions

1. Identify the following terms:

   a. par value
   b. market value
   c. book value
   d. pre-emptive right

   e. preferred stock
   f. convertible preferred stock
   g. maturity date
   h. secured bond

i.   debenture
j.   convertible bond
k.   bond indenture
l.   serial bond
m. sinking-fund bond
n.   bond trustee
o.   callable bond
p.   yield
q.   stock exchange
r.   over-the-counter market
s.   market order

t.   limit order
u.   round lot
v.   odd lot
w. bull
x.   bear
y.   price-earnings ratio
z.   mutual funds
aa. Blue-Sky laws
bb. Securities Act of 1933
cc. Securities Exchange Act
      of 1934

2. What is common stock?

3. How are common stocks valued?

4. How are preferred stocks different from common stocks?

5. "Bondholders are creditors—not owners—of the corporation." Explain.

6. How are bonds retired?

7. Discuss the three major goals of investors.

8. Compare different types of securities with the three basic investment objectives.

9. How does the New York Stock Exchange operate?

10. How does an investor go about placing an order for a common stock?

Discussion questions and exercises

1. Evaluate the pro and con arguments to the controversial issue that appears in this chapter.

2. Ask a local stockbroker to talk to your class about setting up an investment program.

3. Assume that you have just inherited $20,000 from a rich aunt, but that her will stipulates you must invest all of the money until you have completed your education. Prepare a report on how you would invest the money.

4. Record for thirty days the daily price movements of a group of three to five common stocks. At the end of this period prepare a brief report on what you think influenced the price movements in these issues.

5. Assume that you are an investment counselor, and are asked to set up some general investment goals for the following individuals:
   a. a fifty-six-year-old retired Army officer
   b. a forty-year-old divorcee
   c. a wealthy nineteen-year-old college student
   Assume that all have adequate current income and about $30,000 to invest. Prepare a short report outlining the proposed investment goals for each person.

Case 16-1

The Shah (Almost) Makes the Going Great!

Pan American World Airways was in a shaky financial position in early 1975. The firm had experienced six continuous years of losses that totaled $256 million. Pan Am owed nearly $400 million in loans from U.S. insurance companies and many people were predicting that the airline would soon be in bankruptcy court.

Pan Am investigated several possible solutions to its problems, including mergers with other U.S. airlines. Nothing happened as a result of these efforts until the Shah of Iran announced a $300 million deal. Iran planned to loan Pan Am $245 million for ten years at 10.5 percent interest with no payments due until three years later. Most of this money was to be used to pay off Pan Am's creditors. The insurance companies, in turn, were to accept 51¢ on each dollar owed them as payment in full. The Shah also planned to buy a 55 percent interest in Pan Am's profitable Intercontinental Hotels subsidiary for another $55 million. Pan Am was to give the Shah the option of buying up to 13 percent of the company's stock at $2.50, at a time when the stock was being traded for about $4 per share. An Iranian representative was to be seated on Pan Am's Board of Directors, but was not to be allowed to vote on matters concerning international relations.

In July 1975 the Iranian government announced that it was canceling the deal. The airline's poor financial condition, reduced oil revenues, and pressing domestic needs were cited as reasons for the decision.

Questions

1. What is Pan Am's current financial position?
2. Should foreign investors be allowed to invest in U.S. companies?
3. Do you think Iran made a wise decision in canceling the deal with Pan Am?

Source: Todd E. Fandell. "$300 Million Rescue of Pan Am by Iran Is about to Be Effected," *The Wall Street Journal* (May 13, 1975), pp. 1, 17. Reprinted with permission of *The Wall Street Journal,* © Dow Jones & Company, Inc. 1975. All rights reserved. *See also* "Iran Decides Not to Invest in Ailing Pan Am," *Detroit News* (July 21, 1975), p. 2-A.

Case 16-2

British Bonds Battle Inflation

The British government introduced an innovative bond scheme to protect the savings of retired persons. Lump-sum investments of up to $1,200 can be made by Britons of retirement age (sixty-five for males, sixty for females). The bonds have a maturity of five years and pay a bonus if held to maturity. They are exempt from income and capital gains tax. While the bonds will draw no interest, their cash value is adjusted annually on the basis of changes in the retail price index. The bond plan, introduced in 1975, is designed to cope with an inflation rate of nearly 20 percent.

Questions

1. Would Americans be interested in buying an inflation-proof bond? Why, or why not?
2. Do you think it would be advisable for the British government to extend their bond scheme to younger persons?
3. Should the government of the United States consider a plan similar to Britain's? If so, how should it be introduced?

Source: Peter Cole-Adams. "Britain Offers Bond to Battle Inflation," *The Age* (August 8, 1974). p. 6.

17

Risk Management and Insurance

"Nothing is ever gained without risk. You can't steal second base with one foot on first."

—Anonymous

What Chapter 17 Is All About

1. In this chapter you will learn the meaning of risk and the two types of risk faced by individuals and businesses.
2. You should be able to explain and evaluate each of the four methods of dealing with risk.
3. Insurance is based on the Law of Large Numbers. You should be able to explain this law and how it makes insurance possible.
4. Several types of property and casualty insurance exist. Which types are most useful to businesses? Which types are needed by individuals?
5. Which type of life insurance are you most likely to purchase in the next ten years? Which type appears best for your parents?
6. After reading this chapter, you should understand these terms:

risk	health insurance
speculative risk	ocean marine insurance
pure risk	inland marine insurance
self-insurance	fidelity bond
insurance	surety bond
insurable interest	title insurance
insurable risk	credit insurance
Law of Large Numbers	public-liability insurance
mutual insurance company	product-liability insurance
stock insurance company	group life insurance
fire insurance	mortality table
coinsurance clause	term insurance
automobile insurance	whole life insurance
no-fault insurance	cash surrender value
burglary insurance	limited payment life
robbery insurance	insurance
theft insurance	credit life insurance
Workers' Compensation Insurance	endowment

Robert Craig
("Evel") Knievel

In 1974 when Evel Knievel made an unsuccessful attempt to jump across the Snake River Canyon in Twin Falls, Idaho, on his motorcycle, it probably was not the enormity of the leap that attracted so much excitement; more likely, it was the spectacle of the great risk Knievel took that commanded attention.

What makes Knievel undertake his daredevil tricks? Part of the answer is money—royalties paid on toys, accessories, clothing, and from films and television. But another part must be the rewards he gets as a swashbuckling gladiator admired by thousands of fans, reveling in attention, and showing off his courage.

Born in Butte, Montana, where he still lives, Knievel owned his own motorcycle by the time he was a teenager. He was already doing stunts on Butte's main street. He was also in trouble with the law (for snatching purses, stealing, and later on for cracking safes and committing armed robbery) and he even spent some time in jail.

A good athlete, Knievel has been a ski-jumping champion, hockey player, and pole vaulter, as well as a motorcycle jumper. But until he found his niche, Knievel had tried many other ways to earn a living—as a miner, hunting guide, insurance salesman, and motorcycle dealer.

His troupe, Evel Knievel's Motorcycle Daredevils, was formed in 1965, and began riding in 1966. But the troupe broke up quickly, and Knievel decided to work alone.

He has had a number of major accidents and believes he has broken every bone in his body. One of his accidents has left him with a limp. He cannot hedge his risks because his public image and his appeal calls for a real brush with death.

Folk hero or freak, Knievel will probably go on taking risks long after his fortieth birthday, which will occur in 1977.

A small family-owned company in Newark, New Jersey, had been producing and marketing soup for more than a hundred years until the day in 1971 when its name became a household word. The company was the Bon Vivant Soup Company, and the day was July 1, 1971. That day the Food and Drug Administration notified Bon Vivant—and the world—that a New York man had died and his wife was paralyzed from botulism caused by eating a can of Bon Vivant's vichyssoise (pronounced *vishy-swah*) soup.

Although Bon Vivant quickly traced the problem to a single crate of 460 cans of soup, the FDA recalled all of the fifty-two varieties of Bon Vivant soup. Over 4 million cans of soup had been manufactured by Bon Vivant in 1971.[1]

The next month Bon Vivant was in bankruptcy court. A lawyer for the company reported that the total recall of the firm's products resulted in no money coming in with which to pay debts. In November 1972 the company resumed operations under a new name—Moore & Company Soups. The FDA continued to keep a close watch on the company's products as they reached the grocers' shelves in early 1973. The new company manufactured five soups. Vichyssoise was not one of them.[2]

The Concept of Risk

Risk is a daily fact of life—for both the individual and the business firm. Automobile accidents take the lives of 50,000 Americans each year. The tornadoes which struck the Xenia, Ohio, area in 1974 resulted in more than thirty deaths and $1 billion in property damage.[3] Fifteen California physicians each paid more than $1 million in 1974 as a result of malpractice suits.[4] Fires took their toll in lives and property damage.

These catastrophes also affect the business firm. The firm also faces the risk of possible injury to its employees in job-related accidents. Changes in consumer tastes may transform a profitable firm into a bankruptcy case. Finally, the firm may risk loss of business and lawsuits caused by faulty products.

The Watch Industry and Changing Demands

At the beginning of the twentieth century the individual's treasured timepiece was likely to be a pocket watch. Retirement from the company or the railroad was frequently the occasion for presenting the retiree with an engraved (often in gold) pocket watch.

But times changed, and the 1920's witnessed the popularity of new wristwatches. Pocket watches were old fashioned and companies such as Waltham, who were unwilling to convert their production to the manufacture of wristwatches, eventually closed due to lack of demand.* The American of the 1920's and 1930's wore a wristwatch with pride. It typically bore the name of such manufacturers as Bulova or Elgin.

Today's watch market has two major segments. One might be called the *disposable watch market*. Many people have a number of watches for different occasions and may choose a watch to fit their wardrobes when dressing. Their watches are inexpensive—often from $15 to $25—and usually bear a name such as Timex.

The second segment is the *quality market*. Watches designed for this segment are likely to be both luxurious and expensive. Manufacturers stress the accuracy of the timepiece and the good taste of its owner. Prices range from $175 to more than $3,000. Bulova's Accutron and the new digital watches are examples of this kind of product.

*The name Waltham was so well known, however, that the name was sold to another watch manufacturer to use on its products.

RISK DEFINED   **Risk** is *the chance of loss or injury*. The business firm's list of risk-filled decisions is long. The warehouse faces the risk of fire, burglaries, water damage, and physical deterioration. Accidents, judgments due to lawsuits, and nonpayment of bills by customers are other risks.

SPECULATIVE RISK— WHY EVEL KNIEVEL JUMPS

Two major types of risk exist: **speculative risk** and **pure risk.** In the case of **speculative risk** *the firm or individual has the chance of either a profit or a loss.* Purchase of shares of stock on the basis of the latest hot tip results in the possibility of profits—and the risk of potential losses. Expansion of operations in a new market may mean higher profits or the loss of invested funds. Evel Knievel's highly publicized attempt to jump the Snake River Canyon exposed him to the risk of broken bones or even death as the price for failure, and the potential of millions in future earnings as a reward for success.

PURE RISK—WHEN NOBODY WINS

With speculative risk there is both a chance of profit and a chance of loss. **Pure risk** *involves only the chance of loss; there is no chance of gain.* Each driver faces the risk of an accident. If a collision occurs, the owner suffers financial loss. If no collision takes place, he or she does not gain. The financial position remains the same. Insurance is used to offer protection against the financial loss which might result in pure risk.

Dealing with Risk

Since risk is an unavoidable part of business, management must find ways of dealing with it. Recognition of the fact that risk is present is an important first step. Once the presence of risk is recognized, the manager has four available methods of dealing with it:

1. avoiding risk
2. reducing risk
3. assuming the risk through self-insurance
4. shifting risk to insurance companies.

AVOIDING RISK

In Chapter 16 we looked at different types of investors. Some were willing to take high risks as the price of potentially high rewards. Others were unwilling to assume these risks. The same is true for different companies. Some firms are unwilling to risk the costs involved in developing new and untried products. They know that DuPont's attempt to develop a leather substitute called Corfam resulted in losses of more than $100 million. Ford Motor Company's unhappy experiences with the Edsel cost over $200 million.

Companies unwilling to assume risk are content to produce and market products with a stable demand and an adequate profit margin. Such strategies may insure profitability, but they also stifle innovation. Companies whose managers seek to avoid most risk will rarely be leaders in the industry. They are content to be followers. Even though Corfam was a market failure, the DuPont product development record is an enviable one, with such contributions as cellophane, nylon, Dacron, and Teflon.

REDUCING RISK   Many types of risk can be reduced—or even eliminated—through eliminating hazards. Safety programs are often begun to educate employees about potentially dangerous hazards and the proper methods of performing specific tasks. Safety glasses and safety shoes may be required for workers performing certain activities. Danger areas within the factory may be marked with red lines or special caution signs.

Other steps may be taken to reduce risks. Guard dogs and twenty-four-hour security patrols may result in minimizing burglaries. Installation of fire retardant building materials and an automatic sprinkler system will better protect a warehouse from fire. Preventive maintenance lessens the risk of defective machinery. Careful credit checks allow managers to make better decisions concerning which customers should be extended credit.

All of these actions may result in reducing the risk involved in business operations. They do not, however, eliminate risk. Preventive maintenance greatly reduces the possibility of a plane crash due to mechanical problems, but such disasters do occur. The risk of loss—even though reduced greatly—is still there.

ASSUMING THE RISK THROUGH SELF-INSURANCE   Instead of purchasing insurance against certain risks *some multiplant, geographically scattered firms may accumulate funds to cover losses.* This is called **self-insurance.**

A department store chain, Federated Department Stores, owns 125 stores in cities throughout the United States. Included in the chain are such famous stores as *Abraham & Straus* and *Bloomingdale's* in New York, *I. Magnin* in San Francisco, *Foley's* in Houston, *Filene's* in Boston, *Sanger-Harris* in Dallas, *Burdines* in Miami, *Shilito's* in Cincinnati, and *Gayfers* in cities along the Gulf Coast. Rather than purchase fire insurance for the various stores, the firm's management may choose to self-insure. Since the stores are large in number and scattered throughout the United States, self-insurance or establishment of a fire reserve fund may be cheaper than paying insurance premiums.

The alternative of self-insurance may be a realistic choice for large multiplant companies, since the likelihood of several fires is small, and the likelihood of a fire can be calculated. For the single-plant firm a single fire may prove disastrous. Contributing $200 each year to a reserve fund for potential fire damage of $500,000 to the firm's only manufacturing facility would not be considered adequate by most managers. As a result smaller firms with concentrated facilities and the possibility of being forced out of business by a major fire or accident usually shift the risk to others through the purchase of insurance.

Insurance Provides Protection against Risk

SOURCE: *The Wall Street Journal*, April 8, 1975. Reprinted with permission from *The Wall Street Journal.*

SHIFTING THE RISK TO INSURANCE COMPANIES

Although steps may be taken to avoid or reduce risk, the most common method of dealing with it is to shift the burden of the risk to others in the form of **insurance.** This is the *process by which a firm (the insurance company) for a fee (the insurance premium) agrees to pay another firm or individual (the insured) a sum of money stated in a written contract (the policy) if a loss occurs.* Insurance is, therefore, the substitution of a small known loss (the insurance premiums) for a larger unknown loss which may or may not occur.

Insurance Basics

Insurance companies are professional risk-takers. They serve society by accepting the risk of loss or damage to businesses and individuals. Three basic principles operate in insurance:

1. the concept of insurable interest
2. the concept of insurable risks
3. the Law of Large Numbers.

INSURABLE INTEREST

In order to purchase insurance an applicant must demonstrate that he has an **insurable interest** in the property or life insured. This is an *insurance concept that requires that the policyholder must stand* to suffer financial loss due to the occurrence of fire, accident, or lawsuit. However, for life insurance a relative may have an insurable interest even though no financial loss would occur in the event of the insured's death.

Key executive insurance

A businessperson can obtain fire insurance for property. An individual can purchase life insurance for herself or himself or members of the family. Since top managers are important assets to a firm, the corporation may purchase key executive insurance. But a businessperson may not purchase insurance to cover damage to the property of competitors. Nor can an individual purchase an insurance policy on the life of the President of the United States. In both cases an insurable interest is not present.

INSURABLE RISKS

A risk must meet a number of requirements in order for an insurance company to provide protection against its occurrence:

1. The likelihood of loss must be *predictable*. Insurance companies know how many fires will occur each year, how many people of a certain age will die, how many burglaries will occur, and how many traffic accidents and job-related injuries take place. Knowledge of the number of occurrences of each loss and the average size of the loss allows the company to determine the amount of premiums necessary to repay those companies and individuals who suffer losses.

2. The loss must be financially *measurable*. In order to determine the amount of premium income necessary to cover the costs of losses, the dollar amount of losses must be known. For this reason life insurance policies are purchased in specific dollar amounts, eliminating the problem of determining the value of a person's life. As Table 17-1 indicates, many health insurance policies list the dollar value of specific operations. Some policies have no schedule of benefits for operations, but pay 80 or 100 percent of the cost.

Table 17-1

Examples of Operations and Medical Procedures Covered by One Blue Shield Insurance Policy and Sample Payments for Each

Operation or Medical Procedure	Surgical Benefits	General Anesthesia Benefits
Appendectomy (removal of appendix)	$225	$40
Cholecystectomy (removal of gall bladder)	335	65
Gastrectomy (removal of stomach)	525	105
Tonsillectomy	85	15
Cataract extraction, bilateral	465	90
Obstetrical delivery	135	30
Caesarean section delivery	270	55

SOURCE: Blue Cross and Blue Shield of Oklahoma.

3. The risk *must be spread over a wide geographic area.* An insurance company that concentrates its coverage in one geographic area risks the possibility of a major catastrophe affecting most of its policyholders. A major hurricane in Louisiana, a California earthquake, or a Midwest tornado might bankrupt the company.

4. The insurance company has *the right to set standards for accepting risks.* The company may have to refuse insurance coverage to persons with histories of heart disease or persons in dangerous occupations—such as fire fighters, test pilots, and crop dusters. Or the company may choose to insure these persons at considerably higher rates, due to the greater risks involved. In the same manner fire insurance rates may be different for residences and commercial buildings.

THE LAW OF LARGE NUMBERS

Insurance is based on the law of averages (or statistical probability). Insurance companies have studied the occurrence of death, injuries, lawsuits, and all types of hazards. From their investigations they have developed the **Law of Large Numbers**, which is a *probability calculation of the likelihood of the occurrence of hazards on which premiums are based.* They also use *actuarial tables to predict the number of fires, automobile accidents, plane crashes, and deaths that will occur in a given year.*

Table 17-2 is one of these actuarial tables. It indicates the number of deaths per thousand persons that will occur this year for each age category, and the number of additional years each person is expected to live. For the eighteen-year-old age category, deaths average slightly less than two per thousand. The eighteen-year-old is expected to live another fifty-two years.

No one can predict which two persons will die, but the insurance companies know that an average of two per thousand will die this year. Armed with this knowledge, the company can determine the size of premium necessary to pay the beneficiaries of the policies when a claim arises. The longer the life expectancy, the lower the premiums paid. The same type of calculation is also made to determine premiums for automobile or fire insurance. The Law of Large Numbers is the basis for all insurance premium calculations.

Types of Insurance Companies

Insurance companies are typically categorized on the basis of ownership. Two types of companies exist: *mutual companies and stock companies.*

MUTUAL COMPANIES

A **mutual insurance company** is actually a type of cooperative. The *insurance company is owned by its policyholders.* The mutual company is chartered by the state and governed by a board of directors who are elected by the policyholders.

Table 17-2
Mortality Tables

Age	Deaths per 1,000	Expectation of Life (years)	Age	Deaths per 1,000	Expectation of Life (years)
0	7.08	68.30	50	8.32	23.63
1	1.76	67.78	51	9.11	22.82
2	1.52	66.90	52	9.96	22.03
3	1.46	66.00	53	10.89	21.25
4	1.40	65.10	54	11.90	20.47
5	1.35	64.19	55	13.00	19.71
6	1.30	63.27	56	14.21	18.97
7	1.26	62.35	57	15.54	18.23
8	1.23	61.43	58	17.00	17.51
9	1.21	60.51	59	18.59	16.81
10	1.21	59.58	60	20.34	16.12
11	1.23	58.65	61	22.24	15.44
12	1.26	57.72	62	24.31	14.78
13	1.32	56.80	63	26.57	14.14
14	1.39	55.87	64	29.04	13.51
15	1.46	54.95	65	31.75	12.90
16	1.54	54.03	66	34.74	12.31
17	1.62	53.11	67	38.04	11.73
18	1.69	52.19	68	41.68	11.17
19	1.74	51.28	69	45.61	10.64
20	1.79	50.37	70	49.79	10.12
21	1.83	49.46	71	54.15	9.63
22	1.86	48.55	72	58.65	9.15
23	1.89	47.64	73	63.26	8.69
24	1.91	46.73	74	68.12	8.24
25	1.93	45.82	75	73.37	7.81
26	1.96	44.90	76	79.18	7.39
27	1.99	43.99	77	85.70	6.98
28	2.03	43.08	78	93.06	6.59
29	2.08	42.16	79	101.19	6.21
30	2.13	41.25	80	109.98	5.85
31	2.19	40.34	81	119.35	5.51
32	2.25	39.43	82	129.17	5.19
33	2.32	38.51	83	139.38	4.89
34	2.40	37.60	84	150.01	4.60
35	2.51	36.69	85	161.14	4.32
36	2.64	35.78	86	172.82	4.06
37	2.80	34.88	87	185.13	3.80
38	3.01	33.97	88	198.25	3.55
39	3.25	33.07	89	212.46	3.31
40	3.53	32.18	90	228.14	3.06
41	3.84	31.29	91	245.77	2.82
42	4.17	30.41	92	265.93	2.58
43	4.53	29.54	93	289.30	2.33
44	4.92	28.67	94	316.66	2.07
45	5.35	27.81	95	351.24	1.80
46	5.83	26.95	96	400.56	1.51
47	6.36	26.11	97	488.42	1.18
48	6.95	25.27	98	668.15	.83
49	7.60	24.45	99	1,000.00	.50

SOURCE: Institute of Life Insurance. *Life Insurance Fact Book 1975*, pp. 108–109. Reprinted by permission from the Institute of Life Insurance.

Unlike the stock company, the mutual company earns no profits for its owners. Since it is a nonprofit organization any surplus funds remaining after operating expenses, payment of claims, and establishing necessary reserves are returned to the policyholders in the form of dividends or they may be used to reduce premiums.

Mutual companies are found chiefly in the life insurance field. Although they account for slightly less than 10 percent of the approximately 1,800 life insurance companies in the United States, mutual companies have sold more than half of all the life insurance in force. As Table 17-3 indicates, such major life insurance companies as Prudential, Metropolitan, John Hancock, and New York Life are mutual companies.

STOCK COMPANIES

Stock insurance companies are organized similarly to firms such as General Motors, RCA, and Pillsbury—they are *insurance companies operated for profit.* Stockholders do not have to be policyholders; they have invested funds in the stock company in order to receive dividends from company earnings. Profits earned by the company will come from two sources:

1. insurance premiums in excess of claims and operating costs
2. earnings from company investments in stocks, bonds, and real estate.

Table 17-3
The Twenty Largest
Life Insurance
Companies in the
United States*

Company	Assets in $ millions	Life Insurance in Force (in $ millions)
1. Prudential (Newark)	35,819	218,270
2. Metropolitan (New York)	32,728	215,901
3. Equitable Life Assurance (New York)	17,558	108,995
4. New York Life	13,002	69,971
5. John Hancock Mutual (Milwaukee)	11,822	81,350
6. Aetna Life (Hartford)**	9,430	79,040
7. Northwestern Mutual (Milwaukee)	7,344	28,679
8. Connecticut General Life (Bloomfield)**	6,950	45,333
9. Travelers Life (Hartford)**	6,373	68,581
10. Massachusetts Mutual (Springfield)	5,397	27,009
11. Mutual of New York	4,397	21,530
12. New England Mutual (Boston)	4,261	19,407
13. Teachers Insurance & Annuity (New York)**	3,813	3,325
14. Connecticut Mutual (Hartford)	3,375	14,418
15. Mutual Benefit (Newark)	3,105	20,677
16. Bankers Life (Des Moines)	2,928	16,727
17. Penn Mutual (Philadelphia)	2,779	11,741
18. Lincoln National Life (Fort Wayne)**	2,746	30,256
19. National Life & Accident (Nashville)**	2,241	13,668
20. Western & Southern (Cincinnati)	2,212	11,729

*Companies are ranked on the basis of assets.
**Indicates stock company. The other 14 are mutual companies.

SOURCE: *Fortune,* July 1973. Reprinted with permission from *Fortune.*

The major difference between stock and mutual companies is that stockholders are seeking profits from the stock insurance company. Even though stock companies attempt to earn profits for their owners, there is no clear indication that their premiums are greater than those of mutual companies. Although mutual companies dominate the life insurance field, the majority of all other types of insurance is written by stock companies. The efficiency of a particular company appears to depend on the abilities of its management.

Lloyd's of London—The Insurers Who Break the Rules

The concept of insurable risks and the Law of Large Numbers are rules to live by for most insurance companies. The typical insurance company requires that the likelihood of loss must be predictable, that the risk be spread over a wide geographic area, and that standards of acceptable risk be established. But Lloyd's of London is hardly a typical insurance company.

Lloyd's is actually not an insurance company at all, but an *association* of individual insurers who agree to insure risks that are not acceptable to more conventional insurance companies. The association has a colorful history that spans nearly three centuries since it began operations in a London coffeehouse in 1689.

Although the main business of Lloyd's is marine insurance, it is best known throughout the world for providing insurance against extremely unusual risk. Lloyd's has insured such body parts as Jimmy Durante's nose and Marlene Dietrich's legs. A Fat Lady in a circus once discovered she was losing weight and took out a policy to protect her career against such a disaster.

Most of the major bridges in the United States are insured by Lloyd's. Since the bridges are usually built by the issuance of bonds, the insurance covers not only damages to the bridges but also losses in revenue that the tolls would have provided.*

Lloyd's has paid off on numerous claims involving extremely large sums of money. When the *Titanic* sank in 1912, Lloyd's lost $3 million (a huge loss for that time). Hurricane Betsy resulted in a $100 million loss in 1965.†

*Denzil Stuart. "Report from London: Lloyd's Non-marine Risks," *Best's Review* (November 1969), p. 48.
†"Lloyd's of London Wants $," *Forbes* (September 15, 1974), p. 77.

Types of Insurance

Although literally hundreds of different types of insurance policies are available for purchase by individuals and business firms, they can be conveniently divided into two broad categories:

1. property and casualty insurance
2. life insurance.

Type of Insurance	Protects Against
Fire insurance	Losses due to fire
Automobile insurance	Losses due to automobile theft, fire, or collision. Claims resulting from damage to other property due to collision or injury, or death of another person resulting from an automobile accident
Burglary, robbery, and theft insurance	Losses due to the unlawful taking of the insured's property, either by force or by burglaries
Workers' Compensation Insurance	Medical expenses and partial salary payments for workers injured on the job
Health insurance	Medical and surgical expenses and lost income due to sickness or accidents
Marine insurance	Losses to property which is being shipped from one location to another
Fidelty, surety, title, and credit insurance	Misappropriation of funds (fidelty bonds); failure to perform a job (surety bond); failure to repay loans (credit insurance); loss due to a defective title to land or other property (title insurance)
Public liability insurance	Claims against property owner for injuries or damage to property of others caused by falls, malpractice, negligence, or faulty products

PROPERTY AND CASUALTY INSURANCE

Eight types of property and casualty insurance exist. Table 17-4 lists and briefly discusses the purpose of each type.

Fire insurance

Every thirteen seconds a fire starts somewhere in the United States. Fires will cause more than $2 billion in property losses this year. Many businesspeople and individuals purchase **fire insurance** as *coverage for losses due to fire and—with extended coverage—losses from windstorms, hail, water, riot, and smoke damage.*

Fire insurance rates will vary according to the risks involved. Homes and buildings located in cities with adequate fire protection have lower rates than those in rural areas. Frame buildings result in higher rates than brick or metal structures.

Since standard fire insurance policies protect only against damage by fire or lightning, policyholders commonly purchase added coverage to protect them against such hazards as windstorms, hail, water, riot, and smoke damage. This *supplementary coverage* is called **extended coverage.**

The Coinsurance Clause Since most fires result in less than total destruction, many businesspeople insure their property for less than its total value. A $100,000 building might carry insurance of $50,000.

Since insurance companies extend coverage on the entire building and receive premiums on only a fraction of the value of the building, they protect themselves by including a **coinsurance clause** in the policy. The clause *requires that the insured carry fire insurance of some minimum percentage of the value of the property* (usually 80 percent) *in order to receive full coverage of a loss.*

The coinsurance clause works this way. If the owner of a $50,000 building suffers a $20,000 fire loss, the amount of the damage that the insurance company will repay depends upon the value of the fire insurance policy. Should the owner have $30,000 in fire insurance, the insurance company will pay only three-fourths of the damage. Why? Since the coinsurance clause requires the owner to have a minimum of $40,000 insurance (80 percent of the $50,000 market value of the building), the $30,000 policy amounts to 75 percent of the required insurance. The insurance company calculates its share of the loss as:

$$\frac{\text{Amount of insurance carried}}{\text{Amount of insurance required}} \times \text{Loss} = \frac{\text{Insurance company's share}}{\text{of the loss}}$$

$$\frac{\$30,000}{\$40,000} \times \$20,000 = \$15,000.$$

The remaining $5,000 of the loss must be absorbed by the insured. In most states the coinsurance clause does not apply to residential property.

Automobile insurance

The National Safety Council regularly advertises to inform the American public of the risk involved when driving automobiles—and with reason. Automobile accidents have killed more Americans than all the battle deaths in our Armed Forces since the Revolutionary War. Every seven seconds someone is injured in an automobile accident. Every ten minutes someone dies in an automobile accident. The automobile injury toll last year was 5 million Americans.

Most **automobile insurance** *includes coverage for losses due to automobile theft, fire, or collision, and claims resulting from damage to the property or persons of others involved in an automobile accident.* The automobile owner protects against these risks through the purchase of comprehensive fire and theft, collison, and liability insurance.

Comprehensive coverage protects the insured's car against damage caused by fire, theft, hail, falling objects, and a variety of other perils. Contents of the car are also usually covered if the car is locked. In recent years insurance companies have been forced to exclude stereo tape decks (or to issue special policies at a separate premium) due to the ease of their detachment from the car and their attractiveness to thieves.

Collision insurance pays for damage caused by collision with another vehicle or a stationary object. Most collision insurance policies list a deductible amount ranging from $50 to $200 or $300, which the insured must pay.

Liability insurance covers both property damage and bodily injury. Bodily injury liability insurance is usually stated on the policy as $5,000/$10,000, $20,000/$40,000, or even $100,000/$300,000, and higher. The first amount listed is the maximum amount the insurance company will pay for the injury or death of one person. The second amount is the maximum amount the insurance company will pay in a single accident. Property damage liability insurance covers any damage to other automobiles or property caused by the insured's automobile. Liability insurance also typically includes a *medical payments endorsement,* which will pay hospital and doctor bills up to a specified amount for any persons injured in the insured's car.

Uninsured-motorist insurance covers the policyholder if he or she is injured in an accident by a driver who has no liability insurance and the second driver is at fault. This type of insurance also protects the insured against losses caused by hit-and-run drivers.

No-Fault Automobile Insurance

As automobile insurance premiums soared and the delays in settling insurance claims lengthened, states began to look for new ways of insuring motorists. In 1971 Massachusetts became the first state to enact a **no-fault insurance** plan. These *state laws require that claims payments by the insurance company of the policyholder be made without regard to fault and limit the right of victims to sue.* Florida, Connecticut, New Jersey, Michigan, New York, Utah, and Kansas quickly followed. Nearly half of the states now have some version of the no-fault plan.

Although the laws are not identical, all of them have these features:*

1. Insurance is required for all drivers of private automobiles. Each motorist must carry liability insurance to cover medical costs resulting from accidents involving himself or herself and other passengers in the car.

2. Payments for economic losses are made, without regard to fault, to any driver, passenger, or pedestrian injured in an auto accident. Payment of claims is made by the insurance company of the policyholder, not by the company of the person who is ruled at fault.

3. All victims are automatically limited in their right to sue. As a rule lawsuits are barred except in cases where medical expenses exceed a set amount—which varies from state to state—or when the accident results in death, dismemberment, disfigurement, or certain other serious injuries.

Proponents of no-fault insurance argue that it will lead to lower premiums. Although it appears to be too early to make a final judgment, premiums have been reduced somewhat in those states with laws that limit the right to sue. Figure 17-1 shows the lower premiums being collected by ten companies under "no-fault" in New York City.

*"No-Fault Insurance: Biggest Boost Yet," *U.S. News & World Report* (February 11, 1974), p. 72.

Should No-fault Automobile Insurance Be National?

Almost half of the states in America have adopted no-fault insurance for automobile drivers. The proposition presented by Professor Robert E. Keeton of the Harvard Law School and Professor Jeffrey O'Connell of the University of Illinois Law School eliminates any requirement that the victim in an automobile accident prove that the injury was the fault of another person. But it also limits the amount of damages that an accident victim can be paid.

Under no-fault insurance, claims are paid promptly and are not astronomical in amount. The supporters of no-fault insurance say that it provides an orderly and fair handling of injury claims. Under other insurance systems, there is a good deal of wastefulness and cruelty. For example, when an injured person sues for damages, he or she may be awarded a fortune or may get no money at all and may even have to pay court costs as well. Or, a victim might exaggerate the extent of the injuries or inflate the medical bills related to the injuries in order to receive larger payments; and insurance premiums for the policyholder would surely rise.

When a lawsuit is the only way to recover money spent on getting well after suffering injuries in an accident, the process is costly and time consuming, as crowded court calendars will attest. No reimbursement, however great, can modify the victim's pain and suffering, so it is best that the insurance claims be taken care of quickly and efficiently.

Those who do not want to see no-fault insurance enacted for the country as a whole see it as a threat to private enterprise. For these critics the high cost of no-fault insurance is a penalty that a careful driver must pay along with drivers who are more of a risk. The fact that drivers can buy medical coverage with their automobile insurance, and that this coverage can be purchased regardless of fault protects insurance holders who have big medical bills as the result of an accident. It is an option for the individual and gives the person freedom of choice, depending on personal judgment.

If a person is seriously and/or permanently injured and, as a result, has lost his or her earning power, the relatively small judgment awarded under no-fault insurance leaves such a person in a poor financial position, often for the rest of his or her life, and it affects the injured person's family as well. In cases in which suits are brought and won, large amounts of money can be gained to compensate for this loss of earning power.

Figure 17-1
New York City Auto
Insurance Premiums
before and after
"No-fault"

SOURCE: Reprinted from *U.S. News & World Report* (February 11, 1974), p. 72. Copyright 1974 U.S. News & World Report, Inc.

Burglary, robbery, and theft insurance

Although burglary, robbery, and theft are all crimes, they each have different meanings, and the insurance rate for each crime is different. The act of taking property from an unlocked building is theft, not burglary. *Coverage for losses due to taking property by forcible entry* is provided by **burglary insurance. Robbery insurance** provides *coverage for losses due to the unlawful taking of property from another person by force or the threat of force.* **Theft** (or larceny) **insurance** gives *coverage for losses due to the unlawful taking of property.* Theft insurance, therefore, is the most expensive of all insurance coverages for crime.

Workers' compensation insurance

Workers' Compensation insurance is established by state laws in all fifty states. This is *insurance provided by employers under state law to guarantee payment of medical expenses and salaries to employees who are injured on the job.*

Premiums are based on the company's payroll. Rates depend on the hazards present on the job and the safety record of the employer. Payments are usually set at a fraction of the employee's regular wage (usually one-half to two-thirds of the weekly salary). A waiting period of a few days to two weeks is usually provided to discourage salary claims for minor accidents.

Health insurance

One out of every seven Americans was hospitalized in 1974. Without insurance, family incomes can be cut off, a lifetime of savings can

409   RISK MANAGEMENT AND INSURANCE

be wiped out, and a family can be left with huge debts.[5] Because of these severe risks, 90 percent of all Americans have some form of **health insurance** which provides *coverage for losses due to sickness or accidents.*

Most business firms offer health and accident insurance for their workers as a part of their fringe benefits programs. Such insurance typically covers:

1. hospital, surgical, and other medical expenses
2. loss of income for a certain period of time
3. specified payments for the loss of an eye, a hand, or a foot
4. death benefits, if death results from an accident.

Health insurance is sold by regular insurance companies and by nonprofit associations such as Blue Cross and Blue Shield.

The federal government has become increasingly involved with health insurance through the Medicare and Medicaid programs, and through the disability provisions of the Social Security Act. More than 21 million persons are covered by Medicare.[6] It also appears likely that Congress will pass a national health insurance law in the near future.

Marine insurance

Marine insurance is the oldest form of insurance, dating back at least five thousand years ago as a means of insuring ships and their cargoes. **Ocean marine insurance** protects shippers from *losses of property due to damage to the ship or its cargo while at sea or in port.* The second type of marine insurance, **inland marine insurance,** *covers losses of property due to damage while goods are being transported by truck, ship, rail, or plane.*

Fidelity, surety, title, and credit insurance

The **fidelity bond** is used to *protect an employer from the dishonesty of an employee.* Such bonds are commonly used by banks, loan companies, and other businesses to cover cashiers and other employees who handle company funds. The employer is guaranteed against loss up to the amount of the policy.

Surety bonds are *designed to protect a person or company from any losses resulting from nonperformance of a contract.* A building contractor agreeing to construct a new city library may be required to furnish a surety bond that the library will be erected according to specifications and will be completed within the time limit of the contract.

Title insurance *protects the purchaser of real estate from losses which might be incurred because of a defect in the title to the property.* Title insurance eliminates the need for the purchaser to conduct an investigation of legal records to determine the true

"Slow'er down a notch, Mike."

Public Liability Insures Businesses against Claims of Injuries by Their Customers

owner of the property, and the presence of any claims against the property. Title insurance is often purchased when a person buys a new home.

Credit insurance *protects lenders against losses from bad debts.* Most credit insurance policies do not protect lenders against all unpaid debts, since the premiums would likely be too expensive. Instead, such policies usually define normal losses from bad debts and cover any losses in excess of normal losses.

Public liability insurance

Public-liability insurance *is designed to protect businesses and individuals from claims caused by injuries to others or damage to the property of others.* Most homeowners' insurance policies include liability coverage against claims by persons injured by falls or bitten by a pet dog. Businesses purchase such insurance to cover possible injuries to customers in the store. Physicians commonly purchase malpractice insurance to protect themselves against charges of incompetency or negligence. In 1975 premiums on malpractice insurance for some surgeons in California cost as much as $25,508 annually.

Product-liability insurance *is designed to protect businesses from claims for damages resulting from the use of the company's products.* This insurance covers such occurrences as a druggist who is sued by a customer who claims that a prescription was prepared

Type of Insurance		Percentage of Total Annual Premiums
Automobile		42.3
Liability	26.5	
Physical damage	15.8	
General liability		6.7
Fire and allied lines (extended coverage)		8.9
Homeowners multiple peril		9.6
Farmowners multiple peril		.5
Commercial multiple peril		6.2
Workers' Compensation		11.7
Marine		4.2
Inland marine	2.6	
Ocean marine	1.6	
Surety and fidelity		1.7
Burglary & theft		.5
Miscellaneous		7.7
Total		100.0

SOURCE: *Insurance Facts 1974.* Reprinted by permission of the Insurance Information Institute.

improperly, or a manufacturer accused of producing and selling unsafe products.

Relative importance of each type of property and casualty insurance

Each type of property and casualty insurance has been developed to protect individuals and businesses against specific types of losses. As Table 17-5 indicates, automobile insurance is the most frequently purchased type of property and casualty insurance, followed by workers' compensation and homeowners' insurance. The rankings are based on the amount of annual premiums paid by policyholders.

LIFE INSURANCE Life insurance is different from all of the other types of insurance coverage described in this chapter. Life insurance deals with a risk that is certain—death. The only uncertainty is the time when it occurs. Life insurance is a common fringe benefit in most firms, since its purchase provides financial protection for the family of the policyholder and, in some instances, an additional source of retirement income for employees and their families. An immediate estate is created by the purchase of a life insurance policy. Because the need for financial security is great in most families, approximately two out of every three Americans are covered by life insurance. In 1974 some 145 million people were covered by 1.8 trillion dollars of insurance. As Figure 17-2 indicates, the average amount of life insurance coverage per American family was $26,500— more than five times as great as in 1950.

Figure 17-2
Life Insurance per
Family in the United
States: 1930–1974

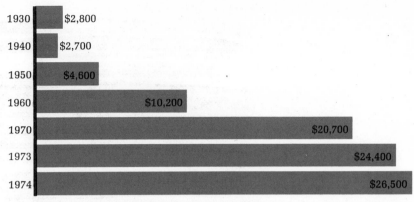

1930	$2,800
1940	$2,700
1950	$4,600
1960	$10,200
1970	$20,700
1973	$24,400
1974	$26,500

SOURCE: *Life Insurance Fact Book* (New York: Institute of Life Insurance, 1975), p. 24. Reprinted by permission from the Institute of Life Insurance.

Group or individual insurance

Life insurance policies may be purchased on an individual basis for almost any amount. Unlike property and casualty insurance, the life insurance purchaser is limited only by the amount of premiums he or she can afford to pay providing the purchaser qualifies medically. Insurance companies have paid as high as $8 million in death benefits on a single policy.[7]

Most businesses purchase employee life insurance on a group basis as a company fringe benefit. Employees may be required to contribute a portion of the cost of the insurance, or the employer may pay the total cost. **Group life insurance** for company employees is typically written under a *single master policy*, and covered employees are not normally required to undergo medical examinations. Since selling costs and administrative expenses are much lower for group insurance, this type is usually much cheaper than individual insurance.

The mortality table is the basis for life insurance

The **mortality table** was first introduced in Table 17-2. It is based on past experience of large numbers of policyholders, and is *used to predict the number of persons in each age category who will die in a given year.* Once this is known, the premiums for a life insurance policy can be calculated to provide sufficient income to pay death benefits, operating expenses, and profits (if the company is a stock company).

Insurance premiums for a forty-year-old will normally be greater than for a twenty-year-old, since the number of deaths per thousand increases from 1.79 to 3.53. As the age of the insured increases, the length of expected future life decreases and life insurance premiums rise.

Types of life insurance

Four basic types of life insurance are term, whole life, limited payment, and endowment. A policyholder may choose one type or some combination of several of them.

Term insurance *provides protection for the individual for a specified period of years, but it has no value at the end of that period.* It is "pure" insurance with no savings features. Some term policies give the policyholder the right to convert to whole life insurance at a higher rate. Term insurance is most often purchased by young marrieds who want protection in the early years of their marriages against the possibility of an early death of one partner. Term insurance offers this low cost protection for one or two decades until the family has the opportunity to develop financial security through savings and investments.

Whole life insurance is the most popular form of life insurance. This type includes a combination of protection and savings. The *insurance provides protection for the individual who pays premiums throughout a lifetime and also builds up a cash surrender value in the policy.* This **cash surrender value** is *the savings portion of a life insurance policy, which can be borrowed by the policyholder at low interest rates or will be paid to the policyholder should the policy be cancelled.*

Several variations of the whole life insurance exist. Many companies offer **limited payment life insurance,** which *is a variation of whole life insurance whereby the policyholder pays all premiums within a designated period, such as twenty or thirty years.* An extreme variation is the **single payment policy,** which consists of *a large premium paid in a lump sum at the time the insurance is purchased.*

A special form of term insurance, called **credit life insurance,** *is often purchased by persons buying a home, or major appliances, which would repay the balance owed on these items should the policyholder die.* The insurance will repay the purchase debt, protecting both the family and the lender. Credit life insurance decreases in value as the loan is repaid. In 1974 more than $100 billion in credit life insurance was in force.

Endowment policies place more emphasis on savings than does whole life insurance. The purchaser of an endowment policy gets *coverage for a specified period,* usually for twenty years or until the age of sixty-five. *After this period the face value of the policy is refunded to the policyholder.* Endowment insurance is considered forced saving and is commonly used as a portion of a family's retirement income plan.

Which type of life insurance policy is best?

The answer to the question, "What type of life insurance policy is

Bought at Age	Straight Life	Limited Payment (20 years)	Endowment (20 years)	Renewable-Convertible Term (5 years)
18	$11.95	$20.15	$43.17	$ 5.35
20	12.54	20.93	43.20	5.38
25	14.27	23.11	43.43	5.50
30	16.60	25.83	43.68	5.68
40	23.32	32.87	45.20	7.96
50	34.51	43.06	48.91	14.21

*Rates shown are approximate premium rates for nonparticipating life insurance policies for men. Rates for women are somewhat lower because of women's somewhat lower mortality. Rates of participating policies would be slightly higher, but the cost would be lowered by annual dividends. The premium rates shown here are per $1,000 of protection if the policies were purchased in units of $10,000.

SOURCE: *Policies for Protection* ((New York: Institute of Life Insurance, 1975), p. 7. Reprinted by permission from the Institute of Life Insurance.

best?", must be, "It depends." Table 17-6 compares the typical annual premiums for $1,000 worth of insurance for each of the four types of life insurance policies.

Each individual must carefully study his or her personal situation with the aid of a qualified insurance agent. Such factors as costs of different policies, the insured's age, family responsibilities, health, and future expectations must be considered. While Table 17-6 provides an illustration of cost comparisons among the different types of life insurance, each person must determine the proper balance between savings and protection that is best for the family.

Summary

Risk is a part of the daily life of both the individual and the business firm. Risk comes in different forms: property damage, dishonesty, death, injury to employees or customers, sickness, lawsuits, and nonpayments of debts. Individuals and businesses must develop methods of dealing with risk.

The four methods of dealing with risk are:

1. avoiding risk
2. reducing risk through proper management and elimination of hazards
3. assuming risk through self-insurance
4. shifting risk to insurance companies.

Insurance is based upon the concepts of insurable interest, insurable risks, and the Law of Large Numbers. Insurance companies are professional risk-takers who operate by charging premiums that are large enough to repay insurance claims and cover operating expenses.

Insurance may be divided into two categories. *Property and casualty insurance* includes:

1. protection against fire
2. protection against automobile accidents
3. protection against burglary, robbery, and theft
4. Workers' Compensation
5. health
6. marine
7. fidelity, surety, title, and credit
8. public liability.

Life insurance may be purchased by individuals or on a group basis by employers at lower rates than for individuals. Four basic types of life insurance are available. Term insurance provides pure protection for a specific period of time. Whole life insurance provides a combination of protection and savings for the policyholder, who pays premiums throughout a lifetime. Limited payment insurance is similar to whole life, except that the policyholder pays all premiums within a designated time period. Endowment life insurance policies are a type of forced savings which provide the policyholder with protection for a specified time period and then return the face value of the policy to the policyholder.

Each type of life insurance has merits and shortcomings. The choice of the best type or types must be made by considering such factors as age, size of the family and the ages of its members, health, and future job expectations of the individual.

Review questions

1. Identify the following terms:
    a. risk
    b. speculative risk
    c. pure risk
    d. self-insurance
    e. insurance
    f. insurable interest
    g. insurable risk
    h. Law of Large Numbers
    i. mutual insurance company
    j. stock insurance company
    k. fire insurance
    l. coinsurance clause
    m. automobile insurance
    n. no-fault insurance
    o. burglary insurance
    p. robbery insurance
    q. theft insurance
    r. Workers' Compensation Insurance
    s. health insurance
    t. ocean marine insurance
    u. inland marine insurance
    v. fidelity bond
    w. surety bond
    x. title insurance
    y. credit insurance
    z. public liability insurance
    aa. product liability insurance
    bb. group life insurance
    cc. mortality table
    dd. term insurance
    ee. whole life insurance
    ff. cash surrender value

gg. limited payment life
insurance

hh. credit life insurance

ii. endowment

2. Explain the concept of risk as it relates to business.
3. What methods are available to the manager for dealing with risk?
4. Discuss the three basic principles of insurance.
5. Identify the various types of property and casualty insurance that exist.
6. Describe the relative importance of each type of property and casualty insurance.
7. How is life insurance different from other types of insurance?
8. Identify and describe the four basic types of life insurance.
9. What types of insurance should a small family-owned bakery carry?
10. Why does group insurance cost loss than individual insurance policies?

Discussion questions and exercises

1. Evaluate the pro and con arguments to the controversial issue that appears in this chapter.
2. Insurance companies typically charge higher automobile insurance rates for people under twenty-five than they do for older persons. Do you think this is a fair policy? Why do you think insurance companies charge higher rates for young persons? Can you think of any situations where younger people receive more favorable insurance rates than older ones?
3. Interview an executive at a local firm about its employee insurance program. Then report what you found out to the class. Can you suggest any possible improvements in the company's insurance program?
4. Ask a local insurance representative to describe to your class the types of policies his or her firm offers.
5. Prepare a term paper on the role that insurance organizations play in U.S. society.

Case 17-1

Medical Malpractice Insurance

Malpractice insurance is carried by medical doctors to protect them from lawsuits by former patients who allege that the doctor's treatment led to some avoidable injury or loss. Malpractice insurance pays for damage awards that may result from these lawsuits. Similar types of insurance are carried by lawyers, certified public accountants, and others involved in providing professional services.

A major nationwide insurance crisis began in 1975. Lawsuits for medical malpractice cases had resulted in rapidly rising payments to former patients. Awards amounting to several hundred thousand dollars became common in these cases. As a result, the insurance companies raised their malpractice insurance rates, with some physicians paying over $20,000 a year in premiums. But as the risks mounted, some insurance companies refused even to issue new insurance or to renew existing policies.

The malpractice insurance crisis resulted in doctor strikes in California, New York, and elsewhere. State legislatures began immediate consideration of the problem. Some states decided to limit damage awards in medical malpractice cases. Others became involved in insuring physicians.

Questions

1. What is the current status of the medical malpractice controversy?
2. How did your state approach the malpractice insurance crisis? Do you agree with your state's solution?
3. Could similar insurance crises in medicine and other professions occur in the future? How can these problems be avoided?

Case 17-2

Equity Funding Life Insurance Company

During the 1960's, Equity Funding was one of the hottest stocks on Wall Street. Life insurance companies were fashionable for investors, and Equity Funding was believed to have great growth potential. But in March of 1973 Laurence Baker of the California Insurance Department handed an Equity Funding official a seizure order and announced: "We're taking over Equity Funding Life Insurance Company. We're going to sweep the floor."

Why did the California Insurance Department take such a drastic step? Later indictments alleged that some Equity Funding personnel entered nonexistent life insurance policy-holders into its computer-based recording system, and then later sold these policies to other insurance companies. If these indictments are proved correct, Equity Funding will surely become one of America's best-known financial scandals.

Questions

1. What is the current status of the Equity Funding case?
2. How is the insurance industry regulated in your state?
3. How can scandals, which might be similar to the Equity Funding allegations, be prevented?

Source: Raymond L. Dirks and Leonard Gross, "You're Making a Terrible Mistake," *M.B.A.* (April 1974), pp. 38–42. Copyright © 1974 Raymond L. Dirks and Magella, Inc. From *The Great Wall Street Scandal* by Raymond L. Dirks and Leonard Gross. Used with permission of McGraw-Hill Book Company.

Careers in Finance, Banking, Investments, and Insurance

All enterprises require assorted financial services. So do private individuals. This means that there is a wide array of potential career fields for people interested and qualified in the area of finance. These careers are exciting and challenging, and also provide excellent advancement possibilities into top management.

The Bureau of Labor Statistics has projected annual job openings to 1985. Their forecast for some selected jobs in finance, banking, investment, and insurance appear below:

Job Projections to 1985

Career	Latest Employment (1972 estimate)	Annual Average of Job Openings to 1985
Bank officers	219,000	13,600
Credit officials	114,000	7,500
Economists	36,000	1,500
Insurance agents and brokers	385,000	16,000
Securities sales workers	220,000	11,900
Underwriters	61,000	2,500

SOURCE: *Occupational Manpower and Training Needs* (Washington, D.C.: Bureau of Labor Statistics, 1974).

Here are some of the careers in finance, banking, investments, and insurance that are available to you:

Finance Director
: The Finance Director is the chief financial officer of any organization. This person has overall responsibility for all aspects of the finance function. Sometimes this person is called "Vice-president of Finance" or "Treasurer."

Financial Analyst
: A Financial Analyst is someone who studies and analyzes financial data. Reports are then

prepared for management that outline various financial strategies that can be taken by the firm. Financial analysts are very important in any enterprise.

Banker

Banker is a general term that applies to a number of jobs within a bank. Most top bank executives have had experience in all aspects of bank management and operations. Banking is a prestigious, rewarding career field.

Stockbroker

A stockbroker is an agent in the purchase and sale of securities, such as common and preferred stocks and bonds. These people work for a brokerage house. They provide information and advise clients on their investments. Stockbrokers execute buy and sell orders for securities.

Portfolio Manager

Portfolio managers are financial consultants to investors. They supervise investments, and often have legal authority to buy and sell securities for a client. Individuals, pension funds, banks, trust funds, colleges, insurance companies, and private foundations all employ portfolio managers.

Underwriter

Underwriters evaluate insurance applications in regard to the risks involved for the insurer. Underwriters specialize according to types of insurance, such as life and casualty. After assessing the insurance application, the underwriter assigns the proper rate (price) to the new policy. If the risks are too great for the insurer, the underwriter will reject the application.

Insurance Agent

Insurance agents are insurance consultants and sales representatives. They evaluate one's insurance needs and recommend the correct type of coverage. If the prospect agrees, they complete the sales transaction. Insurance agents can work either directly for a company or represent several companies as independent agents.

VI Quantitative Tools of Management

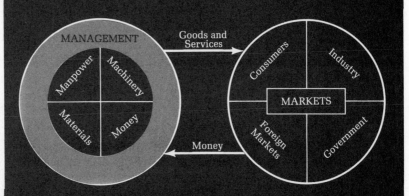

MANAGEMENT

Manpower Machinery

Materials Money

Goods and Services →

← Money

MARKETS

Consumers Industry

Foreign Markets Government

SOURCE: United Press International

18

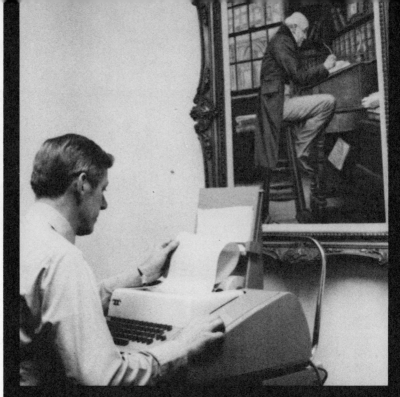

The Role of Accounting

Never ask of money spent
Where the spender thinks it went.
Nobody was ever meant
To remember or invent
What he did with every cent.

—Robert Frost

Though this be madness, yet there is method in it.
—William Shakespeare

SOURCE: James Nolan, American Institute of Certified Public Accountants from *Getting Acquainted with Accounting* by John L. Carey, Houghton Mifflin Co., 1973.

What Chapter 18 Is All About

1. In this chapter you will be introduced to the functions of accounting and the role accounting plays in a business.
2. Accounting serves a number of interested parties—both inside and outside the firm. You will be able to identify these parties and show how accounting information is used by each of them.
3. Three key accounting statements are used to show the financial status of a firm. You will be able to explain briefly how each statement is used.
4. You will also be introduced to a number of financial ratios used in interpreting financial statements. After reading the chapter you should be able to explain to the owner of a small business the purpose of each ratio.
5. After reading the chapter you should understand these terms:

accounting	statement of changes in financial
certified public accountant (CPA)	position
assets	working capital
equities	current ratio
liabilities	acid test ratio
owners' equity	inventory turnover
accounting equation	earnings per share
balance sheet	debt to net worth ratio
income statement	ratio of net income to sales

Abraham Briloff

Abraham Briloff has held the title of Professor of Accountancy at The Baruch School of the City College of New York since 1966. Briloff has a doctorate from New York University and a CPA in New York, and a very down-to-earth mind and a sense of humor.

A dyed-in-the-wool New Yorker, Briloff was born, educated, and still lives in New York City. He began his teaching career in the city high schools in the accounting department.

Briloff has also served as a special consultant to the New York City Council in a study of price trends and to the Federal Trade Commission in a study of the growth of conglomerates. He is a member of a number of learned societies, including the American Institute of CPA's and the American Association for the Advancement of Science. As treasurer and a member of the Board of Directors of The Baruch College Fund, he applies the problems of accounting in a very practical way.

Enormously prolific as a writer, Briloff is the author of four books and over fifty articles. Among the latter are "The Homebuilder's House Is Not in Order" and "The $200 Million Question." He has written for the *Financial Analysts Journal, Barron's*, the *CPA Journal*, the *Financial Times* of London, *Forbes*, and *The Wall Street Journal*. His 1972 book, *Unaccountable Accounting*, tackled the problem of dubious accounting methods and the measures needed for reform.

A frequent speaker and lecturer, Briloff addresses many business schools and professional organizations throughout the United States.

Simon Reynolds carried a leather attaché case with him to the first meeting with the president and chief officials of Computer Controls, Inc., the reportedly fast-growing company he was considering for acquisition as the fourteenth subsidiary of Reynolds Enterprises. He shook hands with everyone at the meeting and quickly went to his seat at the head of the long polished oak conference table. He immediately opened the attaché case and produced a folder with one typewritten page inside.

"Gentlemen, let's come right to the point. Here is the information I need immediately."

The list was a short one:

1. Did Computer Controls earn a profit last year?
2. What was the taxable income for the year?
3. How did Computer Controls raise money last year, and how was it used?

4. What were the production costs of the firm's major products?
5. What were the costs involved in marketing the products?
6. How profitable and efficient were each of the three major divisions of Computer Controls?
7. What is the overall financial position of the company?
8. How did last year's operations and current financial position compare with plans that were made by management at the beginning of the year?

The president of Computer Controls breathed a sigh of relief. "Thank goodness we've got a good accounting system."

What Is Accounting?

Accounting is the language of business. It can formally be defined as *the process of measuring and communicating financial information to enable interested parties inside the firm and outside groups to make informed decisions.* Accountants are responsible for gathering, recording, reporting, and interpreting financial information which describes the status and operation of a firm and which aids in decision making. Three tasks must be accomplished by accountants:

1. score-keeping
2. calling attention to problems and opportunities
3. aiding in decision making.

Accounting for Whom?

Who are those interested parties—both inside and outside the firm—aided by accounting? *Inside* the firm accounting information aids *management* in planning and controlling daily operations, as well as in long-range planning. *Owners* of the firm rely on accounting data to decide how well the firm is being operated. *Union officials* use accounting data in contract negotiations.

Outside the firm *potential investors* use accounting information to help them decide whether to invest in the company. *Bankers and other creditors* must make decisions on whether or not to lend money to a firm, and accounting information gives them an insight into the company's financial soundness. Accounting records are also used for determining credit ratings. Such *government agencies* as the Internal Revenue Service use accounting information to evaluate the company's tax payments for the year.

Accounting versus Bookkeeping

Too many people make the mistake of using the terms *accounting* and *bookkeeping* interchangeably. The terms are not synonymous.

**"And then I found an accountant who rendered unto
me that which was Caesar's."**

Professional Accountants Can Make Major Contributions to the Success
of a Company

SOURCE: *The Wall Street Journal,* May 16, 1973. Reprinted with permission from *The Wall
Street Journal.*

Bookkeeping is the *chief clerical phase of accounting.* Bookkeepers are primarily responsible for the systematic recording of
company financial transactions. They provide the data that the
accountant uses.

Accounting is a much broader term. The 500,000 accountants
in the United States are responsible for developing accounting
systems for classifying transactions, developing methods of summarizing transactions, and interpreting financial statements.

Accountants are decision makers; the bookkeeper is trained
primarily for the largely mechanical tasks of record-keeping. Trained
accountants hold positions as chief executives in many of the
largest companies and in top-level government offices.

The Certified Public Accountant—
Accounting Professional

A **certified public accountant (CPA)** has proven his skills through the completion of a number of rigorous tests. Although requirements vary from
state to state, most states require applicants to have a college degree with
a major in accounting and at least two years of experience with an accounting firm. In order to obtain the CPA certificate, the *applicant must
pass a comprehensive three-day examination covering law, accounting
theory, practice, and auditing.* The CPA has the same professional status
within his or her field as attorneys in law or physicians in medicine. Approximately 130,000 accountants are registered CPAs.*

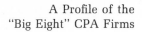

A Profile of the "Big Eight" CPA Firms

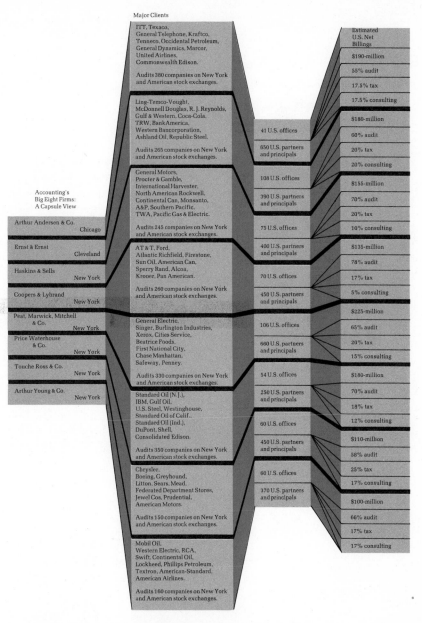

Major Clients

ITT, Texaco, General Telephone, Kraftco, Tenneco, Occidental Petroleum, General Dynamics, Marcor, United Airlines, Commonwealth Edison.

Audits 380 companies on New York and American stock exchanges.

Ling-Temco-Vought, McDonnell Douglas, R. J. Reynolds, Gulf & Western, Coca-Cola, TRW, BankAmerica, Western Bancorporation, Ashland Oil, Republic Steel.

Audits 265 companies on New York and American stock exchanges.

General Motors, Procter & Gamble, International Harvester, North American Rockwell, Continental Can, Monsanto, A&P, Southern Pacific, TWA, Pacific Gas & Electric.

Audits 245 companies on New York and American stock exchanges.

AT & T, Ford, Atlantic Richfield, Firestone, Sun Oil, American Can, Sperry Rand, Alcoa, Kroger, Pan American.

Audits 260 companies on New York and American stock exchanges.

General Electric, Singer, Burlington Industries, Xerox, Cities Service, Beatrice Foods, First National City, Chase Manhattan, Safeway, Penney.

Audits 330 companies on New York and American stock exchanges.

Standard Oil (N.J.), IBM, Gulf Oil, U.S. Steel, Westinghouse, Standard Oil of Calif., Standard Oil (Ind.), DuPont, Shell, Consolidated Edison.

Audits 350 companies on New York and American stock exchanges.

Chrysler, Boeing, Greyhound, Litton, Sears, Mead, Federated Department Stores, Jewel Cos, Prudential, American Motors.

Audits 150 companies on New York and American stock exchanges.

Mobil Oil, Western Electric, RCA, Swift, Continental Oil, Lockheed, Phillips Petroleum, Textron, American-Standard, American Airlines.

Audits 160 companies on New York and American stock exchanges.

Accounting's Big Eight Firms: A Capsule View

- Arthur Andersen & Co. — Chicago
- Ernst & Ernst — Cleveland
- Haskins & Sells — New York
- Coopers & Lybrand — New York
- Peat, Marwick, Mitchell & Co. — New York
- Price Waterhouse & Co. — New York
- Touche Ross & Co. — New York
- Arthur Young & Co. — New York

41 U.S. offices
650 U.S. partners and principals

108 U.S. offices
390 U.S. partners and principals

75 U.S. offices
400 U.S. partners and principals

70 U.S. offices
450 U.S. partners and principals

106 U.S. offices
660 U.S. partners and principals

54 U.S. offices
250 U.S. partners and principals

60 U.S. offices
450 U.S. partners and principals

60 U.S. offices
370 U.S. partners and principals

Estimated U.S. Net Billings

$190-million
55% audit
17.5% tax
17.5% consulting

$180-million
60% audit
20% tax
20% consulting

$155-million
70% audit
20% tax
10% consulting

$135-million
78% audit
17% tax
5% consulting

$225-million
65% audit
20% tax
15% consulting

$180-million
70% audit
18% tax
12% consulting

$110-million
58% audit
25% tax
17% consulting

$100-million
66% audit
17% tax
17% consulting

NOTE: Unlike the thousands of publicly held corporations they audit, CPA firms are organized as partnerships. Data on revenues, operating costs, and other significant financial figures are not a matter of public record and traditionally have been closely guarded secrets. The table represents *Business Week's* estimates of Big Eight operations, together with other important dimensions of the nation's best-known accounting firms.

SOURCE: Reprinted from the April 22, 1972 issue of *Business Week* by special permission. © 1972 by McGraw-Hill, Inc.

The CPA certificate is not required for accountants, but only CPAs can officially express an opinion on the accuracy of a firm's financial statements. This official opinion is required of all publicly-held corporations, and is usually required by any lending agency. In Canada, the

United Kingdom, and Australia, these accounting professionals are called chartered accountants (CAs).

*John L. Carey. *Getting Acquainted with Accounting* (Boston: Houghton Mifflin Company, 1973), p. 1.

The Accounting Process

The basic data used in accounting are financial transactions between the firm and its employees, suppliers, owners, bankers, and various governmental bodies. Weekly payroll checks result in cash outflows for the compensation of employees. A payment to a supplier results in the receipt of needed raw materials for the production process. Prompt payment of bills preserves the firm's credit rating and its ability to obtain future loans.

As Figure 18-1 indicates, these transactions must be recorded, classified, and summarized in order to produce financial statements for the firm's management and other interested parties.

THE ACCOUNTING JOURNAL— STOREHOUSE OF FINANCIAL TRANSACTIONS

Each financial transaction is recorded in chronological order in a book called a *journal.* The journal can take the form of a listing prepared by hand or the form of computer printouts in firms with computerized accounting systems. A sample page from a journal is shown in Figure 18-2.

The accounts listed in Figure 18-2 should be familiar, since they were discussed in Chapter 15 as sources or uses of funds. The July 1st purchase of land and a building cost $30,000 and reduced the cash account by that amount of money. The July 25th payment of $1,000 by Arnold Wilson on his account increased the amount of cash on hand by that amount.

In practice, the transactions work much like your checking account. Each check you write or deposit you make reduces or raises your checking account balance. The check or deposit is recorded in your checkbook for your records. The bank also keeps a record of each deposit made and each check written. The bank's records are usually maintained by computers, and a bank statement is provided to each depositor at the end of each month. Journal

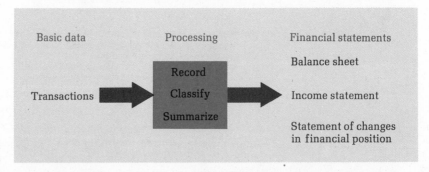

Figure 18-1
The Accounting Process

Figure 18-2
Sample Page from an
Accounting Journal

General Journal				Page 1
1976				
July	1	Land	5,000	
		Building	25,000	
		Cash		30,000
		To record purchase of land and building for cash.		
	5	Furniture	8,000	
		Accounts Payable —Oakleigh Furniture Co.		8,000
		To record purchase of furniture on account.		
	10	Accounts Payable—Oakleigh Furniture Co.	5,000	
		Cash		5,000
		To record payment on account.		
	20	Accounts Receivable—Arnold Wilson	1,800	
		Sales Revenue		1,800
		To record sale of merchandise on account.		
	25	Cash	1,000	
		Accounts Receivable—Arnold Wilson		1,000
		To record collection on account.		

entries reflect changes in a company's accounts in the same way. A cash sale increases the cash account while reducing inventory. Purchases of stationery, for instance, increase the supplies account and reduce cash.

Assets

As was explained in Chapter 15 the **assets** of a business are *everything of value found in the business.* Cash, accounts receivable and notes receivable (amounts owed to the business through credit sales), land, buildings, supplies, and marketable securities are all examples of assets.

Equities: Liabilities and Owner's Equity

Equities are *claims against the assets of a business.* The two major classifications of individuals who have equities in a firm are the **creditors** (*liability holders*) and the **owners.**

The **liabilities** of a business are *everything owed to creditors.* Liabilities are the claims of the firm's creditors. When the firm makes credit purchases for inventory, land, or machinery, the claims of the creditors are shown as *accounts payable* or *notes payable.* Wages and salaries owed to employees also represent liabilities known as wages payable.

Figure 18-3
The Accounting
Equation Shows the
Relationship between
Assets and Equities

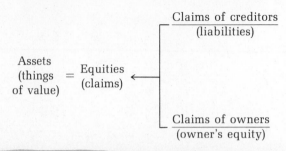

The **owner's equity** represents *the proprietor's, the partners', or the stockholders' claims against the assets of the firm, or the excess of all assets over all liabilities.*

The Accounting Equation

Since equities, by definition, represent the total claims against assets, then *assets must equal equities.* This relationship is shown in Figure 18-3.

Figure 18-3 shows the basic **accounting equation,** which reflects the financial position of any firm at all times:

$$Assets = Liabilities + Owner's\ equity.$$

Business assets *owned* equal the *sources* of those assets. The equation can be modified slightly to reflect the form of ownership of the firm. For a corporation the equation would be:

$$Assets = Liabilities + Stockholders'\ equity,$$

and in a partnership the equation would be:

$$Assets = Liabilities + Partners'\ equity.$$

Accounting Statements

The relationship expressed by the accounting equation is used to develop the three primary accounting statements:

1. the balance sheet
2. the income statement
3. the statement of changes in financial position.

THE BALANCE SHEET

A **balance sheet** *shows the financial position of a company as of a particular date.* It is like a photograph capturing the status of the company's assets and equities at a moment in time.

Balance sheets should be prepared at regular intervals to provide information to management concerning the financial position of the firm. Most firms prepare balance sheets at least once a year, and often for each month or quarter.

"Hold it, gentlemen, hold it! I had it the wrong way around. It isn't <u>assets</u> that are in excess of ninety-seven million. It's <u>liabilities</u>!"

Figure 18-4 shows the balance sheet for Armstrong Cork Company. The basic accounting equation is illustrated by the three classifications. The assets total must equal the liabilities and stockholders' equity total.

As the figure indicates, assets are divided into current and long-term assets. Current assets consist of cash and other assets that can be readily converted into cash or are expected to be used in the operation of the business within one year. Current assets are usually listed in order of their expected **liquidity**, or *the speed at which they could be converted to cash.* For Armstrong Cork the current assets are cash, marketable securities, accounts receivable, and inventory. Prepaid expenses, the final current asset, are services, such as insurance, that have already been paid for but have not yet been used up.

ARMSTRONG CORK COMPANY AND SUBSIDIARIES
Consolidated Balance Sheet

ASSETS	1974 (000)
Current assets:	
Cash	$ 7,855
Short-term securities (at cost, which approximates market)	128
Accounts and notes receivable (less allowance for discounts and losses: 1974–$7,036,000; 1973–$5,892,000)	104,840
Inventories	197,503
Prepaid expenses	9,203
Total current assets	319,529
Long-term receivables	33,670
Property, plant and equipment (at cost, less accumulated depreciation and amortization: 1974–$223,559,000; 1973–$206,233,000)	363,624
Sundry assets and investments, at cost or less	17,232
	$734,055
LIABILITIES AND STOCKHOLDERS' EQUITY	
Current liabilities:	
Notes payable	$ 34,850
Current installments of long-term debt	3,187
Accounts payable and accrued expenses	61,681
Federal and foreign income taxes	1,460
Total current liabilities	101,178
Long-term debt	143,495
Deferred income taxes	28,763
Minority interest in foreign subsidiary	2,821
Stockholders' equity	457,798
	$734,055

STOCKHOLDERS' EQUITY	1974 (000)
Preferred stock, $3.75 cumulative, no par value. Authorized 161,821 shares; issued 161,522 shares (at redemption price of $102.75 per share)	$16,596
Voting preferred stock. Authorized 1,500,000 shares	—
Common stock, $1.00 par value per share. Authorized 60,000,000 shares; issued 25,930,860 shares	25,931
Capital surplus	46,909
Retained earnings	377,657
	467,093
Less treasury stock, at cost:	
Preferred stock, $3.75 cumulative–43,373 shares	3,986
Common stock–192,782 shares	5,309
	9,295
	$457,798

Net property, plant and equipment are assets to be used over a long period of time (generally more than a year) in the operation of the business. These fixed assets include such items as land, factories, and machinery. Long-term receivables are debts of the firm's customers that are not due to be repaid within the next twelve months.

Liabilities, like assets, are also divided into current and long-term claims. The term **current liabilities** is used to identify *those claims which will be repaid within a one-year period.* Accounts payable and notes payable are the liability counterparts of accounts receivable and notes receivable. **Accounts payable** represent *credit purchases by the firm which must be repaid within a one-year period.* **Notes payable** are *loans represented by a written document such as an IOU for a longer period of time than one year.* The portion of the notes payable due in the current year is listed as a current liability. Notes payable due after one year are included on the balance sheet as a long-term liability.

Federal and foreign income taxes are listed on the balance sheet as both current and long-term liabilities. Since profitable firms are required to pay a sizable portion of their estimated income taxes every three months, the $1.46 million current liability on the balance sheet is the remaining portion still to be paid by Armstrong Cork.

In order to encourage manufacturers to keep their plant equipment modern and efficient, tax regulations permit companies to put off certain tax payments to a future date. The $28.8 million in deferred income taxes represents the tax obligation that will come due later than twelve months in the future.

Stockholders' equity (shown in Figure 18-5) represents the claims of the owners of the firm. Since Armstrong Cork Company is a corporation, the term stockholders' equity is used rather than owner's equity or partners' equity.

When the stock of the corporation has a stated amount on the stock certificate called the par value, this par value times the number of shares of stock outstanding is shown in the stockholders' equity portion of the balance sheet. Since the common stock of Armstrong Cork Company sold at a premium over the $1 par value when it was issued, an account called capital surplus (also known as paid-in capital in excess of par) is also listed on the balance sheet. The two amounts when combined represent the total contributions made by the stockholders over time to the corporation.

The profits of the corporation may be distributed to the stockholders in the form of cash dividends, or they may be retained by the corporation and reinvested. These *retained earnings* can be used for expansion, growth, and can be invested in such assets as land and buildings. The retained earnings of $377.7 million represent the accumulated earnings of Armstrong Cork Company that have been left in the firm.

A corporation may decide to repurchase some of its own stock. Such stock is called treasury stock. If the corporation receives approval from the Securities and Exchange Commission, it may purchase its stock on the open market for such uses as an employee stock purchase program. Armstrong Cork currently holds $9.3 million of treasury stock.

THE INCOME STATEMENT

While the balance sheet reflects the financial position of the company at one specific time, the **income statement** *reflects the operations of the company over a period of time.*

The purpose of the income statement (also called a statement of earnings) is to show the profitability or unprofitability of a firm during a period of time such as a year, a quarter, or a month, and to provide basic data to help the investor analyze the possible reasons for such results. The income statement is even sometimes called a *profit and loss statement.* Figure 18-6 shows the 1974 income statement for Armstrong Cork Company.

The income statement summarizes the income and expenses of the firm over a period of time. The basic format of the income statement is the deduction of costs and expenses, including taxes, from

Figure 18-6
Income Statement for Armstrong Cork Company, for Year Ended December 31, 1974. Percentage figures in the last column have been added to show approximate proportion of sales income represented by each item.

ARMSTRONG CORK COMPANY AND SUBSIDIARIES Consolidated Statement of Earnings		
CURRENT EARNINGS	1974 (000)	
Income:		
Net sales	$889,309	100.0
Other income (expense), net	(2,143)	(.2)
	887,166	99.8
Costs and expenses:		
Cost of goods sold	626,382	70.4
Selling and administrative	151,696	17.1
Depreciation and amortization	30,367	3.4
Interest expense	12,332	1.4
	820,777	92.3
Earnings before income taxes:	66,389	7.5
Federal and foreign income taxes	28,600	3.2
Net earnings	$ 37,789*	4.3
Net earnings per share of common stock	$ 1.45*	

*Reflects change to LIFO method of valuing material content of virtually all domestic inventories not previously on LIFO and change in accounting for foreign exchange fluctuations. Effect of changes for LIFO and foreign exchange was to reduce net earnings by $12.8 million, or $.50 per share, and $2.0 million, or $.08 per share, respectively.

income in order to determine the net profit of the firm for that time period. The equation for the income statement is:

$$\text{Income} - \text{Expenses} = \text{Net profit (or loss)}.$$

Income from sales shows the total sales to customers during the accounting period. Sales represent the major source of income for the company. Other income (or expense) represents net profit (or loss) from such transactions as the sale of machinery, rent received from property, and interest earned on investments during the period.

In order to determine the profit earned for the year, the expenses involved in producing the goods that were sold must be deducted from income. Next, the selling and administrative expenses of the period must be deducted from income. These expenses include advertising, sales commissions, officers' salaries, and rent.

Deduction of these expenses from income leaves income before taxes. Once taxes are deducted, the net profit (or loss) for the period is determined. For Armstrong Cork, the net income for 1974 was approximately $37.8 million, or $1.45 per share of common stock.

LIFO versus FIFO: Why Companies Are Making the Switch

More and more firms switched to the LIFO method of inventory accounting during the inflationary period of the mid-1970's. Among the ranks of major firms who made the change were Du Pont, Firestone Tire & Rubber, Armstrong Cork, and Eastman Kodak.

LIFO (last-in, first out) is a method of inventory valuation by which the cost of goods sold is based on the most recent purchases of raw materials and component parts used in producing these goods. By using recent prices, the cost of goods sold reflects the higher prices that must be paid to purchase new raw materials. Use of the LIFO method reduces profits (since it increases the cost of goods sold), but proponents of the method argue that it provides a more correct statement of profits than is the case with FIFO.

In previous years FIFO (first-in, first-out) was used, and the assumption was made that the first raw materials purchased would be the first used in producing finished goods. However, as raw materials increased in cost, use of the FIFO method produced higher profits. Many accountants felt that these higher profits were unrealistic, since they ignored the need to replenish inventories at higher costs; and so the switch in inventory valuation methods was made.

A switch from FIFO to LIFO can reduce profits considerably, but it has another important effect. Reduced profits increase the amount of cash available to a firm, since income taxes are also lowered. The example below shows the effect of a switch in inventory valuation methods on profits. The example assumes an 8 percent rate of inflation and a tax rate of 50 percent.

	FIFO method	LIFO method
Sales	$100,000	$100,000
Cost of goods sold	75,000	81,000
Profits before taxes	25,000	19,000
Income taxes	12,500	9,500
Net income after taxes	$ 12,500	$ 9,500

THE PERCENTAGE OF NET SALES INCOME STATEMENT HELPS IN MAKING COMPARISONS

The use of percentages based upon net sales points up the important expense items on the income statement. The percentage figures also assist investors and financial analysts in comparing the income statement with similar statements for previous periods. The percentages may in some instances make comparison of company operations with other firms in the industry easier, and aid in comparisons of company figures with industry averages.

STATEMENT OF CHANGES IN FINANCIAL POSITION

The statement of changes in financial position is of more recent origin than the income statement or the balance sheet, and is required for almost all companies. Since 1970 the Securities and Exchange Commission has required this statement as part of the annual registration information for all companies listed on organized stock exchanges. It must also be included as part of the accounting information for firms whose financial statements are audited by public accounting firms. As its name indicates, the **statement of changes in financial position** is designed to *explain the financial changes that occur in a company from one accounting period to the next.* The 1974 statement of changes in financial position for Armstrong Cork Company is shown in Figure 18-7.

Working capital is *the difference between current assets and current liabilities.* In effect, working capital represents the source of assets available to keep the business operating during the months ahead.

As Figure 18-7 shows, working capital is created from a number of sources. Much of it typically comes from company earnings. Another source is cash received from creditors and through the issue of stock. The payment of dividends to stockholders, and payments for new plant, property, and equipment represent uses of working capital.

The statement of changes in financial position acts as a link between the present and preceding year's balance sheets. It provides interested parties with an insight into how the firm's operations are being financed and what its funds are being used for. For these reasons the statement of changes in financial position has earned its status as one of the three key accounting documents.

Figure 18-7
Statement of
Changes in Financial
Position for Armstrong
Cork Company for
the Year Ended
December 31, 1974.

ARMSTRONG CORK COMPANY AND SUBSIDIARIES
Consolidated Statements of Changes in Financial Position

	1974 (000)
Funds became available from:	
Operations:	
Net earnings	$ 37,789
Add items not requiring funds:	
Depreciation and amortization	30,367
Deferred income taxes	2,481
Portion of $4,037,000 loss on foreign exchange	
($2,691,000 in 1973) related to long-term debt	5,313
Other items	136
Total from operations	76,086
Long-term borrowings	58,149
	134,235
These funds were used for:	
Capital additions to property, plant and equipment	68,804
Dividends to stockholders	23,606
Other items	1,941
	94,351
Increase in working capital	$ 39,884
Changes in working capital consist of:	
Increase (decrease) in current assets:	
Cash and short-term securities	$ (8,502)
Receivables	4,315
Inventories	48,494
Prepaid expenses	4,005
	48,312
Increase (decrease) in current liabilities:	
Notes payable and current installments of long-term debt	23,179
Accounts payable and accrued expenses	(1,629)
Income taxes	(13,122)
	8,428
Increase in working capital	$ 39,884

Interpreting the Financial Statements

Once the financial statements have been produced from the accounting data collected for the period, the accountant must interpret these statements. The fact that a firm earned a profit for the past year is of interest—but of equal interest is *the profit it should have earned.* Over the years a number of techniques have been developed for interpreting financial information in order to aid management in planning and evaluating the operations of the company from day to day and month to month.

One common method of interpreting income statements has already been discussed. This is the practice of converting the various costs and expenses on the income statement as percentages of sales. When the cost and expense items are shown in percentage form, they can quickly be compared with the income statements of previous periods or with other companies in the industry, as we have seen. In this way, unusually high or low expenses will be apparent to management, and corrective actions may be taken should this prove necessary.

A second method of interpreting financial statements is through ratio analysis. By comparing the company ratios to industry standards, problem areas can be pinpointed. Among the most commonly used ratios are:

the current ratio

the acid test ratio

inventory turnover

earnings per share

total debt to net worth ratio

the ratio of net income to sales.

CURRENT RATIO

The **current ratio** *compares current assets to current liabilities.* This ratio is designed to measure the ability of the company to pay its current debts as they mature. The current ratio of Armstrong Cork Company is computed as:

$$\text{Current ratio} = \frac{\text{Current assets}}{\text{Current liabilities}} = \frac{\$319,529,000}{\$101,178,000} = 3.2 \text{ to } 1.$$

This means that Armstrong Cork Company has $3.20 of current assets for every dollar of current liabilities.

The current ratio is one of the most widely used balance sheet ratios. *In general, a current ratio of 2 to 1 is considered to be financially satisfactory.* This rule of thumb must be considered along with other factors, such as the nature of the business, the season of the year, and the quality of the management of the company.

ACID TEST RATIO

The **acid test ratio,** or **quick ratio,** measures *the ability of the firm to meet its current debt on short notice.* This ratio does not include inventory or prepaid expenses. Only cash, marketable securities, and accounts receivable—all highly liquid assets—are included.

The current balance sheet of Armstrong Cork Company lists the following quick assets: Cash ($7,855,000), marketable securities ($128,000), and accounts and notes receivable ($104,840,000). The acid test ratio is computed in this manner:

$$\text{Acid test ratio} = \frac{\text{Quick assets}}{\text{Current liabilities}} = \frac{\$112,823,000}{\$101,178,000} = 1.1 \text{ to } 1.$$

Since *the typical minimum acid test ratio is 1 to 1,* Armstrong Cork Company appears to be in a good short-term credit position.

INVENTORY TURNOVER

The **inventory turnover** rate indicates *the number of times the merchandise moves through the business.* It is calculated by dividing the cost of goods sold by the average amount of inventory. For a retail jeweler, for instance, the inventory turnover may be calculated as:

$$\frac{\text{Inventory}}{\text{turnover}} = \frac{\text{Cost of goods sold}}{\text{Average inventory}} = \frac{\$285,000}{\$120,000} = 2.4 \text{ turns.}$$

The turnover rate can then be compared with industry standards and used as a measure of efficiency. For a jewelry store, 2.4 turns is above average. For a supermarket, the turnover rate should be about 20. In general, the higher the turnover rate, the less warehouse space needed and the greater the number of sales being made.

EARNINGS PER SHARE

One of the most commonly watched ratios in business is **earnings per share.** This ratio indicates *the amount of profits earned by a company for each share of common stock outstanding.* As Figure 18-6 indicates, the 1974 earnings per share for Armstrong Cork Company is $1.45.

$$\text{Earnings per share} = \frac{\text{Net earnings} - \text{Provision for preferred dividends}}{\text{Average number of common shares outstanding}}$$

$$= \frac{\$37,789,000 - 443,000}{25,738,000} = \$1.45.$$

The $1.45 earnings figure can be compared with earnings per share in previous years to provide some indication of earnings growth at Armstrong Cork. It can also be compared with the earnings per share of other firms in the industry to evaluate the relative performance of the firm.

DEBT TO NET WORTH RATIO

The **debt to net worth ratio** is designed to measure *the extent to which the operations of the company are financed by borrowed funds.* It indicates the amounts of funds contributed by creditors as compared with the total funds provided. The debt to net worth ratio for Armstrong Cork Company is computed as:

$$\text{Debt to net worth ratio} = \frac{\text{Total liabilities}}{\text{Stockholders' equity}} = \frac{\$276,257,000}{\$457,798,000} = .60.$$

RATIO OF NET INCOME TO SALES

The **ratio of net income to sales** measures company profitability by *comparing net income and sales.* For Armstrong Cork Company, the ratio of net income to sales is computed as:

$$\text{Ratio of net income to sales} = \frac{\text{Net income}}{\text{Sales}} = \frac{\$37,789,000}{\$889,309,000} = 4.3 \text{ percent.}$$

Does the Corporate Financial Statement Reflect Economic Reality?

Since a corporation is owned by stockholders, it would seem that corporate management owes them a frank disclosure of its plans and strategies, not only for the present, but also for the future of the corporation.

Accounting methods are as old as civilization itself. They were developed originally out of a need to keep track of grains and sheep, and later the system was expanded to maintain tax records and to record and evaluate costs. Accounting is both a means of determining the profitability of an enterprise and a way of attesting to the accuracy of financial statements issued by a firm. Given this ancient background, it is no wonder that the accounting system tends to be kept intact: the system has worked before; why should it not continue to do so.

Because of concern in the business community over the problem of inflation, some professionals see a need for specific changes in the accounting system in order to take a closer look at real profits. This would mean dealing with changes brought on by the erosion of the U.S. dollar so that the general price level, as well as the value of resources and obligations, are taken into account when financial statements are drawn up. Such statements would give corporate management up-to-date information about their firm's financial position and would allow investors to have a more realistic look at corporate profits and losses.

A corporation's long-term assets, when these are not adjusted for current changes in the dollar, reflect an inaccurate monetary position of the firm. Planning cannot be conducted in a sensible manner if unrealistic financial statements are used. Unexpected losses that could have been predicted simply throw planners into a panic.

Yet, if adjustments for a more realistic corporate picture are made, and a financial statement is issued on that basis, the corporation's profit and loss position will be distorted in the marketplace. If a corporation is compared with its competitors, who do not make such an adjustment, it will look much less appealing as an investment relative to other firms. Even though an explanation of the meaning of a relatively low or no-growth year accompanies the statement, stockholders and even the board of directors might feel shaky about the future of the corporation and doubtful of its management's ability.

This 4.3 percent ratio of net income to sales is approximately the same as the national average of 4 to 5 percent. Similar profitability ratios can be computed by comparing the net income of a company to assets or net worth.

Summary

Accounting is the language of business. Its purpose is to supply financial information for use in planning and evaluating the operations of a firm. Accountants are professionals who are responsible for the recording, classifying, summarizing, reporting, and interpreting of the financial transactions of a firm.

Accounting data are grouped into three basic classifications: assets, liabilities, and owners' (or stockholders') equity. Assets are things of value owned and used in the business. Cash, accounts and notes receivables, inventory, land, buildings, and machinery are all assets. Liabilities are claims against the assets by the creditors of the firm. The owners' claims on the assets are called owners' (or stockholders') equity. The relationship between the assets of a firm and the claims against those assets is shown by the basic accounting equation:

$$\text{Assets} = \text{Liabilities} + \text{Owners' equity.}$$

Financial information is summarized in three key accounting statements: the balance sheet, the income statement, and the statement of changes in financial position. The balance sheet can be thought of as a photograph showing the assets, liabilities, and owners' equity of a firm at one point in time. The income statement is a motion picture designed to show the profitability of a company over a period of time such as a month or year. By subtracting the expenses from the income, the income statement reveals the amount of profit (or loss) for that accounting period. The statement of changes in financial position explains the financial changes that occur from one accounting period to the next. It focuses on the sources and uses of funds in the firm.

Financial statements may be interpreted through the use of percentages or ratios. Such ratios as the current ratio, the acid test ratio, inventory turnover, earnings per share, the debt to net worth ratio, and the ratio of net income to sales are commonly used. These assist the manager and other interested parties by making possible the comparison of current company financial information with that of previous years and with industry standards.

Review questions

1. Identify the following terms:
   a. accounting
   b. certified public accountant (CPA)
   c. assets
   d. equities
   e. liabilities

f. owners' equity
g. accounting equation
h. balance sheet
i. income statement
j. statement of changes in financial position
k. working capital

l. current ratio
m. acid test ratio
n. inventory turnover
o. earnings per share
p. debt to net worth ratio
q. ratio of net income to sales

2. Who are the major users of accounting information?
3. Distinguish between accounting and bookkeeping.
4. Explain the concept of equities. What are the two chief types of equities?
5. What are the major differences between the balance sheet and the income statement?
6. Distinguish between current and long-term assets.
7. Briefly explain these concepts:
   a. stockholders' equity
   b. paid-in capital in excess of par
   c. treasury stock
8. What are the major advantages of showing the various items on a firm's income statement in percentages based upon net sales rather than showing the actual figures involved?
9. Relate the statement of changes in financial position to the other two chief financial statements.
10. Explain the techniques used by accountants in interpreting financial statements.

Discussion questions and exercises

1. Evaluate the pro and con arguments to the controversial issue that appears in this chapter.
2. Interview an accounting professor at your college or university. Determine the major differences between the certified public accountant (CPA) and other types of accountants.
3. Review the material on the Securities and Exchange Commission (SEC) in Chapter 16. Write a brief report explaining why the SEC would require firms to file an annual statement of changes in financial position.
4. Interview a college placement officer. Determine the demand for accountants in your area and in a brief report explain the reasons for this demand.
5. List each of the ratios covered in this chapter. Explain the *value* of each ratio from the point of view of the decision maker.

Case 18-1

Beatrice Foods Company

Beatrice Foods Company is a highly diversified manufacturer with headquarters in Chicago. Its product lines include dairy products (Meadow Gold, yogurt, dehydrated food items, franchising for Weight Watchers soft drinks); grocery products (LaChoy, Miracle White, Clark Candy, and others); specialty meat products, warehousing, manufacturing, life insurance, and chemicals. The financial statements for the year ended February 28, 1975, are shown below:

Consolidated Balance Sheet
February 28, 1975

Assets

Current assets:	
Cash	$ 70,486,967
Marketable securities, at cost which approximates market	18,264,308
Receivables, less allowance for losses, $14,940,249	382,898,991
Inventories	502,448,387
Prepaid expenses	23,062,448
Total current assets	997,161,101
Investment in unconsolidated subsidiary	39,679,890
Plant and equipment:	
Land	32,185,562
Buildings	275,822,206
Machinery and equipment	513,806,686
	821,814,454
Less accumulated depreciation	331,940,479
	489,873,975
Investments and other assets	31,206,268
Intangible assets	100,249,139
	$1,658,170,373

Liabilities and Stockholders' Equity

Current liabilities:	
Accounts payable and accrued expenses	$ 352,557,233
Current portion of long-term debt	11,210,702
Income taxes	38,210,702
Total current liabilities	401,978,030

Debentures and notes	230,735,000
Other long-term debt	43,904,345
Deferred credits and other noncurrent liabilities	87,615,721
Minority interests in subsidiaries	22,488,047

Stockholders' equity:
  Preference stock (without par value)
    Authorized 2,500,000 shares. Issued 341,235 shares
    at stated value with aggregate liquidation
    preference of $33,558,180   9,233,016
  Common stock (without par value)
    Authorized 100,000,000 shares. Issued
    77,413,117 shares at $1.85 stated value   143,214,266
  Capital surplus   34,887,006
  Earnings invested in the business (earned surplus)   684,369,937

                            871,704,225

Less 136,754 shares of common stock in treasury at stated value   252,995

Stockholders' equity   871,451,230

                            $1,658,170,373

Statement of Consolidated Earnings
Year Ended February 28, 1975

Income:	
Net sales	$4,191,763,971
Other income, including equity in net earnings of	
unconsolidated subsidiary	12,006,062
	4,203,770,033
Costs and expenses:	
Cost of sales	3,176,581,688
Selling, administrative, and general expenses	682,112,049
Depreciation expense	52,389,139
Interest expense	27,895,719
	3,938,978,595
Earnings before income taxes	264,791,438
Provision for income taxes	126,000,000
Earnings after income taxes	138,791,438
Minority interests in net earnings of subsidiaries	4,027,272
Net earnings	$ 134,764,166

SOURCE: Used by permission of Beatrice Foods Company.

Questions

1. Calculate the following ratios for Beatrice Foods Company:
   a. current ratio
   b. acid test ratio
   c. earnings per share
   d. debt to net worth ratio
   e. ratio of net income to sales
2. What would you conclude about the company from your analysis?

Case 18-2

The Fiscal Year

A fiscal year is a twelve-month, 365-day period used for accounting and budgeting purposes. It does not necessarily correspond to the calendar year. For instance, a fiscal year for Beatrice Foods is March 1st to February 28th of the next year. Many companies, nonprofit organizations, and government units use July 1st as the beginning of their fiscal years. Still others use dates such as October 1st.

Questions

1. Find out why many firms and organizations use a fiscal year rather than the calendar year in their accounting systems.
2. Interview someone in the business office of your college or university. Inquire whether your institution uses a fiscal year in its accounting system. If so, determine the reasons for choosing the fiscal period. If not, find a business organization that uses a fiscal year and find out why.

19

The Role
of Computers

*"Between 1970 and 1980 the most important industry in the world,
after oil and automobiles, will be computers."*

—Jacques Maisonrouge

*"Collecting data is much like collecting garbage. You must know in
advance what you are going to do with the stuff before you collect
it."*

—Mark Twain

What Chapter 19 Is All About

1. In this chapter you will be introduced to computers and the functions they perform in the business world of the 1970's. You should be able to identify the elements of a computer system and the function of each.
2. Software is one of the most expensive aspects of computers. You should be able to explain what software is and identify the most commonly used programming languages.
3. Computers have shortcomings as well as advantages in their use. You will be able to describe the major limitations of computers.
4. Computers use binary arithmetic rather than decimal numbers. You should be able to explain how binary arithmetic works and why it is appropriate for use by computers.
5. After reading this chapter, you should understand these terms:

minicomputer	binary arithmetic
computer	program
input	flowchart
memory	programmer
arithmetic	FORTRAN
control	COBOL
output	PL/1
computer hardware	remote terminals
software	time-sharing

Thomas J. Watson, Jr.

Watson was born in Campbell, New York, in 1874. His strict Methodist father wanted him to study law, but the young man wanted to get a job and earn a good salary. He agreed to spend a year at the Elmira School of Commerce, and then clerked two more years in a music-sewing machine store, and later became a cash register sales representative.

Conservative in dress, Watson was dignified and a little shy, but that did not stop him from being a super sales representative. The motto "Think," which he first used to raise morale at National Cash Register, while he was the company's sales manager, and later introduced at IBM, has sprouted thousands of offshoots since he told a sales meeting "'I didn't think' has cost the world millions of dollars."

In forty-two years at IBM, serving as its president and chairman, Watson watched the company grow from 1,200 employees to 274,000, with customers in over one hundred countries around the world. Watson's belief in research and training has spurred the company's expansion and its development of new business machines.

His position as honorary president of the International Chamber of Commerce and as trustee of the Carnegie Endowment for International Peace are indications of Watson's conviction that peaceful solutions to world crises can be found through "sound economics between countries." A leader in employee benefits planning, under Watson's direction IBM employees receive medical coverage, insurance, and a pension plan. Women at IBM have been encouraged to grow with the firm.

Watson died a month after his son became chief executive of IBM.

Computers are such awesome machines! Their blinking lights, whirring reels, and chattering printouts produce a mystique that results in both admiration and distrust from people who don't really understand them. But whether we like or dislike them, we cannot ignore them.

A generation or two ago, who had even heard of computers? Today, who hasn't? Computers are everywhere. As tools of the greatest technological revolution in our lifetime, they make our airline and hotel reservations, keep a record of inventory on hand at the local department store, monitor cardiac care patients in hospitals, figure payrolls, check our credit, control scientific experiments, calculate our bills at some supermarkets, forecast trends in the economy, and even help educate schoolchildren.*

*Most computers in operation today are *digital* computers that manipulate numbers by adding, subtracting, multiplying, or dividing. A second type, the *analog* computer, uses continuous data—such as pressure, temperature, or voltage in scientific or engineering applications. Digital computers are more suited for business uses and are discussed in this chapter.

Computers Come in All Shapes and Sizes

Some computers need large rooms to hold all of their parts. Others fit on the top of an executive's desk. The earliest computers contained vacuum tubes and were gigantic beasts. The invention of solid state circuitry reduced their sizes greatly. New technological advances have made possible the development of **minicomputers,** *small machines about the size of a cash register used by scientists and business decision makers for solving numerous problems.* Today, there are about 70,000 general-purpose computers in operation—and hundreds of thousands of minicomputers as well.

The Minicalculator—Friend of Students, Business Decision Makers, and Shoppers

The slide rule died with the introduction of *minicalculators— pocket-sized machines that could almost instantly add, subtract, multiply, or divide.* The first pocket calculators were expensive, but their prices plummeted as competitors—and technological breakthroughs—emerged. Over eight million people bought minicalculators in 1973, and 1974 sales passed the ten million mark. By 1975 these pocket calculators were appearing in college classrooms, neighborhood supermarkets, and even in elementary schools. Prices on some models have dropped below $20 at a number of discount outlets. Industry sources predict that by the end of the decade a very simple calculator could be marketed for $10.

The minicalculator has features similar to the minicomputer, but usually lacks the ability to store and retrieve data from memory files. But sophisticated models, such as the Hewlett-Packard HP-65, contain memory, a 200-year calendar, buttons to push when calculating bond yields and annuities, and separate programs for developing forecasts and for statistical calculations. Retail prices will usually vary with the number of features provided by the calculator.

Well-known companies in the minicalculator industry include Texas Instruments, the Royal Division of Litton Industries, and Hewlett-Packard.

What Is a Computer?

The computer may be known by different names: IBM 1130, 360, 370, or System/3; CDC; Burroughs; National Cash Register (NCR); Honeywell; and UNIVAC. **Computers** can be defined as *electronic machines that accept data and manipulate it mathematically to solve problems and produce information.* Computers, in reality, function much like the human brain. Instructions and data are

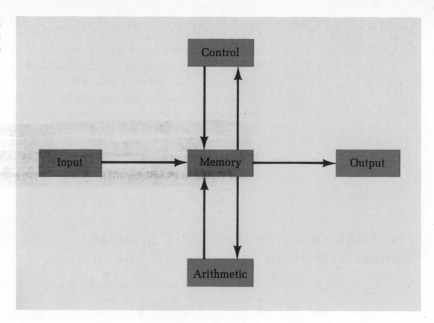

Figure 19-1
The Basic Elements
of the Computer

received; the data is processed; and the information user is provided with solutions to problems or answers to questions.[1]

ELEMENTS OF THE COMPUTER

Each computer system is made up of five basic elements:

1. input
2. memory
3. arithmetic
4. control
5. output.

These are shown in Figure 19-1.

INPUT—"READING" DATA INTO THE COMPUTER

The **input** portion of the computer is responsible for *converting incoming data into a form that the computer can understand*. Data may be "read" into the computer in a number of forms: punched cards; machine-readable magnetic letters, such as those found at the bottom of checks; punched-paper tapes; magnetic tapes and disks; *Optical Character Recognition* (such as the raised letters on credit cards); and typewritten instructions on a special keyboard attached to the computer.

The punched card has traditionally been the most commonly used device for inserting computer data and is still widely used. But punched cards are easily bent or torn (and sometimes carry the warning "Do not fold, spindle, or mutilate."), and they take up a great deal of storage space. In recent years magnetic tapes and disks; teletype terminals; and visual display devices called *cathode ray tubes* (CRTs), which display data on a television screen, have been

QUANTITATIVE TOOLS OF MANAGEMENT

Figure 19-2
Computer Input Methods

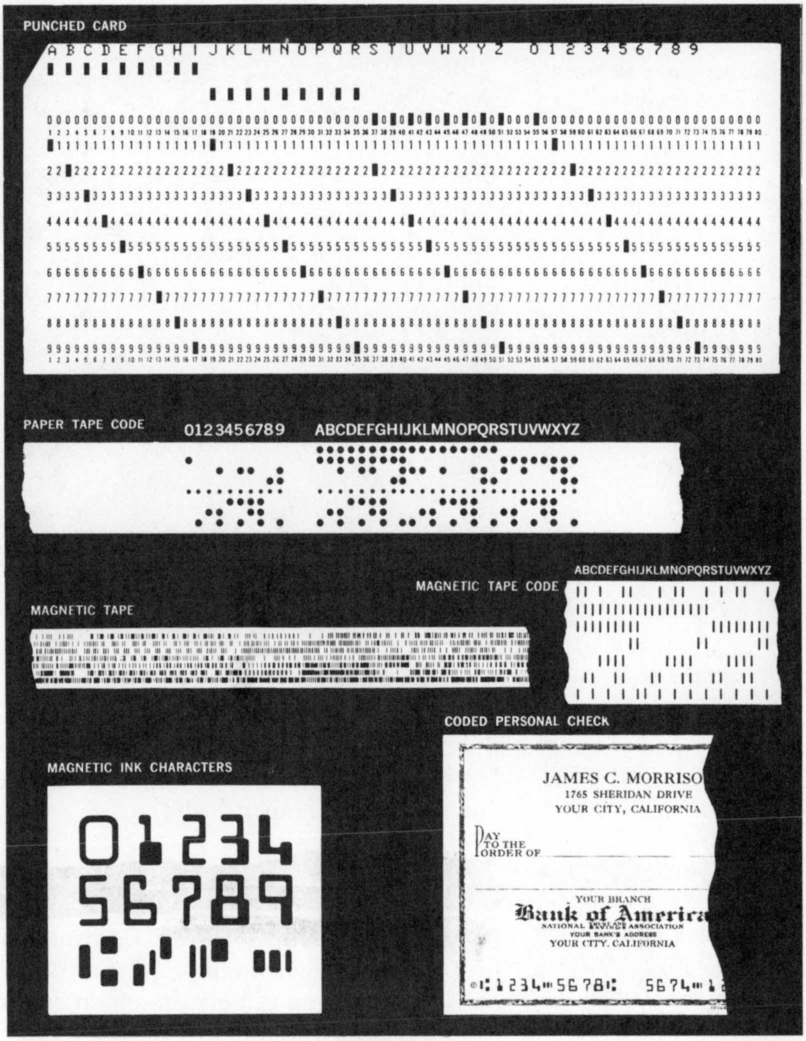

SOURCE: Courtesy of General Electric Company.

increasingly used as input devices. Figure 19-2 shows many of the ways information may be fed into the computer.

**MEMORY—
STOREHOUSE
OF THE COMPUTER**

The **memory,** or storage unit, is the heart of the total computer system. This is *where information is stored.* The memory element of the computer serves as its filing cabinet, where it stores both information for solving a problem and instructions on how to use the information that is stored there.

**ARITHMETIC—
THE COMPUTER'S
ADDING MACHINE**

The **arithmetic** unit is *where all calculations take place.* When adding, subtracting, multiplying, or dividing is required, the necessary data moves from the memory unit to the arithmetic unit. Once

453 THE ROLE OF COMPUTERS

Figure 19-3
The Elements of a
Computer System in a
Modern Installation

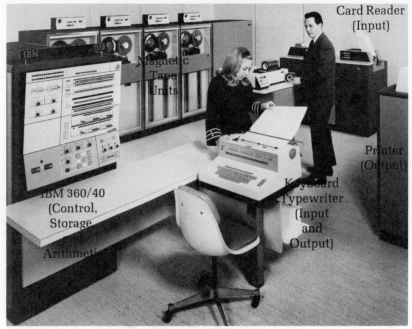

Card Reader
(Input)

Magnetic
Tape
Units

Printer
(Output)

IBM 360/40
(Control,
Storage
and
Arithmetic)

Keyboard
Typewriter
(Input
and
Output)

SOURCE: Courtesy of International Business Machines Corporation.

the calculations have been performed, the answers are then transferred back to the memory unit. The arithmetic unit is like a minicalculator, only much faster.

**CONTROL—
DIRECTOR
OF COMPUTER
OPERATIONS**

The **control** unit is responsible for *directing the sequence of operations, interpreting coded instructions, and giving the right commands to guide the computer.* Control simply means doing things in
proper order. The computer must be guided every step of the way in
solving a problem or performing an assignment, such as computing
the weekly payroll and printing paychecks. The control unit directs
and coordinates both the input and the output elements of the computer system, moves data to and from memory, and directs the
activities of the arithmetic unit. When incoming instructions are
not in the proper form, the control unit rejects them.

**OUTPUT—WHERE
THE ANSWERS
COME FROM**

The **output** unit *takes answers from the computer once the problem
has been solved.* Often output is in the form of a computer printout.
In some cases punched cards or paper tape are produced, especially
when the data will be reused. Output may also be recorded on magnetic tapes or disks. And, in some cases computer output even takes
the form of the spoken word.

Figure 19-3 shows how the elements of a larger computer system look in actual operation.

HARDWARE AND SOFTWARE

Computer hardware consists of *all of the elements of the computer system* shown in Figure 19-3—the input devices; the machines that store data, process it, and perform the required calculations; and the output devices that produce the results for the information user. Computer hardware, therefore, includes all of the machinery and electronic gadgets that make up the computer installation.

Of equal importance in the effective use of computers is computer **software.** Software consists of the *instructions, or computer programs, that tell the computer what to do.* Computer languages and computer programming represent software.

Strengths and Weaknesses of Computers

ADVANTAGES OF COMPUTERS

The major advantages of using computers are:

1. Computers are *fast.* Calculations that may have taken weeks when done by hand can be done in seconds by the computer. In ten seconds a person can add 4,826 to 2,739 and produce an answer of 7,565. In that same time a computer can add a million four-digit numbers. IBM's 3800 system high-speed printer can print at speeds of up to 13,360 lines per minute.

2. Computers are *accurate.* People make mistakes, especially when they are tired. The computer never gets tired—or bored. If programs have been properly written, the chances of a computer mistake are almost nonexistent.

3. Computers can *store large quantities of information in a small space.* Whole rooms filled with filing cabinets can be replaced by a few computer memory tapes. Bulky records of employee information, sales invoices, accounting records, and inventory records can be converted to compact computer storage.

4. Computers can make *great volumes of data available for management decisions.* The information retrieval function of computers allows the manager to retrieve any bit of stored information in less than one second.

5. Computers can *perform much of the mechanical, often boring, routine work of recording and maintaining incoming information.* These tasks are performed accurately and tirelessly, freeing people to handle more interesting and challenging assignments.

LIMITATIONS OF COMPUTERS

Although computers provide management with a number of benefits, they also have a number of limitations:

1. Computers are *expensive.* Major computer systems may cost $100,000 or more per month to lease. Large sums of money are also required to develop the necessary programs used in computer systems.

"Oh, you press the button down.
The data goes 'round and around,
Whoa-ho-ho-ho-ho-ho,
And it comes out here."

SOURCE: Drawing by Lorenz; © 1967 The New Yorker Magazine, Inc.

2. **Computers can make *disastrous mistakes when programmed in-correctly.*** About ten years ago a computerized defense system almost tried to shoot down the moon. About the same time an amazed magazine subscriber received 700 copies of a magazine issue in the mail. And a charge card customer realized that the only way he could prevent the computer from continuing to bill him for $0.00 was to send the store a check for $0.00.[2] All of these mistakes were caused by computer programming errors. The programs contained "bugs," and the resulting output was "garbage." The computer term for such mistakes is GIGO—*Garbage in, Garbage out.*

3. **Computers may become *a management crutch rather than a tool in decision making.*** Computers cannot think, and their output is only as good—or as bad—as the information that is fed in. The final judgment in making a decision must remain the responsibility of the manager.

4. ***Too much reliance on computers may alienate customers by ignoring the human element.*** Computerized bills are sometimes incorrect. Often when the customer writes a letter of protest, the message is ignored and the computer continues to send out letter after letter threatening legal action if a bill is not paid. One com-

puter letter mailed from a Charleston, West Virginia, hospital puts out this message:

"Hello, there, I am the hospital's computer. As yet, no one but me knows that you have not been making regular payments on this account. However, if I have not processed a payment from you within 10 days, I will tell a human who will resort to other means of collection."[3]

A federal law went into effect in 1975 requiring creditors to answer a customer's inquiry about a charge within thirty days. If the bill is not explained or corrected within ninety days, the charge will be forfeited if it is $50 or less. In addition, the customer can sue for damages and collect a minimum of $100 from any firm that violates the law.

"Now then, what makes you feel that we're dehumanizing you 624078?"

SOURCE: *The Wall Street Journal*, April 22, 1974. Reprinted with permission from the artist, Eli Stein and *The Wall Street Journal*.

Computer Letters—Personalizing "Impersonal" Communications

Direct mail letters have long been used for mail-order sales, political campaigns, and fund-raising drives. But recipients have long ago realized that a letter addressed to "Occupant" does not bring good news. As a result, many people categorize such letters as "junk mail" and discard them unopened.

Today's marketer, political candidate, or fund raiser can purchase mailing lists containing prime prospects for just about anything. Lists are available for such categories as expectant mothers, new car purchasers, biochemists (and any other occupational category), previous political campaign or charitable organization donors, credit card holders, even people who previously responded to a "FAT LEGS?" advertisement.

High-speed computers can then produce personalized letters in any type style, with secretarial initials, personal post scripts, and such personal references in the body of the letter as the town in which the addressee lives, her name, or even businesses within her shopping area. Finally, a machine-produced signature is added which will smear when the recipient puts a moist finger on it. For a few cents, a computerized "personal" letter can almost duplicate in seven-tenths of a second a hand-typed letter that might have cost the sender three dollars or more to produce.

But mistakes can creep in. A 1972 campaign letter from Senator Edmund S. Muskie asked a "Miss Soc" to complete the enclosed form and make a contribution. The computer-printed letter was addressed to *Miss Ouri Histor Soc* and somehow was delivered to the place for which it was intended—the Missouri Historical Society.*

Dow Jones & Co., the publisher of *The Wall Street Journal,* once received the following "personalized" letter: "Dear Mr. Jones: How would you and the rest of the Jones family like to see a brand-new car parked in front of the Jones household at 22 Courtlandt Street?" [which is corporate headquarters].†

If an individual wants his or her name removed from a mailing list—or added to one—a letter addressed to the Direct Mail/Marketing Association will accomplish this. The organization, located at 230 Park Avenue, New York, New York 10017, reports that 20,396 persons asked to have their names removed in 1973, while 5,306 wanted their names added.

The Computer: How It's Changing Our Lives (Washington, D.C.: U.S. News & World Report, Inc., 1972), p. 73.
†"Mailing-list Brokers Sell More than Names to Their Many Clients," *The Wall Street Journal* (February 19, 1974), p. 1.

How to Talk to the Computer

One major advantage of computers is speed. An English mathematician named William Shanks devoted one-third of his life to computing π to 707 decimal places (only to make a mistake at the 528th place). Today's modern computer can duplicate Shank's work (without error) within five seconds.[4] Computers can process data so rapidly that scientists had to dust off a little-used time measure called a *nanosecond,* which is defined as one-billionth of a second!

BINARY—THE YES-NO LANGUAGE OF THE COMPUTER

The actual processing of data within the computer is much like the operation in a $29.95 calculator. Like most minicalculators, the computer can add, subtract, multiply, and divide.* But there is one important difference: While the calculator uses the decimal system of the digits 1, 2, 3, 4, 5, 6, 7, 8, 9, and 0, the computer uses the simple yes-no system of binary arithmetic.

Binary arithmetic is *a special counting system that uses two digits*—0 *and* 1. While decimal numbers are built on a base of 10, binary numbers are on a base of 2. The base 10 means that when

*The computer "multiplies" by adding at incredible speeds. "Division" is accomplished by subtracting at a blinding pace.

Table 19-1
Converting Decimal
Numbers to Binary

Number	Binary number
1	000001
4	000100
7	000111
12	001100
20	010100
33	100001

you move a digit one space to the left and add a zero, it is worth ten times as much. With binary numbers, every time a number is moved one space to the left, it is worth two times as much.

The question arises how do you count to two, without a digit 2? The answer is that the value of a binary number increases by two times as it is moved one space to the left. To produce a two in binary, simply move the 1 one space to the left and add zero. So, 10 in binary is the same as 2 in decimal—except that it doesn't *look* the same. Table 19-1 illustrates how decimal numbers can be converted to binary.

In addition to decimal numbers letters of the alphabet and symbols can also be written in binary. The binary code for the letter *A* is 010001; the code for the $\pm$ sign is 110000. Each digit—either a 1 or a 0—is called a *bit* (for binary digit). All information moves through the computer one bit at a time.

Since binary exists in yes-or-no states, the computer can quickly accept incoming information simply by opening or closing an electrical circuit. A 1 is indicated when the circuit is on; a 0 is indicated when the circuit is off. Magnetizing to the left or the right produces the same results for other computers.

PROGRAMMING— TELLING THE COMPUTER WHAT TO DO

When solving a problem the computer can do nothing without a detailed set of instructions. It can follow instructions, but *it cannot think*. These detailed instructions are called the computer program. A **program** is *a set of instructions developed by computer personnel that tells the computer what is to be done, how to do it, and the proper sequence of steps*. The computer then follows these directions step-by-step until the job is completed.

Before developing specific programs for solving problems or obtaining information, the programmer outlines the logical steps needed to arrive at the correct solution to the problem. The problem to be solved is analyzed and broken down into its component parts.

An effective method of accomplishing this is through drawing a **flowchart**. A flowchart is a *pictorial description of the logical steps to be taken in solving a problem*. The symbols, arrows, and lines showing the step-by-step processing of information, activities,

Figure 19-4
Flowchart for Issuing
Airline Tickets

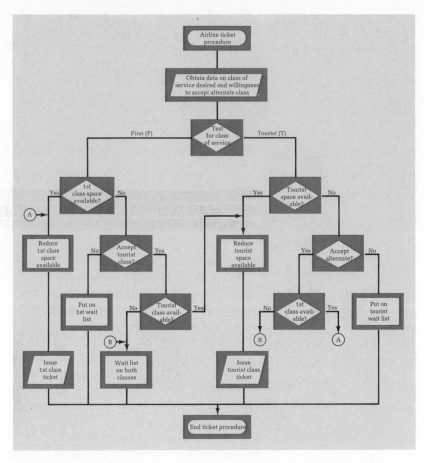

SOURCE: Reproduced by permission from Gordon B. Davis, *Computer Data Processing* (New York: McGraw-Hill, 1973), p. 233.

and decisions involved in issuing airline tickets is illustrated by the flowchart in Figure 19-4.

COMPUTER
LANGUAGES

The **programmer** (*the computer specialist who tells the computer what to do*) uses the flowchart to design programs that contain instructions telling the computer how to handle each step in a process. But a problem arises. The computer does not understand English. Computer programmers earn their salaries by writing instructions to the computer in a symbolic language which it can convert into binary. Although the language of the computer is binary arithmetic, a number of programming languages have been developed to enable the programmer to communicate with the computer in English and algebraic symbols. Three of the most commonly used computer languages are FORTRAN, COBOL, and PL/1.

FORTRAN (FORmula TRANslation) is a widely used computer language. It was originally developed to solve mathematical equations, and it continues to be the dominant scientific computer language. FORTRAN is also sometimes used for business purposes.

COBOL (COmmon Business Oriented Language) was designed specifically for business problems. It avoids the use of symbols and algebraic notations, and uses English words and sentences instead.

PL/1 (Programming Language 1) is a more recent computer language designed for use in both scientific and business environments. Although PL/1 was developed by IBM in 1966, and is currently used mainly on IBM computers, it can be used on other computer systems as well.

CONVERSATIONAL PROGRAMS— ALLOWING THE NOVICE TO USE THE COMPUTER

A number of special programs have been developed to assist the manager, who does not have the necessary training in writing computer programs, to use the computer in decision making.

What makes conversational programs possible are specially designed FORTRAN or COBOL programs. These programs supply instructions to the computer as to how to respond to specific questions that may be asked by the manager-user.

Rather than taking a program to the computer center, executives may have access to **remote terminals.** *These are machines that look like typewriters, and are connected to the main computer installation. They are, however, located in a site physically removed from the computer itself.* The user-manager can type in instructions and receive replies on either a display screen (CRT) or in the form of typewritten output. Figure 19-5 illustrates how conversational programs might be used by showing a series of questions by a business student and the computer responses to these questions.

The Role of Computers in Business

Every area of business has felt the impact—and value—of computers. Banks, insurance companies, manufacturing firms, retailers, utilities, government agencies, airlines, accounting firms and departments, securities firms and stock exchanges, transportation companies—all have found important uses for computers. The following examples illustrate some of their many uses.

RECORD HANDLING

One of the earliest and most widespread uses of computers in business is for storing and processing records. In such repetitive work as payroll accounting, inventory records, and billing the speed and accuracy of the computer can be put to good use. Information on file in the computer memory can also assist management by supplying data on sales in each geographic region, for each product and brand, and the types of customers who are making purchases.

Figure 19-5
Conversation between
Student and Computer

Computer: YOU ARE A MANAGEMENT CONSULTANT CALLED IN TO ADVISE A TOY COMPANY ON A PROPOSAL TO CHANGE THEIR SCHEDULE OF PRODUCTION. IN THE PAST THE COMPANY'S PRODUCTION SCHEDULE HAS BEEN SEASONAL, REFLECTING THE HIGHLY SEASONAL PATTERN OF SALES. THE COMPANY IS CURRENTLY CONSIDERING THE ADVANTAGES OF RISKS INVOLVED IN A POSSIBLE SHIFT TO A LEVEL SCHEDULE OF PRODUCTION OVER THE YEAR. YOUR JUDGMENT IS BEING SOUGHT. ASK FOR THE INFORMATION YOU WANT BY TYPING IN ITEMS FROM THE VOCABULARY YOU HAVE BEEN GIVEN . . . BEGIN YOUR INVESTIGATION AS SOON AS YOU ARE READY.

Student: MACHINE MAINTENANCE COSTS?

Computer: THE ESTIMATED MACHINE MAINTENANCE COSTS ARE $23,000 FOR SEASONAL PRODUCTION AND $10,000 FOR LEVEL PRODUCTION.

Student: PRO FORMA* INCOME STATEMENT?

Computer: YOU HAVEN'T GOT ALL OF THE DATA NEEDED TO MAKE UP THE PRO FORMA INCOME STATEMENT. YOU DON'T KNOW THE COST OF GOODS SOLD.

Student: COST OF GOODS SOLD?

Computer: THE COST OF GOODS IS 60% OF LAST YEAR'S SALES.

Student: PRODUCTION VOLUME?

Computer: THE PROJECTED PRODUCTION VOLUME? THAT'S YOUR PROBLEM. TELL ME WHEN YOU KNOW.

Student: INCOME TAXES?

Computer: DO YOU MEAN FEDERAL INCOME TAXES?

Student: YES.

Computer: THE PROJECTED TOTAL SALES FIGURE IS $1 MILLION. WOULD YOU LIKE TO SEE THE PROJECTED MONTHLY SALES ALSO? . . . NOW THAT YOU HAVE OBTAINED THE PRO FORMAS, YOU CAN STATE YOUR DECISION FAVORING EITHER SEASONALLY VARYING PRODUCTION OR LEVEL PRODUCTION THROUGHOUT THE YEAR—WHENEVER YOU'RE READY. MEANWHILE, TYPE "HELP" IF YOU BECOME TROUBLED BY ANY OF YOUR FINDINGS.

Student: DIRECT LABOR COSTS?

Computer: THE ESTIMATED DIRECT LABOR COSTS ARE $217,000 FOR SEASONAL PRODUCTION AND $170,000 FOR LEVEL.

Student: HELP!

Computer: WHAT FINDINGS BOTHER YOU? IS IT YOUR PRO FORMA INFORMATION?

Student: YES.

Computer: YOU CAN HAVE REVISED PRO FORMAS IF YOU THINK OF SOMETHING THAT WOULD CHANGE THEM. WHAT NEW FACTOR IS RELEVANT?

Student: OVERTIME COSTS.

Computer: IT'S FORTUNATE THAT YOU HAD SECOND THOUGHTS HERE. THE OVERTIME AMOUNTS TO $60,000 FOR SEASONAL PRODUCTION AND NONE FOR LEVEL. THESE NEW DATA SHOULD CHANGE YOUR PRO FORMAS AND HAVE VERY SIGNIFICANT EFFECTS ON YOUR DECISION . . .

Student: SEASONAL PRODUCTION.

Figure 19-5
(continued)

Computer:	NOW THAT YOU HAVE MADE A DECISION, LET'S CONSIDER IT IN THE LIGHT OF THE RELEVANT FACTS . . . CONSIDER THESE PRO FORMAS CAREFULLY. THEN TELL ME—ARE YOU STILL HAPPY WITH YOUR CURRENT DECISION?
Student:	YES.
Computer:	TELL ME AGAIN, JUST TO BE SURE THAT I UNDERSTAND, *WHICH* PRODUCTION SCHEDULE DO YOU RECOMMEND?
Student:	SEASONAL PRODUCTION.
Computer:	LET'S CONSIDER A HYPOTHETICAL QUESTION. IF YOU WERE GUARANTEED THAT YOU WOULD NOT BE CAUGHT WITH A LOT OF UNSALABLE INVENTORY, WOULD YOU CHANGE YOUR DECISION TO ONE IN FAVOR OF LEVEL?
Student:	NO.
Computer:	THEN LET'S CONSIDER WHETHER OR NOT WE ARE AGREED ON AMOUNT OF SAVINGS THAT WOULD RESULT. ASSUMING ALL THE INVENTORY WERE SOLD, HOW MANY THOUSANDS OF DOLLARS IN SAVINGS WOULD RESULT FROM GOING TO A LEVEL PRODUCTION SCHEDULE?
Student:	110.
Computer:	THAT'S ABOUT RIGHT. THE ACTUAL VALUE, DETERMINED FROM DIRECT LABOR COSTS, OVERTIME COSTS, WAREHOUSING COSTS, AND MACHINE MAINTENANCE COSTS, IS $108,000. THAT'S A LOT OF MONEY. DOESN'T THIS CHANGE YOUR DECISION?
Student:	NO.

*Estimated or projected.

SOURCE: From *Introduction to Computer Data Processing* by Margaret S. Wu, © 1975 by Harcourt Brace Jovanovich, Inc., and reproduced with their permission.

AUTOMATION OF PRODUCTION

Computers have also taken over some production jobs that formerly were performed by hand. Continuous process operations, such as a petroleum refinery, may run entirely by computers. At each stage of the refining process, information is fed into a computer on pressure of flows, temperature, and the like. This information is then used by the computer to send instructions to machinery that will change the temperature, increase or decrease the pressure, or take whatever action is needed to control the refining process.

Ford, General Motors, and Chrysler use about one thousand computers in their operations. Each automobile may have as many as 15,000 component parts, and computers are used to make certain that the right part is in the right place at the right time. Other computers test the engines, carburetors, distributors, and other machine parts.

In other industries computers are at work monitoring glass manufacturing plants, blast furnaces, paper machines, pulp digesters, nuclear power plants, and inventory on hand in warehouses.

Figure 19-6
An Advertisement
Tracing the History of
the Computer

Blaise Pascal   *Gottfried Leibniz*   *Charles Babbage*   *Herman Hollerith*

From Abacus to Computer

Most of us think of the computer as being the unique product of twentieth century technology. Yet many of the elements which are inherent in today's computers are centuries old. The abacus, developed about 3,000 years ago, was the first digital counting machine. Since then, many other "machines and engines" were developed—all of which led to the ultimate development of the modern electronic computer. Here are just a few:

The Arithmetic Machine—1642

In the seventeenth century Blaise Pascal developed the first true calculating machine, using a technique which still is used in modern computers. A leading mathematician and philosopher in France, Pascal conceived his arithmetic machine in 1642 when he was only 19. The machine was operated by dialing a series of wheels bearing the numbers 0 to 9 around their circumferences.

The Calculating Machine—1694

Just over fifty years later Gottfried Leibniz, also a renowned mathematician and philosopher, devised a crude machine to mechanize the calculation of mathematical tables. His calculating machine was the first machine to multiply and divide directly. More complex than Pascal's arithmetic machine, it was designed to mechanize the calculation of trigonometric and astronomical tables.

The Difference Engine—1822

This was the first of several difference engines built in the nineteenth century. Developed by Charles Babbage, a British mathematician, it accumulated differences to produce tables for navigation, astronomy and even insurance. It was capable of generating tables to a 20-place accuracy. Out of his work on the difference engine, Babbage came up with the first idea for a computer, a machine which could handle any sort of mathematical computation automatically. His "analytical engine", although never built, included all those essential parts of a computer: a stored program, an arithmetic unit and a section for data entry and output.

The Census Machine—1890

Dr. Herman Hollerith, a statistician from Buffalo, N.Y., solved a problem of major importance for the U.S. Census Bureau when he designed his electric tabulating machine in the 1880's. The problem was this: at the rate the population was growing, the eleventh census in 1890 would be obsolete before it was tabulated. Hollerith's machine solved the problem by being able to tabulate the massive amount of data electrically. The machine consisted of three parts: a tabulator which used a clock-like counting device (shown), a sorter box with compartments which were electrically connected to counters in the tabulator, and a pantographic punch, one of the first devices used to punch data onto cards.

The year 1890 marks the date the first major statistical machine was built and put into large-scale use. It was this invention of Hollerith's that launched the information-handling revolution. Afterward, many others followed who also made significant contributions leading to the development of the computer in the 1940's.

IBM

Source: Reprinted by permission of IBM.

RETAILING APPLICATIONS

In many clothing stores an unusual price tag is attached to suits, dresses, and sportswear. The tag shows the price, but also includes a number of punched holes and numbers. When the article of clothing is sold, the salesperson tears off the tag and deposits it in a special box. At the end of the day these tags are collected and taken to the computer center.

Such tags are actually computer cards identifying the article of clothing, its cost, color, the store, and the department. Processing of the card allows inventory in the store to be automatically controlled

Figure 19-7
How Computerized
Check-outs Work

At Pathmark supermarket in New Jersey, electronic checkout equipment speeds customer lines, keeps track of inventory and cuts labor costs.

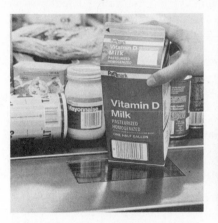

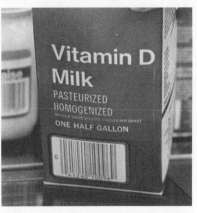

Clerk passes item over scanner which reads code. Computer matches code with the store's price.

Price symbol is series of printed lines that identify the product's name and price.

without having to resort to frequent counting. When inventory reaches a certain level, new shipments may automatically be made to stores, minimizing the possibility of running out of popular items.

Many cash registers have been replaced by computer terminals. The terminals calculate each sale and also maintain records of the store's inventory level for each item carried.

COMPUTERS IN THE SUPERMARKET

The latest application of the computer at the supermarket is the computerized checkout. Those printed lines shown on the milk carton in Figure 19-7, called the *Universal Product Code,* are actually magnetic symbols which can be "read" by the optical-scanning device of a computer. As cashiers pass each item over the electronic reader, the computer instantly displays and records the sale and gives the customer a detailed receipt. Although use of the system is expensive (between $100,000 and $150,000 per store) and is opposed by both the retail clerks union (who fear job losses) and consumer groups (who fear shopper exploitation if supermarkets stop marking prices on individual items), many supermarket chain executives argue that the new system is a worthwhile investment. One industry spokesman has stated that the new system will cut food costs by more than a $100 million a year.[5]

OTHER COMPUTER APPLICATIONS

We have already mentioned the many uses that banks, credit card companies, stockbrokers, securities exchanges, and accountants have for computers. Often the individual is affected by computers without ever knowing it.

If, for example, you decide to make a trip by plane, your seat will probably be selected from an inventory by a computer in an automatic reservation system. To pay for your computer-recorded ticket, you might use a computer-checked credit card or a check that will be handled by a computer at your bank. You may drive to the airport in your computer-designed car over computer-designed roads and computer-controlled traffic intersections. At the airport you will take your seat in a computer-designed airplane. It will be flying with the aid of a computer-compiled weather report and a computerized ground traffic control system. If the plane is a Boeing 747, a computer coupled to the craft's autopilot might be steering the plane automatically—as you sit there in your suit made of cloth cut by a computer, reading a newspaper set in type by a computer.[6]

Computer Dating: Can a Machine Play Cupid?

Computer dating began in 1965 when two Harvard undergraduates developed a program called *Operation Match*. A $3 fee entitled a participant to a minimum of five dates with "compatible" persons selected by the computer. The idea proved successful beyond all expectations and, in the first nine months of operation, over 90,000 college students had dated persons who had been selected for them by the computer.

The idea quickly swept the country and the service expanded. In addition to matching curious college students for fees of five to ten dollars, dating services grew to a business of matching lonely persons of all ages. As the services grew, so did the fees. Several large companies operating nationwide charged fees as high as $1,000.

People who sign up for a computer dating service will typically fill out a lengthy and involved personal data form to determine such information as age, sex, race, creed, weight, education, and income. In addition, the form asks for more detailed information through such questions as: "Are you fickle or steady?" "Do you associate with churchgoers?" "Do you like camping, jazz, animals, cars, novels, marketing, soccer, peace marches, children, Wall Street, physics, fashion, poker, politics, drugs, situation comedies, psychotherapy, etc., etc.?"*

The information is then stored on computer tape or disks. When an applicant requests use of the service, his or her information is compared with the stored information on hundreds or thousands of other applicants.

International Compatibility, a large computer dating service operating in major cities throughout the United States, bases "compatability" on 33 out of 64 possible areas. Problems arose in the first few years of operation when such factors as age, religion, and height were not among the 33 points that matched. In fact, several law suits developed due to mismatches.[†] These services receive letters from both satisfied and irate customers. Here are two of them:

Dear Sir:

Jeffrey and I are celebrating our first wedding anniversary thanks to your beautiful computer, which made it all possible.

One thing we have discovered after one year. Boy, did we both lie when we filled out our questionnaires!

Sandra and Jeffrey W.

Dear Gentlemen:

Your computer was right. Mitzi W. and I like all the same things. It is truly remarkable. We like the same food, we both like the opera. Mitzi likes bike riding and so do I. I like dogs, and so does Mitzi.

Actually, there was only one thing we didn't like—each other.

Dwight J.

Perhaps the only safe thing that can be said about computer dating is that it "will keep introducing the kind of people who seek dates through computers to the kind of people who seek dates through computers."

*Alan C. VanDine. "Romeo and Univac," *Saturday Review* (May 11, 1968), p. 8.
†Linda Mason. "Trap for the Lonely," *The Nation* (May 4, 1970), pp. 530–532.

Source: From *Dear Dating Computer,* copyright © 1968, by Bill Adler, reprinted by permission of the Publisher, The Bobbs-Merrill Company, Inc.

What's Ahead for Computers?

Few people doubt that the next twenty-five years of computer technology will be just as significant as the past quarter-century. Technological developments will undoubtedly make them faster and cheaper. In 1952 it cost $1.26 to do 100,000 multiplications on an IBM computer. Today this number can be done for a penny. That same IBM computer could do about 2,000 multiplications a second in 1952. Today's computer can multiply at the rate of two million a second!

Minicomputers—small in size and inexpensive in price—will grow rapidly to service firms which cannot afford the larger installations or do not need the capabilities of larger computers.

Minicomputers will also probably replace the current use of **time-sharing.** Time-sharing is *the linking of several companies through remote terminals (usually teletypewriters) to a large central computer.* Companies whose volume of data to be processed is too small to allow them to afford their own computers can share the costs with other, similar users through dividing the use of a computer owned by a time-sharing company. The time-sharing firm also provides many of the necessary computer programs, reducing the software expenses of the user. Time-sharing is often found on college campuses, where numerous buildings are linked by input-output teletypewriters to a central computer.

While time-sharing services continue to be popular, both the size and the price tags of minicomputers continue to decline. In time, most small firms may own their own computer hardware.

Software expenses are often the chief cost item in a computer facility. New means will be found in the future to communicate with computers. Future users may be able to communicate directly with the computer through special pens or through voice commands. Early strides in this direction have already been made.

In a number of colleges instructors report grades by making appropriate pencil marks on their grade sheets. Special computer input devices called optical character recognition (OCR) equipment "read" this information, store it, and print out grade reports.

Voice-input systems are still primitive, but they are already being used in a number of business activities. Bank tellers, for example, might use a special terminal to call the computer to determine whether a check should be cashed. The communication exchange goes something like this:

Computer: THIS IS THE EZ SYSTEM. WHO ARE YOU?

Teller: 201 [teller's number]. 15 [branch number].

Computer: ENTER TRANSACTION CODE.

Teller: 03 [checking account inquiry].

Computer: ENTER CHECKING ACCOUNT NUMBER.

Teller: 805-257-0.

Computer: BALANCE ON CHECKING ACCOUNT NUMBER EIGHT ZERO FIVE DASH TWO FIVE SEVEN DASH ZERO IS ONE ZERO SEVEN DOLLARS AND ZERO FIVE CENTS.*

*Elias M. Awad. *Business Data Processing* (Englewood Cliffs, N.J.: Prentice-Hall, Inc., 1975), pp. 315–316.

Some computers are also learning to talk. One, developed by Bell Laboratories, has a 1,500-word vocabulary. The voice is not a tape recording but the result of a computer program that uses mathematical functions to represent the position of the tongue, lips, and palate in humans. The program is used to generate electronic speech signals that may be heard over a telephone or loudspeaker.

By removing the person in the middle (the computer programmer) between the user and the computer, such voice input and output systems may someday make the computer an integral part of every manager's arsenal of decision-making tools.

Do Computer Data Banks Violate the Right to Privacy?

The rights of the individual are basic to the American way of life. Yet, in order to run the country, and especially to help predict trends so that provisions can be made for a more comfortable future, government and private sources are constantly gathering data about the American people.

The Bureau of the Census and the Internal Revenue Service are just two of the governmental sources of information about people. For example, if government planning ten years ahead requires that more facilities for the aged and fewer elementary schools be built, then planners need information about the population.

Along with health and medical information and records from the armed forces and data from the courts, the United States has gathered and stored data for over 1 billion individuals. With the gathering and storing of this information about individuals, and the development and ability of computer technology to handle such masses of material has come a concern on the part of legislators, professionals of all kinds, and the general public that their privacy is being invaded and that somehow this must be stopped. How is the individual to be protected from the machine?

One answer seems to be in the number and kinds of controls that are enforced. There is real concern over the accuracy of stored information. The only way of insuring such accuracy, say critics, is to allow an individual to see his or her records and to make a formal complaint or to correct inaccurate information. The person also should have the right to amend a statement in the records if the requested correction is not made.

Another concern is that the individual be informed as to who is using a file by means of a log which could be reviewed by the person concerned. Such logs could be published, for example, in places where the subject would be most likely to see them. Some feel that the individual should also have the right to refuse access to his or her records.

Others object that controls of this nature make some purposes of data gathering invalid. For example, an employee would have the right to review the boss's evaluation of him or her once the evaluation became a part of the employee's permanent record. In such a case the boss may not give his or her real thoughts, leading to a bland, inaccurate evaluation, if the employer's main concern is with not rocking the boat. Then, the privacy of the evaluator would be invaded.

The cost of protecting records and of training employees to do so is very great, and the enforcement of protection is difficult, especially in a private company.

Summary

Computers provide business firms with the ability to collect, analyze, store, and process information at a speed and accuracy unparalleled in history. The main elements of the computer are the *input devices,* which feed data into the computer; *memory,* which stores data and instructions for later use; *arithmetic,* which processes the data; control, which directs the sequence of operations, interprets instructions, and gives the proper commands to guide the computer; and *output,* which produces the requested information. These five elements represent computer hardware.

Software consists of computer languages and programs that tell the computer what to do. The most frequently-used programming languages are FORTRAN, COBOL, and PL/1. Special conversational programs have been developed to allow persons with no programming abilities to use the computer.

In addition to speed and accuracy computers provide the following advantages over hand methods of data processing: They can store large amounts of data in a small space; they can quickly make this data available for decision makers; and, by performing the mechanical, routine, boring work of recording and maintaining incoming information, they free people for more challenging work.

The major limitations of computers are cost (both for hardware and programming); computer mistakes caused by faulty programming; the tendency for management to over-rely on computers as a crutch rather than as a tool in decision making; and the potential for alienating customers by ignoring the human element in customer relations.

Computers have made contributions in every facet of business: banking, finance, marketing, manufacturing, accounting, personnel, securities markets—even the supermarket. Their contributions will increase in the future as faster and less expensive computers are developed. Continued development of minicomputers will allow smaller firms to utilize computerized operations. Software developments will increase and software expenses will continue to decline if direct communication through voice input and output systems is refined and perfected.

Review questions

1. Identify the following terms:

a. computer	g. output
b. minicomputer	h. computer hardware
c. input	i. software
d. memory	j. program
e. arithmetic	k. binary arithmetic
f. control	l. flowchart

m. programmer
n. FORTRAN
o. COBOL

p. PL/1
q. remote terminals
r. time-sharing

2. Describe each of the five basic elements of the computer.
3. What are the major advantages of computers?
4. List the primary weaknesses of computers.
5. What is a nanosecond? What does this term imply about computer technology?
6. Distinguish between binary arithmetic and the decimal system.
7. How are flowcharts used by computer programmers?
8. What is meant by a computer language?
9. Select four or five areas of business. Can you think of at least two computer applications in each area? List them.
10. What types of advancements in computer technology can be expected in the years ahead?

Discussion questions and exercises

1. Evaluate the pro and con arguments to the controversial issue that appears in this chapter.
2. Discuss how a computer is (or could be) used in the operation of your college.
3. Draw a flowchart showing how you study for examinations in this course.
4. Convert the following decimal numbers to binary arithmetic:

104	21
16	39
11	50

5. Interview a local business executive on the subject of how he or she uses a computer in making business decisions. If a computer is not being used, find out how it could be used in the business and the problems that prevent it from being used now.

Case 19-1
Computer Crimes

In their book, *The Computer Survival Handbook,* Wooldridge and London describe a number of instances where the computer has been used to defraud unsuspecting companies. Among the wrongdoers who used a computer rather than a gun or knife were:

The programmer at a large bank who was responsible for calculating interest on savings accounts. Instead of dropping off fractions of pennies, he simply added them to his own account and the bank's books balanced. Even fractions of a penny add up when savings accounts number in the tens of thousands, and the programmer was able to retire a wealthy man. He now resides in Rio de Janeiro.

The programmer in charge of payrolls at a major company who decided to trim a few cents off each check and add them to his own. Although the books balanced, this programmer was not so lucky. He now resides at the state penitentiary.

The army programmer who created an entirely new (although imaginary) military base staffed by 200 imaginary people. He then opened 200 checking accounts for their paychecks and the money rolled in. Everything went so smoothly that it took him several months to realize that he would probably never be caught *as long as the base continued to operate.* He had become—in a few months—a self-made millionaire, but could think of no way to close the base! An accidental bombing, mass food-poisoning, or 200 desertions all seemed too unbelievable. So finally he simply turned himself in.*

Questions

1. What characteristics of the computer make it vulnerable to such crimes?
2. Suggest several procedures for preventing similar occurrences at other firms.

*Susan Wooldridge and Keith London. *The Computer Survival Handbook: How to Talk Back to Your Computer* (Boston: Gambit Inc., 1973), pp. 160–161.

Case 19-2
Ecology and the Computer

Michigan's Department of Natural Resources (DNR) is in charge of the state's environmental and natural resources programs. The Department has made frequent use of a computer in monitoring industrial discharges of waste water, as well as the condition of the state's many lakes. The federal Environmental Protection Agency is now using some aspects of the DNR system.

The DNR is currently studying other ways to use the computer in order to protect the environment and the state's natural resources. Possibilities include computer programs to track the state's deer herd and to determine the best combination of gamefish to stock the Great Lakes.*

Questions

1. Can you think of other examples where the computer can be used to protect the environment? List them.
2. What other government departments can use computers in their work? How?

*James L. Kerwin. "DNR Uses Computer to Aid Environment," *Detroit News* (March 30, 1975), p. 5-C.

20

Management Information

"If it would take a cannon ball 3 1/3 seconds to travel four miles, and 3 3/7 seconds to travel the next four, and 3 5/8 to travel the next four, and if its rate of progress continued to diminish in the same ratio, how long would it take to go fifteen hundred million miles?"
—Arithmeticus
Virginia, Nevada

"I don't know."

—Mark Twain

"There are three kinds of lies: lies, damned lies, and statistics."
—Benjamin Disraeli

What Chapter 20 Is All About

1. After reading this chapter you should be able to explain the purpose of a management information system and how it functions in a firm.
2. You should be able to distinguish between primary and secondary data, and explain the strengths and limitations of each.
3. Several methods of collecting survey data exist. You should be able to identify each method and suggest situations when each method should be used.
4. You should be able to explain how the mean, median, and mode are calculated and when each measure should be used.
5. After reading this chapter, you should understand these terms:

management information system (MIS)	census
	sample
internal data	statistics
external data	array
secondary data	frequency distribution
primary data	mean
observation method	median
survey method	mode

George Gallup

George Gallup received his Ph.D. in psychology in 1928 at the age of twenty-seven from the University of Iowa. His thesis was commissioned by the Des Moines *Register;* it was a study of reader interest in newspapers and magazines. Gallup went on to teach journalism and psychology at the University of Iowa, Drake, Northwestern, and Columbia.

Gallup's first surveys were done for his mother-in-law, while she was running for secretary of state in Iowa. His professional application of psychological research methods led him to select a random sample, the size of which was determined by the laws of probability. He came up with a forecast that pointed to a Democratic landslide in the 1934 congressional elections, although political pundits sneered at his results. When the public voted for Franklin D. Roosevelt's New Deal that year, Gallup was proven to be correct.

On October 20, 1935, Gallup founded the American Institute of Public Opinion in Princeton, New Jersey, and began to publish the Gallup Poll. This was a weekly survey of opinion in the United States on questions of social, economic, and political interest of the moment. Since that time the Gallup Poll has established branches in thirty-two other countries where public opinion is surveyed.

Before Gallup developed his Poll, politicians received feedback only through their workers and from letters sent to their offices. Because the representation of this audience was limited and prejudiced, politicians generally got poor advice. With the Poll, a greater number of people have been heard from in a more accurate way.

Describing his organization as fact finding, accurate, and rigorous, the plus-seventy-year-old Gallup maintains that the Poll is not in the business of prediction but of research and keeping score.

T he chief task of the manager is decision making. Managers earn their salaries by making effective decisions which allow their firms to solve problems as they occur. Managers must also anticipate and prevent future problems. All too often the manager is forced to make decisions with limited information, with inadequate facts. If effective decisions are to be made, a system must be developed to insure that this information is available when it is needed and in a form that is suitable for analysis by the decision maker.

The Role of the Management Information System

Someone once defined the recipe for effective decisions as "90 percent information and 10 percent inspiration." In order to obtain relevant information for decision making, most large and medium-

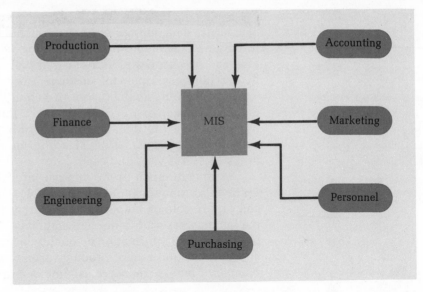

Figure 20-1
The MIS Provides
Decision Information
for All Parts of
the Organization

Production

Accounting

Finance

MIS

Marketing

Engineering

Personnel

Purchasing

sized firms establish a systematic approach through the installation of a management information system (MIS).

"What are the storage costs for Model 24?"
"What is the sales potential for our brand in the Chicago territory?"
"How much is Allison accomplishing so far?"
"How do our wage rates compare with similar firms in Sacramento?"
"How many units of Model 24 are there in the Kansas City warehouse?"

These represent a few of the hundreds of questions asked every day in a business operation. An effective information system aids decision making by having such information available for the business executive. The **management information system** can be defined as *an organized method of providing past, present, and projected information on internal operations and external intelligence for use in management decision making.*[1]

As Figure 20-1 indicates, the MIS can assist decision making in all major areas of the organization.

Collection of Information

The heart of any management information system is *information*. Decision-related information is needed in almost every company activity—both for internal operations and also for being kept informed about changing consumer demands and the actions of competitors. Finally, information on government regulations and possible legislation is required for the firm to be able to present its viewpoint on public issues.

477 MANAGEMENT INFORMATION

Internal data are *data generated within the organization*. A number of internal data sources exist. A tremendous amount of useful information is available from accounting records. Here data can be obtained on changes in accounts receivables; comparisons of sales by territory, salesperson, customer, or product line; inventory levels; loans outstanding; cash on hand; profitability of particular divisions; customers; or product lines. Financial records provide important insights into business operations. And, since they are collected on a regular basis, this information can be added to the firm's MIS at a very low cost.

Although much of the internal information is financial, other kinds of information inputs are available. The personnel department can supply data on employee turnover, and they may collect information on worker attitudes and employee suggestions. Quality control can supply information on quality levels of materials purchased and the rejection rate of products produced by the firm. Customer complaint letters can serve as another information input.

How Sears Satisfies
Its Internal Information Needs

To see how the Sears MIS works, let's follow a coffeepot as it heads for a Sears store. When the coffeepot is shipped from the warehouse, an automatic ticketmaker produces a ticket indicating the color, stock number, price, and department number in the store. When a customer takes the coffeepot to the register, the Sears clerk either keys the numbers into the register or uses a special reading wand.

The data is then stored in the store's minicomputer until nighttime, when it is automatically transferred to one of Sears' twenty-two regional data centers. There one of the thirty-three large IBM computers processes the information. The customer's credit account is charged (if a charge sale is made), sales and tax information are entered into the accounting department's records, and the salesperson's commission record is credited to the payroll department.

Sales data are also sent to the coffeepot department's inventory management system. If the day's coffeepot sales reduce the department's inventory below a predetermined amount, the computer automatically prints a purchase order, which is sent to the department manager the next morning. If the manager decides to purchase additional coffeepots, the reorder goes to the warehouse for shipment.

At the same time the sales data are channeled to a central data-processing department in the Chicago headquarters. Here all sales information for the entire Sears operation are compiled. The network of 30,000 registers, 640 minicomputers, and 33 large computers allows Sears managers to monitor sales by store, region, department, and product on a daily basis.*

*For a more detailed description of the Sears system *see* "How Giant Sears Grows and Grows," *Business Week* (December 16, 1972), pp. 54–55.

Much of the information for the firm's MIS will come from **external data.** These represent *data generated outside the firm.* This information will be of two types: primary or secondary.

Secondary data—fast and inexpensive

An extremely important source of management information is the use of **secondary,** or *previously published,* **data.** Although considerable secondary data is available internally, even more is available from external sources. So much secondary data is available at little or no cost that the information manager faces the problem of being overwhelmed by thousands of volumes of collected data.

Government Sources The various levels of government are the nation's most important source of secondary data. The most frequently used government sources are census data. Although the Bureau of the Census spent slightly more than one dollar per person in conducting the 1970 Census of Population, the information is available for use without charge at local libraries, or it can be purchased for a nominal fee on computer tapes for instantaneous use.

The Census of Population is so detailed for large cities that breakdowns of population characteristics are available by city block. Data is available on age, sex, race, citizenship, educational levels, occupation, employment status, and income.

The Census Bureau also conducts a Census of Housing, which provides such information as the value of homes in a particular geographic area, the number of rooms, type of structure, race of occupants, and the year the home was built. This information is used by numerous governmental agencies and such departments as the Department of Labor; the Department of Health, Education and Welfare; and the various operations of the Department of Housing and Urban Development. Such information can also be used by shopping center developers to analyze potential customers, or in plant location studies to determine available skills in a community and the number of available workers.

Other government reports include the Census of Business, the Census of Manufacture, the Census of Agriculture, the Census of Minerals, and the Census of Government. So much data is produced by the government each year that most firms should purchase the guidebook, *Catalog of U.S. Census Publications,* in order to keep abreast of current publications.

Other government sources include the *Statistical Abstract of the United States,* the *Survey of Current Business,* the monthly *Federal Reserve Bulletin,* and the *Monthly Labor Review.*

State and city governments are other important sources of information on employment, production, and sales activities within a particular state or city.

Private Sources A number of private organizations provide information for business decision makers. Trade associations are excellent resource centers for their members. They often publish journals or newsletters containing information on production costs in the industry, suggestions for improving operations, and wage surveys in the industry. Advertising agencies continually collect information on the audiences reached by various media such as magazines, television programs, and radio.

Several national firms offer information to business firms on a subscription basis. The *A.C. Nielsen Company* collects data every sixty days on the sales of most products stocked in food and drug stores. *Sales Management* magazine publishes an annual *Survey of Buying Power* which provides detailed information on population, income, and retail sales in cities and counties for each state in the United States and in the Canadian provinces. Moody's, Dun & Bradstreet, and Standard and Poor's provide financial information on a subscription basis. The chief source of information concerning construction activities is provided by the Dodge Corporation.

Secondary data—advantages and disadvantages

The use of secondary data offers two important advantages over the use of primary data:

1. lower cost
2. less time is involved in locating and using secondary data.

Even though some secondary data may have to be obtained on a subscription basis, its cost is invariably less than it would have been had the firm collected the data itself. A considerable amount of time is involved in determining the information needs, identifying the sources of data, preparing collection instruments, training researchers, collecting, and interpreting the data—all activities that are performed in obtaining primary data.

But the use of secondary data is subject to two important limitations. *First,* the data may be *obsolete.* The data provided by the 1970 Census of Population is already obsolete for such areas as southern California, Alaska, and Florida due to the substantial increases in population in these areas since 1970. *Second, the classifications of secondary data may not be usable for the firm.* Since the secondary data was originally collected for a specific purpose, it may not be in a usable form for a particular decision maker. In either case, the firm may be forced to collect primary data.

Collecting primary data

Primary data is *information collected for the first time for use in solving a business problem.* Most primary data is collected by one of two methods: observation or surveys.

The Observation Method **Observational studies** are conducted by *actually viewing (either by visual observation or through mechanical devices) the actions of the respondent.* The quality control department often uses the observation method in checking for defective products. Traffic counts may be used to determine the best location for a new fast-food franchise. Television ratings are usually determined by the Nielsen Audimeter which, when attached to a television set, records the times when the set is turned on and the channel is being viewed.

The Survey Method Much primary data cannot be obtained through mere observation of actions of a person or machine; the researcher must ask questions. When information is needed concerning *employee, supplier, or customer attitudes and opinions,* the **survey method** must be used.

Information is rarely gathered from all sources during a survey. If *all sources are reached,* the results would be called a **census.** But unless the number of sources is quite small, the costs are too great to contact everyone. Instead, the researcher selects a *representative group* called a **sample.** If the sample is chosen in such a way that every member of the population has an equal chance of being selected, it is called a *random,* or *probability,* sample. A quality control check of every hundredth part of an assembly line may give the production control engineers a representative sample of the overall quality of the work. A random choice of student names from the list at the registrar's office will provide a probability sample of students at your college.

Three kinds of surveys exist:

1. telephone
2. mail
3. personal interviews.

Telephone interviews are cheap and fast for obtaining small amounts of relatively impersonal information. Since many firms have leased WATS services,* a survey of suppliers' opinions on a proposed payment plan could be conducted quickly and at little expense. Telephone interviews must be limited to simple, clearly worded questions. Such interviews have two limitations. *First,* it is extremely difficult to obtain personal information from respondents and, *second,* the survey may be prejudiced, since two groups will be omitted—those households without telephones and those with unlisted numbers.

Mail interviews allow the researcher to conduct national studies at reasonable costs. Whereas personal interviews with a

---

*Wide Area Telephone Service, a telephone company service which allows a business firm to make unlimited numbers of long-distance calls for a fixed rate per state or region.

**"In the first place, my good man, I'm
hardly an average American."**

Opinion Polls Use the Survey Method

SOURCE: *The Wall Street Journal*, November 21, 1974. Reprinted with permission from *The Wall Street Journal*.

national sample may prove too costly, the researcher can reach each potential respondent with the price of a first-class stamp. Costs may be misleading, however, since returned questionnaires for such a study may average only 15 to 25 percent, depending upon the length of the questionnaire and respondent interest. Unless additional information is obtained from those persons not responding through a telephone interview or other method, the results are likely to be biased, since there may be important differences between the characteristics of the nonrespondents and those persons who took the time to complete and return the questionnaire.

The *personal interview* is the most expensive and most time-consuming survey method. It calls for trained interviewers, competitive pay, and expenses involved in traveling to the location of the respondent. But it is typically the best means of obtaining detailed information. The interviewer can explain questions which might be confusing or vague to the respondent. The flexibility of this method, combined with the detailed information which can be collected, often more than offsets the time and cost limitations.

Are Television Ratings Accurate?

Local television stations can collect information about the habits of their viewers through such methods as telephone surveys and diaries (week-long listings of viewers' habits in certain time periods). But network television ratings are done nationally and by machine, specifically by the Neilsen Audimeter. This device consists of a timer set to local time, a cartridge of film, and a lamp that lights up, exposing the film when the set is turned on and a channel is selected.

Network income is based partially on the ratings of its shows, and, therefore, the three major networks compete for the largest audience for each segment of the broadcasting day and particularly for prime time in the evening.

In 1963 the House Commerce Committee investigated the Nielsen rating system and broadcast ratings in general for about two months. As a result of this investigation, the broadcasting industry began some self-policing by establishing the Committee on Nationwide Television Audience Measurement (CONTAM).

The Neilsen Television Index samples about 1,200 homes across the nation, retaining each family in the sample for about three years. The family mails the film cartridges to the company once a week and is paid 50 cents every time it inserts a new cartridge in the television set.

When the House committee began its investigation, it was discovered that the sample design had not been updated since the late 1940's and that replacements for families that had dropped out had been very casual indeed. Some families had stayed in the sample for over a decade. Many of the sets surveyed were in a janitor's or superintendent's home in a building; they were easy to reach because someone was usually at home. Some sets had been broken and had not been repaired.

Since the investigation, although the procedures followed by the Nielsen Company have been improved, the industry has discovered that the problems of the ratings system are built into this kind of study. Many families simply refuse to participate in a ratings study or do not answer an inquiry from the Nielsen survey, and this distorts the sample. Since the ratings are based on households and since many households have more than one set, and only one set is monitored, even sample locations give inaccurate information. The Nielsen Audimeter will register even when a set is going without its picture—if it is broken, for instance. Also, sets in such places as dormitories, bars, or country clubs where groups of people view programs are not counted in the sample, although many people are often involved.

How Fisher-Price Determines
Consumer Reactions to Its Toys

Fisher-Price is the nation's largest maker of toys for children under six. For this reason it is not surprising to discover that its research and development building is actually a state-licensed nursery school located at the firm's East Aurora, New York, headquarters. The nursery school is run by trained teachers paid by the company. As in any nursery school, the kids fingerpaint, sing, eat snacks, and read stories.

And they do other things. For Fisher-Price, the most important part of the school is the free-play time, where the 3- and 4-year-olds become toy-testers for the firm's proposed new toys. There they bang, poke, kick, accept—and sometimes reject—the new toys dreamed up by the firm's designers.

A new group of kids comes in every six weeks to make certain that one group's whims aren't forced on a nation of toy buyers. In the nursery, the kids are never asked such direct questions as "How do you like this toy?" or "Isn't this a cute doll, Bratina?" Instead, teachers make elaborate notes during free play and sometimes call designers to observe through one-way windows.

Children's inputs often cause changes in successful toys. One such toy is the jack-in-the-box, a toy business staple item. Fisher-Price built one a few years ago and tested it in the nursery school. But the teachers reported an unusual occurrence. After pressing the button to make "Jack" pop out of his box, the children invariably would gather round and talk to him. "Is it dark in the box?" they would ask and then, assuming the role of Jack, give each other answers. So the teacher suggested making Jack's jaws move. Designers spent another year building a lever-operated mouth, a squeaky voice, and a turntable head for the figure.

Source: Jim Hyatt. "At One Toy Company, the Guys in Research Are 3 and 4 Years Old," *The Wall Street Journal* (December 20, 1971), p. 1. Reprinted with permission of *The Wall Street Journal,* © Dow Jones & Company, Inc. 1971. All rights reserved.

INTERPRETATION
OF RESEARCH
FINDINGS

Considerable expertise is required in collecting primary data. Many firms have research departments staffed with specialists in designing questionnaires, training interviewers, developing representative samples, and interpreting the findings of the research study. Other companies hire specialized research firms to handle specific projects.

It is extremely important that the information user and the researcher agree upon the studies to be conducted—and precisely how they will be conducted. Too many research studies go unused because managers view the results as too restricted due to lengthy discussions of research limitations or the use of unfamiliar terms such as "confidence limits" and "Type II errors." Recommendations should be included in the written report when primary data is collected and reported. Whenever possible, an oral report should be given so that the written document can be explained, expanded, or clarified. This increases the possibility of its use by management.

Statistical Analysis of Management Information

Our world is filled with statistics. The distance from earth to the sun is 93 million miles. The average family has 2.1 children. Heart disease is the number one cause of death. The movie *Ben Hur* attracted the largest number of viewers (85.6 million) among all films

Managers Should Be Familiar with *Basic* Statistical Concepts

SOURCE: By permission of John Hart and Field Enterprises, Inc.

ever shown on television. (*The Godfather,* with 84.4 million, was a close second.) The Brothers Guinness made their fortunes by amassing thousands of statistics and publishing them as the *Guinness Book of World Records.*

When viewed as individual items such as a basketball scoring average or the quarterly earnings per share of a corporation, statistics refer to a collection of numerical data about some event, object, or individual. A broader definition of **statistics** is *the collection, analysis, interpretation, and presentation of information in numerical form.* This definition includes the first, more limited, concept of statistics.

It is not an overstatement to say that *statistics—*like accounting—*are the language of business.* Although business executives are not expected to be statistical experts, they must possess some familiarity with the basic concepts and terms used in this field.

HOW STATISTICAL ANALYSIS WORKS

Table 20-1 is an example of secondary data from Dun & Bradstreet. The table shows the profits earned by different types of wholesalers as a percentage of their total sales.

Table 20-1 is an example of an **array.** This is *a listing of items by size, either from the smallest to the largest or the largest to the smallest.* In order to increase the meaning of the statistics, it is common practice to group the data into a **frequency distribution.** This *shows the number of times each item appears in the data.*

Table 20-1
Net Profits of
Selected Wholesalers

Kind of Business	Net Profit as a Percentage of Net Sales*
Confectionery	.6
Groceries	.7
Tobacco products	.7
Meats and meat products	.8
Beer, wine, and alcoholic beverages	1.1
Clothing and furnishings, men's and boys'	1.1
Drugs, drug proprietories, and sundries	1.1
Electrical appliances, TV, and radio sets	1.6
Paper and paper products	1.6
Dairy products	1.7
Furniture and home furnishings	1.7
Hardware	1.8
Footwear	1.9
Tires and tubes	1.9
Petroleum and petroleum products	2.0
Automotive parts and supplies	2.3

*After provision for federal income taxes.

SOURCE: Reprinted by special permission from "The Ratios of the Wholesalers," *Dun's Review* (October 1974), pp. 113, 116. Copyright 1974, Dun & Bradstreet Publications Corporation.

Figure 20-2
Frequency Distribution

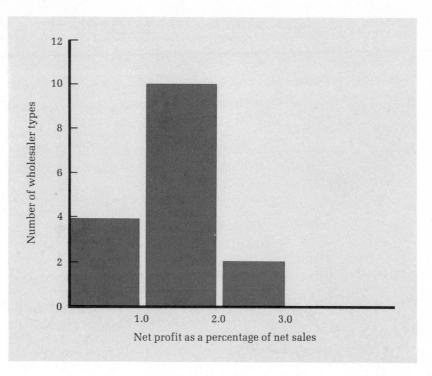

Figure 20-2 illustrates the frequency distribution for the data contained in Table 20-1. The figure graphically displays the frequency distribution of wholesalers and net profits. It is helpful in summarizing the data in Table 20-1, and points out that most of the wholesalers earned net profits between 1 and 2 percent of sales.

THE MEAN, MEDIAN, AND MODE

The arithmetic **mean,** or average, is perhaps the most widely used statistical measure. It is calculated by *summing all observations and dividing by the number of observations.* The mean net profit as a percentage of sales for the selected wholesalers in Table 20-1 is 1.4 percent (the 22.6 total divided by the 16 types of wholesalers).

A second commonly used measure is the **median,** *the middle score in the distribution.* The median is the value which lies above half of the observations in the distribution and below the other half. Since Table 20-1 contains an even number of observations, the median lies between the eighth and ninth observations, or 1.6 percent.

A third measure is the **mode,** *the most frequently observed value.* The mode in Table 20-1 is 1.1 percent.

Each of these measures has its limitations. Although the mean is the most commonly used measure, it is subject to distortions when extremely low or high numbers appear. Median income figures are frequently used, since the presence of a few millionaires will distort "average" income figures if the mean is utilized. A travel agent may be interested in using the mode to plan a package vacation tour for the next season. By knowing last year's most popular vacation area, the agent may be able to meet the desires of the firm's clients better.

Presentation of Data

It is not enough that data be collected, analyzed, and interpreted. If it is to fulfill its role as decision-oriented management information, it must also be presented in a form which allows the decision maker to understand and use it.

The proper form for presentation of data may vary from one executive to the next, or from department to department. In some cases computer printouts may be the proper form. Copies of financial reports, such as an income statement, may be sufficient for other users. In other cases statistical information should be presented in tabular or pictorial form. Data can be effectively summarized and represented in graphic form by preparing a line chart, bar chart, pie chart, or pictograph. Examples of these charts are shown in Figure 20-3. These pictorial summaries serve to insure the use of the information by the decision maker.

Figure 20-3 Examples of Graphic Presentations of Data: (a) Line Chart; (b) Bar Chart; (c) Pie chart; and (d) Pictograph.

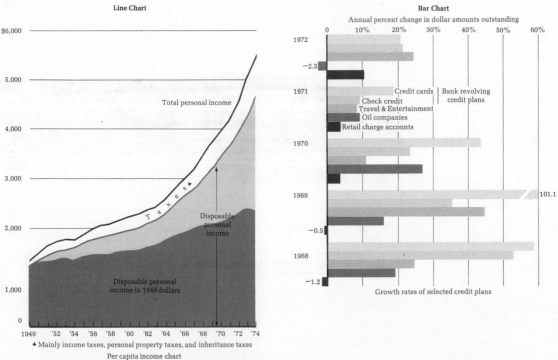

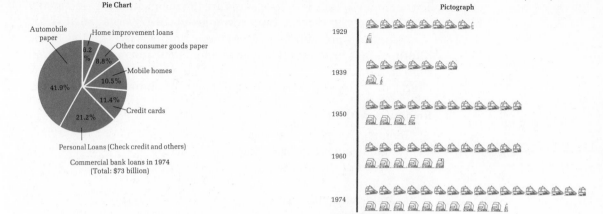

Pie Chart

Automobile paper

Home improvement loans

Other consumer goods paper

6.2%

8.8%

Mobile homes

41.9%

10.5%

Credit cards

11.4%

21.2%

Personal Loans (Check credit and others)

Commercial bank loans in 1974
(Total: $73 billion)

Pictograph

1929

1939

1950

1960

1974

RAILROADS = 50,000
TRUCKS

SOURCE: *Road Maps of Industry.* Reproduced by permission of The Conference Board.

Summary

Information is a vital element in management decisions. Effective decisions cannot be made without answers to questions about the internal operations of the firm and the environment in which it operates. Progressive companies are currently involved in introducing and perfecting planned management information systems (MIS). This will allow them to obtain organized methods for providing past, present, and projected information on internal operations and external intelligence for use in making decisions. Such information systems should aid all areas of the organization—production, accounting, marketing, personnel, purchasing, engineering, and finance—in their decision-making responsibilities.

A great deal of the information in the firm's MIS is generated from internal information. Much of this comes from accounting records. Other internal information comes from production, personnel, employee suggestions, and other internal sources.

External information is information collected outside the firm. It can be divided into two types: primary and secondary. Secondary data is that which has been previously published. Important sources include federal, state, and local governments and firms that supply information on a subscription basis.

Primary data is information collected for the first time for use in solving a business problem. Primary data may be obtained through observation or through surveys. Surveys can be conducted by telephone, mail questionnaires, or personal interviews.

Statistical analysis is used in interpreting data obtained from research investigations. Statistics involves the collection, analysis, interpretation, and presentation of information in numerical form.

Three common statistical measures are the mean, median, and mode; they indicate the central values in a group of observations.

Effective presentation of research findings is essential if the information is to be useful in management decision making. Pictorial representations of data in the form of line charts, bar charts, pie charts, or pictographs are effective means of summarizing findings.

Review questions

1. Identify the following terms:
   a. management information system (MIS)
   b. internal data
   c. external data
   d. secondary data
   e. primary data
   f. observation method
   g. survey method
   h. census
   i. sample
   j. statistics
   k. array
   l. frequency distribution
   m. mean
   n. median
   o. mode
2. Explain the role of the management information system in contemporary business.
3. Identify the internal sources of information.
4. What are the major external sources of information?
5. Distinguish between primary and secondary data and explain the strengths and limitations of each.
6. Discuss the two chief methods of collecting primary data.
7. Identify the three methods of collecting survey data. Give an example of when each method might be used.
8. Assume that a class of fifteen students received these grades on a business examination:

100	88	82	76	76
96	86	82	76	72
92	84	78	76	66

   a. What is the mean grade in this class?
   b. What is the median grade in this class?
   c. What is the mode for this class?
9. Assume that a local supermarket reported these monthly sales figures during 1976:

Month	Sales	Month	Sales
January	$ 90,000	July	70,000
February	85,000	August	80,000
March	90,000	September	105,000
April	100,000	October	100,000
May	105,000	November	130,000
June	105,000	December	140,000

a. What is the mean monthly sales for this store?
  b. Would the median and mode be useful figures for the super-market manager to calculate? Why, or why not?
10. How should data be presented to management?

Discussion questions and exercises

1. Evaluate the pro and con arguments to the controversial issue that appears in this chapter.
2. Interview a local businessperson. Ask this manager what types of information he or she needs every day. Find out how the manager obtains this information.
3. Prepare a report using the following to present your data: a line chart, a pie chart, a bar chart, and a pictograph.
4. Prepare a brief report on the use of statistical analysis in business.
5. Conduct a survey of students on your campus concerning some current controversial issue. Then analyze the data you collect.

Case 20-1
The Political Pollsters

Every election year is filled with reports of political pollsters who try to tell us who is going to win the various elections. Political opinion polls are usually conducted by recognized research firms that specialize in this activity. The Louis Harris and Gallup polls are two of the best-known polls in the United States.

Some political pollsters are employed by newspapers and magazines to provide this information for their readers. Some polls are done for syndicated columns, and some are commissioned by national television networks. Still other pollsters are hired by the politicians themselves to assess a campaign and devise new campaign strategies.

Most people are amazed by two aspects of political polling. First, the pollsters are usually correct, although there have been a few embarrassing mistakes:

One large-scale poll picked Alf Landon as the Presidential winner over Franklin Roosevelt in 1936.

A Chicago newspaper carried the headline "Dewey Defeats Truman" in 1948.

Second, the political pollsters base their findings on research involving a sample of only a few thousand people. These small samples are then used to represent the viewpoints of millions of U.S. citizens.

Questions

1. Why are the political pollsters so accurate when they base their conclusions on such small samples? Explain.

2. Do you know anyone who has ever been sampled in a political opinion poll? What election or matter did the poll concern?

3. Suppose you had been hired to do the political polling for a candidate for the governorship of your state. What type of research plan would you set up?

Case 20-2

"What Did You Get on the Test?"

"What did you get on the test?" is a common phrase in college hallways. Students usually respond with letter grades like "A," "B," "C," and so forth. These letter grades are often used to represent the numercial scores achieved by students.

But did you ever consider how your grade is determined? Grading is essentially a research assignment for your instructor. A group of twenty-five students were enrolled in an "Introduction to Business" class where *Contemporary Business* was the assigned textbook. They took a fifty item objective question examination. Consider the following scores which were achieved by these students:

Students	Score	Students	Score
Student 1	100	Student 14	72
Student 2	98	Student 15	70
Student 3	92	Student 16	70
Student 4	88	Student 17	70
Student 5	86	Student 18	68
Student 6	84	Student 19	66
Student 7	82	Student 20	66
Student 8	78	Student 21	64
Student 9	74	Student 22	60
Student 10	74	Student 23	56
Student 11	74	Student 24	48
Student 12	74	Student 25	46
Student 13	72		

Questions

1. Calculate the mean, median, and mode for this distribution of scores.
2. What letter grade would you assign to each of these scores?

Careers in Accounting, Computers, and Research

Accounting, computers, and research offer considerable career opportunities for business students. People with accounting training are found in high positions throughout most organizations. Accounting entry-level jobs are plentiful and provide real challenges for graduates. Computers require professional personnel to assure that management gets the information that is required for critical decisions. Business researchers are also important in several areas of industry: They secure and analyze the data upon which decisions are based.

The Bureau of Labor Statistics has projected annual job openings to 1985. Their forecast for some selected jobs in accounting, computers, and research appear below.

Job Projections to 1985

Career	Latest Employment (1972 Estimate)	Annual Average of Job Openings to 1985
Accountants	714,000	41,900
Actuaries	5,500	500
Computer service technicians	45,000	4,100
Electronic computer operating personnel	480,000	27,000
Mathematicians	76,000	8,100
Programmers	186,000	13,000
Statisticians	23,000	1,700
Systems analysts	103,000	8,300

SOURCE: *Occupational Manpower and Training Needs* (Washington, D.C.: Bureau of Labor Statistics, 1974).

Here are some of the careers in accounting, computers, and research that are available to you:

Public accountant

Public accountants are independent business persons who provide accounting services to other firms and individuals. Public accounting services range from the setting up of accounting systems to the preparation of tax forms. "Certified Public Accountant" (CPA) is the professional certification for public accountants.

Auditor	Auditors are public accountants who check the accuracy and validity of accounting records and procedures. If these records and procedures conform to recognized standards, the auditor certifies them in a public statement.
Cost accountant	Cost accountants are involved in accounting for the costs of producing the firm's product and operating the enterprise. They gather, analyze, and report cost data for management.
Programmer	A programmer is the person who gives commands to the computer through specialized computer languages. This person is able to select meaningful information out of the data stored in a computer.
Systems analyst	A systems analyst is a well-trained computer expert. This person develops the various computer-based information systems that are needed in an organization. A systems analyst determines what information is required and how best to obtain it.
Statistician	Statisticians apply statistical procedures to data in order to assess its validity and reliability, to analyze, predict, and evaluate. Statisticians are needed in quality control, marketing research, production control, finance, and other areas.
Actuary	Actuaries calculate insurance risks. By using statistical methods, actuaries determine the likelihood of death at a certain age, or the possibility of a casualty loss under given circumstances. Once these risks are calculated, actuaries help determine what insurance rates are necessary to cover such risks.

VII Additional Dimensions

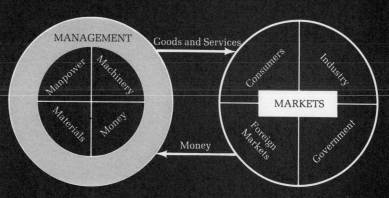

MANAGEMENT

Goods and Services

Manpower Machinery

Materials Money

Consumers Industry

MARKETS

Foreign Markets Government

Money

SOURCE: United Press International.

World Business

We want to participate in the growing opportunities abroad.
—Anonymous Executive

What Chapter 21 Is All About

1. This chapter will explain the importance of world business.
2. You will learn about the concept of international business, and why countries tend to specialize in certain goods.
3. Different levels of involvement in world business will be identified and explained.
4. You will understand the various obstacles to effective world business.
5. Multinational economic integration, the role of the multinational corporation, and the status of the United States as a foreign market will become familiar to you.
6. After reading this chapter, you should understand these terms:

exporting	comparative advantage
importing	tariffs
balance of trade	Kennedy Round
balance of payments	quotas
devaluation	embargo
revaluation	exchange control
exchange rate	cartels
absolute advantage	FCN

Asa Griggs Candler

Asa Griggs Candler was forty years old when, through a complicated and almost incidental series of purchases, he became the sole proprietor of the soon to be organized Coca-Cola Company. He had been a farm boy until he apprenticed himself to a pharmacist early in 1870 in Cartersville, Georgia. Sleeping in the back of the pharmacy at night, he worked all day and read medical books in his free time. Three years later, with only $1.50 in his pockets, Candler came to Atlanta to work without pay in George J. Howard's pharmacy.

By 1882 Candler had his own drugstore, but he decided to spend all his time promoting and selling Coke. The company was incorporated that year and began a growth pattern which was to continue from that day on. Beginning with sales of about 9,000 gallons, Candler could point with pride to sales of over 20 million gallons before his death in 1929. The mystique of the Coca-Cola formula has been maintained by passing it down by word of mouth from father to son, with only a handful of people in on the "most closely guarded secret" in American industry.

Because of an aggressive advertising and promotional policy and low overhead (for instance, only thirty employees were in the home office when the company was doing millions of dollars worth of business), Candler saw Coke sales climb. It was during his years as president that the unique distribution system of bottled Coke was begun. The first large bottling plant opened just before the turn of the century.

Candler left the company in 1916, and although he retained an interest in the business through his family, he owned only a few shares of stock when he died.

Ford Motor Company has manufacturing plants in Europe. British Petroleum operates throughout the world. Japanese imports have a sizable portion of the Pago Pago automobile market. Abu Dhabi, Iran, Oman, Saudi Arabia, and Venezuela export their most precious natural resource to the oil-starved industrialized nations of the rest of the world. All of these situations illustrate that business activities are not limited by national boundaries. World business is a fact of life in today's society.

The Importance of World Business

Everywhere one looks there is evidence of the growing importance of world business. The United States is both a seller and a purchaser in the world marketplace. Most firms in the United States—like their counterparts elsewhere—view the globe as their market. Over 15,000

Table 21-1
Importance of Foreign
Markets to Some
American Companies

Company	Percent Sales Abroad	Year
DuPont	23.7	1973
General Motors*	16.1	1973
Chrysler*	36.3	1973
International Harvester	30.0	1974
Abbott Laboratories	35.3	1973
Warner Lambert Pharmaceuticals	37.0	1973
Singer	42.0	1973
IBM	46.8	1973
U.S.M. Corporation	53.3	1974
Heinz (H.J.)	41.6	1973
NCR	49.3	1973
Pfizer (Chas.)	51.9	1973
Caterpillar Tractor	49.7	1973
Colgate Palmolive	52.3	1973

*Excludes Canada.

U.S. firms are engaged in some type of international business activity.[1]

Some U.S. companies are heavily dependent on their ability to sell their products overseas. The importance of foreign markets is shown in Table 21-1. For a manufacturer like Caterpillar Tractor, almost one of every two sales dollars comes from customers in other countries.

Foreign trade is important to the United States from both the **exporting** (*selling abroad*) and **importing** (*buying foreign goods and raw materials*) viewpoints. The United States is both the largest exporting nation and the largest importer in the world. But foreign trade is still relatively less critical to the United States than it is to such countries as the United Kingdom, Belgium, or New Zealand, who are heavily dependent upon international trade. Some leading trade partners of the United States are shown in Table 21-2.

World business allows a nation to sell abroad products not

Major Suppliers	($ Millions)	Major Customer	($ Millions)
1. Canada	$21,924	1. Canada	$19,932
2. Japan	12,338	2. Japan	10,679
3. West Germany	6,324	3. West Germany	4,986
4. Venezuela	4,671	4. Mexico	4,855
5. United Kingdom	4,061	5. United Kingdom	4,574
6. Mexico	3,390	6. Brazil	3,089
7. Italy	2,585	7. France	2,942
8. France	2,257	8. Italy	2,752
9. Brazil	1,700	9. Australia	2,173

SOURCE: *Survey of Current Business* (August 1975), pp. S-22, S-23.

Table 21-3
Some Leading
Commodities in U.S.
Foreign Trade—1974

Exports	($ Billions)	Imports	($ Billions)
Grains and cereal preparations	$10.3	Petroleum and products	$24.3
Chemicals	8.8	Automobiles and parts	10.3
Motor vehicles and parts	7.9	Electrical machinery	5.3
Electrical machinery	7.0	Iron and steel	5.1
Soybeans	3.5	Chemicals	4.0
Construction machinery	3.1	Nonferrous metals	3.9
Iron and steel	2.6	Sugar	2.2
Coal and related products	2.5	Metal ore	1.8
Textiles	1.8	Textiles	1.6

SOURCE: *Survey of Current Business* (August 1975, pp. S-22, S-23, S-24.

needed domestically. It also allows a country to import items not produced or in short supply locally. New Zealand imports 100 percent of its motor vehicles. The United States imports a large part of its oil supply.

Some leading exports and imports for the United States are shown in Table 21-3.

The Concept of International Business

International business activity is the result of several factors—some economic, others political or traditional. A starting point for understanding international business is the concepts of balance of trade and balance of payments.

BALANCE OF
TRADE

A nation's **balance of trade** is *determined by the relationship between its exports and imports.* A favorable balance of trade is when a nation's exports exceed its imports. This means that—other things being equal—new money would come into the country's economic system. An unfavorable balance of trade, by contrast, occurs when imports are greater than exports. The net money flow would be outward—other things being equal.

BALANCE OF
PAYMENTS

A country's balance of trade plays a key role in determining its **balance of payments,** *the flow of money into or out of a country.* But other factors are also important. A favorable balance of payments means that there is a net money flow into the nation; while an unfavorable balance of payments means a net money outflow.

The balance of payments is also affected by factors other than the balance of trade. Tourism, military expenditures abroad, investment abroad, and foreign aid all affect a nation's balance of payments. A money outflow caused by these factors may erase the money inflow from a favorable balance of trade and leave a nation with an unfavorable balance of payments.

"At least he still has confidence in the dollar."

Some People Do Not Understand the Concept of Devaluation

SOURCE: *The Wall Street Journal,* April 23, 1975. Reprinted with permission from *The Wall Street Journal.*

During the past two decades the United States has often had an unfavorable balance of payments. The net dollar flow was sometimes negative even in years when there was a favorable balance of trade. Foreign claims on U.S. currency led to the devaluation of the U.S. dollar in the early 1970's. **Devaluation** occurs when *a nation reduces the value of its currency in relation to gold or some other currency.* Devaluation of the dollar has the effect of making U.S. goods cheaper abroad, and making trips to the United States cheaper for foreign tourists. **Revaluation,** a less typical case, is when *a country adjusts the value of its currency upward.* In both cases the nation adjusts its **exchange rate,** the rate at which *its currency can be exchanged for other currencies or gold.*

Specialization between Countries

Argentina has vast grazing lands, while the Netherlands is an industrialized nation with almost no available space for raising beef. Hong Kong's 4.1 million people live in a small area that has become one of the most urbanized territories in the world. Hong Kong has become a world trader, as well as a source of foreign exchange for the People's Republic of China. Kuwait has rich oil fields, but few other industries or resources.

All of these situations suggest that nations are usually better off if they specialize in certain products or commercial activities. By doing what they do best, nations are able to exchange the production not needed domestically for foreign-made goods that are needed. Kuwait could set up manufacturing industries, but it has opted for specializing in oil production. This allows a higher standard of living than would be possible through diversified business enterprises. But specialization by countries sometimes produces odd situations. A classic example was when Britain's Conservative Party issued T-shirts with the party slogan "Put Britain First." Later, it was discovered that the T-shirts were made in Portugal.[2] In a similar situation are the number of "Buy American" stickers that can be found on the rear bumpers of Volkswagens and Toyotas.

The concepts of absolute and comparative advantage play a crucial role in the specialization between countries.

ABSOLUTE ADVANTAGE CONCEPT

A country has an **absolute advantage** in the marketing of a product if it is *the sole producer, or can produce it for less than anyone else.* Examples of absolute advantage are rare since few nations are sole producers and economic conditions rapidly alter production costs.

COMPARATIVE ADVANTAGE CONCEPT

A more realistic approach toward international specialization is that of **comparative advantage.** This concept says that *a nation has a comparative advantage in an item if it can produce it more efficiently than alternative products.* Nations will usually produce and export those goods in which they have the greatest comparative advantage (or least comparative disadvantage), and import those items in which they have the least comparative advantage (or the greatest comparative disadvantage).

Table 21-3 suggests how the comparative advantage concept is applied in the United States. The export commodities tend to be those in which there is a comparative advantage over the trading partners. Being a highly industrialized nation, with good natural resources, the United States tends to export manufactured items and natural resources, such as coal. By contrast, countries with low-cost labor tend to specialize in products that require a significant labor content—such as textiles, shoes, and clothing.

THE SELF-SUFFICIENCY ARGUMENT

Some countries refuse to specialize their productive efforts because they want to be self-sufficient. The Communist nations have typically followed this pattern. Israel is another example. Rhodesia was forced into this position because of world reaction to its racial policies. Still other nations follow the self-sufficiency viewpoint only for certain commodities that they regard as strategic to their long-run development. The United States, for instance, has decided it wants to be self-sufficient in regard to energy sources by about 1980.

In most cases nations seek to be self-sufficient for military reasons, fear of economic reprisals from other countries, and because of nationalism. Countries that follow the self-sufficiency argument usually see noneconomic reasons as being more important to the national welfare than the economic advantages of specialization.

Levels of Involvement in World Business[3]

World business involvement is often an evolving process for many firms. A company usually starts exporting on a small scale, and then expands its overseas efforts as management gains confidence and the ability to operate well abroad.

There are five separate levels of involvement in world business. These can be identified as:

1. casual, or accidental, exporting
2. active exporting
3. foreign licensing
4. overseas marketing by the firm
5. foreign production and foreign marketing.

CASUAL OR ACCIDENTAL EXPORTING

Some firms may sell abroad without ever knowing it. U.S. buyers for foreign companies or distributors may be buying the firm's goods and sending them overseas, while the firm considers these domestic sales. U.S. purchasers may export a supplier's goods for inclusion as part of an item manufactured overseas.

This sort of casual exporting probably occurs in a large number of firms, but it does not represent any real commitment to international trade. Some firms may see such occasional exporting as a way to unload an unexpected surplus or some obsolete inventory.

ACTIVE EXPORTING

For various reasons a firm may decide to enter the export market. This will require the investment of some company resources—capital and managerial effort. The export operation may be handled within the organization by an "export manager"; or the company may elect to engage an outside organization to handle this activity.

Active exporting is distinguished from casual exporting by the company's commitment to seek export business. In some cases active exporting actually evolves from the firm's experience in casual exporting.

FOREIGN LICENSING

The firm may decide to license foreign manufacturers to produce its product, rather than to export. Licensing may prove more practical than exporting because of the high costs of shipping goods abroad, the high tariff barriers or trade restrictions, or nationalistic preferences for locally produced goods. Licensing may also provide competitive advantages, such as local market knowledge and the distribution capabilities of the licensee.

OVERSEAS MARKETING BY THE FIRM This level of world business involves setting up a foreign sales office or marketing subsidiary abroad. The product may come from plants, licensees, or contract manufacturing in the United States, but foreign marketing is now controlled more directly by the U.S. firm through its physical presence in the market.

FOREIGN PRODUCTION AND FOREIGN MARKETING The ultimate degree of world business involvement is when a firm engages in its own foreign manufacturing and marketing operations. Acquiring an existing producer in a foreign market is a popular and quick way of entering such a market. Other firms may decide to form their own organizations in the country.

Obstacles to World Business

Various obstacles, or barriers, to effective world business exist. Some are minor and can be overcome easily. Others are nearly impossible to bridge. The key point is that business executives must expect, and learn to handle, a multitude of problems in attempting to reach international markets.

ECONOMIC, SOCIETAL, AND CULTURAL OBSTACLES Economic conditions and societal and cultural attitudes often influence world business. The economic status of some countries makes them less (or more) likely candidates for international business expansion. Nations with low per capita income may be poor markets for expensive, industrial machinery, but good markets for agricultural hand tools. These nations cannot afford the technical equipment necessary in an industrialized society. The International Bank for Reconstruction and Development estimates that the poorer countries will require a cash injection of up to $18.3 billion by 1980 to even reach moderately acceptable growth rates.[4] Wealthier countries can prove to be prime markets for the products of many U.S. industries, particularly those involved with consumer goods and advanced industrial products.

Many American products have failed overseas simply because the firm tried to use the same business strategy that was successful in the United States. The Campbell Soup Company suffered heavy losses in attempting to market tomato soup in the United Kingdom before discovering that the British prefer a more bitter taste.[5]

U.S. products do not always meet the needs of foreign consumers. The products of U.S. automobile manufacturers have traditionally been called "Yank Tanks" by Australians, who must travel vast distances on narrow roads. Similarly, some foreign products do not meet the needs of Americans. Japanese machine-tool producers found that U.S. firms, with higher labor costs, used machines more intensively and could afford less time for maintenance. This required that the Japanese alter both their product and service programs.[6]

In some cases U.S. industry has not done a good job of doing research in the market for an overseas product. One U.S. tire manufacturer built a plant in France because it felt that exporting had given them sufficient knowledge of the French market. But French driving habits had changed while the plant was being built and this forced the firm to make costly production adjustments. Later, the firm hired an international marketing research director; and before it built an Italian plant a detailed marketing analysis was conducted.[7]

This example suggests the importance of economic, societal, and cultural factors for the success of world business. Business managers desiring to operate in an overseas market must consider such environmental aspects before undertaking a project.

TARIFFS AND TRADE RESTRICTIONS

World business is also affected by tariffs and related trade restrictions. **Tariffs** are *taxes levied against products imported from abroad.* Some are based on a set tax per pound, gallon, or unit. Other tariffs are figured on the value of the imported product. Tariffs may be classified as either revenue tariffs or protective tariffs. Revenue tariffs are designed to raise funds for the government. Most of the revenue of the infant U.S. government came from this source. Protective tariffs are designed to raise the retail price of imported products, and are usually higher than a revenue tariff. In earlier days it was believed that a country should protect its "infant industries" by using tariffs to keep out foreign-made products. Some foreign goods would enter, but the addition of a high tariff payment would make domestic products competitive. Recently it has been argued that tariffs should be raised to protect employment and profits in domestic U.S. industry.

The General Agreement on Tariffs and Trade (GATT), an international trade accord, has sponsored six *major tariff negotiations that have reduced the overall level of tariffs throughout the world.* The latest series, the so-called **Kennedy Round,** took place between 1964–1967. While the general movement has been toward tariff reduction, economic downturns always bring calls for economic protection of domestic industries.

There are other forms of trade restrictions. **Quotas** *set limits on the amount of products in certain categories that may be imported.* The objective of import quotas is to protect local industry and employment and preserve foreign exchange. The ultimate form of a quota is an **embargo,** *the complete ban of certain products.* In the past the United States has prohibited the import of products from some Communist countries.

Foreign trade can also be regulated by **exchange control** through a central bank or government agency. Exchange control means that *firms gaining foreign exchange by exporting must sell this foreign exchange to the central bank, or agency, while importers must buy foreign exchange from the same organization.*

The government can thus allocate, expand, or restrict foreign exchange according to existing national policy.

POLITICAL AND LEGAL OBSTACLES

Political factors influence international business. Colgate's popular Irish Spring soap was introduced in England with a political name change. The British know the product as Nordic Spring.[8] Washington's Jewish community asked a Jewish newspaper to publish a list of Dutch products so that they could reward the Netherlands for its refusal to condemn Israel while under Arab pressure.[9]

Many nations try to achieve political objectives through international business activities. Like it or not, firms operating abroad often end up involved in, or are influenced by, international relations. American companies have been boycotted, burned, bombed, and banned by people who objected to U.S. foreign policy. South African and Rhodesian firms have seen the markets for some of their products dwindle as a result of their governments' racial policies. A dynamic political environment is a fact of life in world business.

Legal requirements complicate world business. Liquor sales in Sweden must go through a government monopoly.[10] The Netherlands requires that candy commercials on television carry tooth decay warnings.[11] Many nations have *local content laws* specifying the portion of a product that must come from domestic sources. These examples suggest that managers involved in international business must be well-versed in legislation affecting their specific industries.

The legal environment for U.S. firms operating abroad can be divided into three dimensions:

1. U.S. law
2. international law
3. the legal requirements of host nations.[12]

Firms in the United States are subject to a comprehensive set of U.S. business legislation which is outlined in Chapter 23 of this book. International operations are also subject to various trade regulations, tax laws, and import/export requirements. One of the best-known U.S. laws is the Webb-Pomerene legislation of 1918, which exempted combinations of U.S. firms acting together to develop foreign markets from antitrust laws. The intent was to give U.S. industry economic power equal to that possessed by **cartels**, *the monopolistic organizations of foreign firms.* Companies operating under the Webb-Pomerene law must not reduce competition *within* the United States, and must not use "unfair methods of competition."

International law can be found in the treaties, conventions, and agreements that exist among nations. The United States has many **"Friendship, Commerce, and Navigation" (FCN)** treaties with other countries. FCN treaties include many aspects of commercial relations, such as the right to conduct business in the treaty partner's domestic market. The International Monetary Fund has been set up to lend foreign exchange to nations that require it to conduct international trade. This facilitates the whole process of world business.

Other international business agreements concern international standards for various products, patents, trademarks, reciprocal tax treaties, export control, international air travel, and international communications.

The legal requirements of host nations affect foreign marketers. Jaguar sedans were withdrawn from the American market because of U.S. safety standards. Ghana sets gross profit margins. Other nations limit foreign ownership in their business sectors.

People in world business realize the critical importance of obeying the laws and regulations of the countries within which they operate. Even the slightest violations of these legal requirements are setbacks for international business generally, and should be carefully avoided.

Multinational Economic Communities

Several multinational economic communities have been formed since World War II.[13] Probably the best known of these associations is the European Economic Community (EEC), or the Common Market. Many of these groupings have strong political, as well as economic, ties among the participants. The various regional groupings are shown in Table 21-4.

Three basic formats for economic integration exist. The simplest approach is a **free trade area,** where the participants agree to free trade of goods among themselves. All tariffs and trade restrictions are abolished between the nations involved. A **customs union** establishes a free trade area, but also establishes a uniform tariff for trade with nonmember nations. The EEC is the best example of a customs union. A true **common market,** or **economic union,** involves a customs union, and also seeks to bring all government regulations affecting trade into agreement. The EEC has been moving in the direction of an economic union.

Regardless of the approach that is followed, it seems certain that multinational economic communities will play a significant role in world business during the next decade. U.S. firms invested heavily in Western Europe in the 1960's basically because of the attraction of larger markets offered by the EEC. Multinational economic integration is forcing management to adapt its operations abroad to meet the format requirements, and it is likely that the pace will accelerate in the future.

Table 21-4
Regional Economic Groupings

Membership and Date of Origin

1. ANCOM: Andean Development Corporation (also called the Andean Common Market), September 1967—Bolivia, Colombia, Chile, Ecuador, Peru.
2. Arab Economic Unity Agreement, April 30, 1964—Iraq, Jordan, Kuwait, Syria, U.A.R. (Egypt); other signatories—Sudan, Yemen.
3. ASEAN: Association of South East Asian Nations, August 1967—Indonesia, Malaysia, Philippines, Singapore, Thailand.
4. BENELUX, November 1960—Belgium, Luxembourg, the Netherlands.
5. CACM: Central American Common Market, 1960—Costa Rica, El Salvador, Guatemala, Honduras, Nicaragua.
6. CARIFTA: Caribbean Free Trade Area, January 1966—Antigua, Barbados, Dominica, Grenada, Guyana, Jamaica, Montserrat, St. Christopher-Nevis-Anguilla, St. Lucia, St. Vincent, Trinidad, and Tobago.
7. CMEA: Council for Mutual Economic Assistance (also called COMECON), 1949—Albania, Bulgaria, Czechoslovakia, East Germany, Hungary, Mongolian People's Republic, Poland, Romania, USSR; partial participant—Yugoslavia.
8. East African Community, December 1967—Kenya, Tanzania, Uganda.
9. EEC: European Economic Community, January 1, 1958—Belgium, France, West Germany, Italy, Luxembourg, the Netherlands, United Kingdom; associated members—(in Europe) Greece, Turkey, Israel, Spain; (in Africa) Burundi, Cameroon, Central African Republic, Chad, Congo (Brazzaville), Congo (Democratic Republic), Dahomey, Gabon, Ivory Coast, Madagascar, Mali, Mauritania, Niger, Rwanda, Senegal, Somalia, Togo, Upper Volta.
10. EFTA: European Free Trade Association, May 1960—Austria, Denmark, Norway, Portugal, Sweden, Switzerland, United Kingdom; associate member—Finland.
11. LAFTA: Latin American Free Trade Association (also called ALALC), February 1960—Argentina, Bolivia, Brazil, Chile, Colombia, Ecuador, Mexico, Paraguay, Peru, Uruguay, Venezuela.
12. NORDEK: The Nordic Council, 1952—Denmark, Iceland, Norway, Sweden.
13. OCAM: *Organisation Commune Africaine et Malgache*, February 1965—Cameroon, Central African Republic, Chad, Congo (Brazzaville), Congo (Democratic Republic), Dahomey, Gabon, Ivory Coast, Madagascar, Niger, Rwanda, Senegal, Togo, Upper Volta.
14. ECUWAS: Economic Community of West African States, 1975—Dahomey, Gambia, Guinea Bissau, Ivory Coast, Liberia, Mauritania, Niger, Nigeria, Sierra Leone, Togo, Upper Volta, Mali, Guinea, Senegal, and Ghana.

SOURCE: Vern Terpstra. *International Marketing* (New York: Holt, Rinehart and Winston, Inc., 1972), pp. 45–46. Copyright © 1972 by Holt, Rinehart and Winston, Inc. Reprinted by permission of Holt, Rinehart and Winston, Inc.; *The Detroit News* (May 29, 1975), p. 5-C.

The Multinational Corporation

When IBM developed the System/360 computers they followed a completely multinational approach by giving their United Kingdom, French, and German subsidiaries major responsibilities in the project. This international specialization speeded the overall task, and generated enthusiasm in the participating subsidiaries.[14]

A **multinational company** *operates in several countries, and literally views the world as its market.* The development of the IBM 360 is an example of how this concept operates effectively.

Ideally, the multinational corporation should standardize its product lines to maximize its production efficiency. Parts manufacturing should be done where it is most economical, and sales efforts should be concentrated where the market is growing fastest.[15]

Ford Motor Company has discovered that there are also many problems in managing a multinational enterprise. Ford of Europe, the umbrella organization for an integrated manufacturing/marketing operation in Europe, is headquartered in Warley outside of London. There are large manufacturing plants in Britain and Germany, with smaller factories in Belgium, France, Ireland, the Netherlands, and Portugal. The organization has had to face British complaints that German-designed parts were too precise, German complaints that strikes in Britain delayed shipments, and the like. Still, Ford is number two in Europe behind Fiat, and remains committed to the multinational approach.[16] It seems likely that most major U.S. companies will follow the example set by Ford and others and continue to develop an international approach to their operations.

Multinational corporations have become so dominant in some foreign markets that they are now the object of close political and economic scrutiny. Research studies have shown that multinationals usually make higher profits overseas than do their local competitors.[17] Canada and Australia—among others—have shown some concern over the dominance of the multinationals. These firms will probably come in for even closer observation in the years ahead.

U.S. multinationals have been attacked on several grounds. The Interfaith Center on Corporate Responsibility, an organization sponsored by Protestant and Catholic churches, has accused multinational corporations of exploiting African labor. Some mining operations in Africa, the Center claims, pay about two-thirds of the total wages to white workers who make up only slightly over 20 percent of the labor force. The Center's project director has also said that IBM should cease operations in South Africa because its computers help strengthen the *apartheid* system.[18]

It seems likely that the multinational corporation will continue to be criticized in several areas. Some criticism may be justified; other criticism certainly is not. Companies operating abroad must be sure that they act as fairly and responsibly overseas as they do at home. To do otherwise is to court disaster in international markets.

The United States as a Foreign Market

The United States is a "foreign market" to many other countries. All the coffee, crude rubber, diamonds, and bananas in the United States are imported from abroad. There is heavy dependence on foreign sources for a variety of other goods and services. The Japanese have now achieved a considerable share of U.S. electronics

"Oh-oh."

Some Foreign-produced Items Have Become Very Expensive in Recent Years

SOURCE: Reprinted by permission of *Advertising Age,* March 18, 1974.

and small car markets. Foreign steel has also made inroads into the United States.

Foreign sellers can employ any of the five levels of international business involvement noted earlier in this chapter. Most Americans are surprised to learn of the amounts of direct investment made by foreign companies in the United States. Japanese-owned and managed companies are currently operating in California, Wisconsin, Washington, New York, Texas, and other states. Kuwait owns an island off the South Carolina coast. Arab investors have purchased office buildings in Manhattan and a share of one of Detroit's biggest banks. And Texans were shocked when a Saudi Arabian sheik wanted to buy the Alamo for his son.[19] Figure 21-1 shows the industries and the locations of foreign firms operating in the United States.

Many foreign nations actually conduct or coordinate their sales efforts in the United States through an agency or corporation of their own governments. Agricultural and primary products are often marketed in this way.

Americans have shown a preference for some foreign products over their domestic competitors. The Datsun 280Z, Porsche, MGB, Triumph, Toyota Celica ST, and Fiat 124 Spider have dominated the U.S. sports car market. English china, Sony, and French wine all have sizable shares of the U.S. market. Some foreign products are sold in the United States because of their quality images—such as Swiss watches. Others sell on the basis of a price advantage over domestic competition. The desire for foreign products is even reflected in where we dine, as ethnic restaurants become more popular than ever before.

Arab Investment in the United States

Since the end of World War II there has been an increasingly international aspect to business. The boundaries of a country are not necessarily the boundaries of a large firm. Markets are worldwide, as are the supplies of raw materials and partially finished products. Big business in the United States has steadily invested in the world market to a startling total of over $100 billion. Becoming number one in a given industry in the United States has limited further expansion of some large corporations and has led them to move into European, Asian, and Latin American industries. Just as U.S. companies have invested abroad, so now the member nations of the oil-producing Arab states are seeking to put money into the United States. It is estimated that the sum of this investment is almost $70 billion.

There are some dangers in such large investments by a united group of foreign powers, and these dangers must be guarded against. For example, no such investments should be allowed in areas sensitive to national security. Corporations that deal in weaponry, nuclear power, or with strategic industries must be kept free from foreign control. Furthermore, there should certainly be no policy-making decisions by Arab nations or individuals in such crucial areas as defense, transportation, and communications. It is important that the United States maintain control over its own markets both at home and abroad, and that Arab investments not be allowed to influence that control.

Another important consideration should be with whether the investors are individuals or governments, or whether influence on the foreign policy of the United States through an Arab lobby might alter that foreign policy and U.S. relationships throughout the world. If this were the case, the United States relationship with Israel would certainly be jeopardized.

Yet Arab money could well support American business in such a way as to promote free trade and peace for the United States in its relations with the rest of the world. By investing in companies in the United States, Arabs are strengthening the economy, creating more jobs for U.S. workers, and lending U.S. corporations funds with which to improve their technology.

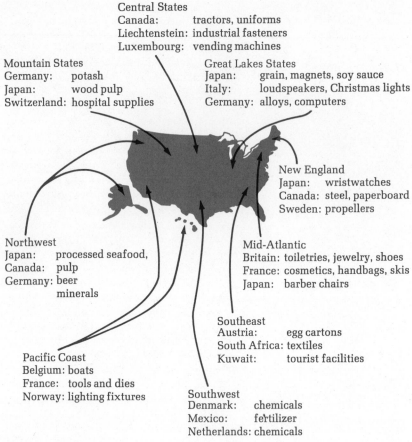

Figure 21-1
Industries and Locations
of Foreign Firms Doing
Business in the
United States

Central States
Canada: tractors, uniforms
Liechtenstein: industrial fasteners
Luxembourg: vending machines

Mountain States
Germany: potash
Japan: wood pulp
Switzerland: hospital supplies

Great Lakes States
Japan: grain, magnets, soy sauce
Italy: loudspeakers, Christmas lights
Germany: alloys, computers

New England
Japan: wristwatches
Canada: steel, paperboard
Sweden: propellers

Northwest
Japan: processed seafood,
Canada: pulp
Germany: beer
               minerals

Mid-Atlantic
Britain: toiletries, jewelry, shoes
France: cosmetics, handbags, skis
Japan: barber chairs

Southeast
Austria: egg cartons
South Africa: textiles
Kuwait: tourist facilities

Pacific Coast
Belgium: boats
France: tools and dies
Norway: lighting fixtures

Southwest
Denmark: chemicals
Mexico: fertilizer
Netherlands: chemicals

SOURCE: Reprinted from *U.S. News & World Report.* Copyright 1974 U.S. News & World Report, Inc.

Americans Flock to Ethnic Restaurants

The National Restaurant Association estimates that 37,400, or 11 percent of all U.S. restaurants, feature the foods of other countries. Americans in increasing numbers are trying *pogogi* (the highly seasoned Korean "fire meat") or *saganaki* (the flaming cheese appetizer from Greece). Fayetteville, North Carolina, now has a Vietnamese restaurant that serves soldiers and their Vietnamese wives from nearby Fort Bragg. Foreign travel experiences, informality, and relatively low prices have all contributed to the rise of ethnic restaurants in the United States.

Many ethnic restaurant managers report that they have had to modify the original dishes to meet American tastes. Rocky Aoki, owner of Benihana of Toyoko, Ltd., which operates sixteen restaurants in the U.S., says: "Americans wouldn't touch raw fish. If I served it, I'd go broke." So Aoki's restaurants feature "Japanese style" steak, chicken, and shrimps. He admits it is not completely authentic, but points out that restaurants back home in Japan are starting to copy him. Chris Liakouros of Chicago's Parthenon says Greek food should be greasy and cooked in fat. "But that would make my customers sick, especially on hot days," he says.

The failure rate for ethnic restaurants is high, with up to 50 percent failing in the first two years. Jory Graham, a restaurant columnist for the *Chicago Sun-Times,* says: "Not many of these places can afford to advertise. Most depend on favorable newspaper reviews and word of mouth, but that takes time, and by then it's often too late."

Source: Adapted from David M. Eloner, "Travel, War, Boredom Spur Rise in Openings of Ethnic Restaurants," *The Wall Street Journal* (September 7, 1973), pp. 1, 12. Reprinted with permission of *The Wall Street Journal,* © Dow Jones & Company, 1974. All rights reserved.

Government policy, and even public opinion on imports, has varied over time. Rising unemployment in the 1970's led to calls for higher tariff walls and severe import restrictions to protect U.S. industry and its employees from imports made with "cheap" foreign labor. This economic protection argument has been voiced by both corporate management and labor union executives. The import market has often been used to accomplish economic and political objectives. For example, the Australian government once revalued its dollar upward to attract "cheaper" imports in an attempt to combat severe inflation.

It appears likely that imported goods will grow in importance in the United States in the future. The long-run trend seems to be toward increased world trade. The reduction of some trade barriers between the Eastern and Western power blocs illustrates this trend.

Summary

World business is growing in importance. The United States is both the biggest exporting nation and the biggest importer in the world. Over 15,000 U.S. firms are engaged in some type of international business activity.

Chapter 21 discusses the concept of international business, including the balance of trade (the relationship between exports and imports) and the balance of payments (the difference between inward and outward cash flows). Specialization between countries is examined in the context of the concepts of absolute and comparative advantage, as well as the self-sufficiency argument.

Levels of involvement in world business include:

1. casual, or accidental, exporting
2. active exporting
3. foreign licensing
4. overseas marketing by the firm
5. foreign production and foreign marketing.

Obstacles to world business can be classified as:

1. economic, societal, and cultural obstacles
2. tariffs and trade restrictions
3. political and legal obstacles.

There has been a movement toward multinational economic integration in many parts of the world. Three basic approaches exist:

1. free trade area
2. customs union
3. a common market, or economic union.

Discussions of the multinational corporation and the United States as a foreign market conclude this chapter.

Review questions

1. Identify the following terms:

a.	exporting	i.	comparative advantage
b.	importing	j.	tariffs
c.	balance of trade	k.	Kennedy Round
d.	balance of payments	l.	quotas
e.	devaluation	m.	embargo
f.	revaluation	n.	exchange control
g.	exchange rate	o.	cartels
h.	absolute advantage	p.	FCN

2. Is it possible for a nation to have a favorable balance of trade and an unfavorable balance of payments? Discuss.
3. Distinguish between the concepts of absolute advantage and comparative advantage.
4. Outline and discuss the five possible levels of involvement in world business.
5. Explain the difference between a revenue tariff and a protective tariff.
6. What is the Webb-Pomerene Act?
7. Describe the three basic formats for multinational economic integration.
8. What is a multinational corporation?
9. Describe the growth of the United States as a "foreign market" for overseas competitors.
10. What types of products does the United States export? Import?

Discussion questions and exercises

1. Evaluate the pro and con arguments to the controversial issue that appears in this chapter.
2. Prepare a report on the use of import quotas and embargoes by the United States since its founding.
3. Prepare a report on the operation of the International Monetary Fund.
4. Set up a classroom debate on the topic: "What are the social responsibilities of a multinational business?"

5. Prepare a report on the operations of a multinational corporation based in a country other than the United States. Does this company seem to operate in the same general manner as U.S. multinationals? Why, or why not?

Case 21-1

Living with *"La Mordida"*

Multinational corporations inevitably encounter the twin problems of payoffs and bribes. Mexicans use the term *"La Mordida"*—The Bite—to describe this practice, common in many business systems.

Most U.S. firms have corporate policies prohibiting the payment of bribes for any purpose. Industries like airlines and defense suppliers also face governmental regulations against bribery. But *"La Mordida"* is commonplace in the cultures of many nations.

One vice-president of a U.S. airplane manufacturer was told by a top South American official that a recent airplane crash was the fault of the aircraft, not pilot error as the evidence showed. The official indicated that a $100,000 payment was necessary for the courts to reach a verdict of pilot error. The U.S. executive refused payment, and a local distributor put him on the next flight out of the country. The corrupt official was later replaced by his government.

Questions

1. What would you have done if you had been the U.S. executive described in the case?
2. Why do you think *"La Mordida"* is an accepted aspect of some business systems?
3. Suppose you were chief executive of a large multinational. How would you handle this problem?

Source: James C. Makens. "U.S. Marketers Should Be Aware of and Able to Deal with International Problems of Payoffs and Bribes; The Mexicans Call It "La Mordida"—The Bite," Reprinted from *Marketing News* (April 25, 1975), p. 8, a publication of the American Marketing Association.

Case 21-2

The French Table Water Market*

Despite tests showing that some popular table waters do not meet government standards for municipal water systems, the French remain the world's largest consumers of bottled water. They also often pay higher prices for table water than ordinary wine. The typical French citizen drinks slightly over 60 litres of mineral water annually (a litre equals 1.057 quarts) compared to about 110 litres of wine. A 7½ ounce carafe of red table wine costs about 30 cents in a Paris café, while the French must pay about 56 cents for bottled water.

Bottled water marketers are able to maintain this sizeable price differential largely because of French concern about kidney and liver trouble, and a distrust of tap water. Many French water advertisements argue that tired kidneys and livers require daily baths of mineral water.

Questions

1. Suppose you were a U.S.-based mineral waters distributor. Would you consider France to be a good overseas market? Why, or why not?
2. What level of business involvement would you choose if you were seeking to enter the French table water market?
3. Develop a promotional strategy for a firm entering the French table water market.

*This market is described in the *Detroit Free Press* (March 10, 1974), p. 9-A.

22

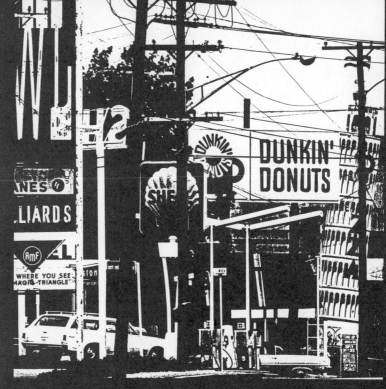

Small Business and Franchising

"It is more admirable to be in business for yourself than to work for somebody else."

—H.L. Mencken

What Chapter 22 Is All About

1. This chapter will explain the important role played by small business in our economy.
2. You will learn what a small business is and where small businesses are found.
3. You will understand how small businesses differ from larger firms in terms of their strengths and weaknesses.
4. You will find out what franchising is, what problems are associated with franchising, and what franchising means for the potential owner of a small business.
5. You will learn of the problems facing the small business—including the minority-owned business—and some ways to overcome these problems.
6. After reading this chapter, you will understand these terms:

small business	minority-owned businesses
franchise	Small Business Administration (SBA)
franchisee	Office of Minority Business
franchisor	Enterprise (OMBE)

Ray A. Kroc

SOURCE: McDonald's Corp.

If anything could replace the bald eagle or apple pie as a symbol of the United States it might well be the hamburger. Throughout the world the burger and french fries *are* the American way of eating. Ray Kroc knew this when he founded the McDonald's restaurant chain. And he also knew that the people of the United States wanted quality, service, and cleanliness—the "Q.S.C." motto that has left its mark on every McDonald's store.

Kroc was a high-school dropout who lied about his age in order to join the Red Cross ambulance corps in World War I. When he returned to his native Chicago after the war, he became music director of a pioneer radio station and played piano in a band. The team of Sam and Henry, whom he hired for $5 a show, later became famous as "Amos 'n Andy."

With Chicago as a base, Kroc made forays into Florida for the about-to-bust real-estate boom, and became midwest sales manager for the Lily-Tulip Cup company. Later he took a job as exclusive sales representative for a milk-shake mixing machine. Eight mixers were purchased by the McDonald brothers for their California hamburger restaurant. Kroc realized that such places would use a lot of his mixers, and so he started a chain of hamburger restaurants under a royalty arrangement with the brothers.

As one of the creators of the modern fast-food industry, Kroc began licensing independent restaurant owners. His corporation only trains licensees and establishes and enforces standards; it does not sell supplies to licensees. There are 3,000 McDonald's restaurants throughout the United States, Canada, Asia, Australia, and Europe, and there are plans for still further expansion.

Small business has always played an important role in the economy of the United States. The independently owned and operated business represents one of the areas where individuals can "do their own thing" in business. Owning and operating one's own business is part of the American business heritage. Research has shown that many Americans dream of someday owning a business they have created.

There are about twenty million small businesses in the United States, including some 12 million farmers and about 8 million individual business firms. When one considers that the total number of *all* business firms in the United States is about 8.4 million, it is easy to understand the importance of small businesses. Less than one-half of 1 percent of all U.S. businesses employ as many as 2,500 people. Yet over 51 percent of the nation's business employment, and over 43 percent of its privately produced output, comes from small businesses.[1]

Even the president of General Motors Corporation would be reluctant to drive very far from home if there were no service stations available to repair cars or to fill gas tanks, or a restaurant at which to stop if one gets hungry. This executive also knows that many General Motors plants, like those of any large company, would quickly have to close without the literally thousands of suppliers who furnish everything from brake linings to tools and dies. If thousands of dealers—all independently owned small businesses— were not in existence, General Motors would face an almost impossible job of trying to carry out the many activities performed by these dealers.

Small business was operating even in Colonial days, so it is pretty evident that small businesses are here to stay. The small business is the backbone of business.

What Is a Small Business?

What is small depends on one's point of view. A "small" steel company might be considered a major corporation in some other industry. The classic illustration is American Motors with sales of well over $1,000,000,000. In most industries American Motors would be considered large, but in the automobile industry it is small compared to Ford, Chrysler, and General Motors. The Small Business Administration once classified American Motors as "small," thus permitting the then ailing firm to enjoy special advantages in bidding on government contracts.

The number of employees on the payroll is probably the most widely used yardstick for classifying small businesses. Less than a hundred employees is a common cutoff point. Most people would consider a **small business** to be one with few employees, low sales volume, and limited assets. The owner is usually directly involved in the management as well as the operation of the business, and may not have had much training or experience in business. Probably the most workable definition of a small business is the one suggested some years ago by the Committee for Economic Development. To qualify as a small firm under their definition, a business must have at least two of the following four characteristics:

1. Management of the firm is independent. The managers are typically also the owners.
2. Capital is provided by one individual, or a small group of people.
3. The area of operations is mainly local, with workers and owners living in one community. However, the market for the product or service need not be local.
4. The size of the firm is small relative to the industry. This measure can be in terms of employees, sales volume, or assets.[2]

Where Are Small Businesses Found?

Small businesses are found everywhere in the economy. The retailing and service industries represent the largest share of all small firms. But in fields like communication, transportation, and public utilities, the investment in plant and equipment is generally so sizeable that only large firms can operate profitably. Small businesses usually are abundant in those industries where:

1. initial capital requirements are low
2. managerial experience is not too important
3. the market is localized
4. technological requirements are minimal.[3]

A look at a few industry classifications will suggest where small businesses are to be found.

Mining   It is often surprising to many people when they learn that small mining companies are a large part of the total mining activity in the United States and in many nations throughout the world. Companies with less than one hundred employees account for 45 percent of the total employment in the mining industry. There are thousands of small coal mines operated with only a few employees.

Manufacturing   Because of the large amount of initial capital required for most production facilities, large firms predominate in manufacturing. But one can find hundreds of thousands of small firms, including everything from small furniture and clothing manufacturing plants to cabinet shops and soft-drink bottling plants. Even in a large-scale industry like automobile manufacturing, small firms play a vital role. While three giant companies dominate the automobile industry, thousands of small businesses—tool and die shops, machine shops, and parts manufacturers—are needed so that the giants can function.

Wholesaling   The wholesaling of consumer and industrial products is basically a small business activity. Wholesale firms with less than one hundred employees account for more than 75 percent of all the people employed in this industry. The small wholesaler's function is primarily that of serving as a middleman between the manufacturer and the retailer or industrial purchaser. The wholesaler performs the marketing activities of assembling, storing, and distributing the products, which might include groceries, machinery, drugs, appliances, or hardware.

Retailing   In spite of the fact that there are many large department stores, mail-order houses, chain stores, and discount stores, small

Retailing Offers Many Small Business Opportunities

SOURCE: Courtesy of Sidney Harris and *The Saturday Evening Post.*

firms dominate retailing. Firms employing nineteen or fewer employees account for about 40 percent of the total employment in retailing. Small retailers are to be found for nearly every type of product or service. These include clothing stores, service stations, restaurants, independent grocery and meat markets, hardware stores, jewelry stores, ice-cream parlors, vending machine businesses, and music stores. A drive down any commercial street, or a walk through any shopping center, will reveal a long list of small firms engaged in retailing.

Service Almost half of the labor force is employed in the service industries, and about forty cents of every consumer dollar is spent for services. Due to the ease of entry and relatively small initial investment, service industries abound with small businesses. Service firms are varied and numerous. Some broad categories which would include a high percentage of small businesses are:

Personal services—such as barber and beauty shops, laundries, funeral homes, and dry cleaners

Amusement and recreation services—such as theaters, golf courses, indoor tennis courts, and dance bands

Lodging services—includes hotels, motels, and trailer camps

Repair services—includes such diverse businesses as watch, television, upholstering, and automobile repair shops

Business services—such as accounting firms, private employment agencies, answering services, management consultants, and collection agencies.

How Small Businesses Are Different

All of the major firms in the United States were at one time small businesses. It is reasonable to expect that many of today's small firms will become tomorrow's industrial giants. At the same time it is not correct to assume that small firms are just like large firms—only in smaller versions. The small business is quite distinct from the large firm, and many small companies go out of business because they try to imitate the "giants."[4]

Strengths of Small Businesses

A small firm frequently has a competitive advantage over a large firm *because* of its smallness. A few of these distinct advantages are discussed below.

MANAGEMENT FLEXIBILITY One feature of the modern business environment is change. Change in the form of new products, markets, machines, and techniques has become a fact of life for all businesses. In general, the smaller the company, the faster it can adapt to change.

A large firm is likely to be weighted down with procedures and tradition. Any major decision must pass through several layers of management before change can occur. In most independently owned and operated businesses the lack of several management levels leads to quicker decisions and more flexibility in operation. If a local retailer learns of a new product line that is likely to sell in the area, the retailer can make the decision to place an order in a matter of hours. Large retailers with hundreds of stores might take weeks, or even months, to make a management decision of this nature.

SENSITIVITY TO LOCAL NEEDS A local businessperson is in a good position to adapt a business to local peculiarities. National firms, because they must appeal to large regional or national tastes, often find themselves unable to penetrate certain local markets, especially when a local firm has made a more direct appeal to the customer.

Many customers will buy from a firm because of a close personal relationship with the owner or employees established over the years. Especially where product and price differences are slight, the personal touch of the local businessperson can be the most important competitive distinction. The local owner of a business is in an ideal situation to study the preferences and customs of the local market, and then make the necessary adjustments in the business.

LOWER OPERATING COSTS While the larger firm has certain economies of scale, in general the typical small business faces lower operating costs. For example, Edwin L. Anderson, the President of the Atlanta-based Johnson Manufacturing Company (a small maker of switch gear), says that his firm's biggest advantages are low overhead and flexibility.[5] The small firm may use family labor which can be more productive and cheaper than rates paid to other members of the labor force. And since the organization structure is simpler, problems of communication are easily resolved and at a lower cost in personnel and materials in a small firm. The impact of a decision is also quickly seen, and corrective action can be taken if necessary.

The small firm can usually operate at lower costs due to a relatively smaller investment in plant and equipment, less administrative cost, and fewer employee benefits to be paid. It should also be noted that since the top executive of the small firm probably owns part or all of the business, this person is likely to work harder and with more personal involvement. Such an involvement can have a positive effect on employee morale and productivity.

Weaknesses of Small Businesses

Large firms share many of the weaknesses of small firms. Most business failures that occur every year could be avoided if the firm were properly managed. But, in addition to the problems that face all businesses, there are certain disadvantages inherent in small firms. Three of the more common ones are discussed below.

FINANCING Many small businesspersons feel that their businesses would be successful if they just had adequate funding. But since the chances of survival are much less for small firms, the chances of getting necessary capital and credit are much less than for large firms. The smaller firm has only limited access to the money markets that are open to larger firms. Capital for expansion usually has to come from personal funds or from profits retained in the business.

Since the small firm normally has a lower credit rating, lenders are reluctant to provide funds. If they do, interest rates tend to be higher than for large, established businesses. Borrowing from friends or relatives frequently ends with the friends or relatives desiring to manage the business. The final result is often broken friendships, hard feelings, and poorly operated businesses.

LACK OF MANAGEMENT ABILITY AND DEPTH

Since many small businesses can be started by almost anyone who has the initial capital, numerous small firms are owned and operated by individuals lacking the necessary education, training, and personality needed for business success.

Running a small business means becoming somewhat of an expert in many fields—such as advertising, accounting, purchasing, personnel, and selling. In a very small business the owner will have to help out at the worker level. In a very large firm top management would have a staff of experts to perform these diverse activities. The owner of a small business may end up being a "jack of all trades and master of none." There is a common temptation to emphasize those activities that the owner feels most comfortable doing, whether this is selling or solving production problems in the shop, at the expense of the other necessary functions—especially the management function.

The small business has another unique problem related to management succession. If the original owner retires or dies, the management of the business is frequently taken over by the heirs. It is not unusual to find the heirs lacking in the qualifications needed to operate the business. This problem is not as likely to occur in a large firm where there is depth of management and development programs that are intended to fill projected vacancies in the organization.

DIFFICULTY IN OBTAINING AND KEEPING PERSONNEL

Many Americans prefer working for a large corporation which offers higher wages, more fringe benefits, and more job security than most small firms do. This means that the small business is sometimes at a disadvantage when it comes to securing competent employees. One small manufacturer, Atlanta Stove Works, Inc., reports that up to 40 percent of its labor force turns over *several* times a year.[6] Also, since opportunities for promotion are relatively limited in the smaller firm, college graduates and other qualified personnel are likely to become dissatisfied unless they see some clear promise of growth and development for themselves.

Recruiting, training, and keeping qualified employees is a problem for all firms, large or small. It becomes even more critical in the small firm where the owner lacks expertise or fails to see the significance of running a sound personnel program.

"But dear, suppose you did flunk the aptitude test . . . you own the company."

Some Small Businesses Have Difficulty in Hiring Competent Employees

SOURCE: Reproduced by permission of the Masters Agency.

Many Small Businesses Don't Make It!

A study of 81 new small businesses found that only 41 survived for two years. Four failed in the first few weeks. Eighteen lasted for 18 months, and another 18 survived for 21 months. Of the 41 survivors; 12 were classi-fied as marginal survivors, 21 as limited successes, 5 as potentially profit-able firms, and only 3 as profitable enterprises.

Source: The First Two Years: Problems of Small Firm Survival and Growth (Small Business Administration, 1961). Reported in *Strengthening Small Business Management* (selection from the paper of L.T. White), Joseph C. Schabacker, ed. (Small Business Administration, 1971), p. 36.

Franchising Opportunities in Small Business

To many people, franchising is one of the last frontiers for the in-dependent businessperson. To its critics, it is a gimmick to separate small businesspersons from their life savings—and worse. But it cannot be denied that franchising is one of the most rapidly growing business arrangements today, and it does offer an opportunity for individuals with limited funds and experience to own and operate their own businesses.

Statistics illustrate both the significant size and rapid growth of franchising. The Bureau of Domestic Commerce reveals that franchised businesses now account for almost one-third of all retail sales.

WHAT IS FRANCHISING? To the customer, the locally-owned and operated business run under a franchise agreement would appear to be part of a large chain. In many cases each local business operating under the franchise agreement has an identical store front, trademark, equipment, and standardized services, products, and business procedures.

It is not easy to define what a franchise is because the term is used to describe widely differing business agreements. In general a **franchise** is *a legal agreement by which a* **franchisee** *(or dealer) agrees to conduct a business in accordance with certain methods and terms specified by the* **franchisor** *(parent company).* Companies engaged in franchising give the dealer the right to use its name and product or service. Franchisors frequently add their own merchandising techniques and management counseling. In return, the franchisor gets a fee for the use of the franchise name (McDonald's charges $60,000), and receives a royalty or other form of payment for the duration of the relationship.

A franchise may simply be a contract to sell a product, method, or service within a geographical area with some nominal payment involved. Most franchise agreements, however, emphasize a continuing relationship between the parent company, or franchisor, and the individual owner, or franchisee. Under the continuing relationship concept, the franchisee is actually an independent businessperson who contracts for a "package" business.[7]

The package may include such services as:

1. location analysis and assistance
2. store development aid, including lease negotiation
3. store design and equipment purchasing
4. initial employee and management training
5. continued management consultation
6. advertising and merchandising assistance
7. standardized operating procedures
8. financial assistance in the establishment of the business.

SCOPE OF FRANCHISING Franchising has been around for a long time. As far back as 1898 the first "independent dealer" was established to sell and service electric and steam automobiles. However, franchising has experienced rapid growth only within the past twenty-five years. Ninety percent of all franchise companies in existence today started after 1954.

Franchise opportunities are now available in every conceivable type of business, including such well-known categories as motels, car rentals, laundry and dry cleaning, auto service and supplies,

Should Tying Contracts in Franchise Agreements Be Prohibited?

Franchise operations, from car rental agencies to fast-food chains, have sprung up in the last decade in the United States at a great rate. The convenience of leasing equipment or of buying ready-cooked foods has a special appeal in both boom and bust economies. Avoiding big investments in money, time, and energy have great attraction for the public and for the franchise owner and operator as well. With a known name and product, national advertising, and training, plus other kinds of backup, franchises have become popular for the potential investor as a way to avoid the corporate life and yet acquire some of the advantages of a sizeable business.

Legislators concerned with how profits are made by a person who acquires a franchise and how the business is regulated by the parent company have taken a close look at franchise contracts. Some franchises include accounting and tax services and the rental or purchase of equipment as part of the deal. But whether or not the purchase of supplies used to run the franchise is tied to the parent company has caused some serious questions to be raised.

In some cases buying supplies from the parent company results in premium prices for the products. The parent company may then be making a profit on such sales in addition to taking a percentage of the earnings as part of the franchise agreement. Certainly, required buying of this kind takes away the power of the dealer to make decisions.

Some people, including federal law enforcement agencies, see such purchase requirements as representing restraints on trade, unless the dealer is selling a product made from a special formula (for example, soft ice cream). Recently the courts have limited the rights of companies to supply franchise dealers exclusively.

Yet, if centralized purchasing and billing allows the parent company to pass lower prices on to its dealers, requirements for such purchases make sense, since savings do occur. Even if the parent company is making a profit from these purchases, the savings to the dealer may still be substantial. Centralized purchasing can also help to maintain quality control of the product.

The question of whether or not a dealer should be allowed to carry competing products or offer services and goods other than those authorized by the parent company has not yet been settled by law.

fast foods, and specialty eating places, of which there are hundreds of different systems.

Franchises are also offered in somewhat less well-known types of small businesses—petshops, duplicating services, diet programs, and art galleries, for example. Newer franchise opportunities include everything from campgrounds to mobile dog-grooming centers. Nearly 500,000 businesses now operate under a franchised system.

Fast Food Franchises Go International

A U.S. Agriculture Department study predicts that the leading American fast-food franchises will more than double their outlets overseas by 1979. The study forecasts that foreign fast food sales will soon exceed $2 billion annually, compared to a $9 billion domestic market. Japan is expected to be the main target for the expansion of American fast-food franchises. Japan is followed by Australia, Europe, and Canada.*

WARNING: Not all overseas fast-food franchises succeed. All of the eleven Kentucky Fried Chicken outlets opened in Hong Kong failed within two years. "Finger-licking good" chicken didn't make sense to fastidious Hong Kong residents, who often have hot towels with their meals in order to clean their hands.†

*Bernard Brenner. "Fast-food Boom Abroad," The Detroit News (March 10, 1975), p. 9-A.
†Kentucky Fried Chicken's failure in Hong Kong was reported in "Colonel's Chicken Flops in Hong Kong," an AFP wire story; and in International Newsletter (May 5, 1975).

FRANCHISING AND THE SMALL BUSINESSPERSON   It is estimated that if franchising did not exist, 52 percent of the franchisees would not otherwise be self-employed.[8] These people would be working for someone else rather than owning their own small businesses. The history of franchising is full of individuals who gave up their jobs and became successful small businesspersons. Richard Cooper, age twenty-nine, hit a pedestrian with his bike in New York's Central Park. The pedestrian turned out to be a lawyer for Weight Watchers International. Cooper and the lawyer became friends, and Cooper eventually gave up his job and bought Weight Watchers' Chicago franchise. Cooper was worth $10 million by the time he was thirty-four.[9]

A number of newly franchised businesspeople lack the expertise and experience to properly evaluate the franchise agreements which govern their business ventures. As a result, many small businesspeople become discontented and leave franchising. As might also be expected in any rapidly expanding field, several companies have failed. Broadway Joe's, Minnie Pearl's, and Dizzy Dean's Beef and Burger are all examples of franchise organizations that have failed.

Franchising is not a "get rich quick" deal, and it does not guarantee success or big profits with little effort. As in any type of business venture, the return on owning a "good franchise" is related directly to the amount of time and money the small businessperson invests.[10]

Problems Facing the Small Business

All businesses, large or small, involve some risk. Small businesses, however, have a much greater risk than do large ones. Over 73 percent of the businesses failing in 1972 had less than $100,000 in liabilities. Furthermore, over 30 percent of the businesses had less than $25,000 in debts.[11]

Each year about 450,000 to 500,000 new businesses (almost all small) are started. Over half of the new small businesses are retail operations of some type, including restaurants. Unfortunately, the very conditions that make it easy for someone to go into business also make overcrowding inevitable in most industries, and only the firms with a good product or service and the necessary management skills can survive. Every day 1,100 new small businesses open, but 1,000 small businesspersons close their doors permanently.[12]

The chances for success in a small business varies by industry and by the lines of business within an industry. For example, retailing, which has a high proportion of small businesses, always has a high failure rate. But there is a great deal of variability among the lines of business within retailing. One study showed that women's ready-to-wear and cameras and photographic supplies stores had higher failure rates than did shoe stores.[13]

SPECIAL PROBLEMS OF THE MINORITY-OWNED BUSINESS

The U.S. Census shows that minority groups in the United States comprise about 17 percent of the total population. Minorities, however, own only about 4 percent of the nation's businesses. Of the total number of businesses owned by minority groups, about half are black-owned, about a third are owned by Spanish-speaking minorities, and the remainder are owned by other minorities. The failure rate is higher for minority-owned small businesses than for white-owned businesses.

In most respects the problems of minority-owned businesses are the same as those of white-owned businesses. However, there are some problems that are unique to minorities, and others that are unique to black minorities. For example, because of the overall lower incomes of minority groups, fewer minority families are able to get the necessary funds to purchase or start anything other than a small marginal business. Many have difficulty in securing funds from lending sources. Many minority individuals, particularly blacks and American Indians, lack business or managerial experience. Minority individuals sometimes have a negative attitude toward business and seldom view it as the means of achieving community status and economic betterment.

In an effort to overcome some of the problems facing minority-owned small businesses, a number of private and public programs have come into existence. While it is beyond the scope of this book to discuss all of these efforts to increase minority participation in the economy, two government programs deserve mention.

The **Small Business Adminstration (SBA)** has provided *financial assistance to minority-owned businesses through various loan and funding programs.* Technical and management assistance programs have also been made available through the SBA. The **Office of Minority Business Enterprise (OMBE)** under the Department of Commerce also provides help to minority businesses. OMBE gives *assistance such as business research, technical help for contractors, and management development programs to minority businesses.*

OVERCOMING THE PROBLEMS OF SMALL BUSINESS

Having seen the scope of small business, discussed its strengths and weaknesses, and considered some of its problems, it is possible to develop some ideas for overcoming these problems and weaknesses. Every small businessperson must realize that hard work alone is no guarantee of success, nor can it make up for a lack of training and experience as a business manager. In addition, the person starting a business can prevent failure by avoiding the following common pitfalls of new ventures:

The Common Pitfalls of New Businesses

1. starting with inadequate capital
2. choosing a poor location
3. putting too much into fixed assets
4. failing to plan and formulate goals
5. keeping inadequate financial records
6. failing to follow modern management practices.[14]

The successful small business is likely to be one which is based on a good product or service that is available in the necessary volume at a low enough cost so that, after adding a profit, it can be competitively priced. There must also be a big enough market to allow the necessary sales volume to be reached. If all this is true, the small business has a good chance of success and of taking its place as part of the economy of the United States.

Summary

Owning and operating one's own business is still part of the business heritage of the United States. Small businesses were operating successfully in the United States long before the Declaration of Independence was signed, and are still considered to be the backbone of the business system.

There are some 8 million independently-owned and operated firms out of a total number of 8.4 million businesses in the United States. In most industries 90 percent of the firms employ less than one hundred people. While small businesses are found everywhere in the economy, they are distributed disproportionately throughout various industries. They are abundant in those industries where initial capital requirements are low, managerial experience is not so important, the market is of a localized nature, and technological requirements are minimal. The retailing and service industries have the largest share of all small firms.

A small business is not merely a miniature version of a large firm. On the contrary, the small business is quite distinct from the large firm. Some of the advantages, or strengths, of the small firm are management flexibility, sensitivity to local needs, and lower operating costs. At the same time, small firms have certain disadvantages. Three of the more common ones discussed in the chapter are related to problems of financing, lack of management ability and/or depth, and staffing problems.

Franchising is often cited as one of the last opportunities for the individual desiring to own a small business. A franchise is a legal agreement by which a franchisee (or dealer) agrees to conduct a business in accordance with certain methods and terms specified by the franchisor (parent company). Most franchise agreements emphasize a continuing relationship between the franchisor and the local business, and provide for a package of services. Ninety percent of all franchise companies in existence today started after 1954. Franchise opportunities are now available in nearly every type of business. But franchising is not a "get rich quick" deal, and it does not guarantee success or high profits.

All businesses are risky. But small businesses have a much greater risk than do large ones. This chapter examined some of the problems facing the small business. Special reference was made to some unique problems facing minority-owned businesses. The chapter concluded with some practical suggestions for overcoming the problems of small businesses.

Review questions

1. Identify the following terms:
   a. small business
   b. franchise
   c. franchisee
   d. franchisor
   e. minority-owned businesses
   f. SBA
   g. OMBE
2. Identify the various definitions of small business discussed in this chapter.
3. In what sectors of the economy is small business most important? To what do you credit its strength in these areas?
4. Does the existence of giant corporations make it difficult for small businesses to get started and succeed?
5. Identify the strengths of small businesses.
6. Identify the weaknesses of small business.

7. Outline the role of franchising in our economy.
8. Why are the problems of small businesses different from those of big business?
9. Describe the special problems of the minority-owned business.
10. List the common pitfalls of new businesses.

Discussion questions and exercises

1. Evaluate the pro and con arguments to the controversial issue that appears in this chapter.
2. It has been said that the small business, by defending itself against failure, can insure its own success. In what ways do you agree or disagree?
3. Contact some small businesses in your area. Make up a list of specific problems they face. Are any of these common problems?
4. Visit the owner of one or more local franchise businesses. Ask these people why they decided to buy a franchise rather than start a business of their own. Find out what problems (if any) they are having with their franchises.
5. Prepare a two-page report on the services available from the Small Business Administration and from the Office of Minority Business Enterprise.

Case 22-1
The Birth of Holiday Inn

In 1951 [Charles Kemmons] Wilson packed his family into a car and drove to Washington, D.C., for what turned out to be a fateful vacation. The family stayed in motels, but all were costly, cramped and uncomfortable. Wilson sensed a need for decent accommodations for the growing number of motorists and says that "as soon as I got back to Memphis, I decided to build a motel that had all the things we missed." The draftsman who designed it, Eddie Bluestein, scrawled a title across the bottom of the plans: Holiday Inns. He got the name from an old Bing Crosby movie that he had seen the night before.

Wilson borrowed $300,000 from a bank, and in 1952 the first Holiday Inn opened on Summer Avenue, one of the main approach roads to Memphis. Business was so strong that within 20 months he built three almost identical inns on other roads leading into the city. "You just had to go by a Holiday Inn to get into Memphis," he says.

Questions

1. If you had faced this decision in 1951, do you think you would have made the same decision Wilson did? Why, or why not?
2. Why do you think Holiday Inn has proved to be such a successful franchise?
3. Can you identify any new possibilities or areas where franchises might be successful today?

Source: "Rapid Rise of the Host with the Most," *Time* (June 12, 1972), p. 79. Reprinted by permission from *Time,* The Weekly News magazine; © Time Inc.

Case 22-2
Small Business's Profitability

Small businesses are not always successful enterprises. Many fail, with only three out of ten remaining in operation for more than a year. Profits are also low. Ninety-eight percent of all businesses are small- or medium-sized firms. Yet these businesses generate less than 28 percent of the total profits earned by U.S. companies.

Questions

1. Why do small businesses earn such a small proportion of the total profits of industry in the United States?
2. What can be done to help small businesses be more successful?
3. Who should be responsible for helping small business? Government? Large corporations? Small businesspersons themselves? Explain your answer.

Source: Michael L. Johnson. "Small Businessmen: More Rags than Riches," *Industry Week* (July 29, 1974), p. 36.

23

Chicago Tribune
THE WORLD'S GREATEST NEWSPAPER

~ Thursday, November 21, 1974

Morning **Final** Sports
★★★★

9 Sections   15¢

Justice Dept. moves to break up A.T.&T.

Biggest trust case in history

By Bill Neikirk

Chicago Tribune Press Service

WASHINGTON — Undertaking the biggest antitrust case in its history, the Justice Department asked the federal courts Wednesday to break up the American Telephone & Telegraph Co., the world's largest privately owned corporation.

The government filed a 15-page civil complaint in Federal District Court here accusing the giant firm of monopolizing telecommunications service and equipment in the United States.

Specifically, the Justice Department asked the court to require A.T.&T. to divest itself of Western Electric Co. Inc., its wholly owned subsidiary that manufactures the telephones and all communications equipment used in the nationwide Bell Telephone System.

WESTERN ELECTRIC is one of the largest U.S. corporations, with sales of more than $7 billion last year, the department noted. A.T.&T. has assets of more than $67 billion.

In addition, the suit sought

AP Wirephoto

John DeButts, chairman of A.T.&T.:

"Our obligation to the public as well as to our investors and employes requires us to do all we can to see that that [the break-up] doesn't happen. And we are confident that, when the consequences are made plain, it won't."

William Saxbe, attorney general of the United States:

"I am fully aware of the service that the Bell System has provided. Nevertheless, I believe the law must be enforced. We have carefully considered the possible impact of this litigation and the requested relief."

Main target of suit
Western Electric's biggest plant here

Business and Our Legal System

"Anyone who sells butter containing stones or other things (to add to the weight) will be put into our pillory, then said butter will be placed on his head until entirely melted by the sun. Dogs may lick him and people offend him with whatever defamatory epithets they please without offense to God or King. If the sun is not warm enough, the accused will be exposed in the great hall of the gaol in front of a roaring fire, where everyone will see him."

—Edict of Louis XI, King of France
A.D. 1481

What Chapter 23 Is All About

1. In this chapter you will learn the meaning of law and the nature of business law.
2. The structure of the judicial system will be explained in this chapter.
3. You will learn what the major aspects of business law are.
4. You will learn how competition is regulated in the United States.
5. Key federal business regulations will be explained.
6. After reading this chapter, you will gain a basic understanding of these terms:

law
common law
statutory law
business law
judiciary system
trial courts
appellate court
appellant
administrative agency
contract
consideration
capacity
Uniform Commercial Code (UCC)
property
tangible personal property
intangible personal property
real property
agent
principal
tort
negligence
products liability
bankruptcy

Chandler Act (1938)
negotiable instrument
endorsement
patents
trademarks
copyrights
Sherman Anti-Trust Act (1890)
Clayton Act (1914)
tying contract
interlocking directorates
Robinson-Patman Act (1936)
Celler-Kefauver Act (1950)
Federal Trade Commission
  Act (1914)
Pure Food and Drug Act (1906)
Wheeler-Lea Act (1938)
Fair Packaging and Labeling
  Act (1967)
Consumer Credit Protection
  Act (1968)
Fair Credit Reporting Act (1970)
Environmental Protection
  Act (1970)

John Sherman

While his brother, General William Tecumseh Sherman, was marching through Georgia, John Sherman was acting as chairman of the Senate Finance Committee in the North and was helping to develop the financial measures that were adopted during the Civil War and the Reconstruction period.

Born in Lancaster, Ohio, in 1823, Sherman studied law and was admitted to the bar when he was twenty-one years old after having dropped out of school at fourteen. A delegate to the Whig national convention on two occasions, Sherman was elected to Congress in 1854. A year later he helped to organize the Ohio Republican party, and six years later he was elected to the Senate. As a Senator he took a moderate position on Reconstruction, and, after earlier opposition, voted to impeach President Andrew Johnson.

He had a great influence on the fiscal policy of the United States, and it was increased further when President Rutherford B. Hayes appointed him Secretary of the Treasury in 1877, after he had acted as Hayes' campaign manager. In 1881 Sherman was re-elected to the Senate, where he served for the next sixteen years.

As the sponsor of the Sherman Anti-Trust Act in 1890, the Senator's name gave the bill prestige, although he only helped to draft it and was not the main author. In that same year Sherman also worked on the Sherman Silver Purchase Act, which regulated the purchase of silver and the issuance of Treasury notes based on the metal. Because he never fully supported the act, Sherman voted for its repeal three years later.

Named Secretary of State by President William McKinley in 1897, Sherman served in the post about a year. He died at the turn of the century, having been one of the most influential political figures on U.S. fiscal policy during his lifetime.

Businesses must operate within the legal system of federal, state, and local governments in the United States. Executives are not expected to be attorneys, but they should be aware of the various legal requirements that affect their management decision making. Business law is playing an increasingly important role in the free enterprise system.

What Is Law?

Law can be defined as *rules and regulations set by government and society either in the form of legislation or customs.* Laws are enforced through a judicial system. It consists not only of legislation and legal decisions but also arises from state and federal constitutions that originally established the forms of government. In a broad sense law is any rule or custom which if not followed and obeyed by citizens will subject them to legal consequences and sanctions.

This broad body of principles, regulations, rules, and customs that governs and effects control over the actions of all citizens, including business, is derived from several sources. **Common law** is that *system of unwritten law based on custom or court decisions that developed in early England and was adopted in North America.* Today, the term common law refers to the body of law arising out of judicial decisions interpreting, affirming, and enforcing this unwritten law inherited from England.

While common law still plays an important role in the legal system, the primary source of law in modern society is the statutory enactments of the fifty state legislatures of the United States, as well as the statutory laws passed by Congress. The **statutory law,** or written law, *includes state and federal constitutions; legislative enactments; treaties of the federal government; and ordinances of towns, cities, and other local governments.* More and more law is passing from unwritten, or common law, into the category of statutory or "codified" law, as legislative bodies enact new codes in most areas of legal and governmental concern.

Statutory law should not be regarded as a body of fixed and unchanging rules and regulations. While statutes must be drawn in a precise and reasonable manner to be constitutional and thus enforceable, the courts are frequently called upon to interpret the intention and meaning of language in the statutes. These rulings result in the statutory law being expanded, contracted, modified, or even nullified altogether.

Law also changes as the nation and society change. No system of law, either written or unwritten, is rigid. Law reflects the beliefs of the people it regulates, and both the courts and the legislatures of the nation reflect this fact. Laws are constantly being added, repealed, or modified as the requirements of society and government dictate.

The Nature of Business Law

In a broad sense all law is business law because all business entities—whether organized as corporations, partnerships, or proprietorships—are subject generally to the entire body of law in the same manner as all other citizens are subject to it. But in a narrower and more usual sense, **business law** consists of *those branches or areas of law which most directly and specifically influence and regulate the planning and carrying out of various types of business activity.* The term business law includes all law which is of concern to business. The particular areas of legal emphasis will vary widely from business to business and from industry to industry. Laws affecting small proprietorships are different from those governing large corporations. The legal interests of the automobile industry will differ from those of real-estate developers.

The thrust of some laws, such as the Internal Revenue Code or the National Labor Relations Act, are national and universal in scope. These are laws written by Congress. Numerous federal laws exist which regulate only one industry, such as oil and gas drilling or television communications. State and local laws have the same characteristics in this regard as do federal laws. Some state statutes effectively regulate all business conduct in a state, regardless of the size or nature of the enterprise. Workers' Compensation law governing payments to workers for injuries incurred on the job is an example. Other state statutes narrowly control only certain businesses or business activities, such as the so-called "Blue laws" which regulate the extent to which business—particularly retailers—can operate on Sundays.

The importance of law in all aspects of business is evident. No owner, manager, or employee can conduct any type of business activity without reference to law in some regard. All business decisions must be made with this legality in mind. Some decisions will involve in-depth legal planning and review; while other, more routine, business decisions take place with only implied or subconscious reference to the law. Business decision makers build up and gain experience and expertise in applying legal considerations to their decisions and activity in much the same manner as any other business management skill is developed—through constant use and refinement. When legality cannot be determined through the experience and judgment of the businessperson, other professionals—such as lawyers, government employees, and elected officials—must be consulted. The more complex the business objective, the more complex the role of law will be in most instances.

The Judicial System

The branch of government charged with the responsibility and authority to hear controversies between parties and to apply the body of law to these disputes in order to reach an enforceable decision is our **judiciary,** or court, **system.** This judiciary system is comprised of several types and tiers of courts, each with specific jurisdiction, depending on the size and nature of the matter to be resolved. Court systems are organized at the federal, state, and local levels. There is also a large group of administrative agencies operating at various levels of government. Administrative agencies often have some limited judicial functions, although they are more properly regarded as belonging to the executive or legislative branches of government.

"LAST WEEK I'M RUNNING AN ELECTRONICS PLANT IN OHIO — TODAY I'M A HOLY MAN IN KASHMIR. WHAT WON'T MY TAX LAWYER THINK OF NEXT?"

Legal Advice Is Essential in Many Aspects of Business

SOURCE: Reproduced by permission of Sidney Harris.

TRIAL COURTS   At both the federal and state levels there are courts known as courts of general jurisdiction that hear a wide range of cases. Unless a legal matter is relegated by law to another court, or to an administrative agency, the court of general jurisdiction is empowered to hear it. The majority of legal cases, including criminal and civil matters, are heard by these courts. Within the federal system these courts are known as the *United States District Courts,* and there is at least one such court in each state. In the state court systems the general jurisdiction courts are known as *circuit courts,* with one to each county in most states. Some states call these general courts by other names, such as *superior courts* or *common pleas courts.*

The state judiciary systems also have a wide range of courts of lesser or specific jurisdiction. These courts hear only a certain size or type of case as set forth by statute or constitution. In most states these courts are inferior to the circuit or general trial courts in the sense that appeals of decisions in these lesser courts must go to the general jurisdiction courts for resolution. Examples of such lesser courts are *probate courts,* for settling a deceased person's estate, and *small claims courts,* where people can represent themselves in suits over small damage claims. Only specific matters are heard in these courts, and their jurisdiction is limited.

APPELLATE COURTS

Both the federal and state systems have a network of **appellate courts** that hear appeals from the general trial court level. These *appeals usually take place when the losing party in the general court feels that the case has been wrongly decided by the judge and/or jury.* A Swiss attorney filed an appeal with that nation's Supreme Court to annul a decision of a lower court because one of the judges fell asleep during the hearing.[1]

The appeal process allows a higher court to review the case and correct any lower court error complained of by *the party making the appeal,* known as the **appellant.** The federal appeals system, together with that of most states, consists of two tiers of courts. The federal intermediate level of appellate courts is called the *U.S. Circuit Courts of Appeal,* and each such federal court of appeal hears cases from the U.S. District Courts of several states. The intermediate level of state appellate courts—if it exists—is known as the *Court of Appeals* or *District Court of Appeals* in most states.

Appeals from the federal intermediate appellate court level may go to the highest court of the land, the *U.S. Supreme Court.* The highest court in each state, usually called the *State Supreme Court,* hears appeals from the state courts of appeal. In states without such courts the State Supreme Court hears appeals directly from the trial courts. Parties not satisfied by the verdict of a State Supreme Court may appeal further to the U.S. Supreme Court, if grounds for such an appeal exist and if the U.S. Supreme Court considers the case significant enough to be heard.

While the great majority of cases are resolved by the system of courts just outlined, there are certain highly specialized cases that require the expertise of special courts. Such cases are consigned to special courts by constitutional provision or statute. Examples of such courts in the federal system are the *U.S. Tax Court* (for hearing tax cases) and the *U.S. Court of Claims* (for hearing claims against the U.S. government itself). Similar specialized courts exist in many of the state judicial systems.

ADMINISTRATIVE AGENCIES

Administrative agencies—also known as bureaus, commissions, or boards—are organized at all levels of government. Their powers and responsibilities are sometimes derived from constitutional provi-

"I'm pleased that you've reached a unanimous verdict, but I'm wondering what became of the twelfth juror?"

Our Court System Relies on the Unanimous Judgement of a Selected Group of Citizens

SOURCE: "Off the Record," by Ed Reed, reprinted courtesy Register and Tribune Syndicate.

sions, but usually come from state or federal statutes. They are *empowered to hear and decide a broad range of legal questions.* These agencies conduct hearings or inquiries rather than trials; but the parties are often represented by attorneys, evidence and testimony are given, and regulations are applied by the administrative agency in reaching its legally binding decision.

Examples of federal administrative agencies with far-reaching powers are the Federal Trade Commission, the National Labor Relations Board, and the Federal Power Commission. Examples at the state level would include state power or public utility commissions, boards which govern the licensing of various trades and professions, and other state regulatory bodies. At the local level there are zoning boards, planning commissions, boards of appeal, and other administrative agencies concerned with such matters at the city or county level.

The decisions of most administrative agencies can be appealed to the courts of general jurisdiction or to other specified appellate courts. Many businesses have regular contact with federal, state, and local administrative agencies, even though they have little contact with the regular court system.

Important Aspects of Business Law

Most legal areas affect business, like all citizens, in some manner—either directly or indirectly. But certain specific legal subjects are so vital to business enterprise that every businessperson should understand their roles in the legal framework.

LAW OF CONTRACTS
The law of contracts is an important aspect of business law due to its overall effect on most aspects of business operation. Contract law is the legal foundation upon which the normal course of business dealings is constructed.

A **contract** is defined as *an agreement between two or more parties to do, or not to do, a particular thing.* The key element is that there must be an agreement between the parties as to the act or thing specified. In order for such an agreement, or contract, to be valid and enforceable through the courts, there are other required elements. There must be consideration furnished by each party to the contract. **Consideration** is *the value or promise or other benefit that a party provides to the other party or parties to the contract.* There is legal consideration for a contract when *A* agrees to work for *B* and *B* agrees to pay *A* a certain salary. The contract is just as valid if *B* actually pays *A* for the work at the time *A* agrees to work, rather than *B* merely agreeing to pay at that time. Similarly, there is valid consideration even if no promises are exchanged, but *A* merely works for *B* and *B* merely pays *A* for the work.

In addition to consideration, there must be a *legal and serious subject matter* if the contract is to be enforceable. Agreements made in jest or agreements relating to purely social or frivolous matters, or pertaining to the commission of crimes or other acts against public policy, are not enforceable as legal contracts. An agreement between two competitors to fix the prices for their products would not be enforceable as a contract because of the illegal subject matter and because the performance of such an agreement would constitute a crime.

The last element of a legally enforceable contract has to do with the parties themselves. Each party to a contract must have the capacity to make the contract. **Capacity** relates to *the legal and mental qualifications of the party to enter into agreements.* The law will not permit certain persons, such as those judged to be mentally unstable, to enter into legally enforceable contracts.

Contracts arise in almost all types of business transactions and dealings. The great majority of these contracts are created and carried out by the enterprise without special effort or difficulty on the part of either of the contracting parties. Much of this success can be attributed to the consciousness of contract law and its implications in business. Activities giving rise to legal contracts would include:

1. agreements with employees regarding employment and compensation
2. agreements with suppliers and vendors regarding purchases of · raw materials or supplies
3. agreements with customers regarding sales of products and/or services
4. agreements with labor unions regarding employees
5. agreements with government units regarding regulated activities
6. agreements with insurance carriers regarding insurance coverage of all types
7. agreements with advertising media or channels of distribution regarding promotion and/or marketing of products and services.

LAW OF SALES   The **law of sales** is in reality an offspring of the law of contracts. But a sales agreement, or sales transaction, is a special kind of contract and is one which takes place at all levels of the economic system millions of times each day. The law of sales is applicable to *the sale of goods or products for money or on credit.* Sales, as an economic transaction, can involve the sale of services or real estate, as well as goods, but the law of sales is only concerned with the *transfer of tangible personal property.* The law of intangible personal property and of real estate will be examined in a later section.

    The parties to business sales are concerned not only with the entire body of general contract law but also with the specifics of sales law. In fact, sales law has evolved in a separate manner, going back to the ancient English law consisting largely of the customs of merchants and including a system of merchant courts to resolve disputes. Many of these commercial legal customs and practices came to the United States as part of the common law. U.S. business found that growing industrialization and commercial development brought with it a need for predictability and uniformity in commercial law generally, and especially in the law of sales.

    The **Uniform Commercial Code (UCC),** originally drafted in 1952, *is a comprehensive commercial law that has been adopted in all states except Louisiana. The UCC covers the law of sales as well as other specific areas of commercial law.*

    The law of sales in Article Two of the UCC specifies when a contract of sales has been entered into by seller and buyer. Ordinarily such an agreement is based upon the express conduct of the parties and is usually in writing. Under the UCC enforceable sales contracts must generally be in writing if goods over $500 in value are involved. The formation of the sales contract is quite flexible, in the sense that certain missing terms in the written contract, or other ambiguities, will not prevent it from being legally enforceable. A court will look to past dealings, commercial customs, and other standards of reasonableness in evaluating the existence of a legal contract.

Such variables will also be considered by a court when either the buyer or seller is seeking to discover and enforce his or her rights against the other party if a sales contract has not been performed, has been only partially performed, or where performance or the goods has been defective or unsatisfactory. The UCC provides remedies in such cases, consisting largely of money damages for the injured party. Rights of the parties to have the contract specifically performed, to have the contract terminated, to reclaim the goods or have a lien against them are also defined precisely.

Article Two sets forth the law of warranty for the sales transaction. There are two basic types of warranties. Express warranties are specific representations made by the seller regarding the goods. Implied warranties are those imposed on the seller by law automatically. Unless such implied warranties are disclaimed by the seller in writing, they automatically arise in favor of the buyer should the goods prove to be defective. Other provisions of the UCC Article Two govern rights regarding acceptance, rejection, and inspection of the goods by the buyer; the rights of the parties during manufacture, shipment, and delivery; and the passing of title to goods and the legal significance of sales documents—such as bills of lading and the placing of the risk of loss in the event of destruction or damage to the goods during manufacture, shipment, or delivery.

Two decades of court interpretation of the UCC provisions have substantially cleared up the inevitable ambiguities and problem areas that exist in any new statutory law. On balance, the UCC has been a step forward in sales law.

LAW OF PROPERTY   The law of property is not only an important part of the free enterprise system but it is also a key feature of our democratic way of life. **Property** refers to *the unrestricted right to possess and use something.* Property rights are guaranteed and protected by our form of government.

Property can be divided into several categories. **Tangible personal property** consists of *physical things such as goods and products.* Every business is concerned with tangible personal property—machines, equipment, supplies, and delivery vehicles.

Intangible personal property is property *most often represented by a document or other instrument in writing,* although it may be as vague and remote as a bookkeeping or computer entry of some type. Certain intangible personal properties are well known to everyone, such as personal checks and money orders. Other types of intangible property are less widespread in use, but are important to the businesses or individuals who own and utilize them. Examples are stocks, bonds, treasury bills and notes, letters of credit, and warehouse receipts. Mortgages are technically intangible personal property.

The other major branch of property law is that of **real property,** or *real estate.* Some real property customs and principles have been formalized in statutes. There is also case law to guide real-property owners in their transactions and conduct. All businesses have some concern with real estate law because of the need to own or occupy the space or building where the enterprise is conducted. The real estate needs of national retail store chains or major manufacturing companies are indeed considerable. Some businesses are created to serve the real estate needs of customers or other businesses. Real estate developers, builders and contractors, architects, real estate brokers, and mortgage companies are concerned with various aspects of real property law.

THE LAW OF AGENCY

The **law of agency** concerns *every relation,* business or otherwise, *where one person acts for or represents another by the authority or consent of the latter person.* The **agent** is *the person who acts for another person. The person the agent acts for* is known as the **principal.** While the agency relationship can arise as simply as one family member acting for and on behalf of another, this legal concept is most closely associated with business agency relationships. This is true because all types of firms conduct business affairs through a broad variety of agents, partners, directors, corporation officers, and sales personnel.

The law of agency governs the principal-agent relationship. This body of law is based on common-law principles, as they were expanded and modified by case decisions in the state and federal courts. Relatively little of agency law has been enacted into statute. This body of law is used to determine when the agency relationship exists between parties. It is important because the principal is generally bound by the actions of the agent.

The legal basis for holding the principal liable for acts of the agent is the Latin maxim of *respondeat superior,* which, loosely translated, means: "let the master answer." In agency law cases the courts must decide the rights and obligations of the various parties. Generally the principal is held liable where there was an agency relationship and the agent had some general authority to do what he or she did—even if the agent went somewhat far afield. An agent is always liable to the principal for any damages caused to the principal in these cases. Principals have no responsibility for the acts of persons who are not agents.

THE LAW OF TORTS

The word **tort** is an old English term that refers to *a private or civil wrong inflicted upon one person by another.* While criminal law is concerned with crimes against the state or society, tort law is concerned with correcting or compensating injured persons who are the victims of noncriminal wrongs. An act, such as assault, may constitute both a crime and a tort, and the wrongdoer may be held liable for both. The law of torts is also closely related in business to the law of agency, because the business entity, or principal, may be held liable for the torts committed by its agents in the course of business dealings. A California couple filed a claim against a Las Vegas hotel when a performing horse fell on their table and caused injuries to them in the midst of a nightclub act.[2]

Many torts, such as an assault, are intentional actions carried out by the wrongdoer. Sometimes the violator will argue that while his or her actions were intentional, the damages caused were not intended. Examples of intentional torts are embezzlement, trespass, slander, libel, and fraud. Business can become involved in tortious behavior through the actions of owners or employees. The retail supermarket clerk who manhandles a suspected shoplifter and holds the suspect in the manager's office for questioning may have committed a tort if his or her conduct against the suspect is excessive or otherwise unjustified. The store owner, under agency law, could be held liable for any damages or injury caused to the suspect.

The other large body of tortious conduct, which is not based upon intentional acts, is **negligence.** This tort is based on *carelessness or reckless disregard where someone has a duty to take due care and where neglect of this duty causes injury to someone else.* Businesses are held liable for the negligence of employees or agents under the principles of agency law. The furniture store delivery truck driver who kills a pedestrian while on a route has created tort liability for the employer, if the accident results from negligence. Similarly, an airline is liable if a plane crashes because of faulty maintenance, pilot error, or other negligence.

A branch of tort law known as **products liability** has been developed by both statutory and case law to hold business liable for its negligence in the design, manufacture, sale, and use of products. If a defectively bottled beverage explodes or shatters thereby injuring a consumer, the company will be held liable for negligence. Some states have extended this theory of tort to cover *all types of injuries caused by products, whether the manufacturer was proven negligent or not.* This legal development is known as **strict products liability.**

Careful supervision of employees and careful conduct by employees in their duties is the best way to avoid most tort liability. However, with tort damages running higher and higher, most firms have turned to liability insurance to protect the business from tort liability.

Even the U.S. Consumer Product Safety Commission has been affected by this area of law. The commission had to recall 80,000 lapel buttons promoting safe toys because of sharp edges, high-level lead content in the paint, and clips that could break off in a child's mouth and be swallowed.[3]

BANKRUPTCY LAW **Bankruptcy** refers to *the inability to meet financial obligations.* In earlier days people who did not pay their bills were thrown into debtor's prisons as punishment. But modern society recognizes that bankruptcies are to be expected in a free-enterprise economy, so provision has been made for an orderly handling of excessive debts. Bankruptcy allows the person or firm to get a fresh start.

The **Chandler Act** (1938) is *federal legislation under which bankruptcies are now handled.* Bankruptcies can be classified as either voluntary or involuntary. A voluntary bankruptcy is where individuals or firms decide they can no longer meet their obligations, so they ask the court to judge them bankrupt. In an involuntary bankruptcy the firm's creditors petition the courts to declare a bankruptcy. Federal district judges decide the validity of bankruptcy petitions. If they agree, the matter is forwarded to a bankruptcy court. The creditors are brought together, and they decide on a trustee who liquidates and then distributes the assets of the bankrupt firm.

The law sets forth the priority of claims against a bankrupt's assets. The ranking of claims is:

1. court expenses
2. employee wages earned prior to the bankruptcy action
3. expenses involved in disposing of the assets
4. tax claims
5. any priority debts set by law.

Any remaining funds are then used for proportionate payments to the bankrupt's creditors.

NEGOTIABLE
INSTRUMENTS Business has a need for certain types of *commercial paper that can be transferred from one person or firm to another.* This form of commercial paper is known as **negotiable instruments.** Checks, the most common form of negotiable instruments, are actually cash substitutes.

Several rules must be followed if an instrument is to be negotiable:

1. The instrument must be in writing and signed.
2. There must be an unconditional promise or order to pay a given amount of money.
3. The instrument has to be payable on demand or at a specified future date.
4. A negotiable instrument must also state that it is payable to order or to bearer.

Checks and other commercial paper are *transferred when the payee signs the back of the instrument*. This transfer process is known as **endorsement** and can be done in four ways:

1. Blank endorsement. The payee simply signs his or her name on the back of the instrument. This makes the check payable to the bearer, so it should only be used when the instrument is being given directly to the next holder.
2. Restrictive endorsement. When banking by mail, it is wise to endorse checks "For Deposit Only." If the check is lost or stolen, it cannot then be cashed, only deposited in your account. This is known as a restrictive endorsement because it limits the negotiability of the check.
3. Qualified endorsement. If you endorse a check received from a third party to someone for payment of a debt, you are still responsible for the debt if the check proves uncollectible from the first payee. To avoid this liability, it is sometimes wise to use "Without Recourse" as part of the endorsement. Such an endorsement limits your liability to the third party.
4. Special endorsement. A check with the notation "Pay to the Order of Ira Siegel (signed) Theodore Sultan" is a special endorsement. This form of endorsement limits the negotiability of the instrument to Ira Siegel.

PATENTS, TRADEMARKS, AND COPYRIGHTS

Patents, trademarks, and copyrights are important legal protection for key business assets. Du Pont's patents, Pabst Brewing's Blue Ribbon, and the copyrights of publishers are some of the major intangible assets possessed by these firms. Patents, trademarks, and copyrights are carefully guarded by their owners.

Patents *guarantee inventors exclusive rights to their inventions for seventeen years, provided the inventions are accepted by the U.S. Patent Office*. Scientists working for a firm are usually required to assign any patents resulting from their work to their employers. Patent owners sometimes license the use of the patent to others for a fee. After seventeen years, patents expire and anyone can use them.

Trademarks (and brand names) are *words, symbols, or other designations used by businesses to identify their products*. The *Lanham Act* (1946) provides for federal registration of trademarks. Registration of a trademark means that the firm will have exclusive rights to it for as long as they desire. However, if a trademark becomes the generic term for a class of products, then the registrant loses this important protection. Aspirin, nylon, kerosene, linoleum, and shredded wheat were once the exclusive properties of their manufacturers, but they became generic terms, and now anyone can use them.

Copyrights are filed with the Library of Congress. They are granted for a twenty-eight-year period and are renewable once. Copyrights can be *used to protect from unauthorized use anything that is written, drawn, designed, or illustrated.* They can offer important safeguards in many areas of commercial activity.

Regulation of Competition

Government, acting through law, influences and regulates business in many ways. One aspect of this process is the government regulation of competition. Effective and continuous competition is the cornerstone of the free-enterprise economy. Americans have generally advocated minimum interference by government with commerce, and the *laissez-faire* doctrine (or "hands off" policy) was in effect during the first one hundred years of the existence of the United States. Laissez faire was ideal for the rapid growth of the nation—geographically, politically, and economically. But as the nation developed and matured, economic abuses and an overconcentration of economic power crept into the free-enterprise system. Monopolization of certain basic industries resulted. Mergers of powerful groups of companies or industries further concentrated economic power and caused additional abuses that led directly to government intervention.

When government regulation of business competition and other commercial activity came about in the late 1800's, it took two broad forms. The first was through the concept of the regulated industry. The second was by enacting statutes concerning competition. In a regulated industry competition is either eliminated altogether or is limited, and close government regulation of the company or industry in question is substituted for the market controls of free competition. Regulated industries have already been mentioned in connection with the body of administrative law and agencies that have been created for this purpose by various governmental units. Examples of such industries include all of the public utilities, as well as other industries which are closely tied to "the public interest." In these industries competition is restricted or eliminated because it tends to become wasteful or excessive. Only one telephone company is permitted to serve a given geographical area or market with its product or services. The large capital investment required to operate an airline route, or to construct a pipeline or electric transmission line over great distances, or to build and operate a nuclear power plant makes this type of regulation economically reasonable. But the lack of competition can sometimes cause deterioration in services and performance.

The second broad form of regulation pursued by government has been the enactment of a series of statutes affecting competition and commercial practices of various kinds. Such statutory laws exist at both the state and federal levels, but the most effective and widespread regulation has resulted from the federal statutes. The first effort to regulate competition by the federal government came with the **Sherman Anti-Trust Act** of 1890. This law was drawn in a broad and general manner. *It prohibits every contract or conspiracy in restraint of trade and declares as illegal any action which monopolizes or attempts to monopolize any part of trade or commerce.* This act is enforced by the antitrust division of the U.S. Department of Justice. Violators are subject not only to criminal fines or imprisonment but also to civil damage suits by competitors or other parties injured by the unlawful acts. In some cases the government will allow the accused enterprise to enter into a **consent order** where *the enterprise agrees voluntarily to cease the conduct the government is alleging to be an antitrust violation.*

Another major federal statute is the **Clayton Act** of 1914, which *forbids trade restraints such as tying contracts, interlocking directorates, and certain anticompetitive stock acquisitions.* A **tying contract** is one where *the seller forces the buyer to purchase a secondary, relatively undesirable product.* The copy machine company that forces buyers to also purchase its paper and supplies is an example. **Interlocking directorates** exist where *companies that are supposedly competitors have identical or overlapping boards of directors.* The acquisition of stock by one company in another is a way of effecting a merger, and this is forbidden of competitors under certain circumstances.

The **Robinson-Patman Act** of 1936 *outlaws price discrimination between purchasers of like quality and quantities of products where such discrimination injures competition or tends to create a monopoly.* Such discrimination in price is allowed where the seller does it in good faith to meet competitive pricing, or where the seller can justify different prices as arising out of the different costs of serving various customers. The **Celler-Kefauver Act** of 1950 amends the Clayton Act by *outlawing monopoly or overconcentration of competitors in an industry by means of a major asset purchase by one competitor of another.*

A major statute is the **Federal Trade Commission Act** of 1914. *This law created the Federal Trade Commission (FTC) as a federal agency and gave it broad powers to prevent business entities of all types and sizes from engaging in unfair methods of competition.* The powers and investigative ability of the FTC have grown rapidly over the years. Today it is a vigorous and aggressive "watchdog" agency of the federal government. It may sue wrongdoing enterprises or persons, or enter into consent orders with alleged violators who agree to cease the questionable practices. The role and authority of the FTC has grown greatly in the modern economy. It is now the major regulatory and enforcement agency in the area of competitive practices.

There is still room for improvement in the regulation of business. Aggressive competition keeps prices down to the lowest level possible, but in some areas competition is not as intense as it might be. The head of the Justice Department's Anti-Trust Division estimates that ineffective competition costs U.S. consumers as much as $80 billion a year.[4]

Other Business Regulations

Hundreds of business law volumes can be found in any legal library. No businessperson can expect (or can be expected) to know all of the federal, state, and local regulations pertaining to business. Management should view the legal profession as partners in these matters. Executives should know the basic legal principles affecting business, but when in doubt, they should consult an attorney.

In addition to the legislation mentioned earlier in this chapter, and elsewhere in *Contemporary Business,* there are some specific federal laws with which the businessperson should be familiar. These include:

1. *Pure Food and Drug Act* (1906), which prohibts the adulteration and misbranding of foods and drugs. The legislation was strengthened by the *Food, Drug, and Cosmetic Act* (1938) and the *Kefauver-Harris* drug amendments (1962) which resulted from the so-called thalidomide babies.
2. *Wheeler-Lea Act* (1938) amends the Federal Trade Commission Act to further outlaw "unfair or deceptive acts or practices" in commerce. This act gives the Federal Trade Commission jurisdiction over false or misleading advertising.
3. *Fair Packaging and Labeling Act* (1967) requires that certain information be disclosed on packages or labels. This information includes product identification, the name and address of the producer or distributor, and quality information.
4. *Consumer Credit Protection Act* (1968), known as the Truth in Lending Act, requires lenders to specify the exact interest charges that a borrower will have to pay. This law affects banks, loan companies, and other sources of consumer credit.
5. *Fair Credit Reporting Act* (1970) allows people to see credit reports prepared about them. The person can also request that incorrect information be changed.
6. *Environmental Protection Act* (1970) set up by the Environmental Protection Agency (EPA) with the authority to deal with various types of pollution.

Many specific state and local regulations are important to businesses operating in various areas. Management must be aware of these laws and their business implications if the firm is to succeed in the competitive marketplace.

Access to Credit Reports

The concept of credit has taken on a new meaning for individuals in the United States. "Plastic money," the credit charge cards carried by so many people, is becoming a new kind of monetary system. It is even conceivable that paper and metal money might go completely out of style in the future, leaving people with a card or number against which all their needs would be charged. With this practice, even check writing could fall victim to a complicated computer system that would transfer funds automatically from a buyer's to a seller's account.

The system of checking business credit through references, ratings, reports, and recommendations is complicated. A firm such as Dun & Bradstreet earns its unique position through careful and reliable issuing of credit information. Other credit agencies also exist, such as local industry councils, which try to make information available to a limited membership.

Should credit reports be readily available to any supplier before credit is extended in order to prevent cheating? And, if so, who or what should make the decisions about giving out credit information, and where should such data be kept?

The seller of raw materials, goods, and services must be paid for the supplies provided to a firm or individual if the economy is to be ongoing. Without credit, many customers would be unable to make purchases or products, which would in turn slow the flow of merchandise or stop it altogether. The same need for credit applies to the original seller. "Cash on delivery" is very risky and physically unmanageable, if the amounts involved are large enough.

Even with a superior credit department in a firm and with outside credit agencies, not all of the information about a customer can be made available. Rumor must be discounted in evaluating a firm's or an individual's debt position, which means that credit information must come from a reliable source.

However, even if it were possible to know a firm's exact financial position at any one time, the gathering of data would be enormously expensive and time consuming. Information from one source, though reliable, might describe a one-time experience or might even have changed the way the firm operates in the present. If this is so, such data can do real harm to the customer and jeopardize a business.

The privacy of the individual and of the firm, so that they can both function, often depends on strategies that can succeed only if these are kept from competitors. Such strategies require that access to credit reports be limited.

Summary

Law can be defined as the rules and regulations set by government and society either in the form of legislation or custom. Business law consists of those branches or areas of law which most directly and specifically influence and regulate the planning and carrying out of various types of business activity. Business law is administered through a series of trial courts, appellate courts, and administrative agencies that exist at all levels of government.

Aspects of business law that are particularly important to executives are the law of contracts, law of sales, Uniform Commercial Code, law of property, law of agency, law of torts, bankruptcy, negotiable instruments, patents, trademarks, and copyrights. All of these are examined in detail in the chapter.

Government and law are also involved in the regulation of our competitive economic system. The Sherman Act, the Clayton Act, the Robinson-Patman Act, the Celler-Kefauver Act, and the Federal Trade Commission Act all have an effect on the regulation of competition.

Chapter 23 concludes with a brief description of other important laws with which the businessperson should be familiar. These include: the Pure Food and Drug Act, the Wheeler-Lea Act, the Fair Packaging and Labeling Act, the Consumer Credit Protection Act, the Fair Credit Reporting Act, and the Environmental Protection Act.

Review questions

1. Identify the following terms:

   a. law
   b. common law
   c. statutory law
   d. business law
   e. judiciary system
   f. trial courts
   g. appellate court
   h. appellant
   i. administrative agency
   j. contract
   k. consideration
   l. capacity
   m. Uniform Commercial Code
   n. property
   o. tangible personal property
   q. real property

   r. agent
   s. principal
   t. tort
   u. negligence
   v. products liability
   w. bankruptcy
   x. Chandler Act
   y. negotiable instrument
   z. endorsement
   aa. patents
   bb. trademarks
   cc. copyrights
   dd. Sherman Anti-Trust Act
   ee. Clayton Act
   ff. tying contract
   gg. interlocking directorates
   hh. Robinson-Patman Act
   ii. Celler-Kefauver Act

jj.	Federal Trade Commission Act	nn. Consumer Credit Protection Act
kk.	Pure Food and Drug Act	oo. Fair Credit Reporting Act
ll.	Wheeler-Lea Act	pp. Environmental Protection Act
mm.	Fair Packaging and Labeling Act	

2. Trace how business law has evolved over the years.
3. Why is an understanding of business law important to business-persons?
4. Describe the organization of the U.S. judicial system.
5. Explain the law of contracts.
6. Discuss the law of sales.
7. Why is the law of property so critical in the free-enterprise system?
8. What is meant by the law of agency?
9. Explain the concept of negotiable instruments.
10. How is competition regulated in the United States?

Discussion questions and exercises

1. Evaluate the pro and con arguments to the controversial issue that appears in this chapter.
2. Set up a classroom debate on the question: "Should attorneys be required to have some training in business administration?"
3. Discuss the following question: "Does business law help or hinder management?"
4. Prepare a two-page report on a legal requirement affecting some aspect of business. Choose a regulation not discussed in this chapter.
5. Ask an attorney to speak to your class concerning a law career and, in particular, a legal practice dealing with business matters.

Case 23-1
Age Discrimination in Business

A 1967 federal law protects against job discrimination toward employees or employment candidates between the ages of forty and sixty-five. This legislation was designed to guard against discrimination in favor of younger, usually lower-paid employees or applicants. There are now hundreds of legal cases being processed that allege age discrimination by business firms. The number of complaints and damage awards has grown steadily. Some of the nation's leading companies have been accused of age discrimination in hiring and retention decisions.

Questions

1. What type of management decisions are affected by this law?
2. Do you agree with the age discrimination law?
3. Can you think of any other situations where businesses have or might discriminate in favor of younger people? What is your evaluation of these situations?

Source: The issue of age discrimination is discussed in "The Courts Interpret Old-age Discrimination," *Business Week* (February 24, 1975), p. 91.

Case 23-2
Warranty Plans for New Homes

Britain has an interesting law requiring homebuilders to guarantee new homes according to a complex 300-page set of standards. A $35–$60 fee for the guarantee is included in the purchase price of the home. The regular warranty coverage is for two years, but buyers are protected against dry rot, roof collapse, foundation flaws, and building materials failure for ten years. Australia, New Zealand, Holland, Canada, South Africa, Spain, and West Germany have introduced, or are considering, similar legislation. The National Association of Home Builders has introduced such a plan in the United States.

Questions

1. What is your reaction to these warranty programs?
2. Can you think of any drawbacks to these plans?
3. Could a warranty program of this nature be used in other industries? Where? How?

Source: Robert Deindorfer. "Repairs are Really on the House," *Parade* (April 21, 1974), pp. 17, 20.

24

The Future of American Business

"The greater thing in this world is not so much where we stand as in what direction we are going."

—Oliver Wendell Holmes

SOURCE: Painting by Folon. Courtesy Armistead Miller Wallace Inc. Collection.

What Chapter 24 Is All About

1. In this chapter you will learn why it is so difficult to predict the future.
2. You will learn about the accelerating pace of change.
3. The current trends affecting business in the United States are explained in this chapter.
4. You will gain an appreciation of the challenges that will confront management in the future.
5. After reading this chapter, you will understand these terms:

population explosion   technology
Third World   automation
life style

His Highness Sheikh
Sabah Al-Salim
Al-Sabah

SOURCE: Embassy of the
State of Kuwait.

Located at the head of the Persian Gulf, Kuwait's land mass is smaller than Vermont or New Hampshire, but most of the land is filled with 20 percent of the world's oil riches. In June of 1961 Kuwait became independent from Great Britain and established a constitutional monarchy. The ruling family is called Al-Sabah, and the present Emir, or ruler, was selected in 1965. As chief of state, the Emir appoints both his cabinet and the prime minister, but a fifty-member National Assembly is elected by males over twenty-one years of age.

Although oil was discovered in Kuwait in 1938, it was not produced in large quantities until after World War II, when Kuwait became the world's second largest oil exporter. Half the profits of the foreign-owned oil companies active in Kuwait are turned over to the Sheik, who has used them, as did the Sheik who reigned before him, for the education and welfare of the people and for modernization and industrialization of the country.

As a member of the ruling family, Sheik Al-Sabah had been active in foreign and domestic affairs before he became Emir. His government has joined the Arab States' boycott of western nations and has supported Egypt against Israel. Although its major export is a single resource, oil, Kuwait has a favorable balance of trade; so much so that startingly large investments in foreign real estate and in foreign companies have been made. Among these are the purchase of a thirty-square-mile island off the coast of South Carolina; the Manhattan Tower in Paris, which is judged to be worth about $100 million; 14 percent of the shares in Daimler-Benz; and the St. Martins Property Corporation, Ltd., an English real-estate firm.

The United States supplied about 13 percent of the goods imported by Kuwait in 1974, second in volume only to Japan. This includes about $100 million in aircraft and armaments.

One thing that most people will agree on is that we all hope for a better future. Some argue that we should return to an earlier era such as the early 1900's, when millions of automobiles did not clog the streets and highways, factories did not belch torrents of smoke into the air, and people lived a simpler carefree life.[1]

But the evidence shows that things were not as good in earlier days as many of us have been led to believe. In fact, the standard of living has risen rapidly over the years. Many items cost a smaller proportion of our earnings today than they did in the "good old days." Table 24-1 shows how long a typical factory worker would have to work today to buy various items as compared with the work hours required fifty years ago.

Table 24-1
The Growth of an
American Worker's
Buying Power

One way to measure change in American living standards over the years is to compare how long a typical factory employe would have to work at different times to buy various goods and services. Here are "worktimes" a half century ago and today, based on prices and after-tax earnings for each period:

To Buy This—	A Worker Would Have to Put in—	
	50 Years Ago	Today
New car	41½ weeks	26½ weeks
Year's cost at state university	31 weeks	15 weeks
Steamship fare, New York to Europe	6 weeks	3 weeks
Rail fare, Washington to Atlanta	1 week	1½ days
Gas range	138 hours	61½ hours
Electric clothes washer	120½ hours	54 hours
Electric sewing machine	101½ hours	22 hours
Vacuum cleaner	59½ hours	13½ hours
Hair dryer	27½ hours	4½ hours
Toaster	8½ hours	3½ hours
Man's shoes	7½ hours	7 hours
Electric coffee percolator	8 hours	5 hours
Lady's wool skirt	6½ hours	3 hours
Man's dress shirt	3 hours	2½ hours
Oranges, dozen	49 minutes	19 minutes
Potatoes, 10 pounds	30 minutes	19 minutes
Coffee, pound	48 minutes	20 minutes
Milk, half-gallon	31 minutes	12 minutes
Butter, pound	57 minutes	15 minutes
Margarine, pound	33 minutes	11 minutes
Eggs, dozen	53 minutes	13 minutes
Bread, pound	10 minutes	6 minutes
Round steak, pound	38 minutes	27 minutes
Chicken, whole, pound	39 minutes	9 minutes

SOURCE: Reprinted from *U.S. News & World Report* (February 10, 1975), p. 30. Based on data supplied by the U.S. Departments of Labor and Health, Education and Welfare and on various industry sources. Copyright 1975 U.S. News & World Report, Inc.

Even during the rapid inflation of the 1970's wages have generally kept pace with rising prices. Admittedly, you have to work 2 hours and 20 minutes longer than you did in 1965 to pay an attorney to make out your will—so you can leave all your hard-earned possessions to a relative. However, this is more than offset by the fact that you now only have to work 336 hours instead of the 408 hours and 10 minutes required ten years ago to pay for your own funeral.[2]

Anyone living in the late 1970's realizes that we have not yet reached utopia. Society in general, and business in particular, faces many problems. While the standard of living has improved, many people argue that the quality of life has not kept pace. These critics say that there is more to life than just acquiring material possessions. Few disagree!

"DO I HAVE TIME TO BOWL A GAME?"

It Is Often Difficult to Predict How Future Events Will Influence Our Lives

SOURCE: Copyright, 1975, Universal Press Syndicate. Reproduced by permission.

The Problem of Prediction

The typical American's impression of earlier times is an excellent illustration of how difficult it is to predict future trends. If society cannot correctly assess what has already happened, how can business management forecast its future direction?

During the 1970's Detroit sadly missed the mark on its forecast of small-car demand. With small-car sales more than 50 percent of the total automobile market, U.S. manufacturers later admitted that their predictions were not adequate. The automobile companies have had to take some drastic actions to get smaller cars on the market. The industry failed to recognize changing consumer tastes. The trend toward smaller cars actually began in the mid-1960's, but received a big push when the oil shortage of the 1970's occurred.[3]

The calculator industry is another example of a situation where some firms had not correctly predicted the future. Bowmar Instrument Corporation, the second largest minicalculator manufacturer in the United States, began bankruptcy proceedings in 1975. The cause—poor forecasting! Bowmar began to increase its production of pocket calculators and enter new markets—such as microwave ovens and digital watches—at the same time that increased competition was driving down the price of calculators.[4] But Bowmar's failure was not unique. Several other calculator producers failed as the prices of some models dropped to less than 50 percent of their previous levels.

All businesspersons are required to predict future conditions for their industries and companies. No one should underestimate the problems involved in this important task.

The Accelerating Pace of Change

Prediction is also difficult because of the accelerated pace of change. Business is no longer able to assume that what happened yesterday or today will be true tomorrow. Alvin Toffler's bestseller, *Future Shock,* pointed out that man's 50,000 years of existence can be divided into 800 lifetimes of about 62 years each. Man spent the first 650 of these lifetimes in caves. Writing has existed for only the last 70 lifetimes. Most of the products used today were developed within the present lifetime.[5]

Things are changing rapidly even within our own lifetimes! Modern management must deal with an endless parade of crisis situations—inflation, shortages, and the rapid growth of technology. Most people agree that change is inevitable, and that its pace is quickening. France's President Giscard d'Estaing has observed:

The world is unhappy. It is unhappy because it doesn't know where it is going and because it senses that if it knew, it would discover that it was heading for disaster. . . . The crisis the world knows today will be a long one. It is not a passing difficulty. It is actually the recognition of permanent change.[6]*

Today's management must be well trained and ready to deal with the accelerating pace of change in contemporary business.

Current Trends Affecting American Business

There are several current trends in society that are influencing business. Effective managers must recognize these trends, determine how they affect their businesses, and develop appropriate strategies for dealing with the changed environment.

POPULATION
CHANGES

At the present growth rate the world's population will be 6.6 billion by the year 2000, compared to its current 4 billion. The so-called **population explosion** is a well-documented fact. There were 250 million people on earth when Christ was born. It took until 1650 to double the planet's population. Another two centuries passed before the population doubled again. The rate of growth has risen rapidly since that time.[7]

The population of **Third World** nations (*those countries that are not politically aligned with either the East or West*) is rising at 2.4 percent annually, primarily because of improvements in health and sanitation and high birth rates. This rate compares with only .9 percent annually in more developed nations.[8]

Population growth—both in the United States and abroad—has always meant expanding markets for business. But this assumes

*Reprinted from "Into a New Era—How Your Life Will Change," U.S. News & World Report (March 3, 1975), p. 34. Copyright 1975 U.S. News & World Report, Inc.

"DIRECTIVES FROM THE GOVERNMENT, MEETINGS WITH THE UNION, DISPUTES WITH SUPPLIERS'—IT'S GETTING MORE AND MORE DIFFICULT TO MAKE BUBBLE GUM THESE DAYS."

Many Factors Influence the Production of Bubble Gum

SOURCE: Reproduced by permission of Sidney Harris and the *Milwaukee Journal.*

that purchasing power will keep pace with the growing population, and this has not always been the case in poorer nations. Several reports have noted that the gap between rich and poor countries has widened in recent years.

Population changes will vary from state to state, and the differences can be a significant factor in business planning. Figure 24-1 shows how each state's population will change.

LIFE STYLE CHANGES

Life style refers to *the way a person lives. It includes work, leisure time, hobbies, interests, and personal philosophy.* A person's life style may be dominated by work, with little time left for social activities. Another person may spend much time and effort in pursuing a hobby, recreational activity, or personal philosophy.

There is little doubt that life styles are changing, and that this

Figure 24-1

How Each State's
Population Will
Change—Projected
Population Change from
1973 to 1990

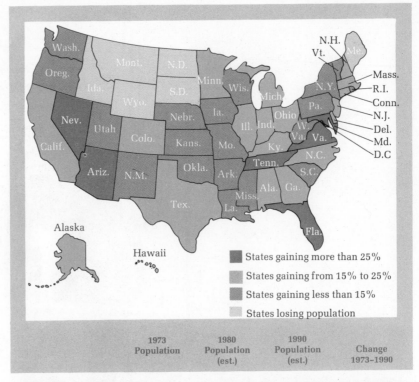

| States gaining more than 25% |
| States gaining from 15% to 25% |
| States gaining less than 15% |
| States losing population |

	1973 Population	1980 Population (est.)	1990 Population (est.)	Change 1973–1990
Alabama	3,539,000	3,747,000	4,090,000	Up 15.6%
Alaska	330,000	333,000	391,000	Up 18.5%
Arizona	2,058,000	2,226,000	2,701,000	Up 31.2%
Arkansas	2,037,000	2,087,000	2,271,000	Up 11.5%
California	20,601,000	22,403,000	24,982,000	Up 21.3%
Colorado	2,437,000	2,586,000	2,890,000	Up 18.6%
Connecticut	3,076,000	3,358,000	3,710,000	Up 20.6%
Delaware	576,000	627,000	707,000	Up 22.7%
D.C.	746,000	750,000	750,000	Up .5%
Florida	7,678,000	8,926,000	10,978,000	Up 43.0%
Georgia	4,786,000	5,147,000	5,907,000	Up 23.4%
Hawaii	832,000	848,000	979,000	Up 17.7%
Idaho	770,000	708,000	738,000	Down 4.2%
Illinois	11,236,000	12,091,000	13,056,000	Up 16.2%
Indiana	5,316,000	5,784,000	6,364,000	Up 19.7%
Iowa	2,904,000	2,913,000	2,993,000	Up 3.1%
Kansas	2,279,000	2,228,000	2,281,000	Up .1%
Kentucky	3,342,000	3,609,000	3,982,000	Up 19.2%
Louisiana	3,764,000	3,744,000	3,937,000	Up 4.6%
Maine	1,028,000	972,000	992,000	Down 3.5%
Maryland	4,070,000	4,473,000	5,275,000	Up 29.6%
Massachusetts	5,818,000	6,267,000	6,876,000	Up 18.2%
Michigan	9,044,000	9,743,000	10,645,000	Up 17.7%
Minnesota	3,897,000	4,119,000	4,553,000	Up 16.8%
Mississippi	2,281,000	2,328,000	2,450,000	Up 7.4%
Missouri	4,757,000	5,071,000	5,439,000	Up 14.3%

	1973 Population	1980 Population (est.)	1990 Population (est.)	Change 1973–1990
Montana	721,000	670,000	665,000	Down 7.8%
Nebraska	1,542,000	1,499,000	1,557,000	Up 1.0%
Nevada	548,000	616,000	761,000	Up 38.9%
New Hampshire	791,000	843,000	919,000	Up 16.2%
New Jersey	7,361,000	8,080,000	8,923,000	Up 21.2%
New Mexico	1,106,000	1,055,000	1,131,000	Up 2.3%
New York	18,265,000	19,352,000	20,946,000	Up 14.7%
North Carolina	5,273,000	5,736,000	6,465,000	Up 22.6%
North Dakota	640,000	579,000	563,000	Down 12.0%
Ohio	10,731,000	11,651,000	12,609,000	Up 17.5%
Oklahoma	2,663,000	2,762,000	2,993,000	Up 12.4%
Oregon	2,225,000	2,335,000	2,537,000	Up 14.0%
Pennsylvania	11,902,000	12,649,000	13,416,000	Up 12.7%
Rhode Island	973,000	1,032,000	1,115,000	Up 14.6%
South Carolina	2,726,000	2,819,000	3,122,000	Up 14.5%
South Dakota	685,000	655,000	648,000	Down 5.4%
Tennessee	4,126,000	4,557,000	5,191,000	Up 25.8%
Texas	11,794,000	12,167,000	13,580,000	Up 15.1%
Utah	1,157,000	1,160,000	1,310,000	Up 13.2%
Vermont	464,000	482,000	519,000	Up 11.9%
Virginia	4,811,000	5,295,000	6,135,000	Up 27.5%
Washington	3,429,000	3,550,000	3,806,000	Up 11.0%
West Virginia	1,794,000	1,832,000	1,845,000	Up 2.8%
Wisconsin	4,569,000	4,737,000	5,013,000	Up 9.7%
Wyoming	353,000	331,000	334,000	Down 5.4%
UNITED STATES	209,851,000	223,532,000	246,039,000	Up 17.2%

Note: Population estimates by U.S. Census Bureau assume birth rates will remain near recent levels.

SOURCE: Reprinted from *U.S. News & World Report* (July 15, 1974), p. 57. Copyright 1974 U.S. News & World Report, Inc.

will have an impact on the way business operates in the years ahead. Several factors are causing life style changes in U.S. society. First, there is more leisure time than ever before. The work week is now less than forty hours, as compared to seventy hours a century ago. Some experts believe the work week will be twenty-five hours or less before the year 2000.[9] Several firms have adopted four-day work weeks with longer hours each day. Others have cut the number of hours worked each week. Reduced work schedules mean increased leisure time for the average American.

Fewer children means smaller families and a different life style. Many young married couples have either decided on a childless marriage, or have postponed childbearing. This trend has forced many businesses to modify their competitive strategies. Gerber Products Company, who used to advertise "Babies are our business—our only business," has had to expand its product lines. New Gerber products include ketchup and single-serving adult foods.[10]

Americans are well-educated and relatively prosperous. These advantages give the freedom to question and examine a way of life. In some cases inquiries of this nature have led to personal life style changes. The youth of the 1970's are more independent, better educated, and perhaps more individualistic than in past generations.

Business is just now beginning to realize how a person's life style can influence their behavior as employees, consumers, and members of modern society. Management would be well advised to monitor life style changes in the future.

ECONOMIC CHANGES

The 1970's have seen sweeping economic changes that will alter the course of U.S. business. Oil boycotts, inflation, unemployment, recession, and energy resource allocation have all had a profound impact on American lives. People are more conscious of how economic factors affect everday life now than they did a decade ago.

Some people are alarmed by the high unemployment and double-digit inflation of the 1970's. Others fear economic domination by Japanese and German firms or the oil-rich Arab states. But statistics show that the United States is still the world's wealthiest nation and an effective competitor in the world marketplace.

Recent economic adjustments show how important it is for a businessperson to thoroughly understand the competitive system. No firm is far removed from the basic economic changes that occur in society. Effective managers must be aware of current economic events that may affect their businesses.

TECHNOLOGICAL CHANGES

Technology can be defined as *the knowledge and scientific procedures, techniques, and equipment that are applicable to industrial situations.* New technology is being introduced at a rate far faster than that of even a decade ago. Technological changes mean that production methods must be updated, employees retrained, and management thinking restructured.

Technological changes require people changes. Today's education will be outdated within ten years after graduation. People can become occupationally obsolete as a result of technological change. Society has begun to emphasize life-long education and training so that people can remain productive for more than a few years.

Some people worry that technology is out of control. Perhaps there are even a few who believe that mortals will someday be the slaves of computers or of "super machines." Most business executives believe that technology has always been (and will continue to be) a way of improving the standard of living and the quality of life. But most executives will also point out that technological improvements will fail to win public support if it results in substantially higher costs. Ford President Lee A. Iacocca puts it this way: "What good is it in 1980 to have the cleanest, safest, least damageable car if no one can afford it?"[11]

Is Technology Out of Control?

At the present time societies of all types exist side by side. There are wandering tribes in Africa and Australia, farming communities in India and China, and the supermechanistic nations of Europe and the United States. During this century in the United States, especially after World War II, we have seen rapid change and increasingly sophisticated technologies. The growth of urban areas has altered the lives of the poor and of minorities; and the small farm community has almost disappeared in the wake of large, scientifically operated farming industries.

Sociologists have expressed a deep alarm over the loss of values and the disintegration of society in the United States. They point to statistics on crime, to loss of jobs through automation, particularly for the elderly; to the harm done to the environment (through strip mining, for instance). These critics predict chaos and the loss of integrity and justice if Americans do not check their demands for power and for noncooperative "me-first-ism." A disregard for others is also attributed to businesses where the drive for ever greater profits seems to carry with it a neglect of the rights and needs of individual citizens. The critics see this disregard spreading as the business community breaks away from national boundaries into a world market.

Yet, just as a washing machine gave the housewife more leisure and less backbreaking work, advanced technology can be made to free people for more productivity and time for thought. The statistics of crime and corruption in the past may not be impressive, but we should remember that they were not scientifically gathered and should be questioned. If old jobs are disappearing, new jobs are coming into existence.

Planning is the key to both good management and a better society. Reliance on research methods, which goes hand in hand with developing technology, can teach business and government what will be needed for the future good of the American people. Because business is composed of profit-making enterprises, it will adjust to such new demands quickly. Government must also learn to make these adjustments.

Although the problems of today still need to be solved, they can be viewed as a challenge that advanced technology will help to define and answer.

SOCIETAL
CHANGES

Contemporary Business outlines many of the societal changes that are taking place today. All of these trends affect the way business operates.

Many societal changes affecting business involve either the issue of social responsibility or the quality of life. The public wants socially responsible decisions from executives, and has begun to protest actions that do not comply with this thinking. Admittedly, the public in the United States has not gone as far as some Brazilian travelers did a few years ago. After their train broke down, two other trains passed without noticing their plight. The 3,000 upset passengers responded by burning three carriages, wrecking another twelve, and barricading an adjacent track.[12] But U.S. citizens have filed lawsuits against producers of poor products, picketed supermarkets, boycotted certain firms, and demanded stronger legislation to control certain business practices.

There is also increasing concern about the quality of life. Most still seek more material possessions, yet there is great interest in living fuller, personally rewarding lives. Individuals must decide on the life style that is right for them.

BUSINESS
STRATEGY
CHANGES

Business strategy has changed over the years. These changes have had a direct effect on how firms operate today. Some of these changes are:

Computer-based management information systems which have been instituted so that executives can cope with the mass of statistics and data needed to make complex decisions.

Automation which refers to *replacing jobs with machines, provided the machines can do a task faster or cheaper than humans.* Petroleum refineries are examples of large operations that have relatively few workers. Most experts note that new workers are required to make the new machines, so that the labor force stays constant. The problem is that the displaced workers may not be qualified or trainable to handle the new jobs.

Cost control programs which are very important, especially during periods of inflation or sales declines. Accountants and other managers must find new ways to hold down the rising costs of doing business.

Increased attention which must be given to *supply sources.* U.S. businesses have experienced several energy and raw materials shortages in the past. As a result, management has had to devote more attention to acquiring the energy and materials necessary to the operation of their firms.

Management must realize the *attitudes and problems of a modern workforce.* The labor force is composed of a multitude of different groups—groups that may require different managerial approaches.

Now, more than ever, management must be sure that leadership styles match the work situation.

Tomorrow's Challenge

Many of today's problems will be present tomorrow. But management must also watch for the new challenges that will appear. Some of today's problems may seem slight when compared to the complexities to be faced in the future!

Tomorrow's challenges require preparation today. Business executives must learn to adapt to events that may be unheard of at the present time. Management must be flexible and prepared to meet new situations with business strategies designed for the future. This approach requires a sound education. Qualified executives are those with a solid understanding of the business system and those who can adapt to change.

The only thing constant about U.S. business is change! Change is a vital part of everyday business life. Change was yesterday's challenge; it is also today's challenge—and it will be tomorrow's challenge!

Summary

It is very difficult to predict the future of U.S. business. In some cases we do not even have correct impressions of what has already happened. Prediction is difficult because of the accelerating pace of change.

Current trends affecting U.S. business are:

1. population changes
2. life style changes
3. economic changes
4. technological changes
5. societal changes
6. business strategy changes.

All these changes have had a significant impact on the way business operates in the late 1970's. The only thing constant about U.S. business is change. Change is tomorrow's challenge; and it requires management preparation today.

Review questions

1. Identify the following items:
   a. population explosion
   b. Third World
   c. life style
   d. technology
   e. automation
2. What do most Americans mean when they talk about returning to an earlier era?

3. Why is it difficult to predict the future course of U.S. business?
4. What can be learned from the automobile industry and Bowmar Instrument Corporation examples given in the chapter?
5. Describe how the accelerating pace of change affects business.
6. Identify the current trends affecting business.
7. Why are population changes particularly significant for Third World nations?
8. Reread the section on "Life Style Changes." How have the life styles of college students changed over the past few years?
9. Identify the economic changes that affect business.
10. What business strategy changes have occurred in recent years?

Discussion questions and exercises

1. Discuss the pro and con arguments to the controversial issue that appears in this chapter.
2. The personality profile in this chapter is an example of someone who has influenced the future of U.S. business. Pick another person and prepare a brief, one-page report on how your choice has affected U.S. business.
3. "The only thing constant about U.S. business is change." Comment.
4. A study by the University of Southern California's Center for Future Research forecasts that by 1983 automobiles will be barred from the downtown areas of major cities. The study also forecasts that in twenty years all of California's major cities will have free public transportation.*

    If these forecasts are accurate, how will business be affected? Can this study be used in future business planning? How?
5. Prepare a two-page report on what you see as "The Future of U.S. Business."

*Ray Hebert. "Californians Peer into Future," *Tulsa Daily World* (March 9, 1975).

Case 24-1
The National Commission on the Financing of Post-secondary Education

The future of U.S. business will probably depend on the success of the generation of managers now enrolled in collegiate business courses. A study by the National Commission on the Financing of Post-secondary Education found that 83 percent of today's students believe that curricula should be designed to make college students more employable and that on-the-job training or internship programs would make education more valuable.

When asked to name the single most important reason for their college enrollment, the students replied:

Reason	Percentage replying
Self-development	34%
Employability	25%
Income	16%
Sociability	14%
General skill development	9%

Questions

1. What are the implications of this study for contemporary business?
2. What are the implications of this study for your particular college?
3. Do you think your generation of managers will be well trained for its tasks? Discuss.

Source: Financing Post-secondary Education in the U.S., a publication of the National Commission on the Financing of Post-secondary Education (December 1973).

Case 24-2
Homemakers—1984

Kenyon & Eckhardt, a New York advertising agency, has conducted a research study on how homemakers will function in 1984. The research shows that the percentage of *superhomemakers* (women whose home is their life) will decline from a current 40 percent to 20 percent. Realistic homemakers will increase from 40 to 60 percent of all homemakers. A *realistic homemaker* maintains a comfortable home and enjoys cooking, but shares household chores with other family members. *Escape artists,* who view all housework negatively, will continue to hold about 20 percent of all homemakers.

Herbert Zeltner, a Kenyon & Eckhardt vice-president, points out:

There have been marked shifts in what women find important . . . they still care about feeding their families well, but now they also care about having time to go to work or just plain enjoy themselves.

These changes in attitudes are shown in hard statistical figures:

women are having fewer children; more married women are continuing to work through childbearing years whether or not they have children; women's educational levels continue to increase . . . all of which say that increasingly the home will be only one place where women will look for fulfillment.

Questions

1. Do you agree with the conclusions reached in the Kenyon & Eckhardt study? Why, or why not?
2. How would these changes affect U.S. business?
3. Identify the implications of this study for:
   a. a manufacturer of washing machines and dryers
   b. the life insurance industry
   c. your local community college.

Source: Marsha May. "What Housewives Will Be Like in 1984," *National Enquirer* (December 31, 1974), p. 4.

Careers in World Business, Business Law, and Small Business

World business, business law, and small business all offer career opportunities. World business includes many careers both at home and abroad. Many people are employed in all phases of international commerce. Attorneys assist management and often become actively involved in the operation of a firm. Some lawyers work directly for companies, but most contract their services to business. Law offices are examples of small businesses. Franchise outlets, most retailers, and service stations are other examples of small businesses.

The Bureau of Labor Statistics has projected annual job openings to 1985. Their forecast for some selected jobs in world business, business law, and small business appear below.

Job Projections to 1985

Career	Latest Employment (1972 Estimate)	Annual Average of Job Openings to 1985
Economists	36,000	1,500
Lawyers	303,000	16,500
Merchant Marine Officers	15,000	200
Shipping and receiving clerks	451,000	13,800
Traffic agents and clerks (civil aviation)	59,000	7,000

SOURCE: *Occupational Manpower and Training Needs* (Washington, D.C.: Bureau of Labor Statistics, 1974).

Here are some of the careers in world business, business law, and small business that are available to you:

Importer	Importers are individuals who buy foreign products and then resell them in their home country. It is an interesting field because of the many new product ideas with which importers are involved.
Export manager	These people direct the foreign sales of a company. They are responsible for marketing, distribution, financing, and after-sale servicing. Export manager is an important position because foreign sales represent a significant proportion of many firm's revenues.
International manager	When a company has multinational operations a separate international unit is usually set up. The manager, or chief executive, for this unit has overall responsibility for these operations.
Attorney	Most legal firms are extensively involved in business problems. Some attorneys work directly for a firm, but most are independent contractors. Since so much of an attorney's work is in business law, it is advisable for these people to have a business as well as a legal education.
Owner/Manager	The ownership and management functions are often performed by the same person in a small business, where people can "be their own boss." This is a rewarding experience for many people.

Appendix A
Career Development—
A Life-long Approach

SOURCE: Bob Mader/Tom Stack & Associates

Career development must be a lifelong endeavor. Statistics show that most workers will change jobs at least four times during their full-time working years. This does not mean just changing from Employer *A* to Employer *B* (same job, different organizations), but actually performing different kinds of work. Change is a normal part of an individual's career development.

People are constantly searching for better ways to perform the work which is in demand. The process of discovering the most effective and efficient ways to structure and define real jobs is a time-consuming task. While it takes considerable effort to improve the way a job is performed, the rewards are significant.

Preparing for a Career Cluster of Related Business Jobs

How should you approach your career development, especially in terms of getting an **entry-level job?** (An entry-level job is your *first full-time employment.*) First it is necessary to identify what the likely *demand* will be for a given kind of work. Since supply and demand forces from the marketplace will determine what kind of jobs and how many jobs will be available, you should become aware of future employment projections and trends.

Suppose you are interested in teaching in a public-school system. It is important to know that some areas of teaching are faced with an oversupply of trained people. A U.S. Labor Department study shows that by 1985 there will be an oversupply of chemists, food scientists, geologists, historians, lawyers, life scientists, meteorologists, newspaper reporters, physicists, political scientists, psychologists, and teachers. On the other hand, the Labor Department expects a strong demand in 1985 for accountants, land clerks, tellers, computer programmers, stenographers and secretaries, typists, receptionists, cashiers, and bookkeepers.[1]

Even in an employment area where the supply of workers exceeds the demand, many qualified individuals will be able to obtain employment. But some people will have to accept alternative forms of employment. Students would be wise to select and prepare for several related jobs in a given career cluster which offers positive employment opportunities.

The notion of a **career cluster,** or *group of related jobs,* is not difficult to understand. Changing technology and changing demands for goods and services make it difficult to estimate what the future employment opportunities for a specific job will be. It is far easier to estimate job opportunities in a group, or cluster, of related occupations.

Each specific job in a career cluster requires certain unique knowledge and skills. One should be sure, however, that he or she is well prepared in the common core of knowledge and skills which

**"What do you mean you
still want to be a cowboy?"**

Not Everyone Agrees on the Correct Approach to Career Development

SOURCE: *The Wall Street Journal,* June 12, 1974. Reprinted with permission from *The Wall Street Journal.*

will help them to gain entry-level employment in one of several related jobs.

The U.S. Office of Education has identified fifteen very broad career clusters.[2] These clusters include such areas as business and office, marketing and distribution, marine science, and health. Not only do business and office, and marketing and distribution represent career clusters, business knowledge and skills are required in all career clusters! For example, in the hospitality and recreation, health, and transportation clusters, most jobs require some basic understanding of effective management, sound accounting practices, legal concepts, and marketing skills. In most colleges the business curriculum is organized around several key courses. These courses usually include: accounting, management, marketing, business law, economics, statistics, and computers.

Such business courses deal with the common knowledge required of any meaningful entry-level business position. Students can then acquire more specialized knowledge by taking advanced classes in each of these areas. This knowledge, along with a positive attitude, will provide the initial flexibility needed for many kinds of business jobs. Fresh knowledge can be acquired at any time, if you have an attitude which values personal and professional improvement.

Many business jobs are in high demand. If you have a good general background in the basic business subjects, you can gain entry-level employment in several areas. You should emphasize the development of a rich foundation of basic concepts which apply to the entire career cluster.

Employment Trends

Several general employment trends and facts are important to college students. First, there are many challenging employment opportunities in the *service-producing industries*. The Bureau of Labor Statistics divides service-producing industries into these areas:

1. transportation
2. public utilities
3. trade
4. finance, insurance, and real estate
5. services
6. government.

Goods-producing industries include:

1. manufacturing
2. contract construction

3. mining
4. agriculture.

These classifications are somewhat arbitrary. But it is easy to comprehend the difference between a physical good and an economic service. Examples of physical goods range from a house to bread. Although services are not quite as apparent, they can be just as valuable and important. Transportation, for example, includes all the jobs which involve moving people and/or things from one location to another. Airlines, common truck carriers, buses, and ships are just a few specific elements within this category. Trade industries would include retail and wholesale employment. Finance, insurance, and real estate industries are everywhere. Services would include employment in several areas not included in any other category. The hospitality field (hotels, motels, and restaurants) would be included in the service area; so would dry-cleaning, shoe repair, and private education. Government includes local, state, and federal workers.

Manufacturing is still the largest employer of workers—larger than any other single industry. About 27 percent of all workers are employed by manufacturing concerns.

According to the U.S. Bureau of Labor Statistics, the work force of three industries will grow by more than 30 percent in the decade of the 1970's:[3]

1. services   39 percent
2. contract construction   37 percent
3. government   33 percent.

Three other industries will show an employment growth rate of over 12 percent:

4. trade   18 percent
5. finance, insurance, and real estate   15 percent
6. manufacturing   13 percent.

Business careers are available in every industry. Accountants, managers, computer programmers, and salespeople are required in every segment of the business world. The employment growth of business jobs is expected to represent over 50 percent of the total employment growth in the labor force during the 1970's!

Knowing Yourself Is a Part of Career Development

Numerous studies show that in order to become successful in a particular job, a person needs to enjoy and value the tasks required by the job. While there are some individuals who do not really enjoy and value their particular jobs, it makes sense to select a line of work which provides job satisfaction.

In addition to analyzing the demand for employment, you must also understand yourself:

How well do you know yourself?

Do you understand your likes and dislikes?

Why do you value certain things, and not others?

In what school activities have you succeeded? Failed?

Can you explain why you failed at certain tasks?

How much do you fear failure?

Are you really interested in the feelings of other people or do you just like to go through the motions of collecting friends?

If you had a choice, would you select a job which primarily involved working with other people, as opposed to working with data or creative ideas?

The process of self-understanding will enhance your career development. In addition to self-understanding, one must also understand the job requirements. The career development goal is to obtain a proper match between an individual and the requirements of a particular job.

Most people need help in both kinds of analysis—self and job. As a college student you will find a wealth of information and personal assistance in your school's library and at the counseling and guidance center. During recent years there has been a major trend toward career education. Most schools now have material relating to:

1. the awareness of self in relationship to potential careers
2. the development of an awareness of available careers
3. an awareness of relevant factors to be considered in employment decision making
4. the development of acceptable job attitudes.

Most schools also maintain a career guidance or placement office. The personnel there can be very helpful in your career decisions.

Obtaining the Right Position

What is the best way to find a good job? Perhaps there is not a single best way. However, there are some basic principles which one should attempt to follow.

Guideline #1 Identify as many job openings as possible.

Be resourceful! Your success depends on gathering as much information as possible. Register at your school's placement office. Establish a credential file, including letters of recommendation and supporting personal information. You should become familiar with how the placement office conveys employment information. Most placement offices send out a monthly list of new job vacancies, so be sure your correct name and address is on this mailing list. If possible, personally visit the placement office at least once or twice a month. Check what new job information is available. Meet the people who work in the placement office—secretaries and career counselors. They can prove invaluable in your job search.

PREPARING YOUR CREDENTIAL FILE

Most credential files include the following information:

1. at least three letters of recommendation from people who know you—professors, parttime employers, and others
2. a typed outline of all academic courses completed, along with corresponding grades, dates, and instructors, or an official transcript
3. a personal information form—which usually includes name, address, age, and marital status
4. sometimes—a statement of personal philosophy and career goals
5. information about your early life, extracurricular activities, and the like.

The last four items on this list are usually prepared on special forms provided by the placement office. These forms must be completed neatly and accurately. The typing, punctuation, spelling, grammar, and writing style should be perfect. Employers are extremely interested in the student's ability to communicate in writing. The written narrative of your credential file should be clear, logical, precise, accurate, and perhaps creative. Give yourself ample time to write several drafts and to polish the final copy. Never write the narrative parts of your credentials when you feel upset or rushed for time. Let other people read and criticize your work.

Prepare a copy of the final credential file for your own use. This may be very important to you in terms of preparing similar information for other employment sources. If you cannot personally deliver the completed forms to the placement office, be sure to check that your file is in order. Your official letters of recommendation are very important. Be very selective in securing credential recommendations. It is usually wise to include a business professor on your list of references. The people you ask for recommendations should be familiar with both your strengths and your career objective(s).

Always *personally* ask people if they will write a favorable letter of recommendation for you. In addition, be prepared to give these individuals a brief outline of your academic preparation along with information concerning your entry-level job preferences and your career objectives. Periodically check with the placement office to see if your letters of recommendation have been received. Give your references a couple of weeks before you politely follow up on tardy references. One purpose of giving your reference a brief outline of your plans is that this approach often produces a faster response.

OTHER EMPLOYMENT SOURCES

The second step in the process of identifying job openings involves seeking out additional placement and employment agencies. This includes other educational placement offices, as well as private and public employment agencies.

If you live in an urban area there are several public colleges and universities located within a fifty-mile radius. The other schools will not permit you to establish a credential file with their placement offices unless you have completed some course work there. However, there is nothing unethical about visiting the placement offices of these colleges and reading their bulletin boards.

If you have completed formal academic course work with more than one college or university, check with them about setting up a credential file there. Some colleges have a reciprocity agreement that permits a student who has completed course work at several schools to establish a credential file with each placement office with certain information being shared between all offices. Under this arrangement official letters of recommendation can be sent from one placement office to another.

Commercial or private employment agencies can be very effective in helping a person obtain employment. These agencies often specialize in certain types of jobs. For example, it is not uncommon to find commercial employment agencies handling only accounting or managerial jobs or marketing jobs. Privately-owned employment agencies perform several services—for both the employer and the candidate—that are not provided elsewhere. For example, some private agencies will interview, test, and screen job applicants.

Many commercial agencies have established a very good relationship with employers who are looking for a particular type of worker. In turn, these agencies can offer candidates valuable counseling advice on how to "market" their employment skills to employers.

Be sure you find out the exact details of the agreement between the candidate and the commercial employment agency. These services can be expensive. Many charge between 5 and 10 percent of the first year's salary of a person who obtains a job as a result of these services. A $10,000 salary and a fee of 7 percent would equal an employment fee of $700. Who is responsible for paying this fee—employer or employee? No blanket rule exists, so be sure to find out the details if you go to a private employment agency.

State employment agencies can be quite effective in providing employment leads. However, in many states these public agencies process unemployment compensation along with other kinds of work. Because of this mix of duties, some people view state employment agencies as providing services for semiskilled or unskilled workers. But the state agencies also list jobs in many professional categories.

Other sources which can help identify job openings include:

1. newspaper employment advertisements (The Sunday edition of a metropolitan newspaper is often a rich source of job leads.)
2. trade journals or magazines
3. college professors and administrators
4. community organizations, such as the Chamber of Commerce
5. friends.

Another approach is to conduct a systematic survey. It would include the identification of all the organizations where you think you would like to work. Mail a letter of inquiry and your resumé to these companies. If possible, these two documents should be addressed to a specific person who has the authority to hire new employees. The letter of inquiry should ask briefly about employment opportunities for a particular line of work. It should also ask for a personal interview.

PREPARING YOUR RESUMÉ

Regardless of how you identify job openings, you must learn how to develop and use a resumé.

Guideline #2 A resumé is you!

A **resumé** is *a written summary of your personal, educational, and professional achievements.* It is a very personal document! Items such as educational background, work experience, career preference, major interests, and personal information should be included in a resumé.

The primary purpose of a job resumé is to highlight important information about your qualifications. Vital statistics—such as your name, age, address, and telephone number—should also be included. In general, a resumé for a person seeking entry-level employment should only be one page in length. Information in a job resumé should therefore be as concise as possible. The physical layout of the data is also vital. *Ease of reading* is the primary requirement. *Attractiveness* is a close second.

There are several acceptable ways of preparing a job resumé. Some resumés will use narrative sentences to explain exact job duties and career goals. If one uses the job resumé along with the credential file, a lengthy resumé is not needed. You must remember that the resumé should be designed around your own needs and objectives. An example of a very simple job resumé follows.

RESUMÉ

Personal Information

Name	Albert A. Belskus
Address	4300 West Alton Street, Apt. B
	Warren, Michigan 40999
Telephone	(300) 777-1324
Date of birth	January 30, 1955
Height and weight	5' 8''; 180 lbs.
Physical condition	Excellent
Marital status	Single

Education

Essex County Community College	Associate of Arts degree in Business (1975)
Motor State University	Bachelor of Business Administration (1977)

Combined Grade Point Average is 3.01

Business Experience

Town Center Motel Post Road Dearborn, Michigan 40001	Room Clerk (1972–1974)
Big Harvey's Restaurant Monroe Avenue Warren, Michigan 40002	Assistant Shift Manager (1974–1975)
St. Anthony's Hospital First Street Detroit, Michigan 40000	Assistant Supply Manager (1975 to date)

References

Complete credential files are available from either:

Placement Center Essex County Community College Troy, Michigan 40003	Placement Center Motor State University Detroit, Michigan 40000

Additional References

Professor Edward Van Allen Business Department Essex County Community College Troy, Michigan 40003	Professor C. Carson Jones Department of Management Motor State University Detroit, Michigan 40000
Ms. Helena Steinoretz Manager, Town Center Motel Post Road Dearborn, Michigan 40001	Mr. Lawrence Poulson Supply Manager St. Anthony's Hospital Detroit, Michigan 40000

Guideline #3 Rank your list of job opportunities.

Your efforts to identify potential job opportunities should yield several prospects. Obviously you will prefer some prospects over others. The following factors should be taken into consideration when arranging your list from most preferred to least preferred:

1. type of work involved
2. type of company
3. type of industry
4. opportunity for advancement
5. salary range
6. image of the company
7. growth opportunities of the company
8. company's financial position
9. geographical location.

The factor you consider most important in your ranking of job opportunities depends on your own values. One word of caution: Do not consider just the starting salary. Remember, you are concerned with your entire career progression and not just the first year!

A number of information sources are useful in ranking job prospects. Annual reports, financial summaries, and other data can usually be obtained from libraries, stockbrokers, and placement offices. In addition, officials at your placement office or employment agency may be familiar with the companies on your list. If possible, try to visit the premises of these companies for first-hand impressions of the firm. Ask people what they know about the desirability of working for the company in question. Much information can also be obtained from a personal interview.

THE PERSONAL INTERVIEW Almost all companies require a personal interview before someone is hired. A basic goal of your job search is to obtain personal interviews with prospective employers.

Guideline #4 If you think that employment with a particular company is desirable, then do your homework for the personal interview.

Homework for the personal interview includes obtaining essential information about the company. Consider items such as:

1. historical background information
2. key financial data (assets, profits, dividends, position in the industry)
3. the goods and/or services produced by the firm
4. the firm's competitors
5. organizational structure

6. number of employees
7. reputation in the community

This information is useful in several ways. First, it will help you gain a feeling of confidence during the personal interview. Second, this information might prevent you from making an undesirable employment choice. Third, interviewers often try to determine how much an applicant knows about the company to determine interest level. Candidates who do not make the effort to obtain such information are often eliminated from further consideration.

Where do you get this preinterview information? First, check with your placement office or employment agency. They should be able to tell you something about the company and also provide published material. Second, check with some of the business instructors at your school. Third, go to the library and investigate the company in the standard financial guides. Ask your librarian for help. Fourth, contact a stockbroker and ask for information about the company. Fifth, ask friends who have dealt with the company, either as customers or as workers. Sixth, contact the local Chamber of Commerce office where the company is located. These techniques should produce all the information you will need.

Guideline #5 Evaluate employment information in terms of your career objectives.

You must relate employment information to employment goals. When all of the facts and figures are combined in a meaningful way, does the package help you realize your career goal?

Information pertaining to this question must be evaluated carefully. While no employment opportunity will satisfy your every expectation, it is important to understand to what extent job opportunities will correspond to your career objectives.

Guideline #6 Be prepared to ask questions in a clear and concise manner during the personal interview.

Guideline #7 Be prepared to give personal and career information in a clear and concise manner.

Interviewers report that many students fail during the interview process for two reasons:

1. inadequate preparation for the interview
2. lack of confidence.

Both factors prevent effective communication. Remember that the interviewer will first determine whether or not you can communicate effectively. You should be specific in answering and asking questions. Do not fear to express your concerns and questions in a clear and positive manner.

INTERVIEWER
TACTICS

Most people who conduct initial employment interviews work in the personnel division of an organization. They are in a staff position, which means that they can make recommendations to other managers concerning which individuals should be employed. Line managers get involved in interviewing at a later stage of the hiring process. In many instances the decision is made by a group selected from the personnel department and the immediate supervisor of the prospective employee. In other cases the decision is made entirely by the immediate supervisor. Rarely does the personnel department have sole hiring authority.

Interviewers use various techniques to elicit required information for employment decisions. If you are interested in a job as a supervisor, the company wants to have some idea of how you can cope with conflict. Since the handling of personal conflict is an important phase of the supervisor's job, the interviewer could use a stress interview to determine how much pressure you as an individual can handle. The **stress interview** puts *pressure on the interviewee by creating a crisis situation.* The interviewer might begin with a harsh criticism of your academic record or lack of practical experience. You might also be faced with a series of rapid-fire questions about how you would handle a hypothetical situation. It is important to retain your composure and communicate in a clear and precise manner.

Another technique, which is more common than the stress interview, is for the interviewer not to talk very much during the interview. This type of **open-ended** interview is *designed to study the thought processes of the interviewee.* The open-ended interview forces you to open up and talk about yourself and your goals. If you appear unorganized, the interviewer may eliminate you as a possible employee. When faced with this type of situation, be sure your thoughts are expressed clearly and that the conversation is kept on target—the employment opportunity in relationship to your career objectives. In an open-ended interview you should talk for about ten minutes, then ask some specific questions of the interviewer. Listen very carefully to the responses. Remember, if you are prepared for a job interview, it will involve a mutual exchange of information.

If the initial interview was satisfactory, you will be invited to come to the company for another interview at a later date. Sometimes you will also be asked to take a battery of intelligence or aptitude tests. The most important aspect of how you perform on various employment tests is the effectiveness of your written communication. Most students do very well in these tests, since they have plenty of practice in college to sharpen their testing skills.

THE EMPLOYMENT DECISION

Now let's consider the actual hiring interview. By this time the company will know a lot about you from your credential file, resumé, and initial interview. You should also know a lot about the company. The primary purpose of the second interview is to determine whether you can work effectively with your potential superior and peer group.

If you create a positive impression during your second interview you are likely to be offered employment. Again, your decision to accept the employment offer should depend on the closeness of the match between career opportunities and your career objectives. If there appears to be a good match, your work is just beginning!

Your career development is a lifelong process. It includes gaining a broad general preparation for employment, establishing specific career objectives, identifying market demand, analyzing yourself, conducting a formal job search campaign, and successfully performing every unique job assignment. The success of your career progression will depend both on your human relations skills and the ability to apply yourself to a particular work situation.

No list of career information sources can ever be complete. But the following sources may be helpful in your career planning. Additional sources of information can be obtained from your college's placement office.

Sources of Career Information

Accounting Careers Council
National Distribution Center
P.O. Box 650
Radio City Station
New York, N.Y. 10019

Administrative Management
   Soc.
Willow Grove
Pennsylvania 19090

Air Transport Assoc. of
   America
1000 Connecticut Avenue
Washington, D.C. 20036

American Advertising
   Federation
1225 Connecticut Avenue, N.W.
Washington, D.C. 20036

American Association of
   Advertising Agencies
200 Park Avenue
New York, N.Y. 10017

Bank Personnel Division
American Bankers Assoc.
1120 Connecticut Ave., N.W.
Washington, D.C. 20036

American Bar Assoc.
Information Services
1155 E. 60th Street
Chicago, Ill. 60637

American Council on Ed. for
   Journalism
c/o Milton Gross
School of Journalism
University of Missouri
Colombia, Missouri 65201

American Economic Assoc.
1313 21st Ave. South
Nashville, Tenn. 37212

American Fed. of Labor and
   Congress of Industrial
   Organizations
815 16th Street, N.W.
Washington, D.C. 20006

American Hotel and Motel
   Assoc.
388 7th Avenue
New York, N.Y. 10019

Amer. Institute of Certified
   Public Accountants
1121 Avenue of the Americas
New York, N.Y. 10036

Amer. Institute of Planners
917 15th Street, N.W.
Washington, D.C. 20005

American Management Assoc.
135 W. 50th Street
New York, N.Y. 10020

American Marketing Assn.
Suite 606
222 South Riverside Plaza
Chicago, Ill. 60606

Amer. Soc. for Personnel
   Administration
52 East Bride St.
Berea, Ohio 44017

Amer. Statistical Assoc.
810 18th Street, N.W.
Washington, D.C. 20006

Assoc. for Computing
   Machinery
1133 Avenue of the Americas
New York, N.Y. 10036

Assoc. of Industrial Advertisers
41 East 42nd Street
New York, N.Y. 10017

Assoc. of University Programs
   in Hospital Administration
1755 Massachusetts Ave.
Suite 500
Washington, D.C. 20036

Bureau of Labor Statistics
Occupational Outlook Service
U.S. Dept. of Labor
Washington, D.C. 20212

Careers
Washington, D.C.
20202

College Placement Council,
   Inc.
P.O. Box 2263
Bethlehem, Pa. 18001

Council on Hotel, Restaurant,
   and Institutional Education
Statler Hall, Cornell Univ.
Ithaca, N.Y. 14850

Data Processing Management
   Assoc.
505 Busse Highway
Park Ridge, Ill. 60008

Direct Mail Advertising Assoc.
230 Park Avenue
New York, N.Y. 10017

Education Director
National Restaurant Assoc.
1530 North Lake Shore Drive
Chicago, Ill. 60610

Educational Institute
American Hotel and Motel
   Assoc.
221 West 57th St.
New York, N.Y. 10019

Financial Executives Institute
633 Third Avenue
New York, N.Y. 10017

Institute for Certifying
Secretaries
1103 Grand Ave.
Kansas City, Mo. 64106

Institute of Internal Auditors
170 Broadway
New York, N.Y. 10038

Institute of Life Insurance
277 Park Ave.
New York, N.Y. 10017

National Assoc. of
Accountants
505 Park Ave.
New York, N.Y. 10022

National Assoc. of Bank
Women, Inc.
60 E. 42nd St.
New York, N.Y. 10017

National Assoc. of Insurance
Agents, Inc.
96 Fulton St.
New York, N.Y. 10038

National Assoc. of Life
Underwriters
1922 F. St., N.W.
Washington, D.C. 20006

National Assoc. of Purchasing
Management
11 Park Place
New York, N.Y. 10007

National Assoc. of Wholesaler-
Distributors
1725 K. St., N.W.
Washington, D.C. 20006

National Automobile Dealers
Assn.
2000 K. St., N.W.
Washington, D.C. 20006

National Consumer Finance
Assoc.
1000 16th St., N.W.
Washington, D.C. 20036

National Retail Merchants
Assoc.
100 West 31st St.
New York, N.Y. 10017

National Secretaries Assoc.
616 East 63rd St.
Kansas City, Mo. 64110

National Soc. of Public
Accountants
1717 Pennsylvania Ave., N.W.
Washington, D.C. 20006

National Vocational Guidance
Assoc.
1607 New Hampshire Ave.,
N.W.
Washington, D.C. 20009

Office of Econ. Opportunity
Washington, D.C. 20009

Public Relations Soc. of
America, Inc.
Careers
845 Third Avenue
New York, N.Y. 10022

Sales and Marketing
Executives, International
630 Third Avenue
New York, N.Y. 10017

Securities Industry Association
20 Broad Street
New York, N.Y. 10005

Society of Actuarials
208 South La Salle Street
Chicago, Ill. 60604

Soc. for the Advancement of
Management
1412 Broadway
New York, N.Y. 10036

U.S. Department of Commerce
Employment Information
Center
Room 1050
14th and Constitution Avenue
Washington, D.C. 20030

Appendix B
Articles You Should Read

This appendix contains a list of materials that represent worthwhile reading for the beginning business student. As you increase your knowledge of contemporary business, you will want to read additional materials in each of these areas.

Business and its environment

Banks, Louis. "The Mission of Our Business Society," *Harvard Business Review* (May–June 1975), pp. 57–65.

Buskirk, Richard H., and James T. Rothe. "Consumerism—An Interpretation," *Journal of Marketing* (October 1970), pp. 61–65.

"Can Capitalism Survive?" *Time* (July 14, 1975), pp. 52–63.

Fox, Harold W. "Pollution: The Priceless Problem," *Business and Society* (Spring 1971), pp. 4–9.

Gray, Elisha, II. "Changing Values in the Business Society," *Business Horizons* (August 1968), pp. 21–26.

Leighton, David S.R. "The Internationalization of American Business—The Third Industrial Revolution," *Journal of Marketing* (July 1970), pp. 3–6.

Netschert, Bruce C. "Energy vs. Environment," *Harvard Business Review* (January–February 1973), pp. 24–28 ff.

Raymond, Robert S., and Elizabeth Richards. "Social Indicators and Business Decisions," *MSU Business Topics* (Autumn 1971), pp. 42–46.

"Small Business: The Maddening Struggle to Survive," *Business Week* (June 30, 1975), pp. 96–104.

Management

Drucker, Peter. F. "Managing for Business Effectiveness," *Harvard Business Review* (May–June 1963), pp. 53–60.

——. "New Templates for Today's Organizations," *Harvard Business Review* (January–February 1974), pp. 45–53.

Greiner, Larry E. "What Managers Think of Participative Leadership," *Harvard Business Review* (March–April 1973), pp. 111–117.

Hanan, Mack. "Make Way for the New Organization Man," *Harvard Business Review* (July–August 1971), pp. 128–138.

Herzberg, Frederick. "One More Time: How Do You Motivate Employers?" *Harvard Business Review* (January–February 1968).

Koontz, Harold. "The Management Theory Jungle," *Academy of Management Journal* (December 1961), pp. 174–188.

Levinson, Harry. "Asinine Attitudes toward Motivation," *Harvard Business Review* (January–February 1973), pp. 70–76.

Luthans, Fred. "The Contingency Theory of Management," *Business Horizons* (June 1973), pp. 67–72.

McGregor, Douglas M. "The Human Side of Enterprise," *Management Review* (November 1957), pp. 22 ff.

Mintzberg, Henry. "The Manager's Job: Folklore and Fact," *Harvard Business Review* (July–August 1975), pp. 49–61.

"The Office of the Future," *Business Week* (June 30, 1975), pp. 48–84.

Marketing

Backman, Jules. "Is Advertising Wasteful?" *Journal of Marketing* (January 1968), pp. 2–8.

Davidson, William R. "Changes in Distributive Institutions," *Journal of Marketing* (January 1970), pp. 7–10.

Kotler, Philip. "Behavioral Models for Analyzing Buyers," *Journal of Marketing* (October 1965), pp. 37–45.

Kotler, Philip, and Sidney J. Levy. "Broadening the Concept of Marketing," *Journal of Marketing* (January 1969), pp. 10–15.

Levitt, Theodore. "Marketing Myopia," *Harvard Business Review* (July–August 1960).

Oxenfeldt, Alfred R. "Multi-stage Approach to Pricing," *Harvard Business Review* (July–August 1960), pp. 125–133.

Pessemier, Edgar. "New Product Ventures," *Business Horizons* (August 1968), pp. 5–7, 9–16, 18–19.

Thompson, Howard A. *The Great Writings in Marketing* (Plymouth, Mich.: The Commerce Press, 1976). Thirty-eight classic marketing articles with retrospective comments by the authors.

Finance

Anthony, Robert N. "The Trouble with Profit Maximization," *Harvard Business Review* (November–December 1960), pp. 126–134.

Byrne, R., A. Charnes, A. Cooper, and K. Kortanek. "Some New Approaches to Risk," *Accounting Review* (January 1968), pp. 18–37.

Donaldson, Gordon. "Financial Goals: Management vs. Stockholders," *Harvard Business Review* (May–June 1963), pp. 116–129.

Hertz, David B. "Investment Policies that Paid Off," *Harvard Business Review* (January–February 1968), pp. 96–108.

Hunt, Pearson. "Funds Position: Keystone in Financial Planning," *Harvard Business Review* (May–June 1975), pp. 106–115.

Levitt, Theodore. "Dinosaurs among the Bears and Bulls," *Harvard Business Review* (January–February 1975), pp. 41–53.

Searby, Frederick W. "Return to Return on Investment," *Harvard Business Review* (March–April 1975), pp. 113–119.

Quantitative tools

Ackoff, Russell L. "Management Misinformation Systems," *Management Science* (December 1967).

Axelrod, Joel N. "14 Rules for Building an MIS," *Journal of Advertising Research* (June 1970).

Burnett, Gerald J., and Richard L. Nolan. "At Last, Major Roles for Minicomputers," *Harvard Business Review* (May–June 1975), pp. 148–156.

Chou, Ya-lun. *Statistical Analysis.* (New York: Holt, Rinehart and Winston, 1975), Ch. 1.

Goldstein, Robert C., and Richard L. Nolan. "Personal Privacy versus the Corporate Computer," *Harvard Business Review* (March–April 1975), pp. 62–70.

Huff, Darrell. *How to Lie with Statistics* (New York: W. W. Norton & Company, 1954), Chs. 1 and 2.

Weston, Frank T. "Adjust Your Accounting for Inflation," *Harvard Business Review* (January–February 1975), pp. 22–29, 146.

Notes

Chapter 1

[1]C. Northcote Parkinson. *Big Business* (Boston: Little, Brown and Company, 1974), pp. 34, 36.

[2]Arch Booth. "Big Business: Straw Man," *Marketing Times* (January-February 1975), p. 9.

[3]Noted in Parkinson, p. 34.

[4]The term *five M's of Management* was first suggested by L. T. White, a leading small business proponent. See Joseph C. Schabacker (ed.), *Strengthening Small Business Management: Collections from the Papers of L. T. White* (Washington, D.C.: Small Business Administration, 1971), p. 21.

[5]Copyright © 1975, U.S. News and World Report, Inc.

Chapter 2

[1]Ralph E. Winter. "Furor over a Plant on Lake Superior Is Warning to Industry," *The Wall Street Journal* (August 25, 1974); James L. Kerwin. "Reserve Mining Case Far from a Solution," *The Detroit News* (March 19, 1975), p. 3-C.

[2]*Ibid.*

[3]William Hieronymus. "Worried about Image, Business Makes Effort to Sell Itself to Public," *The Wall Street Journal* (June 12, 1973), pp. 1, 17.

[4]"A Happiness Index," *The Wall Street Journal* (January 20, 1972), p. 1.

[5]*A National Study of Roadside Litter* (Research Triangle Park, N.C.: Research Triangle Institute, October 1969), p. 13.

[6]*The Age* (August 13, 1974), p. 1.

[7]Leonard L. Berry. "Marketing Challenge in the Age of the People," *MSU Business Topics* (Winter 1972), pp. 7-13.

[8]Farish A. Jenkins, Senior Vice-president of National Biscuit Company, discusses these rights in "Business, Government, and Consumer," *Journal of Business,* Vol. 8 (South Orange, N.J.: Seton Hall University, December 1969), pp. 25-29.

[9]*The Wall Street Journal* (April 11, 1974), p. 1.

[10]*The Wall Street Journal* (December 27, 1973), p. 1.

[11]As noted in *Natural History* magazine (October 1973).

[12]This study is discussed in Max Ways, "Business Faces Growing Pressures to Behave Better," *Fortune* (May 1974), p. 310.

[13]These levels have been suggested by Professor William Lazer of Michigan State University.

Chapter 3

[1]Marcowitz's story is told in Frederick C. Klein. "Launching a Business in These Risky Times Is a Frustrating Task," *The Wall Street Journal* (November 6, 1974).

[2]Max Ways. "Business Faces Growing Pressure to Behave Better," *Fortune* (May 1974), p. 316.

Chapter 4

[1]It should be pointed out that management writers differ on both the number of management

functions and the specific lists of functions. Writers who choose to define the specific functions more narrowly include such functions as staffing, communicating, motivating, innovating, coordinating, and evaluating. Each of these functions must be accomplished by managers. The four functions listed here are assumed to encompass these more specific functions.

Chapter 5

[1]C. Northcote Parkinson. *Parkinson's Law and Other Studies in Administration* (Boston: Houghton Mifflin Company, 1957).

[2]Robert Townsend. *Up the Organization* (New York: Alfred A. Knopf, Inc., 1970), p. 134.

[3]Keith Davis. *Human Relations at Work* (New York: McGraw-Hill Book Company, Inc., 1967).

Chapter 6

[1]Stuart Chase. *Men at Work* (New York: Harcourt, Brace & World, 1941), pp. 21–22.

[2]Abraham H. Maslow. "A Theory of Human Motivation," *Psychological Review* (July 1943), pp. 370–396.

[3]Richard Bach. *Jonathan Livingston Seagull* (New York: The Macmillan Co., 1972), pp. 30–31.

[4]Douglas McGregor. *The Human Side of Enterprise* (New York: McGraw-Hill Book Company Inc., 1960), pp. 33–34.

[5]McGregor. Pp. 47–48.

[6]Frederick Herzberg. *Work and the Nature of Man* (Cleveland: The World Publishing Company, 1966).

[7]Peter Drucker. *The Practice of Management* (New York: Harper & Brothers, 1954), pp. 128–129.

[8]Charles R. Walker and Robert Guest. *Man on the Assembly Line* (Cambridge, Massachusetts: Harvard University Press, 1952), p. 19.

[9]William J. Paul, Jr., Keith B. Robertson, and Frederick Herzberg. "Job Enrichment Pays Off," *Harvard Business Review* (March-April 1969), p. 61.

[10]"Workers Don't Give a Damn? Chrysler Thinks They Do, If—," *Ward's Auto World* (June 1972).

[11]"The Plant that Runs on Individual Initiative," *Management Review* (July 1972).

[12]Robert N. Ford. *Motivation through the Work Itself* (New York: American Management Association, 1969), p. 188.

[13]M.D. Kilbridge. "No Workers Prefer Larger Jobs?" *Personnel* (September–October 1960), pp. 45–48.

[14]William E. Reif and Peter P. Schoderbek. "Job Enlargement: Antidote to Apathy," *Management of Personnel Quarterly* (Spring 1966), pp. 16–23.

[15]*Detroit Free Press* (December 2, 1973), p. 14-F.

Chapter 8

[1]The Homestead battle is described in Jeremy Brecher. *Strike!* (San Francisco: Straight Arrow Books, 1972) pp. 53–63.

[2]Quoted in Campbell R. McConnell. *Economics* (New York: McGraw-Hill Book Co., 1975), p. 754.

[3]This section is adapted from Heinz Kohler. *Economics: The Science of Scarcity* (Hinsdale, Ill.: The Dryden Press, 1970), pp. 449–451.

Chapter 9

[1]Three interesting books on the life of Henry Ford and the Ford Motor Company are: Keith Seward. *The Legend of Henry Ford* (New York: Rhinehard, 1948); Reynold M. Wik. *Henry Ford and Grass Roots America* (Ann Arbor: University of Michigan Press, 1972); and Alan Nevins. *Ford Motor Company* (New York: Charles Scribner's Sons, 1954).

Chapter 10

[1]Committee on Definitions. *Marketing Definitions: A Glossary of Marketing Terms* (Chicago: American Marketing Association, 1960), p. 15.

[2]Some of the discussion in Chapter 10 follows that in Louis E. Boone and David L. Kurtz. *Contemporary Marketing* (Hinsdale, Ill.: The Dryden Press, 1974).

[3]Robert J. Keith. "The Marketing Revolution," *Journal of Marketing* (January 1960), p. 36.

[4]Thomas T. Semon. "Family Income and Spending Capacity," *Journal of Marketing* (April 1962), pp. 26–30.

[5]*The Wall Street Journal* (April 4, 1974), p. 1.

[6]*Marketing Definitions: A Glossary of Marketing Terms*, p. 17.

[7]Peter Vanderwicken. "P&G's Secret Ingredient," *Fortune* (July 1974), p. 77.

[8]*Ibid.* p. 79.

[9]Barry R. Linsky. "Which Way to Move with New Products," *Advertising Age* (July 22, 1974), p. 46.

[10]William B. Mead. "What's in a Name Brand," *Money* (February 1974), p. 40.

[11]E.B. Weiss. "Private Label? No, It's Now 'Presold'—Wave of the Future," *Advertising Age* (September 30, 1974), p. 27.

Chapter 11

[1]E.B. Weiss. "What Lies Ahead in Retailing for the Abandoned Gas Station," *Advertising Age* (October 21, 1974), p. 62.

[2]Committee on Definitions. *Marketing Definitions: A Glossary of Marketing Terms* (Chicago: American Marketing Association, 1960), p. 10.

[3]This list appears in Richard H. Buskirk, Donald J. Green, and William C. Rodgers. *Concepts of Business* (San Francisco: Rinehart Press, 1972), p. 151.

[4]*Ibid.*, pp. 181–182.

[5]Thomas Enrich. "Down-east Look Helps Maine Outdoor Store Build National Business," *The Wall Street Journal* (December 5, 1973), pp. 1, 14.

[6]*Parade* (December 9, 1973), p. 5.

[7]The Wheel of Retailing, originally proposed by M.P. McNair, is discussed in Stanley C. Hollander. "The Wheel of Retailing," *Journal of Marketing* (July 1960), pp. 37–42.

[8]Stanley C. Hollander. "The Wheel of Retailing,"

Journal of Marketing (July 1960), pp. 37–42.

[9]The growth of the video game market is traced in Stephen Sansweet. "Sophisticated Cousin of Pinball Machine Entrances the U.S.," *The Wall Street Journal* (March 18, 1974), pp. 1, 25.

[10]E.B. Weiss. "The Hypermarché Marches into U.S. Mass Retailing," *Advertising Age* (December 30, 1974), p. 20.

Chapter 12

[1]Leo Greenland. "Advertisers Must Stop Conning Consumers," *Harvard Business Review* (July–August 1974), p. 24.

[2]A. Richard Immel. "Try as They Might, Folks in Oregon Can't Deter New Residents," *The Wall Street Journal* (May 22, 1974), pp. 1, 22.

[3]"Marketer of the Year Wells Tells Uncola Story, Blast Consumerists," *Marketing News* (April 1974), p. 8.

[4]*Advertising Age* (September 16, 1974), p. 2.

[5]*Advertising Age* (September 30, 1974), p. 76.

[6]Comparative advertising is discussed in Michael J. Connor. "Naming Names of Rivals in Ads Is Catching on but Spurs Controversy," *The Wall Street Journal* (December 26, 1973), pp. 1, 17; Greenland, pp. 19–20.

[7]*Executive's Digest* (June 1971), p. 4.

[8]*The Wall Street Journal* (December 6, 1973), p. 1.

[9]*The Wall Street Journal* (September 14, 1971), p. 1.

[10]Howard Stumpf. "P.O.P. Grows 8% Annually in Decade," *Advertising Age* (September 30, 1974), p. 71.

[11]"Reminders from the IRS," *Specialty Advertising Report,* vol. VII, no. 4, p. 4.

[12]Walter A. Gaw. *Specialty Advertising* (Chicago: Specialty Advertising Association, 1970), p. 7.

Chapter 13

[1]"Food was 11¢ a Day in 1776," *The Press* (February 11, 1974), p. 3.

[2]Robert W. Lanzillotti. "Pricing Objectives in Large Companies," *American Economic Review* (December 1958), pp. 921–940.

[3]*The Age* (October 5, 1974), p. 1.

[4]These examples are from Lanzillotti, pp. 924–927.

[5]William J. Baumol. "On the Theory of Oligopoly," *Economics* (August 1958) pp. 187–198. *Also see* William J. Baumol. *Business Behavior, Value and Growth* (New York: The Macmillan Company, 1959).

[6]This example is from Lanzillotti, pp. 924–927.

[7]*The Wall Street Journal* (March 21, 1974), p. 1.

[8]Examples are from William Guttmann. "You Can't Beat Inflation," *The Age* (September 28, 1974), p. 11.

[9]Roy Macartney. "American Rides Inflation Blow," *The Age* (September 9, 1974), p. 9.

[10]Ronald G. Shafer. "Inflation Is Eroding the Ability of Many to Buy Own House," *The Wall Street Journal* (September 3, 1974).

[11]Byron Klapper. "Encouraged by Lenders and Retailers, More People Use Credit and Regret It," *The Wall Street Journal* (August 17, 1974), p. 24.

[12]William Wong. "Sugar Industry Revels in Record Prices; Some Consumers Switch to Substitutes," *The Wall Street Journal* (September 26, 1974), p. 28.

[13]*The Wall Street Journal* (May 16, 1974), p. 1.

[14]Bill Hieronymus. "How a Firm is Jolted by Inflation, and Acts to Blunt the Damage," *The Wall Street Journal* (August 23, 1974).

[15]Steven Grover. "In Throes of Postage Hikes, Publishers Shrink Product, Hike Prices, Cry Doom," *The Wall Street Journal* (March 20, 1974), p. 36.

[16]Wong, p. 28.

[17]"Pricing Strategy in an Inflation Economy," *Business Week* (April 6, 1974).

[18]The examples in this section are from "Pricing Strategy in an Inflation Economy," p. 434.

[19]Peter Vanderwicken, "P&G's Secret Ingredient," *Fortune* (July 1974), p. 78.

[20]The Du Pont, Dow, Wella-Balsam, and Alberto-Culver examples are from "Pricing Strategy in an Inflation Economy," p. 434.

[21]James H. Myers and William H. Reynolds. *Consumer Behavior and Marketing Management* (Boston: Houghton-Mifflin Company, 1967), p. 47.

Chapter 14

[1]"Creeping Inflation," Federal Reserve Bank of Philadelphia *Business Review* (August 1957), p. 3. Quoted in Campbell R. McConnell. *Economics* (New York: McGraw-Hill Book Company, Inc., 1975), p. 289.

[2]David Lindsey and Edwin G. Dolan. *Basic Macroeconomics: Principles and Reality* (Hinsdale, Ill.: The Dryden Press, 1974), p. 121.

[3]*Electronic Money . . . and the Payments Mechanism* (Boston: Federal Reserve Bank of Boston, 1973), p. 10.

[4]Lawrence S. Ritter and William L. Silber. *Principles of Money, Banking and Financial Markets* (New York: Basic Books, 1974), pp. 385–386.

[5]Board of Governors of the Federal Reserve System. *The Federal Reserve System: Purposes and Functions* (Washington, D.C.: U.S. Government Printing Office, 1967), p. 1.

[6]"How Safe Are Your Bank Deposits?" *U.S. News & World Report* (October 21, 1974), p. 63.

[7]"Franklin National Fizzles Out," *Time* (October 21, 1974), p. 56.

[8]*See Electronic Money . . . and the Payments Mechanism.*

Chapter 15

[1]"Companies Gain Funds by Speeding Intakes and Slowing Outgoes," *The Wall Street Journal* (July 31, 1974), p. 1.

Chapter 16

[1]"Time to Shop Around," *Time* (June 30, 1975), p. 63.

[2]*1974 Mutual Fund Fact Book* (Washington, D.C.: Investment Company Institute), p. 5.

[3]*Ibid.*, p. 9.

Chapter 17

[1]Mary Bralove. "Sales of Canned Gourmet Soups Fall Sharply after Death Laid to Bon Vivant Vichyssoise," *The Wall Street Journal* (August 3, 1971), p. 32.

[2]"Bon Vivant Changes Name and Resumes Operations," *The Wall Street Journal* (November 15, 1972). p. 19.

[3]"Insurers Tote Up the Tornadoes' Toll," *Business Week* (April 13, 1974), p. 30.

[4]"Lawsuits: A Growing Nightmare for Doctors and Patients," *U.S. News & World Report* (January 20, 1975), p. 53.

[5]*Decade of Decision* (New York: Institute of Life Insurance, 1972), p. 30.

[6]*Source Book of Health Insurance Data* (New York: Health Insurance Institute, 1974), p. 11.

[7]This case is described in Jonathan Kwitny. *The Mullendore Murder Case* (New York: Farrar, Straus and Giroux, 1974).

Chapter 19

[1]*The Computer: How It's Changing Our Lives* (Washington, D.C.: U.S. News & World Report, Inc., 1972), p. 12.

[2]*The Computer: How It's Changing Our Lives*, p. 73.

[3]*The Journal of Insurance* (March/April 1975), p. 17.

[4]Donald H. Sanders. *Computers and Management* (New York: McGraw-Hill Book Company, 1970), p. 16.

[5]"Grocery Checkout by Computer—What It Means to Shoppers," *U.S. News & World Report* (December 30, 1974), p. 56.

[6]*The Computer: How It's Changing Our Lives*, p. 14.

Chapter 20

[1]Walter J. Kennevan. "MIS Universe," *Data Management* (September 1970), p. 63.

Chapter 21

[1]Some of the discussion in Chapter 21 follows that found in Vern Terpstra. *International Marketing* (New York: Holt, Rinehart and Winston, Inc., 1972).

[2]*The Age* (October 4, 1974), p. 1.

[3]This section is based on Terpstra, pp. 11–14, 297–298.

[4]*The Age* (September 24, 1974), p. 17.

[5]Louis E. Boone and David L. Kurtz. *Contemporary Marketing* (Hinsdale, Ill.: The Dryden Press, 1974), p. 169.

[6]Terpstra, p. 233.

[7]This example can be found in Vern Terpstra. *American Marketing in the Common Market* (New York: Praeger, 1967), p. 120.

[8]*The Detroit News* (February 28, 1975), p. 1.

[9]*The Wall Street Journal* (February 15, 1974), p. 8.

[10]"International Product Manager Has Tough Task Even When His Product Has Spirit(s)," *Marketing News* (May 15, 1974), p. 8.

[11]Bud Gordon. "TV Candy Commercials Must Carry Tooth Decay Warning," *National Enquirer* (December 31, 1974), p. 10.

[12]Terpstra, pp. 122–144.

[13]*Ibid.*, pp. 42–48.

[14]*Ibid*, pp. 155, 261.

[15]William M. Carley. "A Giant Multinational Finds Unified Activities Aren't Easy to Set Up," *The Wall Street Journal* (February 20, 1974), p. 1.

[16]*Ibid.*, pp. 1, 24.

[17]William T. Ryan. "Multinationals Moving in While Africans Seek Capital, Know-How," *Marketing News* (September 1, 1974), p. 4.

[18]Valerie Christian. "Internationals Hit on Morals," *The Age* (July 18, 1974), p. 19.

[19]*The Detroit News* (January 24, 1975), p. 3-A.

Chapter 22

[1]From Thomas S. Kleppe. *The Vital Majority*, Diane Carson, ed. (Washington, D.C.: Superintendent of Documents, U.S. Government Printing Office, 1973), Introduction.

[2]These features are suggested in *Meeting the Special Problems of Small Business* (New York: Committee for Economic Development, 1947), p. 14.

[3]J. Fred Weston. *The Financing of Small Business* (New York: The Macmillan Co., 1967), p. 46.

[4]Lawrence A. Klatt. "Problems of the Small Business," *Managing the Dynamic Small Firm: Readings* (Belmont, Calif.: Wadsworth Publishing Co., Inc., 1971), pp. 25–49.

[5]Michael L. Johnson. "Small Businessmen: More Rags than Riches," *Industry Week* (July 29, 1974), p. 40.

[6]*Ibid.*, pp. 37–38.

[7]Lawrence A. Klatt. *Small Business Management* (Belmont, Calif.: Wadsworth Publishing Company, Inc., 1973), pp. 141–150.

[8]Selby D. Hunt. "The Socioeconomic Consequences of the Franchise System of Distribution," *Journal of Marketing* (July 1972), p. 32.

[9]*U.S. News & World Report* (February 25, 1974), p. 48.

[10]Lawrence A. Klatt. "Franchising," *Managing the Dynamic Small Firm: Readings* (Belmont, Calif.: Wadsworth Publishing Company, Inc., 1971).

[11]*The Business Failure Record* (New York: Dun & Bradstreet, Inc., 1973), p. 6.

[12]*Strengthening Small Business Management* (selections from the papers of L.T. White), Joseph C. Schabacker, ed. (Small Business Administration, 1971), p. 16.

[13]*The Business Failure Record*, p. 5.

[14]These are suggested in Klatt. *Small Business Management,* p. 10.

Chapter 23

[1]*The Age* (October 7, 1974), p. 1.
[2]The Age (September 9, 1974), p. 1.
[3]*The Age* (November 23, 1974), p. 1.
[4]*U.S. News & World Report* (November 25, 1974), p. 47.

Chapter 24

[1]"The 'Good Old Days'—Or Were They?" *U.S. News & World Report* (February 10, 1975), pp. 28–31.
[2]Gary F. Schuster. "We're Better off Now," *The Detroit News* (February 11, 1975), p. 1.
[3]Gregg Conderacci. "Detroit's Estimates of Small-car Demand Badly Missed Mark," *The Wall Street Journal* (March 18, 1974), p. 1.
[4]"A Price War Staggers Bowmar," *Business Week* (February 24, 1975), p. 28.
[5]Alvin Toffler. *Future Shock* (New York: Random House, Inc., 1970), p. 14.

[6]Quoted in *U.S. News & World Report* (March 3, 1975), p. 34.
[7]Andre Van Dam. "The Future of Industry's Growthmanship," *Business and Society* (Fall 1974), p. 26.
[8]Ray Vicker. "Population Growth Is Still a Key Problem in Many Poor Nations," *The Wall Street Journal* (October 23, 1974).
[9]Ella Mae Howey. "Business in the Year 2000," *Carroll Business Bulletin* (Fall 1974), pp. 18–19.
[10]"A Conversation with Gerber's John Suerth," *Advertising Age* (February 3, 1975), pp. 29, 32, 34.
[11]What Are the Cars in Detroit's 'New' Future," *Family Weekly* (July 28, 1974), p. 9.
[12]*The Age* (October 18, 1974), p. 1.

Appendix A

[1]"Oversupply of College Grads Feared," *The Detroit News* (March 16, 1975), p. 16-A.
[2]"What's Job Clustering All About?," *The Occupational Outlook Quarterly* (Winter 1973).
[3]*Jobs for the 1970's: Slide Series* (U.S. Department of Labor, Bureau of Labor Statistics).

Glossary

Absolute advantage Situation where a country is the sole producer of a product, or can produce it for less than anyone else.

Accountability Act of holding a manager liable for carrying out activities for which he or she has the necessary authority and responsibility.

Accounting Process of measuring and communicating financial information to enable interested parties inside the firm as well as outside groups to make informed decisions.

Accounting equation *Assets* (things of value) equals *liabilities* (claims of creditors) plus *owners' equity* (claims of owners).

Acid test ratio A ratio designed to measure the ability of the firm to pay its current debt on short notice. It is calculated by dividing cash, marketable securities, and accounts receivable by current liabilities.

Administrative agencies Agencies organized at all levels of government empowered to hear and decide a broad range of legal questions.

Advertising Nonpersonal sales presentation usually directed to a large number of potential customers.

Age Discrimination in Employment Act Federal law passed in 1967, and designed to prevent discrimination in firing or refusing to hire workers over the age of forty.

Agency shop Employment agreement whereby any qualified employees may be hired, but nonunion workers must pay the union a fee equal to union dues.

Agent The person who acts for another person.

Agent wholesalers Independent wholesalers who take possession but not legal title to the goods. Agent wholesalers typically act as some type of sales agent.

Alien corporation A corporation organized in another nation, but operating in the United States.

American Federation of Labor (AFL) A national union made up of affiliated individual craft unions.

Analog computers Computers that use continuous data—such as pressure, temperature, or voltage—in scientific or engineering applications.

Antitrust laws Laws that prohibit attempts to monopolize or dominate a particular market.

Appellant The party making an appeal in law.

Appellate courts Courts that hear appeals from the general trial court level.

Apprenticeship training Training programs in which new workers serve as apprentices to trained employees for a period of two to four years.

Arbitration The process of bringing in a third party, called an arbitrator, who renders a binding decision in a labor-management dispute.

Arithmetic element The portion of the computer system where all calculations take place.

Array A listing of items by size, either from the smallest to the largest or largest to the smallest.

Assets Everything of value found in a business.

Authority The power to act and make decisions in carrying out assignments.

Autocratic leaders Leaders who make decisions on their own without consulting others.

Automation Replacing people with machines, provided the machines can do the task faster and cheaper.

Automobile insurance Coverage for losses due to automobile theft, fire, or collision, and claims resulting from damage to the property or persons of others involved in an automobile accident.

Balance of payments The relationship between a nation's inward and outward money flows.

Balance of trade The relationship between a nation's exports and imports.

Balance sheet The financial statement that measures the assets, liabilities, and owners' equity of a firm as of a particular date.

Bankruptcy Inability to meet financial obligations.

Bear An investor who expects stock prices to decline.

Binary A system of counting that uses the two digits 0 and 1.

Blue laws Regulation of the extent to which businesses—particularly retailers—can operate on Sundays.

Blue-sky laws Early state laws regulating securities transactions.

Board of directors The governing authorities of corporations. A board elects the firm's officers. Most states require a minimum of three directors, and at least one annual meeting of the board.

Bond Long-term borrowing by corporations or government agencies.

Bond indenture The legal contract containing all provisions of the bond.

Bonus Addition to a time or piece wage to provide incentive for employees to increase productivity.

Book value Assets minus liabilities minus the value of any preferred stock.

Boycott Attempts to stop the purchase of goods or services from a company.

Brand names Names used to identify products.

Breakeven point The level of sales that will cover all of the company's costs.

Bull An investor who expects stock prices to rise.

Burglary insurance Coverage for losses due to taking property as a result of forcible entry.

Business All profit-directed economic and commercial activities that provide goods and services necessary to a nation's standard of living.

Business law Those branches, or areas, of law which most directly and specifically influence and regulate the planning and carrying out of various types of business activity.

Callable bond Bonds with provisions allowing the issuing corporation to redeem them prior to their maturity date, if a premium is paid.

Canned sales presentations Memorized sales talks.

Capacity The legal and mental qualifications of the party to enter into agreements.

Capital The funds necessary to finance the operation of a business.

Capital items Those industrial products that are relatively long-lived, and that usually involve large sums of money.

Cartels Monopolistic organizations that are permitted in some foreign countries.

Cash discount Reduction of purchase price of products, provided the purchaser pays for the goods within a specific time period.

Cash surrender value The savings portion of a life insurance policy which can be borrowed by the policyholder at low interest rates, or will be paid to the policyholder should the policy be cancelled.

Cathode ray tube (CRT) A televisionlike device for displaying data from a computer installation on a screen.

Celler-Kefauver Act (1950) Federal law that amends the Clayton Act to outlaw monopoly or overconcentration of competitors in an industry by means of a major asset purchase by one competitor of another.

Census Collection of data from all sources.

Centralization The practice by which managers disperse very little authority throughout the organization.

Certificates of deposit Short-term notes issued by commercial banks.

Certified public accountant (CPA) An accountant who has met state certification requirements concerning college degrees and experience, and who has passed a comprehensive examination covering all major aspects of accounting.

Chandler Act (1938) Federal legislation under which bankruptcies are handled today.

Check Piece of paper addressed to one's bank on which is written a legal authorization to withdraw a specified amount of money from one's account, and to pay that amount to someone else.

Classroom training Training programs using classroom techniques to teach new employees difficult jobs requiring high levels of skill.

Clayton Act (1914) Federal antitrust legislation forbidding trade restraints—such as tying contracts, interlocking directorates, and certain anticompetitive stock acquisitions.

Closed shop Employment agreement whereby management agrees not to hire nonunion workers.

Closing That part of the sales presentation at which a salesperson actually asks the prospect for the order.

COBOL (COmmon Business-Oriented Language) A computer language designed for business problems.

Coinsurance clause Requirement that the insured carry fire insurance of some minimum percentage of the value of the property in order to receive full coverage of a loss.

Collective bargaining Process of negotiation between management and union representatives for the purpose of arriving at mutually acceptable wages and working conditions for employees.

Commercial paper Short-term promissory notes issued by major corporations with very high credit standings.

Committee organization Organizational structure where authority and responsibility are jointly held by a group of individuals rather than by a single manager.

Common carriers Shippers who offer to perform services for the general public within a particular line of business. Common carriers are required to furnish regular service.

Common law System of unwritten law based on custom or court decision that developed in early England and was adopted in North America.

Common stock Class of stock having only a residual claim (after everyone else has been paid) to the firm's assets; common stockholders have voting rights in a corporation.

Communism An economic theory developed by Karl Marx during the nineteenth century. Marx believed that the people should own all of a nation's productive capacity, but conceded that the government would have to operate businesses until a classless society could evolve.

Comparative advantage A nation has a comparative advantage in an item if it can produce it more efficiently than alternative products.

Comparative advertising The practice of making direct comparisons with competitive products in an advertisement.

Competition The battle between businesses for consumer acceptance.

Computer hardware The physical equipment that makes up the elements of the computer installation.

Computer software A set of programs, procedures, and instructions that tell the computer what to do.

Computers Electronic machines that accept data and manipulate it mathematically to solve problems and produce new information.

Congress of Industrial Organizations (CIO) A national union made up of affiliated individual industrial unions.

Consideration Value, or promise or benefit, that a party provides to the other party or parties to the contract.

Consumer Credit Reporting Act (1968) Federal law, known as the "Truth in Lending Act," that requires a lender to specify the exact interest charges that a borrower will have to pay.

Consumer goods Those products and services purchased by the ultimate consumer for his or her own use.

Consumerism Trend toward consumers becoming more activist; willing to take action against what they see as abuses in the business system.

Containerization Packaging into a form that is relatively easy to transfer.

Contract An agreement between two or more parties to do, or not to do, a particular thing.

Contract carriers Shippers who transport goods for hire by individual contract agreement.

Control element The portion of the computer system responsible for directing the sequence of operations, interpreting coded instructions, and giving the right commands to guide the computer.

Controlling The management function involved in evaluating the organization's performance to determine whether it is accomplishing its objectives.

Convenience goods Those products the consumer seeks to purchase frequently, immediately, and with a minimum of effort.

Conversational programs Special computer programs designed to assist users with no special computer training.

Convertible bond Bond with the option of being converted into a specific number of shares of common stock.

Convertible preferred stock Preferred stock with the option of being converted into common stock at a stated price.

Cooling-off laws Laws that permit a consumer to cancel a sales contract within a certain period of time.

Cooling-off period The right given to the President of the United States under the Taft-Hartley Act to ask for an eighty-day court suspension of strikes that endanger the national health and safety.

Cooperatives Organizations where private ownership is maintained but all of the owners band together to collectively own and operate all or part of their company.

Copyrights Protection of one's right to something that is written, drawn, designed, or illustrated. Copyrights are granted for a twenty-eight-year period and are renewable one time.

Corporations Form of business organization considered separate legal entities apart from their owners.

Cost-push inflation Inflation resulting from rising costs that are passed on to the consumer.

Countervailing powers A term used to describe big business, big labor, and big government.

Craft union A labor union consisting of skilled workers in a specific craft or trade.

Credit insurance Insurance designed to protect lenders against losses from bad debts.

Credit life insurance Special form of term insurance purchased by persons buying a home, auto, or major appliances which would repay the balance owed on these items should the policyholder die.

Critical path The sequence of operations in the PERT diagram that requires the longest time for completion.

Cumulative voting Practice allowing smaller stockholders to have a greater influence on the selection of the board of directors. If three director positions are to be filled, cumulative voting allows small stockholders to cast three times their shares for one position, rather than apportioning their votes among the three positions.

Currency Two components of the money supply—coins and paper money.

Current assets Items of value which are expected to be converted into cash or used up within a period of one year.

Current ratio A ratio designed to measure the ability of the firm to pay its current debts as they mature. It is calculated by dividing current assets by current liabilities.

Debenture Bonds backed by the reputation of the issuing corporation, rather than by specific pledges of assets.

Debt capital Funds provided by borrowing.

Debt to net worth ratio A ratio designed to indicate the extent to which company operations are financed by borrowed funds. It is calculated by dividing total liabilities by stockholders' equity.

Decentralization The practice by which managers disperse large amounts of authority to subordinates in subsidiary firms.

Delegation The act of assigning part of the manager's activities to subordinates.

Demand curve A schedule of amounts that will be purchased at different prices.

Demand deposits The technical term for checking accounts.

Demand-pull inflation Inflation occurring when there is too much money relative to the products available.

Democratic leaders Leaders who involve their subordinates in making decisions.

Departmentalization The subdivision of work activities into units within the organization.

Devaluation When a nation reduces the value of its currency in relation to gold, or some other currency.

Digital computers Computers that manipulate numbers by adding, subtracting, multiplying, or dividing.

Directing The accomplishment of organizational objectives by guiding and motivating subordinates.

Discount rate Interest rate charged by the Federal Reserve System on loans to member banks.

Dispatching That phase of production control that issues instructions to each department on what work is to be done and the time allowed for its completion.

Dividends Payments from earnings of a corporation to its stockholders.

Domestic corporation A firm is considered a domestic corporation in the state where it is incorporated.

Earnings per share The amount of profits earned by a company for each share of common stock outstanding. It is calculated by dividing net earnings (or net profits) by the number of common shares outstanding.

Ecology Relationship between people and their environment.

Electronic banking Computerized systems of reducing check-writing through electronic depositing and withdrawal of funds.

Embargo Complete ban of certain products.

Employers' associations Cooperative efforts of employers to present a united front in dealing with labor unions.

Endorsement The process of transferring a negotiable instrument.

Endowment Type of insurance policy providing coverage for a specified period. After this period the face value of the policy is refunded to the policyholder.

Energy crisis The annoyances and inconveniences caused by the declining supplies of some energy source.

Entrepreneurs Risk-takers in the free enterprise system.

Environmental Protection Act (1970) Federal act that set up the Environmental Protection Agency (EPA) with the authority to deal with various types of pollution.

Equal Employment Opportunity Commission (EEOC) A federal commission created to increase job opportunities for women and minorities and to assist in ending job discrimination based on race, religion, color, sex, or national origin.

Equities Claims against the assets of a business.

Equity capital Funds provided by the firm's owners through purchases of stock.

Esteem needs A person's need to feel a sense of accomplishment, achievement, and respect from others.

Exchange control Requirement that firms gaining foreign exchange by exporting must sell this foreign exchange to a central bank, or government agency, while importers must buy foreign exchange from the same organization. The government can thus allocate, expand, or restrict foreign exchange according to national policy.

Exchange rate The rate at which a nation's currency can be exchanged for other currencies or gold.

Expense items Usually less expensive industrial products than capital items, consumed within a year of their purchase.

Exporting Selling abroad.

External data Data generated outside the organization.

Factor Financial institution that will purchase—at a discount—the accounts receivables of such retailers as furniture and appliance dealers.

Factors of production The basic inputs into the free enterprise system. These include land, labor, capital, and entrepreneurship.

Fair Credit Reporting Act (1970) Federal law that allows people to see credit reports prepared about them. The person can also request that incorrect information be changed.

Fair Packaging and Labeling Act (1967) Federal law that requires certain information be disclosed on packages or labels. This information includes product identity, the name and address of the producer or distributor, and quality information.

FCN ("Friendship, Commerce, and Navigation" treaties) Treaties covering many aspects of commercial relations between countries.

Featherbedding A labor practice where workers are paid for work not done.

Federal Deposit Insurance Corporation (FDIC) A corporation that insures bank depositors' accounts up to a maximum of $40,000, and sets requirements for sound banking practices.

Federal Reserve System System of controlling banking in the United States through twelve Federal Reserve regional banks controlled by the Board of Governors.

Federal Trade Commission Act (1914) Federal law that created the Federal Trade Commission as a federal agency and gave it broad powers to prevent business entities of all types and sizes from engaging in unfair methods of competition.

Fidelity bond Bond used to protect an employer from the dishonesty of an employee.

FIFO **(First In-First Out)** Method of inventory accounting that assumes the first inventory purchased and still on hand is the first sold when determining cost of goods sold.

Finance The business function of effectively obtaining and using funds.

Fire insurance Coverage for losses due to fire and—with extended coverage—losses from windstorms, hail, water, riot, and smoke damage.

Fiscal year A twelve-month period other than a calendar year used for accounting purposes.

Five M's The basic resources of any firm—management, manpower, materials, money, and machinery.

Fixed assets Items of value which are not expected to be used up or converted into cash within a one-year period.

Fixed costs Those costs that remain stable regardless of the sales level achieved.

Floor-planning The practice of retailers handling expensive items—such as automobiles, furniture, and appliances—of obtaining funds through assigning title to their inventories to financing agencies in return for short-term loans.

Flow chart A pictorial description of the logical steps to be taken in solving a problem.

Follow up That phase of production control that spots problems in the production process and informs management of needed adjustments.

Foreign corporation If a firm expects to do business in states other than its state of incorporation, it is called a foreign corporation in those other states.

Form utility The creation of utility through the conversion of raw materials and other inputs into finished products or services.

FORTRAN **(FORMULA TRANSLATION)** A widely used computer language.

Franchise Legal agreement by which a franchisee (dealer) agrees to conduct a business in accordance with certain methods and terms specified by the franchiser (parent company).

Franchisee The dealer, or representative, under a franchise agreement.

Franchiser The parent company under a franchise agreement.

Free enterprise system A system whereby businesses operate in a dynamic environment in which success or failure is determined by how well they match and counter the offerings of competitors.

Free rein leaders Leaders who believe in minimal supervision and who leave most decisions to be made by their subordinates.

Frequency distribution A listing, or graph, of the number of times each item appears in a group of data.

Fringe benefits Nonmonetary employee benefits—such as pension plans, health and life insurance, sick-leave pay, credit unions, and health and safety programs.

Functional organization Organizational structure based on technical authority for each work activity or function.

General partnerships Partnerships established when all partners carry on the business as co-owners. All partners are liable for the debts of a general partnership.

Grapevine The informal communications network found in most organizations.

Grievance Employee or union complaint that management is violating some provision of the union contract.

Hardware (*See* computer hardware).

Hawthorne studies A series of investigations that led to the development of the human relations approach to motivation by revealing that money and job security are not the only sources of employee motivation.

Health insurance Coverage for losses due to sickness or accidents.

Human resources management (*See* Personnel Management).

Importing Buying foreign goods and raw materials.

Income statement The financial statement that measures the income, expenses, and profits of a firm over a period of time.

Industrial distributors Wholesalers of industrial goods.

Industrial goods Products purchased to be used, either directly or indirectly, in the production of other goods for resale.

Industrial park Planned site locations providing necessary zoning, land, shipping facilities, and waste disposal outlets.

Industrial Revolution The shift to a factory system of manufacturing that began in England around 1750–1775.

Industrial union A labor union consisting of all of the workers in a given industry, regardless of their occupations or skill levels.

Inflation Rising prices or the decreased purchasing power of a nation's currency.

Informal organization A self-grouping of employees in the organization possessing informal channels of communications and contacts.

Injunction A court order prohibiting some practice.

Inland marine insurance Coverage for losses of property due to damage while being transported by truck, ship, rail, or plane.

Input element The portion of the computer system that is responsible for converting incoming data into a usable form for the computer.

Institutional advertising Promotion of a concept, idea, philosophy, or good will of an industry, company, organization, or governmental entity.

Insurable interest An insurance concept that requires the policyholder to stand a financial loss due to the occurrence of fire, accident, lawsuit, or death.

Insurable risk Requirements which a risk must meet in order that an insurance company provide protection against its occurrence.

Insurance The process by which a firm (the insurance company) agrees that for a fee (the insurance premium) it will pay another firm or individual (the insured) a sum of money stated in a written contract (the policy) if a loss occurs.

Intangible personal property Property most often represented by a document, or other instrument in writing, although it may be as vague and remote as a bookkeeping or computer entry of some type.

Interlocking directorates A practice existing when companies that are supposedly in competition have identical or overlapping boards of directors.

Internal data Data generated within the organization.

Inventory control Balancing the need to have available supplies of inventory on hand to meet demand with the costs involved in carrying inventory.

Inventory turnover The number of times the average amount of a firm's inventory is used (or sold) each year.

Investment Company Act of 1940 Federal law that brought the mutual funds industry under the jurisdiction of the Securities and Exchange Commission.

Invisible hand Term used by Adam Smith to describe how competition regulates the free enterprise system.

Job analysis A systematic, detailed study of jobs consisting of identifying and examining each job's elements and characteristics and the requirements of the person assigned to the job.

Job description A document which describes the objectives of a job, the work to be performed, the responsibilities involved, skills needed, the relationship of the job to other jobs, and its working conditions.

Job enrichment Giving the workers more authority to plan their work and decide how it is to be accomplished; allowing them to learn new, related skills or trade jobs with others.

Job evaluation Method of determining wage levels for different jobs by comparing each on the basis of skill requirements, education, responsibilities, and physical requirements.

Job specification A document which describes the special qualifications required of a worker who fills a particular job.

Joint ventures Types of partnerships where two or more people form a temporary business for a specific undertaking.

Judiciary system Term that refers to a system of courts.

Kennedy round A series of tariff negotiations that took place between 1964–1967.

Key accounts Major customers of the firm.

Labor Everyone who works for a business.

Labor union A group of workers who have banded together to achieve common goals involving the key areas of wages, hours, and working conditions.

Laissez-faire "Hands-off" business-government doctrine.

Land All types of real property.

Landrum-Griffin Act (1959) Federal legislation requiring regularly scheduled elections of union officers by secret ballot and increased regulation of the handling of union funds.

Lanham Act (1946) Federal law providing for registration of trademarks.

Law Rules and regulations set by government and society either in the form of legislation or customs.

Law of agency Law that concerns every relation, business or otherwise, where one person acts for or represents another by the authority or consent of the latter person.

Law of large numbers Probability calculations of the likelihood of the occurrence of hazards on which insurance premiums are based.

Law of supply and demand An economic law that says market price is determined by the intersection of the supply and demand schedules.

Layoff Temporary job dismisals due to business slowdowns.

Leverage The technique of increasing the rate of return on investment through the use of borrowed funds.

Liabilities Claims of the creditors of the firm.

Life style The way a person lives. It includes their work, leisure time, hobbies, interests, and personal philosophy.

LIFO (Last In-First Out) A method of inventory accounting that assumes that the most recently purchased inventory is the first sold in determining cost of goods sold.

Limit order An investor request that a stock purchase or sale be made at a specified price.

Limited partnership A partnership composed of one or more general partners and one or more limited partners. A limited partner is one whose liability is limited to the amount contributed to the capital of the partnership.

Limited payment life insurance A variation of whole life insurance whereby the policy holder pays all premiums within a designated period, such as twenty or thirty years.

Line of credit An agreement between a commercial bank and a business firm that states the amount of unsecured short-term credit the bank will make available to the borrower—provided the bank has enough funds available for lending.

Line organization An organizational structure based on a direct flow of authority from the chief executive to subordinates.

Line-and-staff organization An organizational structure combining the direct flow of authority present in the line organization with staff departments who serve, advise, and support the line departments.

Liquidity The speed at which items may be exchanged for money.

Lockout A management strike to bring pressure on union members by closing the firm.

Maintenance factors Such job-related factors as salary, working conditions, and job security which must be present in order to avoid worker dissatisfaction but which are not strong motivators when they are present.

Maloney Act of 1938 Federal law authorizing self-regulation of the over-the-counter securities operations.

Malpractice insurance A type of public liability insurance designed to protect physicians, attorneys, and teachers against losses due to charges of incompetency or negligence.

Management The achievement of objectives through people and other resources.

Management functions The activities of management in accomplishing the objectives of the firm. Management functions include planning, organizing, directing, and controlling.

Management Information System (MIS) An organized method of providing past, present, and projected information on internal operations and external intelligence for use in management decision making.

Management by Objectives A program designed to improve employee motivation through participation in setting individual goals and in knowing in advance precisely how employees will be evaluated.

Management pyramid The hierarchy, or levels, of management in an organization.

Mark-up The amount that is added to cost to determine the market price.

Market order Investor request that a stock purchase be made at the current market price.

Market segmentation The process of taking the total market and dividing it into groups with similar characteristics.

Market share The percentage of a market controlled by a certain company or product.

Market targets Groups of consumers toward whom the firm decides to direct its marketing effort.

Market value The price at which a stock is currently selling.

Marketing The performance of business activities that direct the flow of goods and services from producer to consumer, or user.

Marketing channels The paths that goods—and title to those goods—follow from producer to consumer (American Marketing Association definition).

Marketing concept A business philosophy that says a firm should adopt a company-wide consumer orientation with the goal of achieving long-run profits.

Marketing mix A term used to describe the four elements of a marketing strategy: product strategy, distribution strategy, promotional strategy, and pricing strategy.

Marketing research Systematic gathering, recording, and analyzing of data about problems relating to the marketing of goods and services.

Materials handling The moving of items within the customer's warehouse, terminal, factory, or store.

Maturity date The date at which a loan must be repaid.

Mean (or average) A statistical measure calculated by summing all items and dividing by the number of items.

Median The middle score in a series of items.

Mediation The process of bringing in a third party, called a mediator, to make recommendations for the settlement of labor-management differences.

Medium of exchange The function performed by money in facilitating exchange and eliminating the need for a barter system.

Memory element The storage unit of the computer from which information can be retrieved when needed.

Merchant wholesaler An independent wholesaler who takes legal title to goods.

Merger When one firm buys the assets and liabilities of another company.

Metric system A standard of weights and measures based upon the decimal system of tens and multiples of ten.

Middle management The second level of the management pyramid, including such executives as plant managers and department heads.

Middlemen Organizations that operate within a channel of distribution.

Minicomputers Small, cash-register-sized computers for use by scientists and business decision makers in solving problems not requiring the storage or processing capacity of larger computers.

Minority-owned businesses Firms owned and operated by racial or ethnic minorities in the United States.

Mixed economies Economies where there is a mix of socialism and free enterprise.

Mode The most frequently observed value in a series of observations.

Money Anything which is generally accepted as a means of paying for goods and services.

Monopolistic competition An industry where a few less firms (than would exist in perfect competition) produce and sell products that are different from those of competitors. Monopolistic competition also gives the firm some power over the price it will charge.

Monopoly A market situation where there is only one firm in the industry.

Morale The mental attitude of employees toward their company and their jobs.

Mortality table The table used to predict the number of persons in each age category who will die in a given year.

Motivational factors Such job-related characteristics as the work itself, recognition, responsibility, advancement, and growth potential, which are the key sources of employee motivation.

Motives Inner states that direct the individual toward the goal of satisfying a felt need.

Mutual funds Companies that sell shares of stock in their own companies in order to raise money to invest in the securities of other firms.

Mutual insurance company An insurance company owned by its policyholders.

Nanosecond One-billionth of a second.

National bank A commercial bank chartered by the federal government.

Near-money An asset, such as a savings account, that is almost as liquid as a checking account but cannot be used directly as a medium of exchange.

Need The lack of something useful.

Negligence A tort based on carelessness or reckless disregard where someone has a duty to take due care and where neglect of this duty causes injury to someone else.

Negotiable instrument Commercial paper that can be transferred from one person to another.

No-fault insurance State laws requiring claims payments by the insurance company of the policyholder without regard to fault, and limiting the right of victims to sue.

Norris-La Guardia Act (1932) Early federal legislation aimed at protecting unions through greatly reducing management's ability to obtain injunctions to halt union activities.

Objectives Guideposts for managers in defining standards of what the organization should accomplish in such areas as profitability, customer service, and social responsibility.

Observation (*See* Observational method).

Observational method Studies conducted by actually viewing the overt actions of the respondent.

Occupational Safety and Health Act of 1970 (*See* OSHA).

Occupational Safety and Health Administration (OSHA) Federal administering body created by the Occupational Safety and Health Act of 1970 to assure safe and healthful working conditions for the U.S. labor force.

Ocean marine insurance Coverage for losses of property due to damage to the ship or its cargo while at sea or in port.

Odd lot Purchase or sale of less than one hundred shares of stock.

Odd pricing Practice of using uneven prices, such as $1.99 or $2.99.

Office of Minority Business Enterprise (*See* OMBE).

Oligopoly A market where there are few sellers.

OMBE The abbreviation for the Office of Minority Business Enterprise in the U.S. Department of Commerce. OMBE is a federal agency that provides help to minority-owned businesses.

On-the-job-training An employee training program based on the new worker actually performing the work involved under the guidance of an experienced employee.

Open market operations The technique of controlling the money supply by purchase and sale of government bonds by the Federal Reserve System.

Organization A structured process in which people interact to accomplish objectives.

Organization chart The formal outline of the authority and responsibility relationships in an organization.

Organizing The means by which management blends human and material resources through the design of a formal structure of tasks and authority.

Output element The portion of the computer system that takes answers from the computer once the problem has been solved.

Outside directors Members of the board of directors of a corporation who are not employed by the firm.

Over-the-counter market Trading of unlisted securities outside the organized securities exchanges.

Owners' equity Claims of the owners of the firm (or the *excess* of all assets over all liabilities).

Ownership utility Utility created when marketers arrange for the transfer of title from seller to buyer.

Paid-in capital in excess of par The difference between the par value of shares of company stock and the price paid by the original stockholders.

Par value The value printed on stock certificates of some companies.

Parkinson's Law "Work expands so as to fill the time available for its completion."

Partnerships Associations of two or more persons who operate a business as co-owners by voluntary legal agreement.

Patent A guarantee to inventors of exclusive rights to their inventions for seventeen years, provided the inventions are accepted by the U.S. Patent Office.

Penetration price policy The practice of pricing a new product low relative to substitute items in order to secure wide market acceptance.

Perfect competition A situation where all of the firms in an industry are so small that none of them can individually influence the price charged in the marketplace.

Personal selling A promotional presentation made on a person-to-person basis with a potential buyer.

Personnel management The recruitment, selection, development, and motivation of human resources.

PERT Program Evaluation and Review Technique is a scheduling technique designed for such complex products as ships or new airplane designs.

Physical distribution That aspect of the distribution system which refers to the actual movement of goods from producer to user.

Physiological needs The primary needs for food, shelter, and clothing that are present in all humans.

Picketing The practice of workers marching at the entrances of an employer's plant as a public protest against some management practice.

Piece wage Employee compensation based

upon the amount of output produced by the worker.

PL/1 (Programming Language 1) A computer language designed for use in both scientific and business environments.

Place utility Utility created by having the product available to the consumer at a convenient location when the person wants to buy.

Planned obsolescence Where products are made less durable than they might otherwise be.

Planning The management function of anticipating the future and determining the courses of action to achieve company objectives.

Plastic money The use of credit cards as substitutes for cash.

Pollution The tainting or destroying of a natural environment.

P.O.P Abbreviation for point-of-purchase advertising.

Population explosion The term refers to the rapid growth in the world's population in recent years.

Positioning The promotional strategy of concentrating on specific market segments rather than trying to achieve a broad appeal.

Pre-emptive right The right of current stockholders to purchase a proportionate share of new stock issues.

Preferred stock Stock whose owners are given preference in receiving dividend payments, but who do not normally have voting rights.

Price A product or service's exchange value in the marketplace.

Price-earnings ratio The current market price divided by the annual earnings per share.

Price lining The offering of merchandise at a limited number of prices, rather than pricing each item individually.

Primary data Data collected for the first time for use in solving a business problem.

Prime interest rate The lowest rate of interest charged by commercial banks for short-term loans to major corporations with extremely high credit standings.

Principal The person for whom an agent acts.

Private brands (often known as house, distributor, or retailer labels) Products that are not identified as to manufacturer, but carry the retailer's label.

Private carriers Shippers who carry their own property in their own vehicles.

Private property A person's right to own, accumulate, buy, sell, and will property under the free enterprise system.

Probate courts Courts that settle a deceased person's estate.

Product advertising Nonpersonal selling of a good or service.

Product liability insurance Insurance designed to protect businesses from claims for damages resulting from the use of the company's products.

Product life cycle A series of stages from initial appearance to death that all products pass through. The stages of the product life cycle are introduction, growth, maturity, and decline.

Production The use of people and machines to convert materials into finished products or services.

Production control A well-defined set of procedures for coordinating people, materials, and machines in providing maximum production efficiency.

Production era The early part of the twentieth century when business managers concentrated almost solely on the firm's production tasks.

Products liability A branch of tort law that holds business liable for any negligence in the design, manufacture, sale, and use of its products.

Profit The difference between revenues (the firm's receipts) and expenses (the company's expenditures).

Profit and loss statement (*See* Income statement).

Profit-sharing A type of incentive wage program where a percentage of company profits are distributed to employees involved in producing those profits.

Program A detailed set of instructions for performing some operation written in some language suitable for input to a computer.

Programmer A person who designs, writes, and tests computer programs.

Programming The process of writing computer programs.

Promissory note A traditional bank loan whereby the borrower signs a note stating the terms of the loan, including its length and the interest rate charged.

Promotion The upward movement in the organization to positions of greater authority and responsibility and higher salaries.

Promotional strategy The function of informing, persuading, and influencing a consumer decision.

Property The unrestricted right to possess and use something.

Prospects Potential customers.

Proxy A statement authorizing someone else to vote your shares at a corporation's annual meeting.

Public liability insurance Insurance designed to protect businesses and individuals from claims caused by injuries to others, or damage to the property of others.

Public ownership Some governmental unit or its agency which owns and operates a particular organization on behalf of the population served by that unit.

Purchasing Acquiring materials and supplies needed in the operation of a firm.

Pure Food and Drug Act (1906) Federal law that prohibited the adulteration and misbranding of food and drugs.

Pure risk A type of risk involving *only* the chance of loss.

Qualifying That part of the sales presentation that determines whether a prospect has the financial ability and the authority to buy.

Quality control The measurement of output against established quality standards.

Quick assets Highly liquid assets—such as cash, marketable securities, and accounts receivable—that are available to meet current debt on short notice.

Quotas Limits on the amount of products in certain categories that may be imported.

Ratio of net income to sales A profitability ratio designed to measure the relationship between net income and sales. It is calculated by dividing net income by sales.

Real property A legal term referring to real estate.

Reciprocity An extension of purchasing preferences to those suppliers who are also customers.

Remote terminal A typewriterlike machine connected to the main computer installation but located in a site physically removed from the computer.

Reserve requirement The percentage of a bank's checking and savings accounts that must be kept in the bank or as deposits at the local Federal Reserve District Bank.

Respondeat superior A Latin maxim meaning "let the master answer."

Responsibility The obligation of a subordinate to perform assigned duties.

Retailer The final member in the distribution channel.

Revaluation An upward adjustment in the value of a nation's currency.

Revolving credit agreement A guaranteed line of credit.

Right to work laws State laws outlawing the union shop.

Risk The chance of loss or injury.

Robbery insurance Coverage for losses due to the unlawful taking of property from another person by force or threat of force.

Robinson-Patman Act (1936) Federal law that outlaws price discrimination between purchasers of like quality and quantities of products where such discrimination injures competition or tends to create a monopoly.

Round lot Quantities of one hundred shares.

Routing That phase of production control which determines the sequence of the work throughout the plant.

Safety needs The human need for job security, protection from physical harm, and avoidance of the unexpected.

Salary Employee compensation calculated on a weekly, monthly, or annual basis.

Sales branches Manufacturer-owned wholesalers who stock the items they distribute and process orders from that inventory.

Sales offices Manufacturer-owned wholesaling operations that do not maintain inventory but are sales offices for providing close local contacts with potential purchasers.

Sample A representative group.

Savings and Loan Association A financial institution that pays interest on time deposits and lends money for residential construction and commercial purposes.

SBA The abbreviation for the Small Business Administration, a federal agency that provides assistance to small businesses.

Scheduling That phase of production control which is involved in developing timetables that specify how much time each operation in the production process takes.

Scrambled merchandising The trend for retailers to diversify by adding dissimilar products to their merchandise lines.

Secondary boycott Refusal by union members to buy or handle products produced by another union or worker group.

Secondary data Data that has been published previously.

Secured bond A bond backed by specific pledges of company assets.

Securities Act of 1933 Federal law designed to protect investors through requiring full disclosure of relevant financial information by companies desiring to sell new stock issues to the general public.

Securities Exchange Act of 1934 Federal law creating the Securities and Exchange Commission (SEC) to regulate the national stock exchanges.

Self-actualization needs The need for fulfillment, for realizing one's potential, for totally using one's talents and capabilities.

Self-insurance The practice by some multiplant, geographically scattered firms of accumulating funds to cover possible losses.

Separation Resignations, retirements, terminations, and layoffs.

Serial bonds The issue of a large number of bonds which mature at different dates.

Sherman Anti-trust Act (1890) Federal anti-trust legislation that prohibits every contract or conspiracy in restraint of trade and declares as illegal any action which monopolizes or attempts to monopolize any part of trade or commerce.

Shopping goods Products purchased only after the consumer has made comparisons of competing goods on such bases as price, quality, style, and color in competing stores.

Sinking-fund bonds Bonds where the issuing corporation makes annual deposits of funds for use in redeeming the bonds when they mature.

Skimming price policy The practice of pricing a new product relatively high compared to substitute goods, and then gradually lowering the price.

Small business The term used to refer to firms with few employees, low sales volume, and limited assets.

Small Business Administration (*See* SBA).

Small claims courts Courts where people can represent themselves in suits over small damage claims.

Social needs The desire to be accepted by members of the family and other individuals and groups.

Social responsibility When management considers social effects as well as economic effects in its decisions.

Socialism An economic system which believes that the government should own and operate all basic industries. Private ownership would still exist in smaller businesses.

Software (*See* Computer software).

Sole proprietorship An organization owned, and usually operated, by a single individual.

Span of control The optimum number of subordinates a manager can effectively manage.

Specialty goods Those products that have no reasonable substitute in the mind of the buyer.

Speculative risk The type of risk where the firm or individual has the chance of either a profit or a loss.

Stagflation A term used to describe the dual economic problems of high unemployment and a rapidly rising price level.

State bank A commercial bank chartered by an individual state.

Statement of changes in financial position The financial statement designed to explain financial changes that occur in a company from one accounting period to the next.

Statistics The collection, analysis, interpretation, and presentation of information in numerical form.

Statutory law Written law that includes state and federal constitutions; legislative enactments; treaties of the federal government; and municipal ordinances of towns, cities, and other local governments.

Stock Shares of ownership in the corporation.

Stock exchange The locations at which stocks and bonds are bought and sold.

Stock insurance company An insurance company operated for profit.

Stock turnover The number of times the average inventory is sold annually.

Stockholders Those people who own the shares of a corporation.

Stockholders' equity The claims of the owners of the corporation.

Store of value The function performed when money is used to store accumulated wealth until it is needed for new purchases.

Strict product liability The branch of tort law that holds a manufacturer responsible for all types of injury caused by its products whether the manufacturer was proved negligent or not.

Strike A temporary work stoppage by employees until a dispute has been settled or a contract has been signed.

Subchapter S corporations Those corporations

that can elect to be taxed as proprietorships, and still maintain the advantages of
incorporation.

Subsidiary When a corporation's stock is either
wholly- or majority-owned by another
corporation.

Supervisory management The third level of
the management pyramid, including supervisors.

Supplementary unemployment benefits (SUB)
The United Auto Workers Union's version
of the guaranteed annual wage whereby
laid-off UAW members may qualify for
payments amounting to 95 percent of their
take-home pay.

Supply curve A schedule that shows the
amounts that will be offered in the market
at different prices.

Surety bond A bond designed to protect a
person or company from any losses resulting from nonperformance of a contract.

Survey method Studies conducted by asking
respondents to answer questions in order
to obtain information on attitudes, motives, or opinions.

Taft-Hartley Act (1947) Federal legislation designed to balance the power of unions
and management by prohibiting the closed
shop and a number of unfair union
practices.

Tangible personal property Physical things,
such as goods and products.

Tariffs Taxes levied against products imported
from abroad.

Technology Knowledge and scientific procedures, techniques, and equipment that are
applicable to industrial situations.

Term insurance Insurance providing protection for the individual for a specified period
of years, but which has no value at the
end of that period.

Termination Permanent job losses resulting
from inability to perform the work, repeated violation of work rules, excessive
absenteeism, elimination of jobs, or the
closing of company facilities.

Theft insurance Coverage for losses due to the
unlawful taking of property.

Theory X Traditional managerial assumptions
that employees dislike work and must be
coerced, controlled, or threatened in order
to motivate them to work.

Theory Y Newer set of managerial assumptions
that workers do not dislike work and that,
under proper conditions, they will accept

and seek out responsibilities in order to
fulfill social, esteem, and self-actualization
needs.

Third world nations Those countries not politically aligned with either the East or West.

Time deposits The technical name for savings
accounts.

Time-sharing The linking of several companies
or organizations through remote terminals (usually teletypewriters) to a large
central computer.

Time utility Utility created by having the product available when the consumer wants
to buy.

Time wage Employee compensation based
upon the amount of time spent on the job.

Title insurance Protection for the purchaser
of real estate from losses which might be
incurred because of a defect in the title to
the property.

Top management The highest level of the management pyramid, comprised of the president and other key company executives.

Tort A private or civil wrong inflicted upon
one person by another.

Trade credit Sales or purchases on credit or
open account.

Trademark Words, symbols, or other designations used by a business to identify its
products.

Transfer Horizontal movements in the organization at about the same wage and same
level in the organization.

Treasury bill Short-term U.S. Treasury borrowings, usually for 91 or 182 days.

Treasury stock Stock that was originally issued
to company stockholders and later reac-
quired by the issuing corporation.

Trial courts Courts that exist at both federal
and state levels to hear a wide range of
cases.

Turnover (*See* Inventory turnover).

Tying contract A contract where the seller
forces the buyer to purchase a secondary
relatively undesirable product.

Uniform Commercial Code A comprehensive
commercial law that has been adopted in
all states except Louisiana. It covers the
law of sales as well as other specific areas
of commercial law.

Union shop An employment agreement whereby any qualified employees may be hired,
but they must join the union within a
specified time period.

Unit of account The function performed when

money serves as a common denominator for measuring the value of all products and services.

U.S. Court of Claims   Federal court that hears claims against the U.S. government.

U.S. tax courts   Federal courts that hear tax cases.

Unitizing   A physical distribution term that refers to combining as many packages as possible into one load that is usually handled by a forklift truck.

Universal Product Code   A series of magnetic symbols placed on grocery items that can be read by the optical-scanning device of a computer at supermarkets with computerized checkouts.

Utility   The want-satisfying power of a product or service.

Variable costs   Those costs which change with the level of production.

Voice-input computer systems   Computers that have been programmed to respond to spoken instructions.

Wage   Employee compensation based on the number of hours worked.

Wagner Act (1935)   Federal legislation which made collective bargaining legal and required employers to bargain with the elected representatives of their employees.

Wheel of Retailing   A concept that explains how the retail structure is continually evolving as new retailers enter the market by offering lower prices through a reduction in services. These new entries gradually add services and raise prices as they grow.

Wheeler-Lea Act (1938)   Federal law that amended the Federal Trade Commission Act to further outlaw "unfair or deceptive acts or practices" in commerce.

Whole life insurance   Insurance providing protection for the individual who pays premiums throughout his lifetime and also builds up a cash surrender value in the policy.

Wholesalers   Distribution channel members who sell to retailers, other channel members, or industrial users, but only occasionally and in small amounts to ultimate users.

Workers' compensation insurance   Insurance provided by employers under state law to guarantee the payment of medical expenses and salaries to employees who are injured on the job.

Working capital   Funds used in the daily operation of the business generated through company earnings, loans, or the sale of stock.

Yield   Income received from securities.

Zero population growth   That point where live births equal the current death rate.

Name Index

Subject Index